THE DIARY OF
SAMUEL PEPYS

THE DIARY
OF
SAMUEL PEPYS

A new and complete
transcription edited by

ROBERT LATHAM
AND
WILLIAM MATTHEWS

VOLUME XI · INDEX

Compiled by
ROBERT LATHAM

HarperCollins*Publishers*

University of California Press
Berkeley and Los Angeles

Published in the UK by
HarperCollins*Publishers*
77-85 Fulham Palace Road
Hammersmith, London w6 8jb
www.**fire**and**water**.com

UK paperback edition 1995
Reissued 2000

Published in the USA by
University of California Press
Berkeley and Los Angeles, California

First US paperback edition 2000

1 3 5 7 9 8 6 4 2

First published by Bell & Hyman Limited 1983

ISBN 0 00 499031 5 (UK)
ISBN 0 520 22716 6 (USA)

Library of Congress Catalog Card No. 70-96950

Printed and bound in Great Britain by
Clays Ltd, St Ives plc

CONTENTS

PUBLISHER'S NOTE

The publication of Volumes X (the *Companion*) and XI (*the Index*) marks the completion of the eleven-volume edition edited by the late Robert Latham and the late Professor William Matthews.

Professor Matthews' main work as Joint Editor was the transcription of the original manuscript of the *Diary* in the Pepys Library at Magdalene College, Cambridge. He had arrived at the end of this immense task shortly before his death in 1975 but sadly did not live to see the completion of publication.

Mr Latham had borne the responsibility alone for the *Companion* and *Index* volumes. He started work on the eleven-volume edition in 1950. Since that time he held academic posts in England, the USA and Canada, and from 1972 until 1982 was Fellow and Pepys Librarian at Magdalene College, Cambridge. Throughout these years he spent an enormous amount of time on the research required for this edition and the publishers are deeply grateful to him for the scholarly dedication and skill he brought to this massive undertaking. Mr Latham died in January 1995.

PREFACE

In this volume an index is provided to the text of the diary, the principal footnotes and the editorial introduction. It does not cover the *Companion* (volume X) which is designed to be in most respects self-indexing.

References to everyday or recurrent events, such as attendance at the office or at church, are not indexed if Pepys makes no more than a passing mention of them. Other omissions are indicated in the head-notes to the entries, and in this preface under *Places*.

An attempt has been made to avoid excessive use of that bane of indexes – the unbroken run of numerals. In avoiding that extreme I may have been guilty of using more words than is usual in an index. This has often been necessary for the sake of clarity. It has also been due to an attempt to catch something of the diary's flavour – hence the use of Pepys's own phrases where briefer ones could easily have been substituted. Here and there, as in the entry on the diary itself, it is hoped there are passages which will not only serve the reader who is looking for references but may also give pleasure to the reader who wants to browse.

Persons

Where the diary is the only authority for the spelling of a surname it appears in that form. In other cases it is spelt in the form used, or used most often, by its owner (if that is known), or in the standard books of reference, with Pepys's spelling (if substantially different) added in brackets. Occasionally, as with Will Hewer, all Pepys's variants are recorded.

Brief identifications are added in many cases, and are always given – if the information is available – in those cases where no identification is given either in the footnotes to the text or in the *Companion*.

The longer entries are divided into sections and sub-sections arranged in logical rather than alphabetical order. Thus the section 'misc[ellaneous]' may come last, and that on 'public affairs' may precede that on 'private life'. Within the sections and sub-sections the order in which the references are given is usually that of the diary, though occasionally a thematic order has seemed preferable. 'Social' is a subject-category borrowed from Dr de Beer's index to Evelyn – a model to all indexers. Pepys's sociability gives the category a special value, but it should be added that its use is limited to those occasions about which he reports nothing beyond the social encounter itself. If he has at those points a statement about any other subject, the reference is omitted from 'social' and entered under another heading such as 'news from' or 'business with'. Where he records, as he so often does, what was eaten or drunk on those occasions the reference is repeated in the entries 'Food' and 'Drink'.

The treatment of Pepys and his wife has called for special measures. A small number of references to Pepys has been gathered under his name, covering events before the diary period. For the rest it has been taken for granted that the diarist is himself the subject of his diary. References to him are therefore distributed throughout the index. Some entries (e.g. 'Clerk of the Acts') are devoted exclusively to him; others such as 'Dress' include references to him which are signalled by a prefatory '(P)'; while certain large subjects have two distinct entries – e.g. 'Tangier' and 'Tangier (P)'. A list of the principal entries relating directly to Pepys is given below at page xiii.

A different policy has suggested itself for his wife. She is indexed for the most part under her name, but other references to her (marked 'EP') are entered elsewhere, principally under the subjects to which cross-references are given in the headnote to her entry.

It is probable that the index, like the diary itself, is unfair to Elizabeth. There are many occasions when Pepys takes his wife's presence for granted and does not accord her a mention.

Places

London and Westminster are treated similarly to Pepys, since – almost as much as Pepys himself – they may be assumed to be omnipresent in the text. Streets, buildings and other places within the two cities are indexed under their names except for those grouped as taverns or theatres. The entries 'London' and 'Westminster' are confined to listing events and corporate affairs.

No attempt is made to include passing references to well-known streets such as the Strand.

Subjects

Many subjects are dealt with under group headings rather than individually. Animals for instance are mostly impounded in a single entry. Similarly with other topics – books, naval stores, pictures, plays, sermons and so on. The longer lists of items are usually arranged alphabetically; the shorter ones in the order of their appearance in the diary. In the case of certain subjects (books, prices, plays, ships, taverns) some editorial information (specified in the headnotes) has been added.

Extensive use has been made of subject-entries in order to make accessible the mass of information which the diary contains, even though in many instances this involves the repetition of material to be found elsewhere in the index under other entries. 'Parliament' and 'Privy Council' for instance carry many of the references given in 'Navy' and 'Navy Board'.

Format

The form of reference to volume- and page-numbers, different from that used elsewhere in this edition, has been chosen as the most convenient for note-taking.

Asterisks and daggers are occasionally added to the references to convey editorial information. Their meaning is explained in the head-notes.

The sub-heading 'also' is used for minor but substantive references, and is distinct from 'alluded to' which introduces passing mentions only.

The tilde (~) indicates material tangential to the main subject of the entry – in the case of persons, often a servant or relative.

PRINCIPAL INDEX ENTRIES CONCERNING PEPYS

ACKNOWLEDGEMENTS

My wife Linnet has shared in the making of this Index. I laid down the ground plan, but she involved herself in every process of its construction. She read aloud the entire text of the diary while I took notes – discussing with me, as we went along, exactly what words might best introduce the successive groups of references, and thus converting what might have been a chore into a paper-game. At later stages she undertook innumerable investigations into detail, and checked from the text every reference in the typescript.

My thanks are also due to David and Susan Yaxley who, once the ground plan had been established, read the whole of the diary text and compiled index slips in draft which I found useful as a basis for my own slip-notes.

Various scholars have contributed to parts of the Index. There are several subjects which it would have been impossible to index adequately without the information which only experts can provide. The entry 'Health', for instance, is at some points organised around diagnoses made by Dr C. E. Newman. Similarly Professor W. A. Armstrong helped with 'Theatre', Professor Kerry Downes with 'Whitehall Palace', Professor A. Rupert Hall with 'Science', Dr Richard Luckett with 'Music' and Mr J. L. Nevinson with 'Dress'. The entry 'Prices' is based on a study made by Hugh Walton. I thank them all.

My publisher's editor, Mary Butler, and her assistant Elizabeth Brooke-Smith, have been a tower of strength in the preparation of the book for the press, and have been quick to lighten my task in every way they could.

Once again I express my warmest thanks to Mary Coleman who has typed the manuscript and (with her colleague Aude Fitzsimons) has undertaken much of the checking. I cannot believe that there are many as fortunate as I in having secretarial help of such quality.

Robert Latham

'A man may think a place is missing, when it is only put in another place.'

PEPYS, 8 JUNE 1663 (on Newman's *A Concordance to the Holy Scriptures*)

INDEX

& n. 3; his ships aground off Gibraltar, 6/8 & n. 3, 12; attacks Dutch fleet off Cadiz, 6/13–14 & n., 19; returns to Portland, 6/62 & n. 4; made Rear-Admiral, 6/147; on *Royal James*, 6/287; dispute about pay, 7/93–4 & n.; and about chaplain's groats, 7/97 & n. 1; neglected by Albemarle, 7/178; captures Dutch merchantman, 7/249, 255; complains of Rupert's misgovernment of fleet, 7/332; presses men for winter voyage, 7/355; elected Elder Brother, Trinity House, 7/382; ill, ib.; to be 'land-admiral' at Plymouth, 8/149; engagement with La Roche, 9/96–7 & n.; low reputation in Mediterranean, 9/137; Tangier voyage, 9/272, 274, 427–8 & n.; victuals sent to, 9/382; concludes peace with Algiers Feb. 1669, 9/473 & n. 1; returns, 9/508, 510 & n. 3; to be sent back, 9/513 & n. 2; discusses policy towards Algiers, 9/516; said to be P's enemy, 9/529
SOCIAL: 4/4, 53, 340; 8/140; 9/544, 563
MISC.: house, 4/405; coach, 8/479
ALLUDED TO: 9/276

ALPS, the: 9/206

ALSOP, [Josias], Rector of St Clement Eastcheap 1660–6: preaches, 2/219

ALSOP, [Timothy], brewer to the King: anecdote by, 4/156; court gossip from, 5/56–61 & nn.; victualling contract, 5/196, 199, 204, 210; illness and death, 5/217–18, 221, 223, 224; social: 5/195

AMEIXIAL, battle of: 4/198 & n. 2, 202–3, 215 & n. 1, 220

AMERICA: *see* New England, New Netherland

AMSTERDAM: city gives yacht to Charles II, 1/222 & n. 1; plague in, 4/340 & n. 2, 358; 5/142; quarantine on ships from, 4/399 & n. 2; comet reported, 5/134 & n. 1; bank, 7/252 & n. 4; burgomaster, 8/68; propose cession, 8/108

ANABAPTISTS [*see also* Fanatics]: dismissed from fleet, 1/101, 109 & n. 2; elected to Parliament for London, 2/57 & n. 1 [error]

ANDERSON, Charles, physician, P's contemporary at Magdalene: 1/149–

50; 2/103; ~ his brother, 1/90

ANDREW(S), John, steward to Lord Crew: transactions with P, 1/4, 32, 43, 64, 95; alluded to: 1/313

ANDREWS, John, timber-merchant, Bow: pessimistic about public affairs, 8/377; musical: 6/324–5; 7/422; social: 7/421; 8/483

ANDREWS, ——, wife of the foregoing: expecting child, 6/325; social: 7/421–2; 8/483

ANDREWS, Matt, coachman to Lord Crew: social, 1/18

ANDREWS, [Thomas], merchant, of St Olave's parish: contract for Tangier victualling, 5/223, 226, 236, 263; 6/37, 85, 86, 139, 193, 337; discusses Tangier business with P/Povey, 6/38, 97–8, 105, 130, 185, 201(2); gifts to P, 6/57, 202, 251, 337; accounts, 6/201, 202; in country during Plague, 6/185; P's regard, 6/201–4 passim; to resign victualling to Gauden, 6/203–4, 226–7, 251; receives sacrament, 6/210; also, 8/205; musical: sings, 5/120, 194, 199, 209, 217, 226, 325, 332, 337, 342, 349; 6/24, 27, 32, 39, 44, 55, 73, 80, 88, 98, 125, 131, 219; social: 6/62, 86, 210; 7/413; 8/64, 377; 9/220, 404; ~ his wife [Hester], 5/342; 9/220, 404; his son, 9/404

ANGEL, [Edward], actor: 9/85 & n. 5

ANGIER, John, sen., tailor, P's cousin, of Cambridge: drinks King's health, 1/67; EP visits, 2/180; asks for place, 4/363–4, 409; bankrupt, 4/439; social: 1/69; 2/89; 3/217, 218; alluded to: 2/136; 4/409; ~ his wife, 2/89; 4/430

ANGIER, John, jun.: asks for place, 4/178, 363; to be sent to sea, 4/409; a rogue, 4/439; death, 5/291

ANGIER, Percival, P's cousin, of London: at East India House, 4/384 & n. 4; burial, 6/16; social: 4/364

ANGLESEY, Earl of: *see* Annesley

ANIMALS [For domestic animals and household pets, *see* Household etc.; and under names of owners. Horses are principally indexed under Travel (road). *See also* Entertainments; Games etc.]:
GENERAL: menagerie at Tower, ?1/15 & n. 2; 3/76 & n. 2; noises made by

animals in Rochester, 8/313; P's dislike of cruelty to, 9/154, 203; theories of generation, 2/105 & n. 4, 160
PARTICULAR: baboon [?chimpanzee; gorilla]: from Guinea, 2/160 & n. 3; bears: in Baltic, 4/413; boars: in Baltic, 4/413; bulls: 2/209 & n. 2; 7/245–6; cat(s): P/EP's, 1/325; 8/553; experiments on, 6/95–6; survives Fire, 7/277; colt: allegedly mistaken for sturgeon, 8/232–3 & n.; cows and calves: 3/221 & n. 2; 6/179; deer: in Baltic, 4/413; hunting terms, 8/475; dogs: P tempted to steal, 2/149; kill child, 3/205; P chased/frightened by, 4/131; 7/26; experiments on, 5/151; 6/57, 84; 7/370–1 & n., 373, 389; 9/263 & n. 1; guard dogs, 7/133 & n. 1; sheepdog, 8/339; elephant: hunting of in Siam, 7/251; foxes: hunting of in Baltic, 4/413; frogs: 2/105; horses: manège, 4/120; kidney stones, 4/146; staggers, 8/390; Royal Mews, 5/70–1; performing, 9/297, 301; kitten: experiment on, 6/64; lions: ?1/15 & n. 2; monkeys: performing, 2/166; 4/298; snakes: story of, 3/22 & n. 2; sow, Hamburg: alluded to, 9/420; toad: in drink, 7/290; whale: skeletal remains of, 1/150 & n. 2; fished off Greenland, 4/125; wolves: in Baltic, 4/413
ANJOU, Duc d': *see* Philippe
ANNE of Austria, wife of Louis XIII of France (d. 1666): Bristol's intrigues with, against Mazarin, 4/212 & n. 1
ANNE (b. Hyde), Duchess of York (d. 1671):
PERSONAL: plain, 2/80; proud and extravagant, 3/64; 8/286–7; 9/38; dress, 6/172; portraits by Lely, 3/112–13 & n.; 7/82 & n. 1; her 'silly devotions', 9/164
CHRON. SERIES: birthplace, 6/198 & n. 1; to visit Portsmouth, 4/24; jealous of Monmouth, 4/138; Western progress, 4/321; ill, 4/436, 439; 5/4; to visit Harwich, 6/104; effect of Clarendon's fall on, 8/424, 506; 9/11, 153; reconciled to Coventry, 9/336, 342; receives French ambassador, 9/284; favours French alliance, 9/536;

friendly with Lady Castlemaine, 9/417
MARRIAGE AND FAMILY: marriage, 2/40–1 & n.; also, 1/275, 315, 319, 320; 2/1; 7/261, 354; birth of son, Charles, Duke of Cambridge, 1/260–1, 273; his death, 2/95; death of daughter Princess Mary, 3/75; of son, James, Duke of Cambridge, 4/229; about to lie in, 6/19; birth of son, Charles, Duke of Kendal, 7/201 & n. 2; of son, Edgar, Duke of Cambridge, 8/436 & n. 2; death of grandmother, 2/213; and of mother, 8/570; jealousy, 3/248; dalliance with husband, 4/4; love affairs, 6/302 & n. 1; 7/8, 323; said to have poisoned Lady Denham, 8/8; and (with children) to have pox, 9/154–5 & n.; domineers over husband, 9/342
HOUSEHOLD: maids of honour, 6/41
SOCIAL: at theatre, 2/80, 164; 7/347; 8/167; gives play at court, 7/325; attends Feast at Inner Temple, 2/155; at Durdans, 3/184; Whitehall chapel, 3/42; 9/163–4; Somerset House, 3/191; 5/300; ball at Whitehall, 3/300–1; 7/372; dines in public, 4/407; 8/161; at court lottery, 5/214; in state at Whitehall, 8/33; plays cards on Sunday, 8/70; at Hinchingbrooke's wedding, 9/51; at Deptford party, 9/468–9
ALLUDED TO: 9/344, 407
ANNESLEY (Anslow), Arthur, cr. Earl of Anglesey 1661, politician and Treasurer of the Navy:
CHARACTER: 5/336; 8/301, 327
CHRON. SERIES: appointed to Privy Council, 1/171; opposes motion in Commons to reward Sandwich, 1/178; chairs Council's Admiralty Committee, 5/319; 6/45; at Fishery Committee, 5/336; at Privy Council/Council committees, 8/278, 291; pessimistic about war, 8/288, 291; (untrue) rumour of appointment to Treasury commission, 8/367; manager of conference between Houses, 8/551 & n. 4, 561; rumoured dismissal from Council, 8/571, 596, 600; views on issues in Skinner v. E. India Company, 9/196 & nn.
AS TREASURER OF THE NAVY: appoint-

ment, 8/295 & n. 3, 297, 301, 322;
attends Board, 8/327; 9/39, 196;
anxious to learn from P, 8/334; his
allowance, 8/334-5 & n., 378;
proposals for paying-off fleet, 8/397,
456, 567, 571; active in sale of prize
ships, 8/484; rumoured dismissal,
9/10; promises reforms, ib.; annoys
Duke of York, 9/253, 256, 310;
criticises P, 9/244, 295, 306 & n. 1,
308; 'suspended and discharged',
9/340-1 & n., 346 & n. 3, 357; resists
order, 9/341, 342-3, 344-5, 416;
petitions King, 9/351, 362 & n. 1;
Board's complaints of, 9/428; unspecified business, 8/462; also, 9/42,
67 & n. 3
POLITICAL NEWS FROM: 8/375, 555, 561,
565; 9/8-9, 25, 323
ALLUDED TO: 1/66; 9/145, 209
ANNIS, [Robert], workman, Woolwich yard: to be tried for embezzlement, 3/137 & n. 2
ANSLEY (Annesley), Capt. [Abra-
ham]: appointed Master-Attendant,
Deptford, 9/441 & n. 1
ANSLOW: see Annesley
ANTIGUA, Leeward Is.: captured by
French, 8/38 & n. 1
ANTRIM, Earl of: see Macdonell
ANTWERP: 9/396
APPLEYARD, ——, of Huntingdon:
9/224
APPRENTICES: riots/demonstra-
tions, 1/39 & n. 1, 54; 5/99-100 & n.,
101; 9/129-30 & n., 132, 133, 152 &
n. 2; church attendance, 3/194; in
good seats at theatre, 9/2; affray in
Moorfields between Weavers and
Butchers, 5/222-3 & n.; hard life of
apprentice fisher-boy, 6/241-2
APSLEY, Sir Allen, M.P. Thetford,
Norf.: reports news of battle of
Ameixial, 4/215 & n. 1; drunken
speech in Parliament, 7/416; establish-
ment as Master-Falconer reduced,
8/394-5 & n.; alluded to: 7/73
APSLEY, Sir Anthony [recte Sir
Allen]: 7/73
APSLEY (Appesley), Col. [John]:
accused of forgery, 3/43-4
ARCHANGEL: hemp from, 4/175,
394; map of river, 4/390

ARCHER, Betty, sister of Mary:
admired by P as undergraduate, 2/220
ARCHER, Mary, of Bourn, Cambs.,
later wife of Clement Sankey: at
theatre, 2/220 & n. 4, 226; her portion, 2/220; alluded to: 2/225; ~ her
uncle's house, 2/220
ARCHES, Court of: see Justice,
administration of
ARCHITECTURE, P's taste in [aste-
risks denote the occasions when he
makes a descriptive comment]: admires Audley End House, 1/69-70*;
8/467-8*; disappointed with alterations at Hinchingbrooke, 3/220*;
with Old Wanstead House, 6/102*
& n. 4; and Wilton, 9/230*; admires
Gauden's house at Clapham, 4/244*;
Wricklemarsh, 6/94* & n. 3; Swakeleys, 6/215*; Dagnams, 6/159; Clarendon House, 7/32* & n. 2, 42*; Sir
P. Warwick's new house, 7/64;
Bridewell, 8/6; Belasyse's new house,
9/202; and Goring House, 9/276
ARGIER(S): see Algiers
ARITHMETIC: see Science and mathematics
ARMADA, Spanish [see also Navy,
Royal]: 3/187; alluded to: 8/293
ARMIGER, [William], relation of P:
in pre-coronation procession, 2/82;
attempts to court EP, 2/208; lodges
with Tom P, 3/6; 4/183; social: 1/54,
88; 2/43, 53, 60; ~ his son, 5/71
ARMORER, ——, [? the following]:
claims to have enjoyed favours of
Duchess of York, 4/138
ARMOURER, [?Sir   Nicholas],
Equerry of the Great Horse to the
King: in drunken frolic, 8/446-7 & n.
ARMY [For P's service in, see Mount-
agu, E., 1st Earl of Sandwich.
See also Commonwealth; Militia;
Tangier]:
CHRON. SERIES: Lifeguards routed in
Venner's rising, 2/10; troops sent to
Portugal, 3/48, 63; their conduct in
campaign, 4/215 & nn.; Guards quell
riots by seamen, 7/416; 8/28; by
apprentices, 9/129, 130, 132; blow up
houses in Fire, 7/269; regiments raised
against invasion threats, 7/395; 8/265;
troops moved to Portsmouth and

Portuguese money, 3/102, 103, 114, 115

BUSINESS WITH GOVERNMENT: in Flanders, 6/149–50 & n., 155, 163, 165, 171, 322–3; creditors create difficulties, 6/149–50, 151, 165; is confident of King's backing, 7/215 & n. 2; survives run on banks in Medway crisis, 8/263, 528–9; pays Swedish envoys at Breda, 8/528

HIS NEWS/OPINIONS: on new coinage, 4/396; prospects of war, 5/134; announces Peace of Breda on Exchange, 8/328

PRIVATE AFFAIRS ETC.: new buildings in Lombard St, 4/214 & n. 3; 9/517 & n. 1; buys estate near Brampton, 9/185 & n. 2; new house in London, 9/517 & n. 1; health, 8/557

SOCIAL: 2/119; 3/200; 9/21, 400, 560

BACKWELL, [Mary], wife of Edward: P's admiration, 3/94, 114; 9/21, 185 & n. 2, 400; at St Olave's, 9/508, 514, 555; pride, 9/517; ~ her mother, 9/508, 514

BACON, Capt. [Philemon], naval officer: killed in action, 7/148, 154

BADILEY (Boddily, Bodilaw), Capt. [William], Master-Attendant, Deptford: sale of stores, 2/45; 4/319; narrowly escapes death, 3/173

BAGG, Frank: 2/193–4

BAGSHOT, Berks.: King hunts at, 8/444; 9/302

BAGWELL, [William], ship's carpenter, Deptford: welcomes P's visits, 4/233–4; 5/351; asks for place, 4/266; 5/163, 302; on *Providence*, 7/176; returns to fleet, 7/189, 282; master-carpenter of *Rupert*, 8/39 & n. 1, 95; ~ his father, 6/189; mother, 6/201; 9/469

BAGWELL, ——, wife of William: her good looks, 4/222; P plans to seduce, 4/222, 266; visits, 4/233–4; finds her virtuous, 4/234; and modest, 5/163; asks P for place for husband, 5/65–6, 163; P kisses, 5/287; she grows affectionate, 5/301–2; he caresses, 5/313; she visits him, 5/316, 339; her resistance collapses in alehouse, 5/322; amorous encounters with: at her house, 5/350–1; 6/40, 162, 189,

201, 253, 294; 7/166, 284, 285; 8/39, 95; 9/221; Navy Office, 6/186; 7/351, 380; tavern, 6/20; assignations frustrated, 9/25, 217; P's valentine, 6/35, 226, 294; asks for promotion for husband, 6/39–40; P strains a finger, 6/40; she returns from Portsmouth, 7/96; has sore face, 7/191; returns from Harwich, 9/12, 25; also, 6/158; 7/96, 210, 339; 8/99; ~ servant dies of plague, 7/166

BAILEY, [Francis], shipbuilder: *see* Baylie

BAINES, [Jeremy], P's schoolfellow at St Paul's: 'a great nonconformist', 5/37 & n. 4

BAKER (Barker), Capt. [Richard], Excise Commissioner: 1/14–15 & n.

BAKER, [Roger], purser: dispute with commander, 9/505 & n. 1

BALDOCK (Baldwick), Herts.: P overnight at, 2/148–9; visits church, 2/148 & n. 1; and fair, 2/183 & n. 6; increase of Quakers, 2/149 & n. 1; also, 4/314; 8/475

BALES: *see* Bayles

BALL, Capt. [?Andrew], naval officer: in Four Days Fight, 7/288

'BALL', Betty, actress: *see* Hall, Betty

BALL, [John], Treasurer to the London Commissioners of Excise: proposed as Treasurer for Tangier, 6/94 & n. 1; business with P, 6/130; 8/331; political news from, 8/410; dismissed, 8/557 & n. 3; 9/110; deplores state of country, 9/120; social: 9/331

BALL (Bell), Capt. [?Naphthali], naval officer: in Four Days Fight, 7/150; news from, 7/288

BALL, Sir Peter, Attorney-General to the Queen Mother: Brampton business, 2/28 & n. 2; 3/102, 176 & n. 3; also, 8/22

BALL, Dr Richard, Master of the Temple: preaches at St Gregory's, 3/252 & n. 2; anecdotes of sermons, 9/505–6 & n.

BALLADS [*see* Music: Songs; Musical Compositions]: on Rump, 1/114 & n. 2; 'To all you ladies', 6/2 & n. 1; on Albemarle, 8/99 & n. 2; Arthur of Bradley, 9/460 & n. 5

BALLAST OFFICE: 1/296 & n. 2

BALLOW (Ballard), [Stephen], leather seller: 4/265 & n. 1; ~ his wife, ib.

BALTIC, the (the Sound): convoys, 1/102; 6/328, 331; Sandwich in (1659), 1/141, 180, 285; 4/69 & n. 2; P in (1659), 1/285; 2/185 & n. 5; fishing through ice, 4/412; ships from, 6/202, 248

BALUE, Cardinal [Jean], (d. 1491): death, 9/256 & n. 2

BANBURY, Oxon.: Tom P visits, 3/176, 213; Coventry to take waters, 9/258 & n. 2

BANCKERT, Adriaen, Dutch naval commander: sails north, 6/133 & n. 2; brings fleet home, 6/146; ship burnt in action, 7/229 & n. 5

BANES, [J.]: see Baines

BANES, [? Robert]: on *Naseby*, 1/99 & n. 1

BANISTER, John, court musician: to play at Mitre, 1/25 & n. 4; airs by, 7/171; replaced at court, 8/73 & n. 3; plays theorbo, 9/138; teaches song to Knepp, 9/189; writes out song for P, ib.; also, 9/134, 175

BANISTER, ——: 7/246

BANKER(T): see Banckert

BANKS, Sir John, merchant: his wisdom, 7/24; praises Cromwell, 5/52 & n. 1; advises P on victualling, 6/265; (unspecified) Tangier business, 7/24, 132; report on Dutch raid, 7/162; views on Exchequer as bank, 8/132; complains of Navy Board's debts, 9/149 & n. 2; political views, 9/399; house near Aylesford, 9/495–6 & n.; also, 9/497, 562

BANKS and bankers [*see also* Amsterdam; Backwell, E.; Colvill, J.; Finances (P); Vyner, Sir R.]: loans to government, 3/297 & n. 2; 4/17; King controlled by, 4/176; P's business with, 6/193, 332; 7/195, 196; at risk under monarchy, 7/252; reluctant to lend to government, 6/133, 311; 8/143, 591; Exchequer as bank, 8/131–2 & n.; Treasury's/Downing's hostility, 8/230, 240 & n. 2; run on during invasion scare, 8/263, 270, 275–6, 285, 450; proclamation in their support, 8/285 & n. 3

BANKSIDE [*see also* Taverns etc.:

Falcon]: plague burials at, 6/213; alluded to: 2/114; 7/271

BANNESTER, Bannister: see Banister

BANSTEAD DOWNS, Surrey: horse races and footraces, 4/160 & n. 5, 243, 255

BANTAM, Java: 6/36 & n. 1

BAPTISTA: see Draghi

BAPTISTE: see Musical Compositions: Lully, J.-B.

BARBADOS, W. Indies: attack on St Kitt's from, 7/390 & n. 3, 391; naval action off, 8/430; fire at Bridgetown, 9/243 & n. 2; also, 8/275, 374

BARBARY COMPANY: see Royal African Company

BARBER, [John], purser: 2/207

BARBER: see Barbour

BARBER-SURGEONS' COMPANY: see London: livery companies

BARBER-SURGEONS' HALL, Monkwell St: rebuilding after Fire, 9/292 & n. 5

BARBON (Barebone), Praisegod, republican: petitions Parliament, 1/51 & n. 3; windows broken, 1/54 & n. 4, 65

BARBOUR, [William], clerk in the Navy Office: asks for place, 7/345–6 & n.; news from, 8/280

BARCKMANN, Sir Johan, Baron Leijonbergh, Swedish Resident 1661–72, Envoy 1672–91 (d. 1691): dispute about prizes, 8/21–2 & n., 23, 123 & n. 1, 135–6; his house, 8/22 & n. 1; perspective painting, 9/352; ~ his wife, 7/372; his secretary, 8/23

BARCROFT, [John], Serjeant-at-Arms: 8/86 & n. 3, 92–3 & n.

BARDSEY: see Bawdsey

BAREBONE: see Barbon

BARKELY: see Berkeley

BARKER: see Baker

BARKER, Ald. [William], Baltic merchant: hemp recommended by Batten, 3/155, 157; stories of Baltic, 4/413; at Apposition Day, St Paul's School, 5/37; on hemp trade, 5/63; dispute with Ormond, 8/404, 407, 420 & n. 2; 9/119

BARKER, ——, companion to EP: kinswoman to Fauconberg, 6/235 & n. 4; homely appearance, 6/235;

7/319, 327; improved by good clothes, 7/329; to replace Mercer, 7/299, 303, 304, 314, 319; dismissed, 8/212; musical: P admires her singing, 6/235; 8/165; out of practice, 7/299, 319; learns *It is decreed*, 7/420; 8/36, 50, 54, 142; sings with P/EP, 8/49, 97, 157; learns part-song, 8/113; social: accompanies EP on visits, etc., 7/329, 335, 351, 373; 8/37, 72, 158, 165, 202, 206; runs for wagers, 8/167; alluded to: 7/422

BARKING, Essex: timber shipped from, 3/170

BARKING CHURCH: *see* All Hallows

BARKING CREEK, Essex: ships sunk in, 8/263

BARKSTEAD, John, regicide: arrested, 3/45 & n. 1, 47; hanged, 3/66; treasure allegedly buried in Tower, 3/240–1 & n., 246, 248, 250; the search for, 3/240–2, 244, 250–1

BARKWAY, Herts.: P at, 2/146

BARLOW, [Thomas], former Clerk of the Acts: claims the office, 1/188 & n. 2–193 passim, 198; 2/55 & n. 2; agrees to annuity in compensation, 1/202 & n. 1, 205, 206; annuity paid, 1/305; 2/22, 103; 4/22, 232; P enquires about health, 2/55; supports P's claim to draft contracts, 3/100; gift to Sandwich, 4/323, 397; death, 6/33; payments to executors, 7/40; also, 4/96 & n. 4

BARNARDISTON (Barmston), [George], P's relative, of Cottenham, Cambs.: 8/466 & n. 2

BARNARDISTON (Bernardiston), Sir Samuel: arraigned before House of Lords, 9/192–3 & n.

BARNARD'S INN GATE, Holborn: 8/245

BARN ELMS, Surrey: P/EP visit(s), 7/235; 8/188, 202, 236, 256, 346, 400; 9/128, 271; duel, 9/27

BARNES, [William], of Cottenham, Cambs.: proposed as match for Paulina P, 8/261 & n. 2

BARNET, Herts.: rebels at, 2/8; P and others take waters, 5/200–1; 8/380–2; other visits, 5/64, 233, 299; 7/127; 8/475; 9/224; Red Lion, 5/299; 8/381

BARNET HILL, Herts.: 5/64

BARNETT, Mrs ——, shopkeeper, New Exchange: 9/534; ~ her assistant Betty, 9/534; ? also, 9/263, 511

BARNWELL, Robert, Sandwich's steward: ill, 1/205, 207; 2/3; to see coronation, 2/75; shows P alterations to Hinchingbrooke, 2/183; dies owing money to Sandwich, 3/101, 116; social: 2/135, 183

BARNWELL ABBEY, Cambridge: P visits, 9/213 & n. 1

BARON, Lt-Col. [Benjamin]: news from, 2/58 & n. 5; at Lord Mayor's banquet, 4/354; on Turkish government, 5/30; account of travel in Asia, 5/34

BARON, [Hartgill], clerk in the Privy Seal Office: dispute about clerkship, 1/207 & n. 2, 208, 211, 235, 236; month's service in office, 1/212; fees, 1/247

BARR, Peter, merchant: gift of wine to P, 7/175 & n. 2

BARROW, [Philip], storekeeper, Chatham: efficiency, 4/149; 6/183; discusses faults of yard, 3/154; quarrels with Clerk of Cheque, 3/155; criticises Batten, 4/134; Batten's enmity, 4/149; differences with colleagues, 4/149 & n. 2; 6/183; at launch, 4/225; and muster, 4/228; to visit Isle of Man, 4/240; threatens to resign, 5/5 & n. 1; grievances, 5/47, 50; sends P oysters, 5/88; house, 3/156; and 'antiquities', 4/225; social: 3/153; ~ his niece, 4/225

BARTHOLOMEW FAIR: *see* Entertainments; Fairs and Markets

BARTLET, Nick, servant to Sandwich: 1/33

BARTLET: *see* Berkeley

BARTON, ——, of Brampton, Hunts.: 2/204, n. 2, 205; 3/221, 286–7; 5/298

BARWELL, [John], saddler to the King: social: 3/172; 5/202; ~ his wife, 3/172; her maid, ib.

BASINGHALL ST: plague, 6/144

BASSETT, Sir Arthur, soldier: with Tangier garrison, 5/176 & n. 3; 9/272

BASSUM, John, servant to P's father: P's boyhood memory of, 9/3

wharf, 4/284; ~ almost drowned near Portsmouth, 3/253–4

FINANCIAL BUSINESS: at pays at Treasury Office, 2/227; 4/2, 291–2 & n.; 7/332; works on Treasurer's accounts, 3/240; 5/318; and Creed's, 3/279; 4/11; on commanders' pay, 4/7; also, 6/72; 7/314, 374; 8/20, 200, 274, 510

JUDICIAL BUSINESS: in Field's case, 3/280–1; 4/171, 172, 350, 421–2; at Court of Admiralty, 4/76

OTHER BUSINESS: visits wrecks, 1/313; 6/54; attends launches, 4/102–3; 5/307; visits ships, 4/203–4 & n.; 6/193–4; 7/352; arranges weighing-up of, 8/266, 325; buys Commonwealth arms, 2/69 & n. 2; has Commonwealth figurehead burnt, 4/418 & n. 2, 420–1; angered by pacifist sermon, 2/37; assaulted by seamen, 6/288; abused by seaman's wife, 8/268; part in Carkesse's dismissal, 8/60, 76, 100, 109, 146, 213, 215, 238, 385; unspecified: 1/239, 243, 253; 2/40, 206; 3/21, 22, 24, 62, 101, 146, 203, 229, 272; 4/4, 31, 43, 61, 177, 222, 243, 278, 322, 338; 5/138, 156, 156–7, 274, 299, 342; 6/13, 19, 98, 145, 222; 7/12, 105, 107–8, 115, 162; 8/25, 142, 181, 186, 278

PERQUISITES AND PROFITS [see also Reputation]: chest of drawers from ropemaker, 3/197; granted lighthouse patent, 5/314; 6/3 & n. 4; fails to obtain place in Prize Office, 5/322, 327, 328, 333; buys ketch, 7/105–6; given share in privateer (Flying Greyhound), 7/299, 300–1 & n.; her voyages and prizes, 7/316, 418, 424; 8/1, 8, 17, 180, 344, 349, 351–2, 369, 441–2; dispute with Swedish Resident about prizes, 8/21–2, 23, 27, 128, 130, 135, 135–6, 169; to become sole owner, 8/112; buys out P, 8/341, 385, 462; 9/119; alleged favour to crew, 9/99

RELATIONS WITH COLLEAGUES AND ASSOCIATES: with P: mutually critical, 3/59, 64, 145; 6/92; quarrel about warrants, 3/163–4; mate's appointment, 4/110; contracts, 5/115–16; 7/358–9; supplies, 5/157, 238; un-

specified quarrels, 5/118; 7/232; ally in Field's case, 4/51–4 passim; and in Carkesse affair, 8/101–2, 105; high opinion of P, 8/419; also, 5/45, 341; 7/36; with others: mutual recrimination over Interregnum careers, 2/65; complains of colleagues' malice, 3/171; relations with Pett, 1/240; 4/53–4; 8/100; Warren, 2/78; 4/437; 5/318; Slingsby, 2/202; Waith and officers of Navy Treasury, 3/29; Carteret, 3/59; Mennes, 3/14, 227; 4/194; 5/235, 293; 6/233, 234; Cox, 4/149; Hewer, 4/337; Commissioner Taylor, 5/326, 350; 6/295; Penn, 6/66; 8/217; Brouncker, 7/410; 8/78, 80, 97, 126

REPUTATION: criticised by P for corruption, 3/145; 4/205, 325; 5/120, 121, 131, 143, 182; 6/298; for corrupt collusion: with hemp merchants, 3/101–2 & n.; flagmakers, 3/148 & n. 3; ropemaker, 3/155 & n. 3, 157; tar merchant, 4/182; Cocke, 4/194, 241, 284; Wood, 4/201; 5/117; Castle, 5/83 & n. 3; and Dr Walker, 8/123; criticised by P for inefficiency, 3/59; 4/2, 97, 98, 113; 5/120; 6/284, 330; 7/359; 8/12, 582; said to be more diligent, 3/174; corruption/inefficiency criticised: by Warren, 3/131; 5/131, 143; Capt. J. Allen, 3/155, 157; Coventry, 4/17, 194–5, 196, 341, 397; 5/169; 7/409; 8/570, 571; Carteret, 4/97; 6/74; P. Pett, 4/98; Barrow, 4/134; Hempson, 5/140–1; C. Pett, 5/109; Waith, 5/155; Gilsthorpe, 8/560, and in 'libel', 7/388

OTHER PUBLIC OFFICES: as M.P.: elected for Rochester, 2/55, 57, 58; attends Commons, 4/58; 6/274–5; Trinity House: defeated in election to Mastership, 3/93; elected, 4/185; rebuilds almshouses, 5/116–17 & n.; claims members' exemption from militia, 6/24–5 & n.; power in, 6/107, 298; unspecified business, 2/26; 3/29; dinners at, 2/4; 3/103, 187, 190; 4/209, 343; at Trinity Monday service, 5/172

NEWS FROM: naval: 6/115, 119; 7/151, 156, 225, 228, 395, 415, 416; 8/350;

BATTS, Capt. [George], naval officer: Coventry's high opinion, 4/196; dismissed by Albemarle, 9/5

BAWDSEY, Suff.: P recalls eating oysters, 1/104

BAXTER, [Nicholas], Equerry of the Great Horse to the Duke of York: shows P Royal Mews, 5/70–1 & n.

BAXTER, Richard, Puritan divine and author (1615–91): to preach farewell sermon, 1/251–2 & n.; preaches at St Anne, Blackfriars, 3/92; P buys *Evangelium Armatum*, 4/111 & n. 4

BAYLES (Bales), Tom, lawyer: 7/383

BAYLIE, [Francis], shipbuilder, Bristol: new ship, 9/235 & n. 1

BAYLIE, Maj. [Matthew], Ordnance officer: 9/468

BAYNARD'S CASTLE: King at, 1/178

BEACH, Richard (later kted), naval commander: highly regarded by Coventry, 4/196; by P, 4/432; in command of *Leopard*, ib.; ~ his attractive wife, ib.

BEALE, [Bartholomew], Auditor of Imprests in the Exchequer, and relative of P: attends funeral, 4/432; house in Salisbury Court, 5/7; accountancy methods, ib.; work as auditor of P's Tangier accounts, 6/15; 8/52, 344; 9/58, 202, 477, 478, 479; house and office in Holborn, 9/477, 478; P tips clerks, 9/479; social: 3/279; 6/68

BEALE, [Charles], Deputy-Clerk of the Patents: issues P's patent as Clerk of the Acts, 1/197, 198, 199

BEALE, [Francis], P's landlord in Axe Yard: P's rent, 1/87; alluded to, 1/249; ~ his wife [Alice], 1/249 & n. 1

BEALE, [Simon], shipbuilder: 1/158

BEALE, Simon, Trumpeter to the King: 1/319; 9/317 & n. 3

BEANE, ——, merchant: 4/10

BEARD (Bird), ——, Huntingdon carrier: 1/87; 2/5, 172

BEAR GARDEN, Southwark: P sees bull-baiting, 7/245–6 & n.; and prize-fights, 8/239 & n. 1, 429, 430; 9/516–17

BEAR GARDEN STAIRS: 8/239

BEAR'S QUAY, nr Billingsgate: P visits granaries, 5/179

BEAR STAIRS [P often refers to the jetty as 'The Bear' or 'The Bear at the Bridge Foot': for the tavern of that name, *see* Taverns etc.]: 1/242; 2/114; 5/197; 9/304, 313

BEAUCHAM(P) (Beecham), [James], goldsmith: sells P tankard, 1/292, 296; serves on jury, 4/171; P consults ib., 4/394

BEAUFORT, Duc de: *see* Vendôme, François de

BEAUMONT, [Joseph], Master of Peterhouse and Canon of Ely: preaches at Whitehall, 6/5 & n. 2

BECKART: *see* Bicker

BECKE, Betty, of Chelsea: reputation, 4/270, 281, 303, 388; affair with Sandwich, 4/270–1, 281, 282, 286, 292, 303, 379, 387–8; 5/173–4; lodging in Axe Yard, 4/392; visits Lady Sandwich, 5/179, 184; P's impressions, 5/179; alluded to: 9/455

BECKE, ——, P's cousin: borrows from P, 1/30; visits London, 2/103

BECKE, Mr ——, father of Betty: at Little Chelsea, 4/160; visits Lady Sandwich, 5/179; alluded to: 4/114

BECKE, Mrs ——, mother of Betty: Sandwich lodges at her house, 4/114, 160, 419; also, 5/179; house described, 4/117; banqueting house, ib., 4/160

[?BECKFORD, Peter; Jamaican planter]: 2/6 & n. 3

BECKFORD, Capt. [Thomas], slop-seller to the navy, kted 1677: refuses to undertake victualling, 6/255 & n. 1; gifts to P, 9/81–2, 405; social: 6/329

BECKINGTON, Som.: P visits, 9/232

BECKMAN, Capt. [Martin], military engineer, kted 1685: map of Tangier, 3/37 & n. 2

BEDELL, [Gabriel], bookseller: 1/85

BEDFORD, Lord: *see* Russell, F.

BEDFORD, Beds.: P's visit and comment, 9/224

BEDLAM: (district): bookseller, 5/14; (hospital): Roger P's children visit, 9/454 & n. 1

BEDNALL, Bednell Green: *see* Bethnal Green

BEE, [Cornelius], stationer: dispute over *Critici Sacri*, 9/259 & n. 2

BEECHAM: *see* Beauchamp

BEESTON, [William], actor: in *?The damoiselles à la mode*, 9/307 & n. 1; reads part in *The Heiress*, 9/436 & n. 1

BELASYSE, Sir Henry, son of the 1st Baron Belasyse; M.P. Grimsby, Lincs, kted 1661: on *Naseby*, 1/130; arrested for manslaughter, 3/34 & n. 2; defence printed, 3/35–6 & n.; in brawl at Lord Oxford's, 4/136; killed in duel, 8/363–4 & n., 377, 384; alluded to: 8/454–5 & n.

BELASYSE (Bella(s)es, Bellassis), John, 1st Baron Belasyse, Governor of Tangier 1665–7; Lord-Lieutenant of E. Riding, Yorks., and Governor of Hull:

AS GOVERNOR OF TANGIER: P's low opinion, 7/130; 8/100, 155; appointed, 6/6–7 & n.; asks for P's support, 6/9; supported by committee, 6/18; instructed in duties, 6/22, 25; attempts to reorganise victualling, 6/105; concerned for own profit, 6/306; 7/99; complains of shortage of money, 7/4; returns from Tangier, 7/129; profits 7/130 & n. 2, 265; anxious to increase garrison, 7/130; bills, 7/174, 264; professes friendship for P, 7/185, 320; dislikes Creed, 7/185; meets Excise Commissioners, 7/190, 191; cheated by Vernatti, 7/264 & n. 2, 338; proposal for payment of garrison, 7/320, 321; accounts, 7/330, 338; 8/22, 32, 52–3, 63, 103; passed by committee, 9/199; examined by Exchequer, 9/202, 429, 529; profits in currency exchange, 9/205; tricks Cholmley, 8/45, 100, 127; criticised in committee, 8/61; to resign or be dismissed, 8/103, 111, 117, 127; resigns to become Captain of Pensioners, 8/154, 160; to purchase navy treasurership (rumour), 8/222; supports P in dispute over paymastership, 9/417; unspecified business, 6/13, 27; 7/164, 417, 423; 9/272

MILITARY CAREER IN YORKSHIRE: stories of Civil War, 6/30–1 & nn.; visits Hull to prepare garrison, 7/185 & n. 1, 193, 266; to go to Yorkshire on militia

business, 8/154–5 & n.; offers P help concerning prize ship, 8/345–6 & n.

POLITICAL/COURT NEWS FROM: 7/342–3; 8/74–5, 155; 9/462, 467–8, 472

PRIVATE AFFAIRS ETC.: lodging in Lincoln's Inn Fields, 6/9, 28; new house [? in Bloomsbury Square], 9/202 & n. 2; pictures, 9/202 & n. 4, 434–5; ~ his wife [Anne], 7/171; 9/537; his daughter, 7/171

BELASYSE, John, son of the 1st Baron Belasyse: arrested for manslaughter, 3/34 & n. 2; defence printed, 3/35–6 & n.

BELASYSE, Mary, Lady Fauconberg, (b. Cromwell),wife of the 2nd Viscount: 2/83 & n. 1; 4/181

BELASYSE, Thomas, 2nd Viscount Fauconberg: at theatre, 4/181

BELL, Capt.: *see* Ball, Capt. [?Naphthali]

BELL (Aunt Bell), Edith, sister of P's father: birth-date, 5/360 & n. 1; dies of plague, 6/314, 342; social: 1/205; 2/141, 172; 4/272; alluded to: 1/11

[BELL, William], Rector of St Sepulchre, Holborn: sermon, 5/347 & n. 4

BELL ALLEY, Westminster: plague deaths, 6/132

BELLAMY, [Robert and Thomas], relatives of P and petty-warrant victuallers: debt owed by Navy Board, 4/374 & n. 2; 6/54, 59, 111

BELLAS(S)ES, Bellassis: *see* Belasyse

BELLS, ringing of [*see also* Music: church]: for Monck, 1/52; arrival of Queen, 3/83; peace with Dutch, 8/399

BELLWOOD, Mr ——, formerly clerk to John Turner, lawyer: conceit, 9/463; news from, 9/465

BELL YARD, Lincoln's Inn Fields: gaming house, 2/211–12

BENCE, Ald. [John]: (untrue) story of wife's death of plague, 6/187

BENCE (Bens), ——, [? the foregoing]: 1/323; 2/220

BENDISH, ——, son of Sir Thomas, distant connection of P: 1/259 & n. 1

BENDY, Mrs ——: 5/130

BENIER (Beneere), Tom, barber: shaves P, 3/108, 233; theatre gossip from, 3/233

BENNET, Sir Henry, cr. Baron

Arlington 1665, Earl 1672; Secretary of State 1662–74:
CHARACTER: 4/47 & n. 1; 8/79 & n. 2
AS SECRETARY OF STATE: appointed, 3/226 & n. 2, 227, 237; in search for treasure in Tower, 3/240–2, 244, 284; examines plotters, 3/241; to send soldiers to fight Fire, 7/269; manages peace negotiations with Dutch, 8/68–9 & n.; influence as Secretary, 8/195; papers examined by Committee on Miscarriages, 8/502 & n. 4; intelligence system criticised in Parliament, 9/74 & n. 2, 82; cabinet meets in his chambers, 9/508, 525; opposes French alliance, 9/536 & n. 2; at Cabinet (business unspecified), 5/317; 8/117; 9/473; also, 4/98–9; 7/311; 8/219–20; 9/346, 462, 491; ~ his clerk, J. Swaddell, 9/172
AS TREASURY COMMISSIONER: appointed, 8/223
NAVAL BUSINESS: regard for P, 6/68; informs Duke of York of attack on Dutch, 6/13–14; transmits King's orders to Navy Board, 6/195; 7/20; serves on prize-court, 8/231; blamed for failure to recall Rupert by express, 7/287; urges on Navy Board need for secrecy, 8/126; suggests *Gazette* publish report on Carkesse, 8/216; severe in examination of Commissioner Pett at Council, 8/278; deals with naval business at cabinet, 9/508, 525; also, 7/202
POLITICAL POSITION AND ALLIANCES: King's confidence in, 3/303; 4/137; 5/56; 9/336; fears Parliament, 7/260–1; 9/360; rumoured appointment as Lord Treasurer, 8/96 & n. 2, 118–19, 120, 195; 9/323; unpopularity, 8/304, 342; promotes careers of protégés, 8/185–6 & n.; patron of Ned Mountagu, 4/47; Clifford, 8/289; 9/205; and Sir T. Littleton, 9/341; relations with Buckingham, 8/330, 342, 597; 9/302, 319, 341, 360, 361, 375, 491; allies with Lady Castlemaine, 3/289; joins faction against Clarendon, 4/115, 224; at odds with Coventry, 9/67, 386, 387, 438; and with Duke of York, 9/319, 375, 417, 491; allies with Sandwich, 4/115;

5/208; 6/276, 277, 291; 7/154; 8/190; promotes his pardon, 7/260; allies with Frances Stuart, 4/366
TANGIER BUSINESS: supports P as Treasurer, 6/61–2, 105–6; and Belasyse's proposal on victualling, 6/105; allegedly bribed, 8/127; consulted by P on victualling, 8/294, 318; helps P with memorandum on Algiers, 9/272; attends committee, 4/75; 8/61, 347; 9/316; unspecified business, 6/166
PRIVATE AFFAIRS: said to be crypto-Catholic, 4/48 & n. 4, 224; attempts to arrange sister's marriage, 4/254 & n. 1; attempts to marry Lady Gould, 5/184; marriage, ib.; 7/203 & n. 2; wealth, 8/96 & n. 2; withdraws money from bankers in invasion scare, 8/274; birthplace at Harlington, 6/216; improvements to Euston Hall, 8/288–9 & n.; London house (Goring House), 9/276 & n. 1; commends Montaigne, 9/120; portrait by Cooper, 9/139
SOCIAL: stories of Spain, 8/79; dances well, 9/120; also, 9/118, 293
BENNET, Isabella, Countess of Arlington, wife of the 1st Earl (b. van Beverweerd): marriage, 7/203 & n. 2; at court ball, 7/372; political connections in Holland, 8/68–9 & n.
BENNET, [?John], mercer, Paternoster Row: P buys cloth from, 7/7; 8/341; in Covent Garden, 7/296 & n. 3; alluded to: 7/173
BENNET, [Thomas], of the Ordnance Office: 9/468
BENNET, 'Lady', brothel-keeper: procuress, 1/250; her establishment, 9/218–19
BENS: see Bence
BENSON, [?Benjamin], a Dutchman: at Wights', 5/19, 27
BENSON, ——: alleged letter about sale of places in navy, 4/170
BENSON'S: see Taverns etc.: Bull Head
BENTLEY, Anne (b. Wight), wife of John: marriage, 4/269; social: 3/14, 173; 4/95
BENTLEY, [John], factor, Norwich: marriage, 4/269
BERCHENSHAW: see Birchensha

BERKELEY, Capt. William, kted
1665, naval commander: emissary in
negotiations with Turks, 4/369–70 &
nn.; account of Algiers, 4/386;
accused of avoiding action in Battle of
Lowestoft, 6/129 & n. 5; serves under
Penn, 6/147; offers marriage to
Lawson's daughter, 6/150; illegally
takes prize-goods from Dutch E.
Indiaman, 6/263; portrait by Lely,
7/102 & n. 3; killed in action, 7/169;
body displayed in The Hague, ib. &
n. 3; alluded to: 6/132
BERKENHEAD (Birkenhead), Sir
John (1617–69): P consults about tax
assessment, 3/283 & n. 5
BERKSHIRE HOUSE, Westminster:
occupied by Clarendon (1666–7),
7/375 & n. 1; 8/93; and by Lady
Castlemaine, 9/190 & n. 3
BERMONDSEY: Jamaica House,
8/167
BERNARD, Sir John, son of the
following; succ. bt. 1666; lawyer, of
Brampton Park, Hunts.: family's
electoral interest in Huntingdon,
1/86–7 & n.; elected M.P., 1/87, n. 1,
99; at Brampton church, 3/220; at
Brampton manorial court, 4/309;
arbitrates in dispute about Robert P's
will, 3/265; influence in Brampton
resented, 8/220 & n. 2; ~ his wife
[Elizabeth], 3/220 & n. 1
BERNARD, Sir Robert, Bt, Serjeant-
at-law, Huntingdon: advises P about
Robert P's will, 2/137, 194–5, 205;
3/220–1; presides over Brampton
manorial court, 3/222–3; 4/308–9;
attends arbitration meeting, 3/276;
distrusted by Sandwich, 3/281; retained by P in dispute with Thomas
P, 4/28; arranges disposal of P's
reversionary interest, 5/36, 44; arranges part-payment of Piggot's debt,
5/149, 158; dismissed from recorder-
ship of Huntingdon, 4/30, 62; interest
in Brampton manor, 4/343; ~ his
wife (Lady Digby), 2/137 & n. 5
BERNARD, William, son of Sir
Robert: social: 2/208, 210, 213–14
BERNARDISTON: see Barnardiston
BERNARD'S INN GATE: see Barnard's Inn Gate

BERTIE (Bertus), [Edward]: on *Nase-
by*, 1/134 & n. 5
BERTIE, Montague, 2nd Earl of
Lindsey (d. 1666): in brawl, 4/136
BERTIE (Bertus), [Robert]: on *Naseby*,
1/134 & n. 5
BEST, Mrs —— (Goody Best), of
Gravesend: 8/313
BETHEL, Capt. [?Slingsby], army
officer: given new commission, 8/265;
social: 2/13
BETHNAL GREEN: P visits, 4/200;
5/132; Sir W. Rider's house, 4/200;
7/272, 282, 283; story of blind beggar,
4/200 & n. 6; naval guns heard,
8/254
BETTERTON, Mary ('Ianthe') (b.
Saunderson); actress, wife of Thomas:
P admires in *The Bondman*, 3/58 &
n. 3; 5/224 & n. 2; *The Duchess of
Malfi*, 3/209 & n. 1; Orrery's *Henry V*,
5/240 & n. 3; and *The Rivals*, 5/335 &
n. 1; marriage to Betterton denied,
3/233 & n. 1; her voice, 5/34; acts in
The valiant Cid, 3/273 & n. 1;
'ordinary' performance in *Mustapha*,
6/73; alluded to: 7/347
BETTERTON (Baterton), Thomas,
actor and dramatist: P admires in
The Bondman, 2/47 & n. 2, 56, 207;
Hamlet, 2/161 & n. 3; 4/162; 9/296;
The Duchess of Malfi, 3/209 & n. 1;
Orrery's *Henry V*, 5/240 & n. 3;
9/256–7; *The Rivals*, 5/335 & n. 1;
and *The mad lover*, 9/453 & n. 2; 'the
best actor in the world', 2/207;
sobriety, 3/233; marriage to Mary
Saunderson denied, ib. & n. 1; in
The valiant Cid, 3/273; compared with
Harris, 4/239; in *Mustapha*, 6/73;
laughs in serious part, 8/421; illness,
8/482, 499, 521; 9/63; returns to stage,
9/256; alluded to: 7/347
BETTON(S), Mrs ——: 7/110
BEVERSHAM, [Robert], grocer, Fenchurch St: P orders sugar from,
6/149; dies of plague, 6/298; ~ his
pretty wife, 6/149, 298
BICKER, family of, Amsterdam:
quarrel with House of Orange, 6/147
& n. 1
BICKERSTAFFE [Charles, later kted],
clerk in the Privy Seal Office: in

dispute about clerkship, 1/207 & n. 2, 208, 235, 236; alluded to: 9/474

BIDDLE, ——: 1/85

BIDDULPH, Ald. Sir Theophilus, merchant of Westcombe, Kent: consulted about site for mast-dock, 5/353; and prevention of plague at Greenwich, 6/206, 211 & n. 5; social: 6/208, 338

BIDE, Ald. [John], brewer, Shoreditch: his ale, 8/389 & n. 2, 399, 443, 485

BIGGLESWADE (Bigglesworth), Beds.: P buys stockings, 2/138; P/EP at, 4/313; 5/233

BIGGS, [Thomas], Fellow of Trinity College, Cambridge: chosen taxor, 3/218 & n. 3

BIGGS, [Abraham], Clerk of the Kitchen to the Duke of York: dismissed, 3/214 & n. 1

BILBAO (Bilbo): convoy to, 1/185

BILL (Bills), Lady [Diana]: 7/329

BILLING, [Edward], Quaker: abused by soldiers, 1/44 & n. 2; denounces Hesilrige, 1/50; criticises clergy, 1/279 & n. 1; warns P of parliamentary critics, 8/349

BILLINGSGATE [see also Taverns etc.: Salutation]: 3/150; 8/39; 9/124

BILLINGSLY, [?Richard]: 1/15

BILLITER LANE [see also Taverns etc.: Ship]: 8/156, 345, 443

BILLOP, [Thomas], clerk to Matthew Wren: 9/287, 370

BIRCH, Jane: see Edwards

BIRCH, Col. John, M.P. 1660–91:
CHRON. SERIES: on parliamentary commission for paying off armed forces (1660–1), 1/227, 228, 229; methods criticised, 1/247 & n. 3, 249, 254; at pays, 1/253–4, 255, 262; proposal for reorganisation of naval administration, 7/304; examines Navy Board accounts, 7/305; distrusted by Coventry, 7/310; proposal for rebuilding city, 8/81; to be given regiment, 8/265; on Committee on Miscarriages, 8/502; opinion of P, 9/44, 76–7, 83; lobbied by officers of Navy Board, 9/83, 86–7; praises Cromwell's secret service, 9/70–1 & n.; defends Board, 9/95–6; also, 8/559–60; 9/162

MISC.: stories of fall in land values, 9/44 & nn. 3, 4; proposed purchase of bishops' land, 9/44–5 & n.; views on episcopacy etc., 9/45–6 & n.

BIRCH, Wayneman (Wayneman, the boy), brother of Jane and servant to P:
CHRON. SERIES: enters P's service, 1/250 & n. 3; P beats for lying, 2/206–7; 4/7–8; fighting, 4/12–13; and general misbehaviour, 3/37–8, 66, 116; 4/109, 193; P angry with, 2/239, 295; 4/186; sent to Brampton, 3/141, 145, 151, 200; EP complains of, 3/184, 199, 206–7; P's father refuses to have again, 4/180; to be dismissed, 3/295, 301–2; 4/67, 113; runs away, 4/193, 194, 202, 205; recaptured and dismissed, 4/220; P refuses to take back, 4/252; to go to Barbados, 4/382 & n. 2

AS SERVANT: learns how to put P to bed, 1/251; escorts P/EP in London etc., 1/270, 278, 304; 2/36, 188; 3/289, 292, 293; carries links, 1/290; 2/214; 3/216; 4/30; runs errands etc., 1/325; 3/103, 241; 4/172–3; livery, 3/47, 50, 54, 77; also, 2/79, 174, 241; 3/105, 260–1, 273; 4/15, 71, 171, 177

SOCIAL: sees pre-coronation procession, 2/83; at Vauxhall, 3/95; on country walks, 3/108; 4/112

BIRCH, William, groom, brother of Wayneman: sent for by P, 3/295; attempts to prevent Wayneman's dismissal, 4/67, 202, 252; dies, 8/340 & n. 2; alluded to: 4/113, 194

BIRCHENSHA (Berchenshaw), [John] musician [see also Books]: gives P lessons in composition, 3/8–9 & n., 10, 16, 19, 34, 35; his 'rules', 3/35 & n. 1, 36–7; 5/174–5 & n.; 6/266, 282–3; helps P to compose songs, 3/27, 34–5, 36, 46; his instrumental music, 5/238; house at Southwark, 3/35

BIRCHIN (Burchin) Lane: 5/105

BIRD, [Theophilus], actor: injured during performance, 3/204

BIRD, Thomas, Rector of Great Munden, Herts.: inscription to, 1/70 & n. 4

BIRD: see Beard

BIRDS [omitting those indexed under

Food]: in St James's Park, 2/157 & n. 1
GENERAL: aviaries, 4/85, 272; 7/182;
8/404
NAMED VARIETIES: blackbird: P's, 4/150,
152; canaries: P's, 2/23; 6/8; cocks
and cockfighting: 2/44; 4/427–8;
9/154; eagle: P's, 5/352; geese: 8/68;
hawks: presented to King by Russian
envoys, 3/268, 297; in Russia, 5/272;
hen: experiment on, 6/84; [mina-
bird]: presented to Duke of York,
5/131–2; nightingales: P hears near
Woolwich, 4/151; 5/130; [?ortolans]:
7/200; parrots: P's, 3/174; also, 2/69;
3/105; 6/60; pigeons: P's at Axe Yard,
1/45, 189; Dr Williams's, 2/176; in
Russia, 5/272; burnt in Fire, 7/268;
sparrow (tame): 7/138; 9/225; starling:
once the King's, 9/99, 208, 209;
swallows: hibernation of, 4/412–13 &
n.; turtle-doves: EP's, 1/232; waterfowl: in St James's Park, 2/157; 3/47;
8/68
BIRKENHEAD: see Berkenhead
BIRTHDAYS: P's, 1/65; 2/42; 3/34;
4/55; 5/62; 6/42; 7/53; 8/77; 9/457;
others', 2/142; 6/285
BISCAY, Bay of: 3/78
BISHOP, Sir 'Edward', recte Richard,
Serjeant-at-Arms: 8/564
BISHOPSGATE: Quaker meeting,
5/285
BISHOPSGATE ST [see also St
Botolph; Taverns etc.: Bull; Great
(Old) James]: harpsichord maker,
2/40, 44; Fire, 7/277–8; house blown
up, 8/119; terminus for Cambridge
coaches, 9/207, 209, 213, 306; alluded
to: 2/26; 7/368
BISHOP'S STORTFORD (Stafford),
Herts.: P at, 8/466–7; 9/209, 213;
Reindeer inn, 8/466–7; 9/209
BLACKBORNE (Blackeburne), [Rob-
ert], Commonwealth Admiralty offi-
cial:
CHRON. SERIES: fears restoration of
King, 1/91; issues P's warrant as
secretary to fleet, 1/94; reports
Restoration imminent, 1/103; advises
P on duties, 1/193; now drinks
healths, 1/263; dealings with P about
Hewer, 2/34, 97; 4/323, 353, 358, 367,
371–2; puritan views, 4/372–7 & nn.;

distrusted by Carteret, 3/5; informs
P of corruption in Navy Treasury,
3/28; sends official papers to Navy
Office, 3/37; low opinion of Penn,
4/375; secretary to E. India Company, 9/410; also, 1/96; 9/485
SOCIAL: 1/173, 174, 211, 213, 268, 301,
303; 2/97
ALLUDED TO: 1/27, 59, 81, 83, 84
~ his wife, 1/213, 215, 217, 218, 227,
268; her kinswoman, 1/227; his
brother, 1/303
BLACKBURY, [Peter], timber merchant: P visits yard, 4/176; consults
about masts, 4/261; also, 3/165; 6/195
BLACKFRIARS: St Anne's Church,
3/92 & n. 1; Fire ruins, 8/6; glasshouse,
9/457 & n. 2
BLACKFRIARS [Stairs]: 1/229
BLACKFRIARS THEATRE: see
Theatres
BLACKHEATH: P drives chariot,
6/213
[BLACK HEATH, Wilts.]: ?9/228 &
n. 4
BLACK LION (mercer's shop), Westminster: 9/454
BLACKE: see Blake
BLACKMAN, Capt. [James], Woolwich: 5/190–1 & n.
BLACKWALL DOCKYARD: P
visits, 5/202; 7/126, 138; 8/84, 124;
new docks, 2/14 & n. 2; petrified
trees, 6/236–7 & n.; Navy Board
plans mast-dock, 5/270; 6/96; prize-
goods to be stored, 6/236; soldiers
embark from, 7/141(3); ships repair-
ing, 8/124, 135; alluded to: 1/280;
3/156
BLAGGE (Blake), [Margaret], Maid of
Honour to the Duchess of York:
9/468 & n. 5
BLAGRAVE, [Thomas], court musician: sobriety, 7/128; P redeems lute
from, 1/91; plays flageolet, 1/180;
pew in Whitehall chapel, 1/313;
3/42; sings, 3/67–8; 5/126, 229, 236,
242; tells P of chapel rules, 5/267;
performance disparaged, 8/529–30;
house, 3/67; 5/107, 126, 229, 242;
recommends Tom Edwards, 5/234;
alluded to: 5/242; ~ his wife, 5/242;
his niece: sings, 3/67–8; 5/126, 242;

proposed as EP's companion, 5/107, 224, 229(2), 230, 236, 242

BLAKE (Blacke), Gen. Robert, military and naval commander (d. 1657): courage, 5/169 & n. 3

BLAKE, Capt. Robert, naval officer (d. 1661): made captain of *Worcester*, 1/109; given command of squadron, 1/119 & n. 3; death and burial, 2/73, 74; also, 1/324; 2/15, 16, 17

BLANCH APPLETON (Blanche Chapiton), Aldgate: 5/18

BLAND, John, merchant, first Mayor of Tangier: P's opinion, 5/266; 9/430; writings on trade and Tangier, 3/157–8 & n.; informs P about mercantile practices, 3/255; 4/10; attends Tangier committee, 4/21, 23; 5/105; foreign news from, 4/198 & n. 2; P acts for in freightage dispute, 4/398, 404 & n. 2, 424, 426; 5/19, 23, 26, 36, 139; provides pieces-of-eight for Tangier, 5/15, 226; in dispute about Portuguese customs dues, 5/43 & n. 2; interest in Tangier victualling, 5/212; anxious for post there, 5/226; at Tangier, 5/265, 270, 287–8, 291; 7/109; dispute with Norwood, 9/392 & n. 1, 430–1 & n.; proposals for civil government of Tangier, 9/430–1; unspecified business, 3/300; 4/13, 14, 18, 198; 5/232; social: 3/188; 4/41, 81, 85, 242; 5/265, 270; ~ his son [Giles], 6/65; his kinswoman: musical, 4/242; 6/28

BLAND, [Sarah], wife of John: her grasp of business, 3/300 & n. 2; 5/266; goes to Tangier, 6/28, 42, 43, 44

BLAND, 'one': 9/175

BLAND, ——, waterman: 9/313

BLANQUEFORT (Blancford, Blancfort, Blanfort): see Duras

BLAYNEY, Edward, 3rd Baron Blayney (d. 1669): commends Montaigne, 9/120

BLAYNEY, [Robert], secretary to Lord Ashley: 9/152

BLAYTON (Payton), [Thomas]: accompanies P to Audley End and Cambridge, 1/66, 68, 69, 71; gift to P on appointment as purser, ?6/190–1; social: 1/210

BLEAU: see Balue

BLENKINSOP, ——: 3/44

BLINKEHORNE, ——, miller, nr Wisbech, Cambs.: 4/311–12

BLIRTON: see Blurton

BLONDEAU, [Pierre], Engineer to the Mint (d. 1672): to introduce improvements, 2/38–9 & n.; stamps for new coinage, 3/265 & n. 2; secret process, 4/70, 147

BLOUNT (Blunt), Sir [Henry], traveller: talks about Egypt etc., 5/274 & n. 1

BLOUNT (Blunt), Col. [Thomas], inventor, Fellow of the Royal Society, of Wricklemarsh, Kent: experiments with chariot design, 6/94 & n. 2, 213; 7/20 & n. 2; house and garden, 6/94 & n. 3

BLOW (Blaeu), John, composer (d. 1708): 8/393–4 & n.

BLOWBLADDER (Blowblather) St: 8/371

BLOYS: see Boys, Sir J.

BLUDWORTH (Bluddell), Sir Thomas, Lord Mayor 1665–6: appointed sheriff, 3/162; presses seamen, 7/187, 190; incompetence, 7/190, 269(2), 280 & n. 4, 393 & n. 2

BLUNT: see Blount

BLURTON (Blirton), Mr ——: tells bawdy anecdote, 2/43; social: 2/125, 193; 3/48

BOATE, Mrs ——: 2/54

BOCKET (BOCHETT), Mrs ——: courted by Dr Child, 1/301 & n. 3; at Sandwich's 1/309; ~ her dirty children, 8/193

BODDILY, Bodilaw: see Badiley

BODHAM, [William], Clerk of the Ropeyard, Woolwich: Penn's clerk, 3/69, 75; clerk to Chatham Chest, 5/122; appointment to Woolwich, 5/231; complains of its cost, 5/231, 248; his stores, 5/325; story of Tom of the Wood, 8/270; inspects batteries with P, 8/284; alluded to: 3/156; 6/189

BODVILE (Brodvill), [John]: case in Lords, 5/140 & n. 1

BOEVE (Bovy), [James], merchant: 9/206 & n. 6

BOIS: see Boys

BOIS-LE-DUC (The Boysse), Netherlands: 8/80

BOLES: see Bowles, [J.]
BOLLEN, [James], Groom of the
Privy Chamber: 2/234 & n. 2
BOLTELE: see Bulteel
BOLTON, [Richard], cornet: preaches
mock-sermon, 9/554 & n. 3
BOLTON, Sir William, Lord Mayor
1666–7: sworn in, 7/346 & n. 2; suspended from Court of Aldermen,
8/562 & n. 1
BOMBAY (Bombaim): naval expedition to, 4/139 & n. 2, 204 & n. 1, 210,
291–2, 299; decay of Dutch trade,
4/139; English government deceived
about, 4/299 & n. 2
BOND, [Henry], teacher of mathematics (d. 1678): instructs P on
timber measurement, 3/105 & n. 2;
5/115
BOND, Sir Thomas, Bt, Comptroller
of the Household to the Queen-
Mother (d. 1685): 1/322 & n. 3
BONFIRES: in celebration of:
Monck's action against Rump ('the
Burning of the Rump'), 1/52 & n. 4,
53; 3/95; 7/136; readmission of
secluded M.P.s, 1/63; Restoration,
1/89, 122, 163; 7/136; arrival of
Henrietta Maria, 1/281–2; Gunpowder Plot, 1/283; 7/358; coronation, 2/87, 88; Queen's arrival, 3/83,
87; King's birthday, 3/95; anniversary
of the coronation, 4/109; 7/109; 9/172;
Queen's birthday, 4/382; Battle of
Lowestoft, 6/123 (at Navy Office);
6/129 (by Dutch at Dunkirk); Four
Days Fight, 7/152, 344; Holmes's
attack on Dutch in Vlie, 7/249; P's
comments: bonfires few for King's
birthday, 3/95; few in city, 7/136,
358; none lit for peace, 8/399
BOOKBINDER, P's [see also Books]:
5/199; 9/32
BOOKER, [John], astrologer (d. 1667):
criticises Lilly, 1/274 & n. 2
BOOKS [see also Booksellers (P);
Languages; Musical Compositions]:
P'S COLLECTION:
   GENERAL: history, vol. i, pp. xxxix,
lxxi–lxxiv; removed from Sandwich's lodgings to Axe Yard, 1/59;
French books bequeathed to EP, 1/90;
collection moved to Seething Lane

and rearranged, 1/232, 241, 268, 302;
dusted, 5/358; put in order, 7/37, 311,
316, 322; 9/24(2); removed to and
from Deptford in Fire, 7/?273, ?276,
?278, ?285, 290–1; missing books
found, 7/290 & n. 3, 292; to be limited to two bookcases, 9/18, 48; shown
to guests, 9/411, 424; P consults
Naudé's book on collecting, 6/252 &
n. 1; books acquired from Holland,
1/140 & nn., 260; and France, 9/431–2
& n.
   BINDING [see also Nott, [W.];
and Richardson, [W.]: ordered, 5/199
& n. 2; 7/41; to be made uniforms,
6/14, 24, 31–2, 33; gilded, 7/243, 266,
303–4, 306, 307, 311; of maps, 5/55;
of plays, 7/104–5; books bought
ready bound, 1/140 & nn., 260; cost,
1/281; 4/240; 6/28; 9/166
   BOOKCASES (presses): made by Simpson, 7/214 & n. 4, 242, 243; delivered,
7/251, 252, 258
   CATALOGUES: books numbered and
listed, 7/412 & n. 2, 416, 417, 419, 421;
8/8, 40(2), 45; 'titled', 9/49 & n. 2, 72;
catalogued, 9/72, 559–60
   OTHER COLLECTIONS: Earl of Peterborough's, 4/270; Wisbech parish,
4/311 & n. 3; Earl of Arundel's, 8/6–7
& n.; Capuchin friary's, 8/26; Fou-
quet's, 9/173 & n. 3; Clarendon's,
9/480
BOOKS AND PAMPHLETS MENTIONED IN
THE TEXT [a single asterisk denotes that
P read or 'looked over' a book, or
part of a book; a second that he comments on it]:
[ALLESTRY, R.], The causes of the decay
of Christian piety: 9/10–11 & n. 2
ALSTED, J. H., Encyclopaedia: 1/275 & n. 4
ARETINO, PIETRO: 4/136–7 & n.
ARISTOTLE: 4/267(2)
[ASHLEY, A., The mariner's mirrour]:
4/240 & n. 1
BACON, F., Sermones Fideles (Faber
Fortunae): 2/102** & n. 1; 5/39**;
7/72**, 129**, 242**, 346; Novum
Organum: 1/140 & n. 4
BARCLAY, J., Argenis: 1/231 & n. 1;
4/369*
BARTAS, DU (trans. Sylvester), Divine
weekes and workes: 3/247** & n. 1

[COTTON, C.], *Scarronides, or Virgile Travesty*: 5/72★ & n. 2

COTTON, SIR R., [*An answer to such motives as were offer'd by certain military-men to Prince Henry . . .*]: 8/547★★ & n. 1, 564★★, 568★★

COWLEY, A., *Naufragium Joculare*: 2/39★ & n. 3; 4/218 & n. 1; [*Verses lately written upon several occasions*]: 4/386★ & n. 3; 6/186★

[*Critici Sacri*]: 9/259 & n. 2

DANIEL, S., *The collection of the historie of England*: 5/247 & n. 2

[DAUNCEY, J., *The history of the thrice illustrious Princess Henrietta Maria de Bourbon, Queen of England*]: 1/275★ & n. 2

[DAVENANT, SIR W.], [*The first day's entertainment at Rutland House*]: 5/40★★ & n. 2; *The Siege of Rhodes*: 5/278★ & n. 4; 6/247★★, 248★; 7/235★★; 9/396★

[DAVIES, J.], *The history of Algiers and its slavery*: 8/582★★ & n. 3, 585★★

DAVILA, E. C. (trans. Aylesbury), [*Storia delle guerre civile di Francia*]: 7/206★★ & n. 4

A Declaration and vindication of the Lord Mayor, aldermen and commons of the city of London in common-councell assembled: 1/122 & n. 3

DENHAM, SIR J., [*Poems and translations*]: 8/380 & n. 2

DESCARTES, R., [*Discours de la méthode*]: 4/263 & n. 2; [*Géométrie*]: 4/263 & n. 2; [*Musicae Compendium*]: 9/148 & n. 4, 167 & n. 3, 400–1★★ & n. 1

[*A Dialogue concerning the rights of His Most Christian Majesty*]: 8/253-4★★ & n. 1

[DOLEMAN, R. (Robert Parsons), *A conference about the next succession to the crown of Ingland*]: 9/480 & n. 2

DRYDEN, J., [*Annus Mirabilis*]: 8/40★★ & n. 3; *Essay of dramatic poesy*: 9/311★★ & n. 2; *The Indian Emperor*: 8/508 & n. 2; *The mayden queene*: 9/29★ & n. 1; *The rival ladys*: 7/210★★ & n. 3, 233★★

DUGDALE, SIR W., *History of St Paul's cathedral*: 1/163 & nn.; 4/410 & n. 4; *Originales Juridiciales*, 7/297 & n. 7; 8/168 & n. 3, 170(2)★★

[EDMONDS, C., *The commentaries of C. Julius Caesar*]: 9/400★ & n. 1

[*Ephemeris Parliamentaria*]: 8/10★★ & n. 2

ERASMUS, *De conscribendis epistolis*: 8/32★★ & n. 4

ESTIENNE, H., *Thesaurus Graecae linguae*: 2/239 & n. 3; 3/3, 290 & n.3; 4/33

[*Evangelium Armatum*]: 4/111★ & n. 4

EVELYN, J., [*Elysium Britannicum*]: 6/289★ & n. 4; *Hortus Hyemalis*: 6/289★★ & n. 6; [*Publick employment and an active life . . . preferr'd to solitude*]: 8/236(2)★ & n. 2; [*Thersander*]: 6/289★★ & n. 5

[*An exact and most impartial accompt of the . . . trial . . . of nine and twenty regicides*]: 1/284★ & n. 4, 286

[*Fair warning: the second part*]: 4/111★ & n. 2

FARNABY, T., *Index Rhetoricus*: 1/140 & n. 5

FISHER, P., [*Epinicion vel elogium Lodovici XIIIIti*]: 1/200 & n. 2; panegyric on Charles II: 1/209 & n. 1

[?FLECKNOE, R., *A letter from a gentleman to the Hon. Ed. Howard, Esq.*]: 9/311★★ & n. 2

[FLETCHER, J.], *The madd lovers*: 5/280★★ & n. 1; *A wife for a month*: 3/286★★ & n. 1

[FLETCHER, J. AND MASSINGER, P.], *The custome of the country*: 5/280★★ & n. 2

FOURNIER, PÈRE G., [*Hydrographie*]: 9/17 & n. 5

[FOXE, J.], *Book of Martyrs*: 9/284 & n. 5, 327

[?FRANCO, N.], *La puttana errante*: 9/22 & n. 1

[FRANZINI, G.], *Las cosas maravillosas . . . de Roma*: 1/49★ & n. 4

FULLER, T., *Andronicus*: 9/543 & n. 2; *The church-history of Britain*: 1/56★ & n. 6, 261★, 308★, 312★, 321★, 322★, 325★; 4/329-30★★ & n., 369★; 7/302★; 8/94★★, 535★, 537★; *The historie of the holy warre*: 2/207★ & n. 1; *History of the worthies of England*: 2/21 & n. 1; 3/26-7★ & n., 34★; 4/410, 411, n. 1; 5/118★ & n. 1; 8/94★★

[MACKENZIE, G., *Religio Stoici*]: 8/162★★ & n. 2

[MALYNES, G., *Consuetudo: vel] Lex Mercatoria*: 8/580 & n. 2

?[MANWAYRING, SIR H., *The sea-man's dictionary*]: 2/53★★ & n. 4

MARIANA, J. DE, [*Historia general de España*]: 9/536–7★ & n.

MARNIX, P. DE, [*Le tableau des differens de la religion*]: 9/428 & n. 3

[MARVELL, A.], *The second advice to a painter*: 7/407–8 & n.; 8/313★; *The third advice*: 7/421; 8/21★ & n. 3, 313★★; *Directions to a painter*: 8/439★★ & n. 3

[MASSINGER, P.], *The Bondman*: 2/106 & n. 4; 7/352★★

MERSENNE, M., [*Harmonie Universelle*]: 9/148 & n. 3, 216★ & n. 1

[MIDDLETON, T.], *The Mayor of Quinborough*: 7/169★ & n. 1

[MIDDLETON, T. AND ROWLEY, W.], *The Spanish gypsy*: 2/123★★ & n. 1

[MILLOT, M. ET L'ANGE, J.], *L'escholle des filles*: 9/21–2★★ & n., 57–8★, 59★★

Missal: 1/281–2★ & n.

MONTAIGNE, *Essays*: 9/120, 121 & n. 3

MONTELION, [*The prophetical almanac for the year 1661*]: 1/288–9★★ & n.

MORE, H., *An antidote against atheism*: 8/13★★ & n.1

MORLEY, T., *A plaine and easie introduction to practicall musicke*: 8/105★★ & n. 2

[NAUDÉ (NAUDEUS), G., (trans. J. Evelyn), *Instructions concerning erecting of a library* . . .]: 6/252★★ & n. 1

[NEWCASTLE, DUCHESS OF, *The life of . . . Duke . . . of Newcastle* . . .]: 9/123★★ & n. 3, 124★★

[NEWMAN, S., *A concordance to the Holy Scriptures*]: 4/174★ & n. 5, 178★ & n. 1; [*Large and complete concordance to the Bible*]: 9/31 & n. 3

OGILBY, J., *Aesop's Fables*: 2/6 & n. 4, 18; 4/154★; 7/48 & n. 1; [*The entertainment of . . . Charles II* . . .]: 7/48 & n. 1

[OLEARIUS, A., *The voyages and travels of the ambassadors from the Duke of Holstein, to the Great Duke of Muscovy, and the King of Persia*]: 4/425★★ & n. 1

[ORRERY, EARL OF], *Mustapha*: 9/241 & n. 4, 242★

OSBORNE, F., *Advice to a son*: 2/199 & n. 1; 3/288★ & n. 2; 4/96★★; 5/27; *Works*: 2/22 & n. 2

OVID, *Metamorphoses* (?trans.): 3/289★ & n. 3

[PALMER, R., EARL OF CASTLEMAINE], *The Catholique apology*: 7/393–4★ & n.

[PARIVAL, J. N. DE], *Les délices de la Hollande*: 4/410–11★ & n.

PENN, W. JUN., [*The sandy foundation shaken*]: 9/446★★ & n. 4; [*Truth exalted*]: 9/327★★ & n. 3

[*The perfect politician: or A full view of the life and actions military and civil of Oliver Cromwell* . . .]: 8/382 & n. 2

PETTY, SIR W., [*A treatise of taxes and contributions*]: 3/286★ & n. 2

[PEYTON, SIR E.], *The divine catastrophe of the kingly family of . . . the Stuarts*: 6/33 & n. 3

PHILIPS, K., *Poems*, 8/380 & n. 1, 439★ & n. 1

Philosophical Transactions: 9/548

PLAYFORD, J., *A brief introduction to the skill of musick*: 8/124★★ & n. 3

[*A plea for limited monarchy as it was established in this nation, before the late war. In an humble addresse to his Excellency General Monck*]: 1/61★ & n. 1

[*Pontificale romanum Clementis VIII* . . .]: 1/18★ & n. 2

[*The poor-whores petition to the most splendid, illustrious, serene, and eminent lady of pleasure the Countess of Castlemaine* . . .]: 9/154★ & n. 1

[PORTER, T.], *The Villaine*: 6/214★★ & n. 3

POTTER, F., [*An interpretation of the number 666*]: 7/46–7★ & n., 355★★, 364★★ & n. 2

POWER, H., *Experimental philosophy*: 5/241(2)★★ & n. 2

QUARLES, F., *Emblemes, divine and moral*: 1/11★ & n. 2

[QUEVEDO VILLEGAS, F. DE], *The visions of Dom Francisco de Quevedo*: 8/256★★ & n. 1

[RANDOLPH, T.], *Cornelianum Dolium*: 1/292 & n. 2, 308★★

[RHODES, R.], *Flora's Vagaries*: 8/463* & n. 5

RIDLEY, SIR T., *A view of the civile and ecclesiasticall law*: 7/112** & n. 2; 119*, 126*

ROSINUS, J., *Antiquitatum romanorum corpus absolutissimum ex variis scriptoribus collect*: 1/243 & n. 3

RUSHWORTH, J., *Historical Collections*: 4/395 & n. 1, 402*, 406*, 408*, 411*, 417** & n. 1, 421*, 434**, 435**; 6/10* & n. 3

RYCAUT, P., [*The present state of the Ottoman empire*]: 8/121 & n. 2, 156 & n. 2, 159**, 166*, 167**, 175**, 199**

SANDERSON, W., [*A complete history of the life and reign of King Charles . . .*]: 1/132 & n. 4

[SANDERUS, A.], *Flandria Illustrata*: 5/38* & n. 6

[SANTOS, F. DE LOS, *Descripcion breve del monasterio de S. Lorenzo el real del Escorial . . .*]: 9/353 & n. 1

SCAPULA, J., *Lexicon Graeco-Latinum*: 5/198 & n. 3, 199, 200

[SCARRON, P.], *The fruitlesse praecaution*: 1/135* & n. 2, 266**, 267*

SCOBELL, H., *Collection of acts and ordinances . . . made in the parliament . . .*: 4/395 & n. 2, 402

SCOT, R., [*The discovery of witchcraft*]: 8/383 & n. 2

[SCUDÉRI, MME DE], *Artamène ou le Grand Cyrus*: 1/312 & n. 2; 7/122; 8/225*; *Ibrahim, ou L'Illustre Bassa*: 9/89 & n. 2, 247(2)*

The second addresse from the gentlemen of the county of Northampton to his Excellency the Lord Generall Monck: 1/73 & n. 1

[SEDEÑO, J.], *Summa de varones illustres*: 9/173 & n. 3

SELDEN, J., *Mare Clausum*: 2/223 & n. 3, 226*, 227*, 234* & n. 1, 235*, 236*, 237*, 238*; 3/6* & n. 1; 4/105 & n. 2, 107 & n. 3

SENECA: 8/507

SHAKESPEARE, *Plays*: 4/410 & n. 4; 5/198 & n. 4, 199, 200; *Hamlet*, 5/320 & n. 4; *Henry IV* part 1: 1/325 & n. 1; *Othello*: 7/255**

SIDNEY, SIR P., [*Arcadia*]: 6/2* & n. 3

?[SMITH, J.], *The sea-man's grammar*: 2/53** & n. 4

SORBIÈRE, S.-J., [*Relation d'un voyage en Angleterre . . .*]: 5/297 & n. 2; 9/206*

[?SOUTHLAND, T.], *Love a la mode*: 4/235* & n. 2

SPEED, J., [his 'geography' (? *A prospect of the most famous parts of the world*)]: 1/254* & n. 5; [*History of Great Britaine*]: 7/290 & n. 3; 8/91**, 387 & n. 3, 498; [*The theatre of the empire of Great Britaine*]: 3/114* & n. 4

SPELMAN, SIR H., [*Glossarium Archailogicum*]: 5/190 & n. 2, 198, 199, 200

SPENCER, J., [*A discourse concerning prodigies*]: 5/165** & n. 1

SPRAT, T., *History of the Royal Society of London*: 8/380 & n. 1, 387

STEPHENS/STEPHANUS: *see* Estienne

STILLINGFLEET, E., *Origines Sacrae*: 6/297** & n. 1; [*A rational account of the grounds of the Protestant religion*]: 7/336** & n. 2

STOW, J., *Survey of London*: 4/410 & n. 4

[STUBBE, E.], *Fraus Honesta*: 4/218 & n. 1

SUCKLING, SIR J., *Aglaura*: 5/263** & n. 1

SWAN, W., *The unlawfull use of lawfull things* (? not published): 2/235 & n. 2

[TATHAM, J.], *The Rump, or The mirror of the late times*: 1/289** & n. 2

TAYLOR, J., [Εὐμβολον Θεολογικόν: *or A collection of polemical discourses*]: 6/312* & n. 3

TAYLOR, S., [*A history of gavelkind*]: 1/63 & n. 4; *The Serenade, or Disappointment* (MS.): 9/546–7 & n.

TESAURO, E., *Patriarchae, sive Christi servatoris genealogica, per mundi, aetates traducta*: 2/22 & n. 3

[*Le testament du defunt Cardinal Jul. Mazarini, duc de Nivernois, premier ministre du roi de France*]: 4/411–12 & n.

[*To his excellency General Monck. A letter from the gentleman of Devon in answer to his Lordships of January 23 . . .*]: 1/34* & n. 3

[*A true and perfect narrative of the great

and signal success of a part of His Majesty's fleet]: 7/252 & n. 2

The tryal of Sir Henry Vane, Kt., at the Kings Bench, Westminster, June the 2nd and 6th, 1662 . . .: 4/40★★ & n. 2

[TUKE, SIR S.], *The adventures of five houres*: 4/165, 167★; 7/248–9★★ & n., 250★★ & n. 2, 255★

? [*Urbium praecipuarum mundi theatrum quintum*]: 5/38★ & n. 5

USHER, J., *A body of divinitie*: 4/127★★ & n. 4

[*The victory over the fleet of the States General . . . begun the 25 of July inst. . . .*]: 7/229★ & n. 1, 230★, 234★

[*A vindication of the degree of gentry in opposition to titular honours, and the humour of riches being the measure of honours. Done by a Person of Quality*]: 4/151★★ & n. 2

[VORAGINE, J. DE, (trans.), *Legenda Aurea*]: 9/161 & n. 1

[*Vox et lacrimae Anglorum*]: 9/65 & n. 2

WAGENAER, L. J., [*Spieghel der zeevaerdt* (trans. Ashley, *Mariner's Mirrour*)]: 4/240 & n. 1; 7/290 & n. 3

WALLER, E., [*Poems etc. written upon several occasions*]: 7/369★ & n. 2

WALSINGHAM, E., [*Arcana Aulica: or Walsingham's manual of prudential maxims . . .*]: 5/10 & n. 2★; 7/161–2★★

[WALTON, I., *Life of Richard Hooker*]: 8/223(2)★★ & n. 2

The way to be rich, according to the practice of the great Audley . . .: 4/22★ & n. 5

[WEBSTER, J.], *The Duchess of Malfi*: 7/352★★ & n. 3, 358★★

[WELDON, SIR A.], *The court and character of King James . . .*: 6/33 & n. 3, 102★★ & n. 8

WILD, R., *Iter Boreale*: 4/285★★ & n. 2; 8/589 & n. 3

WILKINS, J., *Essay towards a real character, and a philosophical language*: 7/12 & n. 6, 148; 8/554; 9/200, 202★, 215★★ & n. 4, 255(2)★, 331 & n. 3, 381★★, 382★★

[WILSON, J., *Andronicus Comnenius, a tragedy*]: 7/181 & n. 2

[WINSTANLEY, W., *The honour of Merchant-Taylors*]: 9/277★★ & n. 2

WREN, M., [*Considerations on Mr*

Harrington's Oceana, or Monarchy Asserted]: 8/414 & n. 3

[WRIGHT, A.], *Five sermons in five several styles*: 9/300★★ & n. 5

BOOKS INSUFFICIENTLY IDENTIFIED: merry pamphlets against Rump, 1/56 & n. 4; P's French books, 1/90; 'little French romances', 2/35★; Spanish books, 2/131; book on improvement of trade, 4/160★ & n. 1; cookery book, 4/272–3★★; French verse, 5/58; little book of law, 5/202; two or three good plays, 5/220; collection of modern plays, 7/103, 104–5, 117; French book on navigation, 9/432★ & n. 1

BOOKSELLERS: losses in Fire, 7/297 & n. 3, 309–10 & n.

BOOKSELLERS (P) [*see also* Allestry, [J.]; Herringman, [H.]; Kirton, J.; Martin, [J.]; Mitchell, Mrs [A.]; Morden, [W.]; Playford, [J.]; Shrewsbury, [W.]; Starkey, [J.]]: parliamentary news at, 8/576–7; foreign booksellers, 4/87; also, 9/309

BOONE, [Christopher], merchant: arraigned before House of Lords, 9/193 & n. 1

BOONE, Col. [?Thomas], cr. Baron Delamere 1661 (d. 1684): 2/60

BOOTH, Sir George: released by Parliament, 1/63 & n. 2, 74

BOOTH, Mr ——: 1/230

[BORDEAUX, Antoine de], French ambassador 1652–60: 1/10 & n. 7

BORDEAUX: Dutch Bordeaux fleet taken, 5/326, 348–9, 354; wine merchants' trick, 7/256; also, 6/177–8; 7/200

[BOREEL, Jan], Dutch ambassador 1667–72: King dines with, 9/451

BOREMAN, [George], Keeper of the Wardrobe, Greenwich Palace: Mennes and Batten lodge with in Plague, 6/208 & n. 1; political news from, 8/401; social: entertains Navy Board and others, 6/208, 233, 237, 275, 280, 285, 288, 293; 7/4; gives music party, 7/15, 16; also, 7/1; ~ his son, 6/299

BOREMAN, ——: account of Vane's execution, 3/109

BOREMAN, Dr [Robert], Rector of St Giles-in-the-Fields: sermon, 8/99

BOREMAN, Sir William, Clerk Comptroller of the Household: consulted about mast-dock, 5/353; measures against plague, 6/211 & n. 5; social: 6/208

BORFETT (Burfett), [Samuel], chaplain to Sandwich: social: 1/210, 285; 8/99

BOSCAWEN, [Edward], M.P. Cornwall: examines Navy Board accounts, 7/305 & n. 2; praises P's parliamentary speech, 9/109

BOSSE, [?A.], painter: copy of P's portrait, 9/261 & n. 4

BOSTOCK, ——, formerly clerk in the Exchequer: social: ?1/319; 2/162–3; 5/30

BOSTON, —— [?the foregoing]: 1/319

BOTELER: see Butler

BOTTOMRY (bummary): risky investment, 4/398 & n. 2; fraudulent claim concerning, 4/401 & n. 3

BOUGHTON, Northants.: Sandwich at, 4/307–8

BOULOGNE (Bullen, Bulloigne): storm near, 3/143; Dutch fleet off, 7/279, 281; alluded to: 8/380 & n. 2

[BOURBON, Henri de, Duc de Verneuil], French ambassador-extraordinary Apr.-Dec. 1665: arrives incognito, 6/76 & n. 1

BOURBON-L'ARCHAMBAULT (Bourbon): Henrietta-Maria takes waters, 6/142 & n. 3

BOURNE, Maj. [Nehemiah], Navy Commissioner 1653–60: 1/197 & n. 1

BOVY: see Boeve

BOW: P/EP visit(s), 1/280; 5/175; 7/113, 117, 120, 124, 151, 208, 240; 8/326, 377, 443, 447; 9/470, 528, 546; dancing meeting, 7/238; girls' school, 8/448, 451; King's Head, 3/169; Queen's Head, 8/112

BOW CHURCH: see St Mary-le-Bow

BOWCOCKE (Brecocke), [Richard], landlord of the Swan, Stevenage: 'the best Host I know', 8/475 & n. 1

BOWES, Sir Jerome, envoy to Muscovy 1583–4: anecdotes of, 3/188–9 & n.

BOWES (? Bewes), ——, shopkeeper: 3/52

BOWLES (Boles), [John], grocer: death and burial, 7/256; ~ ?his wife, 5/166; 7/394

BOWLES, John, of Brampton, servant to Sandwich: accompanies P to London, 8/474–5; explains hunting terms, 8/475; social: 2/105, 108, 138, 183; 8/477, 478, 481; 9/224

BOWLING ALLEY, Westminster: 7/123 & n. 3

BOWMAN, Mr —— [?Edward or Francis, Gentlemen-Ushers to the King]: 2/80 & n. 2

BOWRY, Capt. [John]: ship hired, 4/52–3 & n.

BOW ST: alluded to: 6/1; 9/62

BOWYER, [Elizabeth], wife of Robert: her remedy for cold, 1/85; social: 1/317; 2/21, 113; 3/61; alluded to: 1/166

BOWYER, Mary, daughter of Robert: sends maid to EP, 2/218 & n. 3

BOWYER, [Robert], ('father Bowyer') Usher of the Receipt in the Exchequer: EP stays with at Huntsmoor during P's absence in Holland, 1/84, 85, 131, 166; drowned in riding accident, 5/34; social: 1/229, 286; 2/21, 49, 86, 87, 113, 215, 241; 3/65; alluded to: 1/249, 251, 314, 323; ~ his daughters, 1/317; 2/113; 3/61, 258

BOWYER, William, son of Robert; doorkeeper in the Exchequer: escorts EP to Huntsmoor, 1/89; her valentine, 3/29; simple discourse, 3/145, 299; youthful appearance, 6/235; social: 1/88, 176, 192, 201, 244, 320; 2/232; 3/174; 5/262; alluded to: 1/209; 5/34

BOWYER, [William], tar merchant: supplies, 4/182, 187; gift, 4/182

BOYLE, Lady Anne: see Mountagu, Anne, wife of Edward, 2nd Earl of Sandwich

BOYLE, Lady Henrietta: see Hyde, Lady Henrietta, wife of Laurence Hyde

BOYLE, Richard, succ. as 2nd Earl of Cork 1643; cr. Earl of Burlington 1664: travels to Flushing, 1/?106,

?112; as Lord Treasurer of Ireland, 8/301 & n. 1; house in Piccadilly, 9/321 & n. 1; social: 8/498; 9/131 ~ his wife [Elizabeth]: 8/498; 9/322

BOYLE, Richard, son of the foregoing: killed in action, 6/122

BOYLE, Robert, scientist [*see also* Books]: at Royal Society, 6/36 & n. 5; recommends oculist, 9/248

BOYLE, Roger, Baron Broghill, cr. Earl of Orrery 1660, politician and dramatist [*see also* Plays]: influence with Richard Cromwell, 1/180; and King, 6/301 & n. 2; supports Sandwich, 6/301; 7/54; opposes Ormond, 9/185; as dramatist, 9/522; also, 1/260; 9/276

BOYLE, ——, [?Charles or Richard]: 1/106 & n. 3, 112

BOYNTON, [Katherine], Maid of Honour to the Queen: seasick, 5/306

BOYS (Bloys), Sir John: on *Naseby*, 1/106 & n. 4; supports King, 1/112 & n. 3; carries letters between King and Sandwich, 1/125; also, 1/136

BOYS, [John], wholesaler at the Three Crowns, Cheapside: marriage, 3/163; house burnt in Fire, 5/247–8; ~ his wife: 3/163

BRADFORD, [Martha], housekeeper, Hill House, Chatham 1661–9: P complains to about accommodation, 4/225 & n. 3

BRADLY, ——: at Graveley manorial court, 2/182

BRADSHAW, [John], regicide (d. 1659): Westminster lodgings, 1/13 & n. 4; body exhumed and displayed, 1/309; 2/24, 27, 31

BRAEMS (Brames, Breames), Sir Arnold, merchant: social: 1/293, 323; 2/192; 9/57

[BRAGG, Thomas], chaplain, Portsmouth dockyard: sermon 'full of nonsense and false Latin', 3/72 & n. 1

BRAHAM (Brames, Breame), Sir Richard, merchant: 3/43

BRAHE, Nils Nillsson, Graf, Swedish ambassador-extraordinary 1661: in dispute about striking flag, 2/212 & n. 3; 3/14; state entry, 2/187, 188, 189

BRA(I)NFORD: *see* Brentford

BRAMES, Breame(s): *see* Braems/ Braham

BRAMPTON, Hunts. [*see also* Ball, Sir P.; Barton, [J.]; Bernard, Sir R.; Day, [J.]; Dickinford, ——; Gorham, [M.]; Pepys, Robert; Pigott, [R.]; Prior, ——; Stankes, W.; Taylor, ——]:

P'S ESTATE [for his inheritance from Robert P and the subsequent disputes, *see principally* Pepys, R.; Trice, T.]: attempts to buy Norbury's house and land, 2/124 & n. 5; fails to unite scattered holdings, 8/282–3; income, 4/119 & n. 2, 121; 5/36, 44, 354, 360; his 'Brampton book', 3/48; 'Brampton papers', 4/121, 122; 5/31, 39, 195(3); 8/264

P'S HOUSE: alterations, 2/182–3; 3/94, 97, 219; Sandwich's plans, 3/206, 210; further alterations planned, 8/237, 471; parlour, 8/469; garden and summer-houses, ib.; P sends gold to in Medway crisis, 8/263–4, 272, 273; recovers gold, 8/472–5, 539; thinks of retiring to, 7/315, 332; 8/237, 469; 9/293; to be let, 9/212; also, 7/340

MANOR: sold to Sandwich, 3/102, 176; also, 4/343

MANORIAL COURT: P attends, 3/222, 223; 4/308–9; 5/281, 282, 298; his speech at, 4/308–9; also, 3/48, 199, 206, 208, 209–10, 211, 213, 219, 221; 4/300, 303, 305

PLACES IN: Bull inn, 4/309; church [St Mary's], 3/220; Green, 8/471; Portholme meadow, 2/135; 5/158; 9/210; river, 4/312; woods, ib.

P'S VISITS [for visits by other members of family, *see* under names]: 2/133–9, 180–4; 3/216–25; 4/307–14; 5/294–9; 8/453, 457, 460, 464, 465–75; 9/209–12, 223, 224; cost, 8/479; also, 3/127

MISC.: storm, 3/35, 42; parish feast, 3/144; 4/237

BRAYBROOKE, Robert, Bishop of London 1381–1404: tomb etc., 7/367–8 & n.

BREAD ST: 4/181

BRECOCKE: *see* Bowcocke

BREDA, Netherlands: Charles II at, 1/117; alluded to: 1/129

BREDA, DECLARATION OF: read

in Parliament, 1/118 & n. 2, 122; to
Sandwich's Council of War, 1/123-4
& n.; welcomed by fleet, 1/124, 131;
invoked by King, 4/58 & n. 3; alluded
to: 1/127

BREDA, PEACE OF: see War, Second
Dutch

BREDHEMSON: see Brighton

BREKINGTON: see Beckington

BRENTFORD (Branford, Brainford),
Mdx: P visits Povey's house, 6/198,
214, 266, 267; market day, 1/20;
plague, 6/225; church [St Lawrence],
6/199 & n. 1; inns, 6/199 & n. 1;
7/26; alluded to: 6/216; 7/54; 9/509

BRENTWOOD (Burntwood), Essex:
plague at, 6/181

BRERETON, William, 3rd Baron
Brereton: appointed to Brooke House
Committee, 8/577 & n. 3; his manner,
9/10 & n. 1; plays organ, 9/11

BREST: French troops at, 8/1 & n. 3;
engravings, 9/437

BRETT, Sir Edward, soldier: 1/264

BRETTON (Britton), Dr [Robert],
Vicar of Deptford: P's opinion,
4/175; 6/107; preaches to Trinity
House, 4/185; 5/172; 6/107

BREVINT (Brevin), Daniel, Canon of
Durham (d. 1695): 3/85 & n. 1

BREWER, Capt. [William], painter:
4/15, 187

BREWER'S YARD, Westminster:
1/175; 5/212

BRIAN, Mr ——: 3/217

BRIDE LANE, Westminster: see
Taverns etc.: Black Spread Eagle

BRIDEWELL [see also New Bridewell]:
the house of correction, ?1/167; pressed men in, 7/187, 190, 191; building
described, 8/6; the precinct: ?1/167;
2/116

BRIDGEMAN, John, Bishop of
Chester 1619-52: armorial glass,
3/254 & n. 3

BRIDGEMAN, Sir Orlando, Lord
Chief Baron of the Exchequer 1660;
Lord Chief Justice of Common Pleas
1660-7; Lord Keeper 1667-72: charge
to jury at regicides' trial, 1/263 &
n. 2; appointed Lord Keeper, 8/410-
11 & n.; popularity, 8/410; 9/375; P
admires, 8/421; speech to Parliament,

8/476 & n. 2, 480 & n. 2; opinion on
charge against Clarendon, 8/541;
member of Cabal, 8/585; 9/425;
friendly with Coventry, 9/41; opposes
dissolution of Parliament, 9/360, 375;
attempts reorganisation of Navy
Board, 9/290, 291-2 & n., 321, 503,
550; illness, 9/425 & n. 4; his part in
Coventry's petition for release, 9/475,
491; also, 8/412; 9/106; social:
9/352; alluded to: 3/254

BRIDGES, [Richard], linen-draper,
Cornhill: calico contract, 5/292 &
n. 1, 295, 351

BRIDGES, Sir Toby, soldier: praised
by Albemarle, 5/310 & n. 1

BRIDGEWATER, Lord: see Egerton

BRIEFS (Chancery): frequency, 2/128
& n. 3

BRIGDEN, Dick, haberdasher, Fleet
St: sells sword to P, 1/94; 2/24, 28;
made captain of auxiliaries 2/24; house
damaged in storm, 3/32; social: 3/165

BRIGGS, [Timothy], scrivener: gift to
P, 6/83, 100, 101

BRIGHAM, [Thomas], royal coach-
maker: complains of Duchess of
Albemarle, 1/181 & n. 4

BRIGHTON (Bredhemson, Bright-
hemson), Sussex: Charles II's escape
from (1651), 1/156 & n. 1; 8/74;
alluded to: 7/288 & n. 2

BRISBANE (Brisband, Brisbanke),
[John], naval official: P admires,
6/176-7; talks of spells etc., 6/177-8;
takes P to gambling at court, 9/2-3,
4; news from: 9/66, 86, 179; social:
6/179, 182; 7/326, 388; 8/164; 9/35,
87, 126, 188; alluded to: 7/387

BRISTOL, Earl of: see Digby

BRISTOL (Bristow), Som.: story of
mayor, 3/180; Rupert surrenders
(1645), 5/170 & n. 2; 6/30; ships built,
8/47 & n., 270 & n. 4; 9/235 & n. 1;
P and family visit, 9/234-6 & nn.;
dog-carts, 9/234 & n. 4; Bristol milk,
9/235-6 & n.; Cross, 9/236 & n. 3;
Custom House, 9/235 & n. 3; Horse
Shoe Inn, 9/234 & n. 2, 236; Marsh
St, 9/235; Quay, 9/235; Sun Inn, 9/234
& n. 6, 235; Tolzey, 9/236 & n. 2;
Three Cranes tavern, 9/234 & n. 5

BRITTON: see Bretton

reports rumours of appointments, 9/337 & n. 1; rumoured dismissal, 9/503

CONTRACTS: favours Warren's mast contract, 7/2–3; promotes Cocke's interests, 7/91, 115, 150, 184, 206, 221, 228

DOCKYARD BUSINESS: at Woolwich, 6/205–6; Deptford, 6/184; 7/20–1; Chatham and Harwich, 7/408; 8/296; discharges officers and seamen, 7/410(2)

FINANCIAL BUSINESS: approves P's memorandum on pursers, 7/9, 13, 14; comments on pursers' accounts, 7/106; part in proposed reorganisation of comptrollership, 7/361 & n. 2; 8/11–12, 20, 24, 25, 30, 32, 104, 586; objects to Penn's accounts, 8/50; criticised by Carteret, 8/110; offered half-share in Treasury by Carteret, 8/277; to take charge of Ticket Office, 9/383; also, 7/97; 8/4

PERQUISITES: promised plate by Cocke, 7/90, 91; secret understanding with Warren, 8/12, 31, 106, 115, 177; and Clutterbuck, 9/346 & n. 2

RELATIONS WITH P: their mutual dislike, 6/324; 7/78, 121, 131, 232–3, 258; 8/36, 220; annoys P by alliance with Warren, 8/12, 31, 115; baulked by P in payment of bills, 9/346 & n. 2; supports P in Hayter's case, 9/327, 328; and in Hewer's, 9/391, 394; also, 7/36; 8/342; 9/384 & n. 2

RELATIONS WITH PETT: 8/166, 311

COLLECTIVE BUSINESS (his part in discussions, decisions etc.): contracts and stores: 6/327; 7/68; dockyards: 6/216; financial: 6/74, 78, 203, 273, 327, 329, 336; 7/4, 76, 82, 284, 289, 295, 303, 311, 354; 8/111, 131, 372, 441, 460, 550; 9/109, 146, 174, 222, 445; ships/shipbuilding: 6/233, 281; 7/69; 9/100–1; tickets: 8/393; 9/15; victualling: 9/298, 303, 315, 316; misc. and unspecified: 6/193–4, 199, 200, 201, 211, 222, 334, 339; 7/71, 79, 82–3, 107–8, 304, 305; 8/87, 392, 394, 449, 460, 464, 479, 482, 494–5; 9/121, 130, 133, 150, 190, 454

AS COURTIER: supports Sandwich, 6/324; attends Queen's council as Chancellor, 7/303; cabals with Lady Denham, 7/323; omitted from commission on Duke of York's household, 8/592; also, 6/220–1

MUSICAL: examines claviorganum, 8/25; music meetings at his house, 8/54–7, 64–5; explains nature of sound, 9/147

POLITICAL: has conventiclers arrested, 6/199; views on war situation, 7/409, 411–12; supports attack on Clarendon, 8/401, 410; political news. etc. from: 7/152; 8/6, 424, 480; 9/17, 134, 173, 320, 446

PRIVATE AFFAIRS ETC. [for his liaison with 'Madam' Williams, see Williams, Abigail]: his two mistresses(?), 7/237–8; 8/226; infrequent attendance at church, 9/452; illnesses, 6/150, 156; 7/232–3; 9/223, 544, 546; houses/ lodgings: in Piazza, Covent Garden, 6/2; 7/3, 4; coach-house, 7/224; at Greenwich, 6/204, 226; at Navy Office, 7/26, 296; 8/24, 31, 36, 40, 51; alterations, 8/226; 9/544; household poverty-stricken, 8/226; ~ his footman Tom, 7/232; his maid, 8/314

RELATIONS WITH P [see also above, Navy Commissioner; below, social]: admits P to Royal Society, 3/72 & n. 3; 6/36; their mutual regard, 6/237; 9/287–8; his gifts, 6/168 & n. 3, 212; 7/114, 293; recommends spectacles, 7/419; also, 7/378–9, 390; 8/12

SCIENTIFIC: President of Royal Society, 6/36; 7/96; 8/11; 9/333; at meetings of (business unspecified), 7/51; 9/113, 146, 248, 263; at Royal Society club, 7/148; 9/146–7, 334; as mathematician, 6/8; 9/191; helps to design yacht, 3/164, 188; and coaches, 6/94; 7/20; dismantles and reassembles watch, 6/337; discusses Wilkins's 'universal character', 7/12; his recipe for varnish, 7/147–8; discusses anatomy of teeth, 7/223–4; optics, 7/224, 225; sound, 7/147; visits King's laboratory, 9/416

SOCIAL: drives P in Hyde Park, 6/77; 7/106; 9/151; plays billiards, 6/190; gives birthday dinner, 6/285; and Twelfth Night party, 7/5–6; visits P's house, 7/66–7; Greenwich Palace,

7/105; friary, 8/25–6; godfather to
Carkesse's child, 8/111; at theatre,
8/395, 509; 9/57, 148, 157, 166, 178,
310; Teddeman's funeral, 9/200;
Bartholomew Fair, 9/301; parish
dinner, 9/559; at houses/lodgings of
naval associates in Greenwich and
London: 6/186, 187, 191, 212, 220–1,
222, 228, 334; 7/18, 34, 38, 68, 279,
364; 8/3, 4, 77, 394, 482, 525; 9/34,
214, 283, 410–11, 505; at his house in
Covent Garden, 6/2; 7/36, 40; 8/431;
9/104, 161; his lodgings in Greenwich, 6/204, 213, 217, 226, 227, 232–3,
332, 338, 339; 7/1, 3, 4; Madam
Williams's lodgings, 6/302, 303;
7/77, 92–3, 341; 9/199; taverns etc.,
6/38, 119; 7/43, 63, 74, 329; 8/49; 9/82,
115; elsewhere, 5/238; 7/253, 320;
8/180; 9/183, 198
ALLUDED TO: 9/309
~ his kinswoman, 9/146
BROWNE, [Alexander], drawing
master: gives lessons to EP, 6/98 (2) &
n. 1, 205, 282; to Peg Penn, 6/210; P
jealous of, 6/246; objects to his
presence at table, 7/116, 117; his
painting, 9/261; his *Ars Pictoria*,
9/561 & n. 5; social: 7/134
BROWNE, Sir Anthony, of Weald
Hall, nr Brentwood, Essex: 6/181 &
n. 2 ~ his brother, ib.
BROWNE, Capt. [Arnold], naval
officer: 5/30
[BROWNE, Frances], of the White
Horse, Lombard St: her beauty, 7/68;
commits suicide, 8/82 & n. 1; ~ her
husband [Abraham], 7/68 & n. 3
BROWNE, John, Clerk of the Parlia-
ments: social: 3/89; 9/1; ~ his wife
[Elizabeth], 1/177 & n. 1; 2/15, 16;
3/89; his mother, 3/89
BROWNE, John, Deputy-Storekeeper
of the Ordnance, Chatham: 4/260 &
n. 3, 261; 5/30
BROWN(E), [John], mathematical-
instrument maker, the Minories: sells
P 'White's ruler', 4/84 & n. 2; pocket-
ruler, 4/266, 267; slide-rule, 5/17 &
n. 3, 237; Wren's drawing instrument, 9/537–8 & n., 548; also, 4/434;
5/14
BROWN(E) Capt. [John], naval

officer: to sail to Jamaica, 3/150 & n. 3;
quarrels with purser, 3/284 & n. 1;
accidentally killed, 4/113; social:
2/36, 53; ~ his wife, 2/53; 4/113; his
son baptised, 2/107, 109, 110, 146; his
children, 4/113
BROWNE, [John], Storekeeper, Harwich: 1/196
BROWNE, Sir Richard, Clerk of the
Privy Council: opposes new dock at
Deptford, 3/18 & n. 1; explains
quarantine order, 4/399 & n. 2; discusses freight charges, 4/430; clerk to
Council's Committee for Retrenchments, 8/405, 406; his council work
alluded to, 8/176, 278, 279; 9/350;
political news from, 8/317; social:
at Lord Mayor's dinner, 6/126; also,
8/552; 9/206, 502
BROWNE, Maj.-Gen. Ald. Sir
Richard, kted May 1660, bt July 1660,
M.P. London 1660, Ludgershall,
Wilts. 1661–9; colonel in city militia;
Lord Mayor 1660–1: resumes seat in
parliament, 1/64 & n. 2; proclamation
against repealed, 1/65; at ship's pay,
1/253–4; house, 1/275 & n. 3; his
Lord Mayor's Day, 1/276–7; measures against Venner's rising, 2/8, 11;
against riots, 5/99; 9/466 & n. 1;
consulted about militia assessment,
3/283; sued for arbitrary arrests,
6/126; to pull down houses in Fire,
7/271; also, 5/114; social: attends
Lord Mayor's dinner, 6/126; also,
2/105, 232
BROWNE, Sir Richard, son of the
foregoing: at Lord Mayor's dinner
with father Richard and son Richard,
6/126
BROWNE, Capt. —, of the Victualling Office: takes oath, 3/135
BROWNE, ——, nicknamed Colonel,
of Brampton: 9/212
BROWNE, Mr ——, of St Malo:
7/133
BROWNLOW, [William], P's
schoolfellow: 9/153 & n. 3
BRUANT: see Culan de
BRUCE, Robert, styled Lord Bruce,
M.P. Bedfordshire 1661–3, cr. Earl of
Ailesbury 1664: introduces test bill,
4/136; returns from Flanders, 7/142

BRUMFIELD: *see* Bromfield
BRUNKARD, Brunker(d): *see* Brouncker
BRYAN, Jacob, purser: 8/271–2
BRYDGES, William, 7th Baron Chandos (d. 1677): 3/288 & n. 1
BUAT, van: *see* Culan de
BUCK, [James], Rector of St James Garlickhithe Dec. 1661–86: preaches at St Gregory-by-Paul's, 2/192 & n. 5, 211
BUCK(E), Sir Peter, Clerk of the Acts 1600–25: P's pride in his knighthood, 1/318 & n. 2
BUCKDEN, Hunts.: Robert P's property, 2/183 & n. 3; EP at, 3/148; 7/93; Bishop of Lincoln's house, 9/35 & n. 3
BUCKHURST, Lord: *see* Sackville, Charles
BUCKINGHAM, Dukes of: *see* Villiers
BUCKINGHAM, Bucks.: P visits, 9/224–5; church and school, 9/225 & n. 1; bridge, ib. & n. 2
BUCKLERSBURY (Butlersbury): 1/210; 4/182
BUCKNELL, Ald. [William], kted 1670: 9/507 & n. 4
BUCKWORTH, Sir [John], merchant, Crutched Friars: P's regard, 6/145–6 & n.; ~ his wife [Hester], 5/259 & n. 4; 7/273; his son, 7/273, 419–20; his daughters, 9/533
BUCKWORTH, Hunts.: Backwell's estate, 9/185 & n. 2
BUDD, [David], Admiralty lawyer: 8/27
BUGDEN: *see* Buckden
BUGGINS, [John], of Stukeley, Hunts.: 3/176 & n. 2
BUGGINS, Mrs ——: 5/27, 94
[BULL, Nathaniel], Surmaster, St Paul's School: 2/238 & n. 2
BULLEN: *see* Boulogne
BULTEEL (Boltele), [John], secretary to Clarendon (d. 1669): social: 7/38, 68; 8/394
BUN(N), Capt. [Thomas], naval officer: gift to P, 1/231; helps to design Tangier jetty, 3/238 & n. 2; social: 2/120
BUNCE (Bunch), Sir James: recounts

Cavaliers' grievances, 6/329–30 & n.
BUNTINGFORD, Herts.: P visits, 4/307
BURCHIN LANE: *see* Birchin Lane
BURFETT: *see* Borfett
BURFORD, Mr ——: social: 8/465–8 passim
BURGBY, Mr ——, writing-clerk to the Privy Council: news from, 5/72–3
BURGESS, [William], Exchequer clerk: P visits on Tangier business, 6/235; 8/295, 326, 329, 341, 377, 383, 440; 9/477
BURGLARY, robbery and theft [*see also* Law and Order etc.]:
GENERAL: increase allegedly due to disbanded soldiers, 1/256 & n. 3; Rotherhithe notoriously dangerous, 3/201; and road between Westminster and Kensington, 5/180; thefts by servants, 4/294 & n. 3; by disbanded Cavaliers, 4/374 & n. 1
PARTICULAR CASES: thefts from dockyards and ships: 1/316; 3/137 & n. 2; 4/76–7, 236; 6/184; attempted burglary, 1/305; tankard and cloak stolen from P's house, 2/140; EP's new waistcoat from coach, 4/28; horse stolen, 4/310; looting in Fire, 7/282; shoplifting, 9/285; also, 4/260; 5/10–11, 13; 8/316 & n. 2, 319, 321; 9/51
P'S FEAR OF BURGLARY AND LOOTING: leaves lighted candle in dining room, 3/101; fears looting in Fire, 7/285, 286; and by rioting seamen, 7/415; fears burglars, 1/305; 2/4; 5/201, 281, 282, 296; 6/25; 7/197–8; 8/552, 555
P'S FEAR OF ROBBERY AND THEFT: 2/158; 6/106, 200, 232, 235, 236; meets men with cudgels, 5/193; 9/172; fears attack in ruined streets after Fire, 8/60, 62, 371; 9/4, 8, 55; fears for EP's necklace at theatre, 7/412; fears pickpockets at Queen's Chapel, 8/588; and Bartholomew Fair, 9/313; armed guard on coach, 3/201; carries drawn sword in coach, 8/60, 62
POLICE MEASURES AGAINST: watch warns P of open door, 4/304; also, 7/363–4; 8/589; 9/134(2)
BURLINGTON, Earl of: *see* Boyle, Richard
BURNET, Dr Alexander, P's physician,

Fenchurch St: treats P for stone, 5/1 & n. 3, 191, 211; and ulcer, 5/194, 363; confines himself to house in Plague, 6/124, 125; accused of murdering servant, 6/165, 203; death, 6/203 & n. 1, 204, 226; social: 2/107; 3/178; 5/24; ~ his wife, 5/1

BURNTISLAND (Burnt Iland), Fife: Dutch bombard, 8/202 & n. 1

BURNTWOOD: *see* Brentwood

BURR, John, P's clerk: on voyage to Holland, 1/87; on board *Swiftsure*, 1/95, 96; at Gravesend, 1/98–9; annoys P by absence ashore, 1/103, 111, 116, 133; work for P, 1/111, 117; gifts to P and EP, 1/203, 232; also, 1/94, 104

BURRELL, ——: 1/47

BURROUGHS, [William], clerk to Sir W. Penn: 9/326

BURROWS, Lieut. [Anthony], naval officer: death, 6/336; pay-ticket, 7/168

BURROWS (Borroughs, Burroughs), [Elizabeth], of Westminster, widow of the foregoing: her good looks, 6/163; 7/168, 218; an old acquaintance, 6/336; amorous encounters with P, 7/168, 204–5, 240, 345, 392, 396; 9/158; breaks assignations, 7/380, 385, 386, 387, 392, 393; 8/12, 14, 71, 128; feigns grief for husband, 8/111; social: P's valentine, 9/158; also, 7/134, 232, 262, 394; 8/335, 375–6, 429, 478, 564; 9/118, 129, 142; ~ her children, 6/163; her aunt, 7/386

BURROWS, [John], slopseller to the navy: gift to P, 6/63

BURSTON, [John], chart maker, of Ratcliffe: engraves drawing of Portsmouth, 6/38, 46, 49, 50, 55; P buys engravings from, 6/111; ?9/266, 268

BURT, [Nicholas], actor: as Othello, 1/264; 9/438; in *Cataline*, 8/575 & n. 3

BURTON, [Hezekiah], Fellow of Magdalene College, Cambridge: suggested as tutor for W. Penn, jun., 3/21; also, 1/67, 68

BURTON, [Richard], locksmith, Chatham yard: his wife's gift to P, 7/351

BURY ST EDMUNDS, Suff.: beauty of women at, 4/186

BUSBY, Dr Richard, Headmaster,

Westminster School: his 'devilish covetousness', 8/199 & n. 1

BUSHELL, [Edward], merchant: in dispute about Portuguese customs dues, 5/43 & n. 2

BUTLER, (Boteler), family of: household, 1/217; emigrate to Ireland, 1/209

BUTLER, (Boteler), Frances ('la belle Boteler'), sister of Butler, ('Mons. L'Impertinent'): her beauty, 1/58, 176, 201–2, 208, 217; 2/125; 5/100, 286; 6/84; recovers from smallpox, 1/58–9; goes to Ireland, 1/209; courted by Col. Dillon, 1/217; 2/152; 3/299; 9/311 & n. 4; at Clerkenwell church, 5/286; has left Clerkenwell, 7/75; 9/311; ~ her sister; 1/207, 217; 5/101

BUTLER, James, Duke of Ormond, Lord-Lieutenant of Ireland 1661–9: position and wealth, 5/73, 183; 9/347 & n. 1; engraving of, 8/10 & n. 3; resents Albemarle's appointment as Lord-Lieutenant, 1/228–9 & n.; at coronation banquet, 2/85; visits Portsmouth, 3/70, 71; as Lord-Lieutenant, 3/79; Barker's action against, 8/404, 420 & n. 2; threatened impeachment, 8/518–19 & n.; 9/184–5 & n.; establishment reduced, 9/41 & n. 1; in England, 9/195, 204; influence over King, 9/204–5; dismissal, 9/346–7 & n., 375, 385, 446, 466 & n. 1, 478; to be succeeded by commission, 9/351; social: 2/100; also, 1/300; 8/326; 9/525

BUTLER, Lord John: suitor to Elizabeth Malet, 7/385; at theatre, 8/45

BUTLER, Lord Richard, cr. Earl of Arran 1662: hunts deer in St James's Park, 5/239; dances at court, 6/29; said to have given pox to wife, 6/167–8 & n.

BUTLER, Samuel, author of *Hudibras* (d. 1680) [*see also* Books]: dines with P, 9/265

BUTLER, Thomas, son of Duke of Ormond, styled Earl of Ossory: witness to Duke of York's secret marriage, 2/40–1; challenges Buckingham, 7/343 & n. 3, 350; at court ball, 7/372; quarrels with Ashley, 7/376 & n. 1

BUTLER, ——('Mons. L'impertinent'):

6/79, 152, 161, 163; ~ his pretty kinswoman, 3/197
HOUSES AND HOUSEHOLD [*see also* Navy
Treasury]: lodgings at Whitehall,
1/308; 2/227–8; 7/278; Cranbourne
Lodge, Berks.: description, 6/197 &
n. 4; P visits, 6/195, 197–8; 7/54–7;
King and Duke of York at, 8/446–7;
Deptford: 3/58; 4/254; 6/151, 152,
158, 161, 162, 163, 167, 168, 169, 173,
175, 180, 190; 7/20, 285; dislikes Navy
Board meeting at, 6/173; P stores
goods at during Fire, 7/278; Duke
and Duchess of York and others in
'great room', 9/468–9; house in
Lincoln's Inn Fields: 8/450 & n. 1;
9/109; ~ his cook, 6/178; manser-
vant, 6/293
WEALTH: offers loan to Lady Sandwich,
3/55; aims to acquire by public
service, 6/190; his estate, 8/165; P
invests for him, 8/598
SOCIAL: dines with Coventry, 2/222;
5/11; Batten, 3/148; 5/216; Sheriff
Meynell, 3/200; Lord Mayor, 3/241–
2; 4/341; Foley, 5/308; Cocke, 6/72;
Gauden, 6/172; Mennes, 6/191; at
Africa House, 5/52; sees King touch
for scrofula, 8/161; P/Navy Board
colleagues and others dine with,
2/150, 227; 3/84, 179, 197; 4/254; 5/15,
29, 277; 6/119(2); 7/335; 8/32, 163,
189, 417, 428–9, 458, 482, 492, 598;
9/11, 109, 217, 250; also, 7/89
MISC.: sufferings during Interregnum,
3/60; anecdotes of French inns, 3/204;
and of Nostradamus, 8/42 & nn.;
ignorant of meaning of S.P.Q.R.,
4/217; his movements in Plague,
6/290, 293, 322, 324; sprains ankle,
3/197; takes physic, 8/201–2
ALLUDED TO: 1/99; 2/38
CARTERET, George, grandson of Sir
George, cr. Baron Carteret 1681:
birth, 8/324 & n. 2
CARTERET, Lady Jemima (b. Mountagu), wife of Philip:
CHRON. SERIES: chickenpox, 1/13, 17,
20; to wear surgical collar, 1/36 &
n. 3, 64; father's ambitions for, 1/269;
matches proposed for, 3/84 & n. 1;
4/174 & n. 2; unfashionable appearance, 4/127; improved by jewels and

new clothes, 4/239; at royal christening, 4/237–8; at Brampton to avoid
smallpox, 4/439; 5/32, 74, 95; resents
father's liaison, 5/173–4; marriage
with P. Carteret, 6/29, 55, 66, 71, 136,
137, 138, 141, 143, 148, 153, 155–6,
157–8 & n., 159 & n. 1, 160, 161,
173; jointure, 6/138, 180, 191;
wedding, 6/174–6 passim, 179; Sandwich's joy at, 6/202; Sir G. Carteret's
gifts, 7/358; 8/207, 221 & n. 2;
expects child, 8/149, 208, 277, 279; son
born, 8/324, 355; also, 1/25, 41, 46,
57, 223, 276; 2/43; 3/95; 4/117–18,
123, 126; 6/178, 182; 7/241, 356;
8/145, 164, 598
SOCIAL: plays cards, 1/5, 9, 17, 20, 30,
33, 34; at 'tag, rag and bobtail', 1/78;
on river trip, 2/142–3; 5/180; at
Bartholomew Fair, 2/166; P/EP
visit(s), 7/54, 57, 376, 383; 8/115, 463;
9/109, 112; dines at P's house, 9/115,
116–17; also, 1/23, 26, 47, 54, 56, 57,
71, 74, 87, 95; 2/104; 3/57, 59, 68;
4/83, 181, 263, 274; 5/53, 64, 65, 132,
184, 200, 299, 358; 9/130
ALLUDED TO: 8/32, 115
~ her maid Anne: household business
with P, 1/22, 26, 37, 44, 64, 84; ague,
1/33, 37, 41; quarrels with P, 1/40,
43; is paid off by, 1/189
CARTERET,   Louisa-Margaretta
('Louisonne'), daughter of Sir George:
6/167
CARTERET, Philip, son of Sir
George, kted 1667:
CHRON. SERIES: admitted to Royal
Society, 6/48; match with Jemima
Mountagu, 6/29, 55, 66, 71, 136 &
n. 1, 137, 138, 143, 148, 150, 158, 163,
173; 'modest and good natured',
6/152; lame, 6/159 & n. 1; awkward
as lover, 6/159, 160, 161, 167; wedding, 6/174, 175, 176, 179; proposed
as Navy Commissioner, 6/190; at
Cranbourne, 7/54, 56; marriage portion, 7/241; at Gresham College,
7/389; given estate by father, 8/207,
221 & n. 2; high opinion of Louis
XIV, 8/299, 300; lack of money,
8/600; 9/109; his painting and drawing, ib.
SOCIAL: dines with P, 7/387, 388;

9/116–17; at Whitehall chapel, 8/145; also, 7/356, 383; 8/598
ALLUDED TO: 7/17
CARTERET, Lieut. [Philip], naval officer: 3/153
CARTRITE: *see* Carteret
CARTWRIGHT, [William], actor: as Falstaff, 8/516
CARY, [John], Master of the King's Buckhounds: 4/260
~ ?his wife: 1/157
CARY HOUSE, Strand: Mossom's congregation at, 1/60; P dines at, 8/553–4; ?Royal Society at, 8/555
CASE, Thomas, Presbyterian divine (d. 1682): at Scheveningen, 1/140 & n. 6; sermons mimicked, 1/280 & n. 3; printed sermons, 4/111 & n. 4; Presbyterian manner, 9/31, 190
CASE, [?Thomas], clergyman: preaches at Brampton, 2/183 & n. 5
CASE, ——, of the Rolls Office: 9/483
CASTEL-RODRIGO, Emmanuel de Moura-Cortereal, Governor of the Spanish Netherlands 1664–8: 9/176 & n. 3
CASTELL (Castle), [John], clergyman: sermon, 2/52 & n. 2
CASTLE, Dr [John], Clerk of the Privy Seal: business with P, 1/245 & n. 2; 2/63, 64; 3/61, 80; social: 1/208; ~ his clerk, 3/61
CASTLE, Martha (b. Batten), wife of William: P's dislike, 2/161; 3/28; 4/177; in Navy Board pew, 3/40, 55; marriage, 4/177 & n. 3, 217–18, 236–7; social: P's valentine, 2/36 & n. 2, 42, 44, 192; visits Rotherhithe, 2/45; Dartford, 2/57–8; and Deptford, 3/198; at Dolphin tavern, 2/61, 175, 218; 3/31; sees pre-coronation procession, 2/82; at theatre, 2/193; at Penn's wedding anniversary, 3/4; also, ?1/317; 2/?19, 21, 22, 39, 59, 78, 204, 232; 4/5, 253
CASTLE, [William], shipbuilder, Deptford: marriage, 4/177 & n. 3, 217–18; leagues with Batten, 5/83; hostile to J. Taylor, ib.; to Ford and Rider, 6/170; and to Deane, 7/127–8;

slanders P, 5/131; P's low opinion, 5/312; 6/170; masts unsatisfactory, 5/123; and timber, 5/312, 347; builds *Defiance*, 6/7 & n. 2, 169; 7/69, 119; and *Monmouth* yacht, 7/38 & n. 3; social: 2/69, 78; 4/236–7, 253, 284; 7/115; 8/188–9; 9/26–7; alluded to: 5/116, 337
CASTLE, ——, ?of Huntingdon: Brampton business, 9/451, 452; social: 9/212
CASTLE: *see* Castell
CASTLEHAVEN, Lord: *see* Touchet
CASTLEMAINE, Earl and Countess of: *see* Palmer
CATHERINE OF VALOIS (d. 1437), wife of Henry V: P kisses corpse, 9/457 & n. 1
CATHERINE OF BRAGANZA, wife of Charles II:
APPEARANCE, DRESS etc.: handsome, 3/89, 97 & n. 1, 100; 4/229–30; P's opinion, 3/277; broken English, 5/4; dress, 4/229–30; 9/557; sets fashion, 7/335; portrait by Huysmans, 5/254 & n. 4
CHARACTER: modesty and tact, 3/191, 289; 5/40; pleasant humour, 4/174, 177; piety, 7/384
CHRON. SERIES: marriage, 2/52 & n. 1, 65; dowry, 3/90–1, 99, 100; income/jointure, 4/127 & n. 1; 5/40, 50; her court at Lisbon, 2/185, 189, 197; prayed for in London, 2/211; voyage to England, 2/129, 242; 3/15, 51, 62, 79, 90; preparations for arrival at Portsmouth, 3/64, 68, 70, 71, 78, 80; arrives, 3/83, 87; gifts to, 3/72 & n. 2, 74, 100 & n. 4; at Hampton Court, 3/81–2, 89, 95, 97, 100, 146; at Whitehall, 3/175 & n. 2; attends St James's chapel, 3/202; 5/188; 7/384; 8/588–9; said to be pregnant, 3/217 & n. 2, 290, 303; 4/177 & n. 4; miscarries, 7/48–9 & n.; 9/191, 552, 560 & n. 3; inability to have children, 5/56; 8/269 & n. 2; relations with King affectionate, 3/282; 4/222, 272; 5/4; 8/356; 9/205; worsen, 4/112; 5/20, 56; 8/558; rumours of separation/divorce, 8/422 & n. 3, 438, 518; relations with Lady Castlemaine, 3/147, 234; 4/216, 431; 7/159; with Frances Stuart, 5/40; with

Moll Davis, 9/219; seriously ill of fever, 4/337, 339, 342, 344, 347, 348, 352, 356, 358, 363, 378, 407, 439; 5/4; looks ill, 5/107; takes physic, 7/87; visits Tunbridge Wells, 4/240, 251; 7/214; Bath, 4/292; Oxford, 4/315, 321; movements in Plague: at Salisbury, 6/172; Wilton, 6/189; Hampton Court, 7/46; returns to Whitehall, ib.
HOUSEHOLD: her Maids of Honour: their beauty, 4/230; 7/347; dress, 3/92 & n. 2; 5/188; 7/162, 325; complain of drinking water, 3/92 & n. 3; stories of, 3/177 & n. 1; 4/37 & n. 4, 37–8; some return to Portugal, 3/234–5; attend launch, 5/306; play cards, 7/48; 8/70; visit Tunbridge Wells, 7/214; also, 3/299; 4/142; 5/107; court ill-attended, 3/197, 299; 4/49; physician(s), 3/235; 4/345; closet, 5/188 & n. 3; council, 7/303
SOCIAL AND CEREMONIAL: listens to music, 3/90; 8/534; 9/322–3; entertained by Lord Berkeley, 3/184; Lord Mayor, 4/193–4; Buckingham, 4/238; at court ball, 3/300, 301; 7/371–3; at ambassador's audience, 3/297; banquet at Windsor, 4/113; military review, 4/216; her birthday, 4/382; 7/341 (error), 371–3; at opening of parliamentary session, 5/93; visits fleet, 5/193, 196; at launch, 5/306; 9/101; court lottery, 5/214, 215; plays cards, 7/48; 8/70; dines in public, 8/161, 404, 428; 9/320; receives Duchess of Newcastle, 8/163; also, 4/229–30; 5/163, 348; 8/551, 570; 9/294, 323, 331
AT THEATRE: at Cockpit, 3/260, 273; Whitehall, 7/325, 347; 9/219, 456; Theatre Royal, 8/167; 9/203
ALLUDED TO: 8/464; 9/276
CAVALIERS: alleged plots against Commonwealth, 2/204, 225; 5/264; unjust treatment, 3/42–3 & n.; act for relief of, 3/199 & n. 2; cause indiscipline in fleet, 4/169; unfit for employment, 4/196; importune King, 4/373; danger to law and order, 4/374 & n. 1; grievances, 6/303, 329–30 & n.; manners, 9/478
CAVE, [John], Gentleman of the

Chapel Royal: killed in street quarrel, 5/32 & n. 3
CAVE, ——, of St Bride's parish: boards Tom P's child, 5/114; imprisoned, 5/114, 252–3; demands money, 5/82, 154, 158, 167–8
CAVENDISH, Margaret, Duchess of Newcastle (b. Lucas, d. 1673), wife of the 1st Duke [see also Plays]: eccentric dress and behaviour, 8/163–4 & n., 186–7, 196, 243; attracts crowds, 8/163–4, 196, 197, 209; visits Royal Society, 8/243 & n. 3; house at Clerkenwell, 8/209; Life of husband, 9/123 & n. 3
CAVENDISH, William, styled Lord Cavendish, 4th Earl (1684), and 1st Duke (1694) of Devonshire (d. 1707): on Naseby, 1/134
CAYUS: see Caius
CECIL, Robert, 1st Earl of Salisbury (d. 1612): tomb, 8/381 & n. 5
CECIL, William, 1st Baron Burghley (d. 1598): letters, 8/313 & n. 3
CECIL, William, 2nd Earl of Salisbury (d. 1668): 'simple', 5/298–9 & n.; report of expulsion from Lords, 1/127 & n. 1; ~ his gardener, 1/59; 2/139
CENTEN (Seaton), Capt. Bastiaan, Dutch naval officer: killed in action, 6/122 & n. 5
CERVINGTON (Servington), [Charles], tally-cutter in the Exchequer: 2/241
CHAMBERLAIN, Mr and Mrs ——: their singing, 6/316, 338
CHAMBERLAYNE (Chamberlin), Sir Thomas, Governor of the E. India Company: news of Dutch in India, 5/49–50 & n.; supports war, 5/108–9
CHANCERY [see also Justice, administration of]: Rolls Chapel: P hears case, 1/50 & n. 2; orders stationery from, 1/88–9 & n.; hears sermon, 6/80; examines patents in, 9/480, 483; Six Clerks' Office: P visits for patent as Clerk of Acts, 1/197; about agreement with Barlow, 1/205; and dispute with Trice, 2/210; 4/221, 242, 345, 346, 351
CHANCERY LANE [for buildings,

112, 113, 117, 118, 119, 121, 122, 129, 130–1; overtures from Council of State, 1/84 & n. 2, 103 & n. 2; Declaration of Breda, 1/118 & n. 2, 122, 123–4 & n.; proclaimed in London, 1/131 & n. 1, 132; his stay at The Hague, 1/142–4 passim; report of attempted assassination, 1/143 & n. 2; voyage to Dover, 1/152–8 passim; welcomed at, 1/158 & nn.; invests Monck and Sandwich with Garter, 1/161 & nn.; enters London, 1/163 & n. 5, 165; birthday and restoration day to be celebrated, 1/166 & n. 2; issues pardons, 1/168 & n. 1

AFTER 1660: patronage of trade, 2/228; 4/152; inspects Dunkirk money, 3/265; audience to Russian embassy, 4/4; weakened control over Scotland and Ireland, 5/345–6 & n.; fear for his safety, 6/139; rumour of plot against, 7/365; purchase of Audley End House, 7/68 & n. 2, 71; measures against Fire, 7/269, 271, 279(2), 281; consulted on rebuilding London, 8/81; power increased by Fire and war, 7/307; Privy Purse expenses, 8/331 & nn.; attempts to prevent duel, 9/27; attitude to rioters, 9/130; libel against, 9/154; pardons Rochester for affray, 9/451–2 ARMY: reviews guards, 4/216–17 & n.; 9/308 & n. 2; complains of dead pays, 4/334; orders precautions on news of rising, 4/334; suspected of favouring standing army, 5/56 & n. 5; 8/324, 332, 360–1, 366–7; reduces guards, 9/32 & n. 2 CEREMONIES [*see also* Charles II, court of]: touches for King's evil, 1/182 & n. 1; 2/74 & n. 1; 8/161; dines in public, 1/299 & n. 2; 3/60, 202; 4/407 & n. 3; 5/56; 7/217; 8/161, 404, 428; 9/319–20; the assay of food, 8/428 & n. 1; coronation: triumphal arches, 2/39, 47, 73, 74, 77 & n. 2, 81; new peers, 2/79–80 & n.; procession from Tower, 2/81–3 & nn.; coronation day, 2/83–6 & nn.; commemoration of, by service, 6/87; by bonfires, 7/109; 9/172; birthday and restoration observed, 3/95; 4/163; 5/159, 161; 6/111; 7/135, 136; 9/217, 563; at

service celebrating St James's Day Fight, 7/245; lays foundation stone of new Royal Exchange, 8/496–7 & n.; his contempt for ceremoniousness of Spanish court, 7/201; crown jewels: in Tower, 9/172 & n. 2; jewel presented to, 5/226 DRESS: riding habit, 2/157–8; old fashioned suit, 3/81; periwig, 4/360; 5/126; new anti-French fashion, 7/315, 320–1, 324 & n. 3, 328 FAMILY: in mourning for Duke of Gloucester, 1/246; and Queen of Bohemia, 3/81; meets sisters on arrival in England, 1/252, 254; and Queen Mother, 1/276; escorts Queen Mother and Princess Henrietta to Portsmouth, 2/92, 93; meets Queen Mother in Downs, 3/140; also, 2/11; ~ his affection for his (unnamed) bastards, 5/56; 8/183; their number, 7/100 & n. 2 FOREIGN AFFAIRS AND WAR: caricatured in Holland, 4/400 & n. 2; pleased at victories on W. African coast, 5/283; offered bribe to make peace, 5/348; inspects ordnance, 5/316; proclaims fast day for success, 6/73 & n. 4; and thanksgiving day for victory, 6/132 & n. 1; given account of Four Days Fight, 7/140, 146–7, 151; powers in invasion, 8/260; speech to militia, 8/264; announces peace negotiations, 8/61; motives suspect, 7/323; 8/61–2, 145, 335; his part in negotiations, 8/80, 128, 138, 285, 326; Breda medal, 8/83 & n. 1; believes peace necessary, 8/329–30; protests to France against raids, 9/96–7 & n.; favours French alliance, 9/536 & n. 2; also, 5/355 HEALTH ETC.: unwell, 5/197–9 passim; 6/216; vigour, 1/155, 222; height, 1/159 & n. 2; greying hair, 4/360; also, 4/137 & n. 1 HOUSEHOLD [*see also* Charles II, the Court of]: shortage of money, 1/143; 3/210; 7/414; retrenchments, 3/302; 4/205–6 & n.; loans to, 4/176; income and savings, 5/21; 7/404; alleged income from prize money, 8/446 & n. 3; expenditure criticised, 8/331 & n. 2; shortage of linen, 8/417, 418 MARRIAGE [*see also* Catherine of

serious lords out of favour', 3/227; 4/137; Falmouth, Arlington and Lady Castlemaine, 3/227, 237; the 'confidants of his pleasure', 3/302–3; Muskerry and Falmouth, 5/345–6; Arlington, 4/48; Bristol, Buckingham, Arlington, Ashley and Falmouth, 4/137; Falmouth, 4/138; flatterers and time-servers, 4/197; Lauderdale, Buckingham, Hamilton, Falmouth, Proger and Arlington, 5/56; they exalt his power over parliament and city, 5/60; favour vacillates, 8/342, 356; Buckingham, Bristol and Arlington, 8/182, 532, 533, 597; Buckingham, 8/550, 597; Buckingham, Bridgeman, Albemarle and Robartes, 8/585

PRIVY COUNCIL AND CABINET: attendance at, 6/45; weakness at, 8/421, 427; exchanges winks with Duke of York, 9/69; attends Council/Council committee: for naval business, 7/260, 311–13; 8/111–12, 567; 9/69, 121–2, 317–18, 445, 525; Tangier business, 7/336; 8/82; 9/473; judicial, 8/16, 316–17, 420–1; 9/512; examination of Buckingham, 8/330–1; unspecified business, 4/390; 5/317–18; 6/10–11; 7/26, 353, 374; 8/21, 67, 117, 600; 9/17, 508

PROCLAMATIONS AND DECLARATIONS: Declaration of Breda, 1/118, 122, 123; against drunkenness etc., 1/169 & n. 2; Worcester House declaration, 1/278 & n. 2; 4/243; on hackney coaches, 1/286 & n. 1; to commemorate execution of Charles I, 2/24 & n. 2; on Lent, 2/37 & n. 1; against Irish nonconformists, 2/67 & n. 2; general pardon, 2/84; Declaration of Indulgence, 4/5 & n. 3, 44 & n. 2, 57, 58, 62, 65, 82; for arrest of Bristol, 4/298 & n. 4; for Sabbath observance, 4/313 & n. 2; appointing fast day for success in war, 6/73 & n. 4; appointing thanksgiving for victory, 6/132 & n. 1; ordering removal of Exchequer to Nonsuch, 6/188 & n. 1; declaring war against France, 7/40 & n. 2; appointing fast for war against France, 7/138 & n. 1; establishing new markets after Fire, 7/280–1 & n.; appointing chur-

ches to receive homeless after Fire, 7/281 & n. 1; declaring war against Denmark, 7/335 & n. 2; banishing priests etc., 7/343 & n. 5; for Buckingham's arrest, 8/105 & n. 1, 106, 108; ordering method of payment at Exchequer, 8/285 & n. 3; recalling parliament, 8/297 & n. 2; on seamen's grievances, 8/297 & n. 3

RELIGION:

PERSONAL: receives sacrament kneeling, 3/84; on Christmas Day, 3/293; Easter Day, 7/99; commends preachers, 8/116; attends afternoon chapel only for sacrament, 8/154; jokes about Quakers, 5/12–13; kind to, 8/584–5; mocks enthusiasm of Earl of Pembroke, 9/151 & n. 1

POLICY: Worcester House conference, 1/271 & n. 3, 278, 282–3; proposed indulgence (Oct. 1662), 3/186 & n. 2; attempts indulgence by declaration (Dec. 1662), 4/5 & n. 3, 50, 57, 58, 62, 65, 82; proclamation against priests etc., 7/343, n. 5; alienated from bishops, 8/181 & n. 6; support of toleration and comprehension, (Jan.-Feb. 1668), 9/31 & n. 4, 45, 60; tolerant to nonconformists, 9/181, 277–8 & n., 385 & n. 2, 399, 485; suppresses conventicles, 9/502 & n. 1

SCIENCE: dissects cadaver, 4/48; observes dissection, 4/132; preserves horse's kidney stones, 4/156; as 'founder' of Royal Society, 6/6 & n. 1; mocks at, 5/32–3 & n.; observes comet, 5/348; laboratory, 9/416 & n. 1

SPEECHES: poor speaker, 4/250–1 & n.; 5/112 & n. 4; 9/192; addresses militia, 8/264 & n. 1; speeches to parliament: at opening of sessions (21 March 1664), 5/93; (24 Nov. 1664), 5/329; (12 Oct. 1667), 8/476, 479; at prorogations (19 May 1662), 3/89; (18 Feb. 1663), 4/50; (27 July 1663), 4/250–1; (5 Apr. 1664), 5/112; (8 Feb. 1667), 8/52; (29 July 1667), 8/360–1; (10 Feb. 1668), 9/60; on other occasions: on plots and Triennial Act, 5/93; recommending comprehension bill (10 Feb. 1668), 9/60; on supply (30 March 1668), 9/141

SPORTS: yachting: inspects *Mary*, 1/222
& n. 1; has *Catherine* built, 2/12 &
n. 2, 14, 76, 104; his *Bezan*, 2/177 &
n. 4; has *Jemmy* built, 3/164 & n. 4;
4/64; her race against *Bezan*, 3/188;
designs *Henrietta*, 4/123 & n. 1;
hunting: tires out companions, 2/152;
in St James's Park, 5/239; at Bagshot,
8/444, 446–7; 9/302; also, 1/231 &
n. 3; 7/137; 8/382; running: watches
race on Banstead Downs, 4/255;
horse-racing: at Newmarket, 4/324 &
n. 2; 9/209, 214, 264, 340–1, 473, 535;
on Putney Heath, 8/204; tennis:
flattered by spectators, 5/4; weighs
himself, 8/419; also, 4/435; 5/19;
8/418–19
THEATRE: visits Theatre Royal, 2/164,
174, 194; 5/33; 8/91, 167, 388,
450, 487–8, 509; 9/81, 203, 270,
322; visits Duke of York's House,
2/131, 155, 177; 4/431; 6/73; 8/386,
521; 9/54, 85, 183, 398, 458; Cockpit, 1/297; 2/80; 3/260, 273; Great
Hall, Whitehall, 4/56 & n. 3; 7/325,
347, 423–4; 9/456; court masque,
6/29 & n. 6; and puppet play, 3/216
& n. 1; ∼ closes Theatre Royal,
8/168–9 & n., 173; gives £500 to,
8/575
SOCIAL: poor conversationalist, 9/6,
382, 562; entertained at Speaker's,
1/185; with Lord Mayor, 1/193–4 &
n.; 4/193; Albemarle, 1/297; at
Tower, 1/214; Inner Temple, 2/155 &
n. 2; Durdans, 3/184 & n. 2; Dutch
ambassador's, 9/451–2; entertains
Sandwich, 1/179, 185; entertained by
Peter Pett, 4/219; Buckingham, 4/238;
Carteret, 6/169–70; Duchess of Newcastle, 8/163; attends Lincoln's Inn
revels, 3/2 & n. 4; and court balls,
3/300, 301; 7/371–3; dances well,
3/301; French dancing master, 9/507;
drunken frolics, 8/446–7; 9/336; walks
/rides in park [*see* Hyde Park; St
James's Park]; also, 3/60; 4/95, 123,
229–30; 7/39, 106; 9/118
MISC.: pet dogs, 1/158; 8/421;
starling, 9/99, 208, 209; horoscope,
8/330–1; in coach accident, 9/474;
stops fire, 9/535
CHARLES II, the COURT OF [*see*

also Catherine of Braganza: House-
hold]:
REPUTATION: the diary's evidence, vol.
i, pp. cxxviii–cxxx; extravagance and
immorality, 2/167, 170; 3/83, 271,
293; 4/1, 205; 5/306; 6/266, 267; 7/29,
100, 323, 325, 426; 8/168, 181, 269,
325, 355(2); 9/154, 319; likened to
Hell, 7/228–9; satirised in ?*Third
Advice*, 7/421; in *The change of crowns*,
8/167–8 & nn.; proposed parliamentary petition against, 8/361;
courtiers' wealth and frivolity, 2/5;
4/371; 7/155–6, 325–6; 8/282, 446–7
CEREMONIES: Michaelmas, 3/207–8;
Candlemas, 4/31; St Andrew's Day,
4/401; 9/379; St George's Day and
Garter ceremonies, 4/108 & n. 3;
8/177, 184–5; 9/246 & n. 2; St
James's Day, 7/217; Maundy Thurs-
day, 8/150
CHAPEL [*see also* St James's Palace;
Whitehall Palace]: rules, 5/247
ENTERTAINMENTS ETC.: balls, 3/300–1;
5/56; 7/341, 371–3; lottery, 5/214,
215; masque, 6/29 & n. 6; gaming,
3/293; 9/2–4; cards on Sunday, 8/70;
horseraces, 9/209, 535; hunts, 8/444,
446–7; and theatre: courtiers attend
Theatre Royal, 8/167–8, 450; 9/203,
270, 322; and Duke of York's playhouse, 8/521–2; 9/398
MOVEMENTS [omitting notices of seas-
onal movements between St James's
and Whitehall]: at Windsor, 2/75;
Hampton Court for Queen's arrival,
3/95, 97, 100, 175; Tunbridge Wells,
4/240, 251; 7/228; Bath, 4/287, 288,
292; Avebury (1663), 9/240; Oxford,
4/315, 319, 321, 322; 8/379; movements in Plague: 6/140–1, 141–2 & n.;
7/24, 32, 34; at Salisbury, 6/172; at
Wilton, 6/189
OFFICERS [*see principally* under names]:
Groom Porter, 3/293; 9/2 & n. 6;
King's Falconer, 4/264; failure to
pay, 7/414; 8/176, 183, 367; also,
7/218
POLITICAL: factions: 3/238; 4/117;
7/155; 8/356; Sandwich's account,
6/276–7, 301–2; over Lady Castlemaine, 3/15; 9/190; Monmouth,
3/238, 290; 4/117; Clarendon, 8/406;

and Doll Common, 9/415; courtiers despondent about war, 7/153, 155, 197, 213–14; anxious for peace, 8/62; dislike its terms, 8/399; underestimate Dutch, 8/283
MISC.: in mourning, 7/39 & n. 2; 8/154 & n. 1; fails to help during Fire, 7/298; at launch, 9/101
CHARLES II, King of Spain 1665–7: plain dress, 8/79 & n. 3; Louis XIV's negotiations, 8/107
CHARLES X, King of Sweden 1654–60: gift to Sandwich, 1659, 1/238 & n. 1; 2/49; death, 1/76, 83; ~ his son (Gustaf), 7/289 & n. 2
CHARLES, Duke of Cambridge: see Stuart
CHARLETON, Dr Walter, royal physician (d. 1707): on vegetarianism, 7/223–4 & n.; social: 7/92
CHARL(E)TON, Sir Job, M.P. Ludlow, Salop, 1659–78; Justice Common Pleas 1680–6 (d. 1697): 9/93
CHARMS: see Popular Beliefs etc.
CHARNOCK, [Roger], clerk to Sir P. Warwick: 6/154
CHARTERHOUSE YARD: 2/58
[CHASE, John], royal apothecary: eye-lotion, 9/507 & n. 5
CHATELIN'S: see Taverns etc.
CHATHAM, Kent:
TOWN: Charles II's reception, 1/240; oysters, 3/41; St Mary's church, 3/153, 154; 4/227, 259; plague, 7/42 & n. 1, 253
DOCKYARD [see also Allen, J.; Barrow, P.; Cox, J.; Gregory, E.; Pett, Peter]:
CHRON. SERIES: guard, 2/11; squadron at, 2/62; proposed wet dock, 3/154; 4/225–6 & nn., 259; disputes among officers, 3/155–6; 4/149 & n. 2; 5/47; strikes etc., 8/271–2, 291 & n. 1, 307; launch, 4/225; King/Duke of York at, 5/156; 8/298; use of horses, 6/248; standing officers retained, 7/140; yard fortified, 8/125 & n. 2, 256, 260; Dutch raid, 8/259, 261–8, 271–3 passim, 327, 343, 490, 492, 506, 515; 9/524; discharge of ships by ticket, 8/497, 504, 507, 545; 9/69; proposal for surveyor, 8/391; administration criticised by Duke of York, 9/253 & n. 2; master-attendants

suspended, 9/258 & n. 3; dispute about methods of pay, 9/412
VISITS: by P, 1/172 & n. 4; 2/16, 67–73; 3/152–6; 4/222, 225–8, 258–61; 6/182–3, 194–5, 248; 8/305–11; 9/494, 495, 497, 499, 501; by other officers of Navy Board, 2/112, 116; 3/205, 227; 4/314; 6/83, 144, 197; 7/408; 8/350
HILL HOUSE: said to be haunted, 2/68; 4/227; lease, 4/260 & n. 2; housekeeper, 4/225; Treasurer's chamber, 2/68; 4/258; Comptroller's, 4/258; garden, 3/154; P visits/stays at, 2/68–72; 3/153, 155; 4/225–6, 228, 258–60; 6/182, 194, 249; 9/495; also, 8/309
MISC.: musters, 3/155 & n. 2; 4/228, 259; pays, 1/255; 3/215, 290; 4/222, 225; 8/257; 9/495; sales: of stores, 2/68–9; surveys, 1/204; 2/?112, ?116; ?3/68; 4/118; officers' houses, 2/69; 3/155–6; new ropehouse, 6/182 & n. 3; also, 3/163
CHATHAM CHEST: commission of enquiry into, 3/130 & n. 5, 158, 172 & n. 3, 174 & n. 5, 179, 257, 273; 7/109 & n. 2, 110; abuses in management by Commissioner Pett, 3/274; 5/76, 122; and Batten, 5/122, 141, 196, 301; 6/68, 183; 8/277, n. 2; 9/149–50 & n.; pay advertised in *Gazette*, 7/116 & n. 2; insolvency, 8/277; pays, 8/292, 309–10; alluded to: 2/100
CHATTERIS, Cambs.: P overnight at, 4/312
CHAUCER: P's admiration, 4/184 & n. 1; his copy of the *Workes* bound, 5/199 & n. 2; quoted, 5/237 & n. 4
CHEAPSIDE [see also Taverns etc.: Mitre; Star]: gibbet, 1/28; bonfires, 1/52; Lord Mayor's show, 1/277; 4/356; great laceman, 4/332; riot, 5/99, 100, 101; fire, 5/247–8; Great Fire, 7/275, 277; P visits ruins, 7/289; Three Crowns (shop), 3/163
CHEFFINS: see Chiffinch
CHELSEA [see also Taverns etc.: Swan]: P visits, 4/82, 114–17, 160; 7/235, 240; 8/371; 9/216, 563; Plague, 7/95; places in: church [All Saints'], 4/82; girls' school, 4/45, 59, 82, 112; neat-houses, 2/158 & n. 2; 5/268; 7/235; 8/371; 9/216; ~ Little Chelsea, 4/160

CHELSEA COLLEGE: proposed grant of, to Royal Society, 8/537 & n. 3

CHESHIRE: antiquity of families, 9/280 & n. 2

CHESTERFIELD, Lord: *see* Stanhope

CHESTERTON, Cambs.: P's old walk, 9/212; church (St Andrew's), ib.; ferry, ib.

CHESWICKE, ——, musician: 5/194

CHETWIND (Chetwin, Chetwynd), [James], Chancery clerk: P's regard, 3/275; his office, 1/50; P consults on Garter fees, 1/162; his pictures and lute, 1/182–3; chews tobacco, 2/128; his dog, 3/3; dies rich, 3/275 & n. 2; news from, 1/61; social: at old club in Bull Head, 2/127; 7/375; also, 1/50–3 passim, 74, 80, 92, 95, 244, 248; 3/49

CHEVERTON: *see* Chiverton

CHEVINS: *see* Chiffinch

CHICHELE, Henry, Archbishop of Canterbury 1414–43: portrait, 9/226 & n. 2

CHICHELEY, Sir Henry, of Wimpole, Cambs.: on *Naseby*, 1/130

CHICHELEY, Sir John, naval officer: begs prize-ship from King, 8/508; to give evidence to Committee on Miscarriages, 8/527, 549; social: 7/401; 8/433, 575; 9/281

CHICHELEY, Thomas, kted 1670; Ordnance Commissioner and M.P. Cambridgeshire:

PUBLIC CAREER: appointed to Ordnance Board, 5/316; attends Navy Board, 7/104; 8/215 ['Cholmley' ed.'s error]; attends Privy Council committee, 8/112; reports on gun-trials, 7/183 & n. 1; disappointed of Comptrollership of Household, 8/185 & n. 1; a 'high-flyer' in Parliament, 8/85–6; opposes comprehension bill, 9/112; praises P's parliamentary speech, 9/105; parliamentary news from, 8/501, 527

PRIVATE AFFAIRS ETC.: house in Great Queen St, 9/112 & n. 1; high style of living, ib.; social: plays tennis with King, 8/418–19; also, 5/330; 9/281

[CHIDLEY, Samuel], scrivener: 4/344, 345 & n. 1, 351

CHIFFINCH (Cheffins), Thomas,

Keeper of the Private Closet to the King: death, 7/94

CHIFFINCH (Chevins), William, page of the Bedchamber to the King: shows P King's pictures, 8/403; his lodgings, 9/557–8; social: 9/198, 507, 560; alluded to: 7/374

CHILD, Josiah, merchant, cr. bt 1678: P's regard, 6/255 & n. 1; declines Tangier victualling, ib.; bids for navy victualling, 9/287, 288, 316, 323; proposed appointment as Navy Commissioner, 9/507, 509, 550; complaints of, 9/549, 551; social: 9/543

CHILD, [William], organist: suitor to Mrs Bockett, 1/301 & n. 3; to be made doctor of music, 4/199 & n. 1; plays organ, 1/292 & n. 3, 297; 4/428; 8/145; sets music for P, 1/302, 324; 3/33; 7/227; 8/167; plays lute, 1/324; and viol, 2/39; takes P to rehearsal, 2/41; takes P and EP to service, 7/57–8; social: 1/234, 276, 285; 2/96–7; 7/59–60

CHILDREN, P's attitude to [for his foot-boys, *see* Birch, W.; Edwards, T.; Servants]:

HIS CHILDLESSNESS: disappointed of hopes of children, 1/1; finds new use for nursery, 2/127; considers possibility of childlessness, 3/16; 4/365; 5/277, 281; sorry to have no heir, 8/49; given advice on curing infertility, 5/222; asked to adopt child, 6/37; wishes cousin's boy were his own, 8/442

HIS AFFECTION FOR/INTEREST IN: jokes with, 2/72; enjoys company of Mountagu boys, 2/158; takes children to zoo, 3/76; pleased to see Bridewell children at work, 5/289; children dance to his singing, 9/196; admires child at Lamberts', 2/123; Cocke's boy, 2/218; Sir T. Crew's children, 3/76; Gauden's, 4/244; 'stout witty' Dick Penn, 6/35; roguish wit of young J. Pearse, 6/317–18; 7/70, 100; 8/103, 188; pretty boy in church, 7/169; Buckworth's children, 7/273, 419–20; 9/533; the seven children of Sir S. Fox, 7/406; pretty daughter of Mrs Knepp, 8/57; quick wit of boys on trial, 8/319; 'false tone' of shepherd-

boy reading Bible aloud, 8/338; intelligence of Mountagu twins, 8/472; Princess Mary's dancing, 9/507
CHILLENDEN (Chillington), Capt. [Edmund], soldier: 1/7 & n. 4
CHITTERNE, Wilts.: P visits, 9/231
CHIVERTON, Ald. [Sir Richard]: his hemp, 6/77
CHOLMLEY, Hugh, succ. to baronetcy 1665, engineer, Gentleman-man-Usher to the Queen 1662–c. 79:
PERSONAL: duel, 3/157; 4/47; house in Pall Mall, 8/99 & n. 4; ill, 9/95, 99, 122
TANGIER: appointed to committee, 3/238; attends committee, 5/154; 7/321; distrusts Irish, 5/302; hopes to become Governor, 7/99; 8/45, 103–4, 111, 116–17, 127; victualling business, 6/101–2; 7/121; 8/445, 461, 491; mole business: contracts for construction, 4/13 & n. 1, 26–7, 35–6, 45, 88 & n. 3; his gifts to contractors, 8/592–3; to be appointed Surveyor-General, 9/199 & n. 2, 364; accounts/money for, 5/344; 6/103; 7/18–19, 98–9, 323, 403; 8/63, 77, 205, 212–13, 298, 344, 377, 440–1, 482, 518–19, 522, 592–3, 596; 9/197, 199, 214, 388; also, 9/455; unspecified business: 7/132; 8/106, 205, 449; 9/492
COURT/PARLIAMENTARY NEWS FROM: 5/153; 7/163, 336–7, 403; 8/61–2, 93–4, 100, 106–8, 167, 244, 282, 292, 329–30, 412, 438, 446–7, 478, 482, 518–19; 9/53, 185, 530
OPINIONS: of court, 8/331; government by army, ib.; monarchy's prospects, 8/378; Anglesey, 8/301; Coventry, 8/518
RELATIONS WITH P: P's regard, 8/99–100, 331; 9/326; P opposes him over Tangier mole, 5/303; P's annual retainer from, 6/306; 8/593; also, 7/407 & n. 4
RELATIONS WITH SANDWICH: 5/343; 9/326; gift to, 8/592–3
SOCIAL: 5/215; 7/308, 375; 8/557; 9/22, 328–9, 465, 518
CHRIST CHURCH, Newgate St: P attends service, 7/169; Fire, 7/309
CHRISTENINGS: P/EP godparent(s) at private ceremonies: 2/109(2), 216; 5/176; 6/152; 7/49, 128, 129, 329–30;

8/202, 404–5, 540; 9/260; also, 1/42; 2/171, 230; 4/82–3; 5/265; 6/102; 7/129, 394; 8/438; 9/84; public service, at French church, 3/296; Roman Catholic, 7/329–30; customs: 2/109–10, 216; 4/82–3; 5/200, 211; 7/49, 329–30; 8/202, 405
CHRISTIAN, Prince of Denmark, later King Christian V 1670–99: installed as Knight of Garter, 4/108 & n. 3
CHRISTIANIA, Norway: timber from, 3/118 & n. 3
[CHRISTINA OF BOURBON], Dowager-Duchess of Savoy: court mourning for, 5/18 & n. 3
CHRISTINA, Queen of Sweden 1644–54: 8/164 & n. 1
CHRISTMAS, Mr ——, P's schoolfellow: remembers P as 'a great Roundhead', 1/280; mimics preachers, ib.; social: 2/62
CHRISTMAS [see also Drink; Food; Twelfth Night]: wassail bowl, 2/239; boxes, 4/426; 7/422; 8/589; 9/403; gifts (to P's father), 5/344, 346; wedding, 6/338; Catholic ceremonies, 8/588–9; gambling during, 9/2, 4
CHRIST'S HOSPITAL, Newgate St: P buys fairings at, 2/166; boys attend Spital sermon, 3/57–8 & n.; children boarded out after Fire, 7/17 & n. 7
CHURCHILL, Arabella, Maid of Honour to the Duchess of York and mistress of the Duke (d. 1730): 9/413 & n. 2
CHURCH OF ENGLAND [see also Christenings; Funerals; Nonconformists; Presbyterians; Religion (P); Sermons; Weddings]:
CHRON. SERIES:
RESTORATION 1660–2: disputes between Presbyterian and Episcopalian clergy, 1/204 & n. 2; consecration of bishops, 1/276 & n. 2; Worcester House Conference, 1/271 & n. 3, 278 & n. 2, 282–3; bishops restored to Lords, 2/82 & n. 7, 111, 216; Savoy Conference, 2/141; restoration of lands, 1/152; restoration of services: 1/190 & n. 1; at Westminster Abbey, 1/190, 261, 283, 324; Whitehall, 1/176, 195, 210; St Margaret,

CLARENDON PARK, Wilts.: sold
by Albemarle to Clarendon, 5/61 &
n. 1; dispute over timber, 5/203–6
passim, 210, 212–14 passim, 216, 218,
219, 238, 318, 321; alluded to: 9/321
CLARGES (Clerges), Sir Thomas;
Muster-Master General; M.P. Westminster 1660; Southwark 1666; kted
1660: Sandwich's low opinion, 1/129;
army's envoy to King, 1/128 & n. 2,
129; report on navy's debts, 1/288 &
n. 1; criticises Navy Board, 8/510;
9/62; alluded to: 1/184
CLARKE: *see* Clerke
CLARKE, [Frances], wife of Timothy:
P admires, 1/214; 3/75–6, 99; witty
but conceited, 3/299; 4/14; 5/197; a
poor housewife, 4/142; 8/58–9;
proud, 7/100; 8/157; slanderous anecdote of, 7/100; painted, 8/58; social:
4/88 89, 97; 5/245, 291; 8/101, 421;
alluded to: 3/298; 4/42; ∼ her
cousin, 4/14; her kinswoman,
5/197
CLARKE, [Julian] (Aunt Kite): fatally
ill, 2/172 & n. 2; disposes of property,
2/173 & n. 1; burial, 2/178, 179; P as
executor, 2/179; goods valued, 2/190
CLARKE (Clerke), Capt. Robert,
naval officer: arrests Cavalier, 1/99;
gift to P, 1/104; kindness to P, 1/257;
serves on *Antelope*, 6/19; and *Gloucester*, 7/148; conduct in Dutch raid
criticised, 8/310; criticises sinking of
Monmouth, 8/327–8; social: 1/115;
2/74, 210
CLARKE, [Timothy], royal physician:
CHRON. SERIES: P's regard, 1/134;
5/245; on Dutch voyage ('the Doctor'), 1/134, 135, 136, 145, 153–4,
156, 157; tells P story, *The fruitless
precaution*, 1/135 & n. 2, 266; at The
Hague, 1/138; discusses nature of
tragedy, 1/236 & n. 3; visits Portsmouth, 3/69–72; tells bawdy stories,
3/69; to nominate P as Fellow of
Royal Society, 3/72 & n. 3; at Royal
Society club, 6/36; part in P. Carteret's marriage negotiations, 6/136,
137; criticism of Davenant, 8/59;
writes play, 8/59–60; also, 8/159
AS PHYSICIAN: attends Capt. Ferrers,
2/103; Sandwich, 4/17; and King,

5/197; dissects cadavers before King,
4/132; prescribes for P, 4/407, 441;
experiment with opium, 5/151; discusses arrangements for war wounded, 5/332 & n. 5; also, 7/177; 9/254
COURT NEWS FROM: 1/143; 3/282; 4/19;
7/48–9; 8/35, 47
SOCIAL: entertains P to poor dinner,
8/58–9; also, 1/173, 211, 214; 3/73,
74, 230, 299; 4/14, 142; 8/157; 9/200,
413; ∼ house, 3/76
ALLUDED TO: 1/159; 4/10, 97
CLARKE (Clerke), Sir William, kted
1661, Secretary at War 1661–6:
orders troop movements, 1/86; P
asks favour from, 6/169; news from,
6/280–1 & n.; a 'brisk blade', 7/84;
Sandwich's low opinion, 7/203; fatally wounded in action, 7/147, 149,
154; alluded to: 6/121 & n. 2, 122–3;
9/317
CLAXTON, [Hammond], of Booton,
Norf., P's relative: advises P over
Robert P's will, 2/181; 3/218; social:
2/146, 147
CLAXTON, [Paulina], wife of Ham-
mond, housekeeper to Roger P:
3/219; 4/159
CLAYPOLE, John ('Lord') (d. 1688):
enquires for lease of P's Axe Yard
house, 1/218 & n. 1; ∼ his footman,
ib.
CLAYTON, Sir Thomas, Warden of
Merton College, Oxford 1661–93:
9/352 & n. 2
CLEGGAT, Col. [?Thomas], Greenwich: political news from, 6/286;
social: 6/245, 316
CLEMENT IX, Pope 1667–70: election, 8/336 & n. 1
CLEMENTS [?John], bo'sun: 3/155
CLEOPATRA: alluded to in sermon,
5/97; picture, 9/430
CLERGES: *see* Clarges
CLERK OF THE ACTS, the [i.e. P's
principal activities as Clerk. References to his attendance at the Board
and to his share in its collective decisions are indexed under Navy Board.
See also Royal Exchange; for his
relations with colleagues and associates, *see* under names.]:
GENERAL: career summarised, vol. i,

pp. xxx–xxxv; value of diary's evidence, vol. i, pp. cxx–cxxiv
APPOINTMENT: Sandwich's support, 1/177 & n. 4, 182, 188, 191; is offered £500 to withdraw, 1/185; other offers, 1/210, 216; T. Turner's claims, 1/183–4, 189, 191; 7/31; Barlow's, 1/188 & n. 2, 190, 193, 202 & n. 1; P's warrant and patent, 1/187 & n. 4, 196–9 passim & nn., 201; gives plate to Coventry, 1/191, 192, 193, 322; takes oaths, 1/206, 207; receives commission to tender oaths, 1/204; commissioned captain, 9/481 & n. 1
SALARY AND ALLOWANCES: salary fixed, 1/194 & n. 4, 202, 253 & n. 3, 304 & n. 4; 3/279 & n. 2; receives salary and allowances, 1/210, 304, 305 & n. 5; 2/22 & n. 4, 98 & n. 1; 3/37 & n. 3; 4/20 & n. 4, 283; allowed expenses, 6/203 & n. 3; 9/94 & n. 5
DUTIES: responsibility for petty warrant purveying, 2/54 & n. 1; determines to 'exact' privileges, 3/24; offers to help Comptroller, 4/397–8; 7/421 & n. 2; made Surveyor-General of Victualling, 6/271(2) [see also below, Business: victualling]; presence held necessary at Board's weekly meeting with Duke of York, 7/231
PERQUISITES, PROFITS AND BRIBES [including receipts as Surveyor-General of Victualling. See also Prizes and Privateers]:
ACCEPTS MONEY: £5 from Throgmorton, 1/185; £3 offered by Murford, 1/273 & n. 1; £5 from Capt. Grove, 4/93; £36 from Capt. J. Taylor, 4/408, 414, 423; £50 from Dering, 5/1, 5; £40 from Warren, 5/35; £20 from Capt. J. Taylor, 5/127, 158 & n. 3; £100 from Warren, 5/229–30, 270, 271; £100 from Warren, 6/55, 70; £50 from T. Warren, 6/85, 100; £120 from Capt. J. Taylor, 6/98, 274, 280; £20 from Dering, 6/245 & n. 3; £60 from Gauden, 6/251; £100 from Warren, 6/328; £500 from Gauden, 7/8; £320 from Warren, 7/25; £230 from Warren, 7/85, 89–90, 244; unspecified sum from Gauden, 7/118; £500 from Gauden, 8/44, 250; £10 from

Capt. J. Taylor, 8/102; £250 from Gauden, 8/372; £50 from T. Warren, 8/548; unspecified sum from Capt. Beckford, 9/81–2 & n.; records total receipts, 5/3 & n. 3; 8/37
ACCEPTS OTHER GIFTS: beef and tongue, 1/320; gloves and silver-plate, 4/39; ducks, 4/41; pork, 4/120; blackbird, 4/150; sturgeon, 4/182; eels, 4/220; sugar and orange-flower water, 4/290; shells for EP, 4/293; sugar and venison, 4/361; silver plate, 4/368; wine, 4/405; alabaster statue for EP, 4/409; Japan gown for EP, 4/415; wine, 5/32; gloves for EP, 5/35; silver cup for EP, 5/45; mastiff, 5/51, 52; case of knives, 5/62; tongues and bacon, 5/72; oysters, 5/88; cabinet, 5/152; silver flagons, 5/216, 218, 225(2), 234; cake, 5/259 & n. 1; silver candlesticks for EP, 5/316–17; silver candlesticks etc., 6/57; silver watch, 6/83, 100; diamond ring for EP, 6/190–1; turkeys, 6/338; silver plate, 7/90, 91, 364, 405, 409, 413, 415, 416, 420; wine, 7/175; cake, 7/351; silver plate, 7/407; cake, 8/19; warming-pan, 9/405
MISC.: charges pictures to office account, 4/434; buys books from money saved on office stationery, 5/198; earns £50 by trading in calico, 5/289 & n. 3, 291(2), 295, 331; 6/24 & n. 2; 9/562 & n. 1; has book-presses made in dockyard, 7/214 & n. 4; and tool chest, 7/319; plans to buy prize-ship, 7/79; is given Maybolt for trading, 8/112 & n. 3, 455, 464–5 & n., 477 & n. 2, 478, 479 & n. 1; ship fitted out, 8/503–4; and trades in coal, 8/516, 575–6; sold, 8/601–2; 9/29 & n. 4
HIS ATTITUDE TO GIFTS ETC.: hopes for more, 2/129; 4/74, 359, 363, 364, 377, 426; 5/80, 287, 292, 299, 330–1, 332, 344; 6/54, 59, 77, 111, 162, 184, 208, 271, 335; 7/46, 77, 121, 132, 136, 150, 155, 161, 183, 243, 376, 377, 402; refuses/hesitates to accept, 4/182, 391, 415, 436; 5/1, 229–30; 6/185, 245; 7/35, 119, 138; 8/46, 548/9; his rule, 4/415; remarks on danger of, 4/409; insists government should also gain, 4/303–4, 395–6, 409, 415, 426; 5/5,

134, 239, 291; 6/24, 32, 338; 9/562; attitude to giving receipts, 4/436; 5/271; 6/83; 'mighty merry' with Warren over 'our ... tricks', 7/24; falsifies record, 7/295 & n. 1; nervous of parliamentary enquiry into, 9/73, 81–2, 90, 99, 562 & n. 1

HIS SUCCESS [for his love of work, *see also* Vows. For his repute with others, *see* under names]: his pleasure in work and prospect of wealth, 3/40; 4/66; 6/145, 319; 7/215, 249; 8/246; recognises he was appointed by 'chance without merit' and that 'only diligence' keeps him in, 6/285; growing reputation, 2/51; 3/120, 150, 205, 210, 302; 4/1, 289, 296–7, 386; 5/80; 6/324; less unpopular than colleagues in war crisis, 8/297–8, 302, 315, 490(2); said with Coventry to do all work of office, 3/290; 4/19–20; fears distractions of music and cards, 4/104–5, 107; 8/57; realises severity may make him unpopular, 4/256; upbraids himself for idleness, 5/273, 280, 288, 289; 6/92; 7/62, 65, 126, 136; 8/527; 9/173; fears being thought idle, 4/3; 5/341; 6/89; 8/113, 232, 260, 411, 552, 576; 9/78, 144, 155, 170; unwilling to delegate, 6/272; guilty at going to theatre, 8/171, 173, 552; at neglecting Navy Office for Tangier business, 6/107, 109; expected to become Lord High Admiral's secretary, 8/419; alone attends Duke's meeting about expedition to Algiers, 9/516; also, 3/45, 49, 114, 125, 131, 132, 139, 144, 146, 151, 159, 209, 233, 284; 4/23, 71, 166, 188, 205, 257; 5/30, 31, 62, 173, 227, 285, 305, 360; 6/8, 62, 307; 7/107, 123, 286; 8/77, 204, 311–12, 442; 9/8

HIS OFFICE/CLOSET/STUDY IN NAVY OFFICE: alterations, 3/36 & n. 1, 113, 190; 4/282, 284, 286; 5/143 & n. 1, 144, 145; 6/111; 8/522 & n. 3, 523; cleaned, 3/113; 4/285; 7/124; 8/240; bores holes to see into general office, 3/126, 134; table, 3/158; alters position at, 9/547; engravings in, 6/111 & n. 5, 144; 7/124; temporary office at Greenwich, 6/200, 201, 227; study alluded to, 3/266

OFFICE STATIONERY: orders paper from France, 1/201 & n. 1; acquires file, scissors, etc., 2/171; 3/17, 115; buys memorandum-book, 3/115; has paper ruled, 7/98(2), 100. 101, 105, 110, 115

OFFICE RECORDS [The many occasions on which P 'sorts' his papers are not indexed. *See also* Navy Board: records]:

GENERAL: makes inventory, 1/195; buries papers during Fire, 7/274; demonstrates office methods, 9/527

COLLECTIONS [omitting letters, memoranda etc. written for particular occasions]: Admiral's Instructions, abstract of, 3/148 & n. 1; contract book(s): 3/65 & n. 2, 83, 105, 106; 4/214, 220; 5/117; 6/43; 8/353, 540, 545; 9/43–4; entered monthly, 6/43; neglected, 8/350; carried in pocket, 8/540; bound, 8/551; day books, 5/117 & n. 4; 9/444; letter book(s), 3/281 & n. 2; 7/266 & n. 1; 8/258, 314; mast prices, list of, 3/256; memorandum book(s), 4/241 & n. 3, 421, 423; 5/36; 9/91, 406; collection for history of Navy, 9/501 & n. 2, 502, 506, 507; 'Navy MS' or precedent book: 4/11 & n. 1, 14, 15, 23, 29, 36, 65, 96, 107, 188, 191, 214, 218, 219; borrowed by Coventry, 4/264; 'Navy White Book', 5/116 & n. 1, 287; office notes, 5/174; order books, 8/539 & n. 4, 540; ships, list of, with dimensions, 9/26 & n. 2; tables of naval matters, 7/148; varnished paper book, 7/199, ?304, ?305

HIS CLERKS [*see also* Edwards, T.; Gibson, R.; Hayter, T.; Hewer, W.]: purchase price of a clerkship, 1/194; their right to sign warrants, 3/106 & n. 2, 138, 163–4; 4/72; extra provision for, 5/228 & n. 1; 8/593–4 & n.; their profits, 5/320; P's appreciation of, 8/553; their help with pay tickets, 9/100, 102; dine with P [?working dinners], 8/297, 528, 539–40, 540, 546, 565, 569, 584, 588, 594; 9/8, 26, 42, 79, 100, 110, 125, 126, 137, 145, 147, 158, 164, 166, 167, 168, 178, 198, 201, 207, 209, 216, 221, 223, 307, 310, 312, 314, 327, 339, 342, 357, 381, 408, 413, 416, 437, 458, 481

GENERAL: signs warrants for first time, 1/196; relegates Privy Seal work to second place, 1/219; criticised for absences, 2/236; 9/244; late for meetings, 6/137; 7/231; writes agenda for meeting he cannot attend, 8/340; discusses inefficiency of office, 4/105; instructs Brouncker in office matters, 5/343; arranges for conduct of business in Duke of York's absence, 6/56 & n. 4; brings news of naval actions, 6/197; 7/151; 8/258 & n. 2; favours reform of comptrollership, 7/310, 324–5, 328; his leading part in defence of Board before Council, 8/278 & n. 1, 279, 456; before parliamentary Committee on Miscarriages, 8/350, 350–1, 494 & n. 1, 495, 496, 498, 508, 509–10, 537–8 & n., 545–6 & n., 557, 560 & n. 1, 574 & n. 2; 9/62, 79(2), 80; and before Brooke House Committee, 9/38, 39, 43–4, 47, 73 & n. 2; asked to write Council minutes, 8/279; in good repute with parliament because produces papers, 8/333; suspected of suppressing evidence, 8/538 & n. 1; examined by Brooke House Committee about prize-goods affair, 9/48, 49–50, 56, 64, 68; about tickets, 9/55–6, 79(2) & n. 1, 80; prepares for defence of office in Commons, 9/82(2), 97, 98, 100, 102; makes speech in Commons, 9/97–103 passim & nn.; congratulated on it, 9/103–6 passim, 108, 109, 110, 113(2), 114, 122, 123, 130, 140, 146, 248, 527–8; prepares answers to Committee's charges, 9/168, 169 & n. 1, 254 & n. 2, 562 & n. 1; examined, 9/298; reports proceedings to colleagues, 9/442 & n. 1; writes to Duke of York urging need for reform of office, 8/503; his views on reform, 9/151; drafts Duke's letter criticising conduct of Principal Officers, 9/267 & n. 1, 280–7 passim, 289–91 & nn., 301; defends his conduct, 9/304 & n. 4, 305, 306; prepares Duke's answers to Officers, 9/309, 338, 341, 342, 349, 358–9, 360; prepares defence of existing constitution, 9/321, 474, 477–80 passim, 482–5 passim & n., 489 & n. 2, 501, 519, 521,

523, 524, 547–8 & n.; discusses state of office with Brouncker, 9/400; reforms discussed at cabinet, 9/525–6 & n.; favours appointment of seaman as commissioner, 9/349; drafts instructions to commanders, 9/547 & n. 1, 548, 549, 563; expects/will welcome retirement/dismissal, 5/273; 6/109; 7/77, 172, 185, 235, 298, 315, 332, 348, 349, 350; 8/179, 273, 277, 279, 291, 292, 293, 297–8, 323, 350, 518; 9/76, 86, 99, 102, 293, 295, 369, 373, 380, 503, 529, 551; plans to retire temporarily to Deptford, 9/349, 369; and to reduce his work, 9/386; granted leave of absence, 9/555–6 & n.

LEARNS HIS TRADE: studies Admiral's Instructions, 3/129 & n. 1; Hollond's discourses, 3/145 & n. 1; report of Admiralty Commission of 1618–26, 4/96 & n. 4; learns timber measuring, 3/105 & n. 2, 169 & n. 3; 4/176, 189, 206, 233; and multiplication, 3/128, 131–6 passim & n., 140, 148, 149; practises arithmetic, 3/137, 255, 293; 4/2, 3; studies slide-rules, 4/103, 104 & n. 2, 125, 132, 406, 433; instructed about timber, 3/118–19, 131; about naval architecture and rigging, 3/138, 146, 149, 152, 158, 160, 161, 163; 4/172, 236, 262, 396; 5/143–4, 146–7, 159, 309; studies shipbuilding, 5/108, 109, 162, 176; maps, globes and navigation, 3/178; 4/133–4, 150–1, 206, 390; 5/303; 6/80; pursers' accounts and victualling business, 3/181 & n. 1, 195; 4/28, 226; 6/315 & n. 3, 321 & n. 2; flags, 3/205; sailmaking, 4/7; commerce, 4/10; ropes and cables, 4/310; 5/181; 6/34, 35; storage of masts, 4/420; 5/14–15, 55, 72, 115, 195; examines contracts book of R. African Co., 5/14; learns varieties of tar, 5/80 & n. 3

CONTRACTS [entries in which the word contract occurs are indexed here; many entries indexed under supplies may also concern contracts. See also above, Office records]: asserts right to draft, 3/99–100 & nn.; negotiates/drafts: for timber, 3/112 & n. 2, 114; hemp, 3/114, 116, 120; 6/327 & n. 1; 7/136; masts, 4/61 & n. 2,

303–4 & n.; 5/215–16 & n., 333 & n. 1; 7/2–3 & n.; deals, 4/232 & n. 4, 233; tar, 4/364 & n. 1; 5/136 & n. 3; glazing, 5/44 & n. 4; hammocks, 6/40 & n. 2; plank, 6/99 & n. 6, 185 & n. 2; defends Warren's contracts, 4/326, 421 & n. 3; 7/2–3 & n.; 9/254, 255; criticises Winter's, 4/326; and Murford for alleged breach of, 4/353 & n. 1; makes calculation about Wood's masts, 5/51 & n. 4, 52

DOCKYARDS [for his work at individual yards *see* Blackwall; Chatham; Deptford; Portsmouth; Woolwich]: drafts letter 'of reprehension and direction', 3/164 & n. 5; introduces new call-book, 3/234 & n. 2, 289 & n. 2; 4/14–15; to visit Deptford and Woolwich at least once a week, 4/425; defends his administration, 4/256; proposes employment of workmen in fire-fighting, 7/274

FINANCIAL [*see also* Exchequer; Navy Board; Treasury; Warwick, Sir P.]: *general*: prepares statement on debts for parliament, 1/211, 214 & n. 4, 226 & n. 4, 227, 228, 246 & n. 3, 247, 288 & n. 1; drafts scheme for paying off seamen, 1/309 & n. 5; makes estimates for boats, 3/52; drafts statement of navy estimates, 3/179 & n. 4; prepares answer to Lord Treasurer, 3/250, 258, 261, 280 & n. 1; and account of expenses (1660–2), 4/49 & n. 2; calculates debts, 4/304; introduces new method of accountancy, 5/7; proposes separation of posts of deputy-treasurer and muster-master, 5/8 & n. 1; drafts letter to Lord Treasurer on cost of war, 5/325, 326, 329; inflates estimate, 5/330 & n. 2; to be fully informed by Treasury, 6/46; works on accounts, 6/256 & n. 3, 257 & n. 4; 7/76(2); comments on proposal to pay bills in course, 6/304 & n. 3; and on value of Additional Aid (1665), 6/327, 334; 7/4, 87; presents statements of need for money: to Lord Treasurer, 7/48 & n. 2, 294 & n. 1, 295; to Duke of York, 7/122(2) & n. 1, 205–6 & n., 373 & n. 2, 374(2), 381; 8/138 & n. 2, 274 & n. 3; 9/49, 94; to Cabinet/

Council, 7/311–12 & n.; 8/111(2), 111–12 & n., 114 & n. 3; enquires about loans at Guildhall, 7/72 & n. 2, 76, 88 & n. 2; prepares statement on cost of war for Commons, 7/233, 285–8 passim & nn., 291–4 passim & n., 300, 301–2 & n., 308 & nn., 310, 314; 8/90; compares costs of First and Second Dutch Wars, 7/307 & n. 5, 308; calculates extraordinary charges, 7/310; his imprests authorised by Board, 7/328, 330; prepares accounts for parliament, 7/417; examines petty warrant accounts, 8/50; attempts to get creditors paid, 8/203(2); 9/140, 146, 149; works on report to Treasury Commission on accounts (1660–7), 8/250, 349, 372 & n. 1, 373 & n. 2; consults Treasury about commanders' pay, 8/398; works on Navy Treasurer's accounts, 8/448 & n. 4, 458 & n. 2; drafts Council order about Exchequer certificates, 9/152–3; applies to city for cash, 9/169; ordered by Council to calculate charge of summer fleet, 9/216; reforms storekeepers' accounts, 9/300, 374 & n. 1, 474; defends Board against criticisms from new Treasurers, 9/447; examines old accounts, 9/479; prepares estimates, 9/493–4 & n., 501, 530; also, 4/305, 306; 6/75; 7/77; 8/89, 273, 274, 277, 524; 9/40, 109, 110, 119, 271

pays [*see also* Navy Treasury; and under names of dockyards]: signs tickets, 6/158; 7/366; 8/280; discusses order of pay, 7/308, 327; and methods of expediting, 8/433 & n. 1, 558 & n. 3; inspects Ticket Office, 7/76, 418; to draw up rules for issue of tickets, 9/15 & n. 4

pursers: plans reform of, 6/325, 341; memorandum on, 7/1(3) & n. 1, 2(3), 5, 9, 10 & n. 1, 13; plan adopted, 7/27, 28, 105, 106 & n. 2; offers to help Mennes with pursers' accounts, 7/421 & n. 2; new proposals, 9/459, 460 & n. 2

JUDICIAL/DISCIPLINARY BUSINESS [*see also* Carkesse, [J.]; Field, [E.]]: memorandum on bill empowering Principal Officers as city magistrates,

4/81–2 & n.; part in cases of alleged theft, 1/316; 3/137; 6/184; of damage to buoy, 3/149; and embezzlement, 9/291; in enquiries into loss of *Satisfaction*, 3/213 & n. 1; and surrender of *Prince Royal*, 8/12 & n. 1; courts martial, 9/481 & n. 1, 488 & n. 1, 497–8 & nn., 505, 508, 510–11; also 4/78; 8/386

SHIPS AND SHIPPING: part in fitting out/despatching ships, 2/104, 112 & n. 1, 127; 3/31, 51, 59–60 & n., 63, 119 & n. 3, 150; 4/103–4 & n., 131; 5/136–7, 155, 156 & n. 2, 165, 176, 265, 305, 317, 325; 6/257(2); 7/140, 149, 153 & n. 2, 157 & n. 1, 162, 176(2), 177, 181, 183; 8/124 & n. 4, 257 & n. 3; despatches fireships, 8/263, 266–7, 275, 286; and merchantmen, 8/281 & n. 1, 283, 296; hires ships, 3/81 & n. 2; issues masters' warrants, 4/74; attends launches, 4/102; 5/306; 9/101; arranges transport of troops, 4/285 & n. 3; 8/83, 153; musters ships' companies, 4/432 & nn.; visits fleet, 6/239, 241, 275, 286–7, 299–301 passim; 7/149; puts pressed men under guard, 6/99 & n. 5; issues press warrant, 6/131 & n. 1; ships off pressed men, 7/189 & n. 1, 190 & n. 1, 196 & n. 1; pays them with his own money, 7/187; arranges convoys, 6/296 & n. 3, 300–1 & n.; measures ships, 5/217 & n. 1; 7/69; discusses design of *Defiance*, 6/7 & n. 2; and alterations to *Rubis*, 8/121; inspects ships in building and repair, 5/146–7; 8/124, 135; arranges for weighing ships 8/325; also, 8/419 & n. 1

SICK AND WOUNDED: concern for, 6/245–6, 275; business with Evelyn, 6/278; arranges supplies for prisoners, 7/201 & n. 1; discusses terms of their release, 7/380 & n. 3

SUPPLIES: right to issue warrants for petty provisions, 2/54 & n. 1; 3/106 & n. 2; enquires prices of tar and oil, 3/120; investigates supplies of tar and coal, 3/140; reports on hemp to Duke of York, 3/142 & n. 3, 145, 150; criticises flagmakers, 3/164; 4/151; 5/178; inspects Wood's masts, 3/227; 5/6 & n. 4; prepares accounts of hemp

purchase, 4/49, 57, 58, 72; visits timber yards, 4/103, 176; 5/295–6; makes bargains for tar, 4/181, 184, 187; opposes Cocke's offer of hemp, 4/194 & n. 3; and of timber, 4/241–2 & n.; inspects Warren's deals, 4/201; inspects plank, 4/289; discusses insurance of hemp ship, 4/394–7 passim & nn.; and purchase of Albemarle's timber, 4/435 & n. 3; writes to Coventry about preserving masts, 5/54 & n. 2, 56; and measuring them, 5/77 & n. 1, 78, 123–4; inspects canvas, 5/158 & n. 4; consults Richard P of Norwich about supplying bewpers, 5/181–2 & n.; attempts to find site for new mast-dock, 5/202, 231 & n. 1, 270; 6/96; involved in attempt to buy Clarendon's timber, 5/203–6 passim & nn., 210, 212–14, 216, 218, 219, 238, 318, 319; visits Margett's ropeyard, 5/265; buys Nelson's bewpers, 5/305 & n. 3; inspects Castle's knee-timber, 5/312 & n. 3; visits anchor-smiths, 5/314; negotiates with Ordnance for gunwadding, 5/316; writes to Coventry about stores, 5/327 & n. 1; 6/92 & n. 2; enquires about English hemp, 5/352; gets warrant for King's timber, 6/3 & n. 2; enquires about hammocks, 6/51; consults Attorney-General about carriage of timber, 6/101 & n. 2; insures cargo of Hamburg ships, 6/112; discusses canvas with Cocke, 7/68; orders cork, 7/206 & n. 3; discusses transport of timber, 8/114; puts Cocke's hemp into store, 8/572; also, 5/83, 289

VICTUALLING [*see also* Perquisites etc., above]: accounts, 3/52, 62, 106; 4/304, 322; 8/220; 9/214, 381; visits/ inspects Victualling Office, 3/135 & n. 3; 4/84; 6/269; 7/118, 134, 135, 140, 150, 232, 262, 263, 265; reports to Coventry, 3/144 & n. 2; discusses shortages, 4/363, 364, 371; applies to Lord Treasurer for money, 4/389 & n. 1; tries to hasten out victualling ships, 6/91 & n. 1, 103 & n. 4, 107; supplies for Sandwich's fleet, 6/228–9, 230, 253 & n. 4; disastrous shortages in 1665, 6/275; proposes reorganisation, 6/254–5 & n., 255, 265(2); proposals accepted, 6/266, 275; appointed Surveyor-General, 6/271(2) & n. 3, 279–80, 285, 294 & n. 1; salary, 6/284; 8/250; nominates and instructs surveyors, 6/281 & n. 4, 293–4 & n., 306, 315 & n. 2, 315–16, 329; consults Gauden, 6/294, 325; 7/25(2), 232; 8/43, 44; draws up estimates, 6/323 & n. 2; sends victuals to fleet, 7/117; neglects business, 7/118, 121, 134–5, 139, 217, 220; inspects victualling ships, 7/128; reports on supplies, 7/118, 216–17 & n., 234 & n. 4, 262; 8/78 & n. 3; victuallers miss fleet, 7/252; answers commanders' complaints, 7/265 & n. 6, 266; lacks work, 7/421; fears reorganisation of Comptrollership will further reduce it, 8/35, 36, 37; memorandum on need of cash, 8/110, 118(2) & n. 1; resigns as Surveyor-General, 8/241–2, 250, 253, 356, 357, 367; drafts Gauden's new contract, 8/587 & n. 4; 9/8(2), 47, 297, 298, 312; and Board's memorandum on victualling by contract, 9/315, 315–16 & n.; also, 4/288; 8/43, 112, 344, 432; 9/382, 511

MISC. BUSINESS: studies problem of salutes due to British ships, 2/223 & nn., 229 & n. 2, 233, 236 & n. 3, 242; 3/4; discusses privileges of ships' surgeons, 5/271; and transport of coal for city poor, 6/264 & n. 3, 265(2); unspecified [excluding the innumerable occasions on which P records having worked, discussed business, written letters, or attended a meeting, without specifying the business involved]: prepares business for weekly meetings with Duke of York, 3/192, 198, 203, 207, 214, 229, 247, 271; 4/43; 7/25

CLERKE: see Clarke

CLERKE, Christopher, son of P's Greenwich landlady: suspected of having plague, 6/288, 294; walks to Lambeth with P, 6/310; social: 6/336, 338

CLERKE, Sir Francis, M.P. Rochester, Kent: at meeting of Chatham Chest commission, 3/257; house, 8/311 & n. 5; social: 4/188; ∼ his wife: at

Battens', 4/188; slanders Battens, 5/141

CLERKE, Sarah, daughter of P's Greenwich landlady: dogged by P, 6/332(2); also, 6/279, 294, 332, 333; 7/7, 211, ?236; 8/45, 76

CLERK(E), [Thomas]: see Taverns etc.: The Leg, King St

CLERKE, ——, confectioner: Creed lodges with, 3/174

CLERKE, ——, merchant: referee in freightage dispute, 4/404, 424; 5/23, 36

CLERKE, Mrs ——, of Greenwich, P's landlady Oct. 1665 – Jan. 1666: CHRON. SERIES: agrees with P for lodgings, 6/261 & n. 3, 271, 313; 7/7; P absents himself for fear of plague, 6/288, 294; has Christmas dinner with, 6/338; takes leave of, 7/7; stays overnight with, 7/202; also, 6/295; 7/417; ∼ her little boys, 6/287–8

HER HOUSE: Hewer's room at, 6/233, 251; EP overnight at, 6/251, 279, 282, 296, 313, 314; music and dancing, 6/279, 323–4; Twelfth Night party, 7/6; also, 6/235, 236, 238, 244, 245, 252, 253, 254, 256, 258, 265, 270, 272, 274, 278, 281, 285, 286, 293, 297, 302, 305, 307, 308, 310, 317, 318, 320, 325–6, 329, 332, 333, 335, 339, 340, 341; 7/2, 4, 6

CLERKE, ——, milliner, Fenchurch St: 9/517, 518; ∼ his wife admired by P, 9/460, 518; her father, 9/518 & n. 2

CLERKE, Mr ——, solicitor: in Field's case, 4/51, 52, 53, 55, 57, 193, 201, 350, 411, 427; in dispute with T. Trice, 4/344, 345, 346, 352; consulted by P about Robert P's Exchequer accounts, 6/65; helps P to prepare Tangier accounts, 8/508, 547; 9/22, 91, 155; news from, 8/265; death, 9/381; social: 9/8, 42, 223

CLERKENWELL [see also Theatre: Red Bull]: visits by P/EP, 2/58, 152, 232; 5/285–6; 7/75; 8/209; 9/311; churches: [St James-the-Less], 2/152; [St John's], 5/285–6; 7/75; girls' schools, 2/232; 4/132; New Bridewell, 6/65–6 & n.; prison, 9/130

CLEVES: Mary Princess of Orange married at, 7/250 & n. 1

CLIFFORD, family of: in Fuller's *Worthies*, 5/118 & n. 1

CLIFFORD, Martin, Buckingham's secretary: to mediate between Buckingham and Clarendon, 9/361 & n. 2

[CLIFFORD, Rosamund], (d. ?1176) 'fair Rosamund', mistress of Henry II: alluded to in sermon, 5/97 & n. 2

CLIFFORD, Sir Thomas, M.P. Totnes, Devon, Comptroller and Treasurer of the Household, Treasury Commissioner, cr. Baron Clifford of Chudleigh 1672:
PUBLIC CAREER: origin and estate, 8/185 & nn.; 9/205; at Fishery Committee, 5/294; naval service, 7/288 & n. 3; to be Comptroller of Household, 7/390 & n. 2; attacks Pett in Commons, 8/526; appointed to Treasury Commission, 8/229–30; dealings with Navy Board: about Exchequer certificates, 9/122; victualling contract, 9/303, 316–17; debts, 9/444–5; reform of office, 9/525; and other business, 8/249, 278; 9/501
RELATIONS WITH P: P's opinion, 5/294; 7/288; his regard/support for P, 9/487, 493, 501, 503, 512
RELATIONS WITH OTHERS: ally of Sandwich, 7/54; protégé and ally of Arlington, 8/185, 289; unpopular with colleagues, 9/205; disliked by Coventry, 9/472
SOCIAL: 8/79; 9/118, 352

CLIFFORD, Mrs ('Madam') ——: social: 2/151, 169, 193, 201

CLINKE, ——, a Dutchman: fights with waterman, 1/215

CLOCKS: see Watches and Clocks

CLODIUS (Clod), [Frederick], physician: 1/92, 196; ~ his wife (Mary Hartlib), 1/90 & n. 2

CLOTHIER, [John], rope-merchant, Woolwich: 5/190–1, 253 & n. 1

CLOTHWORKERS' COMPANY: see London: livery companies

CLOTHWORKERS' HALL: P visits, 1/187; destroyed in Fire, 7/278–9; alluded to: 9/245, 518

'CLUB', P's: meets weekly in Cromwell's time, 1/208 & n. 4; 2/127; 4/10; 5/30; 6/147–8; 7/375

CLUN, [Walter], actor: replaced by Lacey, 4/128 & n. 4; murdered, 5/232 & n. 5, 233; his talent, 9/411, 438, 523 & n. 1

CLUTTERBUCK, [Richard], merchant: 5/37

CLUTTERBUCK, [Thomas], consul at Leghorn: 9/346 & n. 2

COAL [see also Newcastle-upon-Tyne: Woodmongers, Company of]: P's domestic supplies, 1/11; 2/179; 3/25–6; 8/187, 435; distributed to poor, 4/410 & n. 2; price, 7/401 & n. 5; 8/98 & n. 5, 187, 285, 295–6 & n., 435; scarcity in war, 8/102, 285, 295–6, 576; mined in Nova Scotia, 8/426 & n. 1; exported to Tangier, 9/249 & n. 2

COBHAM, Kent: 8/184; 9/497

COBHAM, Surrey: 9/273

COCKE, [Anna Maria], b. Solomons, wife of George: her good looks etc., 2/218; 3/143, 152; feared consumptive, 4/235; her valuable linen, 4/283

COCKE, Col. Charles George: his reduced condition, 9/113 & n. 2; ~ his daughter, 4/94–5

COCKE, George (Capt. Cocke), hemp merchant, Commissioner for the Sick and Wounded and Prisoners of War 1664–7:
CHARACTER: P's critical comments, 4/283; 5/51; 6/192, 199, 238–41 passim, 282, 290; well thought of, 5/300; good company, 6/227, 342
NAVY BOARD BUSINESS: contracts for hemp, 3/114 & n. 1, 116, 129–30; 6/327 & n. 1; 7/358–9 & n., 385 & n. 2; proposes to provide anonymously, 7/132 & n. 3, 150, 184, 206, 220–1, 228, 359, 361; hemp criticised, 3/155; 4/194 & n. 3; and timber, 4/241–2 & n.; his tar, 4/364 & n. 1; canvas, 7/68; accounts, 4/49, 57, 58, 72, 141; payments to, 6/312, 313, 327, 328, 329; 7/115; 9/140, 146; rumoured appointment as Surveyor, 4/287 & n. 2; discusses exemptions from press, 6/24–5; unspecified business, 3/152–6 passim; 4/235; 6/216, 279, 307; 7/133; 8/447
CHATHAM CHEST: attends meeting, 3/257

COMMISSIONER OF THE SICK AND WOUNDED AND PRISONERS OF WAR: appointed Treasurer, 5/329 & n. 1; business, 8/112; also, 6/217
HIS SHARE IN SANDWICH'S PRIZE-GOODS: bargains and agreements with P and others, 6/230, 238 & n. 4, 241, 243, 245, 297; acquires certificate from Sandwich, 6/247; goods threatened with seizure, 6/243, 252, 256, 259, 260–5 passim, 269–70; profit, 6/313–14, 327, 328, 329, 334, 340, 341; 7/65; affair investigated by Brooke House Committee, 9/48–50 passim & nn., 57, 61, 63, 66, 72; also, 6/228, 234, 239, 246, 247, 248, 271–2, 272, 312, 318; 7/6
POLITICAL VIEWS ETC.: on Dutch war, 5/35, 105; 6/282; 7/286–7; fears parliament will withold supply, 2/196–7; 8/68–70; pessimism about government and state of nation, 6/210–11, 218, 245; 7/14, 375; 8/125, 409; 9/96; believes active King the only solution, 8/37; on danger of civil war, 8/70; help to Coventry, 9/303; news from, 7/220, 287, 309, 311, 317, 402; 8/18, 24, 37, 68–70, 80, 105, 153, 176, 275–6, 409, 447, 535, 568, 572; 9/278
COMMERCIAL NEWS: about Guinea trade, 4/363; loss of rents in Fire, 7/286 & n. 2; bankers' wartime credit, 8/285
HOUSES: at Greenwich: P visits, 3/142, 143; 6/233, 291, 297; stable, 6/233; garden, 6/291, 297; door by the water, 6/297; in London: 8/441, 497
RELATIONS WITH P: gifts of fish etc., 2/225; 3/81; silver plate, 7/90, 91, 121, 132, 405, 409, 416–17, 420; money, 7/132; lends coach, 7/269; warns against Brouncker, 8/203; asks for loan, 8/598; praises parliamentary speech, 9/105, 113; advises about proposed reform of Board, 9/290; also, 7/305; 8/572; 9/285
SOCIAL: drunk, 2/?232, 238; 3/4; 6/290; atheistical talk, 5/335–6; on river trip, 3/30–1; talks of Poland, 3/154; of Roman history, 4/362; of Cromwell's betrayal of Charles I, 5/335 & n. 2; plays billiards, 6/190; enjoys Mrs Penington's company,

6/273, 297, 299, 308, 310; at Twelfth Night party, 7/6; dance, 7/18; taverns, 2/208, 218, 219, 233; 6/325; 7/68, 74, 89; 8/95; houses/lodgings of associates in London and Greenwich, 2/211, 218–19; 3/10, 88; 5/277; 6/186, 187, 204, 209, 217, 236, 237, 275, 285, 303, 307–8, 311, 313, 317; 7/14, 67, 376; 8/65, 66; 9/410; at his Greenwich house, 3/142, 143; 6/191, 192, 212, 220, 222, 227, 228, 275, 291, 296, 316, 324, 335–6, 339; London house, 7/34, 38, 404, 408; 8/394–5, 441, 497; 9/15; also, 2/220, 223–4; ?4/212; 6/226, 248, 303
ALLUDED TO: 9/286, 501
~ his son: 2/218; at school, 6/223; his black footboy (?Jack) dies of suspected plague, 6/232, 233, 236, 244, 283, 285; his servant Jacob, 6/259; his maid, 7/63
COCKE, [Robert], navy victualler at Lisbon: gift to P, 4/290 & n. 2; accounts, 4/325
COCKE, ——, ?a prostitute, Fleet Alley: P entertained by, 5/225–6
COCKER, [Edward], calligrapher and engraver: P's regard, 5/237–8 & n.; engraves P's slide-rule, ib.; sells him reading glass, 5/290, 291–2
COCKPIT, the: see Whitehall Palace
COCKPIT, the new, King's Gate, Holborn: P at, 9/136, 141, 154
[COENDERS, Rudolf], Dutch naval commander: killed in action, 7/229 & n. 3, 231 & n. 4
COFFEE-HOUSES:
GENERAL: political talk/debate in [see also below, Miles's]: 5/30, 228, 321; 8/304; Presbyterians' bold talk, 4/15; literary/scientific talk, 5/14, 27–8, 37, 108, 123; music, 5/12; in Plague, 7/45; chocolate drunk, 5/329
P VISITS [business talk/transactions not noted]: [Miles's, the 'Turk's Head', New Palace Yard, Rota Club at], 1/13, 14, 17, 20–1, 61, 63, 288; Grant's, 4/64–5; coffee-house(s) near Navy Office [all or most in Cornhill], 1/318; 2/11, 108, 111, 151; 3/2, 35; 4/340, 353, 371, 378, 380, 434, 438; 5/1, 12, 34, 293, 295; in Covent Garden, 5/37 & n. 2 (the 'great' coffee

political/court news from, 7/353–4;
8/11, 86, 368–9, 544, 597; alluded to:
2/97; 9/139; ~ his brother, 1/206
COLLADON (Collidon), Sir John,
physician: patent for smoky chim-
neys, 4/315 & n. 1
COLLAR: *see* Collier
COLLETON (Collidon), Sir John,
merchant: report on Fishery lottery,
5/299–300 & n.
COLLIER, [?John] ('Blacke Coller'):
Hawley's case against, 1/199–200
& n.
COLLINS, [Jerome], surgeon: to sail
with Rupert, 5/275 & n. 1
COLLINS, ——: employed by Brooke
House Committee, 9/43
COLNBROOK, Mdx: 9/243
COLVILL(E), John, goldsmith banker,
Lombard St:
BUSINESS WITH P: Tangier: cashes
tallies, 6/108, 115, 163, 164; 7/214,
242; and bills of exchange, 6/169;
7/66; his accounts settled, 6/204–5,
325; also, 9/265; private: sells salts,
6/131; arranges loan on Treasury
warrants, 7/85, 89–90 & n., 230, 243,
244, 251; advances money for
Paulina P's portion, 9/97; unspecified: 6/184, 297; 9/214
HIS NEWS/OPINIONS: critical of ministers, 7/244; news of Dutch fleet,
6/184; of court and parliament, 7/323;
low view of government credit,
6/268; 7/171; praises P's parliamentary speech, 9/109; also, 6/318
MISC.: credit survives Fire, 7/323;
moves to Lime St after Fire, 7/323;
new house in Lombard St, 9/112
~ his beautiful wife: 6/131–2
COLWALL, [Daniel], Treasurer of the
Royal Society: supports Carkesse in
dispute with Navy Board, 8/555; at
Royal Society, 9/147, 334
COMBERFORD, [Nicholas], chart-
maker, Ratcliffe: P admires his
methods, 4/240
COMETS and meteors: *see* Science
and Mathematics: astronomy
COMINGES, Gaston Jean-Baptiste,
Comte de, French ambassador 1663–
5: at review of troops, 4/217; takes
offence at Lord Mayor's banquet,

4/355; house [Exeter House, Strand],
5/103 & n. 4
COMMANDER, [Henry], scrivener,
Warwick Lane: draws up deed for
Sandwich, 4/343; and P's will, 5/20,
25, 26, 29, 31, 192; negotiates P's
purchase of land etc. for coachhouse
and stable, 8/209, 224, 225, 246, 250
COMMON GARDEN: *see* Covent
Garden
COMMONWEALTH, the:
GENERAL: P reproached for service to,
6/329–30; return predicted, 8/337–8,
390, 556; 9/373; political/military
efficiency, 3/90; 6/45–6; 8/250,
377–8, 390–1
POLITICAL HISTORY: successive régimes
in 1659, 5/8 & n. 2; Committee of
Safety (1659), 1/39, 51; 2/92; Council
of State (1660): clerks dismissed, 1/23;
members chosen, 1/65 & n. 4; appoints Sandwich general-at-sea, 1/71;
orders Cavaliers and disbanded soldiers to leave London, 1/91 & n. 2;
prepares agreement with King, 1/103
& n. 2, 111; also, 1/48
ARMY: high repute abroad, 4/215 &
n. 3; and at home, 4/217, 373–4 & n.;
disbandment, 1/242 & n. 1, 249, 257,
295 & n. 3, 304; political activity:
officers submit to Rump, 1/1, 13, 14;
soldiers mutinous, 1/36 & n. 4, 36–7 &
n., 38 & n. 1, 40 & n. 3, 59 & n. 4;
officers' attempted remonstrance to
parliament, 1/81–2 & n., 88 & n. 1;
soldiers said to be anti-royalist, 1/86;
Dunkirk garrison royalist, 1/101;
army's engagement to support parliament, 1/108 & n. 3; envoy sent to
King, 1/128 & n. 2; also, 1/121
FINANCIAL ADMINISTRATION: coinage,
4/148 & n. 2; efficient collection of
excise, 4/374–5 & n.; revenue, 5/68 &
n. 3
NAVAL ADMINISTRATION: alleged corruption, 1/308; praised, 6/45; compared with Navy Board, 7/307 & n. 5,
308; 9/444, 484 & n. 3; methods,
9/485; creditors to be paid (1663),
4/158–9 & n.; promotion by sanctity,
4/375; Cromwell's expenditure, 5/59
& n. 4
COMPTON, James, 3rd Earl of

Northampton (d. 1681): in Chancery case, 1/48, n. 1; introduces bill banishing Clarendon, 8/565

COMPTON, Sir William, Master of the Ordnance: carries letter from Sandwich to King, 1/129–30; watches gun trial, 3/130 & n. 4; compares contemporary fleet with that of 1588, 3/187 & n. 2; appointed to Tangier Committee, 3/238, 272; attends meetings, 4/21, 23, 269, 335, 338; death, 4/338–9; high repute, ib.; social: 3/242

CONDÉ, Louis II de Bourbon, Prince de (d. 1686): Bristol's falsity to, 4/213, n. 2; bravery, 5/171

CONNY, [John], surgeon: 9/495, 497

CONSTABLE, Lord High, office of: rumour of Albemarle's appointment, 8/269 & n. 3, 270

CONSTANTINOPLE: ambassador sails to, 1/217, 224, 250; peace with Algiers confirmed from, 4/369–70 & n.

COOK, John, regicide: trial, 1/263 & n. 1; head displayed, 1/270

COOKE [Edward], underclerk to the Council of State: 1/25, ?203, ?207

COOKE, Capt. Henry, Master of the Choristers, Chapel Royal: anthems sung/conducted/composed by, 1/220, 260; 2/41; 3/84, 85, 190, 197; 4/428; singing and compositions admired by P, 8/59; claims to have taught Davenant, ib.; at music meeting, 8/532; introduces Tom Edwards to P's household, 5/162, 234, 255; 6/77; social: 1/223; 2/103, 142; 7/412; 8/58; alluded to: 7/383

COOKE, [John], clerk to Secretary Morice: 5/62 & n. 2

COOKE, Capt. [Thomas], Master of the Tennis Court, Whitehall: plays with Rupert, 8/418–19 & n.

COOKE, Mr ——, servant to Sandwich: as messenger, 1/101, 109, 111, 118, 128, 131, 132, 137, 162, 165, 166, 167, 170, 179, 238, 239, 264; 8/582; 9/51; troubles P (? for employment), 1/207 (doubtful reference); repays debt to, 2/109; to negotiate match for Tom P, 3/176, 183, 185, 195, 202, 203, 205, 207, 228, 232, 233; 5/252; at

Brampton and Cambridge, 3/219, 223, 224, 226; 9/212; asks for post at Tangier, 4/66; past kindness to P, 5/252; at Hinchingbrooke, 7/131, 234; social: plays ninepins, 4/160; also, 1/151, 174, 176, ?203, 221; 3/138; 7/83

COOKE, [?Samuel], bookbinder: makes bosses for P's Bible, 1/281

COOKSHOPS and cooks [For cooks named in the text, see Gentleman, ——; Levitt, [W.]; Phillips, [?J.]; Slater, ——; Starkey's; Robinson, ——; and Wilkinson's [W.]. Cooks who were domestic servants appear under the names of their employers]: P dines at Welsh cook's at Charing Cross, 4/12; ?6/40, 79; at other cookshops, 1/14, 195 & n. 3; 2/116, 160, 190, 196, 197; 4/34; 7/320; 9/391, 480, 494, 509; food supplied from, 1/10 & n. 6, 16, 17, 190, 202, 270; 2/89, 146, 234, 237; 3/62, ?251, 293; 4/281, 326, 384; 5/126; 6/75; 7/274; food cooked at, 4/334; 7/199; cooks hired from, 2/28; 3/53; 4/13; 7/388, 389, 392; ?9/423–4; wedding party at, 7/262

COOLING: see Coling

COOPER, Sir Anthony Ashley, cr. Baron Ashley 1661, cr. Earl of Shaftesbury 1672, Chancellor of the Exchequer, Treasurer of the Commission for Prizes, and Treasury Commissioner:

CHARACTER: ability, 4/137, 158–9, 176; 5/174; 6/13; 7/121; 8/231; 9/199; alleged corruption, 6/218; 7/128 & n. 3, 129, 137, 156, 163, 167; 8/445, 446

PRIVATE AFFAIRS: claims Whitehall lodgings, 1/17, 22, 23; house [Exeter House, Strand], 8/445, 553; operated on for abscess, 9/246 & n. 1; portrait by Cooper, 9/139 & n. 3

AS POLITICIAN (GENERAL): appointed to Privy Council, 1/171; enemy of Clarendon, 4/137; 5/34; to be Lord Treasurer (rumour), 4/137–8; ally of Buckingham, 4/137; 9/444–5; quarrels with Ossory, 7/376 & n. 1; opinion on status of judges in Lords, 8/445 & n. 4; to be dismissed (rumour), 8/596 & n. 1, 600; speech on bill establishing Brooke House Committee, 9/8

AS CHANCELLOR OF THE EXCHEQUER: navy business, 4/158–9; 5/321; Tangier business, 6/91(2) [*see also* below]; alluded to: 8/180

AS TREASURER OF THE COMMISSION FOR PRIZES: orders payment to navy, 6/319; resists Navy Board's request for ships, 7/80; accounts, · 7/309; 8/446; quarrels with Board over sale of goods, 8/16, 20, 144; sits as Commissioner of Appeal, 8/231; alluded to: 8/252

AS TREASURY COMMISSIONER: appointment, 8/223, 229–30; low view of colleagues, 8/244; and unpopularity with them, 9/205; proposes method of paying off fleet, 8/456; opposes Navy Board's application for money, 9/152, 171, 174, 444–5; unspecified business, 9/525; alluded to: 8/249

AS MEMBER OF TANGIER COMMITTEE: examines Povey's accounts, 6/13, 14, 15–16, 33, 77–8, 79; 9/371, 449; Rutherford's, 6/95; Yeabsley's, 7/121, 156; bribed by Yeabsley, 7/128, 129, 137; supports his claims, 7/156, 167; 8/445, 446, 461; cool with Peterborough, 7/156, 163; examines Belasyse's accounts, 9/199; approves P's fees, 9/340; attends meetings, 5/174; 6/58; 8/347; unspecified business, 6/71 8/197; 9/152

~ his wife [Margaret], 8/446; for his clerk, *see* Blany, R.

COOPER, [Henry], officer of the King's Works: 1/314; provides seat for P at coronation, 2/83

COOPER, [Richard], sailing master: P's opinion, 4/84; 'one-eyed', 4/133; mate of *Royal James*, 3/128; master of *Reserve*, 3/159, 160; quarrels with Holmes, 4/67, 78, 81; dismissed, 4/84; teaches P mathematics, 3/128, 131–4 passim, 136, 140, 148, 149; ships' rigging etc., 3/138, 149, 152, 158, 160, 161, 163; and cartography, 4/133–4; 5/303

COOPER, Samuel, miniaturist (d. 1672): painting of EP, 9/138 & n. 3, 253, 256, 258, 259, 261, 263, 264, 267, 268, 276–7; its cost, 9/277; other

paintings by, 9/139–40; his house, 9/139 & n. 1; musical and other talents, 9/259–60; good company, 9/256; social: 9/265; alluded to; 3/2; ~ his cousin Jack [Hoskins], 9/265

COOPER, [William], timber purveyor to the Navy Board: report by, 3/169; his dullness, 4/231

COOPER, Maj. ——: 7/68, 404

COPENHAGEN: 1/140; 4/69 & n. 2

COPPIN, Capt. [John], naval officer: transferred from *Langport* to *Newbury*, 1/109; killed in action, 7/154

CORBET, Miles, regicide: arrested in Delft, 3/45 & n. 1, 47–8 & n.; in Tower, 3/47; executed, 3/66

CORBET, Mrs ——: social: 7/362; 8/384, 502; 9/12, 128, 133, 186

[CORBETTA], Francesco, court musician: 8/374 & n. 3

CORDERY, Mr ——: 6/108

CORDERY, Mrs ——: 2/153, 157

COREY, [Katherine], ('Doll Common'), actress: performance in *The scornful lady*, 7/422 & n. 6; quarrels with Lady Hervey, 9/415 & n. 1

CORNBURY, Viscount: *see* Hyde, L.

CORNHILL [*see also* Coffee-houses; Taverns etc.: Globe; Pope's Head; Three Golden Lions; White Bear]: coronation arch, 3/138 & n. 2; Fire, 8/151–2 & n.; Backwell's building development, 9/517 & n. 1; stocks, 1/314; carrefour at conduit, 3/268

CORNWALL, rebellion in (1549): 9/167 & n. 5

CORNWALLIS, Charles, 2nd Baron Cornwallis, Gentleman of the Privy Chamber 1660–d. 73: pimps for King, 9/264

CORNWALLIS, Frederick, 1st Baron Cornwallis, Treasurer of the Household 1660–d. 62: distributes medals at coronation banquet, 2/84; death and funeral, 3/10 & n. 4; character, ib.

CORNWALLIS, [Henrietta Maria, of the Queen-Mother's Household]: 9/23

CORONEL(L), [Sir Augustine], financial agent of the Portuguese government: in dispute over customs dues, 5/43 & n. 2

CORRESPONDENCE (P) [omitting

a few letters vaguely described as 'into the country', 'from the sea' etc.]: GENERAL: neglects, 1/215, 218–19; 7/412; letter-book, 2/7, 10; tears up old letters, 4/9–10; 7/402
FROM P TO: Arlington: (passports) 7/203; Batten: (Field case), 4/153; Belasyse: (prize) 8/345–6 & n.; Sir R. Bernard: (Brampton business) 2/195; R. Blackborne: (Hewer) 4/363; R. Bowyer: (pay) 1/107; (unspecified) 1/105; Mrs Bowyer: (unspecified) 1/128; Brouncker (text given) 7/390; J. Creed: (gift) 4/391; (Tangier accounts) 5/39; Sir G. Carteret: (excuse) 3/205; (Warren's masts) 4/380, 382; Lady Carteret: (plague) 6/212; —— Cooke: (Tom P's marriage) 3/185; Sir W. Coventry: (business) 3/64, 144 & n. 2; (surveyorship of victualling) 8/356 & n. 2; (unspecified) 2/7; Lord Crew: (news of Sandwich) 3/146; T. Doling: (text given; enclosing vote of Admiral's Council) 1/126 & n. 2; Downing: (Hawley) 1/58; (house) 1/74; (Moore as P's deputy) 1/83, 107–8; (news) 1/129; W. Fairbrother: (choice of tutor for W. Penn, jun.) 3/21; Gauden: (apology) 4/251; Mrs Anne Hall: (news) 1/56; T. Hayter: (unspecified) 6/312; T. Hill: (incomplete draft) 9/236–7; Mrs Hobell: (Tom P's marriage) 3/195; Mrs Hobell's mother: (same subject) 3/208; E. Knepp: (signing himself 'Dapper Dicky') 7/5; Sir J. Lawson: (unspecified) 1/230; (ship) 1/249; P. Llewellyn etc.: (a merry letter), 1/116; Mennes: (striking flags) 3/4; Moore: (Exchequer business) 1/107; Mrs J. Pearse: (invitation) 7/16; Sir W. Penn: (allegedly from a thief) 2/164, 169, 170
EP: (money) 1/107, 128; (old love letters; torn up) 4/9–10; (Brampton feast) 4/237; (unspecified) 1/105, 162, 167; 3/152; 4/265; John P (sen.): (highway robbery) 3/34; (Brampton business, money matters etc.) 3/48, 270; 4/36, 87, 127, 141, 142; 5/40, 45, 48; 9/293; (Tom P's courtship) 3/201; (his illness) 5/87; (and death) 5/90;

(visit) 3/213; (gifts) 4/6; 5/52; (Brampton feast) 4/237; (criticising brother John) 5/137; (Pall as servant) 5/152; (Pall's dowry and match) 7/15; 8/539; 9/16–17, 97; (her marriage) 9/108; (parents' ill-health) 8/123, 131; (unspecified) 1/76; 2/141, 143, 145, 195, 230; 3/12, 21, 26, 44, 152; 4/202, 265, 306, 329; 8/166, 173; John P (jun.): (complaint) 3/21; (advice) 3/160–1; (parents' quarrels) 4/96; (invitation) 7/111–12, 293; (unspecified) 3/26; Robert P: (John P, jun.) 1/46; (unspecified) 1/270; Roger P: (unspecified) 9/310; Tom P: (visit to Brampton) 3/213; Tom P the turner: (Robert P's will) 3/48;
T. Povey: (Tangier) 3/291; Balty St Michel: (employment) 9/159; Lord Sandwich: (political news) 1/8, 25, 66, 227–8; 3/110; 5/264, 352; 7/412; 8/464, 466 & n. 4; (apology) 2/95; (purchase of cloth) 2/122; (commission as ambassador) 3/12; (treasure hunt) 3/251; (Lawson's return) 4/6; (liaison with Betty Becke; text given) 4/387–8; (employment for Bagwell) 6/39–40; (prize goods) 6/261 & n. 1; (Howe) 6/303 & n. 4; (unspecified; in cipher) 1/44; (unspecified) 1/11, 24, 27, 32, 47, 52, 56, 57, 59, 63, 230, 231; 2/19, 131, 145, 231; 9/65; Lady Sandwich: (Sandwich's voyage) 3/146; (Four Days Fight) 7/154; (news) 8/49 & n. 1; (asks favour) 8/474; (unspecified) 9/165; Sedgwick: (Graveley business) 2/178; Deb Willet: (farewell) 9/370, 371
TO P FROM: anon.: (K. Joyce) 9/124, 125; J. Angier, sen.: (employment) 4/363–4; Batters: (asks favour) 6/37; Belasyse: (prize) 8/345–6 & n.; Brisbane: (Lord Hinchingbrooke) 7/387; W. Coventry: (thanks) 2/10; (news of voyage) 3/143; (business) 4/134; J. Creed: (news of voyages) 2/154; 3/146; (their quarrel) 4/391; 5/45, 46; Downing: (lawsuit) 1/34; Pagan Fisher: (loan) 1/209; Hawley: (money) 1/33; Hewer: (social) 9/310; Lord Hinchingbrooke (his return from France) 6/169, 183; W. Howe: (Sandwich's coach) 4/430; Jane the

cookmaid: (wages) 6/29; E. Knepp: (signing herself 'Barbary Allen') 7/4; Lambert: (a simple letter) 1/183; Lanyon: (news) 6/8 & n. 2; R. Matthews: (pay) 1/33; Moore: (news) 1/113, 170; (lawsuit) 3/83; J. Pearse: (invitation) 4/10; Mrs J. Pearse: (social) 8/25;

EP: (health) 1/128; (family news) 1/166; (her loneliness) 3/257–8; 4/9; (country life) 4/199; (quarrels with father-in-law) 4/210; (quarrels with Ashwell) 4/262; (journeys) 7/93; 8/272; (stay at Roger P's) 9/310; (unspecified) 1/106, 137; 4/221; John P, sen.: (Brampton business) 2/180, 194, 195; 3/212, 240; 4/15; 7/80; (storm) 3/35; (family news) 3/106; 4/271; 5/154; 6/314; 9/308–9; (employment for relative) 3/119; (Ferrer's fight) 3/196; (Tom's match) 4/12; (Tom's children) 5/154, 158; (household arrangements) 4/180; (Pall's match) 7/78; (illness) 8/119; (J. Trice's difficulties) 8/158; (EP's return) 8/286; (unspecified) 9/18; John P, jun.: (request for books) 1/243; (asks favour) 2/26; (his ordination; in Latin) 7/50; (mother's illness) 8/122, 129; (and death) 8/134; (unspecified; in Latin) 1/137; Paulina P: (mother's illness), 3/103; Robert P: (asks favour) 2/96; (land purchase) 2/117; (unspecified) 1/218; Roger P: (Pall's match) 9/18–19; Tom P: (family news) 3/107; Tom P the turner: (Robert P's will) 3/48;

Sandwich: (shipping), 1/302; (alterations at Hinchingbrooke) 1/313–14; (Lisbon news) 2/209; (Tangier news) 2/221; 3/33 & n. 2; (requests visit) 3/240; (comet) 5/352; (return) 6/41; (Lady Jem's marriage) 6/163, 202; (return) 6/237; (prize-goods) 6/269, 309; (rebuke) 9/217; J. Scott: (Tom P's estate) 5/124, 149–50; (unspecified) 1/22 (in cipher); 1/44 (in cipher); 2/163; 5/225

CORTENAER, Egbert Meüssen, Dutch naval commander: sails from Holland, 6/108 & n. 3

COSIN (Cosens), John, Bishop of Durham 1660–d.72: votes for Clarendon's impeachment, 8/542 & n. 1

COTTENHAM, Cambs.: Pepys family in, 8/261 & n. 4, 274 & n. 2 ~ 'Cottenhamshire', 8/517

COTTERELL, Sir Charles, courtier, (d. 1702): story of Russian diplomatists, 8/428 & n. 3; at Danckert's, 9/504; ~ his son [Clement], ib. & n. 3

COTTINGTON, Francis, 1st Baron Cottington (d. 1652), diplomatist: advises Charles I to seize Spanish bullion, 7/253 & n. 1; stories of disinheriting nephew, 8/566–7 & n.; and of mission to Spain, 9/256 & nn.

COTTLE (Cuttle), [Mark], registrar of the Prerogative Court of Canterbury: house at Greenwich, 6/339 & n. 2; at Twelfth Night party, 7/5; alluded to: 6/334; 7/68; ~ his wife, 7/5

COTTON, Cambs.: 2/148

COUNCIL OF TRADE: see Privy Council

COUNTER, the, city prison (in the Poultry): prisoners sent to, 2/73 & n. 3; 3/44; 5/114; and conventiclers, 4/129; also, 4/421

COUNTRY, Capt. [Richard], naval officer: sails with P to Baltic (1659), 2/185 & n. 5; gift of fruit, 2/185–6

COUNTRYSIDE, P's appreciation of [his visits to the country are indexed under place names]: expresses enjoyment of pastoral scene near Brampton, 3/221 & n. 2; nightingales near Woolwich, 4/151; 5/130; walks/rides: near Rotherhithe, 4/112; Woolwich, 4/149; Epsom, 4/245–9; 8/335–40; Brampton, 4/312; Islington, 5/132–3; 8/175; Kingsland, 8/211–12; and Hatfield, 8/381; river outing, 8/236; journey in West Country, 9/229, 231, 232, 234; and Medway valley, 9/495; would rather take trips to country than own country retreat, 8/339–40 & n.

COURLAND, Duke of [? Jacob, Duke 1642–82]: method of hunting, 4/413–14

[COURTIN, Pierre], French ambassador-extraordinary 1665: arrives incognito, 6/76 & n. 1

COVEL, John, Fellow of Christ's College, Cambridge 1659–82, Master 1688–d.1722: P votes for as vice-proctor, 3/218

COVENANT, the, (the Solemn League and Covenant, 1643): to be reprinted and hung in churches, 1/77 & n. 1; renounced under Act of Uniformity, 3/166; and by M.P.s (error), 4/53 & n. 1; taken by Scottish rebels, 7/397; also, 5/347

COVENT (Common) GARDEN [*see also* Coffee-houses; Taverns etc.: Fleece, Rose]: fire, 3/11; storm, 3/32; puppet plays, 3/80, 90, 216, 254–5; Theatre Royal, 4/34–5 & n.; Plague, 6/150; 7/3; conventicle, 6/199; duel, 8/363; the piazza, 6/2; 7/3, 4, 232; 8/21, 158

COVENTRY, Henry, diplomatist, brother of Sir William: reputation, 8/70 & n. 1, 533; plenipotentiary in peace negotiations, 8/61, 63, 138 & n. 4, 175, 189, 216, 218, 249, 322 & n. 3, 323, 326 & n. 3, 330, 427; defends Clarendon, 8/476 & n. 3, 533 & n. 2, and Penn, 9/165; admires P's parliamentary speech, 9/104; visits brother in Tower, 9/468; social: 5/102

COVENTRY, Sir John, M.P. Weymouth and Melcombe Regis, Dorset: news from, 8/354(2) & n. 2; also, 9/93

COVENTRY, Thomas, 1st Baron Coventry, Lord Keeper 1625–40: portrait, 7/183 & n. 3; judgements criticised, 7/261 & n. 3

COVENTRY, William, kted 1665; secretary to the Duke of York as Lord High Admiral ?1660–67; Navy Commissioner 1662–7, Treasury Commissioner 1667–8; M.P. Great Yarmouth, Norfolk, 1661–79:
CHARACTER: P's regard: 'the most ingenious person I ever found', 3/160; 'my most true friend in all things that are fair', 3/197; 'the activest man in the world', 7/171; also, 3/134, 136, 159–60, 243 & n. 3, 261; 4/3, 20, 267; 7/83, 181; 8/149–50, 251, 270, 348, 591; efficiency, 4/317; 5/167; good humour, 7/131; eagerness to learn, 8/431; admired by others: by Duke of York, 4/194; Carteret, 7/196; Sir S. Fox, 7/322; criticised by King as 'visionaire', 9/386–7; disliked by Creed, 7/168

NAVAL APPOINTMENTS:
AS SECRETARY ETC. TO THE LORD HIGH ADMIRAL: inspects new Navy Office, 1/194; refuses gifts of plate, 1/192 & n. 3, 193, 322(3); 2/7, 10; in dispute about fees, 1/240–1 & n.; influence with Duke, 4/116; 7/79, 163; accompanies to France, 3/139, 143; Hampton Court, 3/157; Bath, 4/287, 288; to country during Plague, 6/142; 7/32; and Portsmouth, 8/171; allies with Lady Denham, 7/323; defines clerk's qualifications, 8/207; criticises corruption of Duke's household, 5/120; temporarily dismissed as household commissioner, 8/592 & n. 1; resigns from Duke's service, 8/409, 410, 413, 414, 416, 420, 424; still consulted, 8/485; also, 3/192
AS NAVY COMMISSIONER: appointed, 3/79 & n. 3, 83, 99; on Exchange for first time, 5/39, 41; attends office after Plague, 7/34; absent from meetings through lack of business, 7/249, 255–6, 360; 8/346; threatens resignation, 7/331; resigns, 8/8 & n. 3, 9, 15, 144; excluded from commission enquiring into financial administration of navy, 8/2
NAVY BUSINESS [as Admiral's secretary, Navy Commissioner and Treasury Commissioner. *See also* below, as M.P.; as Privy Councillor]:
ADMINISTRATION: to reform Board, 3/103; and investigate Principal Officers' expenses, 3/104; initiates enquiry into Chatham Chest, 3/179; views on state of Navy Office, 4/17, 135; 5/120, 177; criticises bookkeeping, 7/235; on reform of navy treasurership, 3/106–7 & n., 107–8, 174, 243; 6/292; 8/334–5, 378; comptrollership, 7/324–5, 328, 380, 413; 8/32, 41; and surveyorship, 8/32; plans reorganisation, 8/391 & n. 4; supports reform plans, 9/205, 253, 293–4; opposes pensions for flag officers, 9/257; favours direct management of victualling, 9/312; also, 9/386

other news of 1666 campaign, 7/181, 224, 228, 288, 304; Dutch raid on Medway: disapproves of reduction of fleet, 8/140; orders fireships, 8/256 & n. 2, 259, 260 & n. 1; discharges ships at Chatham, 8/271 & n. 1; blamed for disaster, 8/298; criticises Deane and Spragge, 8/358, 379; defence against parliamentary criticism, 8/490 & n. 2, 492 & n. 2, 497–8, 524, 536; examined on use of tickets, 8/497; incriminating letter suppressed, 8/507 & n. 1; also, 5/321; 6/112

ACCUSATIONS OF CORRUPTION: criticised for selling offices, 3/104 & n. 3; for selling offices and charging excessive fees, 4/156 & n. 4, 166, 169 & n. 3; defence, 3/243, 4/330–2 & n., 383; 7/306–7; takes salary in lieu of fees, 4/331 & n. 4; 9/92; cases cited, 4/71; 5/231 & n. 4, 235, 248–9 & nn.; to be attacked in Commons, 8/18, 69–70; examined by Committee on Miscarriages, 8/504, 505, 507; to be attacked in Commons, 9/87, 92, 98 & n. 2, 108 & n. 2, 128–9, 169; Sir F. Holles's part in attack, 9/92, 129, 173; and Tatnell's, 9/108; petition against him, 9/87 & n. 2, 129, 173; fears Brooke House Committee, 9/258, 277; accused of treason. 7/242 & n. 1

OTHER APPOINTMENTS:

AS TREASURY COMMISSIONER: appointed, 8/223, 229–30; asks for P's help, 8/230–1; dominates colleagues, 8/398; depressed by lack of money, 8/290, 591; 9/101, 248; reorganises Wardrobe, 9/7; concentrates on Treasury work, 9/316, 447; praises Southampton, 9/448; dismissed, 9/478–9 & n.; also, 9/465

AS TANGIER COMMISSIONER: appointed, 3/171, 238 & n. 3; critical of Povey, 3/177; supports P in disputes, 5/279; 9/418; encourages him to accept treasurership, 6/60, 106; other business: Povey's accounts, 5/48, 52, 123, 124, 127, 132, 135, 139; shipping, 5/177; victualling, 5/210; new commission, 5/229; reduction of garrison, 5/310; and of costs, 8/347; P's report on lack of money, 7/383; reform of

government, 8/160, 201; Belasyse's profits, 9/205; construction of mole, 9/364; puts low value on overseas possessions, 8/347–8; misc. and unspecified business, 3/272, 287; 4/335, 341; 5/168, 204; 6/154; 7/156, 166, 167; 8/210

AS M.P.: opposes motion to farm administration of navy, 7/304; defends Carteret, 7/322; libel against, 7/342; assures House King will disband army, 8/353; speaks in defence of clergy, 9/121 & n. 2

AS PRIVY COUNCILLOR: business: Lord Treasurer's accounts, 7/295; state of navy, 7/312; report on Navy Board, 7/374; on Tangier, 7/383; Navy Treasurer's accounts, 8/449; naval bounties, 8/460–1; manning fleet, 9/121; size of fleet, 9/216–17; unspecified, 7/354; 8/317

ON FISHERY COUNCIL: attends meeting, 3/269–70; anxious for its success, 4/366

RELATIONS WITH P: regard for/kindness to, 2/24; 3/134, 151, 171, 183, 185, 202, 210, 216, 272, 282, 302; 4/39, 232, 289; 6/63, 64(2), 172; 7/26–7, 28, 67–8; 8/420; 9/502–3; with P/Pett dominates office, 3/284, 290; P fears his reforming zeal, 3/83; welcomes it, 3/105; supports P's reform of victualling, 6/279–80; of pursers, 7/1 & n. 1, 5, 9 & n. 3, 10, 13, 28, 106; of office in general, 9/205, 253, 293–4, 312, 523 & n. 2; shows him MSS, 5/177 & n. 2; 9/523 & n. 2; supports claim to purveyorship, 2/54; gives silver pen, 4/263–4 & n., 268; suggests he write war history, 5/177–8; proposes increased pay for his clerk, 5/228 & n. 1; advises on dealing with parliamentary critics, 8/303–4, 524, 560; 9/79, 178; and with Brooke House Committee, 9/42, 79, 117; provides office papers for his defence, 9/255; urges him to lend to government, 8/392, 393; helps obtain *Maybolt*, 8/477; congratulates on parliamentary speech, 9/104–5; urges him to enter parliament, 9/454; when in Tower and afterwards advises on office matters, 9/481, 488, 503–4, 523, 563; P values his favour, 7/248; 8/113, 175, 203, 255; fears he has lost it, 4/27; 6/166; 7/65–6, 67, 69; their talks rare, 8/20, 206; also, 4/135, 136, 140, 322; 8/131, 141; 9/33, 255

RELATIONS WITH SANDWICH: enmity, 2/170; 3/121, 122; criticises in prizegoods affair, 7/10, 27, 34, 41, 52, 67, 68; 9/165; prejudiced report of Battle of Lowestoft, 6/121 & nn., 134, 135 & n. 1, 276, 301; their consequent estrangement, 6/230, 276, 287, 291, 301; friendly, 3/177; 6/139; 8/572

RELATIONS WITH OTHERS: criticises Mennes, 4/97, 219, 341; 8/586; 9/131; and Batten, 4/97, 219, 437; 5/169; defends Batten, 4/194; criticises Carteret, 4/195; 7/43, 65–6, 83; 8/140, 164–5, 179–80, 247, 290, 301; friendly to, 7/325; admires Jolliffe, 5/300; criticises Commissioner Pett, 8/230–1, 278; Deane, 8/358 & n. 1; and Anglesey, 8/567; praises Brooke House Commissioners, 8/586

AS POLITICIAN: made knight and Privy Councillor, 6/137, 141; 'now a great man', 7/248; fears fanatics' rising, 3/186; allegedly disloyal to Clarendon, 4/195–6; believes Catholics and Cavaliers incapable of business, 4/196; impatient with inefficiency, 4/267; unpopular, 8/270, 298, 304, 317–18; 9/41; to be Secretary of State, 8/118–19 & n., 120; distrusted by Clarendon, 6/276; 7/55; low opinion of Clarendon and Southampton, 9/40, 256, 486; high opinion of Falmouth, 9/294 & n. 1; leads attack on Clarendon, 8/409 & n. 2, 410, 413–15 & nn., 417, 504, 506, 507, 550, 560; his MS. account of, 9/475–6; loses favour of King and Duke of York, 8/424, 530, 570, 592; no longer in cabal, 8/585, 597; reconciled to Duke of York, 8/413–15, 485, 486, 535, 550–1; 9/79, 342; dependent on him, 9/336; will accept office only in commission, 8/505; ousted by Buckingham and Arlington, 9/67, 323; weary of office, 9/386–7, 447, 471; satirised in *The country gentleman*, 9/471 & n. 2; challenges Buckingham to duel, 9/462–3 & n.,

467–8 & n., 471 & nn., 472; dismissed from Council and sent to Tower, 9/466 & n. 2, 468, 470, 484; petitions King, 9/475; his dismissal unpopular, 9/478; his visitors at Tower, 9/473, 493; released, 9/490, 491, 493; returns to court, 9/515, 523; dislikes French treaty, 9/536; also, 7/325; 9/417

NEWS FROM [select. Coventry was one of P's main sources of information]: 3/44; 4/347, 352; 5/127, 264; 7/308, 318, 321, 364; 8/20, 397, 570; 9/86–7, 92–3, 279, 290–1, 293–4, 415, 489–90

HOUSES: lodgings in Old Palace Yard, 2/222; in Whitehall Palace (in winter): 1/226 etc.; little new chamber, 3/229; in St James's Palace (in summer): 3/136; his plate, 5/120; picture, 7/183; new closet, 7/227; new house in Pall Mall: 8/504 & n. 5, 507–8, 559; closet, 9/255; round table, ib. & n. 2; chimney pieces, 9/267; dining room, 9/303; hangings, 9/330; surrenders claim to Turner's lodgings in Navy Office, 8/24

SOCIAL: sings on barge, 2/77; gives dinners to naval associates, 2/222; 5/11, 102, 111, 166; dines at Trinity House, 3/103, 187; 5/172; at Africa House, 5/48; with Sandwich, 3/139; Batten, 3/148, 181; 5/216, 357; Sheriff Meynell, 3/200; Foley, 3/266; Mennes, 4/28; Carteret, 5/15; and Chicheley, 9/112; dines impromptu with P, 3/285–6; his amusing stories (alluded to), 4/346, 406; 7/135; at theatre, 8/167; at races with King and Duke of York, 8/203–4

MISC.: reads psalms in shorthand, 2/76 & n. 3; his mistress, 5/7; on varieties of courage, 5/169–71; unwell, 5/81, 223; 7/332; 9/563; defends father's reputation, 7/261 & n. 3; goods removed from St James's during Fire, 7/279; anecdote of Fire, 7/282; keeps diary, 9/475; also, 9/276

ALLUDED TO: 1/313; 2/95, 185; 8/324

~ his clerk(s), 3/138, 237 [*see also* Robson, [T.]]; his footboy, 4/15; 8/260

[COWDREY, Walter], Keeper of

Newgate prison: malpractices, 8/562
& n. 2

COWES, Capt. Richard, naval officer:
gift to P, 1/114

COWES, Isle of Wight: 5/304

COW LANE: coachmakers, 9/333,
352; also, 7/395 & n. 1; 8/464

COWLEY, Abraham, poet: new
book of poems, 4/386 & n. 3; ill, ib.
& n. 4; death, 8/380 & n. 3; repute
8/380, 383 & n. 3; alluded to:
7/400

COWLEY, Thomas, Clerk of the
Cheque, Deptford: tells P of abuses,
3/128; bookkeeping, 3/129, 234; 4/80;
gives P Cowley's poems, 4/386; ~
his clerk, 8/39

COWLING: see Coling

COX, Capt. [John], naval officer;
Navy Commissioner 1669–72; kted
1672: quarrels with Storekeeper,
4/149 & n. 2; alleged bribe to Batten,
5/141; action in Battle of Lowestoft,
8/489–90 & n., 491(2), 492; Guinea
business, 9/350; proposed as Penn's
successor, ib.; appointed Navy Commissioner, 9/441, 499; also, 4/226;
8/188; 9/549–50; social: at Trinity
House as Elder Brother, 7/72; at
parish dinner, 9/559; also, 2/229,
?232; ?4/212; 9/469; alluded to:
9/381

COX, [Thomas], Colonel of city
militia: narrow escape in Venner
rising, 7/190 & n. 4

COYET, Peter Julius, Swedish ambassador-extraordinary 1666–7: intermediary in peace negotiations, 8/80 &
n. 4, 92, 155, 177, 317, 349

CRAFFORD: see Crawfurd

CRAFTS: breadbaking (French), 6/48
& n. 3; heraldic painting, 4/424–5 &
nn.; modelling in plaster, 9/442 &
n. 2, 449, 487–8; jewelry (Woolwich
stones), 8/84 & n. 2; mason's work,
5/63 & n. 2, 449, 487–8; needlework,
2/123; 4/74, 180; picture framing,
9/538; shellwork, 1/148 & n. 2;
4/293, 295, 298–9; 5/45; varnish
and lacquer work, 4/153 & n. 2;
6/97; 7/147–8 & n., 184–5 (imitation
tortoise-shell), 9/531–2 & n.

CRAGG, Mrs —: Betty Martin's

landlady, 8/128, 435; P's valentine,
9/126; social: 8/323; 9/551

CRANBOURNE LODGE, Windsor
Park: P/EP visit(s), 6/197–8; 7/52, 54,
56; rebuilt, 6/197 & n. 4; view from,
6/198; alluded to: 6/190, 191; 8/42

CRANBURNE, —, of Fleet Lane:
association with Tom P, 5/82

CRANFIELD, Anne, Countess of
Middlesex (b. Brett), widow of
Lionel Cranfield, 1st Earl (d. 1670):
her accident at court, 1/181–2

CRANFIELD, Lionel, 3rd Earl of
Middlesex (d. 1674): on *Royal Charles*,
1/156

CRANMER: error for Grindal, q.v.

CRAVEN, William, 1st Earl of
Craven, courtier and soldier: chairman of Fishery Corporation, 5/251,
299–300, 323; 6/53; coxcomb, 6/258;
high opinion of P, 6/197, 239, 305;
covets Navy Treasurership, 7/6, 14;
commands riot troops, 9/129; house
at Hampstead Marshall, Berks., 9/242
& n. 2; also, 6/264, 298; 8/278;
social: at theatre with Queen of
Bohemia, 2/156; at Trinity House
dinners, 4/185; 5/172

CRAWFURD (Crafford), John, 17th
Earl of Crawfurd (d. 1678): on
Naseby, 1/134 & n. 3

CRAWLY, —: 5/114

CREED, Elizabeth (b. Pickering), wife
of John: lacks wedding portion,
1/295; well-bred but fat, 4/308; P plans
match for, 6/18, 21; at court masque,
6/29; courted by Creed, 6/88, 89–90;
marriage, 9/269, 279, 318, 322, 332 &
n. 3, 335; with child, 9/562; also,
5/32, 53; 9/345, 487; social: at P's
house, 5/95; 9/408, 409; on river trip,
5/180; P/EP visit(s), 9/379–80, 430,
519–20

CREED, John, servant to Sandwich
and naval official:

CHARACTER: able but false, 4/11, 192,
197, 198, 204, 206; 5/74, 108, 119,
189, 238, 302; 6/15, 71; 7/156, 242;
8/203; 9/247; mean, 1/223 & n. 2;
disliked by P, 7/310, 381; 9/248, 264;
Sandwich, 2/99; 5/74; Howe, 5/74;
Lord Belasyse, 7/185; and Povey,
9/247; also, 7/167, 168

AS DEPUTY-TREASURER TO THE FLEET:
1660: appointed, 1/85–6 & n.; surrenders secretaryship of fleet to P,
1/83, 84, 87; on *Swiftsure*, 1/96, 101;
and *Naseby*, 1/104, 119, 120; attends
on Prince of Orange, 1/138; accounts,
1/117, 225, ?287, 295, 301, 304; 2/56,
57, 61, 98, 99; expenses, 2/34, 96, 97
1661–2: at Portsmouth, 2/90–4
passim; orders imprests, 2/112, 120;
and ammunition, 2/114; stories of
voyage, 3/90–1; chaffs Gauden about
victuals, 4/245; accounts, 3/94, 100,
112, 124, ?136, ?170, 225, 278–9 &
n., 280; 4/11, 12; fraudulent claim,
4/16; miscalculation of rate of exchange, 4/132 & n. 2; accounts criticised, 4/192, 197; amended with P's
help, 4/105, 198, 202, 203, 205, 207,
213; defended by P, 4/216; approved
by Carteret, 4/218–19; profit, 4/204;
5/22; dispute with P over P's reward,
4/391; 5/39, 43, 45–6 & n., 210, 213;
dispute alluded to, 5/29, 34, 189, 209;
accounts alluded to, 4/233
1664: appointed, 5/119, 189, 210; departure delayed, 5/213, 215; returns,
5/238; succeeded as muster-master by
Howe, 6/54; hopes for place from
Falmouth, 6/71
INTELLECTUAL AND CULTURAL INTER-
ESTS: discusses duodecimal arithmetic,
4/178; P admires his learning, 4/192;
5/256; reads Cicero, 4/202; inspects
microscopes, 5/48; elected Fellow of
Royal Society, 5/51; attends meetings, 5/123; 6/36, 84; 8/528; 9/379; at
Royal Society club, 8/541; his viol,
5/64, 106; buys Daniel's *History*, 5/247
LODGINGS: at Mr Ware's, 2/81; at
Clarke the confectioner's, 3/174; new
lodgings in Axe Yard, 4/341; in the
Mews, 6/60; near New Exchange,
7/279, 423; in Scotland Yard, 8/205;
house in Newport St, 9/431, 519;
moves frequently to evade poll-tax,
8/189, 203
NEWS FROM: 2/154; 3/226–7; 4/68, 283;
6/243; 7/221, 229, 365, 366; 8/322,
342–3, 377, 427, 486, 528, 584–5, 587;
9/70, 137, 177
PERSONAL: his Puritanism, 2/98–9;
9/542–3; association with fanatics,

5/107–8 & n.; 6/15; wealth, 5/338–9;
6/151; large appetite, 2/93; 7/30; love
of chocolate, 2/88; 4/5; 5/64; desk
with bookshelves, 5/64; parrot, 6/60;
story of attempted rape by, 7/46; suggested match with Nan Wright, 5/286;
hopes to marry Sarah Gauden, 7/88 &
n. 4; marries Betty Pickering, 6/88,
89–90, 90; 9/269, 279, 318, 332 & n. 3
RELATIONS WITH P: buys books for,
1/260; discusses personal finances,
2/51; 6/198; 7/197; 8/516; and rise of
statesmen, 4/24; confides in about
love affair, 2/54; proposes P as
burgess of Portsmouth, 2/93; appears
in dream to, 2/226; gift to, 3/139;
consulted by about dress, 4/199, 357;
about Fishery, 4/365; recommends
cook, 4/305, 321; to speak for P with
Buckingham faction, 9/509; advises
P not to attract envy, 9/551; unspecified business with, 3/94, 112, 132; also,
1/284; 9/555
RELATIONS WITH SANDWICH: accompanies on Dutch voyage, 1/96, 101,
104, 138, 168; and French voyages,
2/32–3; 3/146; out of favour, 5/302;
refuses loan to, ib.; lends money to,
8/516, 579; accounts with, 3/136, 170;
unspecified business, 9/177; also, 5/64,
173
AS SECRETARY TO TANGIER COMMITTEE:
appointed, 3/272; salary, 7/381; takes
bribes, 6/221, 242(2), 250; 7/167;
9/244; fails to supply boats, 3/291;
plays tricks with accounts, 7/23; fails
to notify Clarendon of meeting, 8/214;
dealings with governors: Teviot,
4/273, 324; Peterborough, 5/48;
Belasyse, 6/22; 7/330, 338, 423; 9/202;
criticises/examines Povey's accounts,
5/102, 106; 6/14, 15(2), 17, 59, 68;
9/244, 371; advises P about Povey's
offer of treasurership, 6/59, 79, 80, 85,
139; 9/416; accounts, 7/23, 84, 98(2),
172, 175; 9/249; other financial business, 6/70, 90, 91, 108, 112, 119–20,
131, 133, 136, 137, 142; 8/52, 340–1,
348; 9/58, 205, 416, 534; victualling
business, 6/85, 86, 105, 171–2; 7/232,
254; 8/445, 461, 515; other business,
4/45, 333; 5/181, 299; 6/65, 118;
9/249; unspecified business/attendance

at meetings, 4/13, 27, 31–2, 102; 5/97, 105, 124, 139, 154, 210, 339; 6/13, 22, 61, 134, 151; 7/95, 121, 228, 254, 265; 8/61, 210; 9/355, 562; also, 3/238 SOCIAL [on some of these occasions, e.g. visits to dockyards, Creed may have transacted Tangier business]: at Trinity House dinners, 1/177; 3/246; 6/35; coronation banquet, 2/86; walks round Tower, 2/213–14; at funerals, 3/269; 6/114, 127; 8/101; christening, 4/82; visits Epsom, 4/245–9 passim; at Bartholomew Fair, 4/298; 5/265; Lord Mayor's banquet, 4/354–6; visits Greenwich, 5/178; Rochester and Chatham, 8/306, 307, 311–14 passim; sees freaks at Charing Cross, 8/326; prize fight, 8/429, 430; and cockfight, 9/154; calls on P with his bride, 9/408; at Twelfth Night party, 9/409; inhospitable to P and EP, 9/520; at taverns/coffee-houses etc., 1/75, 174, 207, 217, 221, 263, 267, 284, 303; 2/36, 63, 79, 88, 95, 101, 103, 116, 117; 3/94, 152, 248, 298; 4/12, 23–4, 58, 130, 179, 196, 349, 353, 361, 371, 427, 435; 6/115, 251; 9/163, 164, 169; at P's house, 1/173; 2/113; 3/91, 116, 132; 4/32, 40, 55, 133, 141, 157, 164, 188, 214, 266, 389; 5/128, 155, 175, 185, 242, 256, 259, 282, 304, 321, 323, 344; 6/41, 61, 109, 118; 7/131, 168; 8/130, 209, 232, 255, 362, 451, 511, 578; 9/51, 57, 61, 116, 197; at theatre, 1/224, 264; 2/34, 35, 54, 56, 66, 80, 89; 3/260; 4/4, 6, 16, 55–6, 162, 163; 5/240; 6/73, 83; 7/421–3; 8/399, 486; 9/162, 186, 248; at houses of other colleagues and associates, 1/268; 5/257; 6/63, 68–9, 87, 172–3; 7/29–30, 191; 9/130, 165, 176; at Sandwich's lodgings, 2/100; 3/288, 299; 4/5, 21–2, 101, 160; 9/334; at his own, 3/226–7, 281, 282; 4/22; 9/345; walks with P in St James's Park, Whitehall, to Deptford, Woolwich etc., 4/30–1, 37, 87, 113, 131, 151, 286, 297, 348; 5/47, 127, 133, 155, 186, 198, 215, 269; 6/118; 7/144, 148–9, 155, 221, 242, 265, 375, 376; 8/94, 368, 412, 464, 544, 545, 590; 9/141–2, 206–7, 215; on pleasure trips to Hackney/Islington/Vauxhall etc., 5/176, 180–1,

190; 6/74, 136; 7/136, 223; 8/240–1, 249–50; also, 4/124, 125, 142, 163
MISC.: admires France, 2/33; at Backwell's, 3/94; belittles Lawson's achievements, 4/73; proposed as jointsecretary to Fishery corporation, 5/251; at Fire, 7/269, 271; at riot, 9/129–30
ALLUDED TO: 1/190; 9/272, 487
~ his footboy, 4/12; 5/45, 180
CREED, Richard, brother of John: his Puritan views, 1/91 & n. 2; alluded to: 1/86
CREEVEY, Thomas, diarist (d. 1838): opinion of P's diary, vol i, p. lxxxiii
CREIGHTON (Creeton), Robert, Dean of Wells 1660–70, Bishop 1670– d. 72: P admires his preaching, 5/96; comical sermon, 3/42–3 & n.; preaches against nonconformity, 4/92–3; 5/96– 7; and (in King's presence) against adultery, 8/362–3, 366; social: 8/417
[CRÉQUI, Charles Duc de], French ambassador to the Papacy 1662, 1664–5: 4/24 & n. 1
CRESSET, ——, 8/425 & n. 3
CREW, Jemima, Lady Crew (b. Waldegrave), wife of John Crew, 1st Baron: her 'saintly questions', 7/17; also, 1/41; 3/2; 5/209; ~ her page, 8/333
CREW, John, cr. Baron Crew of Stene 1661:
PUBLIC AFFAIRS: his part in return of secluded M.P.s, 1/18, 57, 60, 62; elected Councillor of State, 1/65, 82; and M.P., 1/116; created baron, 2/80; views: on constitution of House of Lords, 1/118, 125–6; contribution of Presbyterian clergy to restoration, 3/290–1; Dutch War, 5/244; 6/6; 7/125, 387; poll tax, 7/387–8; Brooke House Committee, 8/193–5; management of royal finances, 8/195; dissolution, 8/558; Dutch alliance, 9/1, 30; toleration, 9/31; the court, 9/190; also, 8/99, 251
PRIVATE AFFAIRS: new house in Lincoln's Inn Fields, 2/153 & n. 2, 213; ill, 9/265, 268, 550
RELATIONS WITH P: their mutual regard, 2/124–5; 3/55, 265; 7/355–6; 9/1; his advice about fees etc., 1/122 & n. 1; offers bargain of land, 5/196; also, 3/11

RELATIONS WITH SANDWICH: consulted about his lodgings, 1/22; his finances 3/11; 8/405-6, 461-2, 463, 480; his involvement in Tangier, 3/204; his naval command, 5/207; and the prize-goods scandal, 7/17, 219; 9/165, 176, 177; discreet about his liaison, 4/305, 316; to help arrange Hinching-brooke's match, 8/190; advises him how to obtain Lord Treasurership, 8/195; regrets his abandonment of Presbyterian interest, 9/164; also, 3/203

POLITICAL/COURT NEWS FROM: 1/44-5, 65; 3/253, 290-1; 4/126; 8/480, 558; 9/190, 222

SOCIAL: reminiscences of Elizabethan nobility, 2/114; at Lady Catherine Mountagu's christening, 2/171; at Lady Jemima Mountagu's wedding, 6/159-60, 176, 179, 180; P visits/dines with: 1/227; 3/2, 22, 33, 68, 78, 112, 203; 4/44, 239; 6/115; 7/423; 8/333; 9/130, 162(3)

ALLUDED TO: 1/73; house in Lincoln's Inn Fields alluded to [P's visits to servants and others]: 1/4, 5, 14, 15, 20, 25, 32, 43, 56, 64, 71, 73, 77, 79, 83, 89, 90, 91, 94, 173, 174, 176, 177, 178, 180-4 passim, 189, 222, 238, 247, 254, 255, 261, 278, 295, 310, 322, 325; 4/26, 123, 135, 237

~ Jane, servant, 1/20; John, coachman: buried, 1/73

CREW, John, son of the 1st Baron: at Dover with Sandwich, 1/158; social: 2/232; 7/356, 388(2); 8/558; 9/1

CREW, John, son of Sir Thomas: 4/239; 7/357

CREW, Nathaniel, brother of the 1st Baron: inherits estate, 7/423

CREW, Dr Nathaniel, son of the 1st Baron, Fellow of Lincoln College, Oxford; later Bishop of Durham and 3rd Baron: appointed proctor, 4/199; views city ruins after Fire, 7/357; preaches at Whitehall, 8/144-5; social: 3/84; 7/356-8 passim

CREW, Samuel, son of the 1st Baron: death, 2/131 & n. 4

CREW, Sir Thomas, son of the 1st Baron, kted 1660; succ. as 2nd Baron 1679:

PRIVATE AFFAIRS: portraits, 1/28-9 & n.; 4/139; copy of Van Dyck's self-portrait, ib.; prints, 7/211; ill, 3/55, 68; 4/136, 239; also, 1/223; 4/316

PUBLIC AFFAIRS: presents address to Rump, 1/73; on Naseby, 1/135, 151, 154, 161; views on taxation, 7/356; criticises Navy Board's accounts, ib.; views on Louis XIV, 8/335-6; defends Sandwich in Commons, 9/64, 177; regrets Sandwich's abandonment of Presbyterian interest, 9/164

NEWS FROM: political/court: 2/213; 3/78; 4/127; 5/244; 7/376; 8/333, 530, 538; theatrical: 8/334; also, 4/139

SOCIAL: 1/95, 187, 309; 4/305; 5/185; 7/388; 9/115

~ his children, 3/76; two daughters, 8/145; servant Pedro, 2/30

[CREW], Waldegrave; son of the 1st Baron: 1/15, 56, 57

CREW, ——, [?Nathaniel, ?Salathiel], brother of the 1st Baron: 3/253 & n. 2

CRIPPLEGATE [see also Taverns etc.: Cross Keys]: Brampton carrier in, 5/122-3; 6/90, 95

[CRISP, Agnes], daughter of Commissioner Pett: 4/168 & n. 1; 6/262

CRISP, Diana: no better than she should be, 1/237, 239, 246; fails to keep assignation, 1/251, 252; social: 1/91, 94, 226; ~ her old suitor, Meade, 1/219

CRISP, Capt. [Edward]: chosen Elder Brother, Trinity House, 6/84; and Master, 6/298

CRISP (Crips), Laud, brother of Diana: to go to sea, 1/91, 92, 237; his singing, 3/147; 8/65; place in Wardrobe, 8/65; social: 1/90; 7/44; alluded to: 1/93

CRISP, Sir Nicholas, merchant: project for dock at Deptford, 3/18 & n. 1, 29, 30, 32-3; social: 3/188; alluded to: 1/52; ~ his son [Ellis] dies of eating cucumbers, 4/285

CRISP, Mrs ——, mother of Diana and Laud: P lodges with, 1/90-4 passim; plays harpsichord, 1/90; advises on furnishing house, 1/210; also, 1/94; 2/166; social: 1/190, 237

CRISPIN, [Arthur], waterman: gives evidence against H. Brouncker, 8/501

CRITZ (Cretz), Emanuel de, Ser-
jeant-Painter to the King (d. 1665):
shows P royal collection of sculpture,
1/188–9 & n.; copies Lely's portrait
of Sandwich, 1/272, 273, 290, 292,
301–2; other copies, 3/80 & n. 1;
social: 5/84
CROCKFORD, ——, ?porter: 1/92 &
n. 2; 2/87
CROFTON, Zachary, Presbyterian
minister (d. 1672): imprisoned, 2/58–9
& n.
CROFT(S), Herbert, Bishop of Here-
ford 1661–d. 91: his preaching, 1/265;
8/116 & nn.; convert from Catholicism, 8/116 & n. 4; votes for Clarendon's impeachment, 8/532 & n. 3
CROFTS, [?Thomas], clerk in the
Signet Office: 1/208, 211
CROFTS, William, 1st Baron Crofts:
3/149 & n. 5; 9/336, n. 4
CROFTS, Mr: see Scott, James, Duke
of Monmouth
CROFTS, Mrs ——, shopkeeper, of
Westminster: her shop, 9/129, 142;
social: 6/115, 163: 7/392
CROMLEHOLME   (Crumlum),
Samuel, High Master of St Paul's
School: a conceited pedagogue, 6/53;
advises on John P's exhibition, 1/27;
given book for school by P, 2/239 &
n. 3; 4/33, 132–3; 5/38; his drinking a
warning to P, 3/199–200; losses in
Fire, 7/297; also, 1/44; 3/142; social:
2/238; ~ his wife, 4/133
CROMWELL, Elizabeth, widow of
Oliver: 1/248 & n. 1
CROMWELL, Frances, daughter of
Oliver: her impending marriage,
1/248 & n. 1; proposed marriage to
Charles II, 5/296–7 & n.
CROMWELL, Mary: see Belasyse
CROMWELL, Oliver:
CHRON. SERIES: at meetings of Eastern
Association, 3/224 & n. 3; attitude to
Charles I (1648), 5/335 & n. 2; to
Charles II, 5/296–7; story of his
tampering with royal tombs, 5/297 &
n. 2; storm at his death, 3/32 & n. 2;
body exhumed, 1/309 & n. 4; 2/24 &
n. 3, 26–7, 31; effigy hanged, 4/418 &
n. 2, 420; portrait by Simon, 4/70
REPUTATION: praised for: strong govern-

ment, 4/376; promotion of trade,
5/52; 8/426; encouragement of navy,
5/59 & n. 4; Irish settlement, 5/346;
financial credit, 6/78; prestige abroad,
8/249, 332; sobriety of court, 8/355;
and intelligence service, 9/70–1; a
'coquin', 5/264; a 'rogue', 8/355;
biography, 8/382 & n. 2
ALLUDED TO: 1/12; 3/46
~ his family, 5/297
CROMWELL, Richard: downfall,
1/21 & nn. 3, 4; rumours of restoration, 1/74, 76, 79; Sandwich's advice
to in 1659, 1/180; life in exile, 5/296 &
n. 2; 7/94 & n. 6
CROONE, [William], physician: de-
scribes blood transfusion experiment,
7/370–1 & nn.
CROPP, ——, waterman: appointed
government waterman, 1/37 & n. 2;
also, 7/319
CROUCHED FRIARS: see Crutched
Friars
CROW, Capt. [?George], naval officer:
8/266–7
CROW, ——, footman to John
Claypole: 1/218
CROWE, Ald. [William], upholsterer
in St Bartholomew's: denied title of
alderman, 4/404 & n. 1; P/EP inspect(s)
tapestries, 9/329, 330; and beds, 9/333,
334, 356; also, 1/269; 9/362
CROWLAND, Abbot of: P's family
connection with, 8/261 & n. 4
[CROWTHER, Joseph]: unnamed
clergyman who married Duke and
Duchess of York, 2/40–1 & n.
CROXTON, [?Jane], of Salisbury
Court: P consults on flags, 3/205 & n.
1; also, 5/86
CRUMLUM: see Cromleholme
CRUTCHED (Crouched) FRIARS
[see also Taverns etc.: Three Tuns]:
7/152; 9/188, 519
CUCKOLD'S POINT, nr Deptford:
4/50
CULAN, Henry Fleury de, Heer van
Buat: executed, 7/315 & n. 1
CUMBERFORD: see Comberford
CUMBERLAND, [Henry], tailor, of
Salisbury Court: burial, 4/32 & n. 2
CUMBERLAND, Richard, P's con-
temporary at St Paul's and Magdalene,

Bishop of Peterborough 1691–
d.1718: in London, 1/43 & n. 1; P
visits, 1/54; P's regard, 8/118; 9/17,
56 ~ his brother, 8/118
CURLE, Capt. [Edmund], naval officer: gifts to P and EP for captain's
commission, 1/180
CURSITORS' ALLEY, Chancery
Lane: 9/140
CURTIS, Capt. [Edmund], naval
officer: to go to Mediterranean, 1/119
& n. 3; social: 2/33
CUSTIS (Custos), [Edmund], merchant: dispute about freightage, 4/404;
5/23, 36
CUSTOM HOUSE: P visits, 3/163;
new site, 7/280; alluded to: 4/163;
8/566
CUSTOM HOUSE (STAIRS): 3/119,
180; 4/144
CUSTOMS DUES: navy expenses
charged on, 4/206; merchants' cheats
(unspecified), 7/31; farmers of: listed,
3/188 & n. 3; dine with Lord Mayor,
4/341; farm criticised by Treasury,
8/373 & n. 4; officers attempt to
seize prize-goods, 6/256, 258, 259
CUTLER, Sir John, merchant: story
of beer and thunder, 4/365; on commission for repair of St Paul's, 4/430;
social: 4/22, 65, 100, 256
CUTLER, [William], merchant: P's
opinion of, 4/188, 322; 5/136; 6/166,
331; his regard for P, 4/296–7; his
rise, 5/52; contracts for hemp, 3/114,
116; 6/77; for tar, 5/136; discusses
navy victualling, 4/181, 398; breaks
with Cocke, 5/51; opposed by P,
5/352; provides cash, 6/191; bargain
for freight to Tangier, 7/65; unspecified business, 4/296; 5/332, 354;
foreign news from, 4/322; 5/51, 141,
343; house in city, 4/398; in Hackney,
6/331; housing property in city,
5/282–3; social: 4/216; 5/19, 23, 62,
159, 186, 255, 336, 341; 6/25, 83, 166;
~ his wife and mother [?]-in-law,
4/398; 6/331
CUTLER, P's: 8/136, 232
CUTTANCE, Capt. Henry, naval
officer: receives commission for *Cheriton*, 1/121; on *Royal Charles*, 1/160;
also, 1/221

CUTTANCE, Capt. Roger, kted
1665, naval commander:
CHRON. SERIES: supports Mountagu
(Sandwich) as parliamentary candidate, 1/103 & n. 4; loyalty to Mountagu questioned, 1/107; transactions
concerning ships' pay, 1/162, 167;
3/128; part in prize-goods affair,
6/230, 240, 241, 247, 313; 9/91, 402 &
n. 3; at council of war, 6/230; news
from, 6/306–7; 8/549–50 & n.; influence with Sandwich, 7/19; out of
favour with Coventry, 7/34; criticised
by Sir J. Chicheley, 8/549; gifts to
Sandwich and P, 1/57, 130, 232; also,
2/15–16, 16–17
TANGIER: appointed to committee,
3/238; attends meetings, 3/272; 4/319,
335; his design for jetty, 3/238; to
visit, 4/132
SOCIAL: 1/56, 265, 267, 321; 2/22, 23,
45, 49, 72, 74; 3/269; on *Swiftsure*,
1/97, 98; on *Naseby*, 1/113, 114, 119,
123, 141, 159, 160, 164
ALLUDED TO: 1/101, 104, 158, 161, 166,
179
CUTTLE, Capt. [John], naval officer:
killed in action, 6/219, 225; also, 2/33,
50
CUTTLE, lawyer: see Cottle
CUTTS, Sir John, of Childerley,
Cambs.: proposed match with Lady
Jemima Mountagu, 4/174 & n. 2

DAGENHAMS (Dagnams), Essex: P
visits for wedding, 6/175–7; his other
visits, 6/158–61, 167, 180–1; 7/17–18;
gallery, 6/159, 160; gardens, 6/160;
buttery, 6/180; also, 6/163, 173, 188,
193, 225
DAKING (Deking), Capt. [George],
naval officer: discharged, 1/109 &
n. 2, 110; (?the same), 3/50
DALMAHOY (Dormehoy), [Tho-
mas]: on *Naseby*, 1/134 & n. 6
DALTON, [Richard], Serjeant of the
Wine-cellar to the King: buys lease of
P's house in Axe Yard, 1/235, 244–8
passim; social: 4/4
[DALZIEL, Lt-Gen. Thomas]: defeats
Scots rebels, 7/390 & n. 6
DAMFORD, ——: anecdote about,
1/262

DAMPORT: *see* Davenport

DANCING: P dances for first time, 2/61, 71; 7/18; dislikes/disapproves of, 2/212; 4/176; 6/79; admires at court, 3/300–1; 6/29; takes lessons/ practises, 4/111, 122, 124, 126, 129, 132, 133, 134, 141, 149, 150, 153, 161, 265; finds useful for a gentleman, 4/122; Sandwich's dancing-master, 2/117; dancing at court, 3/300–1; 5/56; 6/29; 7/341, 371–3; 9/507; King's French dancing-master, 9/507; dancing schools: in Broad St, 1/253; Fleet St, 2/212; in city, 4/107; Bow, 7/238; at private parties: 6/262, 279, 284; 7/73, 230, 263, 360, 362, 363, 422; 8/28–9, 104, 493, 511; 9/8, 12–13, 42, 128, 134, 172, 227, 458, 464, 511; at schools: 8/392, 396; theatres: 3/32; 8/27, 101, 171, 375, 388, 440, 451, 487; 9/24, 48, 107, 144, 183–4, 219, 420, 459; particular dances: branle, 3/300; 7/372; coranto (courant), 3/300; 4/122, 124, 126; 6/88 & n. 1; 7/372; Cuckolds all a'row, 3/300–1; country, 3/300–1; 4/126, 149, 150, 161; 8/232; 9/464; French, 7/372; jig, 6/79; 7/246; 8/101; 9/120, 219, 464; La Duchesse, 4/141, 265; military, 8/451; 9/459; morris, 4/120; Spanish, 9/440

DANCKERTS (Dancre), [Hendrick], painter (d.? 1680): paintings for P's dining room, 9/421, 423 & n. 1, 434, 487; of Greenwich Palace, 9/438, 445, 465, 485; Rome substituted for Hampton Court, 9/504; painting of Windsor, 9/539; of Tangier, 9/541 & n. 2

DANIEL, [Richard], of the Victualling Office: 1/249; death, 5/286

DANIEL, [Samuel], naval officer: wife solicits commission for, 6/335; 7/417; 8/367; on *Royal Charles*, 7/141; brings news of Four Days Fight, 7/145–7; social: 8/76; alluded to: 6/336

DANIEL, Mrs ——, of Greenwich, wife of Samuel: fondled by Lord Rutherford, 6/274; with child, 6/274, 336; dogged by P, 6/332(2); asks favour for husband, 6/335; 7/417; 8/233, 244, 367; P kisses, 6/336;

7/202; ?brings news of plague, 7/236; fondled by P, 7/417; 8/233, 244, 282; 9/132, 248; tries to borrow money from, 9/306; also, 7/7; social: at Greenwich, 6/315, 333, 338; 7/141; at P's house/office, 7/211, 341; 8/45, 76; 9/265; ~ her son, 7/128; ?her mother-in-law, 7/341

DANVERS, Col. [Henry], Fifth-Monarchist: arrest and escape, 6/184 & n. 3

DARCY, [Marmaduke], Cavalier: on *Naseby*, 1/154, 157; alluded to: 2/29

DARCY, Sir William: Fishery business, 3/269–70 & n.

[DARLING, Edward and Thomas] *see* Taverns etc.: Three Tuns, Charing Cross

DARNELL, [?Richard, jun.], musician: P buys music from, 8/24–5

DARTFORD, Kent: P visits, 2/15, 16, 17, 57, 72; 6/242; 9/495, 499; post-house, 2/17; alluded to: 2/32

DARTMOUTH, Devon: Straits fleet at, 8/345

DASHWOOD, Ald. [Francis]: 6/182

DA SILVA, Don Duarte, merchant: 3/114 & n. 2

DAVENANT, Sir William, playwright and producer [*see also* Musical Compositions; Plays]: reinstates Harris, 4/239 & n. 3, 347; opera *The siege of Rhodes*, 6/284 & n. 1; 8/25, 59; allegedly taught by Capt. H. Cooke, 8/59; criticised by Dr Clerke, ib.; death and burial, 9/156 & n. 1, 158 & n. 3; ~ his sons, 9/158 & n. 4

DAVENPORT, [Frances], actress: leaves stage, 9/156 & n. 2

[DAVENPORT, Hester] ('Roxalana'), actress: leaves stage to live with Earl of Oxford, 3/32 & n. 6, 58 & n. 3, 86; alluded to: 3/273, 295

DAVENPORT (Damport), [?John], of Brampton, Hunts.: social: 2/24, 137, 208, 210, 213

DAVIES, [John], Storekeeper, Deptford: character, 1/286; 4/151; P stays with, 2/12; complains of treatment under Commonwealth, 1/308; his stores, 3/111, 173; bookkeeping, 3/129, 234; in disputes over contracts, 4/73 & n. 2, 151 & n. 1; also, 2/13;

alluded to: 4/318; ~ his wife, 2/12; his kinswoman, 3/129

DAVIES, [Thomas], bookseller and P's schoolfellow: heir to T. Audley, 3/264 & n. 2; knighted as sheriff, 8/497

DAVIS (Davy), [John], clerk to Lord Berkeley of Stratton: P's dislike, 2/26; 3/259; attempted burglary at house, 1/305; news from, 2/10; to go to Ireland, 2/55; alluded to: 1/289, 291, 315; 2/9; 4/408

DAVIS, Jack, son of the foregoing, Navy Office clerk: lends Tower Hill lodgings to P, 3/182, 188–209 passim; alleged fraud by, 4/152; Batten wants dismissed, 5/32; social: ?1/289; ?2/8, 26; ~ his Tower Hill landlord, 3/200

DAVIS, [Jane], ('Lady Davis'), wife of John, clerk to Berkeley: P's dislike, 2/55; 3/259; annoys P by closing door to leads, 1/277; resents EP's neglect, 2/10; to go to Ireland, 2/55; social: 2/25–6; alluded to: 2/114

DAVIS, Mary (Mall), actress: (untrue) rumour of death, 7/102 & n. 1; role in *Richard III*, 8/101 & n. 4; in *Love-tricks*, 8/375 & n. 2; her dancing, 8/101, 375; 9/24, 219; leaves stage to become King's mistress, 9/19 & n. 3, 24 & n. 2, 219, 388, 422, 450; alleged parentage, 9/24 & n. 2

DAVIS, [Thomas], messenger, Admiralty office: 1/103

DAVIS, Mr ——: employs Wayneman Birch, 4/382

DAVY: see Davis, [John]

DAWES, [Henry], merchant: shipping business, 1/267 & n. 4; a slave in Algiers, 2/34

DAWES, Sir [John], merchant: clandestine marriage, 4/121–2 & n., 269, 355; baronetcy, 4/269

DAWS, Mr —— [?identical with Henry Dawes]: 1/147

[DAWSON, William], naval officer: 9/488 & n. 2

DAY, [John], of Leverington, Cambs., P's great-uncle by marriage: P's claim on estate, 4/231 & n. 1, 300 & n. 2, 310–12

DAY, [John], 'old Day', fishmonger: 5/53

DAY, ——, carpenter: 1/78

DEAL, Kent: fleet off, 1/105–34 passim; forts near, 1/105 & n. 3; provisions from, 1/107, 134, 136; P visits, 1/119 & n. 4; Fuller's tavern, 1/119; Poole's, ib.; royalist demonstrations, 1/121(2), 129, 163; naval guns heard, 6/65; plague, 7/241 & n. 3; alluded to: 1/134; 5/212; 6/29

DEAN, Forest of: storm damage, 3/35 & n. 5; (1362), 3/165; ironworks, ib. & n. 1; 'forbid' trees, ib. & n. 2; timber, 4/20; alluded to: 3/114

DEANE, Anthony, kted 1675, shipwright:

CHARACTER: able but conceited, 3/170 & n. 1; 4/124, 176, 236, 381; 5/130; 9/152; a fanatic, 5/203

RELATIONS WITH P: instructs P in timber measurement, 3/151, 163, 169; 4/189–90; demonstrates slide-rule, 4/124; gives P ship model, 3/163 & n. 1, 208; instructs about ships/ship-building, 4/157, 172, 236, 262, 396; 5/29–30, 144, 146, 159, 189, 309; 8/489; 9/250; 'Doctrine of Naval Architecture' written at P's request, 9/531 & n. 1; tells of abuses in yards, 4/19, 79, 219; 8/489; 9/249; gift to P, 6/338; offers money, 9/528; P's gift to, 9/531

NAVY BOARD BUSINESS: rivalry with Petts, 3/170; complains of timber, 4/326; of timber contract, 4/381; and of colleagues, 4/384, 433; to fell Clarendon's timber, 5/203, 205, 210, 214, 238; discusses shipbuilding with Brouncker, 6/281; his *Rupert* praised by King and Duke of York, 7/119, 127; his drawing of, 8/142 & n. 2; and of *Resolution*, 9/262 & n. 4; his calculations of ship's draught, 7/127–8 & n.; his fireship design, 8/358 & n. 1; and gun design, 9/528 & n. 1; also, 5/155, 308–9; 8/39; unspecified business, 4/176, 425; 5/137; 9/175

SOCIAL: 4/141, 318; 5/185; 6/282

DEBUSSY (Debusty), [Lawrence], merchant: his tallies, 6/224 & n. 2; letter of credit, 7/174; poor English, 7/404; ~ his house and fine tapestry, 7/174

DEKING: see Daking

DEKINS: see Dickons, [J.]

finger of my left hand, from a strain that it received last night in struggling avec la femme que je mentioned yesterday)', 6/40; 'I am not, as I ought to be, able to command myself in the pleasures of my eye', 7/110; 'into St Dunstan's church. . . . And stood by a pretty, modest maid, whom I did labour to take by the hand and the body; but she would not, but got further and further from me, and at last I could perceive her to take pins out of her pocket to prick me if I should touch her again; which seeing, I did forbear, and was glad I did espy her design', 8/389

MARRIAGE: 'myself somewhat vexed at my wife's neglect in leaving of her scarfe, waistcoat, and night-dressings in the coach today that brought us from Westminster, though I confess she did give them to me to look after – yet it was her fault not to see that I did take them out of the coach', 4/6; 'Coming home tonight, I did go to examine my wife's house-accounts; and finding things that seemed somewhat doubtful, I was angry, though she did make it pretty plain; but confessed that when she doth misse a sum, she doth add something to other things to make it', 5/283; 'To church in the morning, and there saw a wedding in the church, which I have not seen many a day, and the young people so merry one with another; and strange, to see what delight we married people have to see these poor fools decoyed into our condition, every man and wife gazing and smiling at them', 6/338–9; 'high words between us. But I fell to read a book (Boyle's *Hydrostatickes*) aloud in my chamber and let her talk till she was tired, and vexed that I would not hear her; and so become friends and to bed together', 8/250–1

MONEY: 'talking long in bed with my wife about our frugall life for the time to come, proposing to her what I could and would do if I were worth 2000*l*; that is, be a Knight and keep my coach – which pleased her',

3/39–40; 'it is high time to betake myself to my . . . vows, . . . so I may for a great while do my duty, as I have well begun, and encrease my good name and esteem in the world and get money, which sweetens all things and whereof I have much need', 4/6–7; 'And I bless God, I do find that I am worth more than ever I yet was, which is 6200*l* – for which the holy name of God be praised', 7/348–9; 'but it is pretty to see what money will do', 8/123

MUSIC: 'However, music and women I cannot but give way to, whatever my business is', 7/69–70; 'music is the thing of the world that I love most, and all the pleasure almost that I can now take', 7/228; 'but that which did please me beyond anything in the whole world was the wind-musique when the Angell comes down, which is so sweet that it ravished me; and endeed, in a word, did wrap up my soul so that it made me really sick, just as I have formerly been when in love with my wife; that neither then, nor all the evening going home and at home, I was able to think of anything, but remained all night transported, so as I could not believe that ever any music hath that real command over the soul of a man as this did upon me', 9/94

PLEASURE: 'I do think it best to enjoy some degree of pleasure, now that we have health, money and opportunities, rather then to leave pleasures to old age or poverty, when we cannot have them so properly' 3/86; 'I . . . do look upon myself at this time in the happiest occasion a man can be; and whereas we take pains in expectation of future comfort and ease, I have taught myself to reflect upon myself at present as happy and enjoy myself in that consideration, and not only please myself with thoughts of future wealth, and forget the pleasures we at present enjoy', 7/57; 'We eat with great pleasure, and I enjoyed myself in it with reflections upon the pleasures which I at best can expect, yet not to exceed this – eating in silver plates, and all things mighty rich and handsome about me', 7/388; 'they being gone, I paid the fiddler 3l among the four, and so away to bed, weary and mightily pleased; and have the happiness to reflect upon it as I do sometimes on other things, as going to a play or the like, to be the greatest real comforts that I am to expect in the world, and that it is that that we do really labour in the hopes of; and so I do really enjoy myself, and understand that if I do not do it now, I shall not hereafter, it may be, be able to pay for it or have health to take pleasure in it, and so fool myself with vain expectation of pleasure and go without it', 9/13; 'I did, as I love to do, enjoy myself in my pleasure, as being the heighth of what we take pains for and can hope for in this world – and therefore to be enjoyed while we are young and capable of these joys', 9/134

PUBLIC AFFAIRS: 'But methought it lessened my esteem of a king, that he should not be able to command the rain', 3/140; 'I see it is impossible for the King to have things done as cheap as other men', 3/143; 'He showed me a very excellent argument to prove that our Importing lesse then we export doth not impoverish the kingdom, according to the received opinion – which though it be a paradox and that I do not remember the argument, yet methought there was a great deal in what he said', 5/70; 'While we were talking, came by several poor creatures, carried by by constables for being at a conventicle. They go like lambs, without any resistance. I would to God they would either conform, or be more wise and not be ketched', 5/235; '[He] did . . . inform me mightily in several things; among others, that the heightening or lowering of money is only a cheat, and doth good to some perticular men; which, if I can but remember how, I am now by him fully convinced of', 7/304; 'by bringing over

one discontented man you raise up three in his room', 7/311; 'Most things moved were referred to committees – and so we broke up', 7/321; 'Englishmen on board the Dutch ships . . . did cry and say, "We did heretofore fight for tickets; now we fight for Dollers!"', 8/267; 'some rude people have been . . . at my Lord Chancellor's, . . . and a Gibbet either set up before or painted upon his gate, and these words writ – "Three sights to be seen; Dunkirke, Tanger, and a barren Queen"', 8/269; 'But it was pretty, news came the other day so fast, of the Duch fleets being in so many places, that Sir W. Batten at table cried, "By God!" says he, "I think the Devil shits Dutchmen"', 8/345; '[Coling] told us his horse was a Bribe, and his boots a bribe; . . . and that he makes every sort of tradesman to bribe him; and invited me home to his house to taste of his bribe wine', 8/369

SERVANTS: 'To the office, where . . . I sent my boy home for some papers; where, he staying longer then I would have him and being vexed at the business and to be kept from my fellows in the office longer then was fit, I became angry and boxed my boy when he came, that I do hurt my Thumb so much, that I was not able to stir all the day after and in great pain', 7/19; 'coming homeward again, saw my door and hatch open, left so by Luce our cookmaid; which so vexed me, that I did give her a kick in our entry and offered a blow at her, and was seen doing so by Sir W. Penn's footboy, which did vex me to the heart because I know he will be telling their family of it, though I did put on presently a very pleasant face to the boy and spoke kindly to him as one without passion, so as it may be he might not think I was angry; but yet I was troubled at it', 8/164

SOCIAL OCCASIONS: 'Went to hear Mrs. Turner's daughter . . . play on the Harpsicon; but Lord! it was enough to make any man sick to hear her; yet was I forced to commend her highly', 4/120; 'They have a kins-woman they call daughter in the house, a short, ugly, red-haired slut that plays upon the virginalls and sings, but after such a country manner, I was weary of it, but yet could not but commend it', 4/242; 'We were as merry as I could be with people that I do wish well to but know not what discourse either to give them or find from them', 4/427; 'A very good dinner among the old Sokers', 6/36

SUCCESS: 'There was also [a letter] for me from Mr. Blackburne, who with his own hand superscribes it to S.P. Esqr., of which, God knows, I was not a little proud', 1/96-7; 'Lay very long in bed, discoursing with Mr Hill of most things of a man's life, and how little merit doth prevail in the world, but only favour – and that for myself, chance without merit brought me in, and that diligence only keeps me so', 6/285; 'We had much talk of all our old acquaintance of the College, concerning their various fortunes; wherein, to my joy, I met not with any that have sped better then myself', 8/51; 'my Lord Chan-cellor did say . . . that no man in Eng-land was of more method nor made himself better understood then my-self', 8/60

THEATRE: 'Burt acted the Moore; by the same token, a very pretty lady that sot by me cried to see Desdimona smothered', 1/264; 'I sitting behind in a dark place, a lady spat backward upon me by a mistake, not seeing me. But after seeing her to be a very pretty lady, I was not troubled at it at all', 2/25; 'And it was observable how a gentleman of good habit, sitting just before us eating of some fruit, in the midst of the play did drop down as dead; but with much ado, Orange Mall did thrust her finger down his throat and brought him to life again', 8/516-17; 'It pleased us mightily to see the natural affection of a poor woman, the mother of one of the children brought on the stage – the child crying, she by

force got upon the stage, and took up her child and carried it away off of the stage from Hart', 8/594; 'I was prettily served this day at the playhouse-door; where giving six shillings into the fellow's hand for us three, the fellow by legerdemain did convey one away, and with so much grace face me down that I did give him but five, that though I knew the contrary, yet I was overpowered by his so grave and serious demanding the other shilling that I could not deny him, but was forced by myself to give it him', 9/90

WORK: 'having so many [letters] to write . . . that I have no heart to go about them', 1/215; 'here I had a most eminent experience of the evil of being behind-hand in business; I was the most backward to begin anything, and would fain have framed to myself an occasion of going abroad . . . but some business coming in . . . kept me there, and I fell to the ridding away of a great deal of business . . . and . . . I could have continued there with delight all night long', 7/249

WORKMEN: 'At home all the after-noon looking after my workmen in my house, whose lazinesse doth much trouble me', 1/243; 'All the after-noon at home among my workmen; work till 10 or 11 at night; and did give them drink and were very merry with them – it being my luck to meet with a sort of Drolling work-men upon all occasions', 1/255; 'a poor fellow, a working goldsmith, that goes without gloves to his hands', 8/437

MISC.: 'Lay long; that is, till 6 and past before I rose', 3/190; 'so home to dinner, where I find my wife hath been with Ashwell at La Roches to have her tooth drawn, which it seems akes much. But my wife could not get her to be contented to have it drawn after the first twitch, but would let it alone; and so they came home with it undone, which made my wife and me good sport', 4/97; 'By and by news is brought us that one of our horses is stole out of the Stable; which proves my uncles, at which I was inwardly glad; I mean, that it was not mine', 4/310; 'the fellow coming out again of a shop, I did give him a good cuff or two on the chops; and seeing him not oppose me, I did give him another; at last, found him drunk, of which I was glad and so left him and home', 4/342; 'it is not greatest wits but the steady man that is a good merchant', 5/300; 'where a Trade hath once been and doth decay, it never recovers again', ib.; 'one Mr Tripp, who dances well', 7/362; 'He told me also a story of my Lord Cottington: who wanting a son, entended to make his Nephew his heir, a country boy, but did alter his mind upon the boy's being persuaded by another young heir (in roguery) to Crow like a cock at my Lord's table, much company being there and the boy having a great trick at doing that perfectly – my Lord bade them take away that fool from the table, and so gave over the thoughts of making him his heir from this piece of folly', 8/566–7

DICK (Dike) SHORE: *see* Duke Shore

DICKENSON, Esther ('Widow'): *see* Pepys, Esther

DICKONS (Dekins), [John], hemp merchant: dies of grief, 3/213, 233; social: 3/19

DICKONS, [Elizabeth], ('my Morena'): at St Olave's, 2/192; illness and death, 3/213, 233; alluded to: 3/19

DIGBY, Lady Anne, daughter of the 2nd Earl of Bristol: jilted, 4/208–9 & n.

DIGBY, Capt. [Francis], naval officer, son of the 2nd Earl of Bristol: opinion of 'tarpaulins', 7/333

DIGBY, George, 2nd Earl of Bristol, succ. 1653 [occasionally referred to by his original title of Lord Digby], politician: a Papist, 4/224; 9/17; said to have turned Protestant, 5/58; 9/120; a public danger, 9/120; responsible for failure of Treaty of Uxbridge (1645), 4/212 & n. 1; sells

Irish peerage (1646), 8/126; in France and Flanders during Interregnum, 4/212–13 & nn.; enmity to Clarendon: 2/142; opposes over bill of uniformity, 3/49 & n. 1; brings articles of impeachment against (1663) 4/115, 219–20, 223–5 & nn., 229, 231 & n. 2, 367; 8/445 & n. 4; renews attack (1664), 5/34, 60 & n. 4, 73, 85, 89, 137, 208; influence over King, 4/137; part in scheme for parliamentary management, 4/200, 207, 207–8 & nn., 211 & nn., 213; supports marriage alliance with Parma, 4/224 & n. 1; flees to escape arrest, 4/271 & n. 1, 272, 298 & n. 4; 5/85, 89 & n. 3; Lady Denman supports him, 7/405; his faction, 7/261; appears in Lords, 8/362; recovers King's favour, 8/530, 532, 533, 597; ~ his chaplain, 5/58–9 & n.

DIKE: *see* Dyke

[DILLINGHAM, Theophilus], Master of Clare Hall and Vice-Chancellor, Cambridge: 3/218 & n. 4

DILLON, Col. Cary, succ. as 5th Earl of Roscommon 1685: courtship of Frances Butler, 1/209 & n. 3, 217; 2/152; 3/299 & n. 1; 9/311; duel, 3/171 & n. 1; alluded to: 1/214

DILLON, [William]: hanged, 4/60 & n. 1

DIPLOMATS [for individuals, *see* under personal names]: disputes about precedence among in London, 2/187–9 & nn.; in Paris, 4/419–20 & n.; (rumour of) in Madrid, 8/36 & n. 2

DIVES: *see* Dyve

DIXON, Mr——: matchmaker for Tom P, 4/19, 21

DIXWELL, Col. [Basil], cr. bt 1660, of Broome, Barham, Kent (d. 1668): 1/172, 176, 182

DOBBINS, Capt. [Joseph]: feast as Elder Brother, Trinity House, 6/155

DOCTORS' COMMONS, St Benet's Hill: P visits, 1/229; 2/216; 4/368; 5/351

DOLBEN, Catherine, wife of John: story of, 9/89 & n. 5; ~ her two children, 9/89

DOLBEN, John, Dean of Westminster 1662–83, Bishop of Rochester 1666–83,

Archbishop of York 1683–d.86: sermon before King, 7/245 & n. 4; rumoured suspension, 8/587 & n. 2; slanders against, 8/596 & n. 2; dismissed from court office, 9/53 & n. 2, 89

DOLING, Thomas, messenger, Council of State: news from, 1/14 & n. 4; P's letters to, 1/116, 126 & n. 2; to go to Ireland, 1/311; visits Overton in prison, 1/319; social: 1/37, 38, 80, 92, 95, 174–5, 208, 230, 282

DOLL, milliner at the New Exchange: see Stacey

DOMESDAY BOOK: P to consult, 2/236 & n. 3

DONCASTER, ——, waterman: 3/156

DONNE: see Dunn

DONNE, John, poet (1573–1631): takes holy orders, 9/215 & n. 2

DORCHESTER, Lord: see Pierrepont

DORMEHOY: see Dalmahoy

DORMER, Charles, 2nd Earl of Caernarvon (1632–1709): on value of timber, 8/201 & n. 3

DORRINGTON, [?Francis, ?John], merchant: compensation for loss of ship, 9/69 & n. 1; bid for victualling contract, 9/288 & n. 2

DORSET, Earl of: see Sackville, R.

DORSET HOUSE, Salisbury Court: Clarendon at, 1/173, 184

DOUCE: see Doves

DOUGLAS, James, 2nd Marquess of Douglas (d. 1700): at court ball, 7/372; commands troops, 8/306, 308, 309, 311

DOUGLAS, William, 9th Earl of Morton (d. 1681): 9/534 & n. 2

DOVER, Kent: parliamentary elections, 1/96–7, 111(2), 167, 179 & n. 1, 183; clerk of castle, 1/97; jurats visit Naseby, 1/130; mayor welcomes King, 1/158; Dutch ships brought into, 5/326; Rupert's fleet at, 7/143–5 passim; Governor prepares against invasion, 7/187 & n. 1; squadron to be stationed at, 8/149 & n. 1; Dutch attack feared, 8/327 & n. 1, 328; Duke of York as Lord Warden, 9/280 & n. 4; also, 1/134, 279; 7/300

DOVES(?Douce, ?Dowes), Capt.——: 2/207

DOWGATE [see also Taverns etc.: Swan]: Fire, 7/270

DOWNE(S), [Elkanah], Vicar of Ashtead, Surrey, 1662–d.83: dull sermon, 4/247 & n. 1

[DOWNES, John], actor and writer: in Davenant's Siege of Rhodes, 2/131 & n. 3

DOWNES, [John], regicide: reprieved 3/16 & n. 1

DOWNING, [Frances], b. Howard, wife of Sir George: praises Holland, 1/249; alluded to: 1/153

DOWNING, George, kted 1660, cr. bt 1663; Teller of the Receipt in the Exchequer 1656–60; reappointed 1660; envoy to United Provinces, 1657–60, 1660–7, 1671–2; Secretary to the Treasury Commissioners, 1667–71; M.P. Morpeth, 1660, 1661–79, 1679, 1679–81, 1681

CHARACTER: parsimonious, 1/186 & n. 2; 8/85; rogue, 3/45; vain, 8/425; efficient, 8/238, 240

AS ENVOY TO UNITED PROVINCES: offers P clerkship, 1/18, 31; P writes ciphers for, 1/28, 30, 31; leaves for Holland, 1/23, 25, 29, 31, 33; returns, 1/136 & n. 1, 249; knighted, 1/153; has regicides extradited, 3/44–5 & n., 48; news from, 5/121 & nn.; 6/103 & n. 2; protests against Dutch detaining English cargo, 5/321; assists in relief of English prisoners of war, 7/201 & n. 1, 380 & n. 3; 8/407–8 & n., 425; complains of peace terms, 8/425–7 & nn.; intelligence service, 9/401–2 & nn.

IN EXCHEQUER: as P's master, 1/2 & n. 1, 83, 107–8, 238; offers P council clerkship, 1/22 & n. 5, 35; lawsuit against Squibb, 1/31 & n. 1, 33–6 passim, 40, 45, 48, 49; encourages loans on Additional Aid (1665), 6/322, 327, 330, 334; 7/9, 23, 87, 124 & n. 2; 8/131–2, 397–8, 407

AS M.P.: part in drafting Additional Aid bill (1665), 6/292 & n. 3; 7/122; 8/30; project for leather trade, 8/425 & n. 4; introduces bill for Treasury orders, 8/520 & n. 2; parliamentary news from, 7/380; 8/520

AT TREASURY: appointed secretary, 8/238, 240; Tangier accounts, 8/249

SOCIAL: Christmas dinner for poor neighbours, 8/85 & n. 1; also, 7/215, 216

ALLUDED TO: as chairman of Council of Trade, 2/20; also, 1/10, 67

~ his child, 1/249; his mother [Lucy], 8/85

DOWNING, [John], anchor-smith: P returns *douceur*, 7/119, 138

DOWNING, Capt. [?John], soldier: gives evidence to Committee on Miscarriages, 8/538 & n. 3; social: 7/362, 363

DOWNS, the, off Kent [entries concerning use of roadstead by English warships are not indexed]: Batten's trip to, 4/296; Dutch fleet in, 6/258; Smyrna fleet, 7/404

DOYLY, Sir William, M.P. Great Yarmouth, Norf., 1660, 1661–77: parliamentary commissioner for paying off fleet, 1/255, 286 & n. 2; Commissioner for Sick and Wounded 6/217 & n. 4; 8/407; warrant for bucks, 6/220–1 & n.; 8/248; social: 6/218; 8/224

[DRAGHI, Giovanni Battista] (Seignor Baptista; Seignor Joanni), musician: compositions, 7/352 & n. 4; 8/54–5 & n.; feat of musical memory, 8/55–7 *passim*; ?his singing, 9/322 & n. 2

DRAKE, Mr ——, of Hackney: house and garden, 7/181 & n. 3

DRAMMEN (Dram), Norway: timber from, 3/118 & n. 3

DRAWWATER, Dorothy: 8/468 & n. 2

DRAWWATER, [James]: at P's Twelfth Night party, 1/10 ~ his wife [Jane], b. Strudwick, ib.

DRAYDON: *see* Dryden

DREAMS (P): bedwetting, 1/162; EP's death, 1/285; accident to EP, 2/226; swollen testicle, ib.; plots, 3/250; W. Swan the fanatic, ib.; lawsuit, 4/15; St John's Isle, 4/43; J. Cole, 6/145; Lady Castlemaine, 6/191; fire, 7/287, 296, 299; ?8/87, 128; death of mother, 8/129, 303; defending Navy Board in Parliament, 9/88; reflects on nature of, 6/191; EP suspects him of dreaming of Deb Willet, 9/384, 439

DREBBEL (Dribble), [Cornelis] van: his mine, 3/46 & n. 1; 4/378

DRESS AND PERSONAL APPEARANCE (MEN AND BOYS) [*see also* Prices; Watches etc.]:

GENERAL (P): importance of good linen, 3/216, 228; 8/121; and neatness, 2/199 & n. 1; to dress fashionably, 4/343, 357; 5/269, 302; 6/100; concerned at expense, 2/47, 129; 4/356, 357; 6/104; concerned not to over-dress, 9/551

GARMENTS AND ACCESSORIES:

APRONS: worn by apprentice weavers, 5/222

BANDS: King's lack of, 8/417; (P): 1/85; 3/61, 228; 4/234, 235, 354; 5/128, 139, 338; 6/73, 76; 7/61; lace/fine bands, 3/215, 219–20, 228, 236; 6/100, 128; 9/6; in plain band mistaken for servant, 8/115; band strings, 2/80

BELTS (P): sword belt, 4/80; 7/26, 353; 8/83, 321–2; 9/201, 537

BOOTS (P): riding-boots, 1/279; 2/132; 3/204, 217; 4/28

BREECHES: two legs through one knee of, 2/66 & n. 2; (P): baize linings, 1/268; close-knee'd, 3/106; white linings, 4/130; rabbit skin prevents galling, 5/298; silk, 6/218; camlet, 9/533

CANNONS (tops) (P): 1/156; black silk, 4/357, 400

CAPS: montero, 1/120; toilet, 1/239; Venetian, 1/324; fur, 8/22; (P): fur, 1/31; EP makes, 1/85; velvet studying, 1/120; velvet montero, 1/227, 232; 7/346; nightcap, 6/175

CHEMISE (P): 8/158

CLERICAL: 3/224; surplices, 3/215; cassock, 7/299 & n. 3, 310, 313; catholic priest in lay clothes, 7/329 & n. 3; hair shirt and sandals, 8/26; 'plain country parson dress', 8/118

CLOAKS: silk, 1/14; velvet-lined, 5/241; Colchester bays at Spanish court, 8/79; (P): camlet, 1/190; 7/7, 15; 8/525, 580–1, 599–600; velvet, 3/84; velvet-lined, 4/343, 344, 353, 357, 400; 5/125; lined with moiré, 5/142, 144; with plush, 5/302, 308, 309; cloak-coat, 7/106;

'common riding-cloak', 7/208; cloak made into suit, 1/118; 8/314; to be worn if without sword, 3/241 & n. 2

COATS: children's, 1/250; Duke of York's buffcoat, 6/51; (P): jackanapes, 1/193; velvet, 1/194, 221, 227, 232; 2/81, 100, 231; 7/7, 15, 25; camlet, 1/198; 4/112; camlet ridingcoat, 3/42, 85; short black made from cloak, 1/251; trimmed from EP's petticoats, 2/120; 5/44; short, 5/240; as part of suit, 6/175; 7/353

CODPIECES: 8/421, 596

COLLARS: see scallops

COMB-CASE: 1/239

CRAVATS: 2/229; (P): 1/95; 7/25

CUFFS (hands) (P): 8/412, 440; laced, 6/125, 175; 9/201 & n. 1, 540

DOUBLETS (P): 3/181; slashed, 3/116

DRAWERS: holland, 5/222; (P): 7/280

FACINGS (P): 2/120

FROCK: 3/116

GARTERS (P): 4/131

GLOVES: working goldsmith without, 8/437; (P): buckskin, 1/166; kid leather, ib.

GOWNS (P): Indian, 2/130; 7/85; 8/462; morning, 3/77, 82; shag, 4/357, 360; dressing gown, 8/522

HABIT, RIDING (P): 3/288

HANDS: see cuffs

HANDKERCHIEVES ('han(d)kaychers'): as neckcloth, 7/269; King's lack of, 8/417; (P): (with strawberry buttons), 1/94

HATS: beaver, 2/80; plumed, 1/142; 2/172, 229; cocked, 8/249; (P): montero, 1/92, 227; beaver, 2/127, 203; 3/67, 71; 4/360; low-crowned beaver, 4/274, 280; velvet riding hat, 4/360; hatbands, 1/94, 247; wearing of: at meals, 5/277 & n. 3; during toasts, 7/246; by puritan preachers, 3/207 & n. 3; as mark of respect etc., 2/19 & n. 1; 4/114; 5/205; 6/14 & n. 2, 339; 8/319 & n. 2

JEWELRY: ring with Woolwich stone, 8/84 & n. 2; (P): Portuguese rings, 3/139

LACE: see Textiles etc.

LININGS: see breeches

LIVERY: Sandwich's servants', 2/79; Penn's and Batten's, 3/77; others',

8/115, 186; (P): servants', 3/47, 50 & n. 3, 77; 9/372, 378

MITTENS: fur, 8/22

MONTEROS: see hats

MUFF (P): 3/271

NECKCLOTH (P): 6/175; 8/486

NIGHTGOWNS (dressing gowns): 6/228; 7/378; 9/4; silk, 3/242; (P): 6/175; 7/268, 272

PANTALOONS: 5/255 & n. 1

POWDER (for head) (P): 3/96

RIBBONS [see also Marriage: wedding ceremonies]: green for birthday, 6/285; black for leg (new fashion), 7/324; (P): 9/165, 230

SASH (P): 8/462

SCALLOPS (collars): (P): 3/216, 220, 235

SHIRTS (P): wears two, 7/291; halfshirts, 1/231; 2/195; 4/360; 5/191

SHOES: shepherd's iron-shod, 8/339; (P) [see also Wootton, W.]: first wears buckles, 1/26; 'in shoemaker's stocks', 7/107 & n. 2; shoe strings, 9/188

SLEEVES: butchers', 5/222; (P): laced, 6/125; 9/201

SOCKS: (P): 8/105

STOCKINGS: shepherd's woollen, 8/339; (P): knitted, 1/85; grey serge, 1/94; linen, 1/156; silk, 1/164; 4/80; 9/193, 449 & n. 1.; short black, 1/251; thread, 2/138; 6/334; 8/105; woollen, 2/138; cotton, 6/73; leather, 6/309

SUITS: Sandwich's coronation, 2/83; his gold-buttoned, 4/187; Duke of York's riding, 2/213; silk, 5/24; (P): bombazine, 7/172, 182; 9/215, 217; camlet, 6/104, 106, 114, 125, 152; 8/295, 314, 315; 9/533, 534, 537, 540, 548; cloth: grey riding, 2/120; 3/42, 85, 106, 116; 4/243; moiré lined, 5/142, 144; also, 4/130, 316, 369; 5/125, 302, 308, 309–10, 322; 7/39; farandine, 6/124, 125, 175, 210; silk, 3/190, 196; 2/105; stuff, 6/127–8; 9/197, 201, 210, 540; misc.: with great skirts, 1/3, 38; skirts shortened, 1/121; white, with silver lace coat, 1/38; made from cloak, 1/118; old black new-furbished, 3/54; closekneed coloured suit, 4/105; new fashion (vest, coat, belt, sword), 7/353; changes in September from silk to cloth suit, 8/455

SWORDS: Prynne's basket-hilt, 1/62; (P): rapier stick, 1/95, 138; sword 'refreshed', 2/24; smallsword with gilt handle, 4/80, 105; silver-hilted, 7/353; gilded for May Day, 9/537; wears to escort Sandwich, 1/93; starts wearing 'as manner among gentlemen is', 2/29 & n. 2; 3/241 & n. 2; equips footboy with, 3/77 & n. 2; 9/537

TOPS: *see* cannons

TRAVELLING-CLOTHES: 8/233

TUNICS: (P): velvet, 8/489; laced, 9/201 & n. 2; coloured camlet, 9/540

TURBANS: 7/378; worn by giant, 5/243

VEILS: at synagogue, 4/335 & n. 2

VESTS: new fashion, 7/315; first worn by Duke of York, 7/320; description, 7/324, 328; Louis XIV puts footmen into, 7/379 & n. 4; also, 8/154; (P): first wears, 7/346, 353(2), 362, 366; made from old suit, 8/295, 314, 341, 404; his new laced vest, 9/201; and flowered tabby, 9/533, 540

WAISTCOATS (P) (outer garments): green watered moiré, 1/298; false tabby with gold lace, 2/195; black baize faced with silk, 4/360; thin silk, 7/172; (under garments): leaves off/puts on according to season, 2/116, 195, 198; 3/138; 5/198; 6/67; 7/182; 8/235; 9/175, 180, 400, 549

WALKING STICKS (canes) (P): knotted, 1/104; rattan, painted and gilded, 1/244; buys at cane shop, 5/117; varnished for walking, 7/211; silver-headed Japan, 8/84

COMPLETE OUTFITS (P): 4/105, 400; 6/175; 9/201, 533

FASHION: changes at Easter, 8/63; King's new, 7/315, 320-1; description, 7/324 & n. 3, 328; worn by M.P.s, 7/324; hat 'cocked behind', 8/249; French ambassador's unfashionable dress, 9/284 & n. 3; (P): buys/wears to keep up with: buckled shoes, 1/26 & n. 2; short cloak, 1/260; coat and sword, 2/29; longer hair, 2/97; new coat, 2/203; suit with linings

showing under breeches, 4/130; low-crowned beaver, 4/280; suits in new fashion, 7/353(2); 8/295; suit with shoulder belt for sword, 9/201

COURT/CEREMONIAL/PROFESSIONAL [*see also* clerical, above]: coronation robes, 2/80, 82, 84; regalia, 2/84; costumes at court ball, 7/372 & n. 3; Russian envoys' costumes, 3/297; 8/428; Persian envoy's, 9/17; Garter robes, 8/184–5; academic, 9/544

MOURNING: purple worn by King, 1/246; (P): hat band, 1/247; short black stockings, 1/251(2); rings, 2/74 & n. 2; 3/269; 4/21; belt, 2/203; shoes blacked, 5/90; white gloves, 5/90 & n. 2; servants', 8/134

BEARDS: Spanish fashion, 8/453 & n. 1; (P): shaves off beard/moustache, 3/97; 5/22–3 & n.

HAIRDRESSING: wigs worn at court, 4/136; King and Duke of York start wearing, 4/360; 5/49, 126; and W. Howe, 4/390; Rupert's, 8/146; (P): hair cut by: barber, 2/97; 4/237; 5/352; EP, 5/72; 8/35; 9/424; maids, 8/280; 9/201; and sister-in-law, 9/175; close-cropped, 7/112, 302; because lousy, 9/424; foul with powder, 3/96; combed by maids, 3/96; 6/21, 185; 8/531; 9/20, 37, 48, 73, 109, 277, 328, 337; head inspected, 9/239; finds difficulty in keeping hair clean, 3/96, 196; 4/130; to wear periwig, 4/130, 290, 343, 350, 357, 358, 378; first appearances in, 4/362, 363, 365, 369; periwig cleaned, 5/212; repaired, 6/74; fears to wear one made during Plague, 6/210; refuses to buy infested periwig, 8/133, 146; buys from French wigmaker, 8/136, 137, 138, 146, 177; 9/334; barber to keep in repair, 9/217; catches fire in candle, 9/322; periwig case, 4/363; also, 6/89, 97

SHAVING (P): trimmed by barber, 1/90, 113, 136, 142, 148, 152, 162, 200, 208, 214, 219, 224, 252, 298, 308; 2/32, 76, 97, 112, 135, 180, 241; 3/24, 41, 64, 71, 81, 187, 201, 215, 220, 233, 289, 299; 4/16, 20, 23, 43, 96, 130, 154, 186, 190, 258, 261, 312; 5/246; 6/257, 266, 288, 303, 306, 322, 331, 334; 7/6, 278,

293; 9/234, 496; employs barber on giving up pumice-stone, 3/196; for first time for a year, 6/233; pays barber, 9/225; shaves with pumice, 3/91, 97; shaves off beard/moustache, 3/97; begins using razor, 5/6; shaves off beard/moustache, 5/22–3 & n.; cuts himself, 5/29; shaves after week's growth during Fire, 7/288; shaves himself, 5/52, 55, 87; 6/159, 228, 311; 8/247

WASHING (P): washes regularly, 5/320; washes on hottest day of year, 3/75; and at EP's request, 6/44; washes feet/legs, 3/47; 4/165; 7/172, 206; catches cold, 7/207; ears washed, 6/21; lousy, 9/424

DRESS AND PERSONAL APPEARANCE (WOMEN AND GIRLS):

GARMENTS AND ACCESSORIES:

APRONS: Queen Catherine, 9/557

BANDS: lace, 6/172

BODICE: Nell Gwyn, 8/193; (EP): pair, 4/357

CAPS: Duchess of Newcastle's velvet, 8/186, 196

COATS (EP): velvet, 4/316

CUFFS (EP): laced, 8/392–3, 396

DRAWERS: 9/194; (EP): 4/140 & n. 1, 172

DRESS: lying-in, 6/55; 7/329; 'paysan', 8/375; riding, 6/162; 7/162; travelling, 7/142

DRESSING-BOX: 8/46, 53; (EP): 9/91

FANS (EP): 4/172

FARTHINGALES: Portuguese ladies-in-waiting, 3/92 & n. 2

GALLOSHES: 6/299

GARTERS: valentine gift, 9/449; (EP): valentine gift, 2/40

GLOVES: embroidered, 2/38; white, 2/38; 4/68; 7/344; Jessamy, 7/344; 9/449; (EP): valentine gift, 2/40; painted leather, 4/100; with yellow ribbons, 5/264; perfumed French, 9/427

GORGET: 4/279

GOWNS: velvet, 3/299; 4/2, 400; silver-laced, 5/188; flowered tabby, 9/521; (EP): black silk, laced with black gimp, 2/117; moiré to replace taffeta, 3/298; 4/10, 13; trimmed with point, 4/337; Indian, 4/391; 5/8;

Japanese, 4/415; laced, 5/100, 110, 118; 9/455–6; morning, 5/103; 8/465, 468; light coloured silk, 6/76; similar to Lady Castlemaine's, 7/298; coloured flowered tabby, 7/302; 9/540; cloth, 8/242

HANDKERCHIEVES ('han(d)kirchers'): ('lace', worn as collar), 7/341; 8/576; (EP): 2/211, 212, 214; 7/243, 379; 9/6

HATS: plumed, 4/230; straw, 8/382; (EP): straw, 8/382

HOODS: black, 1/42; (EP): yellow bird's-eye, 6/102 & n. 2; white, 8/124; French, 9/453

JEWELRY: posy ring, 1/39; diamonds and pearls at court ball, 7/371–2; (EP): pearl necklace, 1/240; 6/200–1; 7/108, 111, 112, 113, 412; pendants, 4/100; 5/196; diamond ring, 6/190–1; 9/67–8, 78, 88–9

JUSTE-AU-CORPS: black, 8/187; gold laced, 9/213

LACE: see Textiles etc.; when worn as collar, see above, handkerchieves

MANTLE: frieze, 1/60–1; white flannel, 8/79; (EP): 1/320

MASK [see also below, vizard]: at theatre, 8/71–2; at Vauxhall, 9/220; travelling 2/91 & n. 1; (EP): 5/28

MUFF (EP): 1/320; 3/271; 4/7; 7/39

NECKCLOTH: 8/224

NIGHTGOWN: Lady Castlemaine's, 8/404; (EP): 7/18; 8/210, 424, 458

PATCHES: worn by Dutch ladies, 1/138; shop girl, 3/239 & n. 2; Duchess of Newcastle, 8/186; Peg Lowther, 6/9; 8/196, 197; Lady Castlemaine, 9/186; Lady Sandwich and daughter, 1/269; (EP): first wears, 1/234, 283, 299

PATTENS (EP): 1/27

PETTICOATS: satin, 3/83; linen, trimmed with lace (Lady Castlemaine), 3/87; short crimson (Queen Catherine), 4/229; (EP): paragon, 1/82; trimmed with silver lace, 1/225; 5/239; 8/242; and gold lace, 5/44; sarcenet, trimmed with black lace, 3/65; yellow, 3/85; 5/264; green flowered satin trimmed with gimp lace, 3/125; silk striped, 4/199; silk, 5/114; 7/296; blue, 8/124; laced, 9/400

PINNER: (Lady Castlemaine), 5/126;

moderation, 3/130, 151, 163, 197; 4/235; mixes wine with beer, 4/343, 410; 5/236; relaxes vow during Plague, 6/226; 7/49; alleged to be a drinker, 6/243; drinks sack despite oath, 7/23; and burnt wine, 8/130; first morning visit to tavern for seven years, 9/220

HEALTHS: puritan objections, 2/105 & n. 5; 5/172 & n. 4; French method, 4/189; loyal toast accompanied by gun salute, 1/152; drunk kneeling, 1/121, 122; 2/87; ladies toasted, 2/220; 7/246; 8/130–1

VARIETIES:

BRANDY: 9/103, 498; burned, 8/20

BRISTOL MILK: *see* wine

BUTTERMILK: 5/152

CHOCOLATE: 1/178; 3/226–7; 4/5; 5/64, 139; at coffee house, 5/329

CIDER: 3/300; 4/28, 121; 7/115; 8/315; French, 4/254

COFFEE: 5/76, 77, 105

ELDER SPIRITS: 4/221

GRUEL: 4/40

HIPPOCRAS: *see* wine

JULEP: 1/181

LAMB'S WOOL: *see* ale

MEAD: 8/460

METHEGLIN: 1/72; 7/218

MILK: 4/29; 7/207; 9/224; from milkmaid on Epsom Downs, 8/339; from Keeper's Lodge, Hyde Park, 9/142 & n. 1, ? 154, 175, 184, 222, 260, 533–4

MUM: *see* ale

MUSCADINE: *see* wine

ORANGE JUICE: 9/477 & n. 3

POSSET: 3/274; 4/40, 202, 319; 5/77; sack posset: 1/9, 10, 11; 4/14, 38; 9/13; in Davenant play, 9/134

PURLE: *see* beer

SACK: *see* wine

STRONG WATERS: EP for fainting fit, 4/307; also, 2/24; 4/284; 6/40, 198; 7/157; 8/412, 504, 544; 9/99

TEA: 'cupp of tee', 1/253 & n. 5; also, 6/328 & n. 1; 8/302

WATER: [for spa water, *see* Health]: public supply, 3/92 & n. 3; 4/295 & n. 3; 8/370 & n. 2; also, 4/265; 6/23

WHEY: 3/116; 4/164 & n. 2, 175,

179–80, 286; 5/152; 6/120; 7/170 & n. 4; 8/215; 9/215

WINE: Bristol milk: 9/236 & n. 1; burnt: 7/295, 425; 8/47, 120, 130, 589; canary: 2/211; 6/151; claret: 1/277; 2/25; 4/65, 171; 6/151; 7/175, 375; 8/393; burnt, 5/90; 7/386; 8/124; English: from Walthamstow, 1/317; 8/341–2; Florence wine: 1/324; 2/8; Haut Brion ('Ho Bryan'): 4/100 & n. 4; hippocras ('hypocras'): 4/354; 5/118; Malaga (*see also* sack): 3/14; 6/151; muscadine: 1/296; Navarre: 9/443 & n. 1; Rhenish: 2/125; 8/156; with sugar, 2/38; 3/24; Bleakard, 4/189 & n. 3; sack: with wormwood, 2/9; raspberry sack, 2/212; Malaga, 4/235; 6/151; mulled, 6/266; 7/424; 9/103; anecdote of its killing toad, 7/290; also, 1/57, 230, 292, 308; 2/25, 217, 219, 224; 5/32, 37; 6/224; 7/23, 166; 8/5; 9/227; sherry: 3/14, 180; tent: 4/405; 5/11, 222; 6/151; wormwood: 1/301; 4/25, 58; misc.: wine and sugar, 1/167; 4/179; mulled white, 1/292; wine traders' tricks, 7/256

WINE CELLARS: P orders jointly with colleagues, 3/14 & n. 3; crested bottles, 4/346 & n. 1; pride in stock, 6/151; cellars at Audley End, 1/70 & n. 1; 8/467–8; Whitehall palace, 1/193, 246, 247; 2/175; and at Povey's, 4/18 & n. 2, 298; 5/161

DRUMBLEBY (Drumbelly), ——, flageolet maker, Strand: the best in town, 8/53; supplies flageolets, 8/53, 87; 9/30, 51, 160; recorder, 9/157; moulds for eye tubes, 9/278; ~ his boy, 9/364

DRURY LANE [*see also* Coffeehouses; Taverns etc.: Bear; Theatres]: plague in, 7/72–3; milkmaids in, 8/193

DRYDEN (Draydon), John (1631–1700) [*see also* Plays]: known to P at Cambridge, 5/37 & n. 2; share in authorship of *Sir Martin Mar-all*, 8/387 & n. 1, 468, n. 2; alluded to: 8/363

DUBLIN: Castle Plot, 4/168 & n. 2, 170; packet boat, 4/256; alluded to: 3/162

1/317; helps him rearrange books etc. after Fire, 7/292, 336, 367; gathers May-dew with EP, 8/240; also, 1/59, 251; 3/113, 156; 4/9; 5/13; 8/552; 9/116

SOCIAL: at Twelfth Night supper, 1/10; sees pre-coronation procession, 2/83; at Vauxhall, 3/95; on river trips, 7/235; 8/325; visits previous mistress, 8/315; also, 1/76; 3/115; 8/167, 376, 443; 9/516

~ her mother, 2/162

EDWARDS, Tom, P's servant:

CHRON. SERIES: P given allowance for, 5/228 & n. 2; engaged from Chapel Royal, 5/234 & n. 1, 255; given suit from Wardrobe, 5/234, 245, 246, 251; his schoolboy ways, 5/256, 260, 266; neglects music, 6/7, 77, 86; spoilt by EP, 6/26, 28, 29; P boxes his ears, 7/19, 150; beats, 8/176; scolds, 8/202; courtship of Jane Birch, 9/63–4, 283; to leave P's service, 9/441, 483; marriage, 9/483, 484, 493, 499, 500; leaves Seething Lane, 9/502; gifts to, 9/526 & n. 2, 537; also, 5/329; 8/134, 420

AS SERVANT: accompanies P on visits to dockyards/ships etc., 5/305, 317; 6/103, 119, 128, 228, 286–7, 299; 7/112, 202; 8/165; to Westminster/ Whitehall, 6/35; 9/422, 444, 449; church, 5/256, 267, 285; 6/5; Brampton, 9/207, 209–10, 212–13; reads to P, 7/283; 9/202, 215, 271, 300, 311, 313, 315, 317, 318, 320, 337, 354, 381, 382, 400, 433, 482, 501, 502, 542; helps in office, 6/226; 9/524, 526, 548; helps to stow prize goods, 6/259; arrange books/papers, 7/290; 8/432; 9/354; to secure P's money after Fire, 7/284, 336, 367; escorts P after Deb Willet affair, 9/397; also, 6/143, 205, 217; 7/95, 100, 266, 425; 8/444, 540, 551; 9/331

MUSICAL: talented, 5/258; 266; lute/ theorbo lessons, 5/344; 6/86; 7/182, 226–7, 375; 8/558; teaches Barker song, 8/113; writes down P's compositions, 9/412; sings/plays lute/ theorbo, 5/261, 266, 305, 310, 320, 321, 332, 339; 6/138; 7/68, 338; 8/113, 394, 413, 504; 9/179, 213, 300, 401

SOCIAL: looks for comet with P, 5/355; at Bartholomew Fair, 5/260; Vauxhall, 7/198; Islington, 8/376; at taverns with P/EP, 6/27; 9/445, 516, 538; also, 6/263; 8/590

ALLUDED TO: 9/464

~ his father's death from plague, 6/225, 235

EGERTON, John, 2nd Earl of Bridgewater (d. 1686): appointed to Brooke House Committee, 8/194; at Privy Council committee, 8/278; rumoured appointment to Treasury Commission, 8/367–8 & n.; rumoured dismissal from Privy Council, 8/596 & n. 1, 600

EGLIN: see Edlin

EGLIN(G)TON, 6th Earl of: see Montgomerie

EGYPT: 5/274

ELBOROUGH, [Robert], Curate of St Laurence Poultney, and P's schoolfellow: foolish, 1/178 & n. 3; 4/5, 34; preaches well, 7/235; alluded to: 7/269

ELBE (Elve) river: naval squadron in, 7/71

ELIEZER: see [Jenkins]

ELIZABETH I, Queen of England 1558–1603: Armada fleet, 3/187 & n. 2; embassy to Russia, 3/188–9 & n.; coinage, 4/148; letter from Cranmer (recte Grindal), 4/329–30 & n.; letters from, 6/308 & n. 2; Roman Catholic disloyalty, 7/394; avoids summoning parliament (1588), 8/293

ELIZABETH, Dowager Queen of Bohemia (d. 1662): at The Hague, 1/138 & n. 1, 144; 'debonaire but plain', 1/144; on Naseby, 1/154; at theatre, 2/131, 156; death, 3/28, 81; alluded to: 1/140

[ELKINS, RICHARD], Clerk of the Cheque, Gravesend: news from, 8/349 & n. 1, 350

ELLINGTON, Hunts.: 9/211, 553

[ELLIOTT, James], servant to Lord Middleton: killed in affray, 5/32 & n. 3

ELLIOTT, Capt. [Thomas], naval officer: naval news from, 7/142, 143

ELLIS, [William], Solicitor-General 1654: 1/40

ELVETHAM, Hants.: 4/102

ETHELL, Robert, of Huntingdon:
2/137
ETHEREGE (Etherige), Sir George,
playwright (d. 1691) [see also Plays]:
critical of actors, 9/54
ETON COLLEGE: P visits, 7/59–60 &
nn.
EVANS, [Lewis], harpist: dies in
poverty, 7/414
EVANS, Mr ——, butler to Lady
Wright: 1/29; plays lute, 1/29, 288
EVANS, Mr ——, the tailor: 2/165
EVANS, Capt.: see Ewen(s)
EVELYN, John, diarist:
CHARACTER: P's regard, 6/243, 289–90;
7/26, 29, 49, 112, 297; 9/484
POLITICAL OPINIONS: laments state of
court/nation, 7/29, 297, 406; 8/181–4
passim, 248–9, 278, 377; 9/484; stories
of Louis XIV's power, 8/182–3;
believes republic imminent, 8/556
AS COMMISSIONER FOR SICK AND
WOUNDED etc.: attends on Navy
Board, 6/239, 243; consulted by P,
6/253; proposed infirmary, 7/29 &
n. 1, 49; also, 6/275, 278
HOUSE (Sayes Court, Kent): admired
by P, 6/94–5 & n.; P visits, 6/94–5,
243, 253, 289–90, 331; 7/112; garden,
6/97 & nn., 253 & n. 3; also, 9/449
WRITINGS, INTELLECTUAL INTERESTS
ETC.: impromptu nonsense verse,
6/220; translation of Naudé's Advis
pour dresser une bibliothèque, 6/252 &
n. 1; book on painting, 6/286 & n. 2;
Elysium Britannicum, 6/289 & n. 4;
plays, ib. & n. 5; hortus hyemalis,
6/289 & n. 6; Leicester MSS, 6/308 &
n. 2; collection of paintings, mezzotints etc., 6/289 & n. 3; admires
Clarendon House, 7/32; also, 6/243
MISC.: proposes Thomas P of Hatcham
as J.P., 7/112; news of Plague from,
7/241; scheme for making bricks,
9/314 & n. 3; purchase of land near
Deptford yard, 9/484 & n. 1
SOCIAL: stories of Frances Stuart,
8/342–3; also, 6/217, 218, 291,
324
EVELYN, Mary, wife of John: her
paintings, 6/243
EVELYN, [Richard], brother of John
(1622–70): his house (Woodcote

Park), nr Epsom, 8/338 & n. 1, 339 &
n. 1; ~ his wife [Elizabeth], ib.
EVERTSEN, [Cornelis], jun. Dutch
naval officer (d. 1706): captured in
naval action, 6/81–2 & n.; ~ his
father (d. 1679) ib.
EVERTSEN, [Jan], Dutch Admiral:
his squadron, 6/108 & n. 3; suspected
of disloyalty, 6/122 & n. 6; killed in
action, 7/229 & n. 3, 231, 233
EVETT, Capt. [?Philip, naval officer]:
in search for Barkstead's treasure,
3/242, 246, 248, 256, 285, 286
ÉVORA, Portugal: recaptured by
Portuguese, 4/215 & n. 2
EWELL (Yowell), Surrey: P/EP
visit(s), 4/248, 249; 6/235, 244–5, 304;
soldiers quartered at, 6/245; ~ 'my
Besse' at inn, 6/304
EWEN(S) (Evans), Capt. [Thomas],
naval officer: Elder Brother's dinner at
Trinity House, 3/246 & n. 1; reports
on Tangier mole, 4/319
EXCHANGE: see New Exchange;
Royal Exchange
EXCHANGE ALLEY: coffee-house,
4/162; Backwell's building scheme,
4/214 & n. 3
EXCHANGE ST, Westminster: 7/369
& n. 4
EXCHEQUER, the:
CHRON. SERIES: shortage of cash, 1/117;
Lord Treasurer sworn in, 2/31; proposed payment of Navy Victualler by,
3/106–7, 107–8; attempted reorganisation of expenditure, 3/297 & n. 1;
management of credit under Additional Aid Act and Eleven Months
Tax, 6/312; 8/132 & n. 1, 269, 590;
unsuitability as commercial bank,
8/132; also, 6/65
BUILDINGS: 7/325; Upper Bench, 1/47;
at Nonsuch in Plague, 6/186, 188; and
after Fire, 7/278
COURT OF: Squibb's case, 1/48, 49;
Field's case, 4/51–2, 192–3; Lord
Mayor sworn in, 7/346; distringas
from, 9/535
CLERKS: Monck's gift to, 1/118; new
appointments, 1/128; 2/4; fees, 6/100;
7/398; 8/74; inefficiency, 6/157;
7/125, 126, 168; social: St Thomas's
Day feast, 1/320 & n. 1; 2/236; also,

Tower Hill: market established after Fire, 7/281

FAITHORNE, [William sen.], engraver and printseller: P buys from, 1/174 & n. 2; 3/2; 7/173, 359, 393; 8/10; engraving of Lady Castlemaine, 7/359 & n. 3, 393; instrument for drawing perspectives, 9/513

FALCONBRIDGE: *see* Belasyse, Thomas, Lord Fauconberg *and* Fauconberg, Edward

FALCONER, [Edward] (ed. error): *see* Fauconberg, [Edward]

FALCONER, [Elizabeth], widow of John: formerly his maid, 4/67; claims compensation on his death, 5/231, 248 & n. 2, 249, 253; ill, 5/213; social: 5/155, 192

FALCONER, [John], Clerk of the Ropeyard, Woolwich: marriage, 4/67; gift to EP, 5/45, 47; P inspects ropeyard with, 5/54; illness and death, 5/109, 125, 130, 137, 155, 213, 217, 248 & n. 2; stories of gifts to Penn and Coventry, 5/231 & n. 4, 248, 249, 253; 8/228; social: 2/121, 155, 227; 3/19, 102, 142, 159, 179; 4/103; 5/156, 182, 192; ~ his friend, 5/155

FALMOUTH, Viscount: *see* Berkeley, Sir C.

FALMOUTH, Cornwall: 7/397

FANATICS [P uses both 'fanatics' and 'sectaries' to describe the extreme Puritans. *See also* Anabaptists; Fifth-Monarchists; Nonconformists; Plots and risings, minor]: strength in London, 1/109, 111; 4/373 & n. 3; blame King for persecution, 3/127; rising feared, 3/186, 236, 303; prophesy end of world next Tuesday, 3/266–7; want court and church purified, 3/275; alleged loyalty, 4/373; 5/264 & n. 1; rebel in Yorkshire, 4/391 & n. 1; riot in churches, 9/96 & n. 1

FANCHURCH ST: *see* Fenchurch St

FANSHAWE, Anne, Lady Fanshawe, wife of Sir Richard: 3/126; 7/379–80

FANSHAWE, [Henry], brother of Thomas Fanshawe, 2nd Viscount Fanshawe: seeks place in navy, 9/86 & n. 3

FANSHAWE, [Lyonel], 2/163 & n. 3; 3/57

FANSHAWE, Sir Richard, diplomatist: drafts preambles to patents of nobility, 1/188 & n. 1, 189; ambassador to Portugal, 2/163 & n. 3; 3/2 & n. 3, 57; death, 7/214 & n. 1, 380

[FARRINER, Thomas], King's Baker, Pudding Lane: Fire alleged to have started at his bakery, 7/268 & n. 1; 8/81, 82

FAUCONBERG (Falconbridge etc.), [Edward], Deputy-Chamberlain of the Receipt at the Exchequer: agrees to P's resigning, 1/80; consulted by P, 2/236; alluded to: 7/303, 304, 314, 319; 8/212; social: 1/24; 2/239–40, 241; 6/162, 235; 7/398; ~ his kinsman, R. Knightley; his kinswoman, Barker, EP's companion (qq.v.)

FAUNTLEROY (FONTLEROY), [?Thomas]: 1/294

FAVERSHAM, Kent: 8/358

FAZEBY, Capt. [William], naval officer: 7/141–2

FÉCAMP (Feckam): King lands at (1651), 1/156

FEE LANE: *see* Fleet Lane

FELTON, Sir Henry, Bt, M.P. Suffolk (d. 1690): 6/118

FELTON, [John], assassin of Buckingham: 2/93 & n. 2

FENCHURCH ST [*see also* Taverns, etc.: Mitre]: Plague, 6/124, 128, 225; Fire, 7/276; P shops in, 8/173; 9/322; St Gabriel's church, 6/76 & n. 2

FENN, John, Paymaster to the Navy Treasurer: financial business: with P, 4/422; 6/192(2); 8/259; Penn, 7/65; and B. St Michel, 8/153, 162, 163; also, 7/169, 312; 8/121–2, 177, 281, 285; 9/169, 362, 428; malpractices: 6/40, 117; enquired into by Brooke House Committee, 9/82; rudeness, 7/89; a tool of Backwell, 7/214; P warns Carteret against, 6/190; usefulness to Carteret, 8/48 & n. 1, 180, 327; dismissed, 9/357 & n. 2; news from, 8/299, 354, 416; social: 3/14; 6/187, 198; 7/48, 74, 89, 404; 9/337; ~ his pretty wife, 9/337; his son, 6/24

FENNER, family of: dine at P's father's, 1/266; at funeral, 2/179

FENNER, [Hester], second wife of Thomas: marriage, 3/13, 16; old and ugly, ib.; alluded to: 3/88; 5/85

FENNER, [Katherine], first wife of Thomas: ill, 1/75; 2/144; death, 2/156, 158, 159; social: 1/29, 65, 175, 252, 268

FENNER, [Thomas], P's uncle, of St Sepulchre's parish: at odds with sons-in-law, 1/29; 2/45, 158–9; 4/417; proposes wife for Tom P, 2/163, 165; tells P of Tom's illness and debts, 5/81, 84–5; visits dying Aunt Kite, 2/172–3; attends funeral, 2/178–9; acts as executor, 2/179 & n. 3, 190, 192, 209; 3/161 & n. 3; marries again, 2/205; 3/13, 16, 88; dies, 5/157, 158; also, 2/176 & n. 1; 5/111, 113; social: at P's New Year breakfast, 2/2; P sends venison to, 3/173; also, 1/59, 65, 174, 175, 205, 233, 239, 252, 268, 324; 2/139; 3/62; 4/100, 163; alluded to: 2/159; ~ his sister Utbert, 2/173

FENS, the: P's journey through, 4/310; poverty in, 4/311; mosquitoes, ib. & n. 1; Greatorex's drainage scheme, 4/356 & n. 2

FENSTANTON (Stanton), Hunts.: 2/148

[FENTON, Elizabeth, wife of Maurice]: 2/54 & n. 3

FENTON, one Mrs: 7/232

FERNE, Henry, Master of Trinity College, Cambridge 1660–2; Bishop of Chester 1662 (d. 1662): preaches at Whitehall, 1/237

FERRABOSCO, [?Elizabeth]: proposed as companion to EP, 5/262; her singing, ib. & n. 1; attendant to Duchess of Newcastle, 8/243

FERRER [Jane], wife of Capt. Robert: daughter born and christened, 7/49; social: at Sandwich's birthday dinner, 2/142; visits Lady Sandwich, 2/221; also, 3/94, 281, 299; 4/88, 100, 121, 181; 6/278, 279; 7/118; alluded to: 4/286; 8/508

FERRER, Nan: 5/128

FERRER, Capt. [Robert], soldier, member of Sandwich's household:

CHRON. SERIES: injured in leap from balcony, 2/102–3, 108; to go to Lisbon, 2/228–9; brawl with waterman, ib.; with footman, 3/196, 212; with fellow-servant, 6/306–7; P jealous of, 3/206; has solicited EP for Sandwich, 9/356, 404; serves in King's guard, 4/38; children christened, 4/81, 82–3; 7/49; lends P horse, 4/120, 313; escorts Hinchingbrooke from France, 4/121, 187; promised place in Wardrobe, 5/168, 172, 185; 8/508; serves at sea under Sandwich, 6/278; account of Battle of Lowestoft, 6/127, 128 & n. 3, 137; accompanies Sandwich to Spain, 7/6, 54; stories of Spain, 9/404 & n. 1; Spanish horse, 9/510; also, 2/121, 206; 3/139, 215, 216, 219; 4/429

HOUSES: chamber at Wardrobe, 3/81; house at Westminster, 4/82

NEWS FROM: 1/123; 2/32–3; 4/25, 37, 189, 237–8, 433

SOCIAL: at gaming house, 2/211–12; EP's valentine, 4/42; stays with P at Greenwich, 6/278, 283; 7/6; at theatre: 2/59, 89, 151, 154, 156, 191, 203, 214, 221; 3/230; 4/430–1; also, 1/224; 2/35, 120, 121, 170, 195; 3/92, 94, 133, 226, 266, 281, 288; 4/21–2, 179; 5/138, 202; 6/279; 7/8 ~ his friend, 2/203; 4/87, 179 & n. 2, 189

[FERRI, Baldassare]: sings at Theatre Royal, 9/326–7 & n., 329

FETTERS, [Henry, jun.], watchmaker: 1/246

FIELD, [Edward], informer: informs against embezzler, 3/23 & n. 2; 4/76; detained for slandering Navy Board, 3/23 & n. 2; sues P for wrongful imprisonment, 3/23, 64, 120, 231, 280, 281; 4/15, 16, 34, 192–3; awarded damages, 4/394, 396, 411, 421; sues Batten, 4/153, 171, 172; lawsuits alluded to, 4/51–2, 53, 55, 57, 71, 110, 201, 333, 350, 364, 395, 406, 427; 6/126

FIELDING, Basil: murdered by brother [Christopher], 8/208–9 & n., 319, 321 & n. 3

FIENNES (Fines), [Nathaniel], Presbyterian politician (d. 1669): 1/75 & n. 4

FIENNES, [Maj. William]: action at Tangier (1662), 5/167 & n. 1

£2800, 7/367; takes measures for its safety in Fire, 7/275, 336, 340, 367; during Dutch raid, 8/262–4 passim, 264, 273, 280, 281, 296, 472–4, 487, 539; also, 1/57–8, 168, 178–9, 183; 2/50

CASH AT BANKERS: withdraws £200 from Backwell, 2/76; deposits £2000 with Vyner, 7/34; withdraws it, 7/84, 85; withdraws £2000, 7/196; given advance by Colvill, 9/97; also, 6/193; 7/230, 242; 8/151

CASH ELSEWHERE: at Rawlinson's, 1/221; in Exchequer, 2/19

INVESTMENTS: in bottomry, 1/294; Portuguese trade, 2/76; land, 2/127; 5/196; 8/517; loans to government 5/323; 6/330; 7/85, 88–90 & n., 201–2, 205, 230, 243–4, 251; 8/38, 87, 397, 407, 420 & n. 1

TAXES: assessment/payment: poll-tax (1660), 1/315–16 & n.; (1667), 8/30 & n. 1, 120 & n. 2, 152–3, 192; royal benevolence (1661), 2/167–8 & n.; relief of indigent officers (1662), 3/199 & n. 2, 283 & n. 5, 285; Militia Act (1662), 3/275 & n. 1, 283

FINCH, [Francis], Excise Commissioner: P consults about Tangier, 6/136; political news from, 7/191–2

FINCH, Heneage, 2nd Earl of Winchilsea, ambassador to the Ottoman Empire 1660–9: on *Naseby*, 1/133; to go to Constantinople, 1/217; alluded to: 1/134, 135; 7/326

FINCH, Sir Heneage, Solicitor-General, cr. Earl of Nottingham 1681: eloquence, 5/140 & n. 2, 324; 8/22; 9/529; chairman of Commons' Committee for Public Debts, 1/214; administers oaths to P and Batten, 1/252; entertains King at Inner Temple, 2/155 & n. 2; business with Tangier Committee, 3/172; 4/45; with Navy Board, 9/146 & n. 1, 148; rumoured appointment as Attorney-General, 8/412; speeches in court, 9/85 & n. 2, 529 & n. 2, 531–2 & n.; praises P's parliamentary speech, 9/104, 113, 146; his garden, 5/179 & n. 1; alluded to: 9/122, 340; ~ his son, 9/203; his coachman, 4/431

FINCH, [?William], mercer, the

Minories: ?7/303; 8/224 & n. 5, ?525, 529, 580–1; 9/?136, 221; ~ his pretty wife, 8/224; 9/221

FINES: see Fiennes

FIRE: P's fear, 2/100; 5/249; 6/49; false alarm, at P's house, 6/27; outbreaks: in the Piazza, Covent Garden, 3/11; Lombard St, 3/94; 5/71; Lothbury, 3/296 & n. 4; Wood St, (false alarm), 4/6; Lady Castlemaine's lodgings, 5/27; Cheapside, 5/247–8, 249; Deptford Yard, 5/257; Horse Guard House, 7/362–3 & n.; Westminster, 7/363; Southwark, 7/363; 8/191 & n. 1; Bishopsgate St, 8/119 & n. 3; in city, 8/164, 201; Aldersgate St (arson), 8/316, 320; Durham Yard, 9/534–5 & n.; and Bridgetown, Barbados, 9/243 & n. 2; counter-measures: buckets etc., 5/27, n. 1; houses pulled down, 5/248; blown up, 7/362; 8/119; 9/534–5; fire-engines, 8/191, 320; ~ chimney fires, 8/28; 9/534

FIRE, the GREAT (1666):

GENERAL: 7/267; follows drought, 7/269; P writes up diary entries, 7/282, 318, 402; sermon on, 7/283; fast day for, 7/316 & n. 3; 8/413; 9/297; prophesied by: Mother Shipton, 7/333 & n. 2; Nostradamus, 8/42 & n. 2; anon. prophet, 8/42–3; Tom of the Wood, 8/270; P dreams of, 7/287, 296, 299; fears renewed outbreak, 7/366; 8/28, 87, 126, 128; alluded to: 8/191

ORIGIN: in Pudding Lane, 7/268 & n. 1; attributed by rumour to enemies, 7/275 & n. 3, 277 & n. 2, 279, 366, 405 & n. 3, 406; 8/42; enquiry into by Commons' committee, 7/343 & n. 4, 356–7 & n.; 8/439 & n. 4, 444–5; trial and execution of Hubert, 7/357 & n. 2; 8/81–2

OUTBREAK AND SPREAD: 7/267–79 passim; 8/5; fires persist, 7/288; smoking ruins, 7/393, 401, 406; 8/17, 87, 114; Fish St, 7/268(2), 270; Pudding Lane, 7/268; 8/5; St Magnus Church, 7/268; Steelyard, 7/268, 269; Thames St, 7/270; Dowgate, ib.; Cannon St, ib.; Fish St Hill, 7/272; Tower St, 7/273–4, 274–5, 393; Trinity House, 7/274; Pie Corner, 7/275; Old

5/251, 262; P appointed to committee for raising funds, 5/262; lottery proposed, 5/269 & n. 2, 276, 279, 294, 299–300, 323; 6/53; farthing monopoly, 5/269, 336; voluntary collections, 5/293–4 & n., 304, 304–5, 312; P prepares proposals, 5/314, 315; fears he may neglect Navy Office for, 5/280; unspecified business, 5/202, 214, 260, 269, 276, 281, 315, 341, 348

FISHMONGERS' HALL: 5/269, 276

FISH ST (Old Fish St) [*see also* Taverns etc.: Feathers; Swan]: 7/237

FISH ST (New Fish St, Fish Street Hill) [*see also* Taverns etc.: King's Head; Sun]: P buys lobsters, 1/212; 7/103; gradient, 2/214; 7/103–4; Fire, 7/268(2), 270, 272; rebuilt, 9/285 & n. 1

FISH YARD, the, Westminster: 3/67

FISSANT, Mrs ——: 6/173; ~ her daughter, ib.

FIST, [Anthony], clerk to Sir W. Batten: 8/213–15 passim, 277, 278; 9/259, 394

FITCH, Col. [Thomas]: handles mutiny, 1/36–7; dismissed from command of Tower, 1/39 & n. 2

FITTON, Alexander, cr. Baron Fytton of Gosworth, co. Limerick 1689: suit against Lord Gerard, 9/83–4 & n.

FITZGERALD, Lt-Col. [John], Deputy-Governor of Tangier 1662–6: criticised, 5/302 & n. 1, 344–5 & n.; good company, 9/274; commands Irish regiment, 3/204; favourite of Duke of York, 4/116; of Falmouth, 5/345; financial business, 7/173; 8/76; 9/272; ill at Woolwich, 8/403; returns from Tangier, 9/272; arrested to prevent duel, 9/273; alluded to: 8/61; 9/275

FITZHARDING: *see* Berkeley, Sir C.

FITZROY, Lady Charlotte: daughter of Lady Castlemaine, 6/41 & n. 2

FLANDERS: *see* Spanish Netherlands

FLEET ALLEY: prostitutes, 4/164, 301; 5/219–20, 224, 225–6

FLEET BRIDGE: rebuilt after Fire, 9/223 & n. 1, 258

FLEET (Fee) LANE: 5/101, 220–21

FLEET PRISON: 2/118

FLEET ST [*see also* Taverns etc.:

Devil; Globe; Greyhound; Hercules Pillars; Mitre; Penell's; Standing's]: storm damage, 3/32; Fire, 7/275, 279, 288–9; conduit, 1/3; 5/269

FLEETWOOD, Lt-Gen. Charles, parliamentarian (d. 1692): letter to Rump, 1/34–5 & nn.; reprieved, 3/16 & n. 1; alluded to: 1/21, 76

FLETCHER, Capt. [John], naval officer: 3/150

FLOWER, old Mr ——: 1/307

FLOYD: *see* Lloyd

FLUSHING: peace commissioners at, 8/216; alluded to: 1/131, 132; 7/229, 234

FLY, the: *see* Vlie

FOGARTY (Fogourdy, Fougourdy), ——, Catholic priest: P fears influence on EP, 5/39, 103; news from, 5/40

FOLEY, [Robert], ironmonger to the Navy: provides chest for P, 5/323; and tools, 7/245; provides locks for Brouncker, 8/226; social: entertains Navy Board, 3/266; 5/308; also, 9/157; ~ his man, 4/409; 7/245

FOLEY, [Thomas], ironmaster: endows almshouse, 9/227 & n. 3

FONTLEROY: *see* Fauntleroy

FOOD [*see also* Health: diet]:

MEALS ON SPECIAL OCCASIONS [asterisks denote entries at which dishes are listed]: colly feast, 1/24; Shrove Tuesday club dinner, 1/78*; Lenten dinners, 1/80; 2/50, 73; 4/70, 71; 5/44; P's New Year breakfast, 2/2*; P's Lenten dinners, 2/52*; 4/104*; 5/117*; P's stone feasts, 2/60; 3/53*; 4/95*; 5/98; 6/124*; coronation banquet, 2/85; Lord Mayor's banquets, 2/201, 203; 4/354–6 & nn.; P's dinner for Exchequer colleagues, 2/241; Penn's wedding anniversary dinner, 3/4*; P's Christmas dinner, 3/293*; P's dinner for Mountagu children, 5/180*; club dinners, 6/39, 132; bad dinner given by Sir W. Hicks, 6/222*; P's six-course dinner, 7/388; P's seven-course dinner, 8/4; Downing's dinner for poor neighbours, 8/85*; French tavern dinner, 8/211*; bad dinner given by Penn, 8/371*; breakfast after dancing party, 9/289; also, 1/6*, 29*; 2/228*; 4/14*, 247*,

fee etc., 1/293; gift from Sandwich, 1/292, 293, 298; also, 8/430
AS PAYMASTER-GENERAL: management of funds, 8/16; discusses allocation of excise money, 6/136; 7/92, 133; 8/123–4, 198, 586 & n. 3; 9/197, 199; obtains funds from Excise Office/ Treasury for army, 7/133; 8/112, 193, 198, 199, 572, 586 & n. 3; 9/14, 280, 306 & n. 2
NEWS ETC. FROM: suggests P enter parliament, 7/322; stories of Spain, 8/111; pessimistic about public affairs, 8/149; also, 7/322–3; 8/80, 294
SOCIAL: 1/157, 299–300; 2/21, 22, 29; 3/190, 202; 4/63; 6/114; 9/320
FOX(E), Dr [Thomas], physician: daughter's marriage, 1/141
FRAISER, Dr Alexander, physician, kted ?1667: blamed for death of Princess Mary, 1/323 & n. 1; influence at court, 5/275 & n. 1; attends Rupert, 8/41 & n. 4; Duke of Cambridge, 8/192; Mennes, 8/324; and Duke of York, 8/524; arrested for debt, 9/561 & n. 2
FRAMPTON, Robert, chaplain to Levant Company 1655–70; Bishop of Gloucester, 1680–91 (d. 1708): P admires his preaching, 7/316 & n. 4; 8/21 & n. 1, 32, 34 & n. 1
FRANCE:
NATIONAL CHARACTERISTICS, MANNERS, CUSTOMS etc. [for English imitation of French manners, see Food; Humfrey, P.; Mountagu, E., 1st Earl of Sandwich; Penn, W., jun.]: volatility, 1/10; 2/189; 3/160; 'humours', 6/213; English prefer Spaniards, 2/188 & n. 4; mottoes in taverns, 3/204; and bargaining for meals in, 4/131; hiring of servants, ib.
GOVERNMENT: marshals, 4/213 & n. 1; nobility, 4/416 & n. 1; princes of blood, 4/419–20 & n.; taxation, 5/68; 8/300; praised by Evelyn, 8/181–2; by others, 8/335; 9/352; King's arbitrary powers, 8/300 & n. 5; his achievements, ib.
FOREIGN RELATIONS:
GENERAL: ambassador claims precedence in England, 2/187–91 & nn.; and in Spain (untrue rumour), 8/36 &

n. 2, 37, 42; ambassador affronted at Lord Mayor's banquet, 4/355 & n. 2
WITH THE EMPIRE: 4/340, 439; 8/107
WITH ENGLAND: relations deteriorate, 5/343; 6/165, 270, 307; claims wine from Dutch prize, 5/354; attack on English merchantman, 6/278 & n. 3; attempts mediation, 6/76 & n. 1; war declared, 7/24, 40 & n. 2; quarrel over Charles II's new fashion, 7/324 & n.3, 379–80 & n.; embargo on trade, 7/403 & n. 5; fleet movements (1666), 7/139 & n. 3, 216, 300, 327–8; threatens invasion of England, 7/185(2) & n. 1, 186, 286, 287, 395; and of Ireland, 8/1; suspected involvement in Pentland Rising, 7/384 & n. 2; French victories in St Kitt's, 7/171 & n. 3, 390 & n. 3; fleet sent to W. Indies, 8/2 & n. 1; takes Antigua, 8/38 & n. 1; defeated off Martinique, 8/430 & n. 1; peace negotiations, 7/420; 8/11 & n. 3, 69 & n. 2, 72, 74, 96, 106–7 & n., 113, 128, 151, 170 & n. 5, 212, 244, 289, 294 & n. 4; fleet movements (1667), 8/38, 170, 248, 250, 266; threatens invasion, 8/265, 277, 432, 602; peace proclaimed, 8/399 & n. 1; published, 8/453 & n. 3; renewed threat of invasion, 9/7, 18, 30, 181; fleet movements (1668), 9/26, 141 & n. 3, 250–1 & nn., 251; rumoured demand for salute from English ships, 9/397 & n. 3; anxious for alliance, 9/7 & n. 1; alienated by Anglo-Dutch alliance, 9/35 & n. 4; French intentions uncertain, 9/417; English alliance almost achieved, 9/536 & n. 2
WITH THE PAPACY: quarrel with Alexander VII, 3/253 & n. 3; 4/24 & n. 1, 26, 63 & n. 3; 5/40 & n. 1, 42, 60; 6/156 & n. 1; rumour of establishment of patriarchate, 3/253; influence in election of Clement IX, 8/335–6 & n.
WITH PORTUGAL: peace with, 8/191 & n. 6
WITH SPAIN: designs against, 4/340 & n. 5, 439; said to have hired ships against, 4/407, 420; designs on Flanders, 8/74, 92 & n. 3, 175; on Poland, 8/92, 95; diplomatic prepara-

n. 3; visits gaming house, 2/211–12; refuses to, 4/87; gambling at court, 9/2–4, 71; at inns of court, 9/3
GARDENER'S LANE, Westminster: 5/254
GARDENS:
GENERAL: Evelyn's book on, 6/289 & n. 4; H. May's views, 7/213 & n. 2; English superior to foreign, ib.; roof garden, 2/123; bowling greens/alleys, 3/146, 175; 4/142, 246; 7/213, 217; crinkle-crankle wall, 4/313; maze, 7/182; circular walls, 7/213
PHYSIC GARDENS: Oxford, 9/226 & n. 4; St James's Park, 5/127 & n. 1, 130
PLEASURE GARDENS: Barn Elms, 7/235; 8/188, 202, 236, 256, 346, 400; 9/27, 128, 271; Cherry Garden, Rochester, 8/312; Cherry Garden, Rotherhithe, 5/178, 180; Jamaica House, Bermondsey, 8/167; Mulberry Garden, Hyde Park, 5/140; 9/207 & n. 1, 286, 509, 510; Neat Houses, nr Chelsea, 2/158 & n. 2; 5/268; 7/235; 8/371; 9/216; (New) Spring Garden, Vauxhall, 3/95 & n. 1; 4/243, 249, 251, 262; 5/268; 6/120, 132, 136, 164; 7/136, 198, 294; 8/240–1, 249–50; 9/172, 194, 196, 198, 199, 204, 207, 216, 219(2), 220, 249, 257, 264, 268; (Old) Spring Garden, Vauxhall, 3/95 & n. 1
OTHERS: Arundel House, 2/110; Audley End, 8/467; Brampton: P's, 8/469, 472–5 passim, 539; Clapham: Sir D. Gauden's, 6/172; Greenwich: 'common garden', 4/197, 273; palace garden, 6/212; Hackney: Lord Brooke's, 7/181–2 & n.; Mr Drake's, 7/181; The Hague: Huis ten Bosch, 1/147; Hampstead: Belsize House, 9/281 & n. 4; Hatfield House, 8/381; vineyard, 2/138–9 & n.; Hinchingbrooke, 4/313; 5/298; Kensington: Sir H. Finch's, 5/179 & n. 1; Lincoln's Inn, 4/201 & n. 3; Lincoln's Inn Fields: T. Povey's, 5/161; Marylebone, 9/189; Navy Office, q.v.; Nonsuch Palace, 6/235; Sayes Court: J. Evelyn's, 6/97 & nn. 1, 2, 253 & n. 3; 9/449; Spargus Garden, ?Whitehall, 9/172; Walthamstow: Sir W. Batten's, 2/109; Wricklemarsh: Sir

T. Blount's vineyard, 6/94 & n. 3; York House, 2/102
GARRAWAY, William, M.P. for Chichester, Sussex: good company, 7/306; a discontented Cavalier, 7/310; concern for public interest, 7/310–11; 9/303 & n. 3; criticises navy accounts, 7/305, 317; objects to royal commission of accounts, 8/194 & n. 1, 252 & n. 1; against standing army, 8/352–3; visits Coventry in Tower, 9/303 & n. 3
GARTER, the ORDER of the: investiture/installation: of Sandwich, 1/160–1 & nn.; Albemarle, 1/161; Monmouth, 4/99; Christian, Prince of Denmark, 4/108 & n. 3; Duke of Cambridge, 7/398 & n. 2; election of John George II of Saxony, 9/246 & n. 2; chapters, 2/75; 4/108; knights' stalls etc. in St George's, Windsor, 7/58; feast at Whitehall, 8/177 & n. 1; also, 8/184–5
GARTHWAYT, Mr ——: his stable at Scotland Yard, 1/65, 66
GATEHOUSE, the, Westminster: prison, 4/163; 5/58; 6/115; also, 1/208
GAUDEN, Benjamin, son of Sir Denis: proposed match with Paulina P, 7/46 & n. 1, 88–9
GAUDEN (Gawden), Ald. Sir Denis, Navy Victualler, kted 1667; Sheriff 1667–8:
P's REGARD: 6/254; 7/24; 8/567
AS NAVY VICTUALLER: victuals ships in Downs, 1/241; in river, 2/112; at Nore, 7/332–3; at Plymouth etc., 8/88; keeps ships waiting for provisions, 4/31; gifts to P: beef and tongues, 1/320; 3/291; flagons, 5/216, 218, 234, 271, 301; £500, 7/8; £500 p.a. as Surveyor-General, 8/250; £250, 8/372; warned by P not to reveal gifts, 9/99; accounts [some may relate to Tangier]: 3/62, 103, 105, 106; 4/288, 304, 337, 346; 7/74, 373, 403, 405; 8/47, 208, 220, 245, 322; 9/214, 333, 342, 381, 393 & n. 1, 511; proposal for payment from Exchequer, 3/106–7 & n., 107; short of cash, 4/389 & n. 1; 6/254, 323 & n. 2; 7/9, 25, 88; complains of contract, 4/415, 427; allies with P, 6/254; approves his plan for surveyorship,

6/294-5; instructs about pursers' business, 6/325; granted £5000, 7/377; advised by P on allowances, 8/113, 118(3); criticised by Rupert and Albemarle, 8/513; 9/107, 142; new contract, 8/567 & n. 3; 9/8(2), 47, 252, 253, 288, 312, 315(2), 316 & n. 1, 317-18 & n., 323, 393 & n. 1; Penn a partner, 9/348, 399 & n. 4; also, 2/221; 7/29, 118; 8/344, 382-3; 9/429; unspecified business, 4/89; 6/265; ?7/232; 8/43, 110, ?197; 9/25, 393, 427-8, 429

AS VICTUALLER FOR TANGIER: attends meetings, 3/300; 4/21, 23; 5/97; discusses victualling, 4/26; fails to obtain contract, 5/204, 210, 212, 271; account with Teviot, 5/339 & n. 3; awarded contract, 6/157, 171, 204; accounts [see also 'as Navy Victualler'], 6/251; gifts to P: £60, 6/251; £500 6/322, 324, 325, 341; promises commission, 7/8; £100, 8/35, 36, 37, 44; £250, 8/372; P willing for him to reveal gifts, 9/99; also, 7/402; unspecified business: 6/253-4; 7/24, ?232; ?8/197; also, 5/171 & n. 3

AS ALDERMAN AND SHERIFF: in Fire, 7/277; appointed non-resident Sheriff, 8/432, 458; also, 8/583; 9/33, 111

SOCIAL: entertains associates, 4/337; 7/373; 9/34, 214, 432; visits Coventry in Tower, 9/104; also, 1/187; 2/222; 3/42, 107; 4/26, 242; 5/338; 6/329; 8/348, 374, 584; 9/222

MISC.: house at Clapham, 4/244 & n. 1, 249; 6/172, 312; 7/29; at Smithfield, 9/34; to advise Penn about house purchase, 8/197; news from, 8/269 ~ his children, 2/54; 4/244; 6/172; 7/29-30, 88; his man, 8/267; his clerk, 9/342

GAUDEN, [Elizabeth], Lady Gauden, wife of Sir Denis: 4/244, 245; 9/34; ~ her spaniel, 4/246

GAUDEN, [Elizabeth], widow of John: her conversation, 4/244 & n. 4, 245; alluded to: 4/251

GAUDEN, John, Bishop of Exeter 1660-2, Worcester 1662: death, 4/244 & n. 2; social: 1/187 & n. 3

GAUDEN, [Samuel], son of Sir Denis: 4/245 & n. 1

GAUDEN, [Sarah], daughter of Sir Denis: 6/172; 7/30, 88 & n. 4

GAULTIER (Gotier), Mons. ——: teaches singing, 4/242 & n. 4

GAULTIER, Mrs; the Queen's tire-woman: 9/454

GAYET, Susan: see Guyat

GAYLAND: see Guyland

GEERE, [John]: 1/184 & n. 2

GENOA: terms of doges' appointment, 3/7-8 & n.; alluded to: 8/374, 548

[GENS, Jan de], captain of the Mary: 4/157 & n. 2

GENTLEMAN, Jane, P's servant: recommended, 4/274, 276; enters service, 4/290, 292; deaf, 4/292; angers EP/P, 4/337, 354; wishes to leave, 4/356; accused of lying, 4/361; to leave, 5/101; also, 4/362, 389, 399, 438; 5/9, 71, 185; ~ her father, 4/389

GENTLEMAN, Mr ——, cook: 9/116, 373-4; ~ his wife and son, 9/373-4

GENTRY, the: ignorant of corn trade, 9/1; antiquity of in Cheshire, 9/280 & n. 2; rate of decay, 9/550

GEORGE, P's 'old drawer' at the Sun tavern, King St: 1/229; 2/178; 4/217

GERARD, Sir Charles, 1st Baron Gerard of Brandon, cr. Earl of Macclesfield 1678 (d. 1694): friend of Lady Castlemaine, 4/1; favourite of King, 4/68; enemy of Clarendon, 8/525; sells commission in Life-guards, 4/371; 8/436; 9/308; criticised by King, 4/334; dress, 8/154; dispute with Carr, 8/573-4 & n., 581 & n. 1, 583, 587; 9/31-2, 55 & n. 1, 57; dispute alluded to, 9/85; case against Fitton, 9/83-4 & n.; dispute with Newcastle-upon-Tyne, 9/359 & nn.; praises P's parliamentary speech, 9/106

GERARD, [Jeanne], Lady Gerard, wife of Lord Gerard: slanders Lady Castlemaine, 4/68

GERMAN PRINCESS, the: see Moders

GERMANY [i.e. the territory of the Holy Roman Empire]: advance of

Turks into, 4/315–16 & n., 349 & n. 2, 358

GERMIN: *see* Jermyn

GERVAS: *see* Jervas

[GERY, ——]: 1/126 & n. 3

GHOSTS: *see* Popular Beliefs etc.

GIBBONS, [Charles]: his tennis-court, 1/297 & n. 2

GIBBONS, Dr Christopher, organist (d. 1676): performs at Sandwich's house, 2/103; 3/108, 287; 4/160; to set parts for P, 7/418; inspects organ with, 9/89; promises music for flageolets, 9/271

[GIBBS, Ann], actress ('the little girl'): in *The slighted maid*, 4/56 & n. 2; *Heraclius*, 5/78–9 & n.

GIBBS, Mr ——, clerk: his calligraphy, 8/545–6; 9/21, 330

GIBRALTAR, BAY OF: 6/19

GIBSON, Richard, clerk in the Navy Office:

P'S REGARD: 9/16 & n. 1

AS CLERK: compares costs of Dutch Wars, 8/297 & n. 1; stories of commanders, 9/26; carries gold to Brampton, 8/263–4, 268, 272, 273, 473, 474, 487; works for P, 7/284, 294, 305; 8/212, 373–4, 539, 540; 9/22, 42, 101, 283, 286, 308, 315, 316, 340(2), 342, 344, 358, 360, 394, 478, 500, 511, 521, 524, 547, 548, 556

AS SURVEYOR OF VICTUALLING AT YARMOUTH: appointment, 6/315 & n. 3; 8/367; instructs P on pursers, 6/316, 321; 7/1; also, 7/139

SOCIAL: story of meteor, 9/207–8; accompanies P to Maidstone, 9/495, 497; to Hyde Park, 9/564; also, 9/100, 208, 297, 310, 562

MISC.: house, 8/590; Warren's offer of employment to, 9/16; also, 8/253–4 & n.

GIFFORD, [George], Rector of St Dunstan-in-the-East: his preaching, 4/268 & n. 4; 9/482

GIFFORD, [?Henry]: political news, 1/75–6

GIFFORD, [?Thomas], merchant: Tangier business, 6/27, 28; social: 6/21, 44

GIGERY: *see* Jijelli

GILES (Gyles), Sarah (b. Kite), P's cousin and wife of Thomas: borrows money, 4/154–5; P deposits diary etc. with in Medway crisis, 8/264; social: 5/266; 7/174; 8/448; alluded to: 8/262; ~ her children die of plague, 6/342; also, 2/173; her pretty boy, 8/442

GILES, Thomas, of St Giles's parish, Cripplegate: 5/266; 8/264

GILLINGHAM, Kent: P at, 6/248; Dutch raid, 8/309

GILSTHROPP [?Gilsthorpe], ——, clerk to Sir W. Batten: alleged to have paid for place, 5/141; illness and death, 8/337, 560; accusations against Navy Board, 8/560 & n. 1, 564–5; also, 6/244

GIPSIES: *see* Popular Beliefs etc.

GLANVILL(E), [William], of Greenwich: friend of Cocke, 6/243 & n. 5; stores prize-goods, 6/243, 259, 270; P lodges with, 6/243–4, 245, 288, 290, 293, 294; alluded to: 6/273, 297, 299

GLASCOCK, Charles, relative of P: political views, 1/54 & n. 4; house, 2/83; visits dying brother, 2/144; social: 1/81, 85

GLASCOCK, John, Rector of Little Canfield, Essex, brother of Charles: death, 2/144 & n. 1

GLEMHAM, Henry, Bishop of St Asaph 1667 – d. 70: scandalous life, 8/364–5 & n.

GLYNNE, Sir John, lawyer (d. 1666): unpopularity, 2/87–8 & n.

GOA, India: 2/62

GODALMING (Godlyman), Surrey: P visits, 2/91

GODDARD, Dr [Jonathan], physician: attends Royal Society Club, 6/36; defends doctors leaving London in Plague, 7/21

GODFREY, Sir Edmund Berry, magistrate: arrests royal physician, 9/561 & nn.

GODFREY, [Henry]: dispute with P over debt, 3/34 & n. 1, 80

GODFREY, [Richard]: 4/384–5 & n.

GODMANCHESTER, Hunts.: P visits, 4/307

GODOLPHIN, William, diplomat, kted 1668: arrives from Spain, 9/46 & n. 2; Sandwich's regard, 9/52 & n. 3;

maid for, 4/284; in search for Barkstead's treasure, 3/242; advises P on
coachhouse, 9/39, 46; also, 1/278,
298, 314; 3/199, 264; 4/54, 113, 154,
363; 6/27, 224, 258; 7/202, 305;
8/217; 9/43; ~ his wife [Alice],
8/226; son [William] dies, 4/416 &
n. 2; son [Thomas] christened, 5/176
& n. 1; maidservant: 5/249; 7/124; P
attracted by, 3/126; 8/120
GRIFFITH, ——, courtier: at court
ball, 7/372
GRIFFITHS [Griffin], [William], ward
of Sir W. Batten: 4/296; 8/433
GRIMSBY, Lincs.: M.P.s for, 8/454–5
GRIMSTON, Sir Harbottle, M.P.
Colchester, Essex: chosen Speaker,
1/115–16 & n.
[GRINDAL, Edmund; 'Cranmer' in
error], Archbishop of Canterbury
1576–d. 83: letter to Queen Elizabeth,
4/329–30 & n.
GROCERS' COMPANY: see London: livery companies
GROCERS' HALL: 1/71
GROOME, ——, clerk in the Signet
Office: 1/212
GROVE, Capt. [Edward], river agent
for the Navy Board: character, 4/73
& n. 1; defends P against Exchequer
Court bailiffs, 4/52; appointed shipping agent for Tangier, 4/85, 93; gifts
to P, 4/93, 120; wife's death, 5/38, 42;
match projected with Paulina P,
5/42–3; cowardice in Battle of
Lowestoft, 6/130 & n. 2; social:
4/157, 231, 365, 406; 5/95
GUERNSEY, Channel Is.: garrison,
6/142–3
GUILDFORD, Surrey: P/EP visit(s),
2/93–4; 3/69, 75; 9/273–5 passim;
King visits, 3/86; places: Red Lion
inn, 2/93–4 & n.; 3/69; 9/274–5;
Abbot's Hospital and grammar school,
2/93–4 & n.; 9/273 & n. 3; Holy
Trinity church, 2/94 & n. 2; 9/274 &
n. 1; St Catherine's Hill, 9/275
GUILDHALL (Yildhall): seamen paid
off, 2/45, 50, 53, 55; trials, 3/120;
4/402, 403; 9/382; Lord Mayor's
banquet, 4/354–6; P consults officials,
7/72; 9/33; rebuilt after Fire, 8/583 &
n. 1; 9/545–6 & n.

GUINEA: ships to, 1/313, 316; Anglo-
Dutch rivalry, 5/115, 160; Dutch
intentions, 5/121 & n. 2; conflicting
news from, 5/127 & n. 2; Holmes's
attack on Dutch, 5/160 & n. 4, 283 &
n. 1, 285, 341; de Ruyter's counter-
attack, 5/352–3 & n., 355 & n. 1; 6/42
& nn., 43, 46; English losses, 9/401;
fleets sail to: Dutch: 5/225, 231, 242,
273 & n. 1, 283, 295 & n. 2; English:
5/242, 246, 248, 250, 258, 264, 265,
295; also, 2/160; 4/363
GUINEA COMPANY: see Royal
African Company
GUINEA HOUSE: see Africa(n)
House
GUMBLETON, Mr ——: 9/289, 458
GUNFLEET, the, shoal off Essex
coast: fleet in, 6/99; 7/139, 140;
alluded to: 7/178, 300
GUNNING, Peter, Master of Clare
College, Cambridge 1660; Master of
St John's and Regius Professor 1661;
Bishop of Chichester 1669–75, of Ely
1675–d. 84: his London congregation,
1/42; weekly fast, 1/58; sermons, 1/3
& n. 1, 11, 32, 60, 76; 2/239; admini-
sters communion to Commons,
2/107; active against puritans, 2/147 &
n. 2
GUNPOWDER PLOT DAY:
observation of, 1/283; 2/208; 5/314;
7/358
GUNS, pistols [see also Ships: guns]:
P's pistol, 2/9; his French gun, 8/137
& n. 1; repeater guns, 3/310 & n. 4;
5/75 & n. 1
GUY, Capt. [Thomas], army officer:
1/101; social: 1/116, 182
GUY, Capt. [Thomas], naval officer:
7/344–5 & n.
GUYAT (Gayet), Susan: P takes to
Islington, 9/197; theatre, 9/198–9,
203; and Vauxhall, 9/216; sings with,
9/202, 217
'GUYLAND' ('Gayland', 'Guild-
land') [recte 'Abd Allāh al-Ghailān],
Moroccan warlord: relations with,
3/172 & n. 2; 4/283 & n. 1, 337 &
n. 1; 7/167 & n. 3; overthrown, 7/214
& n. 2; 8/347–8 & n.
GWYN, Nell, actress:
CHRON. SERIES: P's admiration, 6/73 &

HAMILTON, James, Bishop of Galloway 1661–d. 74: besieged in house, 4/130–1 & n., 138

HAMILTON (Hambleton), [James, George and Anthony], courtiers: 5/21 & n. 1; alleged liaisons with Lady Castlemaine, 5/21; 'Hamilton' [?Anthony], a favourite of King's, 5/56; 'Mr Hamilton' at court ball, 7/372

HAMMERSMITH: 9/531, 557

HAMMON(D), [Mary]: 6/212; 7/255 & n. 2; death, 9/161

HAMPSTEAD, Mdx: P visits, 6/155; Belsize House, 9/281 & n. 4

HAMPTON COURT: Queen-Mother at, 2/4; court at: on Queen's arrival from Portugal, 3/89, 95, 97, 99, 100, 127, 146, 150, 157, 175; during Plague, 6/142 & n. 1, 166–7; 7/24, 26; Sandwich and family visit, 2/25; 3/94, 96, 103, 104, 120; P visits, 3/81–2 & n.; 6/153, 154, 156, 166, 171; 7/24–7 passim; Charles I's escape from (1647), 6/316–17 & n.; painting by Danckerts, 9/423 & n. 1, 504; rooms etc.: furniture and pictures, 3/82 & n. 2; chapel, 6/166; council chamber, ib.; garden, ib.; alluded to: 8/430

HAMPTON WICK, Mdx: P's lodgings, 7/26, 28, 29

HANBURY, [?Lucy], of Brampton: 3/220

HANES, Joseph: see Haynes

HANES, Lettice: see Howlett

HANNAM, Capt. [Willoughby], naval officer: in St James's Day Fight, 7/222 & n. 2; Coventry's regard for, 7/409–10 & n.

HANSON (Henson), [Edward]: bullet clock, 1/209

HARBING, ——, a poor fiddler: to marry Jane Welsh, 6/16, 19, 22, 74–5; 7/103

HARBORD (Herbert), Sir Charles, sen.: 3/57

HARBORD (Herbert), Sir Charles, jun.: brings letters from Sandwich to King, 3/57 & n. 1; knighted, 6/275 & n. 3; serves in Tangier, 9/374 & n. 2, 418–19 & n., 422; his painting of Tangier, 9/541 & n. 2; social: at P's dinner for Sandwich, 9/423–4; and

for Hinchingbrooke, 9/552, 553; also, 7/54; 9/345

HARBY (Harvy), Sir Job, Bt, customs farmer, d. 1663: 3/188

HARDING, [John], court musician: sings at party, 1/10–11 & n.

HARDWICKE, old: 5/272

HARDY, Nathaniel, Dean of Rochester 1660–d. 70: at The Hague, 1/144; sermon on death of Duke of Gloucester, 1/245; poor sermon on Fire, 7/283

HARE, Mrs [Alice]: see Taverns etc: Trumpet

HARGRAVE, [Richard], cornchandler, St Martin's Lane: 1/182–3

HARGRAVE, Mrs: see Taverns etc: Dog, New Palace Yard

HARLEY (Harlow), Sir Edward, ex-Governor of Dunkirk: to be Governor of Tangier, 9/492 & n. 2

HARLEY, Maj. [Robert], brother of Sir Edward: at The Hague, 1/147 & n. 2

HARLINGTON, Mdx: P at, 6/216; Arlington's title taken from, ib. & n. 1

HARMAN, Capt. John, kted 1665, naval commander: made rear-admiral, 6/129; serves under Allin, 6/147; convoys ships from Baltic, 6/328; conduct in Four Days Fight, 7/143, 154; voyage to W. Indies, 8/132, 147, 156; (untrue) story of capture of Dutch E. Indiaman, 8/374, 375; victory over French, 8/430 & n. 1; award of bounty to, 8/460–1 & n.; conduct at Battle of Lowestoft, 8/491, 492; 9/80 & n. 3, 142, 158–9; committed by Commons, 9/166–7 & n. 167; released, 9/170; portrait by Lely, 7/102; also, 7/97, 110; 8/130, 149; 9/142

HARMAN, Mary (b. Bromfield), wife of Philip: marriage. 4/345 & n. 2; P admires, 4/265; 5/223, 228, 229, 347; 6/164; 7/15; dies in childbed, 6/125, 152, 164; social: 5/266, 280; ~ her father [Thomas], 6/152

HARMAN, [Philip], upholsterer, Cornhill: P's regard, 7/15, 73; marriage, 4/345 & n. 2; son christened, 6/152; proposed match with

Paulina P, 6/164 & n. 1; 7/15, 23, 73, 78, 81(2); offers marriage to Kate Joyce, 9/127; P orders chairs etc. from, 5/251; 7/256, 286, 289; 9/332(2); social: 5/223, 228, 266, 280; 6/86, 126; 7/398; 9/111

[HARMOND, John], shoemaker: marriage, 7/355 & n. 2

HARPER, James, son of Mary: 1/83; 5/17

HARPER, [Mary], widow, tavern keeper, King St, Westminster [see also Taverns etc.: Harper's]: foolish talk, 1/83; 5/71; recommends maids for EP, 4/274, 276, 290, 297, 305; speaks ill of Pepyses, 5/185; alluded to: 4/341

HARPER, Tom: political news from, 1/48

HARPER, [Thomas], Storekeeper, Deptford: gossips about Brouncker, 8/226; helps P with accounts, 8/350; dies, 9/325, 330

HARPER, Mr —: see Taverns etc.: Harper's

HARRINGTON, Sir James, of Swakeleys, Mdx; M.P. Rutland 1646–53: 6/215

HARRINGTON, James, republican author (d. 1677) [see also Books]: at Rota Club, 1/14 & n. 3, 61; political theories, 1/17 & n. 2, 20

HARRINGTON, William, merchant, of St Olave's parish: stories of fishing in Baltic, 4/412 & n. 3, 413, 414; attends Apposition Court of Mercers' Company, 5/37; death rumoured, 6/296 & n. 1, 305; at parish dinner, 9/179

HARRIS, [Henry], actor:
CHRON. SERIES: conversation, 8/29; 9/12, 138; leaves Duke's Company, 4/239 & n. 3; returns, 4/347, 411; ill, 8/73, 86; criticises Burt's acting, 8/575 & n. 3; and Orrery's *Guzman*, 9/522; portrait painted for P, 9/138, 140, 175, 206, 299
HIS PERFORMANCES: praised in *Henry VIII*, 8/73 & n. 2; P admires in *Worse and worse*, 5/215 & n. 1; Orrery's *Henry V*, 5/240 & n. 3; *The Rivals*, 5/267 & n. 2, 335; *The man is the master*, 9/133–4 & n.; *The

royal shepherdess*, 9/458–9; criticised in *Mustapha*, 8/421 & n. 6; and *She would if she could*, 9/53–4; his singing, 5/267; 9/53–4, 133–4 & n., 195; dancing, 9/458–9
SOCIAL: sings/dances at parties etc., 8/28, 29, 242; 9/13, 128, 134, 175, 289; to learn *It is decreed*, 9/131, 136; P visits at theatre, 9/178; with P and actors at Vauxhall, 9/218–19; also, 5/37; 9/139, 220, 256, 265, 292–3
ALLUDED TO: 9/108, 546

HARRIS, [John], sailmaker to the navy: gives dinner to Navy Board, 2/61; instructs P on sails, 4/7; gift to P, 6/57 & n. 2

HARRISON, Capt. [Brian], Deputy-Master, Trinity House: defeated in Trinity House election, 5/172 & n. 3

HARRISON, [James], doorkeeper at Whitehall Palace: 1/300

HARRISON, [?the foregoing]: social: 1/19, 21–2

HARRISON, Sir John, Customs Commissioner: 3/188 & n. 3

HARRISON, Maj.-Gen. Thomas, regicide: tried, 1/263 & n. 1; executed, 1/265 & nn.; head displayed, 1/269–70

HART, [Charles], actor: liaison with Nell Gwyn, 8/402 & n. 5; with Lady Castlemaine, 9/156 & n. 4; quarrels with Mohun, 8/569 & n. 3; P admires in *The mad couple*, 8/594 & nn.; alluded to: 8/196; 9/438

HART, Capt. [John], sen., naval officer: navy business, 8/283

HART, Maj. [Theo]: criticises Commons' committee, 1/249; administers oaths to P, 1/257; pays P as secretary to Sandwich's troop, 1/304; social: 1/232, 242

HARTLIB, Anne: see Rothe

HARTLIB, Mary: see Clodius

HARTLIB, Samuel, sen., author (d. 1662): 5/30

HARTLIB, Samuel, jun.: business with Lord Holland, 1/216; story of Duke of York's marriage, 2/40; accosts EP, 8/423; social: 1/206; 2/127; also, 1/219(2)

HARVEY, Sir Daniel, merchant: security for loan, 3/157 & n. 3; (erroneous) account of Four Days

HENRY, Duke of Gloucester, son of
Charles I: on *Naseby*, 1/152, 153;
sails to England, 1/154, 157, 158; at
theatre, 1/171; entertained by
Speaker, 1/174 & n. 1; ill with smallpox, 1/240, 243; dies, 1/244, 245, 248;
buried in Westminster Abbey, 1/249
& n. 2

HENRY VIII: portrait: at Audley End
House, 1/70; 8/467 & n. 4; at Barber-
Surgeons' Hall, 4/59 & n. 3; tomb,
7/58 & n. 6; 'King Harry's chair',
1/280 & n. 1; alluded to: 5/69

HENSHAW, Joseph, Bishop of Peterborough 1663–d.79: preaches at
Whitehall, 9/563 & n. 2

HENSON: *see* Hanson

HERALDRY: P's arms, 3/50 & n. 3;
8/128 & n. 1; armorial glass at Great
Lever, Lancs., 3/254; arms etc. of
Duke of Monmouth, 4/107 & n. 2;
5/318 & n. 4; of Royal African Co.,
4/152–3 & n.; hatchments etc. at
funeral, 4/424–5, 427, 432; arms and
title of Sandwich, 5/319; loss of
Heralds' rolls in Fire, 7/410 & n. 3;
book on, 8/422 & n. 4; also, 4/175

[HÉRAULT, Louis], minister of the
French Church, Threadneedle St:
sermons by, 3/296 & n. 2; 5/342

HERBERT, Sir C. sen. and jun.: *see*
Harbord

HERBERT, Capt. [Charles], naval
officer: 6/237, 238

[HERBERT], John, servant to Tom
P: 4/183 & n. 2; servant to P.
Honywood, 5/88, 244, 252; character,
5/241

HERBERT, Philip, 5th Earl of Pembroke (d. 1669): rumoured expulsion
from Lords, 1/127 & n. 1; a founder
of Royal African Company, 1/258 &
n. 2; inefficient in financing Royal
Fishery, 5/294 & n. 1; plays tennis,
9/150; views on Genesis, 9/150–1 &
n.; alluded to: 9/230

HERBERT, William, styled Lord
Herbert, 6th Earl of Pembroke
1669 (d. 1674): suitor to Elizabeth
Malet, 7/385

HERBERT, [William], landlord of the
Swan, New Palace Yard [*see also*
Taverns etc.]: unwell, 8/124; finds P

tumbling Frances Udall, 8/224

HERBERT, Mrs ——, of Newington
Green: 5/132

HERCULES PILLARS ALLEY: 9/42

HERMITAGE, the: 3/163

HERRING, John, Vicar of St Bride,
Fleet St: preaches, 1/26 & n. 1;
extruded, 3/162 & n. 1, 167; farewell
sermon, 3/168; social: 1/229

HERRING, [Michael], merchant: lends
money to Sandwich, 1/56 & n. 5, 72,
75, 80

HERRINGMAN, [Henry], bookseller
at the New Exchange: P visits shop,
8/380 & n. 3, 383, 597–8; 9/248,
367

HERTFORDSHIRE: parliamentary
election, 9/150 & n. 2

HERVEY (Harvey), Sir Thomas, Navy
Commissioner 1665–8:
CHARACTER: 6/119; 7/359–60; 8/531–2
AS COMMISSIONER: appointed, 6/37 &
n. 2; absent during Plague, 7/39;
expects dismissal, 8/293–4 & n.; at
pay, 7/359–60; in Carkesse affair,
8/76, 215; examines Gauden's accounts, 8/322; at Ticket Office,
8/531–2; in enquiries of Committee
on Miscarriages, 8/494–5, 538; 9/80,
83, 84, 103; at launch, 9/100–1;
unspecified business, 8/77, 178, 180,
314–15, 328, 479, 581
HOUSE: to occupy Turner's lodgings,
6/37 & n. 2; 7/105, 296, 359
NEWS FROM: 7/152; 8/328
SOCIAL: 6/77; 7/364; 8/65, 77, 220,
563–4; 9/82, 104, 115

HESELRIGE (Haslerig), Sir Arthur,
Bt, republican politician (d. 1661):
his quarrel with City of London,
1/16 & n. 1, 53 & n. 2, 60; and parliament, 1/50, 74 & n. 4, 81 & n. 1;
raises support against army leaders,
(Dec. 1659), 2/92 & n. 3

HETLEY, [William], of Brampton,
Hunts.: on *Royal Charles*, 1/162, 168;
gifts to P and Howe, 1/182; death,
2/18; property at Brampton, 2/28 &
n. 2; social: 1/163, 177, 324; alluded
to: 1/172

HEWER, [Ann], wife of Thomas: P
meets, 1/268; moves to Islington
after Fire, 7/275; 'well-favoured',

8/24; social: 8/48, 101, 158, 193, 197,
254; 9/417; alluded to: 1/215
HEWER, [Thomas], printer and stationer: P meets, 1/268; dies of plague,
6/225, 235; alluded to: 2/96; 4/106,
114
HEWER, Will, P's clerk in the Navy
Office [P spells the name variously:
Eure, Ewere, Ewre, Hewers]:
P'S OPINION: favourable, 1/202–3;
5/255; 8/207; 9/75, 368–9; unfavourable, 2/199, 201; 3/105; 5/301; 9/53
PERSONAL: ailments, 1/215, 216; 2/96;
4/28, 106, 114, 194, 291; 6/174, 175;
9/242; money etc. stolen, 1/233;2/140;
banking account, 8/263; hears common prayer for first time, 1/245; in
mourning for father, 6/235; suggests
Mercer as EP's companion, 5/229,
257, 258, 265; tries to negotiate her
return, 7/300, 301, 303; admires EP,
9/398; gives her diamonds, 9/7;
criticises P to EP, 8/171; P jealous
of, 5/13, 19, 29, 44, 301; refuses proposal to marry Paulina P, 8/17;
brideman to Jane Birch, 9/500; intermediary in Deb Willet affair, 9/367–
71 passim, 373, 379, 411, 413, 518;
also, 9/19
HIS WORK IN HOUSEHOLD:
    GENERAL: arrives, 1/204; sent to
church, 4/43; misdeeds, 1/219, 254–5;
2/34, 63, 79, 97; 3/35; 4/97, 171, 356,
358, 365; 5/13; P thinks of dismissing,
3/4–5; 4/318, 323; ears boxed, 3/105,
180; 4/166; to lodge elsewhere, 4/358,
363, 367, 371–2, 381, 382
    ERRANDS/MESSAGES: 1/226, 232, 237;
2/10, 191, 212, 221; 3/80; 7/176;
9/405, 420
    ESCORTS/ACCOMPANIES P/EP ON
HOUSEHOLD/NAVAL BUSINESS IN LON-
DON: 1/212, 213, 218, 289, 324; 2/8;
4/435; 9/32, 256, 259, 382–4 passim,
401, 406, 408, 417, 421, 422, 430, 451,
465, 474, 484, 493, 519, 520; on
journeys: Brampton etc., 3/206, 217–
23 passim; 5/200–1; 7/92–3, 137;
8/381, 465, 468, 471–2, 474–5, 479;
9/145, 306, 310; Woolwich, 8/240;
West Country, 9/223, 224, 226, 228–
30 passim, 233, 234; Deptford, 9/335
MISC.: helps with accounts, 1/209;

9/564; puts P to bed, 3/182; reads
Latin testament, 4/189, 190, 193, 204,
236; examined in Latin, 4/271; reads
to P, 9/372, 387, 506; copies words of
song, 9/242; helps to store cash,
7/367; 8/473–4; gives first aid to P's
father, 8/237; in mourning for P's
mother, 8/134; witnesses P's will,
8/266; also, 3/152; 4/166; 6/141;
9/209
HIS MOVEMENTS: his new chamber,
4/320, 323; lodges at Mercers', 5/256
& n. 1; his rooms, 7/152; returns to
P's house in Plague, 6/154, 156, 174,
175; lodges at Greenwich, 6/233,
251; moves to Woolwich after Fire,
7/275, 280; returns to P's house,
7/287; in lodgings again, 9/458 &
n. 2
NEWS FROM: 8/269–70, 297, 538;
9/99–100, 104, 397
HIS WORK IN NAVY OFFICE: allowance,
1/305 & n. 5; 4/353, 358; accused of
leaking information, 3/5; fraud, 4/152;
receiving gift, 9/283; and conspiring
to get contract, 9/288 & n. 2, 389–91
passim, 393, 394; at Deptford, 2/95;
3/111, 180; Portsmouth, 3/69–75
passim; 7/75; Harwich, 6/90; ac-
counts/estimates, 1/226–7; 6/205, 256,
271; 7/305; 8/48, 372; 9/260, 376;
other financial business, 2/54–5; 4/20,
337; 7/25; 8/259; 9/376, 377, 486, 513;
at launch, 5/305; in Carkesse affair,
8/94, 204, 212; inspects sunken ship,
8/293; organisation of office, 9/151;
parliamentary business, 9/99, 102–3;
clerical business (general): writes
shorthand notes, 7/374; 9/480, 483;
also, 3/119; 5/257; 6/108, 109; 7/100;
8/503, 557; 9/344, 478, 479; unspecified business, 6/32, 201, 202; 9/281,
282, 325, 364, 392, 547; ~ Tangier
business, 5/267; 7/255; 9/267, 414
SOCIAL: sees pre-coronation procession, 2/83; on river trips, 3/95; 6/119;
to see E. Indiaman, 4/210; entertains
P/EP and others at lodgings, 6/130;
7/152; 9/458, 459; and Barnet, 8/382;
at riotous party, 7/246; on trips to
Islington, 7/317; and Epsom, 8/337–9
passim; at theatre, 7/423; 8/158, 435,
481, 521; 9/249, 296, 326, 521–2; in

3/219, 220, 223; 4/307, 308(2), 313;
5/298; 8/469–72 passim; 9/211; King
to visit, 4/324; alterations, 1/313–14 &
n., 324; 2/8, 27, 35, 48–9 & n., 79, 135,
183; 3/110, 220 & n. 5; 4/308; 5/298;
8/470; cloister, 2/183; courtyard,
4/313; garden (crooked wall, the
Mount), ib.; 8/472; waterworks, 5/298;
summer house, 8/472; park, 8/472;
grove, ib.; drawbridge, ib.; Nuns'
Bridge, ib.; chapel, 9/211; alluded to:
9/495
HIND COURT, off Fleet St: 1/199
HINDHEAD, Surrey: P and EP at,
9/274
HINGSTON (Hinxton), [John],
organist: sets bass to *It is decreed*,
7/414 & n. 1, 420; court news from,
7/414; P consults, 8/574
HINTON, [Edmund], goldsmith:
6/332
HINTON, [John], physician in ordinary to the King: 6/332 & n. 2
HISTORY: P comments on uncer-
tainty of historical knowledge, 8/99
HOARE, [James], sen., joint-Comp-
troller of the Mint: shows Mint to P
and Mennes, 4/143–8 & nn.; social:
7/22; alluded to: 9/410–11 & n.
HOARE (Whore), [James], jun., Joint-
Comptroller of the Mint: 9/410–11
& n.
HOARE (Whore), [Richard], clerk in
the Prerogative Court of Canterbury:
his calligraphy, 1/132–3 & n.; 6/339
& n. 3; also, 2/145
HOARE (Whore), [William], physician: social/musical, 1/10–11 & n.;
4/18; 5/174; 6/61; ~ his wife
[Hester], 6/61
[HOBART, Sir Richard], Groom
Porter: rebuked in sermon, 3/292–3
& n.
HOBELL, Mrs ——, of Banbury:
proposed wife for Tom P, 3/176 &
n. 1, 183, 192, 195, 201, 207, 210, 226;
match broken off, 3/231 & n. 1, 232–
3; 4/12, 253
HODDESDON, Herts.: P at, 9/213
HODGES, [?Edmund], of Lincoln's
Inn Fields: 2/125
HODGES, [Thomas], Dean of Here-
ford (d. 1672): Lady Sandwich stays

with at Kensington, 5/178 & n. 5
[HODGKIN, Roger], Fifth-monarchist: executed, 2/18 & n. 2
HOGG, Capt. [Edward], commander
of privateer *Flying Greyhound*: captures prizes, 7/418, 424; 8/7, 115–16,
341, 344; his knavery, 8/159 & n. 1,
352, 385; ordered to sea, 8/180;
alluded to: 8/392
HOGSDEN: *see* Hoxton
HOLBEIN: portraits of Henry VIII at
Audley End, 1/70; 8/467 & n. 4; and
in Barber-Surgeons' Hall, 9/293 &
n. 1; work at Nonsuch House attributed to, 6/235 & n. 3
HOLBORN [*see also* Taverns etc.:
Black Swan; Chequer; George]:
subsidence in, 5/82–3 & n.; Fire,
7/282; bearded lady, 9/398; Conduit,
3/148; 9/265, 375, 438; terminus for
Brampton coach, 5/200; and York
coach, 5/234; Cockpit at King's Gate,
9/154; alluded to: 4/44
HOLBORN   CONDUIT   HILL:
8/448; 9/520
HOLCROFT, John, P's cousin: 2/109,
111, 114
HOLDEN (Holding), [Joseph], haberdasher, Bride Lane: P buys hats from,
2/25, 104, 127; 4/274, 280, 300, 411;
alluded to: 7/394
HOLDEN, [Priscilla], wife of Joseph:
to recommend maid for EP, 4/279;
finds nurse for Tom P, 5/82; at his
death and funeral, 5/86, 87, 91; godmother, 7/394 & n. 2
HOLDER, [Thomas], Auditor-General
to the Duke of York and Treasurer of
the Royal African Company: 6/170;
8/27; 9/313 & n. 4
HOLDER [?Holden], ——: 7/394 &
n. 2
HOLE HAVEN, Essex: quarantine
harbour, 4/399 & n. 2; Dutch ship
aground, 8/306
HOLINSHED, ——, tobacconist:
marries widowed Kate Joyce, 9/127,
195
HOLLAND, Gilbert: gift to P, 1/95;
social: 1/94
[HOLLAND, John], Rector of Holy
Trinity, Guildford: 2/94 & n. 2
HOLLAND, Capt. Philip, naval

officer: advises P on perquisites, 1/82; commission renewed, 1/167 & n. 2, 168; political news from, ib.; P pays debt to, 2/116; attempts suicide and turns Quaker, 4/109; social: 1/15, 17, 56, 59, 196, 205; alluded to: 1/313, 316 & n. 2; 3/163; ~ his mother, 2/116; sons, 9/184

HOLLAND, ——, wife of Capt. Philip: a plain dowdy, 2/116; her mother a Quaker, 4/109; social: 1/17, 205

HOLLAND, Earls of: see Rich

HOLLAR, Wenceslaus, engraver (d. 1677): appointed royal scenographer, 7/378–9 & n.; engraving of city after Fire, ib.

HOLLES, Denzil, cr. Baron Holles 1661, ambassador to France 1663–6: Privy Councillor, 1/171; (untrue) rumour of dismissal, 8/596, 600; and of affronts to, 4/419–20 & n., 5/59–60 & n.; plenipotentiary in peace negotiations, 8/61, 63, 138 & n. 4, 175, 189 & n. 2, 216, 218, 249, 352; bewails state of country, 7/370; said to be wise, 8/70

HOLLES, Sir Frescheville, naval officer, M.P. Grimsby, Lincs.: conceited, 8/275, 292, 304; 9/516; service with fireships, 8/256 & n. 4, 272, 275, 379; at odds with Coventry, 8/304; 9/76, 92, 108–9, 129, 173; defends Brouncker in Commons, 9/62; attacks Sandwich, 9/68; his family in parliament, 8/454–5 & n.; Sir J. Smith's enmity to, 9/118; parliamentary news from, 9/135

HOLLES, [Gervase], father of Sir Frescheville: as M.P. for Grimsby, 8/454–5 & n.

HOLLIER (Holliard, Holyard), [Thomas], P's surgeon:
AS SURGEON: treats P for stone, 2/17; 4/327, 345–6; 5/162, 165, 241; colic, 4/280, 328, 329, 332, 345, 385–6; and deafness, 4/319, 320; bleeds P, 3/66, 76–7; his laxative pills, 4/153, 386; and draught, 4/332; consulted about sore, 4/252; general advice, 2/17, 201; 3/10; on diet, 4/280, 345–6, 385–6; treats EP for earache, 3/124; and abscess, 4/379, 382, 383–4, 385; 5/145;

8/584; his bill, 4/435; examines Tom Edwards for stone, 3/329; treats P's father for rupture, 8/110, 213–14, 237; denies efficacy of touching for King's Evil, 1/281; supports claims of naval surgeons, 5/261 & n. 1; also, 9/558
GENERAL: praises Luther and Calvin, 4/386; anti-Catholic, 5/256; 8/586, 587; 9/16; losses in Fire, 8/87 & n. 4; house in Hatton Garden, 8/110
SOCIAL: fuddled, 4/386; 5/309; 9/142; talks Latin, 4/386; 9/142, 279; also, 4/434; 6/9; 7/127; 8/64; 9/72–3, 356, 561

HOLLINS, [John], Fellow of Magdalene College, Cambridge, physician: P visits, 1/67; also: 9/212

HOLLIS: see Hawles

HOLLOND, [John], Surveyor of the Navy 1649–52: scheme for paying off seamen, 1/306 & n. 1, 308; MS. discourse(s) on naval administration, 3/145 & n. 1, 280, 285; 9/489 & n. 2

HOLLOWAY: P at, 2/184

HOLLWORTHY, [Mary], widow of Richard: spurns advances of Spragge, 8/141; reputation for gossip, 8/544; conceited, 9/13; social: 9/220, 245; alluded to: 8/172 & n. 3; 9/433

HOLLWORTHY, [Richard], merchant, of St Olave's parish: dies in fall from horse, 6/296

HOLMES, Gabriel: tried for arson, 8/319–21 passim & nn.

HOLMES, Capt. John, kted 1672, naval officer: P's low opinion, 9/157; wounded, 7/155; under Harman's command, 7/409–10 & n.; marriage, 9/157 & n. 2

HOLMES, Margaret (b. Lowther), wife of John: pretty, 8/241; marriage, 9/157 & n. 2; at Lady Penn's, 7/96

HOLMES, [Nathaniel], Rector of St Mary Staining 1643–62, and preacher to the Council of State (d. 1678): preaches at Whitehall, 1/53; n. 1

HOLMES, Capt. Robert, kted 1666, naval commander:
CHARACTER AND REPUTATION: 2/169; 4/196; 6/129; 7/180, 344, 409–10
CHRON. SERIES: friend of Sandwich, 2/169; fails to enforce salute from Swedish ambassador, 2/212 & n. 3,

222, 229; 3/14; returns from Mediterranean, 4/67; quarrels with sailing master, 4/67, 78, 81, 83, 84, 91–2; violent words against Mennes, 4/92; returns from Tangier, 4/299; voyage to Guinea, 5/160 & n. 4, 341; 6/42 & n. 2; sent to Tower, 6/6 & n. 2, 56; in Battle of Lowestoft, 6/122; resigns commission, 6/129 & n. 2; in Four Days Fight, 7/143; quarrel (?duel) with Sir J. Smith, 7/339–40 & n., 348; 9/107 & n. 3, 118, 123; influence in fleet, 7/158, 178, 332, 333; alliance with Rupert, 7/332; and with Buckingham, 9/382, 467; criticised, 7/204; attack on Dutch ships in Vlie ('Holmes's Bonfire'), 7/247 & n. 1, 257; in St James's Day Fight, 7/344–5; appointed 'land admiral', 8/149; his part in Buckingham – Shrewsbury duel, 9/26–7; also, 7/409–10; 9/148, 352
SOCIAL: 1/317; 2/175, 240; 3/14, 22
MISC.: brings ape from Guinea, 2/160; his advances to EP, 2/237; 3/4; offered king's wife in Guinea, 3/11; objects to brother's marriage, 9/157
ALLUDED TO: 1/176, 182
HOLT, Mr ——, of Portsmouth: 3/70
HOLYARD: see Hollier
HOLYHEAD, Anglesey: 4/256
HOMEWOOD, [?Edward], Navy Office clerk: victualling business, 7/139; social: 3/5
HOMOSEXUALITY: increase of, 4/210; P's innocence of, ib.
HONYWOOD, Col. Henry: good natured, 3/9 & n. 2; killed by fall from horse, 4/25 & n. 2; alluded to: 3/7
HONYWOOD, Michael, Dean of Lincoln: good natured, 3/9; 4/167 & n. 1; 5/192, 233; P's gift to, 4/171–2, 173; alluded to: 3/7
HONYWOOD, Peter: lodges with P's parents, 2/5 & n. 3; demonstrates 'Prince Rupert's drops', 3/9 & n. 3; lame, 5/20; pays allowance to John P, 5/142 & n. 3; 6/49; social: at P's stone feast, 5/98; 6/124; also, 4/167; 5/91; 7/173; alluded to: 3/7
HONYWOOD, Col. Philip, kted ?1662: 1/130; 9/74
HONYWOOD, Sir Robert, M.P.

New Romney, Kent: 1/199 & n. 3; ~ his wife, ib.
HONYWOOD, Sir Thomas: 1/181 & n. 1, 220; ~ his daughter, 1/220
[HOOGSTRATEN, Samuel van] painter (d. c.1678): perspective painting, 4/18 & n. 1, 26; 5/277
HOOKE, [Robert], curator of experiments to the Royal Society [see also Books]: P's admiration, 6/36–7, 95; at Royal Society, 6/36–7 & n.; lectures on comet, 6/48 & n. 1; and felt-making, 7/51 & n. 3; experiments in coach design, 6/94–5; 7/12, 20 & n. 2; borrows book of naval terms, 7/148; explains nature of sound, 7/239 & n. 1; 9/147; and blood transfusion, 7/373; social: 8/64; 9/544
HOOKE, [Theophilus], clergyman, P's contemporary at Cambridge: 2/44
HOOKER, Ald. Sir William, merchant, kted 1666, Sheriff 1665–6: drafts plague regulations, 6/211 & n. 5; story of child saved from plague, 6/212; dirty house, 6/328 & n. 3; supplies tallow, 7/41; criticises Penn, 9/170; alluded to: 8/152
HOOKER (of the Privy Seal): see Hooper
HOOPER, [William], minor canon of Westminster: 2/240 & n. 2
HOOPER (Hooker), ——, of the Privy Seal: 1/208, 212
HOPE, the, reach of the Thames: P at, 5/197(2), 317; 6/287; Coventry at, 7/70; fleet/ships in, 1/98; 2/95; 5/190, 193, 196; 6/65, 103; 8/251, 257, 263, 266, 298, 349; Rupert sails from, 5/291; pontoon bridge, 8/254 & n. 4
HORACE: ode recited, 8/472
HORE (Whore), Philip: dispute about Irish estate, 5/324 & n. 1
[?HORNECK, Anthony], German minister: his preaching, 8/580 & n. 1
HORSE DEALERS: tricks, 4/120; 9/384, 391
HORSE GUARD HOUSE: fire, 7/362–3 & n.
HORSE SAND, off Portsmouth: 2/11
HORSLEY, Mrs —— [also Horsfall, Horsfield]: P admires ('my new Morena'), 5/349 & n. 3; 7/135–6 &

n.; takes to Vauxhall, 7/136; married, ib.; house burnt, 8/168; at theatre, 9/203; her silly talk, 9/204; widowed, 9/322; alluded to: 7/235, 269; ~ her husband, 9/204

HORSLEYDOWN, Bermondsey: P at, 7/22

HOSIER, Francis, Clerk of the Cheque and Muster-Master, Gravesend: gift to P, 8/526 & n. 1; advises on store-keepers' accounts, 9/300 & n. 2, 374 & n. 1; his methods approved, 9/444, 445, 474 & n. 1; ~ his wife, 9/300

HOSIER LANE, Smithfield: 9/521

HOTTENTOTS: stories of, 3/298 & n. 3

HOUBLONS, the brothers, merch-ants, sons of James [see also below]: P's regard, 6/337; 7/36, 39, 370; 9/68; send ships to Tangier, 7/20, 36, 38, 44–5, 45, 64, 98; gift to P, 7/64, 66; unspecified business, 7/52, 371; bewail state of nation, 7/371; discount rumours of invasion, 8/1–2 & n.; social: 6/336–7; 7/368; 8/337; 9/405

HOUBLON, Isaac, merchant, son of James, sen.: 7/270

HOUBLON, James, sen., merchant: 9/68 & n. 3

HOUBLON, James, jun., merchant, son of James, sen.: P's affection for, 6/27, 337; 7/64; sends goods to Tangier, 6/27, 28; news from, 8/151, 162; 9/65, 68; social: 6/63, 336–7; 8/1, 337; ~ his wife [Sarah], 9/65–6

HOUBLON, Peter, merchant, son of James, sen.: at Epsom, 8/337

HOULE: see Howell, W.

HOUNDSDITCH: 5/18

HOUNSLOW, Mdx: P visits, 6/197, 198; Priory, 6/198

HOUSEHOLD GOODS AND DOMESTIC ANIMALS [see also Servants (P)]:

FURNITURE, FURNISHINGS ETC.:

BEDS: press beds at The Hague, 1/139; truckle/trundle beds at inns, 3/75; 4/245; 9/231; at Brampton, 8/470, 474; down bed, 6/218; corded, 8/311 & n. 2; curtains, 4/226; 7/286; (P): green, 2/119; 4/329; red, 3/267; 4/329; settle-bed, 9/464; beds/bed-steads bought, 1/257; 3/261; 4/273;

camlet, 9/330, 334, 356, 367, 368; also, 6/147

CABINETS (P): with secret drawers, 5/152 & n. 2; walnut, 9/405, 406

CARPET, TURKEY (P): 1/232

CHAIRS: joke chair, 1/280 & n. 1; with reading desk, 8/25; turkey work, 8/167; gout chair, 9/215 & n. 3; (P): turkey work, 4/329; set, 7/112; also, 5/251

CHESTS: Duke of York's oriental, 2/79; (P): iron, 5/323; 6/205; 7/272; 8/487; plate, 7/367, 405

CHEST OF DRAWERS: 3/197; (P): 2/130

COUCH (P): 7/112

CURTAINS (P): green say, 2/124

DESK: with secret till, 5/9; with bookshelves, 5/64

HANGINGS FOR WALLS/BEDS: suits of, 5/214–15; 8/470; (P): green serge, 1/269; chintz, 4/299 & n. 1; counter-feit damask, 7/7(2), 10, 14, 19, 24; purple serge, 7/255, 256, 257, 258; tapestry, 8/455; 9/287; 'suit of Apostles', 9/329 & n. 4, 330; also, 9/296

LOOKING GLASS: at Hampton Court, 3/82; 'counterfeit windows', 8/25–6; (P): 5/347, 348; 8/213; 9/423

PRESSES (P): for papers, 2/25; cloaks, 4/353; books, 7/214, 242, 243, 251, 252, 258, 300, 311; 9/18, 48; tools, 7/319

TABLES: with leaf, 6/109 & n. 4; inlaid, 8/128–9; round table with recess, 9/255 & n. 2, 471 & n. 3; (P): side table, 2/110; dining table, 4/6, 14; also, 5/251, 253

P's SILVERWARE: his pride in 7/35, 37, 39; 8/4 (2), 157, 580; basin (engraved), 8/548; candlesticks, 5/47; chafing dishes, 7/10, 34; drudger, 7/34; flagons, 5/216, 225, 234, 266, 301; forks, 5/358; plates, 7/409, 413, 426; porringer and spoons (christening gift), 2/109; salts, 5/266; 7/71; snuff dish, 8/40; snuffers, 1/15; state cup and cover, 5/45, 47; sugar box, 5/358; tankards, 2/140; 5/45, 47; tumblers, 5/302; 8/339

OTHER HOUSEHOLD GOODS: provision of in friary, 8/26–7; tableware at Lord Mayor's banquet, 4/354–5; bath,

9/99, 594; alluded to: 4/234; 8/400; 9/103

[HOWORTH, John], Master of Magdalene College, Cambridge 1664–8 and Vice-Chancellor 1667–d.68: 8/469 & n. 1

HOXTON, Mdx: P visits, 5/272; 9/197, 513; Baumes House, 5/272 & n. 2; 9/197

HUBBARD (Hubbert, Hulbert), Capt. [John jun.], naval officer: reputation, 7/333–4; 8/485–6 & n.; refuses to strike flag to French, 9/560 & n. 2

[HUBERT, Robert]: hanged for starting Fire, 7/357 & n. 2; 8/81 & n. 4

HUDSON, [James], wine cooper: 6/151; 8/265–6

HUDSON, [?John], of Westminster: 1/10, 17

HUDSON, [Michael], chaplain to Chatham Dockyard: his preaching, 4/258 & n. 2

HUDSON, [Nathaniel], scrivener, the Old Bailey: 5/114, 168

[HUGHES], Peg, actress: 9/189 & n. 3

HUGHES, [William], ropemaker, Woolwich: reports on yard, 3/101 & n. 3; dismissed, 3/197; to swear against Coventry, 4/170; a rogue, ib.; also, 5/256–7

HUGHES, ——, housekeeper to Parliament: 7/305

HULBERT: see Hubbard

HULL, Yorks.: garrison prepared against invasion, 7/185 & n. 1; prize ships at, 8/341, 344, 349, 352, 369, 385

HUMFREY, Pelham, composer (d. 1674) [see also Musical Compositions]: returns from France, 8/515 & n. 5; disparages King's music, 8/529–30; conducts at court, 8/532, 534

HUNGARY: Turkish advance into, 4/316 & n. 1, 321, 372 & n. 2

HUNGERFORD, Margaret, Lady Hungerford, widow of Sir Edward: 9/534–5 & n.

HUNGERFORD, Wilts.: P visits, 9/228

HUNT, [Elizabeth], of Axe Yard, wife of John:
CHRON. SERIES: P's regard, 4/3; 6/142; 7/92, 219; ill, 2/15; birth of son, 2/234,

235, 236; fat, 7/52; related to Cromwells, 7/94; returns from Cambridge, 7/219 & n. 2; also, 1/94, 254, 257; 2/10, 35, 53; 3/180; 4/361; 5/174
SOCIAL: at P's house, 1/6, 37, 202–3; 3/36, 75; 4/4, 114, 293, 365; 5/146, 340; 6/37; P/EP visit(s) etc., 1/217; 2/55, 87, 207, 240; 3/7, 51; 4/182, 274, 276; 5/51, 79; in Hyde Park, 4/73; 5/126; at P's stone feast, 5/98
~ her cousin, 5/146

HUNT, [?George], musical-instrument maker, Paul's Churchyard: alters theorbo, 2/201, 203; brings bass viol, 4/104–5; makes viol, 4/282, 284; lends lute, 5/258; alluded to: 2/209

HUNT, [John], of Axe Yard, friend and neighbour of P; sub-commissioner of the Excise:
CHRON. SERIES: P's regard, 4/3; 7/219; political news from, 1/58, 77; troubled at return of secluded members, 1/63 & n. 5; dismissed (temporarily) from Excise, 1/254 & n. 4, 257 & n. 2; 2/53 & n. 2; returns from duties in Cambridge, 7/44, 219 & n. 2; 8/84–5 & n.; prospers, 7/92; informs P of Betty Becke, 4/392; stands bail for Hayter, 6/116
SOCIAL: at P's house, 1/6, 37, 49, 53; 2/216; 3/25, 36, 75, 86, 105; 4/83, 118, 293; 5/72, 174, 340; 7/132; in Hyde Park, 5/126; also, 1/8, 27; 2/67, 87; 3/76, 191; 4/231; 9/165
ALLUDED TO: 4/42; 5/167
~ his kinswoman, 5/174

HUNT, John, son of John: birth and christening, 2/234, 235, 236; EP's gift as godmother, 3/7; also, 4/276, 293; 5/146

HUNT, Mrs ——, of Jewen St, Deb Willet's aunt: her conversation, 8/569; 9/332; also, 9/346, 520

HUNTINGDON, Maj. Robert: intermediary between Charles I and Cromwell, 5/335 & n. 2

HUNTINGDON, Hunts.: P visits, 2/137, 148; 3/220; 4/312, 313; 9/212, 224; at school, 1/87 & n. 4; town waits, 8/474; parliamentary elections, 1/86–7 & n., 99 & n. 1; assizes, 2/145, 148; Sandwich appointed Recorder, 4/30 & n. 1, 62; anecdote about

Mayor, 8/232–3 & n.; Mountagus at
school at, 8/472 & n. 1; places: Crown
Inn, 2/137; 3/220; 4/312; church,
4/313; bridge, 8/220; Chequers Inn,
9/212
HUNTINGDONSHIRE: list of J.P.s,
1/184 & n. 1
HUNTSMOOR, Bucks.: Bowyers'
house, 1/85, 88, 131, 170, 177; alluded
to: 3/65
HURLESTONE, [Nicholas]: elected
Master of Trinity House, 6/107 &
n. 1; dies, 6/298
HUSON: see Hewson
HUTCHINSON, [Richard], Treasurer
of the Navy 1651–60: helps check
accounts, 1/312; his accounts scrutinised, 2/100 & n. 1; paymaster to
Navy Treasurer, 9/357 & n. 1; at
Chatham dockyard, 9/495, 499; his
religious bent, 9/495; also, 1/82, 188
HUYSMANS, Jacob, painter (d. 1696):
reputation, 5/254, 276 & n. 3; P views
his work, 5/254 & n. 4; to paint EP,
5/276 & n. 3; 6/113
HYDE, Anne: see Anne, Duchess of
York
HYDE, Edward, cr. Earl of Clarendon
1661, Lord Chancellor 1658–67 (d.
1674):
PERSONAL: created earl, 2/80; patent
of nobility, 2/75 & n. 3; illnesses,
1/144; 3/290; 5/205, 328, 329; 6/11;
8/181; King's grants, 2/157 & n. 3;
poor, 8/402 & n. 2; rich, 8/592;
ungenerous, 8/418; eloquent, 7/321;
as father-in-law to Duke of York,
8/214, 438; also, 6/252 & n. 1
POLITICAL CAREER [for relations with
colleagues, see under names; for
formal speeches to parliament, see
Parliament]: at Worcester House
Conference, 1/271; daughter's marriage to Duke of York resented, 1/284;
2/40–1 & n.; 4/223 & n. 5; 5/60 &
n. 4; 8/287, 367; accused of cupidity,
2/213; 4/223 & nn.; 6/39, 218; 7/55;
8/185–6, 265, 269, 270, 402, 592;
of selling places, 4/166; and of raising
army, 3/15 & n. 2; proposes proviso
in bill of uniformity, 3/49 & n. 1;
fluctuating influence with King,
3/290, 303; 4/115, 123, 137, 195, 196,

213; 5/73, 345; 9/387; unpopular in
Parliament, 3/290–1; and court, 5/73,
345; Bristol's abortive impeachment
of, 4/219, 223–5 & nn., 229, 231 &
n. 2, 367; 8/445; attempts to obtain
loan from city, 7/174; hostile to war,
7/411; 8/145, 287–8; despairs of its
conduct, 8/330; alleged responsibility
for disasters, 9/40; said to favour
standing army, 8/366–7 & n.; appointed Treasury Commissioner,
8/223; opposes parliamentary appro-
priation of revenue, 8/140 & n. 4;
and Downing's plan for Treasury
bills, 8/520 & n. 2; house attacked by
mob, 8/269, 270; opposes recall of
Parliament in Medway crisis, 8/293 &
n. 1, 506; dismissed, 8/304, 401–2 &
nn., 406, 409–10; 9/476; asks for
common law trial, 8/401–2, 403, 544–
5; his hopes from parliament, 8/432,
434; parliament thanks King for dismissal, 8/476 & n. 2, 479, 480, 482 &
n. 2, 525; impeached for high
treason, 8/427, 478, 502, 506, 507, 509,
518, 521, 522, 523 & n. 3, 526–9
passim, 534, 541–5 passim, 555–6,
557–8 & n.; factions in parliament,
8/532–3, 542, 544, 571, 596; flight and
petition, 8/561 & n. 4, 563, 566, 568,
577; banished, 8/565–6 & nn., 578, 583;
satirised, 9/256; rumours of dismissal
of supporters, 8/596, 597, 600;
9/2, 9–10, 17; rumours of return,
9/153–4, 341, 347, 417, 536; said to
favour French alliance, 9/536 & n. 2
NAVY BOARD BUSINESS: high opinion of
P, 3/171, 172; 5/321; 6/91, 292; 8/60;
criticises him, 7/334; receives P's
papers on navy debts, 1/225, 226;
advises P on treatment of parliament,
1/226; and Board in Field case, 4/52;
his timber, 5/203–6 passim, 210, 212–
14 passim, 216, 218, 219, 238, 318;
hears navy business in Council/
Cabinet, 6/10–12; 7/260, 312, 377;
approves Carteret's replacement,
8/301; unspecified business, 7/242;
8/30
TANGIER BUSINESS: P applies to for
money, 6/154; 7/336; 8/74, 75;
criticises P, 6/277; and committee,
8/61; also, 7/321; 8/60

AT COUNCIL/CABINET MEETINGS (business unspecified): asleep, 7/260, 377; also, 5/317; 6/76, 78, 91, 105, 154; 7/107, 260, 312, 336; 9/425
JUDICIAL WORK: in trials, 1/225; 5/204, 205; also, 1/226, 272
HOUSES [see also Berkshire House; Clarendon Park, Wilts.; Dorset House; Worcester House]: Clarendon House, Piccadilly: building, 6/39 & n. 1; P visits/admires, 6/39; 7/32, 42, 49, 87, 93, 220; 8/175; attacked by mob, 8/269, 270; pictures, 8/175 & n., 346–7; furnishings, 8/207
SOCIAL: 4/173; at Lord Mayor's banquet, 4/355
MISC.: with King at The Hague, 1/144; attends coronation, 2/84; in town during Plague, 6/142; his bookbinder, 9/480
ALLUDED TO: 2/118; 4/61
HYDE, Edward, son of the Lord Chancellor: 4/341
HYDE, Frances, Countess of Clarendon, wife of the Lord Chancellor: plain, 2/80; at court, 8/33; death, 8/570 & n. 2
HYDE, Lady Henrietta, wife of Laurence: marriage, 8/190 & n. 3; social: 9/468
HYDE, Henry, styled Viscount Cornbury, eldest son of the Lord Chancellor; M.P. Wiltshire; succ. as 2nd Earl of Clarendon 1674 (d. 1709): attitude to Clarendon's impeachment, 8/427, 544–5 & n.; expelled from court, 9/53 & n. 2; social: 4/341
HYDE, Laurence, son of the Lord Chancellor, M.P. Oxford University, cr. Earl of Rochester 1681 (d. 1711): marriage, 8/190 & n. 3; speech on Clarendon's impeachment, 8/539 & n. 3; expelled from court, 9/53 & n. 2; social: 4/341
HYDE, Sir Robert, Chief Justice of the King's Bench 1663–5: tries marine insurance case, 4/403–4; ignorant of sea terms, 4/403; death, 6/96 & n. 3; alluded to: 5/73
HYDE (Hide), [?John], of St Olave's parish: 8/224; ~ his brother, 8/225
HYDE PARK [see also Gardens; Mulberry Garden]: May Day parade,

1/121 & n. 1; 2/91; 4/119–20; 5/139; 8/196–7; 9/182, 537, 540–1; 'the Tour': 4/95 & n. 3; first day of, 6/60; also, 6/89; 9/141–2, 143, 555; P complains of dust, 5/130, 139; 6/77; 8/196; 9/136; footrace, 1/218 & n. 1; King/Duke of York review(s) troops, 4/216–17 & n.; 9/308, 557; other visits by King, 5/126; 7/106; 8/288; the (Keeper's) Lodge: P visits for first time in year, 9/533–4; also, 9/142 & n. 1, ?154, 156, 175, 184, 222, 260, 541; other visits by P/EP to Park: for first time in year, 7/106; 9/122, 533–4; for first time in own coach, 9/487; find gates locked, 9/549; also, 3/78, 288; 4/73, 95, 120; 5/100, 130, 138; 7/144, 178; 8/207; 9/154, 168, 170, 269, 270, 282, 504, 515, 530–1, 541–2, 549, 556, 563

'IANTHE': see Betterton, M.
IBBOT, [Edmund], naval chaplain: P's opinion, 1/107; sermons etc. on voyage to Holland, 1/97, 101, 137; believes in extemporary prayer, 1/105; at Delft, 1/145; social: 1/100, 147, 149, 162; also, 1/95, 129
ILFORD, Essex: P at, 3/169; 6/126
IMPERIALE, Cardinal (Lorenzo), Cardinal-Governor of Rome: 4/24 & n. 2
IMPINGTON, Cambs.: P/EP visit(s), 2/136, 147–8, 180; 3/218; 9/253, 301, 306, 309; church and parson, 2/147 & n. 3; Roger P's house, 4/159; alluded to: 9/348
INCHIQUIN, Lord: see O'Brien, M.
INDIA: see East Indies
INDUSTRIES [for shipbuilding, see principally Ships; and under dockyards]: bricks, 9/314 & n. 3; cloth, in England, 5/300; in Spain, 8/79–80 & n. ; felt, 7/51 & n. 3; glass, 9/457 & n. 2; gloves, 8/425 & n. 4; ironworks in Forest of Dean, 3/165 & n. 1; mining in Nova Scotia, 8/426 & n. 1; mint (royal), 2/38–9; 3/265 & n. 2; 4/70, 143–7 & nn.; ropes, 6/34 & n. 3; sails, 4/7; textiles, at New Bridewell, 6/65–6 & n
INGOLDSBY, Col. [Richard]: captures Lambert, 1/115 & n. 1, 117; given commission, 8/265 & n. 5, 323

INGRAM, Sir Arthur, merchant: 6/108; 7/169

INGRAM, Sir Thomas, Privy Councillor: courteous, 7/20; appointed to Tangier Committee, 6/7; financial business, 6/33, 121, 133; 9/371; victualling business, 6/117, 171; attends meetings/unspecified business, 6/58, 61, 166; at Council committee, 8/278; ~ his clerk, 1/186

INGRAM, Mrs ——: 5/304

INNER TEMPLE: Reader's Feast, 2/155 & n. 2; 9/465–6 & n.; revels, 4/32 & n. 1; gaming in hall, 9/3 & n. 1; riot, 9/465–6 & n., 511–12

INNS: see Taverns etc.

INNS OF COURT: see under names

INSECTS: spontaneous generation, 2/105 & n. 4; bees: in Baltic, 4/413; apiary, 6/97 & n. 3; fleas: in P's bed, 5/260; also, 3/70; glow-worms: 8/340; gnats (?mosquitoes): at Brampton, 2/135, 138; in Fens, 4/311 & n. 1; lice: P suffers from, 9/231, 424; lice or nits: in P's hair/periwig, 5/212, 8/133, 146; 9/239, 424; moth: courtiers chase, 8/282

INSURANCE (marine): peacetime rates, 4/395 & n. 3, 394–7 passim; wartime, 5/126; story of fraud, 4/401, 403; also, 6/202, 328, 329; 7/25

INVENTIONS and machines [see also Entertainments: clockworks; Guns; Royal Society; Scientific and Mathematical Instruments; Ships; Watches and Clocks]: calculating machine, 9/116–17 & n.; chimney design (to prevent smoking), 4/315 & n. 1; claviorganum, 8/25 & n. 4; coins with milled edges, 4/147; diving bell, 5/268–9 & n.; false teeth, 5/293; fire-engines, 8/191, 320; fountain pen, 4/263–4 & n., 278; glass apiary, 6/97 & n. 2; glass coach, 8/396, 446; joke chair, 1/280 & n. 1; lamp glasses, 1/273; 5/237, 291–2; lighthouses, 5/314; 6/3 & n. 4; mechanical organ, 2/115–16 & n.; mine, 3/45–6 & n.; 4/378; sawmill, 3/118; smoke jack, 1/273; theatrical machinery, 2/155 & n. 1; 4/126 & n. 2, 182 & n. 3; 7/76, 77; varnish, 4/153 & n. 2; 7/147–8; waterwheel, 1/263–4; windmill, 9/520

IPSWICH, Suff.: 6/217

IRELAND: appointment of Lord-Lieutenant, 1/227–8 & n.; his establishment reduced, 9/41 & n. 1; declaration against nonconformity, 2/67 & n. 2; troops transported to Portugal, 3/85; land settlement, 4/66 & n. 1, 80, 82, 223 & n. 4, 295; 5/61, 324, 346; 9/119; rumour of dissolution of parliament, 4/80; Castle Plot, 4/94 & n. 2, 100, 285 & n. 3; controversy over cattle trade, 7/313–14 & n., 343; free quartering of soldiers, 8/518–19 & n.; Irish as French recruiting agents, 8/601

IRETON, Henry, regicide (d. 1651): body exhumed and hanged, 1/309 & n. 4; 2/24, 27; head displayed, 2/31 & n. 4

IRETON, [?Jerman, of Gray's Inn]: 9/464

IRETON, John, republican (d. 1689): imprisoned after Yarranton plot, 2/225 & n. 1

IRONGATE [Stairs], Little Tower Hill: 7/273

IRONMONGERS' HALL, Fenchurch St: funeral, 3/268

ISACKSON, ——, linendraper at the Key in Cheapside: 1/277

ISHAM, Capt. [Henry]: accompanies Sandwich to Holland, 1/95, 96, 102, 115, 126, 136, 137 & n. 2; to go to Portugal, 2/161, 163; brings letters from Lisbon, 3/51; social: 1/92, 97; 2/142

ISLE OF DOGS, the: P and party spend night on, 6/168; stranded on, 6/175; also, 6/331

ISLE OF MAN, the: 4/240

ISLE OF WIGHT [see also St Helen's Point; Newport]: 7/334; Charles I's escape to (1647), 6/316

[ISLEWORTH, Mdx]: P at, 6/199 & n. 1

ISLINGTON: P/EP visit (their 'grand tour'): 5/132; 6/86; 7/108, 122, 126, 129, 167, 170, 202, 223, 265, 267, 317; 8/211; 9/251, 271–2, 521, 558; plague in, 6/175–6; the fields/ponds: P visits, 3/57, 59; 9/32; boyhood memories, 5/101 & n. 1; Katherine Wheel, 7/167, 261; King's Head ('the old house', 'the great house'): boyhood

memories, 5/101; P/EP visit(s), 2/98, 125; 5/133; 6/112; 7/149, 220; 8/174–5, 219, 234, 296, 344, 390; 9/47, 133, 184, 197, 513; J. Birch's wedding at, 9/500; White Lion, 9/32
ITALY: homosexuality, 4/210; gardens, 7/213
IVAN IV, Tsar of Russia 1547–84: anecdotes of, 3/188–9 & n.
IVY LANE: 9/494

JACKSON, John, sen., of Ellington, Hunts.: P's opinion, 9/56, 57; marries Paulina P, 8/585 & n. 6; 9/17, 18–19, 100 & n. 2; marriage settlement, 9/55, 64–5; P's father to live with, 9/212; also, 9/61, 210, 215
JACKSON, John, jun., P's nephew and heir: vol. i, pp. xxxix, lxxi–lxxii
JACKSON, Paulina (b. Pepys), P's sister and wife of John Jackson sen.:
P'S OPINION ETC.: ill-natured, 1/290; 3/223; 4/3; 5/54; 8/475; 'good bodied' but 'full of freckles', 7/138; old and ugly, 8/471; fatter and comelier, 9/210
CHRON. SERIES: birth date recorded, 5/361 & n. 1; servant in P's household, 1/288, 290–1, 324; 2/1, 4; proud and idle, 2/139; dismissed and moves to Brampton, 2/153, 161/2, 167; 5/234; P's small money gifts to, 2/172; 3/223; 5/268; 8/474; unworthy of becoming EP's gentlewoman, 4/3, 15, 49; father defends, 4/108; and seeks dowry for, 4/366; 5/44; growing old, 4/439 & n. 1; P's hopes of marrying her off, 5/42–3, 152, 183; plans match with Harman, 6/163–4 & n., 170; 7/15, 23, 72, 73, 81–2; match proposed with Ensum, 7/78 & n. 2, 81–2, 86, 91, 104, 170, 405; and with B. Gauden, 7/88–9; P's legacy to, 7/134; stays with P in London, 7/40, 137, 138, 140, 175; match proposed with Hewer, 8/17; with Cumberland, 8/118 & n. 3; 9/17; and with Barnes, 8/261 & n. 2; her match with Jackson, 8/539 & n. 1, 585; 9/16–17, 18–19, 47, 55, 56, 58, 61, 64–5; P provides dowry, 9/16–17, 19, 56, 61, 97; marriage, 9/79, 100, 108; to live at Ellington, 9/211, 212, 293; pregnant,

9/553 & n. 4; also, 1/27, 81; 2/64; 3/103, 106; 4/134, 210; 7/40; 8/280, 314, 470
SOCIAL: at Twelfth Night party, 1/10; christening, 2/125; Woolwich, 7/142; Islington, 7/149, 167; and Hinchingbrooke, 8/471–2; also, 2/40, 54, 160; 3/219; 4/313; 7/169, 172, 174
JACKSON, [?Stephen], merchant: 6/164
JACKSON, ——; 2/148
JACOB, Sir John, Customs farmer: 3/188 & n. 3
JACOB'S: see Taverns etc.
JACOMBE, [Thomas], Rector of St Martin-infra-Ludgate: sermons, 2/74–5 & n.; 3/30 & n. 3; friendship with Jane Turner, 3/30
JAGGARD, [Abraham], merchant: victualling business, 5/53; country house, ib. & n. 3; at Gauden's, 7/29; builds house in Thames St, 9/124 & n. 1; ~ his wife [Sarah], 5/53(2), 54
JAMAICA: ships to, 2/6 & n. 3; new Governor sails to, 3/52, 62–3 & nn.; returns, 4/41 & n. 4; its capture (1655), 3/115; 4/376 & n. 2; privateers at, 8/75 & n. 1; also, 2/56; 3/52
JAMAICA HOUSE, Bermondsey: see Gardens; Taverns etc.
JAMES I, of Great Britain: monopolies 3/159 & n. 2; coinage, 4/148; Mennes's memories of, 6/127; privy purse expenditure, 8/324, 331 & n. 2
JAMES, Duke of Cambridge: see Stuart
JAMES, Duke of York, Lord High Admiral:
CHARACTER: independence, 4/116; industry, 4/367; 5/21 & n. 2, 167, 185–6; 'like to be a noble prince', 5/21; courage and modesty, 5/170–1; good judgement, 7/93–4; unpopularity, 4/24; neglects business for pleasure, 7/320, 323, 350
PERSONAL APPEARANCE ETC.: 'very plain' in nightshirt, 2/79; adopts periwig, 4/360; 5/49; 'better' after voyage, 5/339; adopts King's new fashion, 7/320–1; health: ague, 5/249; smallpox, 8/522(2), 524, 526, 527, 551, 565, 575; venereal disease (rumour), 6/60; also, 9/155

8/485; 9/222, 251, 510, 513; laying up ships after war, 8/357 & n. 1, 374, 419 & n. 1, 448, 460–1; visiting/inspecting ships, 4/103; 7/38, 168; building/launching ships, 5/75, 110, 306, 353; 6/169, 170; 7/119, 127, 193, 201; Heemskerck's design, 9/171; sale of prize ships, 8/485

SUPERNUMERARIES: 9/350–1 & n.

SURVEYS: 7/316

VICTUALLING: 7/216–17 & n., 219–20 & n., 260; 8/78; 9/315–18 passim, 323, 382

MISC. BUSINESS: striking flag, 2/222 & n. 3; Navy Officers' lodgings, 3/66; marine insurance, 4/397

ATTENDANCE AT MEETINGS WITH NAVY BOARD: business unspecified, 3/192, 203, 229, 236, 252, 272, 277, 282; 4/3, 4, 17, 25, 31, 43, 70, 74–5, 83, 88, 102, 106, 113, 123, 132, 133, 177, 192, 198, 216, 260, 269, 278, 330, 340, 369, 383, 401, 407, 417–18, 427; 5/4, 11, 18, 26, 49, 70, 82, 111, 131, 138, 151, 183, 190, 228, 235, 268, 274, 286–7, 293, 342, 349, 356; 6/1, 6, 13, 19, 22, 34, 39, 44, 51, 55, 56, 131, 140; 7/47, 61, 71, 84, 90, 96, 109, 115, 125, 130, 150, 155, 162, 173, 183, 231, 239, 247, 256, 265, 284, 289, 316, 348, 358, 391, 397; 8/1, 9, 25, 41, 57, 109, 131, 142, 164, 169, 198, 204–5, 230, 251, 340, 356, 384, 403, 413, 424, 431, 444, 482, 491, 565, 575, 581, 594; 9/17, 21, 106, 112, 156, 173, 178, 190, 198, 199, 246, 258, 262, 263, 267, 280, 330, 335, 349, 359, 369, 376, 383, 391, 396, 406, 419, 422, 454, 470, 506, 522, 544, 553–4, 559; fails to attend: because hunting: 3/198, 247, 260; 4/167; 7/136–7, 228, 388; for other reasons: 4/204, 213, 360; 5/77, 220; 7/105; 8/403, 551; 9/14

AS NAVAL COMMANDER:

CHRON. SERIES: learns seamanship, 1/125; views on ship design etc., 5/75; voyage to France, 2/122; takes command on *Royal Charles* (1664), 5/286–7, 291, 311, 313, 315, 316, 318; returns, 5/336, 339; takes command on *Prince* (1665), 6/51, 57, 64, 65, 86; returns to Harwich, 6/99, 104; in Battle of Lowestoft, 6/116, 121, 122,

135; returns, 6/125, 126, 128; parliamentary concern over his safety, 6/138–9 & n., 267; at sea again, 6/143, 146; voted gift by Commons, 6/281 & n. 2, 291; lampooned in *Second advice to a painter*, 7/407; parliamentary enquiry into failure to pursue Dutch after Battle of Lowestoft, 8/489 & n. 1, 491–2 & n.; his part in decision to divide fleet (1666), 9/74; low view of French conduct of 1666 campaign, 7/327–8; rumour of his taking command (1667), 8/41–2; his plans for 1667 campaign, 8/97–8 & n.; criticised, 8/306; orders fortification of dockyards, 8/84, 115 & n. 2, 125 & n. 2, 126–7 & n., 171, 173; his part in defence of Medway, 8/256, 263, 264, 298; his respect for Dutch seamanship in Medway, 8/358, 359; at Harwich, 8/317 & n. 4, 324, 328; intends to go to sea (1668), 9/140; instructions to Allin, 9/273 & n. 1; his share in prize-money, 9/290 & n. 1; marine regiment disbanded, 9/347, 351 & n. 1; also, 7/147, 153; 8/90–1; 9/67, 185, 248

RELATIONS WITH SUBORDINATE COMMANDERS: prefers old to new, 3/122 & n. 3; concern for discipline, 5/131; 7/212 & n. 1; supports/praises Sandwich, 2/169; 6/127, 134; 9/244; hostile to, 3/121, 122; 5/133; 7/262; commends Teddeman and Harman, 7/154; differences with Albemarle over commanders, 7/163 & n. 1, 222, 314–15, 334; concern for good appointments, 9/39–40; loses control over during war, 9/39–40, 76; with King adjudicates in dispute, 9/107; insists on Penn having command, 9/131; new instructions to commanders, 9/547, 549, 563; also, 5/207

TANGIER: appointed to committee, 3/238; efficiency on, 5/167, 185–6; map of, 3/37; favours Irish regiment, 3/204; 5/345; objects to treatment of Portuguese, 5/239; criticises Belasyse, 8/61; agrees to reform of government, 8/160; other business: ship hire, 6/27; treasurership, 6/59, 60; victualling, 7/156, 296; money, 9/14–15; mole, 9/199; paymaster of garrison,

9/418, 422; unspecified, 3/272, 282, 300; 4/4; 5/177, 223; 6/58, 134; 7/82, 166, 321; 8/60–1, 347, 459, 521, 591, 600; 9/135, 316, 449

MILITARY CAREER: in Flanders (1658): 5/170–1 & n.; 6/302; 8/75; reminiscences, of, 9/396; rumoured appointment to new army, 3/15 & n. 2; 6/277 & n. 2, 302; 7/395; and as general of land and sea forces, 6/321 & n. 1; commands troops during Fire, 7/269, 271, 273; favours standing army, 8/355, 361, 366–7; reviews troops, 4/216–17 & n.; 9/308, 557 & n. 1; Governor of Portsmouth, 2/199 & n. 2; Lord Warden of Cinque Ports, 9/280 & n. 4

OTHER PUBLIC WORK: patron of R. African Company, 1/258; 4/335; 5/11; 9/350; and of E. India Company, 2/228; profits from wine licences, 9/132 & n. 1, 319 & n. 1; low opinion of new Council of Trade, 9/549 & n. 2

POLITICS [see also below, Court]:
GENERAL: favours papists, 2/38; prefers Irish to English subordinates, 5/345; fears/resents Monmouth's claims, 3/238, 290, 303 & n. 1; 4/123, 138; 5/21, 58; 7/411; 8/434; advises tax by prerogative, 8/292–3; favours government by army on French model, 8/332; political news from, 5/13; 8/186, 384; 9/173–4, 310

RELATIONS WITH KING AND MINISTERS: attitude to Clarendon's dismissal, 8/406, 409, 410 & n. 1, 412, 414, 416, 419, 420, 424, 476, 506; power reduced by, 8/434, 597; relations with King deteriorate, 8/431, 480, 482, 530, 532, 535, 558, 596, 602; improve, 8/568; 9/153; fears Clarendon's impeachment, 8/518; rumours of his own impeachment, 8/532, 533–4; reconciled with Coventry, 9/79, 336; power weakened by Buckingham's rise, 9/340, 341, 361, 373, 472, 550–1, 558; relations improve, 9/319, 490–1

AS PRIVY COUNCILLOR: discusses state of navy, 7/311–13; money for navy, 7/377; 8/112; 9/216, 220; flag-officers' pensions, 9/257 & n. 2; attends cabinet meetings, 8/117, 138,

600; other council meetings, 7/26, 353; 8/111; 9/87, 122

PARLIAMENT: candidate defeated, 7/337 & n. 2; attends Lords, 7/406; 8/46; 9/176; opposes recall, 8/292–3 & n.; members attend on, 8/477; instructions to friends, 8/482

FOREIGN AFFAIRS: relations with Algiers, 3/121–2 & n.; 9/473, 516; favours Dutch war, 5/107, 111, 212, 242, 355; warns Dutch ambassador, 5/264 & n. 4; favours French alliance, 9/536; also, 8/452

COURT: reconciled to Queen-Mother, 2/2–3 & n.; association with Fitzharding and Muskerry, 4/116; 5/345; dislike of E. Mountagu of Boughton, 5/207; laughs at Sir R. Howard, 9/190–1; chides Bab May, 9/336–7; fears King may marry F. Stuart, 8/438; allies with Lady Castlemaine, 9/417; resents disgrace of H. Savile, 9/466, 469, 493; dines in public, 4/407; 8/161; attends Garter ceremony, 8/177; 9/246; and court balls, 3/300–01; 7/372; drunk at Cranbourne, 8/446–7; also, 3/191

MARRIAGE [for his mistresses, see Carnegie, Lady; Chesterfield, Lady; Churchill, Arabella; Denman, Lady; Hamilton, Lady Anne; Stuart, Frances]: rumours of, 1/260–1 & n., 273, 275, 284 & n. 1, 315, 319; publicly acknowledged, 1/320; 2/1; the ceremony, 2/40–1 & n.; dalliance with wife, 4/4; her jealousy, 4/138; his mistresses, 8/6, 286; henpecked (nicknamed 'Tom Otter'), 8/368 & n. 2; 9/342; marriage said to have 'undone the nation', 8/367; alluded to: 7/261; 8/287

FAMILY [see also Stuart]: children, 4/238, n. 1; untroubled by death of son Charles, 2/95 & n. 1; plays with daughter, Princess Mary, 5/268; also, 1/247–8; 2/213

RELIGION: friend of Catholics, 2/38; 'silly devotions', 9/163–4; attends Whitehall chapel, 3/42; 4/31, 401

SPORTS [for his yacht, see Ships: Anne]: plays pell-mell, 2/64; 9/542; hunts, 3/76, 198, 247, 260; 4/167, 192; 7/136–7, 228, 388; 8/382, 446–7;

marriage to Queen Mother, 3/263 & n. 3, 303; 5/57–8 & n.; 8/564 & n. 1; new buildings in St James's Fields, 4/295–6; 7/87–8 & n.; dress, 7/328; reckless gamester, 8/190 & n. 2; fine coach, 8/196; also, 6/316 & n. 4

PUBLIC CAREER: ambassador to France, 1/300, 307; rumoured appointment as Lord Treasurer, 3/227; negotiations with France, 8/107 & n. 1; 9/530 & n. 2, 536; also, 2/33; 8/294

SOCIAL: 2/32; 4/229

JERMYN, Henry, Master of the Horse to the Duke of York; cr. Baron Dover 1685: rumoured marriage to Princess Dowager, 1/320; duel, 3/170–1; attempt at abduction, 5/58 & n. 2; at sea with Rupert, 5/311; affair with Lady Castlemaine, 8/366, 368; wealth, 8/196, 563–4; also, 9/473; ~ his brother [Thomas], 8/563–4

JERSEY, Channel Is.: Carteret's government during Civil War, 3/243 & n. 2; 4/195, 306; Sir T. Allin's flight to (1650), 8/161 & n. 4

JERVAS (Gervas), [Richard], barber, New Palace Yard: trims P, 1/90; 4/130, 290; his man hired for Dutch voyage, 1/90; P inspects periwigs, 4/130, 290, 350; 5/224; 6/74; other visits, 5/246, 257, 260, 267–8, 275, 287, 316, 332, 340; 6/1, 6, 9, 16; 8/177; supplies infested periwig, 8/133, 146; sees diving experiment, 5/268–9; ~ his wife [Grace], 4/261–2; 5/268–9; 6/6, 16; child [Ann] buried, 5/221; mother-in-law, —— Palmer, ventriloquist, 4/261–2

JESSOP, [William], Clerk of the House of Commons 1660: 'an old-fashion man of Cromwell's', 9/44; parliamentary business, 1/29; 2/32 & n. 3; secretary to Brooke House Committee, 9/30 & n. 1, 44, 298

JESUITS, the: Leopold I's reliance on, 4/350 & n. 2

JEWEN ST: Deb Willet lodges in, 9/543; also, 9/332, 520(2)

[JEWKES, Roland], lawyer: tomb, 8/545 & n. 2

JEWS: P attends synagogue, 4/335 & nn.; story of new Messiah, 7/47 & n. 4

JIGGINS: see Jegon

JIJELLI (Gigery), Algeria; captured by French, 5/295 & n. 1

JOHN GEORGE II, Elector of Saxony 1656–80: made Knight of Garter, 9/246 & n. 2

JOHNSON, [Henry], shipbuilder, Blackwall: story of petrified trees, 6/236 & n. 4; repairs ships, 8/135; social: 1/280

JOHNSON, Mrs ——, servant to Sandwich: 1/38

JOHNSON, Mrs ——, sister of Lady Mordaunt: 9/476 & n. 5

JOLLIFFE (Jolly), [George], physician: 4/60 & n. 3

JOLLIFFE, [John], merchant: 5/300

JONES, Anne, of St Olave's parish: social: 7/136; 8/29, 104, 150; 9/197

[JONES, John]: elected M.P. for London, 2/57 & n. 1

JONES, Col. John, republican: impeached, 1/34 & n. 2

JONES, Col. [Philip], parliamentarian: influence over R. Cromwell, 1/180 & n. 4; ~ his son, 2/34 & n. 2, 56

JONES, Sir Theophilus, Scoutmaster-General of Ireland 1661–d.85: 2/173

JONES, ——, a young merchant: 8/76

JORDAN, Joseph, kted 1665, naval commander: in Battle of Lowestoft, 6/122; serves under Penn, 6/147; at council of war, 6/230; poor tactics in St James's Day Fight, 8/354 & n. 3, 357–60; portrait by Lely, 7/102 & n. 3

JORDAN, Mrs —— [?Mary, wife of Joseph]: as godmother, 2/109

JOURNAL: see Diary

JOWLES, Lieut. [Henry], naval officer: P's low opinion, 4/229; 5/1; marriage to Rebecca Allen, 4/229 & n. 1; challenges his captain to duel, 8/140–1; ~ his mother, 4/227

JOWLES, Rebecca (b. Allen), wife of Henry: P admires, 2/68, 71, 72; 5/1; dallies with, 9/495, 497; married, 4/229 & n. 1; churched, 4/227; pleads for husband, 5/1; 8/140–1; social: 2/69, 125, 126, 127; 3/153; ~ her pretty cousin, 9/497

JOWLES, Capt. [Valentine], naval officer: commissioned, 1/100; gift to P, ib.

magistrates allegedly puritan, 5/96–7; use of Latin in proceedings, 7/114 & n. 2

COURTS:

ADMIRALTY: revived, 4/76 & n. 2; cases, 4/76–7 & nn.; prize cases, 8/123 & n. 1, 130 & n. 2, 133–6 passim, 181, 231 & n. 2

ARCHES, COURT OF: in St Mary-le-Bow church, 4/33 & n. 3; proceedings concerning Robert P's will, ib.; dispute between Bishop and Dean of Lichfield, 9/45 & n. 2

ASSIZES, COMMISSIONS OF OYER ET TERMINER ETC.: trial of regicides, 1/263 & nn.; story of attack on judge (1631), 8/428–9 & n.; alluded to: Cambridge, 2/145, 146; 8/484 & n. 2; Huntingdon, 2/145, 148; Maidstone, 3/137

CHANCERY [for P's dispute with Trices, see Trice, T; Pepys, Robert]: Court of Wards, 1/48; in Rolls Chapel, 1/50; in Worcester House, 5/203–4, 205; P hears cases, 1/48(2) & nn., 50; 5/205; Lord Keeper Coventry's decrees, 7/261 & nn.; fees, 8/219; P takes oath, 9/340; bar alluded to, 9/104

CORONERS' INQUESTS: 9/49, 78

COURT MARTIALS (naval): 3/124; 6/104 & n. 4; P as assessor, 9/481 & n. 1, 488–9, 497 & n. 1, 498 & n. 1, 505 & n. 1, 508 & n. 1, 510–11

COURT MERCHANT (Tangier): 8/459 & n. 2

EXCHEQUER: cases, 1/48, 49 & n. 1; 4/51–2, 192–3; P swears affidavit, 1/48; Lord Mayor sworn in, 7/346; commission of rebellion, 4/51 & n. 1; writ of distraint, 9/535 & n. 4

FIRE COURT: established, 7/357 & n. 2; 9/23 & n. 1; case, 8/562–3 & n.

HOUSE OF LORDS [for details, see Parliament]: P attends trials, 1/225 & n. 3; 5/139–40 & n.; also, 5/109–12 passim & nn., 126, 128–9

KING'S BENCH: trials: Sir H. Vane, jun., 3/103–4 & n., 116; Sedley and others, 4/209–10 & nn.; fraud, 4/401–4 passim; 'Col.' Turner, 5/18–19 & n.; Carr, 9/55 & n. 1, 57

MANORIAL [for details, see under places]: P attends at Graveley, 2/181–2; at Brampton, 3/222, 223; 4/308–9; 5/281, 282, 298

PREROGATIVE COURT OF CANTERBURY: 2/160 & n. 1

PRIVY COUNCIL [q.v. for details]: trials, 5/324 & nn.; 8/16 & n. 4; 316–17, 330–1, 407, 420–1 & n.; 9/259 & n. 2, 511–12 & n., 531–2 & n.

QUARTER-SESSIONS: city of London: trials, 4/294 & n. 3; 8/316 & n. 1; 319–21 & nn.; alluded to, 9/382; Middlesex: trials, 3/?34 & n. 2, ?35–6; 5/58 & n. 3

PENALTIES [omitting fines, imprisonment and passing references to executions]:

EXECUTION: by burning, alluded to, 4/144 & n. 1; use of silk ropes, 4/60 & n. 1; corpse on gallows, 2/72–3 & n.; executions witnessed by P/EP: of Barkstead and others, 3/66–7 & n.; Vane, 3/108–9 & nn.; and 'Col.' Turner, 5/23 & nn.; other executions, 1/265 & n. 1, 266 & n. 1, 268–70 passim; 2/18 & n. 2; 4/60 & n. 1; also, 3/19 & n. 1; 9/335

MUTILATION: alleged case of, 8/428–9 & n.

PILLORY: in Holland, 1/146–7 & n.; apprentices in, 5/99, 101; Carr in, 8/583 & n. 3, 587; 9/32 & n. 1, 57; alluded to: 5/128–9

TORTURE: possible use, in treason case, 3/237

JUXON, William, Archbishop of Canterbury 1660–3: death, 4/173 & n. 2; lies in state, 4/188, 214, 217; rebuilds hall at Lambeth Palace, 6/164 & n. 2; ~ his executor, 9/163 & n. 6

KEENE, [?Edward]: 3/148

KELSEY, [John], naval officer: 8/512–13

KELYNG (Keeling), Sir John, Lord Chief Justice 1665–71: ability, 8/321, 484; censured by Commons, 8/483–4 & n., 494, 577 & n. 4, 578, 579 & n. 1; binds over Roger P, 8/484 & n. 2; as President of Fire Court, 9/23; conduct in Buckhurst-Sedley case, 9/336; in Sir E. Godfrey's, 9/561; in other cases, 8/319, 321

KEMBE, Harry, Navy Office messenger: damages awarded against, 3/280; dies, 7/412
KEMPTHORNE, [John], naval commander; kted 1670: in Downs, 8/43; presides over court martial, 9/488, 497 & n. 1, 505 & n. 1
KENASTON: *see* Kinaston
KENDAL, Duke of: *see* Anne, Duchess of York
KENERSLY: *see* Kinnersley
KENNARD: *see* Kinward
KENSINGTON: P visits: Holland House, 1/216 & n. 2; tavern with garden and grotto, 9/166, 170, 203; other visits, 5/178, 180–1; 7/54, 95, 100; Sandwich/Lady Sandwich at, 1/210, 215; 5/174, 178; Queen at, 5/163; duel, 1/20
KENT, [John]: *see* Taverns etc.: Three Tuns, Crutched Friars
KENT, Earl of: *see* Grey, [?Henry]
KENT ST: Plague, 6/279, 297
KENTISH KNOCK, the (the shoal off the mouth of the Thames): 1/254
KENTISH TOWN: 5/233
[KERKHOVEN, D.], Dutch naval commander: 6/108 & n. 3
KERNEGUY: *see* Carnegie
KEVET: *see* Kievet
KIEVET, Johan, Burgomaster of Rotterdam ('Amsterdam'):⁜ in peace negotiations, 8/68–9 & n.
KILLIGREW, Henry, chaplain to the King: preaches at Whitehall, 4/393 & n. 2
KILLIGREW, Henry, Groom of the Bedchamber to the Duke of York: at puppet play, 7/267 & n. 1; banished from court, 7/336–7; in affray with Buckingham, 8/348 & n. 1; bawdy talk, 9/218; attacked by Lady Shrewsbury's footmen, 9/557 & n. 2, 558; also, 3/229–30, 265
KILLIGREW, Sir Peter: on *Naseby*, 1/132 & n. 2
KILLIGREW, Thomas, dramatist, manager of the Theatre Royal and Groom of the Bedchamber [*see also* Plays]:
AS MANAGER OF THEATRE ROYAL: his plans for opera, 5/230; 8/56; and for training actors, 5/230 & n. 3;

love of Italian music, 8/54–7 passim; brings Italian consort to court, 8/56, 65–6; on improvement in theatre, 8/55–6; praises Knepp's acting, 8/55, 430; employs whore for actors, 9/425; warned against putting on satirical play, 9/471
AS GROOM OF THE BEDCHAMBER: frank advice to Charles II, 7/400; repartee with, 8/368 & n. 2; appointed King's jester, 9/66–7 & n.; struck by Rochester in King's presence, 9/451–2 & n.; also, 8/497; 9/558
SOCIAL: 5/27; 8/429–30; 9/200
MISC.: his (joke) letter to Queen of Bohemia, 1/157; early passion for theatre, 3/243–4 & n.; early poverty, 9/256 & n. 4
KILLIGREW, Sir William, dramatist and courtier: at Greenwich and Deptford with King, 6/169
KINASTON (Kenaston), [Edward], merchant: P's high opinion, 8/295; Tangier business, 7/19; 8/251 & n. 1, 292, 295, 369–70, 372
KING, Col. [Edward]: 2/53
KING, Henry, Bishop of Chichester 1642–d.69: sermons, 1/195; 4/69; 6/54 & n. 3
KING, [Thomas], M.P. Harwich, Essex: lends P copy of impeachment against Clarendon, 8/523; social: 9/474
[KING, William], landlord of the Crown, Hercules Pillars Lane: wealth, 9/42 & n. 3
KING, [William], Vicar of Ashtead, Surrey ?1648–62: dull preacher, 4/247 & n. 1
KING, [?William], late of the Treasurers at War: dismissed, 1/82
KING, Dr ——, physician, of Huntingdon: 4/313
KING ST, the city: constructed after Fire, 8/562–3 & n.
KING ST, Westminster [*see also* Taverns etc.: Angel; Axe; Bell; Crown; Fox; Harper's; Leg; Red Lion; Rhenish winehouse; Rose; ?Ship; Sun; Swan; Trumpet; White Horse]: flood, 1/93 & n. 1; traffic block, 1/303 & n. 1; alluded to: 3/201
KINGDON, Capt. [Richard], Comp-

troller of the Excise Office: service under Commonwealth, 6/319–20 & n.; business with, 6/319, 332; 8/16
KING'S CHANNEL, the (off the Essex Coast): Dutch fleet in, 8/256
[KINGSDOWN], Deal, Kent: wager on height of cliff, 1/163
KING'S GATE, Holborn: 9/154, 474
KINGSLAND, Mdx: P's boyhood memories, 5/132 & n. 4; 8/211 & n. 3; P/EP at, 2/180; 5/133, 201; 7/121, 132, 220; 8/174, 211–12, 390; 9/197, 513
KINGSMILL, family of: 5/118 & n. 1
KINGSTON, Catherine, Lady Kingston, wife of John, 1st Baron: alluded to, 2/54 & n. 3
KING'S LYNN, Norf.: as port, 1/179; 2/27, 156
KINGSTON, Surrey: P visits, 3/75; 6/154, 166, 167; 7/28; Quakers to be tried, 4/271; alluded to: 2/202
KINNERSLEY, ——, of the Wardrobe: 2/121
KINWARD (Kennard), [Thomas], Master-Joiner of the King's Works, Whitehall: his work at Hinchingbrooke, 1/314, 324; 2/35; and on Penn's lodgings, 3/28, 31, 41; ~ his servant, 1/314
KIPPS, [Thomas], Seal-bearer to the Lord Chancellor: at Whitehall chapel, 1/195; Chancery business, 1/197, 204; in P's 'old clubb', 2/221; also, 1/44, 184; 2/127
KIRBY, Capt. [Robert], naval officer: killed in action, 6/122
KIRTON, [Joshua], bookseller, Paul's Churchyard [until the Fire often 'my bookseller']: P: buys books/pays bills, 3/105, 290; 4/234; 5/38, 358, 359; 6/70, 151; 7/41, 47, 64; orders books, 1/281–2; 2/239; 5/342, 343–4, 355; 6/109; collects books, 6/28; has books bound, 5/355; 6/2, 14, 28; visits shop, 2/22, 165, 238; 4/342; 5/190; 7/46, 116; lends P money, 7/101; ruined by Fire, 7/297, 309; death, 8/526 & n. 2; ~ his apprentice, 1/53–4, 307; his kinsman, 4/80; 7/309
KITE, Ellen, P's aunt: 4/131; 5/132
KITE, Margaret (Peg), P's cousin: orphaned, 2/172; left legacy, 2/173;

troublesome to P as executor, 2/179, 190, 192; marries weaver, 2/209, 231; husband demands marriage portion, 3/161
KITE, Sarah: see Giles
KITE, Mrs —— (Aunt Kite; 'my aunt the Butcher'): see Clarke, Julian
KIUPRILLI, Ahmed, Turkish Grand Vizier 1661–d.76: death reported, 5/236, 237, n. 1
KNAPP, [John]: solicits for places in navy, 4/407 & n. 1; claims to be royal physician, ib.
KNEPP, [Christopher], horse dealer, husband of Elizabeth: 9/391; jealous of P, 6/323; 7/2; social: 7/16, 369
KNEPP (Knipp), [Elizabeth], actress:
CHRON. SERIES: P meets at Greenwich, 6/320 & n. 5; admires, 6/321; 7/1; she signs letter 'Bab Allen', 7/4; P replies as 'Dapper Dicky', 7/5; gives her money, 7/61; 9/309; and gloves, 7/70; his valentine, 8/86, 100; her unhappy marriage, 7/5, 7; pregnant, 7/133, 173; birth and death of son Samuel, 7/196, 198, 236; P fondles, 7/2; 8/29; 9/170, 172, 188, 189–90, 218; EP's jealousy of, 7/120, 236–8 passim; 8/25, 211, 371–2, 399, 599; 9/1, 108, 436, 469; P vows to see no more, 9/339, 368, 391; avoids in theatre, 9/381, 405
HER PERFORMANCES: T. Killigrew's opinion, 8/55, 430; P admires in *The scornful lady*, 7/422; *The custom of the country*, 8/3; *The Indian emperor*, 8/14 & n. 2; *The humourous lieutenant*, 8/27; *The Chances*, 8/46; *The troubles of Queen Elizabeth*, 8/388–9; *The northern lass*, 8/437; *The Duke of Lerma*, 9/81; *The Storm*, 9/133 & n. 1; *The sea voyage*, 9/201 & n. 1; *The silent woman*, 9/310 & n. 2; also acts in *The Goblins*, 8/28–9, 232; *Flora's Vagaries*, 8/463 & n. 5; *The Surprizal*, 9/166 & n. 2; *The Heiress*, 9/435–6; P admires her singing, 8/3, 27, 46; 9/436; and dancing, 8/388–9; alluded to, 8/196; 9/200, 282, 320
HER SINGING (at parties etc.): P enraptured by, 6/321; sings *Barbara Allen*, 7/1; Italian song, 8/57; English songs, 8/599; with P, 7/44, 69, 92–3, 95, 237, 362; he teaches her *Beauty Retire*, 7/53,

54; and *It is decreed*, 7/369; teaches P *The Lark*, 9/299; also, 6/323–4; 7/341, 343–4; 8/65, 86; 9/128, 131, 189
SOCIAL: dances, 7/73; 9/12–13, 134, 289; introduces P to Nell Gwyn, 8/27; at theatre, 7/347; 8/137–8, 156, 383, 395, 463; 9/12; theatre gossip from, 8/168–9; 9/19–20, 155–6; at Vauxhall, 9/219; also, 7/18, 84, 103–4, 257; 8/598; 9/276
ALLUDED TO: 6/342; 7/3, 15–16; 8/242 ~ her daughter, 8/57; her pretty maid Betty: 9/156; P kisses, 9/201, 320–1
KNIGHT, [John], Surgeon to the King: 3/299; ~ his wife, ib.
KNIGHT, [Mary], singer: P admires her voice, 8/453 & n. 4; 9/299
KNIGHT, Sir John, navy agent, Bristol: 9/235 & n. 2
KNIGHTLEY, [Richard], Rector of Charwelton, Northants., 1663–95: proposed as husband for Lady Jemima Mountagu, 3/84 & n. 1
KNIGHTLY, [Robert], merchant, of Seething Lane: wants churchyard limed during Plague, 7/31; social: 2/239–40; 7/31–2, 278, 280; alluded to: 6/142; ~ Mary, ?his daughter, 9/221 & n. 1
KNIGHTSBRIDGE [*see also* Taverns etc.: World's End]: P visits, 5/181; 6/89
KNIPP: *see* Knepp
KÖNIGSBERG (Quinsborough), East Prussia: stories of, 4/412
KRAG (Kragh), Otte, Danish ambassador-extraordinary to the United Provinces 1659–60: 1/153–4
KUFFELER, Johannes Siberius, inventor: his explosive mine, 3/45–6 & n.
KYNASTON, [Edward], actor: in *The loyal subject*, 1/224 & n. 3; *The silent woman*, 2/7 & n. 4; *The island princess*, 9/441 & n. 4; assaulted for mimicking Sedley in *The Heiress*, 9/435 & n. 3, 435–6

LACEY, [John], actor and dramatist [*see also* Plays]: imprisoned for part in *The change of crowns*, 8/168 & n. 1, 172–3; said to be dying, 8/334 & n. 3; imitated in puppet play, 9/445 & n. 2; P admires in *The French dancing*

master, 3/87–8 & nn.; *Love in a maze*, 3/88 & nn.; 4/179 & n. 3; 8/195–6; 9/177–8; *The Committee*, 4/181 & n. 1; 8/384 & n. 3; *The faithful shepherdess*, 4/182; *The change of crowns*, 8/167–8 & n.; also acts in *The humourous lieutenant*, 4/128 & n. 4; in own adaptation of *The taming of the shrew*, 8/158 & n. 2; dances in *The jovial crew*, 9/411–12 & n.; and in *Horace*, 9/420 & n. 2; alluded to: 7/77
[LAFRERI, Antonio, d. 1577]: print by, 7/102–3 & n.
LAM, Mother: *see* Taverns etc.
LAMB, [James], Canon of Westminster: sermon, 1/261
LAMBART (Lambert), [Rose], Viscountess Lambart (d. 1649), first wife of Richard Lambart, succ. 1660 as 2nd Earl of Cavan: 9/215 & n. 3
LAMBERT, [David], naval officer: lieutenant on *Naseby*, 1/105; P tells of diary, 1/107; his gittern, 1/169; instructs P on naval matters, 1/259; 2/13, 115; married, 2/23; house, 2/116, 123; transferred to 4th-rate, 2/90; captain of *Norwich*, 2/115, 203–4; stories of Lisbon, 2/196–7; sails for Mediterranean, 2/214, 219; and Tangier, 3/67; 4/100–1; social: 1/75, 102, 106, 107, 120, 162, 164, 166, 258–9; 2/23, 25, 49, 101, 196–7, 207; alluded to: 1/27; ~ his wife, 2/123; father-in-law, 2/197
LAMBERT, [James], naval officer: captain of *Anne* yacht, 3/63; killed in action, 6/225
LAMBERT, Maj.-Gen. John, republican (d. 1683): opposes Rump, 1/1 & n. 4; rumoured advance on London, 1/4 & n. 5; support in army, 1/7; indemnity offered to, 1/6, 7; submits to Rump, 1/8; defies Rump, 1/51 & n. 2; to appear before Council of State, 1/74 & n. 3; imprisoned in Tower, 1/81; escapes, 1/108 & n. 1; captured, 1/114–15, 117; sent to Guernsey, 2/204 & n. 1; old lodgings in Whitehall, 5/164; alluded to: 2/92
LAMBERT, ——, servant to Coventry: 4/258
LAMBETH, Surrey [For Lambeth ale, *see* Drink. *See also* Taverns etc.:

theatre, 8/172-3 & n.; affray at prize-fight, 8/239; assault in King's presence, 9/451-2 & n.; by hired bullies, 9/435-6 & n., 441, 471, 557 & n. 2, 558; P fears for EP's safety, 9/549; also, 1/215, 303; 2/30, 228-9; 3/34 & n. 2, 35-6 & n., 196, 212; 5/32 & n. 3; 6/306-7; 7/369 & n. 3, 380; 8/90 & n. 3, 206, 208-9, 319, 321 & n. 3, 348-9 & n.; 9/111 & n. 1, 166, 412 & n. 2, 470 & n. 1

DUELS:
GENERAL: P disapproves, 3/171; proclamations against, ib. & n. 2; bill against, 9/53 & n. 1; serving officers arrested to prevent, 8/140-1; 9/273
PARTICULAR: Chesterfield and Wolley, 1/20 & n. 1; Sandwich and Buckingham (challenge), 2/32-3; Cholmley and Ned Mountagu, 3/157 & n. 2; 4/47; Jermyn and Rawlins, 3/170-1 & nn.; P fears challenge from Holmes, 4/83-4; Seymour and Commissioner Pett (challenge), 7/212 & n. 1; Spragge and Commissioner Pett (challenge), ib.; Ossory and Buckingham (challenge), 7/343 & n. 3, 350; Holmes and Smith, 7/348; Porter and Belasyse, 8/363-4 & n., 377, 384; Buckingham and Shrewsbury, 9/26-7 & nn.; Halifax or Coventry and Buckingham (rumoured challenge), 9/462; Leijonbergh and P (challenge, 1670), 8/22, n. 1; also, 3/53; 4/47; 7/376; 8/173

HIGHWAY ROBBERY: 3/34 & n. 2

RIOTS AND DISORDERS [for seamen's mutinies, see Navy: seamen]: by apprentices, 1/39 & n. 1, 54; 5/99-100 & n.; in churches, 3/178 & n. 2; 9/96 & n. 1; by seamen, 4/292 & n. 2, 294; 6/255, 288 & n. 5, 303; 7/330 & n. 3, 415-16; 8/60 & n. 1, 62-3, 272; fanatics, 6/184 & n. 3; in inns of court, 8/223 & n. 3; 9/465-6 & n.; by mob: for recall of parliament, 8/268; against Clarendon, 8/269 & n. 2; for 'Reformation and Reducement', 9/129-34 passim & nn., 152; ~ in Paris, 8/299-300 & nn.

LAWES, Henry, composer (d. 1662) [see also Musical Compositions]: ill, 1/324

LAWES, William, composer, brother of Henry (d. 1645): see Musical Compositions

LAWRENCE, Goody, P's nurse: house at Kingsland, 5/132

LAWRENCE, [Henry], merchant: to go to Algiers, 1/321 & n. 2

LAWRENCE, Sir John, Lord Mayor 1664-5: gives dinner, 6/126; ~ his father [Abraham], ib.

LAWRENCE, [Samuel]: 4/265; ~ his wife, ib.

LAWSON, [Abigail], daughter of Sir John: her funeral, 2/131-2 & n.

LAWSON, [Isabella], wife of Sir John: at Penn's, 4/23; 5/6, 7; also, 7/264

LAWSON, [Isabella], daughter of Sir John: see Norton

LAWSON, Sir John, kted 1660, naval commander (in 1660 'the Vice-Admiral') and member of the Tangier Committee:
CHARACTER: 1/106, 159; 4/12, 24, 376; 6/138; 7/195; ~ cartoon, 1/45
NAVAL CAREER: under Commonwealth, 1/1, 62, 79 & n. 1; 4/375; 8/125; relations with Sandwich, 1/95, 98, 107; 3/121-2 & n.; agrees to serve King, 1/100, 130; commissioned, 1/110; knighted, 1/254; voyages to N. Africa, 3/79 & n. 2, 89, 121, 263 & n. 4, 271; 4/3-4 & n., 6, 73, 369 & n. 2, 415 & n. 1; 5/141 & n. 4, 295, 299; accounts etc., 4/12, 104, 325, 414-15; his ship blown up, 6/52 & n. 1; wounded in action, 6/122, 129; death, 6/131, 132, 138; funeral, 6/145; family impoverished, 6/150-1; alleged plundering, 6/276; also, 1/249; 4/73; 5/15, 17; 6/10, 11; 7/227 & n. 2
TANGIER BUSINESS: proposals for construction of mole, 4/13, 26-7, 31, 35-6; contract signed, 4/88 & n. 3; new proposals opposed, 5/303, 343; profits, 6/71, 101, 103; 8/593; attends meetings, 4/23; 5/11; 6/61; also, 6/39
SOCIAL: 1/114, 115, 167, 317; 2/66; 4/23, 53; 5/6
ALLUDED TO: 1/134, 153, 159
~ his daughters, 6/150

LAWSON, [?Samuel, son of Sir John]: 6/100-1 & n., 185

LENTHROPP: *see* Leventhorpe

LEONARD, [John], under-clerk to the Council of State: 1/49

LEOPOLD I, Holy Roman Emperor 1658–1705: under Jesuit influence, 4/350 & n. 2; persecution of Protestants, 4/372 & n. 2; Louis XIV's friendly offers, 4/349 & n. 3; 8/107 & n. 2; victory over Turks, 5/236–7 & n., 247

LE SQUIRE, Scipio, Vice-Chamberlain of the Receipt in the Exchequer: P hopes for his place, 1/80 & n. 2

L'ESTRANGE, Roger, kted 1685, journalist: *Intelligencer*, 4/297 & n. 2; fine manners, 5/348; P to provide news, ib. & n. 1; account of Battle of Lowestoft, 6/128, 135 & nn.

LETHIEULLIER, [Anne], wife of John: P admires, 6/316, 328, 338, 339; 7/35, 41, 322

LETHIEULLIER, [John], merchant, kted 1674: 6/328; 7/41

LEVANT (Turkey) Company: convoy, 6/10–12; export of cloth, 6/11–12 & n.; to transport troops to Tangier, 6/20; also, 3/259–60

LEVENTHORPE, Sir Thomas Bt (d. 1679): on *Naseby*, 1/130 & n. 3

LEVER, family of: at Great Lever Hall, Lancs., 3/254

LEVER, [William], Purser-General: gift to EP, 5/316–17; P's 'disservice', 5/317

LEVITT, [William], cook: 9/116

LEWIN (Luein), [?John], of the King's Lifeguard: at P's stone feast, 3/53; also, 3/78

LEWIS (Lewes), Sir John, merchant: 3/50

[LEWIS, John], pilot: negligence, 3/213 & n. 1

LEWIS, [?John], cook: 9/116

LEWIS, [Thomas], clerk, Victualling Office: Chatham Chest (memorandum), 3/130; navy victualling, 3/135; 4/322; 6/325; 7/259, 262, 265; Tangier victualling, 5/210; 6/207; Batten's accounts, 8/561; prize business, 8/582, 584; instructs P in pursers' accounts, 3/181, 195; 4/28; unspecified business, 8/483; news from, 8/267, 475; social: 2/60; 8/180; ~ his daughter, 6/225

LEWIS, Ald. [Thomas], merchant: 3/50

LEWIS, [William], prebendary of Winchester (d. 1667): inaudible sermon, 4/63 & n. 1

LEY, James, 3rd Earl of Marlborough, Governor of Bombay and naval officer: P's regard, 5/30; surrender of Bombay, 4/139; stories of India, 5/30; in government's dispute with E. India Company, 5/76, 230; killed in action, 6/122; funeral, 6/127 & n. 3

LEYCESTER, 'Peter' [Ralph], antiquary (d. 1777): letter about P's diary (1728), vol. i, pp. lxxiii, lxxiv

LEYDEN: 1/148

LIDCOTT, Capt. [Robert], republican army officer: 1/45 & n. 3

LIDDELL, Sir Thomas: 7/142

LIGHTHOUSES: at mouth of Humber, 2/41 & n. 2, 44; at Harwich, 5/314; 6/3 & n. 4

LIGNE, Claude Lamoral, Prince de, Spanish ambassador-extraordinary 1660: arrival, 1/237 & n. 1, 247; departure, 1/260; ~ his sister, 2/38 & n.1

LILLY, [William], astrologer (d. 1681) [*see also* Books]: his astrology criticised by Booker, 1/274 & n. 3; laughed at by P, 8/270 & n. 2; his club, 1/274; social: 1/198–9

LILLY, ——, varnisher: death, 9/534; ~ his wife and brother, 9/534, 538

LILLY: *see* Lely

LIMEHOUSE: P visits, 2/198; 4/287; 5/265; 6/34; floods, 1/95 & n. 2; project for dock, 2/198; herring-boats built, 3/274; ropeyards, 5/265; 6/34

LIME ST: robbery, 5/8–9 & n.; execution, 5/23 & n. 2

LINCOLN, Will, of Cow Lane: hires coach and horses to P, 8/460, 464

LINCOLNSHIRE: magistrate imprisoned, 8/252 & n. 2

LINCOLN'S INN: Christmas revels, 3/2; new garden, 4/201 & n. 3; chapel, ib.

LINCOLN'S INN FIELDS/WALKS [*see also* Taverns etc.: Blue Balls]: P/EP walk(s) in, 1/173; 2/177; 3/112; 4/34, 297; 7/423; 8/422; improved, 4/297; coachhouses, 8/224, 225; riot, 9/129

LINCOLN'S INN FIELDS THEATRE [see also Theatres]: Davenant buried from, 9/158 & n. 2
LION QUAY: 4/273
LIPHOOK, Hants.: 9/274
LISBON: dirt and poverty, 2/197 & n. 1; Sandwich's prints, 4/286 & n. 1; Sandwich at, 2/186, 209; 3/51; Spanish fleet off, 3/110; Stayner's death, 3/249 & n. 1; also, 8/374-5 & n.
[LISLE, Thomas], Master of the Barber-Surgeons' Company: at anatomy lecture, 4/59 & n. 1
LISOLA, Franz Paul de, Imperial Resident 1666-7, 1667-8 [see also Books]: at theatre, 8/383-4 & n.; ~ his wife and pretty daughter [Eleanora], ib.
LISSON GREEN, Mdx: P visits, 1/210; 7/204-5, 240
LITTLECOTE HOUSE, Wilts.: P admires, 9/241-2 & n.
LITTLE SAXHAM, Suff.: King at, 9/336 & n. 4
LITTLETON, [James], merchant: victualling contract, 9/287 & n. 1; appointed cashier to Navy Treasurer, 9/357 & n. 2
LITTLETON, Sir Thomas, M.P. Much Wenlock, Salop 1661-79; Joint-Treasurer of the Navy 1668-71: his conversation, 7/210 & n. 1; on commission of accounts, 8/194, 252; opposes standing army, 8/353; to undertake parliamentary management, 9/71 & n. 2; criticises Navy Board, 9/103-4; appointed Joint-Treasurer, 9/341, 346, 351; claims precedence at office table, 9/365; overbearing, 9/412; critical of Board's constitution, 9/550; Duke of York distrusts, 9/408, 410, 507; at dockyard pay, 9/412, 419; navy estimates and debts, 9/444-5, 447, 493-4, 525; supports Child as Penn's successor, 9/549-50; attends meetings, 9/357, 369, 383, 393
LITTLE TOWER HILL: 4/55
LITTLE TURNSTILE (off Holborn): 9/435
LLEWELLYN, [Peter], clerk to E. Dering, timber merchant: dismissed

from underclerkship to Council, 1/23; on *Naseby*, 1/111, 114; returns from Ireland, 4/295 & n. 2; Irish news from, ib.; Dering's business, 4/422, 436; 5/1, 2, 5; 6/185, 242, 245; dies in Plague, 6/304; social: in mock marriage, 1/175; drunk and amorous, 1/244; bawdy story, 2/43, 50; at Bartholomew Fair, 2/166; in Hyde Park, 3/78; at taverns/cookshops etc., 1/25, 27, 31, 37, 38, 87, 92, 174, 195, 208, 212, 232, 233, 248, 257, 311; 2/193; 5/330; visits/dines with P, 2/39, 201; 3/48; 4/326, 415, 421; 5/7, 26, 78, 106, 270, 281, 294, 308, 351; 6/38, 65, 98; also, 1/26, 59, 86; 2/42, 125, 208; alluded to: 1/116; ~ his brother to go to Constantinople, 1/250
LLOYD, Sir Godfrey, military engineer: on fortifications, 8/126 & n. 2
LLOYD, [Philip], clerk to Sir W. Coventry, kted 1674: dances, 7/362; ?9/128; dismissed for idleness, 8/206
LLOYD (Floyd), Sir Richard, M.P. Radnorshire: 4/77
LLOYD, [Thomas], secretary to the Prize Commissioners: 8/58
LLOYD (Floyd), [William], chaplain to the King 1666, Bishop of St Asaph 1680; Lichfield and Coventry 1692; Worcester 1700 (d. 1717) [see also Books]: sermons, 7/382-3; 8/587 & n. 3; also, 8/541 & n. 1
LLOYD (Floyd), ——, captain of merchantman: 5/30
LOCK(E), Matthew, composer (d. 1677) [see also Music; Musical Compositions]: sings with P, 1/63
LOCK, [Matthew], secretary to Albemarle: political news from, 1/50-1; exorbitant fees, 6/260; 7/323-4 & n.
[LOCKETT, Adam]: see Taverns etc.
[LOCKHART, Sir William], Governor of Dunkirk 1658-60 (d. 1676): 5/62 & n. 2
LODUM, Mrs ——: B. St Michel's landlady, 3/286; niece to be EP's companion, 4/19, 21; social: 4/45
LOGGIN(G)S, [John], chorister Chapel Royal: 8/393-4 & n.
LOMBARD (Lumber) ST [see also

9/531–2 & n.; Parish Clerks': P dines with, 1/19; Skinners': entertains Monck, 1/106; liverymen, 4/21; Watermen's: 3/196 & n. 4; Woodmongers': surrenders charter, 8/520 & n. 4

LONDON BRIDGE: piles for, 5/188; P falls into hole, 5/307; pavers at work, 6/312; pales blown off, 7/22; difficulty of passage through: anecdote of Frenchman's fear, 3/160; tides, 3/52; 6/143, 327; 8/202; also, 1/323; 2/59, 101; 3/68, 198, 260; P shoots at night, 6/143, 156

LONDON GAZETTE, the: see Newspapers

LONDON WALL: Plague, 6/150; P drives by to avoid ruins after Fire, 7/358, 364, 395; 8/448, 451, 458, 459; 9/55, 134, 172; ruins in, 8/6

LONG, [?Israel], attorney: in Field's case, 4/201

LONG, Sir Robert, Auditor of the Receipt at the Exchequer: financial business, 4/81; 6/95, 96; 7/76, 79, 137; 8/102, 205, 576; 9/302, 387; defends Additional Aid, 6/311, 312; submits poll tax accounts, 9/82; story of battue, 7/79; house at Westminster, 4/272; and in Surrey, 6/312 & n. 2; ~ his niece, 4/272; kinswomen, 6/312

LONG ACRE: brothels, 5/50

LONG LANE: Plague, 6/150

LONGRACK, [John], purveyor of timber to the navy: wedding reception, 7/262–3

LONG REACH (in the Thames): 1/95; 7/149

LOOKER, Mr ——, gardener to the Earl of Salisbury: bawdy story, 1/59; shows P Hatfield House and garden, 2/139

LOOSDUINEN, Holland: described, 1/149; monument to 365 children, 1/148–9 & n.

LOOTEN, Jan, landscape-painter (d. ?1681): 9/514 & n. 2

LORIMERS' HALL: funeral, 9/200 & n. 2

LOTTERIES: at court, 5/214–15 & n.; management by Fishery Corporation, 5/269 & n., 276, 279, 294, 299–300 & n., 323; 6/53; Virginia lottery

alluded to, 5/323; P wins books, 7/48 & n. 1

LOUD, ——, page to Sandwich: examined by P in Latin, 1/312; also, 1/300; 2/15, 17; ~ his mother, 1/312

LOUIS XIV, King of France 1643–1715 [for his public policy, *see* France]: admiration for Mazarin, 4/26 & n. 2; love of work, ib.; illness, 4/156–7 & n., 159, 162, 163, 166, 169, 189; reviews guards, 4/189; rumoured assassination, 6/257, 259; shoots partridges, 7/79; his attitude to mistresses, 8/183 & n. 2; gift to Frances Stuart, 8/184 & n. 1; association with Elizabeth Berkeley, 8/338 & n. 1; prints of, 9/427 & n. 1, 451 & n. 1

LOVE, Ald. William: elected M.P. for London, 2/57 & n. 1

LOVELACE, Col. [Francis], of Cannon Row: P consults on tax assessment, 3/285 & n. 1

LOVELL (Loven), [?Charles], lawyer: P consults, 4/22, 33

LOVETT, ——, varnisher: pleasant, 7/124; lazy rogue, 7/258; 8/124, 206; new varnish, 6/97; varnishes paper for P, 6/97; 7/119–20, 124, 130, 184, 198–9, 211, 232, 353; P dissatisfied, 7/151, 258; imitation tortoise-shell, 7/184–5; varnishes prints, 7/185, 409; 8/23, 171, 204, 206; of crucifixion, 7/211, 218, 353; and of St Clara, 7/409; P godfather at son's (Catholic) christening, 7/329; to go to Spain, 8/23; social: 7/134

LOVETT, ——, wife of the varnisher: P admires, 6/97; 7/120, 134, 329; works with husband, 7/130, 198; 8/124; plays lute, 7/134, 199

LOWDER: *see* Lowther

[LOWE, Timothy], of Greenwich: 4/283; 6/242 & n. 1

LOWER (Lowre), [Richard], physician: at dissection of eyes, 9/254–5

LOWESTOFT (Lastoffe): 6/130

LOWESTOFT, BATTLE OF: *see* War, the Second Dutch: naval movements and actions (1665)

[LOWMAN, John], keeper of the White Lion prison: 8/81 & n. 5

LOWTHER (Lowder), Anthony:

Marquess of Antrim, Irish royalist (d. 1682): dispute over his estates, 5/57–8 & nn.

MACE: *see* Maes

MACHINES: *see* Inventions and Machines

MACKWORTH, Mr ——: 1/297; 2/119

MACNACHAN, Col. [Alexander]: 9/534 & n. 2

MADDEN, [John], Surveyor of the Woods south of Trent: 7/263; 8/191; ~ his wife, 7/263

MADDOX, Robert, clerk, Navy Office: 4/226

MADEIRA (Maderas): ships to, 3/47, 51; convoy, 7/316

MADEMOISELLE, governess to Sandwich's daughters: *see* Le Blanc

MADGE, [Humphrey], court musician: sings, 1/10; 3/287; 4/428; recommends singing teacher to P, 2/126 & n. 2; defends English music, 2/150; social: 1/85, 223

MAES (Mace, Mawes), [Iudoco], merchant: in customs dispute, 5/38, 43 & n. 3, 50, 147; Carteret consulted, 5/54–5, 76; escapes arrest, 5/72 & n. 1; case discussed by Privy Council committee, 5/251 & n. 3; social: 5/47, 53, 75, 191

MAGIC: *see* Popular Beliefs etc.

MAGNA CARTA: invoked by Sir H. Vane, jun., 3/109; disregarded by Chief Justice Kelyng, 8/577

MAIDENHEAD, Berks.: P at, 9/234

MAIDSTONE, Kent: assizes, 3/137; P visits, 9/495–6 & nn.; Bell inn, 9/496 & n. 2

MAITLAND, John, 2nd Earl of Lauderdale, cr. Duke 1672; Secretary for Scottish affairs: on *Naseby*, 1/133; hostile to Clarendon, 5/34, 57; influence with King, 5/56, 57 & n. 1, 73; cunning, 5/73; Navy Office business, 7/224; house at Highgate, 7/224–5 & n.; on music, 7/225; belittles Pentland Rising, 7/384; at theatre, 8/196; at Council committee, 8/278; also, 7/220; social: 1/325; 3/241; ~ his wife [Anne], 7/224

MALAGA (Malago), Spain: fleet at, 7/45; alluded to: 6/14

MALET, [Elizabeth]: abducted by Rochester, 6/110 & n. 2; Hinchingbrooke's proposed match, 6/110 & n. 4, 119, 193 & n. 2; 7/56, 260; suitors, 7/385; 8/45; marries Rochester, 8/44 & n. 4

MALLARD, (Maylard, Maylord), [Thomas], musician: plays viol, 1/8 & n. 3, 11; 3/287; 5/25, 64; sets tune for P, 5/18; accompanies Sandwich to Portugal, 3/112 & n. 1; also, 4/428; social: 1/19, 24, 272; alluded to: 4/261; 5/349

[MALYN, Thomas], city Waterbailiff: 6/43 & n. 1

MAN, [William], City Swordbearer: emissary to Monck, 1/1; offers £1000 for Clerkship of Acts, 1/210, 216, 219

MANCHESTER, Lord: *see* Mountagu, Edward, 2nd Earl of Manchester

MANDEVILLE, Lord: *see* Mountagu, Robert

MANLEY, Maj. [John]: 9/497; ~ his wife and daughter-in-law, ib.

[MANNING, Edward], City Remembrancer 1665–6: 7/187 & n. 4

MANSELL [Francis]: pension, 8/74 & also, 1/111 & n. 3, 256

MANUEL, Mrs ——: formerly actress, 8/384; P admires her singing, 8/384, 599; 9/128; social: 9/134, 172, 219; alluded to: 9/156; ~ her husband, 9/134, 172

MAPLESDEN, [Gervase], timber merchant: gifts to P, 4/361 & n. 1

MAPS [*see also* Books]: P examines at Cade's, 3/1; at Dutch shops, 4/350; his maps of Paris, 4/320; 9/286 & n. 1; and of Brest, 9/437; buys books of maps of cities, 5/55; his collection, 7/111, 124, 258, 290; his sea-charts, 7/290, 292; at Navy Office: Northern Seas, 4/390; Tangier, by J. Moore, 5/98 & n. 2; Deptford, 6/111 & n. 5, 144; elsewhere: Portsmouth by Sandwich, 6/38, 46, 49, 50(2); city of London by Hollar, 7/378–9 & n.; Paris by Gomboust, 7/379 & n.; England and Wales by Hollar, 8/255 & n. 2

MARDYCK, Flanders: demolition of fort, 1/250 & n. 2; siege (1657–8), 9/6 & n. 2

MARESCOE, (Morisco), [Charles],

merchant: 6/166 & n. 3

MARGATE (Margetts), Kent [*see also* Drink: ale]: Princess Mary at, 1/252; Dutch fleet off, 6/8, 268

MARGETTS, [George], rope merchant, Limehouse: 5/265 & n. 1

MARGETTS, ——, merchant, of Fenchurch St: 9/518

MARGUERITE de Valois, Queen of Navarre (d. 1549): 9/31 & n. 2

[MARIA-ANNA], Queen Regent of Portugal 1665–75: Duke of York's letter to, 8/452 & n. 1

[MARIA-TERESA], Queen of France, wife of Louis XIV (d. 1683): 4/189; 8/254

MARIUS, Gaius (186–57 B.C.): alluded to in sermon, 5/97

MARKHAM, [?George, ?William], kinsman of Sir W. Penn: marriage, 7/235

MARKHAM, Nan (b. Wright), maid to Lady Penn: marriage, 7/235; P kisses, 7/418; 9/177; allegedly Penn's mistress, 8/322; in Navy Board pew, 8/322, 437; pregnant, 8/371; social: 7/246, 249, 280, 353, 422; 8/29, 274, 284; 9/312, 314

MARK LANE: Fire, 7/268, 276; effigy hanged, 8/89

MARLBOROUGH, Wilts.: P visits, 9/241 & nn.

MARLOW, [Thomas], Navy Office messenger: 6/226, 244; 8/538

MARR(E), Mr ——: at Dagenhams, Essex, 6/180; 7/17

MARRIAGE:

GENERAL: 'fools decoyed into', 6/339; special licence, 9/493; divorce, 2/6 & n. 2

MARRIAGE SETTLEMENTS [asterisks denote entries at which amounts of portions etc. are given]: 2/159*, 242*; 3/3*, 176* & n. 1, 226, 228*, 231* & n. 1, 232*; 4/19*, 159*, 345*; 6/138* & n. 1, 150*, 180* & n. 3, 191* & n. 4, 252*; 7/15*, 73*, 78*, 81*, 88–9*, 104*, 170* & n. 1, 241*, 264*; 8/63*, 118*, 190*, 217*, 300* & n. 2, 365*, 539*; 9/16–17, 51* & n. 4, 55, 56* & n. 5, 61* & n. 1, 97*, 157, 170*

WEDDING CEREMONIES: posy ring, 1/39–40; bridemen, 4/345; 9/500; dinner,

7/262–3; untying ribbons etc., 2/23; 3/22; flinging stockings, 4/38; sackposset, ib.; putting to bed, 6/176; 9/51; music on morning after, 8/66; favours/gifts to guests, 4/218; 8/73, 77, 79; 9/28, 335; mock weddings, 1/27; 4/37–8

WEDDING (P) [*see also* Pepys, Samuel: marriage etc.]: anniversary, 2/194; 6/262; forgets it, 5/294; unsure of number of years of marriage, 7/318

MARRIOT(T), [Benjamin], attorney: the great eater, 1/40–1 & n.

MARRIOTT, [James], housekeeper, Hampton Court: 6/166

MARRIOTT, [Richard], housekeeper, Hampton Court: 3/82 & n. 1

MARROWBONE: *see* Marylebone

MARSEILLES: 8/421

MARSH, [Alphonso], court musician: 2/158 & n. 3; ~ his wife, ib.

MARSH, [George], son of Capt. Richard: 3/72

MARSH, Capt. [Richard], Storekeeper, Ordnance Office, the Tower: house at Limehouse, 2/198; also, 3/72; 91; 4/28; 5/215

MARSH, Thomas, Clerk Assistant, the House of Commons: 4/281

MARSH, [James], cook, Whitehall: P visits, 1/23, 25, 27, 61, 64–5, 87, 92

MARSHALL, Anne (Nan), actress: P admires in *The Indian queen*, 5/33–4 & n.; and criticises, 9/250; alleged parentage, 8/502–3 & n.

MARSHALL, Rebecca, actress: her good looks, 8/433; 9/189; alleged parentage, 8/502–3 & n.; P admires in *The maid's tragedy*, 7/399 & n. 2; *The maiden queen*, 8/235 & n. 2; *The virgin martyr*, 9/93–4 & n.; *Hyde Park*, 9/260; also, 9/156

MARSHALL, Stephen, Presbyterian divine (d. 1655): sermons, 4/111 & n. 4; also, 8/502–3 & n.

MARSHALL, ——, timber merchant: 3/169

MARTIN, Betty (b. Lane), wife of Samuel; linendraper in Westminster Hall and P's mistress:

P'S LOW OPINION: 5/216–17; 8/167, 375–6; 9/552

CHRON. SERIES: sells goods to P, 1/214,

MATTHEWS, Capt. Richard: 1/33 &
n. 3, 88, 163
MATTHEWS, ——, prize fighter:
4/167
MAULEVERER, Sir R[ichard]: joins
King at Breda, 1/117 & n. 1
MAWES: *see* Maes
MAY, Adrian, Groom of the Privy
Chamber to the King: 6/265
MAY, Baptist (Bab), Keeper of the
Privy Purse to the King: news from,
6/121; defeated in parliamentary
election, 7/337 & n. 2; profits, 8/324 &
n. 4; on country gentlemen, ib.,
8/361; supports H. Brouncker, 8/416;
plays tennis, 8/418–19; enemy of
Clarendon, 8/525; alluded to: 8/366,
412; 9/336–7
MAY, Hugh, Paymaster of the King's
Works: P's regard for, 6/200; 9/269;
on garden design, 7/213; on rebuilding of city, 7/384–5; 8/33; his new
buildings at Whitehall, 8/417 & n. 2;
9/251 & n. 4, 269 & n. 3; to examine
P's office papers, 9/417–18, 436; relations with Buckingham, 9/491 & n. 2;
pension, 9/491–2 & n.; social: 9/518,
527–8, 557–8
MAY, ——, landlady of Rochester
tavern: a bawdy jade, 8/312
MAY DAY: maypoles: 1/121, n. 1; at
Deal, ib. (2); The Hague, 1/139 &
n. 3; in Strand, ?8/206; coach parade
in Hyde Park, 1/121 & n. 1; 2/91;
4/119–20; 5/139; 8/196–7; 9/182, 537,
540–1; morris-dancing, 4/120; milkmaids dance, 8/193 & n. 2
MAY-DEW, as face lotion: 8/240;
9/549, 551
MAYER(S), [Robert], purveyor of
timber to the Navy, Woolwich:
4/103 & n. 4, 381
MAYLARD, Maylord: *see* Mallard
MAYNARD, Sir John, King's Serjeant: unpopularity, 2/88 & n. 1;
arbiter in dispute, 4/203; asks Backwell for loan, 8/528–9; ~ his wife
[Jane] dies, 9/141
[MAYNE, Jasper], Canon of Christ
Church, Oxford [*see also* Plays]:
preaches before King on adultery,
3/60 & n. 2
MAZARIN, Jules, Cardinal, French

minister: death, 2/48 & n. 5; influence
on Louis XIV, 4/26 & n. 2; Bristol's
falsity to, 4/212–13 & nn.; will,
4/411–12 & n.
MEADE, ——: 1/219
MEDALS [*see also* Coinage]: of Charles
X of Sweden, 1/238 & n. 1; 2/49;
Breda medal, 8/83 & n. 1
MEDICI, Cosimo de', Grand Duke of
Tuscany (Cosimo III) 1670–1723:
visits London, 9/509 & n. 2, 526, 534;
appearance, 9/509, 515; in mourning,
9/515 & n. 3, 563; firework display
for, 9/563
MEDICINE: *see* Health (illness etc.);
Health (remedies etc.)
MEDITERRANEAN, the (the Straits):
(royal) ships for/from, 1/119 & n. 3,
234; 2/214, 219; 6/192, 286; 7/143;
9/473 & n. 4, 513, 552; piracy, 3/13;
5/41–2 & n., 49; 6/10, 111; 9/724;
Dutch fleet, 6/8, 11; rumours of de
Ruyter in, 5/121, 309, 354; French
enforce salute, 6/278 & n. 3; 9/560 & n. 2
MEDOWS, Mr ——, servant to Lady
Wright: 6/161
MEDWAY, the, Kent: P and colleagues sail up, 6/194; P enjoys views,
9/495; 'land-admiral' in, 8/149; defences: installed, 8/84, 125, 126;
broken by Dutch, 8/260–2 *passim*,
268–9, 310; examined by P, 8/308,
309, 314; alluded to, 8/278, 327; new
defences, 9/57
MEGGOT (Maggett), [Richard], Rector of St Olave, Southwark: his
preaching, 5/356 & n. 2
[MEGGS, Mary], 'Orange Mall' of the
Theatre Royal: theatre news from,
7/264 & n. 3; 8/402; carries messages,
8/395, 598–9; saves theatre-goer from
choking, 8/517
[MELLO, Francesco, Marquez de
Sande de], Portuguese ambassador:
returns to Portugal, 2/128–9 & n.;
ambassador to Holland, 8/251 & n. 3
[MELLO DE CASTRO, D. Antonio
de], Governor of Bombay: refuses to
surrender, 4/139 & n. 2
MEMORY, the faculty of: Tom
Fuller's remarkable gift, 2/21 & n. 2;
also, 5/12
MENDICANCY: beggars near Roth-

erhithe, 4/296; increase after Plague, 7/3; at Bishop's Stortford and Cambridge, 8/469; P gives to, 9/227–8
MENNES (Mince, Minnes), Sir John, Comptroller of the Navy 1661–71, and naval commander:
CHARACTER: fine gentleman and good scholar, 2/210; good company, 3/112; 4/67, 196, 346; 5/227; 8/95; honest, 7/255; P criticises, 5/118, 120, 121; foolish/inefficient/senile, 4/67, 97, 98, 104, 151, 152, 233, 324–5; 5/67–8, 80, 182, 318, 322, 326; 6/226, 228, 309; 7/76, 235, 300, 305–6; 8/12, 550; 9/384, 393, 408, 501; criticised by Sandwich, 3/122–3; 4/196; Coventry, 4/97, 196, 341; 5/218, 313–14; 7/235, 302, 308, 310, 409, 413; 8/570, 571; Commissioner Pett, 4/98; and Brouncker, 6/237
AS COMPTROLLER:
APPOINTMENT ETC.: appointed, 2/206 & n. 4; loses right to draft contracts, 3/99–100 & n.; assistants proposed for, 3/236–7 & n.; 4/61 & n. 1, 66, 67, 71, 75, 397–8; 5/15; 7/421; Brouncker and Penn to assist, 8/20 & n. 2, 24, 25, 30, 38; desires place in Prize Office, 5/328; objects to arrangements for tickets, 9/383; rumoured dismissal/resignation, 7/321, 324, 328, 361, 380; 8/586; 9/100, 337, 386, 555; dismissal recommended, 9/131, 151, 205–6, 400
FINANCIAL BUSINESS: estimates etc.: 5/325, 326; 6/72; 7/48, 311–12; 8/140; 9/80, 174, 220, 444–5; at pays, 3/193, 215, 225, 234, 289, 290; 4/175, 219, 222, 225, 253, 291–2; 7/133, 253, 327, 339; 8/114, 257; works on accounts: Creed's, 3/278–9; 4/215–16; Navy Treasurer's, 3/240; 5/104, 105; 7/305–6; 9/222; R. Cocke's, 4/290 & n. 3, 325 & n. 2; Warren's, 8/550; his carelessness, 4/11; 6/119: 9/394; on commanders' pay, 4/7; investigates Exchequer methods, 5/7(2); and new method of paying bills, 6/336 & n. 2; makes proposals about storekeepers' accounts, 9/444
DOCKYARD BUSINESS (other than pays): visits, 3/205, 280; 4/12, 67, 203–4, 284, 317–18, 389; 5/39; 6/83, 171; 8/95;

launch, 4/102; sale of provisions, 4/319; survey, 5/35; mast-dock, 5/202, 353; 6/96
THE PRIZE-GOODS AFFAIR: responsibility for captured E. Indiamen, 6/234, 236, 242, 262, 273, 280, 286; complains of pillage, 6/249; examines Howe, 6/333–4; allowance, 8/446
OTHER BUSINESS: Field's case, 4/51, 52, 54, 71; slops, 4/74; victualling, 4/84; shipping, 4/204, 227; 6/193–4, 226, 228; 9/251; seamen's riot, 4/294, 295; contracts, 4/326, 380–1, 421; 5/318; 6/38; 7/2; 9/542; burning of figurehead, 4/318, 420; Clarendon's timber, 5/205, 218; gun-wadding, 5/316; wreck, 6/54; Board's Greenwich offices, 6/200, 201; Plague at Greenwich, 6/211; Carkesse case, 8/76, 83, 204(2), 213, 215, 386; Dutch raid on Medway, 8/259, 268, 272, 394; defence of office against parliamentary charges, 8/504; 9/80, 103; Duke of York's proposed reforms, 9/305, 525; also, 6/126–7; 9/327; unspecified: 3/106, 201, 203, 229, 236–7, 252, 265, 272; 4/4, 12, 21, 31, 43, 50, 69, 81, 91, 97, 106, 110, 152, 154, 177, 178, 213, 226, 234, 241, 243, 278, 296, 332, 338, 435; 5/98, 138, 156–7, 157, 228, 241–2, 286, 303, 318, 333, 349; 6/39, 140, 145(2), 203, 222, 233, 334, 339; 7/13, 18, 26, 50, 419; 8/62, 178, 198, 346, 403, 413, 565; 9/5, 156, 251, 267, 315, 316, 428, 508
RELATIONS WITH COLLEAGUES AND OTHERS: failure to collaborate, 5/235; enmity to Commissioner Pett, 3/227; 4/91, 228; 6/104; and to P, 4/161; criticises him for neglect of business, 6/92; supports, 5/238; subservient to Batten, 4/194, 205, 436; 5/108; quarrels with, 5/293; complains of Hayter, 4/97, 100; unjust to Steventon, 4/151; accuses Hewer of fraud, 4/152
AS NAVAL COMMANDER: appointed Vice-Admiral, 2/70 & n. 5; salary, 4/325; on flag honour, 2/229; 3/4, 14; at Council of War, 3/124; reminiscences, 3/252; 4/124 & n. 1; 6/127 & n. 1; enmity to Sandwich, 2/169, 216–17, 229; 3/123
OTHER APPOINTMENTS: Master of

Trinity House, 3/93; 4/185; dines at, 3/190; 4/209; 7/381–2; on Chatham Chest Commission, 3/257; 6/68; Tangier Committee, 3/272; 4/319; 6/139; 9/316; and Royal Fishery, 5/199

HEALTH: lame, 4/314; 8/4; seriously ill, 7/253, 255(2), 261, 289; 8/296, 298, 314, 315, 324; also, 4/120; 5/268; 6/21, 23; 7/405; 9/276

HOUSE/HOUSEHOLD: official lodgings at Seething Lane: upper room used by P, 3/38; to exchange lodgings with Turner, 3/111; affected by P's alterations, 3/193, 194, 195, 197, 199, 205, 216, 231, 244, 252, 255, 261; 5/356; P admires, 3/262; new entry, 3/247, 249, 250; complains of accommodation, 5/278 & n. 3; lodgings at Greenwich: 6/190; leaves Turner's lodgings, 7/296; also, 3/259; 4/51, 278; 6/210; 8/552, 555; ~ his servant George, 6/200; coachman, 9/527

INTELLECTUAL INTERESTS ETC.: visits Mint, 4/143–8; quotes Chaucer, 4/184; his pictures, 4/187, 191, 319; views royal collection, 8/403; recites verse, 4/200 & n. 4; interest in chemistry, 4/218; and anatomy, 4/334; prescribes medicines for P, 4/39, 40, 329; medical attendant at court in exile, 5/242 & n. 2; claims to have translated from Dutch, 5/235

POLITICS: opposes test bill, 4/125; friend of Clarendon, 4/196

SOCIAL: his mirth and mimicry, 6/220; 7/1–2; stories: of sanitation in Portugal, 3/205; longevity, 6/237 & n. 3; ancestor's murder, 8/141; and Sir L. Dyve and others, 8/566–7 & nn.; tells bawdy story, 3/243; his stories entered in P's book of anecdotes, 4/346; 8/95; at christenings, 4/165; 8/540; gives dinner for Clarendon, 4/173; at dinners given by Lord Mayor, 4/341; Carteret, 5/15; Coventry, 5/102, 166; Lieutenant of Tower, 6/56; Sir G. Smith, 6/187; Brouncker, 6/204; 7/1–2; Cocke, 6/220; Hickes, 6/222; Sandwich, 6/273; Penn, 8/3, 77; 9/283, 505; and Gauden, 9/214; gives dinners for colleagues and associates, 5/227, 357;

6/191, 237, 333; lends coach to EP, 6/45; his tiff with Battens, 6/233, 234; dines with P, 7/353; at parish dinners, 8/218; 9/179, 559; theatre, 9/269–70; Bartholomew Fair, 9/301; and taverns, 3/279; 5/308; 6/119; 8/220; 9/115, 222, 359; visits/dines with etc. Batten, 3/189; 4/171, 230, 237; 5/216; 6/220–1; 7/226, 8/376; P visits/dines with etc., 4/28; 5/335; 6/206, 210, 212; also, 4/155, 212, 225; 5/176, 217; 6/141; 7/76; 8/389

MISC.: almost drowned near Portsmouth, 3/283–4; praises beauty of Suffolk women, 4/186; on homosexuality, 4/210; on Spanish stamp tax, 7/332; inspects new Exchange Alley, 4/214; King's bawdy joke against, 5/12; Denham's verses on, 8/380 & n. 2; news from Holland, 7/228; 8/88; assessed for poll-tax, 8/120; foundling on doorstep, 9/304

ALLUDED TO: 3/198

~ his sister, 4/74; 6/233; 8/4; niece, 4/74; 8/4; 9/505

MERCER, Anne, Mary's sister: at dances at P's house, 7/230; 8/28, 493, 511; 9/42; runs for wagers, 8/167; also, 7/200, 246; 8/11, 19; 9/12, 96, 111, 197

MERCER, Mary, companion to EP:

CHRON. SERIES: pretty, 5/360; 8/375; growing fat, 8/508; proposed as companion, 5/229 & n. 2, 256 & n. 1; engaged, 5/257, 265, 267; with EP to Woolwich in Plague, 6/143, 183, 340; returns, 7/7; dress, 6/238; helps rule Navy Office books, 7/63, 100; washes P's ears, combs/cuts his hair, 6/21; 7/95; 8/280; quarrels with EP, 6/205, 206; 7/60, 175, 176; EP's jealousy of, 5/274; 7/228, 238; P fondles, 7/104, 172; dismissed by EP, 7/273; P misses her, 7/294; unwilling to return, 7/298–303 passim; visits EP, 7/360; P fondles/kisses again, 7/364; 8/37, 150; 9/55; EP displeased with, 8/79, 118; P's valentine, 9/67; visits Cambridge with EP and others, 9/306; also, 6/25, 66, 85; 7/138; 9/19, 98

MUSICAL: plays harpsichord/viol, 5/266, 282; sings with P/EP/others, 5/266; 6/138; 7/44, 53, 110, 111, 117, 172,

183, 195, 199, 205, 212, 216, 227, 228, 230, 267; 8/37, 165, 174, 223, 283, 289, 328, 375; 9/14, 85, 120, 179, 196, 197, 199, 201, 202, 204, 216, 217, 221, 249; her talent, 7/228; 8/29; P teaches *It is decreed*, 8/35; 9/14, 16; *Canite Jehovae*, 9/194; and the Lark's song, 9/304; her style of singing, 8/165–6
SOCIAL: at theatre, 5/267, 289, 335; 6/73; 7/412; 8/27, 157, 439–40, 508; 9/14, 19, 54, 85, 100, 189, 195, 198–9, 249, 269, 278, 280–1, 296, 304, 326; visits/shopping etc., 5/301; 6/40, 48–9, 87, 89, 102, 104, 121, 128, 223, 250, 251, 270, 282, 320–1; 7/18, 72, 78, 81, 84, 128, 131, 137, 152, 169, 172, 220; 8/431–2; river trips to Gravesend, Woolwich, etc., 5/305; 6/106, 111, 119; 7/142, 233, 235; 8/346; jaunts to Islington, Bow, Hackney, etc., 6/74, 112; 7/54–5, 108, 113, 126, 129, 133, 167, 170, 181–2, 240, 267; 8/150, 174–5, 296; 9/197, 208, 221, 271–2; at Vauxhall, 7/198; 9/195–6, 198–9, 203–4, 216; and Bartholomew Fair, 9/293, 296, 299; dances, 6/262, 279; 7/43–4, 246, 362; 8/29, 493, 511; 9/12, 42, 289; toasted at Bear garden, 7/245–6; visits P's house after leaving household, 7/200, 374, 403, 419, 421; 8/11, 13, 19, 157, 166, 282, 289, 594; 9/111, 213, 244, 250; also, 7/257, 267; 8/165, 167; 9/278
ALLUDED TO: 7/15; 9/454, 519
~ her sisters, 7/230
MERCER, [Nicola], Mary's mother: ends quarrel between EP and Mary, 7/176; annoyed at Mary's dismissal, 7/273, 300, 301; social: gives parties for naval victories, 7/152, 246; also, 5/257; 6/340; 7/43, 101, 200; 9/110, 111, 197, 276; alluded to: 7/175
MERCER, William, Mary's brother: ?provides fireworks for party, 7/152; makes valentine for EP, 8/62
MERCER, [William], Mary's father: 5/265
MERCER, P's: *see* Finch
MERCERS' CHAPEL, Cheapside: P visits, 2/20; in Fire, 7/277
MERCERS' COMPANY: *see* London: livery companies
MERCERS' HALL, Cheapside: P as

schoolboy at, 2/20; Council of Trade meets, ib.
MERCHANT STRANGERS' COMPANY: *see* London: livery companies
MERCHANT TAYLORS' HALL, Threadneedle St: 7/235
MERES, Sir Thomas, M.P. Lincoln: eloquent, 8/2; supports Buckingham, 8/342
MERITON, [John], Rector of St Michael, Cornhill: his high reputation, 7/365 & n. 3; also, 6/152
MERITON, [Thomas], Rector of St Nicholas Cole Abbey: an 'old dunce', 7/365 & n. 3; preaches well, 7/365; 8/222
MERRETT, Christopher, physician: on anatomy, 3/228 & n. 2; at Dr Wilkins's, 7/12; drunk at Royal Society club, 7/21
MERSTON, Messum: *see* Mossom
MERTON PRIORY, Surrey: bought by Thomas P of Hatcham, 9/207 & n. 2
MERVIN, [John], merchant: 6/164
MESSIAH, the false: *see* Sabbatai Zevi
METEORS: *see* Science and Mathematics: astronomy
MEXICO: coinage, 4/146
MEYNELL (Maynall), Ald. Francis, goldsmith-banker; Sheriff 1661–2: entertains P and colleagues, 3/200; income, 4/17; refuses to lend to Navy, 6/121; advances money to victualler, 6/254; death, 7/315; also, 5/33
MICHELANGELO: paintings copied, 3/80 & n. 1
MICO, [Edward], merchant: Dutch compensation to, 5/52 & n. 1
MIDDLEBURG, Holland: 1/137
MIDDLEBURGH, ——, merchant: 4/396
MIDDLEGROUND, the (shoal at mouth of Thames estuary): Dutch fleet in, 8/359
MIDDLESEX, Lord: *see* Sackville, Charles, 1st Earl of Middlesex
MIDDLESEX, Lady: *see* Cranfield
MIDDLE TEMPLE: Readers' Feast, 6/28 & n. 2, 49 & n. 2; gaming in Hall, 9/3 & n. 1; riot, 9/465–6 & n., 511–12
MIDDLETON, Elizabeth/Jane: *see* Myddelton

MIDDLETON, John, 1st Earl of Middleton, soldier and Governor of Tangier 1668–d.74: character, 8/167 & n. 1, 201 & n. 2, 306, 600–1; 9/326, 328, 551; Lauderdale's hostility, 5/57 & n. 1; conduct in Medway raid, 8/306–7, 311; 9/11; Governor of Tangier, 8/167 & n. 1; payment to, 9/294, 325, 328 & n. 3; to go to Tangier, 9/492, 504; favoured by Duke of York, 9/543, 545; asks for loan, 9/534; ~ his servant, 9/326

[MIDDLETON, John], 'the child of Hales', wrestler (d. 1623): 9/226 & n. 3

MIDDLETON, Col. Thomas, Navy Commissioner at Portsmouth 1664, Surveyor of the Navy 1667:

P'S OPINION: 8/462, 582; 9/500

OFFICIAL CAREER: appointed to Portsmouth, 5/314 & n. 2; at pay, 7/75; reports to Board, 7/333; 8/142; appointed Surveyor, 8/462 & n. 3, 575 & n. 1, 582; at launch, 9/100–01; defends master-attendants, 9/267; replies to Duke of York's great letter, 9/314 & n. 1; allegations against Hewer, 9/388 & n. 2, 390–5 passim; criticised about pay, 9/412; on refitting fleet, 9/425–6; proposals about pursers etc., 9/459, 460 & n. 2; assessor at court martial, 9/488–9, 498, 505, 508, 510–11; at Chatham, 9/494, 495, 499; attends meetings/unspecified business, 7/75, 313, 418; 8/594; 9/335, 410, 430; also, 9/525

SOCIAL: his stories of Barbados etc., 8/275; 9/499–500 & n.; at parish dinner, 9/559; also, 5/1; 9/253, 359

MISC.: coach, 9/206; ill, 9/533

~ his wife, [Elizabeth], death of, 9/444, 452

MILDMAY, Sir Henry, regicide (d.? 1664): his sentence, 3/19 & n. 1; house forfeited, 6/102 & n. 4

MILE END/MILE END GREEN [see also Taverns etc.: Gun; Rose and Crown]: P/EP and others at, 5/201; 6/80; 8/389, 393, 398, 399, 419, 424, 443, 485, 500; 9/88, 177, 180, 202, 221, 254, 255; market established at after Fire, 7/280

MILFORD STAIRS: 2/110

MILITIA, the [see also London]: in Yorkshire, 8/154; in Medway raid, 8/308; favoured by country party in parliament, 8/352–3 & n.

MILK HOUSE, the, Hyde Park: P visits, 9/142, ?154, 156, 175, 184, 222, 260, 533–4, 541

MILK ST: 5/122

MILLER, Lt-Col. [John]: holds Tower for Committee of Safety, 1/39 & n. 2

MILLES, [Anna]: christened, 2/192 & n. 3

MILLES, Daniel, Rector of St Olave's, Hart St 1657–89:

CHARACTER: 1/225; 3/134–5; 8/247–8, 564

CHRON. SERIES: adopts Prayer Book service, 1/282, 289; and surplice, 3/213, 235, 247; to begin catechising, 5/49; leaves parish in Plague, 7/35; chaplain to Duke of York and Rector of Wanstead, 8/241 & n. 1, 247–8; also 2/24; 3/81, 104; 5/125; 8/540; 9/325

SERMONS [an asterisk denotes comment by P. See also Sermons (in main series)]: 1/225, 241, 251*, 270*, 308*, 322*; 2/24*, 26*, 42*, 52*, 59*, 67, 112, 161, 210, 225, 238*; 3/12–13*, 20, 104*, 110*, 132*, 178, 247*, 264, 270*; 4/29*, 30*, 177, 268, 369*, 426*, 433*; 5/49, 356*; 6/131*, 132; 7/35* & n. 3, 112*, 283*, 420*, 425*; 8/51*, 91*, 154*, 437, 535*, 557*, 589*; 9/325, 385, 452, 514*, 548*

SOCIAL: first dinner at P's house in five years, 8/437; P's first visit to, 9/220; his story of suicide, 3/239; at parish dinner, 8/218; 9/179; christening, 8/540; and P's house, 9/24, 184, 219, 260, 406; also, 2/28, 131; 3/22; 9/245

MILLES, [Daniel], son of Daniel and Mary: EP godmother, 8/540 & n. 5; P's gift, 8/544

MILLES, [Elizabeth], daughter of Daniel and Mary: christened, 5/265 & n. 3

MILLES, [Mary], wife of Daniel: family connection with Brampton, 2/28; 8/437 & n. 3; at P's house, 2/28; 9/24, 184, 219, 260, 406; alluded to: 9/245; ~ her (unnamed) daughter, 9/219

MILLET, Capt. [Henry]: book of ships' rates, 6/217 & n. 2; evidence against Commissioner Pett, 8/502

MILLICENT, Sir John, of Barham, Cambs: anecdote of, 3/159 & nn.

MINCING (Minchen) Lane: fire, 9/245

MINNES, Mince: see Mennes, Sir John; Myngs, Christopher

MINORIES, the: 4/84, 434; 7/423; 8/224; 9/204

MINORS, Capt. [Richard], naval officer: E. India Company business, 4/299 & n. 2, 396; 9/37

MITCHELL, Mrs [Ann], bookseller in Westminster Hall:

GENERAL: her illegitimate daughter, 5/9; leaves town in Plague, 6/162; kinswoman as maid to EP, 7/108, 109; asks P to help son, 8/341; also, 7/394; 8/72, 202, 479, 583; 9/99

AS BOOKSELLER: P pays, 1/26, 87; buys newspapers from, 6/162; and book, 8/10; reads pamphlets at, 7/393–4; P/EP visit(s), 1/30, 31, 66, 204, 222, 279; 2/31, 139; 3/296; 4/242, 251; 7/61, 123, 186, 295; 8/47, 68, 177, 440; 9/81, 486

~ her daughter, 9/265

MITCHELL, Betty, (b. Howlett), wife of Michael:

CHRON. SERIES: betrothed to Michael's brother, 5/9; 7/75; marries Michael, 7/75, 81; moves to Thames St, 7/98, 108, 114; to Shadwell after Fire, 7/351; unhappily married, 7/284; 8/479; keeps shop for mother, 8/121

P'S FONDNESS FOR: calls her 'wife', 4/234, 242; 7/75, 89; admires, 5/9, 41; 6/330–1; 7/61, 157, 175, 235, 365; 8/20, 21, 47, 51, 91, 121, 138, 159, 224, 236, 273; 9/548–9; mistakes another woman for, 7/303; 8/400; gifts to, 8/46, 53; kisses/fondles, 7/123, 197, 207, 230, 234, 338–9, 395, 419; 8/32, 46, 53, 110, 511; 9/564; she avoids/is cold to, 7/245, 418–19; 8/34, 68, 70, 440; 9/173

SOCIAL: with husband dines at/visits P's house, 7/206–7, 243, 311, 344, 418; 8/5–6, 166, 289, 412–13, 524; 9/255, 276; P visits, 7/255; 8/37, 58, 146, 151; 9/114, 198, 297, 328; at christen-

ing, 7/394; wedding anniversary, 8/72; also, 7/142, 161, 186, 337; 8/45, 66, 255

ALLUDED TO: 8/52, 504, 514; 9/124, 168

~ her first daughter (Betty) born, 8/53, 177, 186, 199–200, 202, 224; baptised, 8/202; dies, 8/273, 277, 289; her second daughter (Betty) born, 9/260, 264; her maid, 8/54

MITCHELL, [John], flagmaker: supplies, 4/73 & n. 2; gift to P, 4/220

MITCHELL, [Michael], keeper of strong-water house:

CHRON. SERIES: marries Betty Howlett, 7/75, 81; succeeds to brother's trade and house, 7/81, 114; P calls there, 7/157, 234–5; 8/20, 32, 34, 37, 58, 66, 94, 102, 120, 151, 175, 186, 199, 224, 504; 9/198, 249, 297; cashes pay tickets, 7/174–5 & n., 319, 338; employed on cork business, 7/206; house burnt in Fire, 7/268; moves to Shadwell, 7/284, 338; new shop, 7/339; house rebuilt, 8/20; 9/75, 114, 124; relations with wife, 7/284; 8/479, 511; prevents P from seeing her, 8/316; 9/173; out of town, 9/564

SOCIAL: on river, 7/161; 8/34, 66, 68; to Hackney, 7/207; at christenings, 7/394; 8/202; wedding anniversary party, 8/72; at P's house, 7/206, 243, 311, 344, 365–6, 418; 8/5–6, 21, 51, 91, 138, 166, 236, 289, 413, 524; 9/255; also, 7/123; 8/493

ALLUDED TO: 9/99, 161

MITCHELL, [Miles], bookseller in Westminster Hall: at coronation banquet, 2/86; leaves town in Plague, 6/162; garden, 7/123; social: 1/204, 222; 8/68, 72, 202; alluded to: 7/308; ~ his (unnamed) son: betrothed to Betty Howlett, 5/9; 7/75; dies of plague, 7/75; ?alluded to, 6/186; another (unnamed) son: 8/341

[MODERS, Mary], 'the German princess': imposter [see also Plays: The German princess]: in prison, 4/163 & n. 4; tried and acquitted, 4/177 & n. 2

MOFFETT (Muffett), [Thomas], physician and author (d. 1604): story of Dr Caius, 8/543 & n. 2

MOHUN (Moone), [Michael], actor: high reputation, 1/297; his part in

Lacy's quarrel with King, 8/168 &
n. 6; quarrels with Hart, 8/569; P
admires in *The beggar's bush*, 1/297 &
n. 3; in *The Traitor*, 1/300 & n. 1;
criticises in *The Moor of Venice*, 9/438
MOHUN (Moone), Capt. [Robert],
naval officer: ship wrecked off Cadiz,
6/19 & n. 3; reputation for ill-luck,
ib. & n. 4, 6/20
[MOLINA, Antonio Francesca Mesia,
de Tobar y Paz, Conde de], Spanish
ambassador 1665–9: 8/107; 9/544
& n.4
MOLINS (Mullins), Edward, surgeon:
leg amputated, 4/340 & n.1; death,
4/345
MOLINS, [James], surgeon: operates
on Rupert, 8/41 & n.2
MONCK, Anne, Duchess of Albemarle:
LOOKS AND CHARACTER (critical comments): 2/51; 6/324; 7/10, 56 & n. 2,
57, 354; 8/147
CHRON. SERIES: trades in appointments,
1/181 & n. 4, 184; 3/43 & n. 3; 8/219–
20; book fulsomely dedicated to,
1/275 & n. 2; speaks well of P, 4/231;
8/490; slanders Sandwich, 6/324;
7/10; and Penn, 9/138–9; dislikes
Coventry, 7/196; comments on du
Teil's incompetent gunnery, 8/147 &
n. 3; and on division of fleet (1666),
8/148; also, 1/53
SOCIAL: 2/51; 3/79; 6/268
ALLUDED TO: 8/228
MONCK, Christopher, styled Earl of
Torrington, succ. as 2nd Duke of
Albemarle 1670 (d. 1688): said to be
illegitimate, 8/536 & n. 2; also, 7/240
MONCK, George, cr. Duke of
Albemarle 1660, ('the General');
Captain-General of the Kingdom:
CHARACTER: P's low opinion, 1/87;
4/435; 6/68, 298; 7/11, 12, 204, 354;
8/499, 536, 586–7, 591; Sandwich's,
1/125; Blackborne's, 4/372–3; Coventry's, 7/203, 204; satire on, 8/21 &
n. 3; popularity, 7/203, 281; 9/205;
trusted by bankers, 7/178; ballad in
praise of, 8/99 & n. 2; bravery, 8/499
CHRON. SERIES: in Scotland, 1/1; ordered
to London, 1/8 & n. 5, 13; political
intentions, 1/16 & n. 3, 22 & n. 4, 30 &

n. 1, 33, 58, 75 & n. 5, 79, 102, 111;
5/297; arrives, 1/39, 40 & n. 2; attends
on Rump, 1/43 & n. 2; his power,
1/45, 74(2); action against city, 1/46–
51 passim & nn.; requires Rump to fill
vacancies, 1/50 & n. 1, 51 & n. 1, 54 &
n. 2; in city, 1/52, 53, 71; allies with
city, 1/54–5 & n.; addresses to, 1/55
& n.4, 73 & n. 1; allies with secluded
M.P.s, 1/60, 62 & nn.; made general,
1/62; entertained by livery companies, 1/71 & n. 2, 79, 106; made joint
general-at-sea, 1/71 & n. 4, 75; actions
against republicans, 1/81, 84, 109;
elected M.P., 1/109 & n. 1; relations
with Presbyterians, 1/117, 118–19;
granted money, 1/118; welcomes
King at Dover, 1/158; invested with
Garter, 1/161; appointed Treasury
Commissioner, 1/170 & n. 3; patent
of nobility, 1/188 & n. 1; appointed
Lord Lieutenant of Ireland, 1/227–8 &
n., 228–9; in trial of regicides, 1/263;
Overton's plot against, 1/318–19 &
n.; attends coronation, 2/82, 85, 86;
exempted from place bill, 4/136 &
n. 1; at Oxford in Plague, 6/310, 320;
appointed to Treasury Commission,
8/223, 229–30; rumoured appointment as Lord High Constable, 8/269 &
n. 3, 270; sharp practice in Moyer
case, 8/325; godfather to Duke of
Cambridge, 8/438; misunderstanding
with King about Buckingham,
9/27
AS CAPTAIN-GENERAL OF THE KINGDOM:
severity against plotters, 3/237, 252;
quells brawl, 4/136; sends soldiers to
guard pressed men, 6/99; victuals
Guernsey garrison, 6/142–3; discusses
apportionment of money for army,
6/154, 155; 8/591; resents proposal to
make Duke of York general, 6/277 &
n. 2, 321 & n. 1; sent for in Fire,
7/279–80, 281; dismisses Catholic
officers, 7/354; quells seamen's riot,
7/416; sends soldiers to man ships,
8/83, 147; confident of peace, 8/128;
his measures to defend Medway,
8/257–8, 260–1 & n.; blames Lord
Brouncker for disaster, 8/271, 315; is
himself blamed by Coventry, 8/490,
492 & n. 2, 497, 505, 515, 524, 536;

MONTOUTH (?Monteith), [?Patrick]: 9/217
MOONE: see Mohun
MOONE, Mr——, secretary to Lord Belasyse: on Tangier business, 7/18, 66, 403, 417; dines with P, 7/270; political news from, 8/30
MOORCOCK, [John], timber merchant, Chatham: gives cakes to Navy Board, 3/82 & n. 4; 5/259 & n. 1; timber deal, 8/231 & n. 1
MOORE, Frank, EP's cousin: letter to EP, 6/216
MOORE, Frank, Maj.-Gen. Lambert's man: 3/118
MOORE, Henry, lawyer, Sandwich's man of business:
P'S REGARD FOR: 1/261, 291; 2/167; 3/196
CHRON. SERIES: P's deputy in Exchequer, 1/83, 107–8, 238; draws up P's will, 1/90; instructs P in law, 1/283; assists him in disputes over Robert P's affairs, 2/28 & n. 2, 137, 141, 176, 196, 198, 209, 211, 217, 226, 230; 3/7, 16, 31, 33–4, 83, 196, 211, 215, 248; 4/384; other financial/legal business with, 1/103, 316; 2/190–1, 215; 4/90; 5/101; to be appointed to Wardrobe, 3/102 & n. 3; visits Brampton, 4/307, 338; returns to town after Plague, 7/13; clears prize goods with customs, 7/31–2; criticises Lord Keeper Coventry, 7/261; also, 2/74, 157 & n. 2, 217 & n. 4; 3/84; 6/83, 84
PERSONAL: house, 1/17; chamber in Whitehall, 2/120; and in Gray's Inn, 2/217; in love with Jemima Mountagu, 1/20; attends Mossom's congregation, 1/183; on nature of tragedy, 1/236, 239; ill, 3/215, 216, 227, 228, 232, 239, 248, 252, 294, 304; 4/3, 23, 45, 66; grown rich, 5/80; dislikes Creed, 5/302; admires Dr Spencer, 7/133 & n. 3
AS CLERK IN PRIVY SEAL: Sandwich's deputy, 1/173, 205, 225, 238, 247; 3/168; fees, 2/2–3; 4/378; accounts with P, 2/25, 98, 106: at sealing day, 2/149–50; attends on Lord Privy Seal, 2/158, 187, 199, 234, 237; also, 1/245, 307, 318; 2/64
AS SANDWICH'S MAN OF BUSINESS:

Sandwich's kindness, 2/101 & n. 1; arranges investments/loans, 1/294, 297; 6/333; 7/31, 32; 8/579, 580, 581–2; in charge of household, 2/75; accounts [some may refer to Privy Seal business], 3/138, 266, 277; 4/288, 416; 7/45, 199; Sandwich's debts, 5/132, 186, 187, 238–9; 6/33–4; 7/13, 45; sea-fee, 8/405; finances (general), 8/187–8, 199, 516; 9/331, 440; hopes for profits, 4/422; advises P in Becke affair, 4/278, 280–1, 281, 281–2, 381, 382, 383, 385, 389–90, 395, 422; 5/42; sends newspaper story of Sandwich's bravery, 6/123, 128 & n. 3; prize-goods affair, 7/260; 8/499; 9/51, 111; hopes for another command for Sandwich, 8/54; unspecified business, 2/47, 62, 104, 109, 229; 3/40, 69, 92, 99, 102, 103, 114, 115, 132, 207, 272; 4/22, 58, 70, 87, 94, 102, 188, 199–200, 281, 304; 5/202; 7/199; 9/313, 474–5; also, 1/171–3 passim, 322; 3/12, 18; 7/168, 406
POLITICAL NEWS ETC.: expects return of Commonwealth, 8/390–1; fears for nation, 8/530–1; also, 1/45, 60, 71, 113, 171, 263, 273, 278, 303; 4/134, 213, 304; 6/277; 8/125–6, 219, 324–5, 433–4, 436; 9/51–2, 99–100; other news, 2/159, 209; 3/76, 101, 143; 8/377
SOCIAL: EP's valentine, 1/55; watches footrace, 1/218; at theatre for first time, 2/6; demonstrates French method of drinking toasts, 4/189; celebrates end of dispute with Trices, 4/364; at taverns/coffee-houses with P, 1/5, 23, 49, 173, 210, 217–18, 227, 231, 295, 310; 2/49, 50, 79, 89, 105, 158, 167, 191, 199, 211, 235; 3/35, 152, 282; 4/257; 5/246; at P's house, 1/82, 246, 261, 267, 294, 318; 2/5, 40, 173, 177, 217, 226, 231; 3/37, 200, 263, 264; 4/362, 377–8, 379; 5/321; 6/52, 112, 137; 8/325; at Sandwich's houses/lodgings, 1/6, 32, 74; 2/48, 124, 149; 3/62, 83, 89, 117, 139, 285; walks with P, 2/145; 3/57, 162; at theatre, 2/141, 221; 6/4; also, 1/49, 89, 181; 2/35, 66, 97; 3/43, 134; 6/159; 8/259
ALLUDED TO: 1/17, 95; 2/110
~ his kinsman, 3/199
MOORE, Jonas, mathematician, kted

rumoured appointment to Treasury commission, 8/367-8 & n.; imprisons Doll Common, 9/415 & n. 1; also, 1/106, 266; 2/96, 97; 4/229; 8/176, 278

PRIVATE AFFAIRS: quarrels with Ned Mountagu, 4/47; dines with Sandwich, 1/75, 220

ALLUDED TO: 8/544; 9/139, 471

MOUNTAGU, Edward, (often referred to as 'my Lord'), cr. Earl of Sandwich July 1660, politician and naval commander; ambassador to Spain 1665-8; P's patron:

CHARACTER: 'a perfect Courtier', 1/269; secretive, 1/285; brave, 3/149; noble, 4/115; grown 'very high and stately', 5/42; neglectful of business, 4/28; 5/155; 9/374; Teddeman's high opinion, 7/345

PHYSICAL APPEARANCE AND PORTRAITS: moustache, 7/26; Spanish beard, 8/452-3; portrait by Lely, 1/262, 271 & n. 1, 296; copies of, 1/270-3 passim, 284, 286, 290, 292, 296, 301-2; miniature by Salusbury, 2/23; second portrait by Lely, 7/102 & n. 3

AS NAVAL COMMANDER:

UNDER COMMONWEALTH: voyage to Mediterranean (1656), 1/238; to Baltic (1659), 1/23 & n. 2, 80; his Swedish medal, 1/238 & n. 1

VOYAGE TO HOLLAND, March–Apr. 1660, to bring over King: joint general-at-sea, 1/71 & n. 4, 75; prepares to sail, 1/78, 82, 83, 84, 90; embarks, 1/95; civil to Cavaliers, 1/99, 112, 117; opposed by Lawson's captains, 1/100; shifts flag from *Swiftsure* to *Naseby*, 1/101; dismisses Anabaptist, 1/101, 109 .& n. 2; Declaration of Breda etc. read to fleet, 1/123 & n. 2, 124 & n. 1, 125, 126-7, 129 & n. 2; Commonwealth flags etc. replaced, 1/130, 133-4, 136-7; sets sail from Downs, 1/133-5 passim; surrenders command to Duke of York, 1/152; accompanies King ashore at Dover, 1/158; invested with Garter, 1/160-1 & nn.; distributes royal bounty, 1/162, 164; returns to London, 1/171; pay, 1/174, 192; 2/49, 55; voted thanks by Commons,

1/176, 177 & nn.; also, 1/96, 98, 115, 167

VOYAGE TO HOLLAND, Sept. 1660, to bring over Dowager Princess Mary: his orders, 1/234 & n. 4, 239; preparations, 1/236, 241; sets sail, 1/238, 241; returns, 1/254, 258; alluded to: 1/247, 251

VOYAGE TO THE MEDITERRANEAN AND PORTUGAL, 1661-2, to bring over Queen Catherine: preparations, 2/45-7 passim, 62 & n. 3, 77, 79, 95, 99, 103, 104/(2), 108, 112(2), 114, 118, 120, 121, 127; his instructions, 2/118 & n. 3; gift of cloth to Algerines, 2/120, 122, 123, 126; expenses granted, 2/150-1 & n., 163; illness at Alicante, 2/152-4 passim, 163; action at Algiers, 2/184 & n. 2, 185, 189; in Lisbon, 2/185-6; provisions sent, 2/186; sees bull-fight, 2/209 & n. 2; action at Tangier, 2/221 & n. 3; asks for astronomical information, 3/7; ambassador-extraordinary to Portugal, 3/12 & n. 3; puts troops into Tangier, 3/18, 33; news from, 3/21 & n. 2; gifts to wife, 3/25; sends map of Tangier to Duke of York, 3/37 & n. 2; returns, 3/84, 89, 97, 120; report on Queen etc., 3/89, 90-1 & n.; gift from Queen, 3/90; his part in treaty with Algiers, 3/121-2 & nn.; determines fleet's rate of pay, 3/128 & n. 1, 129; his cash/pay/ allowances/accounts, 3/93, 99 & n. 2, 115, 121; 4/101, 104, 113, 114, 116-17 & n., 135, 136, 156, 204; also, 2/167, 242; 3/18, 105

VOYAGE TO FRANCE, July 1662, to bring over Queen Mother: 3/128; in storm, 3/143, 144 & n. 1, 145, 146; bravery, 3/149; returns, 3/148, 149

1664 COMMAND: rumours of, 5/160-3 passim & n., 183; visits fleet, 5/187, 196, 197; made admiral, 5/206, 207 & n. 4; departs, 5/208-9, 211-12; at sea, 5/225, 256 & n. 3; in river, 5/265; returns, 5/299; at sea again, 5/360; also, 5/303-4

1665 CAMPAIGN: at sea, 6/13, 29 & n.1, 35, 39, 41, 50; repute, 6/50; at Nore, 6/64-5; death rumoured, 6/120; in Battle of Lowestoft, 6/121 & nn., 123 & n. 2, 127, 129, 137; his account of,

6/134–5 & n.; newspaper account, 6/128 & n. 3; unfair official account, 6/135 & nn., 149, 276; failure to pursue enemy, 8/494, 550; conduct defended by King, 8/573; returns, 6/134; at sea, 6/141; given sole command, 6/147 & n. 4; proposed joint command with Rupert, 6/148 & n. 2; jealousy of Penn, 6/148–9, 151, 230; fails to intercept Dutch E. Indiamen, 6/165, 178, 184 & n. 2; action in Bergen harbour, 6/193, 195–6 & n., 198; his defence of, 6/229; criticised for failure to capture E. Indiamen, 6/218 & n. 2, 231, 277; 8/494, 515, 538, 550; 9/68 & n. 1; puts out again, 6/205, 208; captures *Phoenix* and *Slothany* etc., 6/219 & n. 1, 223 [*see also* below, The prize-goods affair]; captures warships, 6/223–4 & n.; at Nore, 6/226, 228; lack of provisions, 6/228–9, 229, 230, 239; ability as commander, 6/230; at sea again, 6/275, 278, 287; leaves fleet to go to court, 6/307; 9/70 & n. 1, 87; criticised for failure to engage Dutch in October, 6/291 & n. 1; parliamentary motion against, ib.; criticism dies down, 7/148–9, 168, 376, 406; 8/2; also, 6/247, 300–1

THE PRIZE-GOODS AFFAIR: breaks bulk in *Phoenix* and *Slothany*, 6/219, 223, 226, 230–1 & n., 238–9; his profit, 6/238–9, 240, 241, 297–8, 334, 342; navy's allocation, 6/239; 7/27, 45, 54; distribution of goods authorised by King and Duke of York, 6/247 & n. 3, 264, 269 & n. 2, 318; 9/50; goods declared prize, 6/263–4; his action criticised by Myngs, 6/261, 266; in Commons, 6/262, ?291; in Lords, 7/309, 325; at court, 6/262, 263, 268, 276, 287, 301, 302, 311, 323; 7/6, 8; by Colvill, 6/268; Albemarle, 6/273, 313; 7/31; Coventry, 6/276, 301; 9/165; Penn, 9/165; and Duke of York, 6/287, 291, 302; Cuttance's influence, 8/549; 9/402; bill against breaking bulk, 6/274 & n. 4, 277; recovers King's favour, 6/276, 291, 301, 311, 318, 321; 7/8, 52, 54, 55; 9/67; Rupert's, 6/276; and Duke of York's, 6/311; 7/55–6; pardoned by King,

7/13, 17, 27, 55, 260, 262; exculpated by Prize Commissioners, 7/10, 52; attacked in *Second advice*, 7/407–8; affair investigated by Committee on Miscarriages, 8/485, 486, 494, 499, 521, 527, 572, 576; 9/51, 64 & n. 3, 70; and by Brooke House Committee, 9/87, 91, 92, 96, 111, 135, 165, 204, 363–4; discussed by Commons, 9/?174 & n. 5, 176 & n. 2, 177; alluded to: 7/203, 219, 260–1; 8/517, 530; 9/180

AS VICE-ADMIRAL OF THE KINGDOM: appointed, 1/221 & n. 1, 222, 225, 229, 236; subordinate appointments, 1/188; 5/162–3 & n.; with King on yacht, 1/222; provides ships, 1/249, 300; new barge, 2/110; quarrels with Mennes over flags, 3/122–3; fee, 8/405–6 & n.; attends Navy Board, 1/197, 211; 3/265, 272, 282; 4/12, 31, 418

AS ARMY OFFICER: pay, 1/7 & n. 1; regimental dinner, 1/185; regiment disbanded, 1/242, 295; also, 1/13, 14

AS CLERK TO PRIVY SEAL [*see also* Privy Seal]: takes office, 1/128 & n. 1, 176; sworn in, 1/206, 207; fees, 1/237, 238; appoints P his deputy, 1/205 & n. 3; and Moore, 3/168; also, 1/212

AS MASTER OF THE WARDROBE: appointed, 1/170, 175; visits building, 1/180; attendance, 1/303; P his deputy, 2/113 & n. 2, 116; profits, 3/287; 4/251; poundage, 8/418; is owed £7000, 5/206; accounts, 4/257, 390; 5/208; 8/253; 9/52; advised to surrender place, 8/195; also, 1/258; 5/32

TANGIER: appointed to committee, 3/238; nominates P as member, 3/170, 171, 172; rumoured appointment as Governor, 5/313; 9/387; receives money from contractors, 8/592–3 & n.; visits and reports on, 9/135 & n. 3, 355–6 & n.; other business: victualling, 4/30; mole, 4/35; 5/343; mercantile court, 4/102; Peterborough's accounts, 5/74–5, 140; local paymaster, 9/418, 419, 422; also, 9/326; unspecified, 3/232, 272; 4/97, 123, 269, 408; 5/173; 6/58, 61, 134; 9/340, 364

AS AMBASSADOR TO SPAIN: appointed,

6/320–3 passim & n.; departure, 6/342; 7/6, 52, 57; untrue rumour of recall, 7/354, 406; 8/52; and of quarrel with French ambassador, 8/36 & n. 2, 37, 42; negotiates treaty, 8/45, 107; anecdotes of his embassy, 8/451–2; overspends, 8/461–2; accounts, 8/462; 9/387, 440; return expected, 8/189, 190, 207–8, 476; recalled, 8/511; mediates in Spanish-Portuguese peace negotiations, 8/578 & n. 3; 9/59–60, 80, 222; high repute in Spain, 8/578–9; returns, 9/320

OTHER APPOINTMENTS: Deputy-Lieutenant for Huntingdonshire, 1/310 & n. 5; Master of Trinity House, 2/119; 3/29; 4/185; 5/172; work for Royal Fishery, 3/268–70 passim; 4/365–6

FINANCES [for fees etc. *see* under offices]: state of summarised, 5/206 & n. 1; makes will, 1/94, 95; King's grant to [*see also* Fox, Sir S.], 1/271–2, 285 & n. 4, 288, 290–4 passim, 297; 2/3, 47; 3/121; 4/87–8 & n., 156; 8/530 & n. 3; acquires Brampton manor, 3/102, 176 & nn.; debts, 3/55, 118; 5/186, 187(2), 192, 238–9; 7/56, 370; extravagance/insolvency, 4/37; 7/45; 8/187–8 & n., 444, 463, 470, 480, 516, 517; 9/331; lends money to Calthorpe, 1/4, 6 & n. 3, 24, 36; to Sir R. Parkhurst, 1/310 & n. 2, 311; 2/48; 4/94; Worcester money, 1/56 & n. 5, 57, 80, 91–2; borrows £1000 from T. Pepys, 2/43, 61, 62–3 & n.; 3/17 & n. 1; 5/186, 187; 6/331, 333; 7/13, 14–15, 31–2; from P, 2/61 & n. 5; 4/199–200, 286, 288, 290, 438; 5/42, 131, 211; 6/33–4; again from P, 8/579, 580, 582; P refuses to lend, 7/260; 8/187, 199; his borrowings amount to £7000, 3/92; over £9000, 5/132; £10, 000, 5/206; needs loan of £1000, 4/43, 45–6, 57; and of £2000, 9/321–2

RELATIONS WITH COVENTRY [*see* Coventry, Sir W.]

RELATIONS WITH P:

HIS REGARD FOR: 1/141, 206, 303, 323; 2/49, 113; 3/102, 133–4, 139, 187, 232, 248, 304; 5/74; 6/237, 239(2), 248, 287, 302

AS P'S PATRON: 1/129, 167; P as secretary to regiment, 1/7, 14, 25, 257, 304; and to fleet, 1/77(2); 5/65; deputy in Privy Seal, 1/169–70, 205 & n. 3; and in Wardrobe, 2/113 & n. 2, 116; promises P Clerkship of Acts, 1/184, 185, 222–3; thanked by Duke of York for introducing him, 3/215–16; advises him about Clarendon's timber, 5/202, 203, 206, 207, 208; secures his appointment to Tangier committee, 3/170, 171, 172; and to Royal Fishery, 4/366; 5/76, 79; also, 1/202; 2/121, 192; 4/196

AS P'S EMPLOYER [In the diary period P was primarily Sandwich's man of business; his domestic duties were light after his appointment as Clerk of the Acts, and varied with circumstances.]:

P as domestic steward/man of business [*see also* Andrews, J.; Creed, J.; Moore, H.; Shipley, E.; and above: The prize-goods affair; Finances]: appointment: vol. i, pp. xxii–iii; hopes for profits, 3/133; 4/422; his 'little chamber'/'turret' in Whitehall lodgings, 1/59, 186, 222; 4/22; 8/82; moves from, 2/126; overnight at, 3/187, 199, 301; 5/142; domestic duties: in charge of Whitehall lodgings, 1/24, 64; 3/146; and of servants, 3/288, 293; financial business: accounts, 1/24, 32, 104, 297, 305, 306, 307; 2/37, 56, 57, 67, 97, 106; 3/92–3, 99, 116, 120–3 passim, 124, 126, 133, 136, 138, 139, 266; 4/281, 285, 286, 416; 7/7, 41, 42; supervises Wardrobe finances during Sandwich's absence, 2/112; 3/132, 133–4, 147; 4/58; 8/253, 418; advises him on land purchase, 3/176 & n. 2; negotiates Lady Jemima's marriage settlement, 6/29, 135–6, 137; business with bankers, 6/334; misc.: sends deals to Hinchingbrooke, 1/313–14, 324; 2/8, 27, 35, 48–9, 79; advises him on garden design, 4/313; also, 1/29, 40, 78, 310–11, 312; 2/49; 4/343; unspecified business, 2/3; 3/94, 212, 215, 260, 281, 288; 4/23; 9/211

the Becke affair: P disapproves of Sandwich's liaison, 4/238, 270–1, 278, 281, 282, 286, 292, 301, 303, 313, 379; writes 'great letter of reproof', 4/382,

385–8 passim, its effects on Sandwich and on relations between them, 4/390–3 passim, 395, 396, 397, 402, 407, 408, 421, 422, 427, 428, 429, 437; 5/4, 9, 10, 18, 21–2, 26, 42, 43, 65, 70, 80, 83, 108, 110, 120, 185, 189, 192, 200; relations re-established, 5/76, 161, 203, 211, 225

misc.: gives New Year present, 1/4; advises about Robert P's estate, 1/170; 3/220, 226; 4/42; designs alterations to Brampton house, 3/206, 210; urges P to provide for Pall, 4/366; advises about W. Joyce's arrest, 5/110; and about sale of land, 5/211; concerned for during Plague, 6/231; confides in about his political standing, 7/54–6; P fails to write to in Spain, 9/321; and to pay visit of condolence, 9/474; P distrusts his associates, 9/372, 374 & n. 2; P dines/talks with, 2/54, 56, 79, 115; 3/126, 134; 4/82; 6/54–5, 60; P gives dinner for, 9/420, 423–4; also, 4/313

RELATIONS WITH EP: his regard for, 1/293, 294; 3/206, 210; admires her beauty, 4/186; makes advances to, 9/356

POLITICS [*see also* below, Court]:

HIS VIEWS: on restoration of monarchy, 1/77, 79, 107, 110, 285 & n. 2; Presbyterian discontent, 3/176; state of court and kingdom, 6/248, 277; likely effects of war, 7/55; a 'politique', 3/122

HIS POLITICAL CAREER: under Commonwealth, vol. i, pp. xxii, xxiii–vi; corresponds with King (1659), 1/125 & n. 1, 285; 4/69 & n. 2; takes out pardon, 3/121 & n. 1; returns to London, 1/44, 60, 62; elected to Council of State, 1/65; resumes seat in parliament, 1/72; dines with Presbyterian leaders, 1/75; and Lord Mayor, 1/92; elected M.P. for Weymouth, 1/108(3) & n. 2; and Dover, 1/110–11; resigns on becoming peer, 1/179; electoral influence at Harwich, 1/98 & n. 3; Cinque Ports, 1/93 & n. 2, 94, 96, 97; Weymouth, 1/103 & n. 4, 179; Dover, 1/167, 179 & n. 1; Huntingdon, 1/86–7 & n., 99 & n. 2; supports candidate at Huntingdon (1661), 2/3 & n. 5; opposes Sir R. Bernard's

influence there, 3/281–2 & n.; sworn Privy Councillor, 1/179; raised to peerage, 1/184–5 & n., 187–8 & n., 196 & n. 5; attends Lords, 1/208; 2/107; gifts of plate to Secretary and King, 1/185, 192, 193; 2/5; as judge at regicides' trial, 1/263, 266; exempted from place bill, 4/136 & n. 1; member of King's 'private council', 5/207; fears may be blamed for sale of Dunkirk, 7/55 & n. 4; rumoured appointment to Treasury, 8/195, 217; alliance with Clarendon, 1/173; 2/209–10, 221; 3/33, 122; 4/115, 366; 5/207, 208; 6/148, 291, 311; 7/5, 55; 8/418; relations cool, 6/276–7; with Duke of York and his party, 4/115; relations cool, 5/133; with Arlington, 4/115; 5/208; 6/276 & n. 5; with Albemarle, 6/313; and with Carteret, 6/148; also, 1/66, 68; 2/75; 7/28

POLITICAL NEWS FROM: 1/271; 3/237; 4/24, 57, 115–17, 366–7

COURT: attends coronation, 2/82, 86; advised to avoid court, 3/291; standing at court, 3/304; 5/207; 6/273, 276, 287, 291, 301, 302, 311, 318, 323; 7/5, 26–7, 132; 8/149, 207–8; 9/331, 339, 342; absence from court remarked on, 4/370, 379, 387–8; allies with Lady Castlemaine, 4/13, 115; also, 3/94, 157; 4/115, 239, 255; 5/161

RESIDENCES:

AT MRS BECKE'S, Chelsea: 4/97, 101, 112, 114, 117, 123–4, 160, 278, 281, 286, 402, 419; 5/173

AT LORD CREW'S, Lincoln's Inn Fields: 1/77, 87, 89, 94

HINCHINGBROOKE, Hunts. [for the house, *see* under name]: to entertain King, 4/324; visits, 1/221–3 passim, 234, 310, 312, 320; 2/47, 48, 49, 52; 3/116, ?160, 187, 287, 288, 304; 4/12, 251, 292, 313, 348; 5/32, 36, 64, 185; 7/34; 9/541; also, 1/66; 2/108

AT DEAN HODGES'S, Kensington: 5/184, 192

LINCOLN'S INN FIELDS: takes lease, 5/19–20, 43; P visits, 5/65, 74, 75, 79, 132, 202; admires house and garden, 5/74; christening in dining-room, 7/49; let to Carteret, 8/450

LODGINGS AT THE WARDROBE [P's

numerous visits – mostly social – are not indexed. His first mention of them is at 1/277; his last at 5/316.]: roomy but ugly, 1/291; 'pretty pleasant', 2/97; kitchen, 2/106; dining-room, 3/89; parlour, ib.; Capt. Ferrers's chamber, 3/81

LODGINGS IN WHITEHALL [He had lodgings in the palace from c. 1654 onwards and throughout the diary period – whether the same set is not known. P's numerous visits are not indexed. His first mention of them is at 1/17; his last at 9/553.]: next door to Lady Castlemaine's, 3/215; claimed by A. A. Cooper, 1/17, 22, 23; repaired and decorated, 3/49, 146; King's tennis court in garden, 3/147; damaged by collapse of tennis court, 4/197; Hinchingbrooke's chamber, 8/516; Sandwich's study, 1/22, ?251; stair door, 1/71; ? garden, 1/77, 220; nursery, 1/186, 203; house of office, 1/250; buttery, 2/90; drawing-room, 2/102; little new room, 2/103; great dining-room, 1/287; 3/266; also, 2/121

HOUSEHOLD [see also Lady Sandwich: household; Burfett, ——; Carleton, ——; Creed, J.; Crisp, L.; Ferrers, R.; Loud, ——; [Luffe, E.]; Turner, John]: to have French cook and master of horse, 1/269, 311; angry at servants' improvidence, 2/64; new liveries for coronation, 2/79; footboy (Tom), 1/14, 58; black footman, (Jasper), 1/82, 92, 166; other footmen, 3/196, 212; 4/348; porter, 5/202; Spanish dancer, 9/440; great coach, 1/181; 5/200

PERSONAL:

INTEREST IN ARTS AND SCIENCES: on engravings, 6/50; paints miniature of Charles II, 2/59; plans alterations to P's Brampton house, 3/206, 210; his drawings of Lisbon, 4/286 & n. 1; and of Portsmouth harbour, 6/38, 46, 50; admires Danckerts's view of Tangier, 9/541 & n. 2; musical tastes, 1/298; 4/160; composes three-part anthem, 4/418–19, 428; borrows lute, 1/218; plays and commends guitar, 6/301; plays viol, 1/114 (bass), 285; 2/39, 57;

organ, 1/287, 292, 297; his virginals, 2/121–2; sings, 1/114, 115, 118, 129, 133, 169, 285; 2/57; musical parties, 2/66, 103; 3/255, 287; takes dancing-master on voyage, 2/117; sceptical about ghost, 4/185–6; given loadstone, 4/397; astronomical observations, 5/346 & n. 3, 352; also, 3/7; 4/283

RELIGIOUS VIEWS: a 'sceptic' and favours uniformity, 1/141, 201; 'indifferent', 1/261; prefers homilies to sermons, 1/271 & n. 2

HEALTH: heavy cold, 1/202; bruised foot, 1/254; unwell, 1/262; ill (? malaria) at Alicante, 2/152–3, 154, 163; ill (? recurrent malaria), 4/17, 21, 22, 24, 25, 28, 30, 55, 58, 62, 63, 66, 68, 69, 89; 5/207; takes physic, 1/164, 166; 2/42; 3/92; 9/338

DRESS ETC.: rich new clothes, 1/141; garter dress and insignia, 1/160; 2/49; comb-case, 1/239; toilet cap, ib.; French coronation suit, 2/83; gold-buttoned suit, 4/187; watch, 1/120

LIAISONS: affair with Betty Becke, 4/97, 101, 112, 174, 238 & n. 3, 270–1, 281, 286, 292, 301, 303, 305; neglects attendance at court, 4/370, 379; P's letter of reproof, 4/383, 387–8 (see also Relations with P, above); leaves Chelsea, 4/399–400, 402, 419; still visits her, 5/173–4; affair alluded to, 9/455; liaison with Lady Castlemaine, 5/21; his portrait of, 5/200

CHILDREN [The following references are to children/daughters whose names are not given in the text. See also Mountagu, Anne, Catherine; Edward (Hinchingbrooke); James; John; Oliver; Paulina and Sidney.]: in London for coronation, 2/75; P/EP take to theatre, 2/151–2, 173–4; Tower, 3/76; Hampton Court, 3/81–2; Greenwich, 3/111; to see ship, 6/56, 57; also, 2/165, 170, 206; 3/47, 79, 94, 223

CHILDREN'S MARRIAGES: agrees terms for Lady Jemima's marriage, 6/138, 145, 148, 173; his pleasure at, 6/202; refers Hinchingbrooke's marriage negotiations to advisers, 8/190–1 & n.

SOCIAL: plays ninepins on board ship,

1/131, 142, 162, 164, 169; goes fishing with Vice-Admiral, 1/169; dines with Lord Campden, 1/210; with King, 1/214, 297–8; Manchester, 1/220; Albemarle, 4/187; Peterborough, 4/270; and Povey, 9/345; entertains Ormond, 2/100; officers of Wardrobe, 2/104; and Coventry, 3/138–9; at theatre, 3/211, 216; at Lady Castlemaine's, 3/214–15; 4/238; plays at dice, 4/28; loses £100 at cards, 4/134; at Boughton, 4/307; at Whitehall chapel, 4/401; visits Lady Pulteney, 5/163; and Archbishop Sheldon, 6/239
MISC.: challenges Buckingham to duel, 2/32–3; in search for treasure in Tower, 3/240–4 passim
MOUNTAGU, Edward, styled Viscount Hinchingbrooke, eldest son of Lord Sandwich [often referred to as 'Mr Edward' before July 1660]:
CHARACTER: 'a noble and hopeful gentleman', 6/13; 'a most sweet youth', 6/188; his sobriety, 7/235–6, 358; 8/516
CHRON. SERIES: at school at Twickenham, 1/18 & n. 3, 19, 20; on *Naseby*, 1/133; has audience with King, 1/143–4; visits The Hague, Delft and Scheveningen, 1/143–4, 145, 147–50 passim; at Deal, 1/163; Latin lesson from P, 1/165; returns to London, 1/173; continues education, 2/114 & n. 1, 142, 163; 4/25, 121, 187; suspected smallpox, 2/152, 153, 154(2), 157; false report of death, 3/11 & n. 2; kills page in shooting accident, 4/138; visits Rome, 6/13; returns to England, 6/169 & n. 3, 178, 183; has smallpox, 6/191, 193; P's impression of, 7/47 & n. 2; proposed match with Elizabeth Malet, 6/110 & n. 4, 119, 193 & n. 2; 7/56, 260, 385; marriage with Lady Anne Boyle, 8/190–1 and nn., 208, 216, 252, 377, 418, 469, 498, 598; 9/28, 51; short of money, 8/276, 333; assistance in father's financial difficulties, 8/199, 463, 516, 573 & n. 2, 579, 580; dishonourable advances to EP, 9/356; also, 2/107; 3/291; 6/190; 7/46, 54, 94, 234, 356, 368; 9/318, 321
SOCIAL: plays shuttlecock, 1/15; at theatre, 2/8; sees Lord Mayor's Show,

1/276 & n. 3, 277; at christening, 7/49; visits city ruins after Fire, 7/357–8; dines with P, 7/387, 388–9; 9/109, 115, 116–17, 423–4, 553; also, 9/211, 345
ALLUDED TO: 1/151
MOUNTAGU, Edward, 1st Baron Mountagu of Boughton (d. 1644): ?6/238 & n. 2
MOUNTAGU, Edward, 2nd Lord Mountagu of Boughton (d. 1684): dines with Sandwich, 4/136; ill, 5/154; quarrels with son Edward, 5/244; alluded to: 6/155
MOUNTAGU, Edward (Ned), son of the 2nd Baron Mountagu of Boughton; Master of the Horse to the Queen Mother:
CHRON. SERIES: parliamentary candidate, 1/102 & n. 2, 167; carries letters between Sandwich and King, 1/110 & n. 2, 112, 113; on Dutch voyage, 1/135, 171, 173; manages Sandwich's business during absence abroad (1661–2), 2/118, 121, 163, 185, 186, 195, 197, 206, 229; distrusted by Lady Sandwich and P, 2/163; visits Tangier, 2/186; 3/12 & n. 1., 78; low repute at court, 3/15, 43, 289; 4/47 & n. 1; 5/207, 208; mismanagement of Sandwich's business, 3/29, 55–6; duel with Cholmley, 3/157 & n. 2; 4/47; borrows money from Sandwich, 3/157; dispute with Chesterfield, 3/289–90 & n.; 4/25; quarrel with Sandwich, 4/46–7 & nn., 114–15, 366; 5/207, 208; with father and uncle, 4/47, 187–8; 5/244; to procure Frances Stuart for King, 4/366; tries to make mischief between Sandwich and Clarendon, 4/366–7; rusticated for affront to Queen, 5/153 & n. 2, 155, 244; owes Sandwich £2000, 5/206; killed in action, 6/196
SOCIAL: 1/187; 3/139
ALLUDED TO: 2/142, 191, 193
MOUNTAGU, George, son of the 1st Earl of Manchester (d. 1681): with Sandwich on Baltic voyage, 1/44 & n. 3; custos rotulorum for Westminster, 1/79–80 & n.; M.P. for Dover, 1/167, 179 & n. 2, 183, 228; parliamentary candidate for Huntingdon, 2/3 & n. 6, 4; political news

from, 1/228; 2/142; 3/15 & n. 2;
9/302; death of son in France, 3/11,
15; concern for Sandwich in prize-
goods affair, 8/2, 521; 9/64, 162, 165;
praises P's parliamentary speech,
9/105, 153, 302; advises him on
dealing with parliament, 9/178; social:
1/30 & n. 3; 4/82–3; 9/116; alluded
to: 3/92, 224; ~ his wife [Elizabeth],
3/16, 224; 9/153; his sons and
daughter, 9/153
MOUNTAGU, James, Bishop of
Bath and Wells 1608–16, Winchester
1616–d.18 (d. 1618): tomb in Bath
Abbey, 9/238 & n. 1
MOUNTAGU, James, son of Lord
Sandwich: birth and christening,
5/209 & n. 1, 211
MOUNTAGU, James, of Lackham,
Wilts., 3rd son of the 1st Earl of
Manchester: 8/316, n. 2
MOUNTAGU, Jemima, Countess of
Sandwich (often referred to as 'my
Lady'), wife of the 1st Earl of Sandwich:
CHARACTER: 'so good and discreet a
woman I know not in the world',
5/257; P's esteem for, 2/49; 6/119;
8/469
HER FRIENDSHIP/KINDNESS TO P/EP:
1/264, 266; 2/117, 140, 214, 221, 235,
240; 3/54, 103, 206; 4/199; 5/65, 76;
sends younger sons to P's house to
avoid infection, 2/153, 157, 158; urges
P to spend money on EP, 2/210, 211,
212; scolds for failure to visit, 3/143;
recalls P's service in 1650s, 5/192;
invites him to Hinchingbrooke, 6/176;
grateful for his help as matchmaker,
6/178, 180; looks on P as one of
family, 8/472
CHRON. SERIES: comes to London from
Hinchingbrooke, 1/264; audience of
Queen Mother, 1/282; takes up residence at Wardrobe, 2/95, 97; hears of
husband's illness, 2/154; birth of
daughter Catherine, 2/159, 166, 171,
178; meets Queen Catherine, 3/96,
100; at Hinchingbrooke, 3/143, 144;
returns to London, 5/32, 64; has
measles, 5/132, 135–8 passim, 142,
144–5, 155, 257; at Kensington, 5/174
& n. 1, 178; meets Sandwich's

mistress, 5/179, 184; birth of son,
James, 5/209; dislikes Creed's proposed match, 5/286; 6/15, 88, 90;
hopes for daughter's marriage to P.
Carteret, 6/29, 55, 66, 71; visits
Carterets, 6/148, 149, 151, 152, 153,
155, 156, 157, 161; attends wedding,
6/163, 176; ill from drinking waters,
6/151, 152; at Hinchingbrooke, 7/376;
8/49; pleased with son's marriage,
8/216, 469; forced to sell plate etc.,
8/470; borrows £100 from P, 9/194,
211; also, 2/27, 32, 131, 152–3, 163,
186; 3/11–12, 55, 89, 105; 4/237, 262;
6/110–11
COURT NEWS FROM: 1/319, 320; 2/230;
3/80–1; 5/129, 232; 6/41
HOUSEHOLD: Sarah, housekeeper at
Whitehall: re-employed, 1/175 & n.
6; marries and takes to drink, 3/288,
293; husband a cook, 3/251; 4/334,
342; her 'old services' to P, 3/251 &
n. 2; court news from, 3/146; 4/1,
315, 342; P's amorous encounter with,
3/191; social: 1/194; 2/271, 234, 236;
3/12, 49, 87, 255; 4/5; also, 1/241, 325;
3/288, 299; 4/155, 197; other servants:
new French maid, 1/293; page, 2/15,
16; 3/126; maids: Mary, 2/16; Susan,
2/106; Susan's sister, ib.; Betty, 2/236;
butler Archibald dies, 2/211; new
housekeeper at Wardrobe, 2/232;
keeps poor house in Sandwich's absence, 2/122; 5/316
SOCIAL: at Whitehall chapel, 1/276;
Lord Mayor's show, 1/277; investiture
of peers, 2/79–80; talks of beauty,
1/314; and theology, 2/221; visits
ships at Chatham, 2/15, 16; at
Hampton Court, 2/25; 3/81–2; P's
house, 2/143; gives New Year dinner,
3/1–2; criticises EP's portrait, 3/17; in
Hyde Park, 3/78; at Greenwich,
3/126; shows P alterations at Hinchingbrooke, 4/308; with P/EP: at Hinchingbrooke, 3/219, 223; 8/471; Sandwich's London lodgings, the Wardrobe etc., 1/269, 272, 295, 300, 301,
312; 2/6, 8, 10, 30. 54, 64, 89, 116, 123,
126, 127, 132, 139, 145, 149, 151, 160,
162, 165, 176, 180, 184, 198, 201, 206,
217, 219, 226, 232; 3/6, 16, 21, 25, 33,
47, 49, 51, 57, 60, 64, 76, 92, 94, 102,

108; 5/119, 120, 185, 200, 238, 244–5, 333, 339, 347, 358; 6/5, 13, 17, 115; also, 1/309; 3/83
ALLUDED TO: 1/46; 2/101; 4/176; 7/154
MOUNTAGU, Lady Jemima, ('Mrs'/ 'Lady Jem'): *see* Carteret, Jemima
MOUNTAGU, John and Oliver, twin sons of Lord Sandwich: stay with P and EP to avoid smallpox, 2/153, 155, 157, 158; P examines in Greek and Latin, 8/472 & n. 1; alluded to: 9/335
MOUNTAGU, [Mary], (b. Aubrey) wife of (Sir) William (d. 1700): 3/1; 5/19; 8/598
MOUNTAGU, [Mary], ('Lady Mountagu'): 8/319
MOUNTAGU, Oliver: *see* Mountagu, John
MOUNTAGU, Lady Paulina, daughter of Lord Sandwich:
CHRON. SERIES: given page by Sandwich, 3/95; and parrot, 3/105; sent to Brampton to avoid smallpox, 4/439; 5/74 & n. 1, 95; returns to London, 5/32, 53; resents father's liaison, 5/173–4; frightened at shooting London Bridge, 5/180; 'a proper lady', 8/470; fatally ill, 9/455; death, 9/462 & n. 1; piety, 9/520
SOCIAL: on river trip, 2/142–3; at Bartholomew Fair, 2/166; at theatre, 3/57; also, 3/59, 89; 5/64, 65, 132, 184, 358; 9/211
ALLUDED TO: 5/153; 9/474
MOUNTAGU (Montagu), Ralph, son of the 2nd Lord Mountagu of Boughton, succ. as 3rd baron 1683, cr. Duke of Montagu 1705; Gentleman of the Horse to the Duchess of York (d. 1709): anecdote of, 3/43; alluded to: 3/12, 139
MOUNTAGU, Robert, styled Lord Mandeville, succ. as 3rd Earl of Manchester 1671 (d. 1683): on *Naseby*, 1/157; a gallant, 3/15; visits Louis XIV as ambassador extraordinary, 4/156 & n. 2; at Hampton Court, 7/27; valentine gift to Frances Stuart, 8/184; at Harwich in Medway crisis, 8/255; alluded to: 1/86
MOUNTAGU, Sir Sidney, father of Lord Sandwich (d. 1644): coarse

anecdote about, 1/261; his rise, 1/285 & n. 2; alluded to: 6/238 & n. 1
MOUNTAGU, Sidney, second son of Lord Sandwich (d. 1727):
CHRON. SERIES: stays with P and EP to avoid smallpox, 2/153, 155, 157, 158; education in Paris, 2/114 & n. 1, 142, 163 & n. 4; 4/25, 187; returns, 5/185 & n. 1; ill, 6/225; at Cranbourne, 7/54; returns from Spain, 9/321–2 & n.; welcomed at court, 9/323; to visit Flanders and Italy, 9/552; also, 3/291; 5/200
SOCIAL: sees Lord Mayor's Show, 1/276 & n. 3, 277; at theatre, 2/8; 9/419; dines with P, 9/423–4, 553; also, 9/345, 420, 541
MOUNTAGU, Abbot Walter (d. 1677): prevents duel between Sandwich and Buckingham, 2/33 & n. 1; to take charge of Sandwich's sons in Paris, 2/114 & n. 1; alluded to: 4/211 & n. 2
MOUNTAGU, Sir William, lawyer: given charge of Sandwich's will, 1/94 & n. 2, 95; his legal adviser, 1/271, 294, 310; 2/3; 4/45; loyalty to, 7/54; helps arrange Hinchingbrooke's marriage, 8/190 & n. 4; social: 3/1; 4/136; 8/598; alluded to: 8/22; 9/28
MOUNTAGU, ——, grandson of 1st Earl of Manchester: tried for arson and robbery, 8/316 & n. 2, 319; ~ his mother [Mary], 8/319
MOUNTNEY, [Richard], of the Customs House: 7/12
MOUNT'S BAY, Cornwall: 3/79; 9/320, 321
MOXON, [Joseph], type-founder and instrument maker, Cornhill: his shop, 4/302; P buys globes, 4/302 & n. 3; 5/83, 136; also, 4/350
MOYER, [Laurence], merchant, brother of Samuel (d. 1685): secures brother's release, 8/219–20 & n.
MOYER, Samuel, republican (d. 1683): imprisoned, 2/225 & n. 1; dispute over release, 8/219–20 & n., 325
MOYSE(S), Capt. [Richard], army officer: 1/57 & n. 3
MUDDIMAN, [Henry], journalist: his newsbooks, 1/12 & n. 3; 4/297, n. 2; 6/305, n. 3; at Rota Club, 1/13

MUFFETT: *see* Moffett
MULBERRY Garden: *see* Gardens:
Hyde Park
MULGRAVE, Lord: *see* Sheffield,
John, 3rd Earl of
MULLINER, Goody, of Cambridge:
her stewed prunes, 9/212
MULLINER, ——, butler's man at
Magdalene College: college news
from, 9/212
MULLINS: *see* Molins
MUMFORD, Mrs ——, shopkeeper
in Westminster Hall: 1/66; 6/186
MÜNSTER: *see* Galen, Christopher
Bernard von, Prince Bishop of
MURFORD, [Will], Navy Office
messenger: accompanies P to Bramp-
ton, 8/465, 474–5; and to West
Country, 9/229; nickname, 8/467
MURFORD, Capt. [William], timber
merchant: solicits naval commission
for friend, 1/175, 177, 178, 180; offers
gift, 1/273; projected light-house,
2/41 & n. 2, 44; breach of contract,
4/353 & n. 1; also, 1/80; 2/31, 32;
3/284; ~ his widow, [Bridget], 8/231
MURFORD, Mrs ——, shopkeeper in
Westminster Hall [?identical with
Mrs Mumford]: 1/204, 222
MURREY: *see* Moray
MUSIC [*see also* Books]:
GENERAL:
P'S LOVE OF: 4/48; 6/320–1; 7/69, 228;
9/94; fears its distractions, 4/104–5;
his music room, 5/230; also, 5/12, 235;
8/432
P'S TASTES: vol. i, p. xxi; finds pro-
fessionals spoil 'ingenuity' of domestic
music, 5/226; prefers vocal to instrumental, 5/238, 290; dislikes 'old-
fashion' singing, 1/19 & n. 2; critical
of Ravenscroft's psalms, 5/342; prefers English to French songs, 7/171;
and to Italian, 8/384, 599; critical of
Carissimi, 5/217; admires composition
of Italian songs, 8/54–5, 65; reflects on
relation of words and music, 8/54–5,
64–5, 154; critical of elaborately con-
trapuntal songs/anthems, 8/438, 458,
515; 9/59, 251; dislikes trumpets and
kettledrums, 2/29; 4/355–6; guitar,
2/142; Scottish tunes, 7/224–5; and
bagpipes, 9/131

MUSIC THEORY: P attempts to invent
simpler method of composition,
8/574–5; 9/125, 127 (2), 138, 151(2),
152, 155, 412; studies 'scale'/'gamut',
6/227, 236; 9/151, 159, 161; inquires
about physical nature of sound, 9/147;
his 'music papers', 8/177
P'S COMPOSITIONS [sometimes voice-
line only]: takes lessons from Birchensha, 3/8–9 & n., 9, 10, 16, 19, 35, 36;
studies Birchensha's rules, 3/35, 36–7;
5/174–5 & n.; 6/282–3; practises
'music' (composition), 3/14, 15, 19,
20, 21, 24, 26, 27, 32, 33; 4/212, 213,
219, 220, 221, 266; orders music-card,
7/219; dislikes 'unnecessary' octaves,
7/414 & n. 3; attempts to compose a
song, 2/207; composes airs, 3/26;
7/227; composes/sings/teaches/listens
to: 'Gaze not on swans', 3/27 & n. 4,
34–5, 46; 'Nulla Nulla', 3/35 & n. 1;
'This cursed jealousy', 3/36 & n. 2;
'Beauty Retire', 6/320 & n. 4, 324; 7/2
53, 54, 257, 362, 397; 'It is decreed',
7/91 & n. 4, 104, 223, 257, 366(2), 369,
403, 414, 420; 8/35, 36, 50, 54, 142;
9/14, 16, 131, 136; 'I wonder what the
grave', 8/555 & n. 3; a duo, 6/266; a
bass to 'the lark's song', 9/299 & n. 3,
303; also, 7/418; 8/167
INSTRUMENTAL CONSORTS: King's
twenty-four violins, 2/86; 8/73, 404,
458; music meeting, 5/238; Buckingham's band, 9/12–13; bands for
dancing, 8/29; 9/128, 458, 464; band
of fiddles (alluded to), 8/65
PARTICULAR INSTRUMENTS:
angelica: 1/183
bagpipes: 2/101; 9/131
bandore: 3/224
claviorganum: 8/25 & n. 4
'cymbals' (barber's music), 1/169
dulcimer: P hears for first time, 3/90;
also, 3/118
flageolet: P buys, 8/53, 87, 344; 9/30,
162; has lessons from Greeting,
8/205–6, 223, 237, 286, 325, 329;
9/279; plays (alone), at 'echo', 1/58,
70, 147; also, 1/19, 33, 38, 45, 121,
138; 2/65, 115; 3/53, 80; 4/189;
5/215; 8/224, 253, 272, 273, 277, 326,
327, 344, 376, 384, 385(2), 443; 9/163,
184; (with others), 1/71; 8/224, 235(2),

285; 5/120, 194, 261, 321; 6/138; 7/95, 100; 8/444; 9/202, 219; improvised duets, 1/194; with choir, 1/313; 2/240; 'holy things', 3/67–8; French psalms, 3/99; new tunes, 4/63; sings with EP/Mercer, 7/111; 8/29, 171, 198, 203, 206, 209, 223, 238, 244, 250, 253(2), 289, 327, 328, 340, 344, 351, 380, 390, 429, 437–8, 465, 467–8, 504, 557; 9/13, 14, 35, 55, 58–9, 81, 85, 119, 128, 134, 152, 166, 172, 175, 179, 196, 197(2), 199, 201, 203, 204, 213, 216, 217, 221(2), 227, 249, 250, 261, 269, 273, 300, 320, 513, 552, 555, 563

   also, 1/113, 118, 268, 272, 274; 2/57, 101, 118; 3/86; 5/136, 199, 209, 229, 266, 282, 325, 337, 339, 342, 349; 6/24, 32, 34, 39, 44, 50, 73, 77, 79, 86, 88, 98, 125, 156, 219, 283, 294, 321, 323–6, passim; 7/44, 53–4, 69, 73, 92–3, 95, 110, 113, 117, 172–4 passim, 183, 191, 195, 197, 200, 205, 206, 212, 216, 227, 228, 230, 236, 237, 240, 348, 362

P LISTENS TO OTHERS [see also Musical Compositions]: impromptu part songs, 4/249; part songs in tavern, 4/377; Italian songs, 4/428; 5/217; 8/29, 54, 56, 57, 59, 154; a Dutchman, 5/19; sailors, 6/287; French song, 7/199; Irish songs, 8/29; recitativo, 8/55, 57; 'a boat full of spaniards', 8/325; also, 2/104; 5/53, 126, 242; 6/28, 34, 64, 137, 215, 235, 267; 7/12, 30, 341, 343–4; 8/97, 108, 119, 204, 283, 325, 384, 394, 599; 9/11, 20, 111
CHURCH MUSIC: Bath Abbey: organ, 9/238; Chesterton, Cambs.: bells, 9/212; Hackney church (St Augustine's): organ, 8/150, 174; King's College, Cambridge: organ, 2/135–6 & n.; Norton St Philip, Som.: bells, 9/232; Roman Catholic (general): 8/26; St George's Chapel, Windsor: anthem, 7/58; St James's Palace, Queen's chapel at: choir: P dislikes, 3/202; his opinion changes, 7/87, 99; 8/588; 9/319, 515; eunuchs, 8/154; harsh voices, 8/427–8; also, 9/126; St Olave's, Hart St: long psalm, 2/6 & n. 5; 9/21; new psalm, 4/269; clerk out of tune, 5/320; P hopes for organ for, 8/150 & n. 2; St Paul's Cathedral: poor choir, 5/67; Salisbury Cathedral:

organ, 9/229; Westminster Abbey: organ, 1/283 & n. 1, 324; anthem, 6/18; Whitehall Chapel [see also Cooke, Capt. Henry]: anthems: dull, 1/237; badly sung, 1/265; 7/99; rehearsal, 2/41; with symphonies, 3/190, 197, 293; discontinued in Lent, 4/69; in five parts, 4/393; by Sandwich, 4/418–19, 428; on Ps. 150, 6/5; with wind music, 6/5; 9/163; by Humfrey, 8/515; by Silas Taylor, 9/251; also, 1/195, 220; 3/84, 85; 4/63; 7/99, 245, 383, 409; 8/32, 41, 425, 478; 9/294, 563; organ, 1/176, 195; 8/145; wind music, 9/163; unspecified music, 6/109
COURT MUSIC: French musicians, 1/297–8 & n.; 8/73 & n. 3; musicians unpaid, 7/414; disparaged, 8/529–30; Italian musicians, 8/56–7; 9/322; concerts on occasion of peace, 8/458; on Duke of York's birthday, 9/328; also, 8/456, 532, 534; rehearsal of twenty-four violins, 9/163; violins play during dinner, 8/404; undefined music, 8/456, 458
MILITARY MUSIC: reveilles by drums and trumpets, 7/422; 9/403; drums summon militia, 5/99, 101; 7/362; Scottish march, 8/311; Louis XIV's drums and trumpets, 4/189; Italian trumpet music, 7/352; also, 2/29; 8/496; 9/129
OPERA: T. Killigrew's plans for, 5/230; 8/56
THEATRE MUSIC [see also Dancing]: T. Killigrew on improvement in, 8/55 & n. 3; P's comments on acoustics, 4/128; 9/459; in If you know not me, you know nobody (song to Queen Elizabeth), 8/388; The faithful shepherdess, 9/327, 329; The Heiress, 9/436; Macbeth, 8/171; The man is the maister, 9/134; She would if she could, 9/54; The siege of Rhodes, 1/187; 6/284 & nn.; 8/25 & n. 1, 59 & n. 1; The Surprizall, 9/166; The Tempest (echo song), 8/522 & n. 1; 9/189; (seamen's dance), 9/48; The virgin-martyr (wind music), 9/94, 100, 188; also, 8/396; 9/89
TOWN WAITS: Cambridge, 3/224; 8/469; Huntingdon, 8/474; Bath,

9/233–4; Marlborough, 9/241; Reading, 9/243; Thetford, 9/336

MISC.: tavern/eating house music: harp, 1/15; gittern, 2/17; fiddler, 2/61, 175; harp and violin, 2/89; bagpipes and whistling, 2/101; mechanical organ, 2/115–16; dulcimer, 3/118; barber's music: 1/169; 4/237; dinner party music: 3/187; 8/4; street music: blind fiddler, 6/72; wedding music: 7/263; 8/66; also, 1/25, 59; 2/218, 233; 6/250, 251; 9/172, 313

UNDEFINED MUSIC (?instrumental, ?vocal, ?both): by P: 3/94, 184; 4/212, 213, 219, 220, 221, 266; 7/408, 412; by P with others: 3/108, 287; 5/266, 270, 310, 320; by others: 3/187

MUSICAL COMPOSITIONS:

COLLECTIONS [see also below, Lawes, Henry; Playford, John]: P's new song book, 1/161 & n. 4; his MS. song book, 1/302; French psalms in four parts, 1/140 & n. 3; three-part (?viol) music, 8/24–5; printed books of French songs, 9/428

SONGS AND OTHER COMPOSITIONS:

ANON.: ballads: 'The Blacksmith', 1/114 & n. 2; 'Chevy Chase', 8/56 & n. 3; 'St George' ['George, Duke of Albemarle'], 8/99 & n. 2; 'Joan's placket', 8/283 & n. 1; 'Mardyke', 1/41 & n. 2; 'Shackerley Hay', 6/2 & n. 1; others: 'All night I weep', 8/46 & n. 2; 'Barbara Allen', 7/1, 4, 5; 'La cruda la bella', 2/126 & n. 3; 'D'un air tout interdict', 6/223; 'Go and be hanged', 2/72 & n. 1, 78; 'Full forty times over', 8/466 & n. 3; 'The new droll', 8/5; ['I prithee sweet heart'], 2/72 & n. 1, 78; 'The Queen's old courtier', 9/242 & n. 3; 'S'io Moro', 8/174 & n. 2; 'This cursed jealousy', 3/36 & n. 2

[BANISTER, JOHN], ['Ah, Chloris now that I could sit'], 9/189 & n. 4; ['Go thy way'], 8/522 & n. 1; 9/189

[BREWER, THOMAS], 'Turn Amaryllis', 1/115 & n. 2

CARISSIMI, GIOVANNI, songs by, 5/217

DERING, RICHARD, Cantica Sacra, 3/263 & n. 2; 9/194 & n. 2; 'Canite Jehovae', 9/194 & n. 2

DRAGHI, GIOVANNI BATTISTA, opera by, 8/54 & n. 4, 56

[HILTON, JOHN], 'Come follow, follow me', 7/383 & n. 2

HUMFREY, PELHAM: anthems by, 8/515; 9/563; also, 8/532, 534

[IVES, SIMON], 'Fly boy, fly', 1/59 & n. 1

[?KING, WILLIAM, Poems of Mr Cowley . . . composed into songs . . .], 9/208 & n. 1

[?LANIER, NICHOLAS], 'Hermit poor', 8/56 & n. 2

LAWES, HENRY, ['Ariadne'], 6/303 & n. 1; 'At dead low ebb', 8/165 & n. 2; Ayres and dialogues, 6/27 & n. 3; 'Help, help, O help, divinity of love', 1/169 & n. 3, 302; 7/205; ['The Kisse. A Dialogue'] ('What is a kiss?'), 1/164 & n. 2; ['O king of heaven and hell'] ('Orpheus Hymne'), 1/76 & n. 2; from The siege of Rhodes, 6/284 & nn.; 8/25 & n. 1, 59 & n. 1

LAWES, HENRY AND WILLIAM, [Choice Psalmes], 1/285 & n. 5; 3/281 & n. 3; 5/120, 128, 236

LULLY, JEAN-BAPTISTE, music alluded to, 7/171

LOCK, MATTHEW, 'Domine salvum' (canon), 1/63 & n. 3; Little consort of three parts, 1/114 & n. 1; 3/184; Modern church musick, 8/413 & n. 1; duo music for flageolets, 9/279 & n. 2

PEPYS, SAMUEL: see above, Music

PLAYFORD, JOHN, Catch that catch can (1667), 7/381 & n. 4; 8/168 & n. 4, 171 & n. 2, 174 & n. 2; Dancing Master, ?3/263 & n. 1, 278; English dancing-master, ? ib.; Musicks Handmaide, 4/76 & n. 1; Musicks Recreation, 4/152 & n. 2; Select ayres and dialogues, ? 1/54 & n. 6, 115 & n. 2; ?4/110

PORTER, WALTER, Mottets of two voyces, 5/261 & n. 2

RAVENSCROFT, THOMAS, The whole booke of psalmes, 5/332 & n. 1, 342

[?WILSON, JOHN], 'Great, good and just', 1/32–3 & n.; 'The lark now leaves his watery nest', 9/299 & n. 3, 303, 304

MUSKERRY, Lord: see MacCarty

MUSSEL BANK, in the Medway: 8/310

MYDDELTON, Elizabeth, wife of Richard: P admires 4/200; 7/283

n. 2, 280 & n. 1; 4/302 & n. 1; 5/325,
326, 330 & n. 2; 6/72; 7/294 & n. 1
(totals given); 8/57–8, 372 & n. 1, 373;
and to Parliament, 7/64, 78, 93, 294,
295, 298, 305, 306, 308, 314, 356; 8/71
& n. 1, 303, 351, 448, 449; orders
pursers' accounts etc. 2/29 & n. 1;
examines/passes Navy Treasurer's accounts, 3/14, 240; 4/96–7, 99; 5/104 &
n. 2, 105, 318, 329; 6/119(2), 203;
7/289; 8/141, 169–70, 448, 449, 458,
460; 9/222, 250; examines Comptroller's accounts, 7/76; 8/50; discusses paying off fleet, 3/252–3, 265;
6/149; hopes for money from sale of
Dunkirk, 3/265, 271; assigned
£200,000 p.a. by Exchequer, 3/297 &
n. 1, 302; 4/81; discusses exchange
rate of pieces-of-eight, 4/132, 133;
draws up instructions for paying bills,
6/336 & n. 2; 'libel' against Board's
failure to pay bills, 7/388; allotted
£35,000 from poll tax, 8/57–8 & n.,
89, 90; and £500,000 from Eleven
Months Tax, 8/111–12, 205 & n. 1;
bills sold at 35–40% discount, 8/201;
receives £10,000 from Treasury,
8/252; discusses allocation from Treasury, 8/334; discusses pay tickets, 9/80,
263, 266; and cost of new fleet, 9/220
& n. 2; discusses expenses with Treasury, 9/444–5, 525–6, 530; credit good,
4/405 & n. 1; insolvency alluded to:
2/168; 3/210; 6/208, 211, 266, 273,
291–2, 293, 307, 322, 323, 324, 341;
7/256, 312, 313, 327, 331, 383; 8/66–7,
72, 96–7, 122 & n. 1, 206, 277 & n. 2,
315, 430–1; 9/18, 155, 180; also, 7/64,
78, 93, 383; 9/303

JUDICIAL AND DISCIPLINARY [*see also*
Field, [E.]; Carkesse, [J.]]: Officers
appointed J.P.s, 1/240, 252–3 & n.;
3/231; 4/78, 81–2 & n.; 8/31; commits alleged forger, 3/43–4 & n.;
charges alleged thief, 3/137 & n. 2;
adjudicates in dispute between captain
and purser, 3/284 & n. 1; commits
naval officers to trial for cowardice,
6/104 & n. 4; adjudicates between
captain and master, 4/84; between
captain and lieutenant, 7/380; between commander and Waith of
Treasury, 7/93–4 & n.; investigates

loss of ships, 8/12 & n. 1, 28; investigates charges against dockyard officers
9/258–9 & n., 267 & n. 2

SEAMEN AND OFFICERS: chooses ship's
masters etc., 2/103; 4/72; discusses
establishments, 4/290; 6/339 & n. 1;
(peacetime), 8/448 & n. 2; the press,
5/168 & n. 2; 6/45; 7/188; 8/394;
discharges men etc., 7/327; discusses
riot, 8/62–3

SHIPS AND SHIPBUILDING: hires ships,
1/242; 5/349, 350; (fireships), 7/161;
(for Portugal), 3/63, 72, 85, 196; pays
off ships, 1/245 & n. 1, 246, 247,
249, 283, 288, 308–9; 2/18, 19, 28,
30, 33; 8/396–7; appoints winter
guard, 1/257, 266: 8/485–6; sets out
ships, 2/127; 3/30–1, 125 & n. 2;
5/287 & n. 2; 6/233; 9/101, 121–2,
123, 125, 126, 130, 155, 180, 216–17,
220 & n. 2, 223(2); (for Guinea),
5/246 & n. 3, 248, 265; (fireships),
8/256(2) & n. 2, 259, 260 & n. 2;
(merchantmen), 8/314–15, 316; (for
Mediterranean), 9/424, 425–6, 510,
513 ~ to build ten ships, 7/193 & n. 5,
201; discusses design of masts, 9/5 &
n. 1; and Heemskerck's project,
9/198 & n. 1, 206; values ships, 9/96
& n. 1; also, 5/111, 131

SICK AND WOUNDED: orders money
for, 6/239 & n. 1, 243 & n. 2; approves
proposal for infirmary, 7/49 & n. 2;
discusses relief of prisoners, 7/201

VICTUALLING: examines/passes accounts, 3/41–2 & n., 52, 55, 62, 103,
106; 4/337; 7/74(2), 373, 403, 405;
8/47, 49, 50, 77, 208, 322; 9/250;
inspects victualling office, 3/135 & n.
3; 4/84; obtains cash by sale of prize-
goods, 6/239 & n. 1; discusses P's
report, 7/219–20 & n.; examined by
Council about complaints of Rupert
and Albemarle, 7/259 & n. 1, 260;
concludes new contract with Gauden,
9/252, 253, 261, 263, 287(2) & n. 1, 288
& n. 2, 301, 303(2) & n. 1, 428 & n. 4,
429; decides against direct management, 9/315–18 passim & nn.; prepares supplies for Mediterranean
fleet, 9/508 & n. 2; also, 1/212–13;
4/36, 282; 7/13, 129, 135; 8/245;
9/24–5, 142

NEW BRIDEWELL, Clerkenwell: P visits, 5/250 & n. 4, 289; 6/65–6, & n. 3
NEWBURY, Berks.: P at, 9/242
NEWCASTLE, Duke and Duchess of: see Cavendish
NEWCASTLE UPON TYNE, Northumberland: parliamentary election, 2/76 & n. 1; dispute between city and Gerard, 9/359 & nn.; shipping from/ to, 4/395, 397; 8/263, 285, 602; coals from, 8/426, 435, 576
NEW CHAPEL, Orchard St, Westminster: plague burials, 6/162
NEWELL, ——, clergyman: 3/199
NEW ENGLAND: masts/mastships from, 5/123, 127, 239, 321; 7/395, 397; alluded to: 4/71
NEW EXCHANGE, Strand (the Exchange): shut by King's order, 4/431 & n. 5; P spreads news at, 7/151; makes assignation, 7/385; drafts memorandum, 9/84(2); P/EP shop(s) at: for pendants, 4/100; mercers' and drapers' goods, 4/100; 7/70, 344; 8/104, 322, 424; 9/84, 188, 206–7, 400; dressing-boxes, 8/53; 9/91(2); books, 7/103, 104, 117; 8/380, 383, 387, 439, 508; 9/29, 216, 411, 449; baubles, 7/386; knives, 8/433; also visit(s) (to pay bills, or for unspecified purposes): 1/85, 251; 3/52, 65, 215; 4/58, 100, 124, 164, 286, 290, 324, 332, 336, 341, 357, 363; 5/9, 48, 55, 118, 134, 144, 155, 186, 238, 269; 6/17, 52, 100; 7/124, 131, 208, 256, 367, 369, 425; 8/27, 30, 46, 86, 99, 100, 110, 121, 151, 213, 334, 341, 353, 393, 403, 431, 460, 463; 9/6, 28, 39, 46, 89, 113, 120, 124, 158, 178, 179, 182, 215, 218, 247, 264, 269, 295, 304, 313, 333, 393, 397, 412, 419, 422, 437, 465, 449, 474, 511, 532
NEW EXCHANGE STAIRS: 7/233, 284; 8/517; 9/128
NEWGATE: 9/258
NEWGATE MARKET: P shops in: for grate, 4/409; poultry, 5/264; also, 3/294; 9/268; shambles, 3/283; Fire, 7/277
NEWGATE PRISON: prisoners escape, 8/371; malpractices of keeper, 8/562 & n. 2; alluded to: 4/5; 9/111
NEW HALL, Essex: timber at, 4/435 & n. 3

NEWINGTON, Surrey: P's father married, 5/360; alluded to: 2/91
NEWINGTON GREEN, Mdx: 5/132, ?360
NEWMAN, Col. [George]: 4/260
NEWMAN, Samuel, Puritan divine [see also Books]: foretells his death, 9/31 & n. 3
NEWMAN, ——, barber: 1/15
NEWMARKET, Suff.: King/Duke of York visit(s) races at, 4/324 & n. 2; 9/209 & n. 2, 264, 341, 343, 473 & n. 5, 535 & n. 2
NEW NETHERLAND (N. America): surrender of, 5/283 & n. 2
NEW PALACE YARD, [New York] Westminster [see also Taverns etc.: Crown; Leg; Swan]: soldiers in, 1/40, 43; Quaker meeting, 1/44 & n. 2; also, 3/177; 4/234
NEWPORT, Andrew, Comptroller of the Great Wardrobe: appointed, 9/41 & n. 3; at Exchequer, 9/477; social: 9/112
NEWPORT [Richard]: at Vauxhall, 9/218 & n. 4, 220
NEWPORT, Essex: 8/467
NEWPORT (I. of Wight), TREATY OF (1648): 4/473 & n. 2
NEWPORT PAGNELL, Bucks.: P visits, 9/224, 225 & nn.
NEWPORT ST, Westminster: 9/431
NEWSPAPERS: Muddiman's parliamentary newsbooks, 1/12 & n. 3; P's letters quoted in, 1/126, n. 2; Buckhurst's defence in, 3/35–6 & n.; Scottish news, 4/138 & n. 3; 7/387 & n. 2; Portuguese news, 4/203 & n. 1; P reads first number of The Intelligencer, 4/297 & n. 2; asked to contribute news to, 5/348 & n. 1; Moore's account of Battle of Lowestoft in, 6/128 & n. 3; P pays for newsbooks, 6/162; Oxford Gazette: P reads first number, 6/305 & n. 3; Chatham Chest business in 7/116 & n. 2; Great Fire foretold, 7/405 & n. 3, 406; report on Carkesse case, 8/216 & n. 1; French news, 9/38 & n. 1; P reads newsbooks at Brouncker's, 9/161; Lisbon gazette, 4/215 & n. 1; Dutch gazette, 8/126–7 & n. 1; also, 7/242

during Plague, 6/188 & n. 1; and after Fire, 7/278 & n. 1; P visits, 6/234, 235, 244, 303, 304, 311, 312, 313; alluded to: 7/299

NORBURY, [George], P's uncle: social: 2/215, 220; 4/427; 5/47, 49, 151, 340; 7/115, 134

NORBURY, [Katherine], daughter of George: ? 4/312; 5/61

NORBURY, Mary, daughter of George: ?4/312; 5/61

NORBURY, [Sarah], wife of George: offers to sell Brampton property to P, 2/124 & n. 5; 3/13; social: 2/200, 215, 220; 4/312; 5/140, 340; ~ ?her sister, 4/312

NORE, the: English fleet at, 6/275; 7/123, 223, 304, 326, 332, 355, 360; Dutch fleet at, 8/256, 258, 354, 359; P visits *Royal Sovereign*, 6/188, 194; pay at, 8/144

NORMAN, [James], clerk to Sir W. Batten; Clerk of the Survey, Chatham 1664: new design for storekeeper's books, 5/104 & n. 1; alluded to: 3/164; 5/36, 141

NORRIS, ——, frame-maker: 9/538

NORTH, Catherine, Lady North, wife of Sir Charles: 8/600 & n. 3

NORTH, Sir Charles, kted before 1667, succ. as 5th Baron North 1677; relative of Sandwich: P's opinion, 8/600; on Dutch voyage with Sandwich, 1/138, 142, 153, 159; marriage, 8/600 & n. 3; musical: 1/123 & n. 1, 129; social: 1/135

NORTH, Sir Dudley, succ. as 4th Baron North 1666: defeated in elections for Cambridgeshire, 1/112 & n. 2; social: 1/75

NORTH, [Francis; Lord Keeper (as Baron Guilford) 1682–5]: 9/140

NORTHAMPTON, Earl of: *see* Compton

NORTHAMPTON: floods, 4/139 & n. 1

NORTHAMPTONSHIRE: declaration for free parliament, 1/28 & n. 6

NORTHUMBERLAND, Lord: *see* Percy, Sir Henry, 9th Earl; Percy, Algernon, 10th Earl

NORTON, [Daniel], of Southwick, Hants.: marriage, 6/150 & n. 3; death

and will, 7/264; also, 6/60; ~ his son, 7/264

[NORTON, George], innkeeper at Abbotsleigh, nr Bristol: 1/155 & n. 3

NORTON, [Isabella], (b. Lawson), wife of Daniel: her beauty, 4/23; 5/7; marriage, 6/150–1 & n. 3; widowed, 7/264; also, 6/60

NORTON, Joyce, relative of P: P shows her Parliament chamber, 1/39; buys mourning for Duke of Gloucester, 1/251; gives silver cup to P and EP, 5/47; at Tom P's funeral, 5/90; grown old, 9/425; social: at P's father's, 1/65, 81, 85, 88, 176; 2/40; at P's stone feast, 2/60; 3/53; 4/94–5; 5/98; 6/124; also, 1/10, 72; 2/43, 53; 3/207; 5/87, 166; 5/391; 9/530–1; alluded to: 4/272

NORTON, [Mary], actress: P admires in *Le Cid*, 3/273 & n. 1; in *The siege of Rhodes*, 3/295; P meets, 7/190–1

NORTON, Col. [Richard]: given commission, 8/265 & n. 5; alluded to: 6/150

NORTON, [Roger], King's printer: Chancery dispute, 7/261 & n. 5

NORTON ST PHILIP, Som.: church and tombs, 9/232 & nn.

NORWAY: timber, 3/118 & n. 3; 4/103; sawmills, 3/118; transport of timber, ib.; naval supplies from, 5/333; 6/330

NORWICH, Earl of: *see* Goring

NORWICH: flags from, 5/182 & n. 1

NORWOOD, Henry, Maj./Col., Deputy Governor of Dunkirk 1662, and Tangier 1665–8: carries letters between Sandwich and King, 1/112, 125; at surrender of Dunkirk, 3/272; quarrels with Fitzgerald, 5/344–5 & n.; Tangier business, 6/144; 7/18–20 passim; 8/372; invites P to join in trading venture, 7/23, 24; quarrels with Houblons, 7/38, 45; P's low opinion, 7/99; dispute with Bland, 9/392 & n. 1, 430–1; enemy of Cholmley, 9/455; social: 1/264; 7/38, 44, 61

NOSTRADAMUS (Notredame, Michel de), astrologer (d. 1566): anecdote of, 8/42 & nn.

9/434 & n. 2; P defends Cambridge against, 9/545; the colleges: purge of fellows, 1/227 & n. 1; All Souls, 9/226 & n. 2; Brasenose, ib. & n. 3; Christ Church, 8/379; 9/226; New College, 9/544 & n. 4

OXFORD KATE'S: *see* Taverns etc.: Cock, Bow St

[OXMAN, William], rebel: executed, 2/18 & n. 2

PACKER (Parke), [John], merchant: dispute about Portuguese customs-dues, 5/43 & n. 2

PACKER, [Philip], Deputy-Paymaster of the King's Works: advises Sandwich on alterations at Hinchingbrooke, 2/48–9 & n.; social: 9/527, 559; ~ his ?wife/mother, 1/272

PADDINGTON: P at, 7/204

PAGE, Damaris: her brothel destroyed in riot, 9/132

PAGE, Capt. [Thomas], naval officer: account of Four Days Fight, 7/153

PAGE, [William], of Ashtead, Surrey: P and Creed stay with overnight, 4/245 & n. 3

PAGET, [Justinian], lawyer, of Gray's Inn: makes music, 3/184, 281, 287; 5/119; also, 1/234; 4/367; ~ his son [Justinian, of Gray's Inn], 8/365

PAGET'S: *see* Taverns etc.: Mitre, Mitre Court

PAINTER-STAINERS' Company: *see* London: livery companies

PALACE YARD: *see* New Palace Yard

PALL MALL (the alley for the game): *see* St James's Park

PALL MALL (the street) [*see also* Taverns etc.: Wood's]: Plague in, 6/147–8; Lady Castlemaine's lodgings, 7/159; Sir H. Cholmley's house, 9/122; also, 9/540

PALMER, Barbara, (b. Villiers), wife of Roger, 1st Earl of Castlemaine, cr. Duchess of Cleveland 1670:

PERSONAL: P admires her beauty, 2/174; 3/24, 82, 139, 175–6; 4/63; 5/161, 214; 7/347, 409; 8/33; her clothes on washing line, 3/87; her graciousness to child, 3/175; her dancing, 3/301; and her dress, 4/57;

dreams about, 6/191; plain dress unbecoming to, 7/306; her patches, 9/186; her beauty decays, 4/182; 5/294–5; 7/106

CHRON. SERIES: King associates/ dallies with, 1/199 & n. 4; 2/80; 3/87, 302; 4/1, 13, 30, 342; 5/164; flirts with Duke of York, 1/265; relations with Queen, 3/87, 97, 191, 202, 289; 4/68; appointment to Queen's Household, 3/147 & n. 2; leaves husband to live at Richmond, 3/139 & n. 2; moves into Whitehall Palace, 4/112, 132, 134; at Oxford with King, 4/315; ill, 3/24; pregnancy rumoured, 3/248 & n. 1; 4/1; 7/324; 8/355, 366, 368; and abortion, 5/245; 6/71 & n. 3; quarrels with King, 4/213, 216, 222, 272, 342; 8/331, 333, 334, 355; their reconciliations, 4/238; 5/20, 21; 8/366; to leave court, 8/412, 422 & n. 3, 424; at court but out of favour, 8/431–2, 590; 9/24, 219; friendly to Frances Stuart, 8/288; to Nell Gwyn, 8/402; libel against, 9/154 & n. 1; association with/power over King alluded to, 3/132, 147, 227, 282; 4/136, 137, 174, 206, 238, 256; 6/115–16; 7/8, 159, 404, 409; 8/184, 368, 377; 9/27, 417; debts paid by King, 7/404 & n. 2; 8/324–5; pension, 8/424; grant for children stopped, 8/434 & n. 3; affair with Sir C. Berkeley, 4/38; H. Jermyn, 8/366 & n. 2, 368; and Hart, 9/156 & n. 4; alleged lechery as child, 7/336–7; turns catholic, 4/431 & n. 4; attends Queen's chapel, 8/589

POLITICAL INFLUENCE [*see also* chron. series]: friend of Monmouth, 3/191; distracts King from business, 7/57; supports standing army, 8/361; makes a bishop, 8/364–5 & n.; supports H. Brouncker, 8/416; welcomes Clarendon's fall, 8/404 & n. 1, 415, 427; her part in Nicholas's fall, 8/534; alliance with Buckingham, 8/331, 342; 9/27; and enmity to, 9/336, 342; makes peace between King and Duke of York, 9/153; supports French treaty, 9/536

AT COURT: causes factions, 3/15, 245; envied by court ladies, 3/64; power, 3/237; mocks at maids of honour,

6/41; quarrels with Dowager Duchess of Richmond, 3/68 & n. 4; and Lady Hervey, 9/415 & n. 1; encourages Duke of York's affair with Lady Denham, 7/159; at balls, 3/215, 300; 4/68; 7/373; Garter service, 4/112; lottery, 5/214; masque, 6/29; and court play, 9/24; hunts moth, 8/282; gaming for high stakes, 9/71
CHILDREN: by ?her husband, 3/175; by the King: 8/355, n. 1; birth and christening of Charles (later Duke of Southampton), 3/81 & n. 1, 87, 146; birth of Henry (later Duke of Grafton), 4/315 & n. 2; 5/56; George (later Duke of Northumberland), 7/8 & n. 2; Charlotte, 6/41 & n. 2; also, 8/376
HOUSES ETC.: in King St, Westminster, 1/199 & n. 4; 3/147; Pall Mall, 7/159; Whitehall, 5/164; fire at lodgings, 5/27; aviary, 8/404; Berkshire House, 9/190 & n. 3
PORTRAITS: by Lely, 3/113 & n. 3; version acquired by Sandwich, 5/200 & n. 3; P buys prints, 7/359 & n. 3, 393, 417; 8/23, 124, 171, 206; also, 3/230
SOCIAL: at dinner party, 9/468, 469; mock-wedding to Frances Stuart, 4/37-8, 48; at theatre, 2/139, 164, 174; 3/87, 260; 4/56; 5/33, 77; 6/73; 7/347; 8/46, 225; 9/186, 398; puppet play, 8/409; in Hyde Park, 4/95; 5/126; 6/60; 8/196; 9/282
ALLUDED TO: 8/45
~ her servants: her black boy, 8/33; —— Willson, her woman, 8/288, 325; 9/186; her nurse, 8/288
PALMER, Benjamin: 1/246
PALMER, ——, lawyer [?identical with the foregoing]: 4/277; ~ his wife, ib.
PALMER, Sir Geoffrey, Attorney-General 1660–d.70: advises Sandwich on patent of nobility, 1/187-8 & n.; and P on Clerkship of Acts, 1/194; issues warrant for P's appointment, 1/196 & n. 1; and for Tangier commission, 5/229; P consults, 5/325-6; 6/101; 9/281, 291; rumoured appointment as Chief Justice, 8/412 & n. 2; draws up Tangier charter, 9/149;

house at Hampstead, 9/281 & n. 2; alluded to: 8/67; 9/122
PALMER, [James], Vicar of St Bride, Fleet St, 1616–45: death, 1/11 & n. 4
PALMER, [Roger], 1st Earl of Castlemaine [see also Books]: patent of nobility, 2/229 & n. 1; deserted by wife, 3/139, 146-7 & n.; their mutual indifference, 3/175, 248; said to have entered French monastery, 3/147 & n. 1; returns from France, 6/41, 55-6; their amicable separation, 7/404 & n. 2; alluded to: 1/199 & n. 4
PALMER, Mrs ——: entertains P with bawdy songs and ventriloquy, 4/261-2
PANNIER ALLEY: 7/98, 101(2)
PAPILLON, [Thomas], merchant: victualling contract, 9/287 & n. 1; dispute with excise farmers, 9/532 & n. 2
PARGITER, [Francis], of the Muscovy Company: stories of Russia, 5/272 & n. 1; alluded to: 2/142
PARGITER, [John, sen.], goldsmith: loses by purchase of Crown lands, 2/199 & n. 3
PARHAM, [Richard], of the Fishmongers' Company: Fishery business, 3/269-70 & n.; 5/309; gives P oysters, 5/312
PARIS: famine (1661), 3/200 & n. 2; cleanliness and order, 8/299-300 & nn.; peace celebrations, 9/257 & n. 3; also, 8/74
PARISH CLERKS' Company: see London: livery companies
PARKE: see Packer
PARKER, Capt. [John], naval officer: 1/121
PARKER, [?John], merchant, of Mark Lane: ship retaken from Algerines, 2/221 & n. 3
PARKER, Mrs ——: 8/511
PARKHURST, [John and Catherine]: 9/176-7 & n.
PARKHURST, Sir Robert, of Pyrford, Surrey: borrows £2000 from Sandwich, 1/310 & n. 2, 311, 312; 2/48; 4/94; his prescription for colic, 4/441; social: 5/149
PARLIAMENT: (general):
P'S EVIDENCE, vol. i, pp. cxxxi-iii; his

232, 234 & n. 1; abortive motion to reward Sandwich, 1/178 & n. 2; allocates excise to King, 1/303 & n. 4; orders exhumation of regicides' corpses, 1/309 & n. 4; Committee for disbandment of armed forces: appointment and proceedings, 1/245 & n. 1, 246 & n. 3, 247, 249, 283, 288 & n. 1, 308–9; 2/18 & n. 3, 19 & n. 2, 28 & n. 3, 30, 33 & n. 3, 45 & n. 1, 50; parties: Presbyterians to impose terms on King, 1/117, 118; Cavaliers and Presbyterians, 1/118 & n. 4; Episcopalians and Presbyterians, 1/229; 'factions', 2/1

PARLIAMENT (the Cavalier):
ELECTIONS: Cambridge borough, 2/56 & n. 2; London, 2/57 & n. 1; Newcastle-upon-Tyne, 2/76 & n. 1; bye-elections: court candidates defeated, 7/337 & n. 2; Quakers' candidate, 9/150 & n. 2; expenses, 8/454–5 & n.

FIRST SESSION, 8 May 1661–19 May 1662:
    HOUSE OF LORDS: examines Hutchinson's accounts, 2/100; dispute with Commons over licensing bill, 2/144 & n. 3; bishops resume seats, 2/216 & n. 4; debates Clarendon's proviso to bill of uniformity, 3/49 & n. 1; prayers, 3/61
    HOUSE OF COMMONS: receives communion, 2/107 & n. 1; orders Commonwealth legislation to be burnt, 2/108 & n. 4; bill restoring bishops to Lords, 2/111 & n. 2; benevolences, ib. & n. 4; grants supply, 2/217–18 & n.; lack of government control, 2/141 & n. 3; examines regicides, 2/224 & n. 1; orders fast, 3/10 & n. 2; militia bill, 3/15 & n. 2; hearth tax bill, 3/41 & n. 2, 43, 78; uniformity bill, 3/49; hastens business, 3/85

SECOND SESSION, 18 Feb.–27 July 1663:
    GENERAL: reassembles, 4/49; King's speech, 4/50 & n. 2; King calls on to hasten business, 4/159 & n. 3; prorogation, 4/239, 240, 249–51 & nn.; forms of royal assent to bills, 4/249–50 & nn.
    HOUSE OF LORDS: Bristol's attempted impeachment of Clarendon, 4/222–5 passim & nn., 229 & n. 3, 231 & n. 2;

defeats conventicle bill, 4/249; debates bill on popery, ib.; 'mislays' bill for sabbath observance, ib. & n. 2
    HOUSE OF COMMONS: opposes King's declaration of indulgence, 4/44 & n. 2, 57 & n. 4, 58 & n. 1, 62, 63, 82; to disqualify members refusing to abjure Covenant, 4/53 & n. 1; bill encouraging wearing of English cloth, ib. & n. 2; bill and address against popery, 4/67–8, 90 & n. 1, 92, 95 & n. 2, 249; resumption of crown lands, 4/87–8; to enquire into navy expenses, 4/103; and Queen's, 4/127 & n. 1; bill to disqualify ex-rebels from office, 3/291; 4/125 & n. 1, 126, 136 & n. 1; bill to suppress abuses in sale of offices, 4/156 & n. 4, 166, 169 & n. 2, 190; enquiries into revenue, 4/166, 193 & n. 2; bill to suppress conventicles, 4/159–60, 161, 243 & n. 3, 249; votes supply, 4/183, 187, 191, 205–6 & n., 249–50; votes £200,000 p.a. to navy from customs, 4/206 & n. 3; votes on Temple's attempt to manage House, 4/191–2 & n., 200, 207, 208, 211; Bristol's speech on, 4/207–8 & nn.; fast day for weather, 4/237 & n. 3; bill to enforce sabbath observance, 4/249 & n. 2; parties: court party, 4/57, 58

THIRD SESSION, 16 March–17 May 1664:
    GENERAL: reassembles, 5/88; adjourned and reassembles, 5/93; King's speech on triennial bill, 5/112 & n. 4; act about writs of error, 5/112; joint address against Dutch, 5/131, 135, 137; King's reply, 5/137; conference on conventicle bill, 5/147–8 & nn.; (untrue) rumour of prorogation, 5/151; prorogued, 5/247 & n. 4
    HOUSE OF LORDS: Lady Petre's case, 5/109–12 passim & nn., 126, 128–9; joint address with Commons against Dutch, 5/131
    HOUSE OF COMMONS: triennial bill, 5/93–4, 99 & nn., 102–3; Navy Board enabling bill, 5/99 & n. 1, 104, 105; merchants' petitions against Dutch, 5/107–9 passim, 113, 127, 129 & n. 2; grants £2½m. for war, 5/331 & n. 1; parties: Bristol's faction, 5/89; Presbyterian faction, 5/103, 327–8; King's party, 5/331

of York instructs 'friends', 8/482; 'the country party' attack Kelyng, 8/483–4; 'cavalier' party twice defeated, 9/30; members briefed by Navy Board, 9/79, 80, 83; court party supports Penn, 9/165

PARLIAMENT STAIRS [i.e. jetty]: 1/311; 4/263; 7/240

PARMA, Duchy of: projected marriage alliance with England, 4/224 & n. 1

PARRY, [?Thomas; council clerk]: 3/49

PARSON DROVE, Cambs.: P visits, 4/310

PARSON'S GREEN, Fulham: 8/400

PASTIMES: see Games etc.

PATENT OFFICE, the: clerkship in, 9/372 & n. 2, 492; records, 9/479, 480

PATERNOSTER ROW: P/EP buy(s) silks, clothes etc., 1/82, 298; 4/199; 5/114; 6/114, 125; 7/7; other visits, 3/65, 83; 4/155; 5/145; 7/173, 242; Prerogative Office, 4/300 & n. 1

PAUL'S WHARF: see [St] Paul's Wharf

PAULET, Charles, styled Lord St John, succ. as 6th Marquess of Winchester 1675, cr. Duke of Bolton 1689 (d. 1699): affray, 7/391 & n. 1; caricatured in play, 9/187 & n. 4

PAULET, Isabella Theresa Mary, wife of John, 5th Marquess of Winchester: 9/537

PAYLER, [George], Navy Commissioner 1654–60: 3/197

PAYNE, Nell, P's servant: angers P, 8/209; promoted cookmaid, 8/225; P caresses, 8/274, 276(2), 280, 293, 315; 9/188; dismissed, 8/375, 376; P's designs on, 9/180, 469

PAYNE, ——, waterman: leaves P's service for Lord Chamberlain's, 2/96, 97; has plague, 6/225; child buried, ib; recommends maid to P, 8/328; alluded to: 2/101; 9/313

PAY OFFICE, the: see Navy Treasury

PAYTON: see Blayton

PEACHELL, [John], Fellow of Magdalene College, Cambridge: drinks King's health, 1/68; at tavern, 2/146; his red nose, 8/199 & n. 3; also, 9/212

PEAK, the, Derbyshire: 4/19 & n. 2

PEARSE (Pierce), [Andrew], purser: apprenticed to tavern-keeper, 1/301; on *Naseby*, 1/108, 116; gift to P, 1/232; lives in style, 1/313; to be appointed Muster-Master, 2/99 & n. 1; ill, 2/150; advice on provisioning ship, 2/197–8; social: P first visits his house, 1/312; gives dinners, 1/312; also, 1/23, 75, 115, 151, 173, 174, 187, 301; 2/23, 49, 108; 6/327–8; ~ his daughter, 1/313; son-in-law, 2/150

PEARSE, ——, wife of Andrew: social: 1/301, 313; 2/3, 23, 150

PEARSE, Betty, daughter of James and Elizabeth: grows pretty, 7/341, 399; P's valentine, 8/65, 86; portrait by Hayls, 9/188; social: with mother at P's house, 7/399, 400; 8/157, 502–3; 9/128, 172; also, 7/95, 100, 103; 9/219, 289

PEARSE (Pierce), Elizabeth, wife of James:

P'S OPINION: 'gallant', 1/29; admires her beauty, 1/283; 2/94, 151 & n. 2, 117; 3/299; 6/89, 251, 321; 7/135, 220; 'la belle Pearse', 2/157, 193, 213; 3/51; good complexion, 5/151, 197; 8/235; dislikes her painted face, 8/439 & n. 2, 454, 503; 9/262; and sluttish housekeeping, 2/3; 5/151; 8/439; 9/188

CHRON. SERIES: child christened, 1/234; daughter born, 2/151, 171; churched, 2/185; new house, 5/151; expecting child, 6/89; at Greenwich in Plague, 6/228; hides husband's prize-goods, 6/317, 318; admired by Cocke, 6/318; new house in Covent Garden, 7/16; EP jealous of her, 2/201; 7/120, 122; quarrels with, 7/236–7, 238; acquaintance renewed, 7/322; son [Vincent] born and dies, 7/220 & n. 2, 236; son [John] christened, 8/454 & n. 3; pregnant again, 9/286–7, 289; EP's jealousy renewed, 9/1, 108; P forswears meeting, 9/339, 368, 376, 469; her closet, 5/151; 8/439; also, 1/66, 139, 251; 3/52; 8/156

PORTRAIT BY HAYLS: 7/93 & n. 1, 97, 108, 111, 117, 120, 131; 8/169

SOCIAL: at P's stone feast, 2/60; at Portsmouth, 3/72–4; on river trip, 5/197; at music/dancing parties at Greenwich, 6/284, 320–1, 323; 7/16,

17; at her house in Covent Garden, 7/18, 73, 362–3; 9/128; at P's house, 8/25, 28, 29, 104; 9/12; and tavern, 9/134; at theatre, 5/246; 7/347; 8/27, 64, 101, 383, 511; 9/12, 133, 186; P's valentine, 7/44, 49, 70; visits Kensington, 7/95, 100; and Islington, 7/121–2; at court ball, 7/341, 371–3; court news from, 7/99–100; 8/169; 9/23–4, 311, 320; hears Italian singer, 8/599; 9/172, 219; sees crown jewels, 9/172; at review in Hyde Park, 9/308; at P's house, 1/29, 259; 2/23; 4/14, 89; 5/291; 7/92, 118, 343–4, 399–400, 401; 8/151, 157, 502, 598; P/EP visit(s), 1/215; 2/169; 3/8, 301; 4/73, 124; 5/318; 8/103, 105, 242; 9/218; also, 1/32, 86–7, 96, 214, 312–13; 5/245; 6/49, 294; 7/53, 84, 93, 100, 103–4, 136; 8/58

ALLUDED TO: 6/316; 7/53

~ her servant Mary, 6/317; 7/93, 103, 238, 257

PEARSE (Pierce), James, surgeon; surgeon to the Duke of York 1662; Groom of the Privy Chamber to the Queen 1664; Surgeon-General to the fleet 1665:

CHRON. SERIES: visits regiment, 1/64–6 passim, 68; on Dutch voyage, 1/102, 119, 145, 148, 151, 154; on sea service, 1/186; shows P Somerset House, 3/191; and Whitehall, 5/188; promised place as Queen's surgeon, 3/234–5; dissects cadavers, 4/132; injects opium into dog, 5/151; attends dissection, 9/254; buys place as Groom of Queen's Privy Chamber, 4/255; attends Sandwich, 4/17; Sandwich's favour to, 5/22; his part in prize-goods affair, 6/230, 240, 247, 294, 317, 328, 333; away from London in Plague, 6/321; 7/16; account of Four Days Fight, 7/158; applies for place in hospital, 8/91–2; continued in place as Surgeon-General, 8/198 & n. 1; banking account, 8/270; in privateer business, 8/342; and prize-goods scandal, 9/91; consults P on pay, 8/436; P godfather to son, 8/454 & n. 3; evidence about Battle of Lowestoft, 8/491; treats Arabella Churchill for ?pox, 9/413; also, 1/80, 251; 4/91; 5/131–2,

197; 8/20

COURT/POLITICAL NEWS FROM: 3/157, 227, 234, 248, 289; 4/132, 174, 187, 222, 272, 348, 370, 392, 399–400; 5/4, 20, 33, 40, 50, 245, 275; 6/321; 7/8, 99–100, 314–15, 323–4, 399, 400; 8/47, 192, 235, 253, 270, 297, 334, 376, 403–4, 436, 475, 476, 550–1; 9/204–5, 335–6, 501–2

HIS HOUSE: in St Margaret's churchyard, 1/186, 212, 215; new house [?nr Covent Garden], 5/151; 7/136, 296, 341; 8/169; lets rooms after fire, 7/296

SOCIAL: at P's stone feast, 2/60; his 'foul discourse', 4/436; at music/dancing parties, 6/320–1, 323; 7/16; visits Bear Garden, 7/246; attends court ball, 7/371–3; at Teddeman's funeral, 9/200; Vauxhall, 9/219; and Mulberry Gardens, 9/286; to see execution, 9/335; at taverns, 1/26; 2/49, 89, 108, 117; 9/134, 172; P visits etc., 1/27, 47, 208, 283; 2/3, 48; 4/14; 7/92, 100; 8/28, 65; 9/4, 188, 311; at P's house, 1/29–30, 53, 259; 2/23; 3/138; 5/7, 291; 7/236, 352; 8/20, 64, 104, 157, 502; 9/12, 128, 145, 376; on *Naseby*, 1/103, 105, 107; at theatre, 1/214; 2/60; 7/347; 9/522; also, 1/173, 214, 313; 4/21–2; 8/58, 228; 9/126–7, 289

ALLUDED TO: 1/32, 86, 93, 145, 173, 203, 251, 252; 2/114; 9/293

~ his man, 1/68; brother, 2/149; sister, 5/197; kinswoman, ib.; brother-in-law, 8/104

PEARSE, James, son of James and Elizabeth: P delights in his company, 6/317–18; 7/70, 100; 8/188; portrait by Hayls, 9/188; at school, 9/413; social: with mother at P's house, 7/343; 8/104, 157; 9/12, 128; also, 7/93, 95; 8/599; 9/286, 289; his master, 8/188

PEARSON, John, Master of Trinity College, Cambridge 1662–73, Bishop of Chester 1672–d. 86: 8/337 & n. 2

PEARSON, Richard, Vicar of St Bride, Fleet St 1660–6, Canon of Exeter 1643–4, 1660–d. 68: conducts Tom P's funeral service, 5/91

PEDLEY, [Nicholas], lawyer, kted 1672: elected M.P. for Huntingdon,

1/99 & n. 2; consulted on Brampton business, 9/451–3 passim
PEDRO, 'Seignor', musician: *see* [Reggio], Piero
PEIRS: *see* [Pierce, William]
PELHAM, ——, merchant: sings with P, 9/217, 261
PELLING, [?John], apothecary: city/ court/political news from, 8/264–5 & n., 268, 302–3, 396 & n. 1, 490; 9/29, 114; prescribes tea for EP, 8/302; shows P bladder stone, 9/136; gifts to P, 9/286; also, 9/446, 493; social/ musical: sings with P., 8/340, 413, 429, 437–8, 444, 557; 9/11, 58–9, 152, 250, 261, 320; talks of music, 8/432; visits/dines with P, 8/326, 389, 400, 465, 589, 594; 9/48, 57, 118–19, 128, 138, 143, 144, 244, 255, 260, 271, 326, 354, 364, 411, 461, 526; visits gipsies with EP, 9/278; also, 8/453; ~ his wife, 8/400
PELLING, [John], Rector of Bath (d. 1620): monument in Bath Abbey, 9/238 & n. 4
PEMBERTON (Pemmerton), Francis, lawyer, kted 1675; Judge King's Bench 1679; Lord Chief Justice 1681–3; Chief Justice Common Pleas 1683; Privy Councillor 1682–3 (d. 1697): consulted about prize-goods affair, 9/61, 63; acts for navy creditors, 9/140; alluded to: 9/72
PEMBLETON (Pendleton), ——, of St Olave's parish, dancing master: a 'pretty neat black man', 4/140; teaches EP/P, 4/109 & n. 1, 111, 114; 122–3, 126, 129, 132, 133, 134, 141, 148, 149, 150, 155, 156, 161; arouses P's jealousy, 4/140, 141, 144, 148–9, 150, 153–4, 157–8, 161, 165, 166, 172, 173, 179, 183, 229, 277–8, 278, 281, 285, 291, 300, 318, 337–8, 347, 369; 5/17, 18, 125; social: at P's dances, 7/422; 8/28, 511; 9/12; also, 8/337, 503; alluded to: 8/211; ~ his wife, 4/338, 347, 369
PEMBROKE, Lord: *see* Herbert, P.
PEN: P's silver (fountain) pen, 4/264 & n. 1, 278; P carries pen and ink, 6/312
PENELL'S: *see* Taverns etc.
PENINGTON, Ald. Sir Isaac: death, 6/299 & n. 1

PENINGTON, [Judith], daughter of Sir Isaac: P admires, 6/257, 273, 293; visits/meets, 6/290, 299, 308; dallies with, 6/297, 310, 318–19, 332, 334–5; gift to, 6/307; ~ her dog, 6/290, 293
PENN, Capt. [George], merchant, brother of Sir William: P meets, 2/186 & n. 2; death and burial, 5/229, 230 & n.
PENN, [Margaret], Lady Penn, wife of Sir William:
CHRON. SERIES: 'a well-looked, fat, short, old Dutchwoman', 5/246 & n. 4; returns from Ireland, 5/244, 245; rejoices in husband's success, 6/123; at Woolwich in Plague, 6/185, 209 & n. 1; disagreements with husband, 7/284; 8/241, 436; household's poverty, 8/217; humble origins, 8/226–7, 228; also, 7/151, 259, 311, 365; 8/79
SOCIAL: at party, 6/78; at Sheriff's dinner, 6/79; Batten's, 6/140; 8/423; fireworks party, 7/246; P's dance, 8/28; on outings to Bow, 8/112; Islington, 8/234; Vauxhall, 9/194; and Mile End, 9/202; at christening, 8/403 & n. 1, 404–5; at theatre, 9/310; visits/dines with P, 6/76, 144, 210; 7/189, 209, 249(2), 336, 353, 389; 8/4, 106, 282, 284, 433; 9/311–12; P/EP visit(s) etc., 6/223; 7/96, 190, 219; 8/86; 9/170; in Seething Lane garden, 6/112; 7/170, 183, 197; 9/261, 314; also, 6/111, 241; 7/161, 296, 388; 8/13, 435
PENN, Margaret (Pegg): *see* Lowther
PENN, Richard (Dick), son of Sir William: EP's valentine, 6/35 & n. 4
PENN, William, kted 1660; Navy Commissioner 1660–8:
CHARACTER: able, 1/241; 7/257; good company, 1/241, 262, 280; diligent, 4/66–7; Coventry defends, 6/291; foolish talk, 3/75; 'rogue'/'knave', 3/126, 132, 284; 4/68, 401, 436, 439; 5/16, 68, 144, 341; 6/249, 254; 7/65, 68, 75, 91, 110; 8/36, 75, 103, 150, 204, 229, 253, 352, 442, 595; 9/126; envious, 3/189; 7/211, 212; 8/5, 228; suspected of corruption, 4/151; 5/231, 232, 235, 248–9, 253; 8/227, 228; 'of very mean parts but only a bred seaman', 5/293; poor speaker, 5/357–8;

6/10–11, 230; 8/317; poor company, 7/90; 8/135; lazy, 7/258, 327; 9/47, 285, 377 & n. 3; dissembles illness, 2/10; 8/302; mean, 8/122, 142, 172, 217; others' low opinion of: Mennes's, 4/71; Sandwich's, 6/230; Gauden's, 6/254; Carteret's, 6/291; Albemarle's, ib.; Mrs T. Turner's, 8/75, 226–9; also, 3/134; 4/92; 7/27–8; 8/44; 9/291, 314, 503

AS NAVY COMMISSIONER:

APPOINTMENT, ETC.: 1/191, n. 2; office at Seething Lane, 4/288; assistant to Comptroller, 3/236–7 & n.; 4/61 & n. 1, 62, 65, 66, 67, 71, 75; 7/257, 325, 328, 361 & n. 2, 380; 8/20 & n. 2, 24, 25, 41, 586 & n. 2; demands separate office, 8/30, 40; proves strict, 8/44, 54, 97; lampooned, 7/407; reputation grows, 7/189; resigns on appointment as victualling contractor, 9/326, 348, & n. 3, 349–50 & n., 355, 503, 542; examined by Commons Committee on Miscarriages, 8/494, 501, 561; 9/103

DOCKYARD BUSINESS: pays, 2/45 & n. 1, 94, 237 & n. 2, 238; 3/44, 58, 70, 128, 129, 192, 193 & n. 1, 195, 198; sale, 2/50; musters, 3/73, 214; survey, 5/39; sends workers to help in Fire, 7/276; also, 3/19, 31, 69–75, 192; 6/249

FINANCIAL BUSINESS: general, 1/212–13, 226, 247, 312; 2/30, 33 & n. 3, 50 & n. 1; 3/14, 47; 4/154; 7/303, 305; 8/303, 460, 497; 9/94, 101, 130; victuallers' accounts, 3/41–2, 52, 62, 106; 7/74; 8/50, 322; 9/250; Warren's accounts, 8/550

JUDICIAL BUSINESS: Field's case, 3/64, 281; 4/71; also, 8/394

SHIPPING BUSINESS: visits wreck, 1/313, 315, 316, 319; prepares ships, 1/323; 2/62, 127, 128; 3/30–1, 48, 50, 63; 5/152, 153, 182–3; 7/145, 153, 189, 211, 212, 213, 231, 304, 312, 313, 326, 336, 360; at launch, 4/102–3; hires ships, 5/246; opposes convoy, 6/10–11

VICTUALLING BUSINESS: contract, 9/298; also, 3/40; 7/135, 260, 263, 264

OTHER BUSINESS: council order, 1/191 & nn.; office gallery in church, 1/225, 230; winter guard, 1/257, 266; dock at Limehouse, 2/198; occupation of Tangier, 2/202; despatch of soldiers to Ireland, 4/285; dismissal of Carkesse, 8/76, 97, 101, 103, 178, 204, 213, 215, 386; measures against Dutch raiders, 8/123, 125, 256, 259, 270–1, 282, 314, 317, 325; council's examination of Commissioner Pett, 8/460, 461; discipline in fleet, 9/39; valuation of ship, 9/69; conventions of sea warfare, 9/87–8; manning of fleet, 9/121; against putting admiralty into commission, 9/341; unspecified: 1/209, 214, 239, 242–3, 262; 2/36, 39, 40, 207, 229; 3/40, 48, 62, 76, 86, 106, 111, 192, 203, 207, 298; 4/12, 81, 88, 91, 97, 110, 113, 132, 152, 205, 264, 266, 314, 322, 324, 364, 453; 5/53, 228, 274, 356; 6/1, 13, 19; 7/71, 104, 289, 294, 302, 374, 419; 8/9, 25, 40–1, 111–12, 112, 131, 181, 198, 278, 291, 314–15, 448, 479, 509, 524, 581, 594; 9/21, 106, 150, 160, 190, 303, 306, 315, 359

PERQUISITES: plans to acquire Scottish timber, 7/298, 300, 301; hopes for as assistant to Comptroller, 8/229; part-share in privateer (*Flying Greyhound*), 7/299, 301, 306; her prize, 7/418; 8/115–16, 123, 128, 135, 159; dispute with Swedish Resident over, 8/21–2, 23, 27; suspected of tricking partners, 8/349, 351–2, 369; lends government £500 from her prize, 8/392, 393, 407; gains sole possession, 8/90–1 & n., 112, 441–2, 464, 478–9; deals with Lady Batten's interest, 8/561, 582, 584; 9/147; also, 9/99

RELATIONS WITH P: quarrels with: over purveyorship, 2/54(2) & n. 1; choice of ships' masters, 2/103–4, 108; drafting of contracts, 3/99–100; breadth of canvas, 5/238; pursers' duties, 7/13, 28, 106; office accommodation, 8/30, 35–6, 40; F. Turner, 8/150, 155; Clutterbuck's bills, 9/346; and other matters, 3/75, 101, 117, 123–4, 126; 4/367; 8/75–6; P resists him, 7/71; but must keep in with, 7/189; accuses P of negligence, 7/75; but respects his ability, 8/419; helps him over *Maybolt*, 8/477; criticised in P's memorandum to Duke of York, 9/305, 306, 377; also, 4/362; 8/5; 9/340

3/249; garden-door, 4/11; new dining-room, 4/121; new chimney-piece, 5/7; goods removed in Fire, 7/272, 274; land attached, 8/209; house at Walthamstow, 3/64; 6/102; 8/197, 235, 389, 408; plan to buy Wanstead House, 8/172, 197 & n. 2; Irish estate, 2/200 & n. 1, 201; visits to, 3/79, 123, 126, 132, 134, 151, 181–2; also, 5/183; 9/170

HOUSEHOLD: dishes 'deadly foul', 5/18; mean dinners, 7/287; 8/3, 122, 129, 234, 408; 9/505; bad food, 8/284, 371, 375; 9/202, 283; borrows silver etc. for daughter's wedding, 8/63, 77; housekeeping showy but mean/slatternly, 8/73, 122, 142, 197, 217, 408, 423; 9/84; servants [see also Markham, Nan]: footboys, 2/36; 3/77; 4/177; 7/282, 304, 305; 8/164; Harry (boy), 7/292; Jack (black servant), 2/61; John (ex-coachman), 8/173; Tom (coachman), 8/436; Betty (maid), 3/152; Sarah (once at P's), 3/302; chaplain in Ireland, 5/190

SOCIAL: sings bawdy songs, 1/262; visits Batten at Walthamstow, 1/279, 280–1; 2/78; 8/423; fuddled, 1/321; 2/208; at funerals of R. Blake, 2/74; and Batten, 8/476–7; at christenings, 2/109, 146; 4/165; 8/405; watches pre-coronation procession, 2/82; chariot race with Batten, 2/110; sings with P on roof, 2/115; sees wrestling at Moorfields, 2/127; tankard stolen as joke, 2/164, 169, 170, 175–6, 178; makes Cocke drunk, 2/238; gives dinners on wedding anniversaries, 3/4; 5/3, 6–7; and to Navy Board, 3/217; 5/358; 7/11; dines with Lieutenant of Tower, 4/70; dines with Coventry, 5/102; visits Lawson on deathbed, 6/132; takes P, for his health, on coach ride, 7/208; outings to Islington, 7/261; 9/184; and Mile End, 8/485; 9/88, 202; P stays with in Fire, 7/280, 282, 283, 284; at P's New Year party, 8/4–5; gives favours for daughter's wedding, 8/73, 77; in Hyde Park, 8/196–7; 9/122; at parish dinner, 8/218; Bartholomew Fair, 9/301; taverns, 1/292; 2/30, 54, 61, 78, 173, 185, 192, 200, 219, 227, 233, 239; 3/42,

91; 5/149, 308; 7/63; 8/49, 108, 130, 133, 220; 9/82, 115; at theatre, 2/154, 155, 186, 194, 202, 206, 212, 220, 223, 227, 241; 3/24, 31, 56, 86, 88; 5/232; 6/9, 10; 7/267; 8/129, 138, 195, 235, 384, 386, 388, 402, 421, 443, 521–2, 590; 9/57, 78, 104, 193, 310, 329; in garden at Seething Lane, 1/248; 2/24; 5/81; 7/208; 8/315; visits/dines etc. with P, 1/242, 324; 2/22–3, 29, 126, 143, 192, 218–19; 3/8, 34; 4/315; 7/209–10, 259; 8/106, 260, 284, 433; 9/312; and with Batten, 1/293, 295, 309; 2/90, 125; 8/105, 376; P/EP dine(s) with/visit(s) etc., 2/21, 66, 123, 215, 240; 3/3, 18, 60, 77, 90, 125, 183, 209, 286, 293; 4/12, 23, 28, 45, 171, 278, 338; 5/122, 125; 6/38; 7/190–1, 233; 8/146, 508; 9/149, 174, 177, 179, 187, 191; also, 3/5; 5/128, 240

ALLUDED TO: 8/248, 396

PENN, William, founder of Pennsylvania, son of Sir William [see also Books]:

CHRON. SERIES: sent down from Oxford, 2/206 & n. 3; proposed removal to Cambridge, 3/17 & n. 4, 21; nonconformist opinions, 3/73 & n. 1; returns from France, 5/255 & n. 1; 6/213, 222; French affectations, 5/257; with father in fleet, 6/89; returns from Ireland, 8/565 & n. 1; becomes a Quaker, 8/595 & n. 3; also, 3/47; 6/223; 8/228

SOCIAL: sees pre-coronation procession, 2/82; at theatre, 2/241; 3/1; also, 2/239; 3/5, 132; 5/270

PENNY, [Nicholas], tailor, Fleet St ('my tailor', 7/13 onwards): recommended to P, 7/13; work for/visits by P, 7/15, 16, 172, 346; 8/34, 134, 136, 138, 146, 281, 295, 460, 461, 463, 525, 529, 599; 9/197, 198, 201, 203, 215, 333, 455, 456, 534, 537, 540, 551; makes cloak and cassock for John P, 7/299; alluded to: 9/366, 456; ~ his boy, 8/315

PENROSE, Capt. [Thomas], naval officer: 1/172

PEPPER, [Robert], Fellow of Christ's College, Cambridge: John P's tutor, 2/44; Proctor, 3/217–18; social: 1/68

PEPYS, family of: history, vol. i,

pp. xix–xx; 3/26–7 & n.; 8/261 & nn., 274 & n. 2; decay of, 5/134; P's immediate family listed with birth-dates, 5/360–1 & nn.; lack of hand-some women, 8/365

PEPYS, [Anne], wife of Robert, of Brampton, Hunts., P's aunt: ill of the stone, 1/320–1 & n.; 2/5, 17, 27, 52, 133, 134; sends for P's father in hus-band's last illness, 2/126, 127; trouble-some, 2/134 & n. 1, 137; provisions of husband's will, 2/134 & n. 1, 138, 148; dispute over bond, 2/164; 4/384; 5/353

PEPYS, Anne (Nan), of Worcs.: see Fisher, ——; Hall, ——

PEPYS, Bab and Betty, Roger's daughters, P's cousins: visit London with father, 9/446, 450; comely, 9/453; stay at P's house, 9/453–4, 455, 460; at theatre, 9/453, 454, 456, 458, 459, 476; visit Bedlam, 9/454; Westminster Abbey, 9/456–7; and glasshouse, 9/457; at P's dance, 9/463–5 passim; return to Impington, 9/477; also, 9/475; ~ their maid Martha, 9/454

PEPYS, Charles ('the joiner'), son of Thomas Pepys of London: at reading of Robert P's will, 2/153; his legacy, 4/20, 42–3, 102, 345, 346; 5/157; social: 2/172

PEPYS, Edith, P's aunt: see Bell

PEPYS, Edward, of Broomsthorpe, Norf., P's cousin: dies, 4/421 & n. 2, 425; funeral scutcheons and hatch-ments, 4/424–5 & n., 427; buried, 4/426; 5/10; funeral procession, 4/432; social: 1/54, 60; alluded to: 1/72; 5/76; 8/365

PEPYS, Elizabeth, (b. St Michel), wife of the diarist [see also entries under Dress etc.; Health: Household Goods etc.; Servants. For her relations with the Pepyses, Mountagus, St Michels and others, see under names.]:

PERSONAL: her beauty admired at wedding, 1/196; at theatre, 9/398; by Sandwich, 4/186; by Duke of York, 9/515; pretty wearing black patch, 1/283; in black laced gown, 2/117; in flowered tabby, 9/134; better looking than Princess Henrietta Maria, 1/299;

the only pretty woman in theatre, 9/450; her 'comely person', 6/31; washes before going to court, 1/298 & n. 3; visits bath house, 6/40 & n. 1, 41, 45; spends day getting clean, 9/372; snores, 1/266–7; rides well, 2/180; her watch, 8/51, 146

PORTRAITS: by Savill: 2/218 & n. 4, 227, 233, 234, 235; her dog added, 2/241; altered because unlike, 3/17, 19, 21; hung in dining room, 3/25, 34, 106; P wishes Huysmans to paint, 5/276 & & n. 3; 6/113; by Hayls: 7/43, 44 & n. 2, 48, 52, 53–4, 61, 65, 69, 72; a good likeness, 7/73, 74, 78, 82; improved, 9/292, 297, 299; alluded to, 7/98, 108, 117, 120; 9/138; by Cooper: 9/138 & n. 3, 139, 140, 253, 256, 258–61 passim, 263, 264, 267, 268, 276–7; not such a good likeness, 9/264, 267

CHRON. SERIES:

MAIN BIOGRAPHICAL EVENTS: mar-riage, vol. i, p. xxii & n. 13; early differences and separation, 2/153 & n. 3; 4/277 & n. 1; 5/196 & n. 2; believes herself pregnant, 1/1; 4/365; Uncle Wight's unusual attentions to, 5/14, 16, 24, 55, 65; her child to be his heir, 5/61; he proposes they have child, 5/145–6, 151; death, vol. i, p. xxxv

MOVEMENTS/VISITS TO BRAMPTON ETC: with Bowyers during P's Dutch voyage, 1/84, 85, 88, 89–90; returns to London, 1/131, 166, 177, 178; re-united with P, 1/173; moves from Axe Yard to Seething Lane, 1/199–203 passim; stays with P's father during alterations to house, 2/64–7 passim, 88, 90, 94, 96; with P visits Portsmouth, 2/90–4; rides to Bramp-ton and back, 2/180–4; at Brampton while house altered, 3/134, 140, 141, 144, 145, 148, 151, 182; returns, 3/199, 200, 206, 208, 209; with Tom P while house cleaned, 3/251; with P at Sandwich's lodgings, 3/299, 301; 4/1–6 passim; visits Brampton with Ashwell, 4/174, 176, 178, 179, 180, 183, 184, 199, 210, 212, 262; returns following quarrels, 4/271, 273, 276; visits Brampton with P, 4/306–14; without him, 5/200, 201, 224, 233–4; to stay at home till after Easter, 5/358;

to stay at Woolwich in Plague, 6/128 & n. 2, 134, 140, 143, 147; settles in with two maids, 6/149; P's visits to, 6/151-2, 153, 162, 170, 174, 183, 185, 190, 200, 205-6; joined by P, 6/207-10 passim, 212, 214, 216, 219, 221, 223, 226, 228; he visits from Greenwich lodgings, 6/242, 246, 249-50, 262, 263, 273, 303; she visits him, 6/250-3 passim, 270, 279, 280, 282, 284, 286, 295, 296; P rents rooms for at Greenwich, 6/261 & n. 3, 271; she moves to, 6/309, 313, 314; returns to London, 6/313-16 passim, 318, 341; visits P at Greenwich, 6/320, 321, 324, 326, 327, 338; 7/2, 3, 5, 6; P visits in London, 6/329(2), 332, 340; they return to house in Seething Lane, 7/7; with P visits Cranbourne and Windsor, 7/54, 56-9 passim; visits Brampton to advise on Pall's marriage, 7/86, 91(2), 92, 93, 104; with P camps in Navy Office during Fire, 7/273, 274, 275; sent to Woolwich with his gold, 7/275, 280, 283, 284, 285, 286, 289; takes gold to Brampton in Medway crisis, 8/262, 263, 264, 273; returns to London with account of burying it, 8/279, 280, 281; visits Brampton with P and Deb Willet, 8/453, 465-75 passim; at Audley End, 8/467-8; Cambridge, 8/468-9; at Brampton with Deb and others, 9/98, 125, 143, 144, 180; P visits her there, 9/210-12; and calls for at start of West Country tour, 9/224; visits Oxford, 9/226; Salisbury, 9/229; Stonehenge, 9/229-30; Chitterne, 9/231; Bath, 9/232-4, 236, 238-9; Bristol, 8/234-5; Avebury, 9/240; Marlborough, 9/241; visits Petersfield with P and Deb Willet, 9/273-4; with Deb and Hewer visits Roger P to see Sturbridge Fair, 9/301, 306, 310, 315

PUBLIC EVENTS/LONDON SIGHTS: sees burning of the Rump, 1/53; Queen-Mother and princesses dine in public, 1/297, 299; Queen in presence chamber, 3/299; hanging of regicides' corpses, 2/26-7; pre-coronation procession, 2/83; coronation banquet, 2/85; drinks King's health at bonfire, 2/87; sees alterations in St James's

Park, 2/171; rides in Hyde Park coach parades on May Day etc., 3/78; 5/126, 130, 163; 6/89; 8/193, 197; 9/142-3, 260, 269, 270, 487, 515-16, 530, 533-4, 540-1, 541-2, 549, 556, 563, 564; sees wrestling at Moorfields, 3/93; visits Bartholomew Fair, 4/298; 5/259-60; 8/405, 421, 423; 9/290, 293, 296, 299; synagogue, 4/335; at Col. Turner's execution, 5/23; service in Whitehall chapel, 6/86, 87; visits Clarendon House, 7/220; sees Fire of London, 7/272; and city ruins, 7/291; watches bull baiting 7/245-6; puppet plays, 3/254-5; 7/257, 265, 267; 8/121, 157, 421; 9/296; at court ball, 7/371, 372, 373; meets Nell Gwyn, 8/27; sees block ships in river, 8/293; giant children, 8/326, 500; prize fights, 8/429, 430; 9/516; bearded woman, 9/398; giantess, 9/440; royal tombs in Westminster Abbey, 9/456-7

MISC.: receives gifts from P's business associates, 1/222; 2/225; 4/293, 295, 298-9, 391, 415; 5/45, 47, 316; interprets French for Lady Sandwich, 1/293; attends women friends in labour, 2/150, 151; 8/177(2); 9/260; on bad terms with Lady Batten, 2/161; 3/146, 249-50, 302; 4/71, 426; 5/356; ends estrangement from, 6/46, 95; helps wounded acquaintance after fight, 2/229; importuned by drunk, 4/342; fortune told by gipsies, 9/278; first rides in P's new coach, 9/379; and with his new horses, 9/399-400

RELATIONS WITH P [for the Deb affair, see Willet]:

HER LOVE: troubled at his going to sea, 1/84; rejoices at his becoming Clerk of the Acts, 1/199; frightened at his injured thumb, 7/37; devotion in early hardships, 8/82; comforts him before parliamentary speech, 9/102; rejoices in its success, 9/104; rejects advances from Sandwich and Hinchingbrooke, 9/356, 404 & n. 2; and from others, 9/369; also, 1/131; 2/75; 7/398

HIS LOVE: concerned at leaving her for Dutch voyage, 1/89, 92, 102, 106; happy in wife and estate, 1/166; 3/234; troubled at her absence, 1/317;

2/14–15; pleased to be her valentine, 2/36; 'her care, thrift and innocence', 3/247; distress at her fainting, 4/307; pleasure in her company, 4/291, 403, 406, 435; 7/104, 351; 9/401; lies close to in grief for Tom P, 5/87; joy at her return from Brampton, 5/233–4; thanks God for love and health on wedding anniversary, 5/294; kisses at New Year, 5/359; grieved at her removal to Woolwich, 6/149, 157; and at lodging without her at Greenwich, 6/226; keeps cheerful for her sake in Plague, 6/225; finds 'all things melancholy' in her absence, 7/92; will keep together and 'let the world go hang', 8/97; also, 2/96; 3/206; 4/183, 186; 5/50, 55, 296; 6/262

HIS BEQUESTS/GIFTS/ALLOWANCES TO: wills in her favour, 1/88; 4/433; 7/134; 8/266; gives her pearl necklace, 1/240; lace handkerchief, 2/210, 211, 212, 214; money for Easter clothes, 3/26; 6/48; silk petticoat, 5/114, 118; cabinet, 5/152; diamond ring (£10), 6/190–1; pearl necklace (£80), 6/200–01; 7/108, 111, 112, 113; his gifts to equal those to other women, 8/100; gives her Guillim's *Heraldry*, 8/422 & n. 4; lace handkerchief as New Year gift, 9/6; diamond ring for valentine gift, 9/78, 88–9; *Cassandra* and other French books, 9/365; walnut cabinet as New Year gift, 9/405, 406; clothing allowance (£30 p.a.), 9/406, 408, 412; also, 1/106, 107, 139; 5/155; 7/344; 9/98, 501

THEIR SHARED TASTES/PLEASURES [for his teaching her music etc., *see below*: her accomplishments]: distaste for mock wedding, 1/27; amused by absurd book, 1/275; plan French holiday, 2/35; 4/399 & n. 4; 9/462 & n. 3, 546; dislike of Lady Batten, 3/55; and Penn, 3/117; plan improvements at Seething Lane, 4/300; 7/7; enjoy riding through Brampton fields, 4/312; joy at returning home after absence, 4/314; 7/7; play cards together, 6/3, 221; 7/392

HE CONSULTS/CONFIDES IN: on intentions to live frugally and become a knight, 3/39–40; finances, 5/42–3,

131; quarrel with Creed, 5/48; troubles over prize-goods, 6/242; standing at court, 7/31; plan to live at Brampton, 7/202, 235, 340, 344; fears in Medway crisis, 8/260, 262; giving up victualling post, 8/367

HER HELP/ADVICE: on his health, 4/409, 414; his demeanour to Sandwich, 5/65; helps him to catalogue books, 5/49, 72; cuts his hair, 5/72; 8/35; 9/424; searches him for lice, 9/424; rules pursers' books, 7/63; helps him to pack up goods in Fire, 7/272–3; to dig up gold at Brampton, 8/472; and carry it to London, 8/475; tells Hewer of P's dissatisfaction with, 9/52–3; reads to when ill, 4/40; and to save his eyes, 8/413, 438, 440, 444, 455, 535, 537, 538, 547, 548, 564, 568, 572, 582, 589; 9/11, 61, 241, 242, 247, 255, 277, 281, 305, 325, 328, 331–5 passim, 337, 344, 372, 374–9 passim, 385, 396, 401, 402–3, 416, 426, 429(2), 431(2), 432, 433, 444, 446, 460, 472, 475, 481, 482, 483, 493, 508, 535(2), 541, 542, 545, 547

HIS JEALOUSY: annoyed at stranger kissing her, 2/10; jealous of T. Somerset, 2/165 & n. 2, 170, 172–3; J. Hunt, 2/216; Capt. Holmes, 2/237 & n. 1; 3/4; Pembleton (dancing master), 4/140, 141, 144, 148–9, 150, 153–4, 157–8, 161, 165, 166, 172, 173, 179, 183, 205, 229, 277–8, 285, 291, 300, 318, 337–8, 347, 369; 5/17, 125; Hewer, 5/13, 19, 29, 44, 301; W. Penn, jun., 5/263, 270; Llewellin, 6/38; Browne (drawing master), 6/246; W. Batelier, 7/238; Coleman (fellow traveller in coach), 8/286, 305, 588; H. Sheeres, 9/504, 522, 532, 533, 540, 541; she shows him P. Sydney's letter on jealousy, 6/2; troubled at her staying out late, 9/529, 531; also, 5/18, 64, 111; 6/214, 216

HER JEALOUSY: jealous of E. Pearse, 2/201; E. Pearse/E. Knepp, 7/120, 122; her uncivil behaviour to both, 7/236–7, 238, 322, 341; continuing jealousy of, 8/25, 210–11, 371–2, 399, 599, 600; 9/1, 108, 339, 368, 376, 391, 405, 413, 436, 469–70; jealous of Ashwell, 4/122, 165, 180; Mercer, 5/274; 7/228;

be bleached, 8/383–6 passim, 401; 9/283

RELATIONS WITH UNNAMED SERVANTS [for relations with named servants, *see* Servants in main series]: annoyed with for complaining of Suffolk cheese, 2/191; forgets to buy food for, 2/198; servants spoiled by her familiarity, 4/9; with P hears them read Bible, 4/383; scolds for failing to search beds for fleas, 5/260; buys presents for, ib.; permits to attend Lord Mayor's Show, 5/309; joins in Christmas games, 5/357, 358; 6/4–5; dances, 6/252; cards, 7/358

MISC.: makes caps for P, 1/85; worsted cushions, 4/180; tears up flags for bed linen, 5/48; makes shirts and smocks, 8/187; settles household accounts with P, 3/132, 289; 5/283; 6/46–7; 7/125, 243, 397; 8/444; sets up closet, 4/317, 318, 322, 324, 328, 329; works 'like a horse', 7/14; and a drudge, 7/24; helps clean house, 9/365; to learn to fold napkins, 9/423

HER ACCOMPLISHMENTS:

MUSIC: *singing*: to learn from Goodgroome, 2/190; P teaches song to, 7/111; neglects to teach, 7/228; will learn in return for dancing lessons, 7/300; lessons with Goodgroome, 7/348 & n. 1, 397; sings out of tune, 7/348; 8/89; P teaches her 'It is decreed', 7/420; learning to trill, 8/49, 108, 109; P pleased with progress, 8/119, 171, 203, 204, 209; Goodgroome's neglect, 8/109, 378, 411; sings with P/Mercer/ others, 8/90, 166, 198, 206, 209, 238, 244, 250, 253, 325, 327, 344, 351, 380, 390, 458; in garden, 5/266; 7/117, 172, 183, 195, 212, 228, 230; 8/37, 165, 322, 328; on roof, 3/86; 7/110, 174; in coach, 7/267; 9/513; on river, 8/325, 346; 9/552, 555, 563; in cellars at Audley End, 8/468; *flageolet*: lessons from Greeting, 8/87 & n. 2, 89, 110, 400; fails to practise, 8/146, 205–6, 221(2); P pleased with her progress, 8/96, 232, 291, 295, 396, 430, 433, 434, 435; has lessons to encourage her, 8/205–6; she 'pipes' with him, 8/224, 235(2), 250, 253, 305, 327, 367, 369, 370, 380, 384, 436, 437, 443; resumes

lessons, 9/25, 94, 279; plays to P, 9/280; *misc.*: is taught 'some skill in' by P, 1/232, 233, 239; repeats words of French song 'D'un air tout interdit', 6/223; to learn viol, 7/377

DANCING: wishes to learn, 3/213–14; 4/106, 109; 7/300; lessons from Pembleton, 4/111, 113, 114, 122, 126, 129, 132, 133, 134, 140, 148, 149, 150, 155, 156, 161; at dances/dancing parties, 6/279, 315, 323–4; 7/18, 43–4, 73, 362–4, 422; 8/29, 104, 493, 511; 9/1, 4, 42, 128, 134

DRAWING AND PAINTING: lessons from Browne, 6/98(2) and n.; P's pride in her progress, 6/143, 162, 170, 174, 183, 200, 242; 7/232; 9/25; her talent superior to Peg Penn's, 6/185, 210; her picture of Christ, 6/242; and the Virgin, 7/241, 242, 251, 262; resumes lessons, 7/115; also, 6/303; 7/359; 9/424, 534

OTHER INTERESTS: reading: reads *Polixandre*, 1/35; *Le grand Cyrus*, 1/312; 7/122; *Imposture*, 3/247; with P reads Ovid (trans.), 3/289; *Iter Boreale*, 4/285; Fuller's *Worthies*, 5/118; he reads to her *Life of Henrietta Maria*, 1/275; *The siege of Rhodes*, 5/278; and Chaucer, 7/378; her books separated from P's, 1/268; *misc.*: P teaches her astronomy, 4/43; use of globes/geography, 4/302, 343, 344, 433–4; 5/6, 8, 16, 25–6, 49; arithmetic, 4/357, 360, 363, 364, 378, 402, 404, 406; with P experiments with microscope, 5/241

HER RELIGIOUS OPINIONS: enjoys reading missal, 1/282 & n. 1; P fears her becoming catholic, 5/39 & n. 4, 92, 103, 250; 9/378; she claims to be one, 5/92 & n. 2; 9/338, 385; attributes juggler's tricks to the Devil, 8/234; fasts on Good Friday, 6/66

SOCIAL:

ON RIVER TRIPS: sees wreck of *Assurance*, 1/315, 316–17; dines on *Rosebush*, 2/36; sees royal yachts, 2/179; fleet in the Hope, 5/197; at launch of *Royal Catherine*, 5/305, 307; and *Greenwich*, 7/153; visits the *Prince*, 6/56, 57, 59; on river trips to Hampton Court, 3/81–2; Gravesend,

190, 191, 193; portrait by Hayls, 7/151 & n. 2, 161, 164, 166, 170–1, 173, 184, 199; takes P's gold to Brampton, 8/262, 263, 264, 280–1, 472–3, 474, 539; visits P in London, 3/85, 93–4, 97, 99, 103, 104, 106; 4/89, 90, 92, 93, 95, 98–101 passim, 103–6 passim, 108–12 passim, 114, 118, 274, 276, 280; 7/137–40 passim, 142, 149, 151, 152, 161, 164, 166, 167, 169–76 passim, 306, 308, 309, 311, 313, 316, 317, 318, 329; 8/214, 216, 231, 232, 233, 235; death, vol. i, pp. xxxv–vi; also, 1/72, 220; 2/132, 140; 3/6; 5/104, 118

AS TAILOR: work for P/EP, 1/171, 224, 245, 251, 260, 268, 320; 2/104; advises about hangings, 1/256, 261; supplies cloth to Sandwich for gift to Algerines, 2/122, 126; hopes for place at Wardrobe, 1/201, 203; 2/42 & n. 1, 113; 5/168 & n. 3, 172 & n. 1, 185; 8/508

MARRIAGE: date, 5/360; quarrels with wife, 2/64, 81, 89–90, 111, 160, 183; 'unquiet life' with, 3/207; 4/90, 96; 5/234; grief at her dying, 8/129

RELATIONS WITH P: P's affection, 5/120, 298; 7/137, 164, 175, 306; 8/90, 166, 232, 233, 237; P takes leave of before Dutch voyage, 1/93; gives financial support to, 1/222, 274, 317; 4/127; 5/360; 7/169–70, 173, 318; 8/90, 91; other gifts, 3/33; 4/6; 5/52, 261, 344, 346; 6/149; 8/565; plans alterations with at Brampton, 2/182–3; 8/237, 469, 471; helps/scolds him over accounts, 2/162, 183; 4/87, 106, 108, 119, 121, 141 & n. 3; fears his maintenance becoming a burden, 3/276, 302; 4/106; urges him to live on £50 p.a., 4/119, 280, 308; defends his reputation for paying debts, 5/244, 251–2, 253; hopes to maintain at Brampton, 8/508; vol. i, pp. xxxv–xxxvi; bequeaths money to, 7/134; 8/266; also, 3/119, 219

RELATIONS WITH OTHER CHILDREN:

WITH JOHN: enters at Christ's College, Cambridge, 1/26, 27, 66–9 passim; troubled by P's quarrel with, 5/93, 135, 137; John to stay with at Brampton, 8/14, 48, 49, 471; also, 1/46

WITH PAULINA: troubled at her pilfering, 1/27; agrees to her becoming P's servant, 1/288, 290, 291; and to her leaving, 2/161–2; defends against P, 4/108; attempts match-making for, 7/78, 86, 170; lives with after her marriage, 9/212 & n. 1; also, 4/90; 9/293

WITH TOM: angry with for sleeping out, 1/256; Tom disrespectful to, 2/103; matchmakes for, 2/158, 159, 163, 165; tailoring business handed over to, 2/144; 5/250 & n. 2, 351; also, 3/131; 4/410

HEALTH: sight and hearing deteriorate, 2/103; 7/137; deaf, 8/473; hernia, 4/117–18; 7/104; 8/13, 14, 88, 90, 110, 119, 122, 123, 129, 162; acute attacks of, 4/117–18; 8/237; treatment from Hollier, 8/110, 166, 214, 220; truss, 8/232, 237, 252; unwell, 3/48; 4/100, 310, 312, 313, 321, 348, 358; 5/92, 123

HOUSE in Salisbury Court [see also Langford, [W.]; for his house at Brampton, q.v.]: little room, 1/27, 291; cutting house, 1/84; three storeys, 1/181; burnt in Fire, 7/279

HOUSEHOLD: man Ned, 2/163; John Noble, 5/113; boy, 4/313; 9/210; man, 9/210

SOCIAL: at Twelfth Night parties, 1/10; 2/7; first visits P in Seething Lane, 1/210; wedding anniversary dinner, 1/266; at P's stone feasts, 2/60; 5/98; at K. Fenner's funeral, 2/159; dines with Penn, 8/252–3; at Hinchingbrooke, 8/471–2; visits Greenwich, 4/99; Woolwich, 7/142, 149; Islington, 7/149, 167, 170, 317; at taverns, 1/221, 229, 303; 2/17, 25, 45, 114, 124; at theatre, 8/253; Joyces visit at Brampton, 5/263, 266, 268, 273, 282; with P at Axe Yard, 1/43; and Seething Lane, 1/274, 294, 302; 2/9, 28, 44, 52, 113, 125, 155–6, 157; 3/96, 99; with other London relatives, 1/28, 252; 2/2, 162, 164; 3/94; 4/100, 101, 108; 5/119; 7/140, 169, 172, 174; P/EP visit(s) etc. in Salisbury Court, 1/3, 9, 11, 25–6, 32, 42, 54, 64, 65, 85, 88, 179, 195, 205, 230, 289, 319, 324; 2/40, 47, 65, 66, 67, 75, 89, 152

PEPYS, John, P's older brother (d.

1631): his birthdate and death, 5/361 & n. 1

PEPYS, John, P's brother (d. 1677): EDUCATION: gives speeches at St Paul's School, 1/11–12 & n., 18, 44; gains exhibition, 1/42 & n. 4, 46; enters Christ's College, Cambridge, 1/26, 60, 61, 64–9 passim; transfers from Magdalene, 1/68 & n. 2; P gives him books/money/advice, 1/61, 69, 90, 222, 243; 2/95; 3/33; a good scholar, 2/25; elected a scholar of Christ's, 2/44; P dissuades from becoming moderator, 3/160–1 & n.; takes his B.A., 4/27 & n. 1; has studied Descartes, 4/263; and Aristotle's physics, 4/267; P complains of his idleness, 4/291, 292, 316–17, 439; is ordained and takes his M.A., 7/50 & n. 2, 112, 170
CHRON. SERIES: his birthdate recorded, 5/361 & n. 1; at Brampton, 3/219, 220, 223; with P in London, 4/261–3 passim, 266, 269, 273, 282, 300, 317; complains of EP's unkindness, 4/293; comes to London on Tom P's death, 5/91, 122; P angry with over his 'roguish' letters to Tom P, 5/91, 92, 93, 135, 137, 298; 6/134; his allowance, 5/142 & n. 3; 6/49; P makes up quarrel, 7/111–12, 170; stays with P, 7/281–3 passim, 293, 306, 316, 318, 344, 349, 362, 420, 426; 8/14, 31; wears clerical dress, 7/299, 310, 313; his lack of scholarship, 7/327, 346; helps P store his money and plate, 7/367; and to catalogue his books, 7/419, 421; 8/8, 40(2); 9/559–60; has fainting fit, 8/48–9; returns to Brampton, 8/49; 'melancholy and harmless', ib.; his prospects, 8/471 & n. 2; stays with P, 8/474, 477, 478; 9/553, 555, 563; also, 4/27; 5/157, 261; 8/122, 134, 207, 469; 9/144, 210, 212
SOCIAL: at Twelfth Night party, 1/10; P visits at Cambridge, 2/135, 181; visits Westminster Abbey, 7/322, 323, 345; plays lyra viol, 7/327; and bass viol, 8/40; at theatre, 7/398; 8/481; 9/556; dines at Hinchingbrooke, 8/471–2; also, 1/9; 7/317, 351, 366
ALLUDED TO: 1/81; 8/473

PEPYS, John, P's cousin, of Ashtead,

Surrey, lawyer (d. 1652): house, 3/152 & n. 1; 4/247; 8/338; servants, 4/247; 8/338; marshal to Chief Justice Coke, 9/42 & n. 4; alluded to: 9/383

PEPYS, Dr John, lawyer, Fellow of Trinity Hall, Cambridge, P's cousin (d. 1692): P's opinion, 4/211, 389; advises on Robert P's will, 2/136; arbitrator in dispute, 3/265; recovers from illness, 4/211; also, 2/146, 147; 3/218; 4/389

PEPYS, [Margaret], (b. Kite), P's mother:
CHRON. SERIES: washmaid, 2/31 & n. 2; marriage date, 5/360; children's birthdates, 5/361 & n. 1; argues about religion, 1/76 & n. 3; unwell, 1/230, 233, 244, 245; suffers from stone, 1/283, 302, 310, 314; at Brampton, 2/5, 26, 27; quarrels with husband, 2/64, 81, 89–90, 111, 160, 183; has become simple, 2/111, 153, 160, 171; extravagance, 2/144; moves to Brampton, 2/151, 162, 165, 171, 172; ill, 3/103, 106; quarrels with EP, 3/206; 4/274; unquiet life with husband, 3/207; 4/90, 96; 5/234; quarrels with servants, 5/154; P's gifts to, 4/7; 5/268; begs him to forgive brother, 5/298; 6/134; stays with P, 6/90, 95, 99, 132, 133–4; 'impatient and troublesome', 7/104; P's bequest, 7/134; ill, 8/88, 119, 122, 123, 129, 131; dies, 8/134, 135; P's grief, 8/134; also, 1/54, 75, 93, 203; 5/85
SOCIAL: at Twelfth Night party, 1/10; P's stone feast, 2/60; christening, 6/102; visits Woolwich, 6/111; Islington, 6/112; Gravesend, 6/119; P visits at Salisbury Court, 1/9, 28, 71, 72, 205, 215, 324; 2/65, 67, 139, 141, 169; at Brampton, 3/219, 223; visits/dines with P, 1/29; 2/28, 165; also, 1/252; 2/164; 5/266; 6/107–8, 121, 128, 130
ALLUDED TO: 1/60, 81; 3/167; 9/134

PEPYS, Mary, P's aunt: birthdate, 5/360 & n. 1

PEPYS, Mary, P's sister: birthdate and death, 5/361 & n. 1

PEPYS, Mary, P's cousin; daughter of Thomas P of London: see Santhune, de

PEPYS, Paulina, P's older sister: birthdate and death, 5/361 & n. 1

PEPYS, Paulina, P's younger sister: *see* Jackson, J.

PEPYS, Richard, of Ashen, Essex, P's cousin: 1/252 & n. 3

PEPYS, Richard, draper, of Great St Bartholomew's, P's relative: to supply flags for navy, 5/181–2 & n.

PEPYS, Robert, P's brother: birthdate and death, 5/361 & n. 1

PEPYS, Robert, of Brampton, Hunts., P's uncle:

CHRON. SERIES: lease of Hetley's land, 2/28; business with Sir P. Neile, 2/47; surety for loan to Sandwich, 2/62–3; proposes P buy land at Brampton, 2/117; illness and death, 1/81, 321; 2/5, 27, 126, 129, 130, 132, 133 & n. 2; mourning for, 3/7; also, 1/46, 72, 218; 2/3, 96

HIS WILL: P's expectations, 1/73, 77, 81, 170, 264; its terms, 2/133 & n. 1, 134 & n. 2, 135 & n. 1; estate, 2/134–5, 144; 3/275 & n. 3; P exaggerates its value, 2/140; will discussed, 2/153; proved, 2/160 & n. 1, 162; copied, 3/269; legacies: to P and his father, 2/133 & n. 1; 5/143; Pall, 7/15; the Wights, 4/86; the Perkinses, 8/90, 91; debt to Thomas P 'the Executor', 3/17; 6/100; P's papers concerning estate, 2/140; 3/48, 274, 275 & n. 2; 4/121, 122; land sold to meet debts etc., 4/119 & n. 2; 5/211 & n. 2: 6/100; accounts as tax-receiver (1647), 5/31, 39, 135; 6/65

DISPUTES OVER WILL [*see also* Brampton; Godfrey, [R.]; Goldsborough, Mrs ——; Graveley; Moore, H.; Offord; Pepys, Anne; Pepys, Charles; Pepys, Dr John; Pepys, Roger; Pepys, Talbot; Pepys, Thomas of London; Pepys, Thomas, the turner; Prior, [W.]; Trice, J.; Trice, T.; Stirtloe; Turner, Dr John; Williams, Dr John]; copyhold lands at Brampton etc., 2/135; 4/42–3 & nn.; annuities to Thomas P of London and sons, 3/275 & n. 3; 4/42–3 & nn.; debt to Trices, 2/134 & n. 2; 3/265, 274; 4/384; 5/353; also, 2/134–5, 177, 194–5; 3/7, 27, 34, 48, 80, 83, 96, 100, 219–23 passim,

232, 240, 244, 253, 256, 265, 269, 271, 274, 275, 281, 302; 4/15, 20, 28, 34, 63, 119, 126, 132, 153, 203, 344–5 & n., 351–2, 379; 5/36, 157, 225

PEPYS, Roger, son of Talbot, and P's cousin; lawyer; M.P. and Recorder, Cambridge borough:

CHARACTER: simple and well-meaning, 4/389, 402; 5/351; honest, 9/377

CHRON. SERIES: at Cambridge assizes, 2/146; bound over by Kelyng at assizes, 8/484 & n. 2, 578; advises on dispute over Robert P's will, 2/145, 147; 3/113, 218, 253, 263; 4/28, 34, 35, 41; arbitrator between P and Uncle Thomas, 3/256, 261, 265, 267; 4/42; advises on Robert P's Exchequer business, 5/135; Tom P's debts, 5/149, 250, 351; and land purchase, 8/517; 9/95; advises P's father on Robert P's estate, 5/44, 45; intercedes for Pall, 5/44; and for John, 5/135; offers match for Pall, 8/261 & n. 2; arranges her marriage settlement, 9/18–19, 55, 56, 61 & n. 1, 64–5; P's gifts to, 4/232; 8/393; on committee of Canary Company, 7/314; stories of family history, 8/261 & n. 4, 274; reports slander about Archbishop Sheldon, 8/364 & n. 1; also, 1/195; 8/522; 9/83–4

AS M.P.: election, 2/56 & n. 2; critical of Cavalier M.P.s, 2/147–8; and court, 4/193, 197; 8/33, 274; finds politics distasteful, 4/159–60; his independence, 8/33, 85–6 & n., 512; 9/114–15; helps P in defence before Committee on Miscarriages, 8/493, 496; 9/162; congratulates him on parliamentary speech, 9/113; attends debates on ecclesiastical bills, 4/95; 4/159; journeys to and from London for sessions, 4/66, 242, 402; 8/47, 261, 365, 575; 9/113, 477; also, 9/65

NEWS FROM (mostly parliamentary): 4/65, 90, 159, 200, 229; 8/32–3, 274, 361, 510, 512, 527, 558–9, 579; 9/70, 95, 121, 171, 174, 186–7, 463

PERSONAL: marries third wife, 1/39 & n. 3, 45, 46; enquires for rich widow, 4/159; 7/387; woos E. Wyld, 8/365; marries E. Dickenson, 9/431 & n. 2, 441; health, 5/36–7; 9/450; income,

4/159; borrows £1000 from P, 9/357–8, 369, 375, 377; house at Impington, 3/219; London lodgings, 9/348, 353, 473

SOCIAL: at Trinity House, 4/185; funeral, 5/347; visits court, 8/33, 70; EP's valentine, 9/67; at theatre, 9/429; entertains P/EP, 2/147; 3/219; 9/222, 301, 306, 310, 315, 379, 450, 474; attends P's stone-feast, 6/124; dines with/visits P, 4/94–5; 5/337; 7/391–2; 8/362, 577, 578; 9/57, 116, 167–8, 253, 343, 430, 455, 463–4, 553, 559; at tavern, 9/163; also, 1/54; 2/130; 4/235; 9/68, 461, 475, 552

~ his maid Martha, 9/454; his man Arthur, 9/460

PEPYS, Samuel, of Ireland, clergyman; P's cousin: godfather to J. Scott's child, 2/216 & n. 2; also,3/123 & n. 2

PEPYS, Samuel, the diarist, recollections of early life of [i.e. his life before the start of the diary. The dating implied in the organisation of this section is in some cases tentative. The principal entries in the Index dealing with his life during the diary period are listed above, p. xiii.]:

CHILDHOOD AND YOUTH: put out to nurse in Kingsland, 5/132; carried to see Christmas revels in Temple, 9/3; taken to church, 3/167; plays bows and arrows in Islington fields, 5/101; plays games, 4/433; beats parish bounds, 2/106; carries clothes to father's customers, 9/113

SCHOOLDAYS AND ADOLESCENCE: witnesses execution of King, 1/280; eats oysters at Bardsey, 1/104; his 'first sentiments of love', 4/247; writes anagram on Elizabeth Whittle's name, 1/290; at Ashtead, 3/152 & n. 1; at Durdans, 4/246; cast in female part in play, 9/218; his 'boyish' papers, 5/31, 360; examined for leaving exhibition at St Paul's, 2/20; 5/221–2

UNIVERSITY: at Magdalene College, vol. i, p. xxi; 1/67; 2/220; 3/54 & & n. 1; 5/31, 203, 361; 9/212

MARRIAGE AND EARLY MANHOOD: love letters exchanged with EP, 4/9–10; 5/360; wedding ring, 1/238; marriage ceremonies (1655), 2/194, n. 3; wedding dinner, 7/237; their temporary separation, ?2/153 & n. 3; 4/277 & n. 1; and early privations, 8/82–3; efficiency as Mountagu's servant, 5/192; member of 'club' of government clerks, 1/208 & n. 4; 2/127; 4/10; 5/30; 6/147–8; 7/375; attends Scott's divorce proceedings, 4/254 & n. 2; operated on for stone (1658), 1/1 & n. 1, 97 & n. 3; 3/153; speaks 'privately' of King during Rump, 1/204; visits Baltic fleet as messenger, 1/140, 285; 2/185 & n. 5; pawns lute, 1/91; makes notes on family history and writes out medical charms, 5/360–2

PEPYS, Sarah, P's sister: birthdate and death, 5/361 & n. 1

PEPYS, Talbot, of Impington, Cambs.; lawyer; P's great-uncle: advises on disputes over Robert P's will, 2/136 & n. 1, 181; 3/218; P overnight with, 2/147–8; Clarendon acquainted with, 2/209; 7/71 & n. 1; debts, 9/357; alluded to: 8/85

PEPYS, Talbot, Roger's son and P's cousin: law student at Middle Temple, 8/273–4 & n.; brideman to Jane Birch, 9/500; social: visits/dines with P, 9/167, 343, 519, 559; at theatre, 9/398, 414, 453, 456; Mulberry Garden, 9/510; and Hyde Park, 9/530; also, 9/511, 512

PEPYS, Thomas, of St Alphage's parish, P's uncle:

CHARACTER: P's low opinion, 2/178; 4/305

DISPUTE WITH P OVER BRAMPTON ESTATE: claims copyhold land, 2/135, 137; 139, 151, 153; denied possession by manorial court, 2/182; 3/222–3; disputes over rents, 3/219, 221; 4/15, 20, 28; arbitration attempted, 3/42, 256, 261, 265, 270, 302; enters complaint in Court of Arches, 4/33; out-of-court settlement, 4/34, 35, 36, 42–3 & nn., 72, 86, 119, 206; 6/100; surrenders mortgaged lands, 4/133, 308–9; enquires into J. Day's estate, 4/300, 310, 312; P objects to bargain with daughter, 4/344–5 & n., 346, 351; 5/303; reversionary right, 5/225 &

Deptford, 2/77; Chatham, 3/153, 154; 6/182, 232; and Woolwich, 3/289; dines with/visits P, 2/209; 3/120; 4/21, 45; 5/307; 6/205–6; at taverns, 3/165; 5/329; 6/77; 7/223; also, 2/218
MISC.: ill, 4/168; barber, 6/227
~ daughter [?Agnes Crisp], 4/168 & n. 1; 6/262; daughters, 2/12; step-daughter, 2/12; kinsman, 6/262
PETT [Peter], lawyer, son of Peter: 3/113
PETT, [Phineas], Master-Shipwright, Chatham 1605–29: 8/84 & n. 3
PETT, Phineas, (Capt. Pett), Assistant-Shipwright, Chatham 1660, Master-Shipwright, 1661–80; kted 1680: to be suspended, 1/229 & n. 4, 239, 240; house, 2/69; consulted on masts, 4/287; to join in P's timber deal, 7/298 & n. 3, 300, 301; accused of selling boats, 9/499 & n. 2; dismissed but reinstated, 9/267 & n. 2; social: 2/71
PETT, Phineas, shipwright, son of John: 5/109 & n. 1
PETTUS, Sir John, of Chediston, Suff. (d. 1685): on Naseby, 1/103 & n. 3
PETTY, William, kted 1661, scientist and economist [see also Books]: P's regard, 5/12, 27; 6/38; at Rota Club, 1/14; as T. Barlow's agent, 1/191, 305; 6/33; double-keeled ships: [Invention II], 4/256 & n. 3, 263 & n. 1, 334, 437; 5/24–5 & n., 28, 30, 32, 47; [Experiment], 5/353 & n. 3; 6/35, 38, 63 & n. 1; views on public taste, 5/27–8; and dreams, 5/108; proposed bequests for scientific research, 6/63 & n. 2
PHELPS, Mr —— [?John, Auditor of the revenue at the Exchequer]: 1/47; 2/163; 9/465–6 & n.
PHILIP IV, King of Spain 1621–65: prepares for Portuguese war, 4/349 & n. 5; death, 6/257 & n. 5; mourning for, 7/39; also, 7/55
PHILIPPE, Duc d' Anjou, later Duc d'Orleans (d. 1701): marriage, 1/240 & n. 3; 2/56; anecdote, 2/29
PHILIPS, [?John], cook: 9/116
PHILIPS, —— [?Robert, Groom of the Bedchamber to the King]: 5/279

& n. 1
PHILLIPS, [Henry], Council messenger: 1/123, 126
PHILLIPS, Lewis, lawyer, of Brampton and Huntingdon: character, 9/211; consulted in disputes about Robert P's estate, 2/135, 138, 148, 183, 223, 227; 3/27, 31, 33, 221; 4/34, 45, 221; 5/40; as arbiter, 3/261, 265; consulted about land purchase, 8/282–3; political news from, 4/155; leaves Brampton, 8/220; estate, 8/585; social: 2/137, 210, 213; 9/559; ~ his wife [Judith] dies, 9/211
PHILLIPS, [?Philip]: drawing of yacht, 4/301 & n. 2
PHILPOT LANE: 7/262
PHIPPS, [?Thomas], of Rochester: 7/177
PHYSICIANS, ROYAL COLLEGE OF: 4/156
PICKERING, Dorothy, (b. Weld, Wilde), wife of Edward: social: 5/34; 9/431, 487, 504
PICKERING, Edward (Ned):
CHARACTER: a fool but well informed, 2/170; a coxcomb, 1/101; 4/239, 255; 7/295
CHRON. SERIES: on Naseby, 1/101, 105, 133; carries letters for Sandwich, 1/105, 137, 142, 156; in Holland, 1/144, 145, 150; disappointed of place in Queen's Household, 4/239 & n. 2; dismissed from place at court, 4/255–6 & n.; involvement in Sandwich's love affair, 4/270, 301, 303, 371 & n. 4, 392; 5/22, 184; advises P on coach horses, 9/384, 391(2), 431; house in Lincoln's Inn Fields, 7/423; also, 1/251; 3/72, 212; 6/13; 7/295
COURT/POLITICAL NEWS FROM: 1/101–2; 2/152, 156, 170, 216–17; 3/64; 4/48–9; 5/34
SOCIAL: dines/plays cards etc. with Sandwich, 2/64, 115; 3/7; 4/28, 46; at Bartholomew Fair, 2/166; 4/301; theatre, 5/34; also, 8/181; 9/431, 487
PICKERING, Elizabeth, Lady Pickering (b. Mountagu), wife of Sir Gilbert: solicits Sandwich's help for husband, 1/174, 178 & n. 4; poor lodging in Blackfriars, 1/277; visits P, 9/261–2 & n.; also, 1/179

PICKERING, Sir Gilbert, Lord Chamberlain to Oliver Cromwell: pardoned by Parliament, 1/178 & n. 4; death, 9/334 & n. 1

PICKERING, Gilbert, son of Sir Gilbert: marries heiress, 7/358 & n. 2; rogue, 8/181 & n. 4

PICKERING, John, son of Sir Gilbert: fool, 1/116, 161, 295; on *Naseby*, 1/112, 153, 161; annoys Sandwich, 1/142 & n. 5; proposed match, 1/220–1, 295; also, 2/35

PICKERING, Oliver, son of Sir Gilbert: dies of smallpox, 9/487 & n. 2

PICKERING, Sidney, son of Sir Gilbert: 9/335

PICTURES:

COLLECTIONS [*see* under owners or houses: i.e. Charles II; Clarendon; Crew, Sir T.; Evelyn, J.; Graunt, J.; James, Duke of York; Mary, Princess Dowager of Holland, Povey, T.; Audley End House]

PORTRAITS [*see* under subjects: Albemarle, by Cooper; Allin, Sir T., by Lely; Anne Duchess of York, by Lely; Arlington, by Cooper; Ascue, Sir G., by Lely; Ashley, by Cooper; Berkeley, Sir W., by Lely; Lady Castlemaine, by Lely; Catherine of Braganza, by Huysmans; Charles I, by Van Dyke; by Marshall; Charles II, by Luttichuys; by Lely; Archbishop Chichele, by S. Strong; Cleopatra, artist unknown; Colbert, engr. by Nanteuil: Lord Coventry, ?by S. Stone; Crew, Sir T., ?by Lely; Harman, by Lely; Henrietta-Maria, by Huysmans; by Van Dyck; Henry VIII, by Holbein; anon.; Hill, T., by Hayls: Jordan, Sir J., by Lely; Louis XIV, engr. by Nanteuil; Mary, Princess Dowager, by van Honthorst; Myngs, Sir C., by Lely; Ormond, ?by Loggan; Pearse, Mrs J., by Hayls; Pearse, James jun., by Hayls; Penn, Sir W., by Lely; Sarah Robartes, artist unknown; Prince Rupert, by Lely; Sandwich, by Lely; by Salisbury; Smith, Sir J., by Lely; Stuart, Frances, by Cooper; by Huysmans; Swynfen, ——, by Cooper; Teddeman, Sir T., by Lely;

Van Dyck, self-portrait]; ~ the fashion for portraits *en déshabillé*, 6/335 & n. 1

OTHER PICTURES: cartoons, 1/45; 4/400 & n. 2; *The Four Evangelists* (artist unknown), 1/70 & n. 2; *trompe-l'œuil*, 1/148, 257–8 & n.; 4/18 & n. 1, 26 (by Hoogstraten); 9/119, 352; *The Embarkation of Henry VIII* (artist unknown), 3/292 & n. 4; *Henry VIII and the Barber-Surgeons' Company* (by Holbein), 4/59 & n. 3; 9/293; Dutch drawing, 4/109; etchings of Lisbon and the Tagus (by Sandwich), 4/286 & n. 1; Venetian scene (by Fialetti), 7/60 & n. 2; landscape and still life (artist unknown), 7/81; landscape (by Looten), 9/514 & n. 2; flower-piece (by Verelst), 9/515, 516

MEDIA: on cloth, 1/148; 'paper pictures', 4/320; Evelyn explains mezzotints, 6/289 & n. 3; pastels, 7/359; chalk, ib. & n. 3; ink, 8/181; tempera, 9/434–5 & n., 465

PICTURES (P) [including those acquired for the office. It is not always possible to distinguish prints from other pictures. *See also* Prices.]:

HIS COLLECTION:

GENERAL: hangs/rehangs pictures, 3/3; 5/235–6; 7/122, 258, 409, 417; 9/271, 331(2); also, 8/455; buys pictures at The Hague, 1/148; in London, 1/298; 9/373; buys prints, 1/296; 3/2; 4/434; 5/41; 7/173, 208–9, 409; shown to guests, 9/424; also, 3/1; 7/102

ITEMS: portraits in oil [*see* under artists: P by Savill; by Hayls; EP by Hayls; by Cooper; John P, sen., by Hayls; T. Hill by Bosse after Hayls; H. Harris by Hayls]; other pictures: Dutch landscape, 7/208–9; marine scenes, 7/290, 292; Santa Clara, 7/409; royal palaces by Danckerts, 9/423 & n. 1; Rome by Danckerts, 9/504; drawings: *Resolution* by A. Deane, 9/262 & n. 4; also, 8/142 & n. 2; prints etc.: by Ragot after Rubens, 1/194; *Royal Sovereign*, 4/29 & n. 4, 43; by Lafreri, 7/102–3 & n.; the Thames, 7/290; Lady Castlemaine by Faithorne after Lely, 7/359 & n. 3,

lives 'merrily' at Greenwich, 6/342
ITS SPREAD AND INCIDENCE IN
LONDON AND ENVIRONS: first signs,
6/93; houses marked in Drury Lane,
6/120 & n. 1; reported in city, 6/124,
125, 128, 142, 168, 205-7 passim, 225;
Bell Alley, Westminster, 6/132; near
St Clement's, 6/140; Palace Yard,
6/141; King St, Westminster, 6/141,
163; increases in Westminster, 6/144,
154, 210, 268, 289; reported in
Basinghall St, 6/144; Pall Mall,
6/147-8; Long Lane, 6/150; Covent
Garden, ib.; London Wall, ib.;
Rotherhithe, 6/163, 201; Axe Yard,
6/163; St Olave's parish, 6/171 & n. 2,
175, 329, 335; Islington, 6/175-6;
Dagenhams, 6/181; Deptford, 6/189,
204, 206, 253, 294, 332; 7/236 & n. 3,
239, 241, 285; Woolwich, 6/189, 206,
309; Gravesend, 6/195, 249; Hounslow, 6/199; Greenwich, 6/200, 201,
206, 210, 212, 256; 7/236, 239; St
Sepulchre's, Newgate St, 6/225; near
Tower, 6/251(2); Steelyard, 6/270;
Kent St, 6/279, 297; St Martin's-in-
the-Fields, 6/289; Lambeth, ib.; St
Martin's Lane, 6/304; Chatham, 7/42
& n. 1, 253; Drury Lane, 7/73; the
Swan, Chelsea, 7/95; the Mitre,
Fenchurch St, 7/236, 241, 242; fear of,
6/154, 161, 174, 192; (unspecified)
increase of, 6/143, 164, 171, 206-7,
226, 328; 7/41, 108, 123
ITS SPREAD AND INCIDENCE ELSE-
WHERE: at Salisbury, 6/189; Colchester, 6/307 & n. 2; 7/193; Cambridge,
7/219 & n. 2; 8/468; Deal, 7/241 & n.
3; Petersfield, 8/148
MORTALITY [mostly P's summaries of
statistical returns in weekly bills of
mortality]: P notes worst increase,
6/234; other increases, 6/128, 132-3 &
n., 142, 173, 178, 187, 191 & n. 2,
207-8, 208, 214, 295, 335; 7/9, 14, 17,
52, 71, 80, 91-2, 94, 95, 193; decreases,
6/157 & n. 1, 224-5, 243, 353, 264,
284, 299, 305, 314, 340; 7/2, 21, 32, 63,
110; also, 6/163, 170, 180, 206-7;
bills' unreliability, 6/206-7 & n.
BURIALS: plague-pits, 6/162 & n. 2,
164-5 & n., 207, 213; by day, 6/189,
213, 225; coffin left out all night,

6/201; St Olave's churchyard piled
high, 7/30 & n. 3; attended by infected persons, 7/40-1
ANECDOTES: P's coachman stricken,
6/131; his physician accused of killing
servant, 6/165 & n. 2; P encounters
corpse, 6/192; child rescued from
infected house, 6/212; P meets search-
ers, 6/283 & n. 4; victims beg in street,
6/297; breathe on passers-by, 7/41
FAST FOR: proclaimed, 6/155 & n. 4;
observed, 6/179, 294, 320; 7/37, 68,
91, 150, 151, 193, 231, 306, 359(2)
MEASURES AGAINST: discussed, 6/108,
211, 212; houses shut up, 6/120, 125,
192, 203, 212, 224, 225; fumigated,
6/288; whitewashed, 7/166; pest-
houses, 6/165, 181; pest-coaches,
6/181; bonfires in streets, 6/213 & n.
5; churchyards covered in lime, 7/31;
tobacco, 6/120 & n. 2; plague-water,
6/163 & n. 3; 'good drink', 6/226;
burials by night, 6/189, 199, 282;
(untrue) story of curfew, 6/189
FLIGHT FROM: 6/133, 141-2 & n.; Clarendon, Albemarle and Arlington remain,
6/142; streets empty/shops shut, 6/165,
168, 186, 192, 205, 207, 233, 268, 311;
effect on Royal Exchange, 6/192, 224;
river traffic, 6/233, 293; meetings of
Royal Society, 7/21 & n. 1; physicians
leave, 7/21 & n. 2
CESSATION OF: P notes/hopes for decrease, 6/313, 337, 341; 7/29; decrease
in frosty weather, 6/305, 306; town
fills up, 6/278, 328, 342; 7/3, 18, 38,
52; Brampton carrier resumes, 6/314;
theatres reopen, 7/376-7, 399;
Thanksgiving Day appointed, 7/376 &
n. 2; King's presentations for services
during, 8/196 & n. 3
PLANTS, fruits and trees [For timber
trees used in shipbuilding, see Clerk of
the Acts; Navy Board. See also Food.]:
GENERAL: P admires plantations in
Greenwich Park, 3/63 & n. 4; St
James's Park, 5/127 & n. 1; Wricklemarsh, 6/94; discusses botany with
Evelyn, 6/253, 289
PARTICULAR: cowslips: 4/112; goose-
berries: at Hatfield, 2/139; grapes: in
London, 2/176; Walthamstow, 8/341
-2; lemon-trees: in Hampstead, 9/281;

you know not me, you know nobody, or The troubles of Queen Elizabeth, at TR, Drury Lane, 8/388*† & n. 2; alluded to: 8/387

[?HOLDEN, J.], *The German princess*, at LIF, 5/124*† & n. 2; *The Ghosts*, at LIF, 6/83*† & n. 1

HOWARD, E., *The change of crownes*, at TR, Drury Lane, 8/167–8* & nn.; alluded to: 8/169; *The Usurper*, at TR, Drury Lane, 5/3*† & n. 2; 9/381*† & n. 4

[HOWARD, J.], *The English monsieur*, at TR, Drury Lane, 7/401* & n.; 9/155* *All mistaken, or The mad couple*, at TR, Drury Lane, 8/443*† & n. 1, 594*† & n. 1; 9/269*†

[HOWARD, SIR R.], *The Committee*, at TR, Drury Lane, 4/181*† & n. 1; 8/384*, 508*†; 9/200; *The great favourite, or The Duke of Lerma*, at TR, Drury Lane, 9/81*† & n. 2; alluded to: 9/20 & n. 1; *The Surprisal*, at TR, Drury Lane, 8/157*† & n. 3, 402*, 590*† & n. 3; 9/166*, 182

[HOWARD, SIR R. AND DRYDEN, J.], *The Indian queen*, at TR, Drury Lane, 5/28–9* & n., 33–4*†; 9/250*† & n. 1

HOWARD, SIR R.: *see also* Buckingham, Duke of

[JONSON, B.], *The Alchemist*, at TR, Vere St, 2/125* & n. 1, 154; at TR, Drury Lane, 9/522–3*† & n.; alluded to: 5/232; 9/85 & n. 4; *Bartholomew Fair*, at TR, Vere St, 2/116–17* & n., 127*, 174*† & n. 1, 212*†; at TR, Drury Lane, 5/230*; 9/299†; Great Hall, Whitehall, 9/456†; *Catiline his conspiracy*, at TR, Drury Lane, 8/569, 575*; 9/395*† & n. 1; alluded to: 5/349 & n. 4; 9/20; *Epicoene, or The silent woman*, at Cockpit, Whitehall, [1/297–8]; at TR, Vere St, 2/7*†, 106*; at TR, Drury Lane, 5/165*† & n. 3; 8/168†, 169*; 9/310*; alluded to: 1/171 & n. 2, 309 & n. 2; *Volpone*, at TR, Drury Lane, 6/10*† & n. 2; *Works*, alluded to: 4/410 & n. 4

[KILLIGREW, T., sen.], *Claracilla*, at TR, Vere St, 2/223* & n. 2; at Cockpit, Whitehall, 4/4*† & n. 4; at TR, Drury Lane, 9/476*†; *The parson's*

wedding ('*The parson's dreame*') alluded to, at TR, Drury Lane, 5/289 & n. 1, 294; *The Princess, or Love at first sight*, at TR, Vere St, 2/132* & n. 2;

[KYD, T.], *The Spanish tragedy, or Hieronymo is mad again*, at Nursery, Hatton Garden, 9/89–90*† & n. ; *The Labyrinth*, at TR, Drury Lane, 5/139*†; alluded to: 5/138 & n. 1

LACY, J., *The old troop, or Monsieur Raggou*, at TR, Drury Lane, 9/270*† & n. 1, 271*†

LACY, J.: *see also* Shakespeare

Love's Quarrel, at Salisbury Court, 2/66* & n. 3

[MARLOWE, C.], *Dr Faustus*, at Red Bull, Clerkenwell, 3/93*† & n. 4

[MASSINGER, P.], *The Bondman*, at Salisbury Court, 2/47* & n. 2, 56, 60†; at LIF, 2/207*†, 220 & n. 3; 3/58*† & n. 3; 5/224* & nn.

MASSINGER, P.: *see also* Dekker, T.; Fletcher, J.

[MAYNE, J.], *The city match*, at TR, Drury Lane, 9/322* & n. 1

The merry devil of Edmonton, at TR, Vere St, 2/151* & n. 6

[MIDDLETON, T.], *The Widow*, at TR, Vere St, 2/8* & n. 2

[MIDDLETON, T. AND ROWLEY, W.], *The Changeling*, at Salisbury Court, 2/41* & n. 3; *The Spanish gipsie*, at TR, Drury Lane, 9/107*† & n. 4

NEWCASTLE, WILLIAM, DUKE OF, *The country captain*, at TR, Vere St, 2/202*† & n. 2, 220*; at TR, Drury Lane, 8/386*; 9/198–9*; *The Heiress*, at TR, Drury Lane, 9/435–6*† & nn.; *The humorous lovers*, at LIF, 8/137* & n. 4, 163*; *The humours of Monsieur Galliard* (based upon *The Variety*), at TR, Vere St, 3/87–8*† & nn.; *Sir Martin Marall*: *see* Dryden, J.

ORRERY, ROGER BOYLE, EARL OF, *The Black Prince*, at TR, Drury Lane, 8/487–8*† & n., 498*; 9/144* & n. 1; *The General*, at TR, Drury Lane, 5/281–2* & n., 288–9*† & n.; 9/533*†; *Guzman*, at LIF, 9/521–2*† & n.; *Henry the fifth*, at LIF, 5/240–1*† & nn., 282; 9/256–7† & n.; at Great Hall, Whitehall, 7/424*; 8/487–8*; alluded to: 5/245*; 8/380;

PLOTS and minor risings [for major plots and risings, *see* [Derwentdale Plot]; Dublin; Fire, the Great; Pentland Rising; Venner, T.].: P's scepticism, 2/225; 3/236; Yarranton or Baxter Plot, 2/225 & n. 1; 3/15; fanatics in London, 3/92 & n. 4; Southwark, 3/165 & n. 3; Dorset, 3/236 & n. 1, 237, 239, 240, 245; P dreams of, 3/250; in W. Country, 6/209 & n. 2

PLOUGH, the, Fleet St (shop): 1/71

PLUME, Thomas, Vicar of St Alphege, Greenwich 1658–d.1704: sermons, 6/227 & n. 4, 316; 9/502

PLYMOUTH, Devon: damaged ships return, 7/9; convoy, 7/395; prize-ships, 8/7, 115–16 & n.; squadron, 8/149; victuals for, 8/88, 560; Dutch fleet off, 8/345; French raids, 9/79–80; also, 5/341

POINTER (Poynter), [Thomas], Navy Office clerk: P's clerk for victualling, 6/315, 315–16; 7/266; 9/37; recommended to Mennes, 6/336

POLAND: hangmen, 3/154 & n. 2; French designs on, 8/92 & n. 3; state treasuries, 8/454 & n. 2

POLICE: *see* Burglary etc.

POLITICAL OPINIONS (P) [For his views on the King and the politicians, *see* under names. *See also* War, the Second Dutch.]: approves of Charles I's execution, 1/280; recalls talking 'privately' of King during Rump, 1/204; drinks King's health (Feb. 1660), 1/58, 67, 68, 70; sympathetic to arrested Cavalier (March 1660), 1/99; kisses King's letter to Sandwich (May 1660), 6/237; views on: state of nation, 3/127; parliament, 7/416; 9/326; parliamentary enquiries, 8/292–3, 305, 353, 485; power of King to save nation, 7/197, 350, 371; French military absolutism as model for England, 8/332; new balance of power in government, 8/584; ~ regrets failure to keep abreast of news, 1/219; 2/124

POLLARD, Sir Hugh, Comptroller of the King's Household 1660–d.66: replaced, 7/390 & n. 2

POLLEROON, Poleron: *see* Pulo Run

PONT: *see* Punt

POOLE, Capt. Jonas, naval officer: at Greenwich, 2/121; loses commission, 6/129 & n. 1; social: 2/?112, 186; ~ his wife, 2/186

POOLE, Matthew, biblical commentator (d. 1679): dispute about *Synopsis Criticorum*, 9/259 & n. 2

POOLE, Capt. William, naval officer, kted 1672: ship disabled in action, 6/19; social: 2/121; ~ wife, 3/5; 8/403, 405; boy 3/5; daughter christened, 8/403, 405

POOLEY, Sir Edmund, M.P. for Bury St Edmunds, Suff.: fine gentleman, 5/330; 6/309; discontented Cavalier, 6/303; shows P prize-goods, 6/300; social: 6/285, 303, 324; ~ his wife, 7/240

POOR, the [*see also* Mendicancy]: P's poor box, 3/230; 4/56, 123, 149–50, 431; 5/55, 192, 193, 284; 6/29; 7/205, 401; employs parish girl, 4/282, 283; ragpicker, 2/60; city orphanage, 1/180 & n. 1; at cockfights, 4/428; foundling, 9/304

POORTMANS (Portman), [John], naval official under Commonwealth: supports rise of Penn, 4/375

POPE'S HEAD ALLEY: P shops in, 1/80, 298; 3/17, 115; also, 2/141

POPHAM, Alexander, M.P. Bath, Som. 1661–d.69: house (Littlecote House, Wilts.), 9/241–2 & n.

POPHAM, Sir ―― [?Francis: son of the foregoing; M.P. Bath, Som. 1669–d. 74]: 7/385 & n. 3

POPINJAY ALLEY: 4/279

POPISH PLOT, the: effects on P's career, vol. i, p. xxxvii

POPULAR BELIEFS and customs [*see also* Ashmole, E.; Booker, J.; Lilly, W.; Nostradamus]:

ASTROLOGY: horoscopes, 1/274 & nn.; P buys mock almanac, 1/288–9 & n.; laughs at Lilly's prophecies, 8/270 & n. 2; Buckingham accused of having King's horoscope cast, 8/93–4 & n.; and of being influenced by 'conjurors', 9/373 & n. 2; fear of meteor, 9/208

GHOSTS: P meets, 2/68; 4/227; sceptical of Wiltshire drummer, 4/185–6 & n.;

fears house haunted, 8/553; tells/
listens to ghost stories, 2/68; 4/185,
312; 5/349; 7/256; 9/495
MAGIC: graves sown with sage, 3/70–1
& n.; beer preserved by iron bar,
4/365; Quakers charmed by string,
4/438 & n. 1; P wears hare's foot for
colic, 5/359 & n. 1; writes out charms
for illness, etc., 5/361–2 & nn.; story
of levitation, 6/177–8 & n.; EP's
belief in diabolism, 8/234; gamesters'
superstitions, 9/3
PROPHECIES, AUGURIES AND OMENS:
thunderstorm at coronation, 2/86 &
n. 2; fanatics' choice of day for revolution, 3/186 & n. 1; invasion of
Portugal prophesied, 4/198–9; palm-
istry, 4/234–5; gipsy's warning, 4/284,
296; storm foretelling death, 4/338 &
n. 2; numerology, 7/46–7 & n.; 9/46;
prophecies by Nostradamus, 8/42 &
n. 2; and Tom o'Wood, 8/270; nose-
bleeding, 8/324
A 'RIDING': 8/257 & n. 2
WITCHES: stories of, 7/256; J. Glanvill's
book, 7/382 & n. 2; 8/589
PORTER, family of: two of brothers
in brawl, 4/136
PORTER, Charles, kted 1686; solicitor
to Duke of York: ? in Field case,
3/280; consulted on prizes, 9/61, 63,
146; acts for creditors of navy,
9/140; social: 7/404; 8/284; 9/15,
473
PORTER, Tom, courtier and dramatist [see also Plays]: ? in brawl, 4/136;
duel, 8/363–4 & n., 377, 384
PORTER, ——, P's cousin: visits
P, 3/25; husband arrested, 6/186–7
& n.
PORTERS (street): 1/38 & n. 2; 8/598;
9/364; also, 1/46
PORTLAND, Lord: see Weston
PORTLAND BAY, Dorset: convoy,
6/62
PORTMAN: see Poortmans
PORTMAN, Elizabeth, Lady Portman, wife of Sir William (d. 1673):
9/416 & n. 4
PORTSMOUTH, Hants. [see also
Shales, J.; Steventon, St John;
Tippetts, J.]:
TOWN: description, 2/92 & n. 2; Sand-

wich at, 2/3, 18; Queen Mother, 2/4;
Princess Henrietta, 2/11; Queen
Catherine, 3/64, 71, 80, 83, 84; and
King, 3/86 & n. 1, 89; Queen's gift
from corporation, 3/72 & n. 2, 74; P
made burgess, 2/93 & n. 4; 3/74 & n.
2; places: Red Lion, 2/92; walls, 2/92;
3/71, 72; church (St Thomas's), 3/70;
gates 3/73
GARRISON: 2/11; Duke of York visits as
Governor, 2/199 & n. 2; 4/24; 8/173,
175; chapel, 3/71–2; Government
House, 3/71 & n. 7
HARBOUR: Sandwich's drawing, 6/38 &
n. 2; *London* aground off, 2/11;
shipping, 3/119, 249; 4/3, 369; 5/295,
299, 304, 318, 336, 337, 360; 6/9, 275;
7/333, 334; 8/149, 345; 9/273–4, 510;
prize-ships, 5/326; 7/418; 8/1; King
inspects Petty's ship, 4/334
DOCKYARD: visits by P/colleagues, 2/89,
90–3 passim, 199, 202; 3/65, 66, 68,
70–5 passim, 145, 280; 4/389; 5/152,
153; sale of provisions, 2/93 & n. 1;
pays, 3/65, 66, 68, 70–5 passim & nn.,
289; 4/8, 253; 7/75; chaplain, 3/72 &
n. 1; muster, 3/73; instructions to
officers, 3/73, 80; survey, 4/141; creeks
used, 4/225 & n. 6; Middleton
appointed Commissioner, 5/314;
shortage of victuals, 4/363, 364; ships
fitted out, 5/182; labour troubles,
6/144 & n. 1; fortification, 8/98 &
n. 3, 125, 126; men sent to Chatham,
8/272; disaffection of seamen, 8/282;
proposal for resident surveyor, 8/391;
alluded to: 3/174
PORTUGAL [see also Afonso VI]:
marriage alliance, 2/128–9 & n.; fleet
sent for Catherine of Braganza, 2/189,
198, 231, 242; 3/64, 80, 83; dispute
over Bombay, 4/139 & n. 2; war
against Spain: English troops sent,
3/48, 63, 72, 85, 119, 252–3; sea-
campaign, 3/61, 110; Spanish troops
invade, 4/198, 206; repelled at
Ameixial, 4/198 & n. 2, 202–3, 206,
215; Évora recaptured, 4/215 & n. 1;
French support Spaniards, 8/107–8;
peace with France, 8/191 & n. 6; and
Spain, 9/59–60 & n. , 80 & n. 1, 222 &
n. 4; primitive sanitation, 3/205; also,
2/76

POSTAL SERVICES: management, 7/375 & n. 2; express, 4/306; 6/257, 260, 271(2); 7/2; 8/263-4, 429; 9/74; carrier, 1/15, 36, 46, 57; delayed by floods, 7/328-9; post-boy, 1/32; post-houses: Southwark, 2/15, 231; Charing Cross, 6/197

POST OFFICE, Threadneedle St: P rides post from, 2/133; music-meetings at, 5/238 & n. 2, 290; destroyed in Fire, 7/275; also, 1/53

POTTLE, ——, shopkeeper in New Exchange: 8/53

POULTNY: see Pulteney

POULTRY, the: 1/246; 8/180

POUNDY, [?James], waterman: witness against P in prize-goods affair, 8/531; also, 7/202, 275

POVEY (Puvy), [Thomas],Treasurer for Tangier:

CHARACTER: vain, 4/17-18; 'most excellent in anything but business', 6/215; also, 3/300; 4/297-8; 5/139, 339; 6/13, 24, 63, 87; 7/191

AS TREASURER FOR TANGIER: appointed, 3/177 & n. 1, 238; incompetence, 5/97-8, 102, 106, 123, 124, 127, 135, 139, 154; 6/18, 37, 69-70, 84-5; 7/191, 330; neglects to provide boats, 3/291; loses his papers, 6/65; victualling business, 4/30; 5/212-13, 223; Gauden's gift, 8/37, 44; drafts civil constitution, 4/88-9; freightage business, 5/23, 26, 276, 332, 336-8 passim, 340, 348; accounts criticised, 5/105; 6/13-18 passim, 33, 38, 58-60 passim, 71, 77, 77-8; 8/75; examined, 9/244, 247, 371, 449; part in examining Peterborough's accounts, 5/123, 124, 135, 154, 187, 199, 201-2; 6/68-9; other financial business, 6/100-1, 144, 157, 185, 214-15; 9/416; cheated by Vernatty, 7/342; 8/52; resigns office to P on terms, 6/58-63 passim, 79, 84, 89, 91, 94, 108, 109, 121, 130, 139; accounts with P, 7/19, 51, 71, 74, 83, 321, 335(2), 338; 8/593; 9/341-2; at committee meetings, 3/300; 4/21, 23, 269, 341; 5/11, 97, 139, 204; 7/228; unspecified business, 3/232; 4/21, 31, 394; 6/76, 103, 131, 136, 137, 151, 163; 7/156, 245, 265; 8/286-7; 9/437, 543; also, 6/22, 65-6

AS TREASURER FOR THE MANAGEMENT OF THE HOUSEHOLD OF THE DUKE OF YORK: Duke's debts, 7/191-2; 8/287; dismissed, 8/592 & n. 1; 9/38

POLITICAL/COURT NEWS FROM: criticises court, 6/266, 267; 7/228-9; pessimism, 8/286-7; also, 6/215-16; 8/295, 297, 366-7, 431-2; 9/341-2, 373, 414, 416

HOUSES, WEALTH ETC.: house in Lincoln's Inn Fields: cellar, bathroom etc., 4/18 & n. 2, 272 & n. 3, 298; 5/161 & n. 2, 199, 277; 6/139; 8/128-9; 9/345; aviary, 4/272; grotto, 4/298; 5/161; pictures, 4/18 & n. 1, 26; 5/161 & n. 3, 161-2, 212, 277 & n. 2; house at Hounslow, 6/153 & n. 3, 198, 266, 267; chariot, 6/153, 266; horses, 6/266; forced to economise, 6/267; also, 9/443

PERSONAL: bold dalliance with Mary Mercer, 6/85; unwell, 6/97; leaves London in Plague, 6/154; 7/4

SOCIAL: at court ball, 3/300; Hinchingbrooke, 5/65; at funeral, 6/114; at theatre, 8/435; at his house, 4/17-18, 26, 31, 35, 297; 5/161-2, 276; 6/13, 17, 18, 22, 76, 87, 99; 9/345, 521; elsewhere, 4/242; 5/265, 270, 330, 338; 9/434-5

MISC.: gifts to P, 4/306; 5/269, 274; nominates P to Royal Society, 6/36; attends its meetings, 6/84; 9/379; advises P to enter parliament, 9/376-7; helps choose coach, 9/342, 344, 352; introduces to Danckerts, 9/421; warns against ostentation in dress, 9/551; relations with Creed, 5/338-9 & n.; 6/89-90; 9/244, 247; advises Arlington not to buy Euston, 8/288-9 & n.; also, 5/74

~ his wife [Mary], 4/297 & n. 4; 6/199; his man Dutton's wife, 6/266, 267; his man, 7/229

POWELL, Doll, (b. Lane), of Westminster: P's valentine, 9/121, 126; has baby, 9/486; claims to be Rowland Powell's widow, 9/486, 514; amorous encounters with P: 7/337, 342, 345, 359, 386, 406; 8/3, 39-40, 393, 422; 9/78, 121, 527; misses assignations, 8/111, 113-14; 9/317; fails to find privacy for, 8/193; false modesty,

7/112; chest of drawers, 2/130; dressing-box, 8/53; looking glass, 5/347; 9/423; table, 4/6; tapestry, 5/215; 9/329, 330

HORSES: 6/180

HOUSEHOLD GOODS: bakepan, 3/294; lock, 8/226

JEWELRY ETC.: locket (with diamonds), 9/7; necklace (pearl), 6/201; 7/111, 113; also, 8/433; pendants, 5/196; precious stones: pearls, 3/200; diamonds, 6/300; rubies, ib.; rings, 6/190–1; 9/24, 67, 78, 384; watch, 6/83 & n. 2; 8/51

MUSICAL INSTRUMENTS: flageolet, 8/344; 9/30 & n. 2; harpsichord, 2/44; lute, 1/91; spinet, 9/262; theorbo, 2/203; viol, 4/284

NAVAL SUPPLIES: hemp, 6/75 & n. 2; 7/132 & n. 3, 385 & n. 2; tar, 3/137 & n. 3; timber, 4/326

PICTURES AND PICTURE FRAMES: by Hayls: 7/73, 74, 112, 125; Cooper, 9/138, 139–40, 277; Holbein: 9/293; Verelst, 9/515, 516; also, 3/10, 80, 106; 7/208–9; copies, 1/301–2; prints, 6/111, n. 5; 9/268, 313

PLATE: bowl (christening), 8/548; cistern (copper), 8/424; cups, 4/39–40; 5/45, 47(2); 6/63; (gold), 4/115; dish/standish, 4/39–40; 8/35; salt, 6/132; silver and silver-plate (per oz.), 5/301; tankards, 1/296; 2/5; 5/47

RENTS: for P's and EP's lodgings during Plague, 6/261 & n. 3, 271, 315; for other lodgings, 7/296; rise in after Fire, 7/280

SCIENTIFIC AND MATHEMATICAL INSTRUMENTS: globes, 4/302; magnifying glasses, 1/95; 2/35; microscope, 5/240; pantograph, 9/444; ruler (engraving of), 5/238; telescope, 7/241 & n. 1

SHIP: 5/75 & n. 5

TRANSPORT: horses by ferry, 6/181–2; furniture by lighters, 7/293

MISC.: barber, 9/225, 234; blackbird, 4/150; cat-call, 1/80; fortune-teller, 4/284; glass (for lamp), 5/291–2; (for coach), 9/403; guns (French pistols etc.), 5/75; knife, 1/298; leather case, 5/247, 255; musicians, 2/218; 9/13;

office-paper, 7/101; prostitute, 5/225–6; 9/297; tweezers, 3/115

[PRIDE, Col. Thomas], regicide (d. 1658): corpse exhumed and hanged, 1/309 & n. 3

PRIDGEON: see Prujean

PRIMATE, ——, leatherseller, Fleet St: project to increase royal revenue, 4/425–6 & n.

[?PRIMEROSE, David], minister, French church, Threadneedle St: sermon, 3/270 & n. 4; ~ his sisters, 5/342

PRIN, Monsieur, musician: 8/500 & n. 2

PRINTS: see Pictures

PRIOR, [William], of Brampton: buys houses at Brampton, 2/204–5 & n., 236, 237–8; 3/28, 31, 221, 223, 286–7; 4/309; 5/279; 'a poor painful man', 5/279

PRIOR'S: see Taverns etc: Rhenish winehouse, Cannon Row

PRISONS: see Clerkenwell; Counter; Gatehouse, Westminster; Newgate; Southwark; Whitehall: guardhouse

PRI(T)CHARD, [William], ropemaker: 9/37

PRIVATEERS: see Prizes and privateers

PRIVY COUNCIL, the:

GENERAL: P's evidence, vol. i, p. cxxx; councillors' fee, 1/179; sworn in, 3/75; stationery, 8/182–3

MEETINGS: to sit every day, 8/291; 9/316; in mornings, 9/8; full extraordinary meetings, 9/152–3, 154; committees disorderly in King's absence, 6/45 & n. 6; places of [usually Whitehall or St James's but exceptionally]: Hampton Court, 3/157; 7/26; Worcester House, 5/114; 6/11, 76; 7/107; Clarendon House, 8/21, 67; Southampton House, 8/149; also, 8/151; 9/141

COUNCIL BUSINESS [for the Cabinet and Council of Trade see below. References here are to business in full council and in its other committees, both ad hoc and standing]:

NAVAL: financial (general), 1/231 & n. 4; 7/377, 383–4; grant, 8/112 &

n. 2; accounts, 8/448 & n. 4, 449;
9/445; retrenchments, 8/374 & n. 2,
591; pay, 8/396–7; 9/130; compensation for sunk ship, 9/69; flag-officers'
pensions, 9/257; instructions to Sandwich, 3/90; seamen's riot, 4/294;
committee acts in Duke of York's
absence, 5/315 & n. 1, 318–19, 321,
322, 325, 333, 357–8; criticised by P,
5/332, 333, 357–8; 6/58; standing
committee appointed, 9/67 & n. 3;
impressment of men and ships, 6/45,
91; 8/290; insurance of cargo, 6/104–
5; embezzlement of stores, 6/115 &
n. 3, 118; victualling, 6/142, 143;
9/315–18 passim & nn., 429; Marescoe's tar, 6/166 & n. 3; pursers, 7/28;
Medway disaster, 8/269, 278–9,
287–8, 317, 396–7, 404, 454, 456,
460, 461, 567, 571; committee for
seamen's complaints, 8/297; fitting
out merchantmen, 8/316; Carkesse's
dismissal, 8/379, 385, 386, 388; design
of masts, 9/5–6; acts of war by foreign
ships, 9/87–8; calling in fleet, 9/251;
Anglesey's complaints, 9/253 & n. 2,
256; tickets, 9/263; supernumeraries,
9/350–1 & n.; also, 8/67

JUDICIAL: Lane v. Hore, 5/324 & nn.;
desertion of ship, 8/16 & n. 4; private
case, 8/316–17; Buckingham examined, 8/330–1; Barker's case, 8/404,
407, 420–1 & n.; 9/119; Bee's case,
9/259 & n. 2; the Temple's claim to
immunity, 9/511–12 & n.; excise
disputes, 9/529 & n. 2, 532 &
n. 1; Painter-Stainers' case, 9/531–2
& n.

MISC.: parliamentary bills, 3/85 & n.
2; indulgence to Presbyterians, 3/186
& n. 2; plotters examined, 3/241 & n.
2; disorders in Scotland, 4/168–9 & n.;
Portuguese customs dues, 5/251 &
n. 3; King's new fashion, 7/315 &
n. 1; Tangier, 7/321, 336; 9/14–15,
272; poll-tax commissioner committed, 8/252 & n. 2; patent of Canary
Company, 8/297 & n. 4; peace
terms, 8/328, 329–30, 426; retrench-
ment, 8/391 & nn., 394–5 & n., 405;
treaty with Portugal, 9/59 & n. 3,
222 & n. 4; Anglesey's dismissal,
9/342–3, 344–5; also, 5/58; un-

specified: 4/390; 7/26, 137, 158, 159,
177, 178, 186, 252, 353, 354, 385;
8/67, 80, 86; 9/26, 28, 280

ORDERS IN COUNCIL: constituting Navy
Board, 1/191, n. 2, 193; boats for
Jamaica, 3/52 & n. 3; ships for Portugal, 3/85 & n. 3; inspection of Victualling Office, 3/135 & n. 3; quarantine
regulations in Thames, 4/399 & n. 2;
house for Navy Treasury, Broad St,
5/278 & n. 2; impressment, 6/96;
building ships, 7/193 & n. 5; re-
organising work of Comptroller,
8/20 & n. 2, 24, 25, 30; impressment
of ships, 8/260 & n. 2, 291–2 & n.;
bankers' assignments, 8/285 & n. 3;
petitions to Navy Board, 8/393 & n.
1; government loans, 8/400 & n. 1;
enforcing oaths, 8/425 & n. 2; payment of seamen, 8/454 & n. 1; payment of Tangier garrison, 9/14–15 &
n.; setting out fleet, 9/25(2) & n. 1;
25–6; payment of navy creditors,
9/152, 153–4; storekeepers' accounts,
9/474 & n. 1; also, 8/219 & n. 3

CABINET [meeting usually on Sundays;
also 'cabal', 'cabinet council', 'the
Committee for Foreign Affairs',
'King's private council']:

  COMPOSITION: 4/138; 5/317; 7/312;
8/585

  MEETING PLACES [usually 'at Whitehall' but also]: in the Green Room,
Whitehall, 7/260, 311–12; at Secretary's chamber, Whitehall, 9/427; at
Lord Chancellor's, 8/21; Lord Treasurer's, 8/138; Lord Keeper's, 9/424–6,
Secretary Arlington's, 9/473, 525

  BUSINESS: victualling, 6/266, 275;
7/259, 260; state of navy, 7/311–13;
Tangier, 7/321, 336; 8/82; 9/492;
peace terms, 8/138; preparation of
fleet, 9/424, 425–6, 427–8 & n. 1, 473;
Sandwich's allowances as ambassador,
9/440 & n. 2; constitution of Navy
Board, 9/443, 525–6; supply, 7/311–
12; 8/111(2), 111–12, 114; 9/525;
unspecified, 5/317; 7/260, 374;
8/21

COUNCIL OF TRADE: (of 1660) proposals
for convoys, 2/20 & n. 4; secretary,
5/223; (of 1668) angers Duke of York,
9/549 & n. 2

PRIVY SEAL OFFICE:
GENERAL: warrants issued, 1/197; 3/83; 4/62, 65; 5/61 & n. 1, 79; 6/3, 8; P examines records, 4/188–9 & n.; 9/474, 477, 478; lack of method, 9/478; also, 1/295
P'S SERVICE IN: appointed Sandwich's deputy, 1/205 & n. 3, 206, 207; begins work, 1/208, 212; attends by the month, 1/218–19, 235, 303; 2/226; busy, 1/213, 218–19, 232; 2/235; 3/61; idle in King's absence from town, 1/227, 229, 230; alleged error, 1/245 & n. 2; issues free pardons, 1/310, 312, 316, 317, 320; attends sealing-day, 2/149, 150, 156, 159, 186, 187, 229, 232; misses Navy Board meeting, 2/177; fees: amounts, 1/213 & n. 1, 219, 225, 233, 320; 2/2, 3; divided between Sandwich, P and Moore, 1/237, 238 & n. 4; 2/63, 64; 4/378; decrease, 1/262; 3/80; table of, 2/209, 214; unspecified business, 1/214, 216, 217, 220, 221, 223, 224, 228, 231, 307, 318, 320; 2/64, 66, 79, 149, 150, 153, 157, 171, 175, 177, 199–200, 226, 228, 236; 3/66, 83; official stall in Whitehall Chapel, 3/67; ?5/96; resigns, 3/168; also, 1/173; 2/234; 3/66
PRIZE OFFICE, Whitehall: commissioners appointed, 5/322, 327 & n. 2, 328, 333; T. Hill assistant secretary, 6/21; officers dismissed, 7/78 & n. 1; sale of goods at, 8/14, 16; new office in Aldersgate St, 8/16; case before special commissioners, 8/231 & n. 2
PRIZES and privateers:
PRIZES:
GENERAL: act against breaking bulk, 3/118 & n. 2; revenue from, 7/130, 317; 8/446 & n. 3; dividends, 8/23–4 & n.
PRIZE-GOODS TAKEN BY SANDWICH 1665 [see also Cocke, G.; Cuttance, R.; Howe, W.; Sandwich; Penn]: capture of Dutch E. Indiamen, 6/223, 226; cargoes rifled, 6/230–1 & n. 1; goods stored, 6/236; navy's share of proceeds, 6/239 & n. 1; sold by E. India Company, 6/273 & n. 3, 280–1; P joins with Cocke to buy goods, 6/230, 238–42 passim, 244; P's profit,

6/231 & n. 1, 243, 245; advice from broker, 6/250, 254; 7/140; clears customs, 6/247, 256, 258; sells out to Cocke, 6/314, 327, 328, 341; enquiries by Brooke House Committee (and P's defence), 9/48–53 passim, 57, 61, 72, 118, 163; his narrative, 9/64 & n. 2, 68; also, 6/271–2; 7/6, 65, 80, 305; 8/531
OTHER PRIZES: Dutch ships, 5/341 & n. 1; 7/224, 249, 250, 251 & n. 3, 296–7 & n.; French, 7/350 & n. 1, 352; 9/160; Ostender, 9/96, 97 & n. 1; goods sold contrary to order, 8/14, 15–16 & nn., 20 & n. 2, 58, 144; Rupert's licence for discovery of stolen goods, 8/52; ships sold, 8/484 & n. 3, 485
PRIVATEERS [see also Algiers; Ostend; Tangier; Tunis]:
    The Flying Greyhound: lent to P, Batten and Penn, 7/299, 300–1 & n.; to trade with Madeira, 7/316; prizes: at Plymouth, 8/115–16 & n.; Hull, 8/341 & n. 3, 344, 345, 349, 351–2, 369, 385 & n. 2; Newcastle, 8/435; in Holland, 9/117; St John Baptist, 9/147; other ships: 7/418, 424; 8/1, 7, 8; dispute with Swedish resident, 8/17, 21–4 passim & nn., 27, 123 & n. 1, 130 & n. 2, 133–6 passim, 169, 180, 181, 231; P calculates dividends, 8/232; 9/147; sells out to Batten, 8/341, 385; settles with Batten's widow, 8/462, 477, 483, 561, 569, 579, 582, 584; and with Duke of York, 9/290, 298; asked to lend to government from profits, 8/392, 393; accused of favouring ship's seamen in pays, 9/99; also, 7/360; 8/135, 159, 579; alluded to: 9/168
    OTHERS: French caper, 8/162; Scottish, 8/200; Rupert's Panther and Fanfan, 8/341
PROBY, [Peter], son [-in-law] of Sir R. Ford: 4/354
PROCTOR, [William], landlord of the Mitre, Wood St [see also Taverns etc.]: with son dies of plague, 6/175–6 & n.
PROGER, [Edward], Groom of the Bedchamber to the King: influence, 5/56; news from, 8/429–30 & n.;

RABY, Monsieur ——: French news, 4/25–6 & n.

RADCLIFFE [Jonathan], P's schoolfellow; ?Vicar of Walthamstow 1660–2: sermon, 2/109 & n. 2

RAGOT, [François], engraver: 1/194 & n. 5

RAGUSA, Duchy of: 3/8

RAINBOWE, Edward, Master of Magdalene College, Cambridge 1642–50, 1660–4; Bishop of Carlisle, 1664–d.84: Vice-Chancellor, 4/99; bishop, 5/135 & n. 4; high reputation, 8/365; alluded to: 8/51

[RAINSFORD, Sir Richard], Baron of the Exchequer and President of the Court of Claims, Dublin 1663; Judge in King's Bench 1669–78 (d. 1680): 5/324 & n. 2

RALEIGH (Rawly), Sir Walter (d. 1618): 'sacrificed', 6/6 & n. 2

RAM ALLEY: 9/256

RAMSEY, Mrs ——, of St Bride's parish, Fleet St: bequest, 4/410 & n. 2

RAMSEY, Mrs ——: social: 1/9; 2/141, 143; ~ her grandchild, 1/9

[RAND, Capt. William], Master-Attendant, Chatham: evidence against Pett, 8/461 & n. 3; to be dismissed, 9/258 & n. 3

RANDALL, —— [?identical with the following]: 5/253

RANDELL: see Rundell(s)

RAPHAEL, painter: picture, 3/80 & n. 1

[al-RASHĪD, Mawlāy], Sultan of Morocco 1666–72: 7/214 & n. 2

RATCLIFF, Mdx: P at, 1/287; 3/111; 6/50; 8/248; 9/101; Ratcliff highway, 6/46

RATUIT, Louis, Comte de Souche (General Souche): victory over Turks, 5/228 & n. 2

[RAVEN, John], clerk of Dover castle: 1/97

RAWLINS, Col. Giles, Gentleman of the Privy Purse to the Duke of York: killed in duel, 3/170 & n. 3; also, 3/149

RAWLINSON, Daniel, landlord of the Mitre, Fenchurch St [see also Taverns etc.]: takes charge of cash for Sandwich, 1/84, 221; advises P on investment, 2/117; in country, 7/236

& n. 2; provides wine-bottles, 4/346; closes Mitre in Plague, 7/236, 241; death of servants in, 7/236, 242; political news from, 8/427; social: P visits/dines with, 1/187; 2/109, 207, 219; 3/61, 183, 298; 4/257, 318; 5/47, 235; 6/168, 298; also, 1/245; 2/220; 3/178; 4/335; 5/162; alluded to: 2/170

RAWLINSON, [Margaret], wife of Daniel: death in Plague, 7/236, 241; social: 1/187; 2/170; 3/276

RAWLINSON, Richard, antiquary (d. 1755): vol. i, p. lxxi

RAWLY: see Raleigh

RAWORTH, [Francis], barrister, Gray's Inn: in dispute over Robert P's will, 4/203

[RAY, John], scrivener, of Fleet St: legacy, 3/264 & n. 2

RAYNER, [Edmond], boatmaker at Deptford and Woolwich: P refuses gift, 6/185; his ship, 9/160 & n. 2

RAYNOLDS: see Reynolds

READE, Dr [Thomas], lawyer: loan to government, 8/397 & n. 4

'READER, our': see St Olave's Church, Hart St

READING, Berks.: P visits, 9/242–3 & nn.: Broad Face inn, 9/242 & n. 5

REAMES, Reemes: see Reymes

RED BULL, the: see Theatres

RED CROSS ST: 9/543

REDRIFFE: see Rotherhithe

REEVE(S), [Richard], optical instrument maker, Long Acre: sells/demonstrates magnifying glasses, 2/35; 7/219, 226, 243, 254, 257; 9/261; microscopes, 5/223, 240; 7/226; anchor and loadstone, 5/245; picture-box, 7/254 & n. 3, 257; frame with shutters, 7/254; telescope, 7/238–41 passim, 254, 257; camera obscura, 9/261; reading glass, 9/284; P visits shop, 5/48, 221; gives P scotoscope, 5/240 & n. 1; attempts to borrow from, 5/245; lack of theoretical knowledge, 7/254; social: 9/265; ~ his wife, 9/265; his son [John], 1/95; 2/35

REEVE(S), Ald. [Samuel], upholsterer, Long Lane: 9/329

[REGGIO, Piero], (Pedro), musician: 5/217, 226, 239

against Rupert (1648), 5/169 & n. 1; 8/306

RICHARDS, ——, tailor: 9/218

RICHARDSON, [Sir Thomas], Chief Justice, King's Bench (d. 1635): anecdote of, 8/428–9 & n.

RICHARDSON, [William], book-binder: work for P, 7/243, 303–4, 307; 8/237, 551; 9/24, 32, 46, 547–8; also, 8/71; 9/43

RICHMOND, Duke/Dowager Duchess/Duchess of: see Stuart, Charles/Mary/Frances Teresa

RICHMOND, Surrey: P visits, 3/81; 6/154; Lady Castlemaine at, 3/139; 4/238

RIDER, Sir William, hemp merchant, kted 1661:

NAVY BOARD BUSINESS: consulted about provisioning ships, 2/62; hemp contract, 3/114 & n. 1, 116, 129–30; to insure ship, 4/394, 395, 398; quarrels with Cocke, 5/51; contract for tar and canvas, 5/136 & n. 3, 352; hemp business, 6/77; payments to Carteret, 6/191; also, 4/343; 6/256

TANGIER: appointed to committee, 3/238; helps draft civil constitution, 4/89 & n. 1; and examine Peterborough's accounts, 5/48, 105, 123, 132; at meetings, 3/272; 4/83, 320, 335; 5/11, 97, 124, 135, 139; also, 5/212; 7/65

TRINITY HOUSE: Deputy-Master for Sandwich, 3/18, 29; Batten's attempt to make him Master, 6/107; blamed for sinking ships, 8/270–1; dinners, 5/15, 94, 186; also, 2/4, 26

HIS HOUSE AT BETHNAL GREEN: P admires, 4/200 & n. 5; sends valuables in Fire, 7/272, 282, 283

SOCIAL: dines with P, 1/14; 5/62; gives dinner, 4/200; at taverns, 5/341; 6/25, 83, 145; also, 5/255

MISC.: stories of Genoa, 3/7–8 & nn.; 4/201; Chatham Chest, 3/257; 7/110; arbitrates in dispute, 4/426; 5/15, 19, 36; his rise alluded to, 5/52; diary, 5/98; ill, 5/159; fears issue of war, ib.; Fishery business, 5/336; opposes building of New London, 6/170

ALLUDED TO: 2/193

~ his wife [Priscilla], 4/200

RIDER, Mr ——, merchant: 4/247

RIGA, Latvia (Sweden): yarn/cordage from, 3/101 & n. 3, 5/182; hemp, 4/49, 259 & n. 4

RIGGS, ——, servant to Albemarle: 7/203

RINGSTEAD'S: see Taverns etc.: Star, Cheapside

RIOTS: see Law and Order, offences against

ROBARTES, Sir John, 2nd Baron Robartes, cr. Earl of Radnor 1679; Lord Privy Seal 1661–73 (d. 1685):

CHARACTER: 2/149, 150; 5/73; 8/450

AS LORD PRIVY SEAL: introduces register of fees, 2/214; refuses P a deputy, 3/61; refuses to seal royal pardon, 9/52 & nn.; affixes seal, 2/150, 158, 187, 232–3, 234, 237; 6/83, 84; at Chelsea house, 2/158, 187, 201, 234, 237; unspecified business, 2/228; out of town, 2/170, 171, 175, 236; also, 2/214; 3/66, 168

OTHER APPOINTMENTS ETC.: Treasury Commissioner, 1/170 & n. 3; Lord Deputy of Ireland, 1/227–8 & n.; to be Lord-Lieutenant, 9/452 & n. 2; in cabal, 8/585; 9/427

HOUSES ETC.: Whitehall chamber, 2/150; in Chelsea: P admires, 2/187–8 & n.; visits on Privy Seal business, 2/158, 187, 199, 201, 234, 237; pictures, 2/187; 6/84

SOCIAL: 8/450

ALLUDED TO: 3/66, 168

~ his wife [Laetitia], 9/176, 177 & n. 1; his daughter [Laetitia Isabella], 9/176 & n. 4

ROBARTES, Robert, son of the foregoing: case in Chancery, 5/140 & n. 1; ~ his wife [Sara]: her inheritance, 5/140 & n. 1; P admires, 6/84; 9/176–7; portrait, 6/84

ROBERT, Prince: see Rupert

[ROBERT, Anthony], dancing master: 9/507

[ROBERTS, William], Bishop of Bangor 1637–d. 65: 1/259 & n. 3

ROBERTS, [William], merchant, of St Olave's parish: ship, 8/293 & n. 2

ROBERTS'S: see Taverns etc.: Harp and Ball

ROBINS, [?Judy]: 6/187, 202

ROBINS, Tony, of Westminster: 1/92
ROBINS, Monsieur ——, periwig-maker and proprietor of ordinary, Covent Garden: 8/211
ROBINSON, [Anne], Lady Robinson, wife of Sir John: admired by P, 5/67; 6/290; 7/415; by Cocke, 6/290; wanton speech, 6/290; 7/415; social: 6/268
ROBINSON, [Henry], merchant and author (d. ?1673): claims management of Post Office, 7/375 & n. 2
ROBINSON, Ald. Sir John, Lieutenant of the Tower 1660–79; M.P. London 1660, Rye, Sussex 1661–79; Lord Mayor 1662–3:
CHARACTER: P's low opinion, 4/77–8 & n.; 5/12, 307; 6/299; 8/201; love of food and wine, 7/38
AS LIEUTENANT OF TOWER: account of Vane's trial and execution, 3/103–4 & n., 116; allows search for treasure, 3/241 & n. 1, 242, 286; consulted on exemptions from militia service, 6/24 & n. 3; and on pressed men, 7/200; arranges coal supplies for poor, 6/264 & n. 3, 265(2); shirks duties in Dutch raid, 8/266; also, 4/294; 8/278, 299, 394
AS ALDERMAN AND LORD MAYOR: boasts of influence, 4/77; 5/307 & n. 2; plans new street, 4/77; 8/201; precept about coachmen, 4/77–8 & n.; disapproves of Principal Officers of Navy as city magistrates, 4/78; revives ceremonial at Bartholomew Fair, 4/288 & n. 2
SOCIAL: as Lieutenant of Tower: entertains King, 1/214 & n. 3; Navy Board, 2/51; 5/316; Holmes (on his release), 6/56; Albemarle, 6/268; as Lord Mayor: at Trinity House, 3/103, 187; entertains customs farmers, 4/341; other occasions: P dines with, 4/70, 294–5; 5/67; enjoyment of hunting, 6/295; and singing, 6/311–12; dines with P, 9/410–11; also, 7/11–12, 38, 226, 299; 9/108, 543
MISC.: house in Mincing Lane, 3/241; news from, 5/333; 7/268; quarrels with Capt. J. Taylor, 6/56 & n. 3, 295; as M.P., 9/92–3, 193
ALLUDED TO: 8/394
~ his son [John], 7/268

ROBINSON, Luke, M.P. Scarborough, Yorks. 1645–8, 1660: delegate to Monck, 1/51–2 & n.; royalist speech, 1/122 & n. 2
ROBINSON, Capt. [Robert], kted 1675, naval officer: action against Dutch, 7/424 & n. 3
[ROBINSON, Robert, painter]: see Rogerson
ROBINSON, ——, cook: 2/102 & n. 3
ROBSON [Robinson], [Thomas], clerk to Sir W. Coventry: 7/244; 9/87, 169
ROCHE, DE LA [Peter], dentist: 2/53 & n. 1; 4/97
ROCHESTER, Kent: P visits/passes through, 1/172; 2/68, 70, 72; 3/156; 6/182, 241–2, 249; 8/311; burning of figurehead, 4/420; bridge, 1/172 & n. 5; 8/306; 9/11; cathedral, 2/70 & nn.; 8/311; castle, 6/249 & nn.; 8/311; Salutation tavern, 2/70; Crown inn, 3/153 & n. 1; 6/241–2, 249; 8/307; White Hart inn, 8/311, 312; cherry gardens, 8/312; alluded to: 2/15, 55, 57, 67; 6/256; 7/162; 9/50
RODER: see Rothe
ROETTIER(S) (Rotyr), [John], engraver to the Mint: bust of King on coins, 4/70 & n. 3; his dies, 4/147 & n. 2; engraves Navy Board seal, 7/82–3; Breda medal, 8/83 & n. 1; P admires his work, 4/147; 8/83
ROGERS, [?Matthew], of St Margaret's parish, Westminster: 1/47
ROGERS, ——: 9/58–9
ROGERSON [?Robinson, Robert], painter: 9/420 & n. 1
ROLLS CHAPEL: see Chancery
ROLT, Capt. [Edward], Gentleman of the Bedchamber to Oliver Cromwell: his former greatness, 2/108 & n. 1; P's admiration, 8/29; cornet, 8/323 & n. 1; building works in Whitehall, 9/302 & n. 1; social: sings with Mrs Knepp, 6/320–1, 323; 9/166; and Harris, 9/175; at dance at Navy Office, 8/28, 29; at taverns, 2/119, 120; 9/186, 220; also, 2/121; 7/2, 100; 8/51, 172–3, 575; 9/203, 218–19
ROMAN CATHOLICISM [see also Religion (P)]:
STATUS OF/OFFICIAL POLICY TOWARDS:

Catholics befriended by Duke of York, 2/38; long exclusion from office, 4/196; loyalty in Civil War, 7/394; arrest of priest, 4/44; King's Declaration of Indulgence (Dec. 1662), 4/44 & n. 2, 66; Commons fear admission to office, 4/50 & n. 3, 57; 7/343 & n. 5, 354; 8/6; bill and address against indulgence, 4/67–8 & n., 90 & n. 1, 92 & n. 3, 95 & n. 2, 249; book against, 4/111 & n. 2; accused of causing Fire, 7/343 & n. 4, 356–7 & n.; 8/439 & n. 4; fear of further plots, 7/360, 363, 364–5 & n.; 8/264, 269–70; 9/208; proclamation against, 7/343, n.5; order in council, 8/425 & n. 2, 476 & n. 2; Commons address, 9/104

SERVICES: at ambassadors' chapels, 2/102 & n. 2; 5/103; 9/319; Somerset House, 5/63; 9/319; Queen's Chapel, 3/202; 5/63; 7/87, 99, 107; 8/116, 588–9; 9/319; private baptism, 7/329–30; also, 7/94, 97

RELIGIOUS ORDERS: laymen's dress worn by Capuchins, 7/329; Friary at St James's Palace, 8/26–7 & n.; Jesuit to preach at Queen's chapel, 7/94; Jesuit influence in Holy Roman Empire, 4/350 & n. 2; anecdote of Spanish friar, 8/67

MISC.: prohibited degrees of matrimony, 7/329; converts from, 8/99; sermons against, ?1/32; 4/98 & n. 1; 8/587 & n. 3

ROME: Spanish guide-book, 1/49 & n. 4; Corraro's book on, 4/425 & n. 3; print of triumphal column in, 7/102–3 & n.; building works, 8/26 & n. 1; music, 8/26; painting by Danckerts, 9/504, 539; also, 6/177; alluded to: 6/13; 8/56, 336

ROOTH, Capt. [Richard], naval officer: gift to P, 2/23; child christened, 2/110; ill, 3/91; alluded to: 4/205; ~ ?his wife, 3/19; 4/45

ROS (Roos, Rosse), de: disputed barony, 8/22 & n. 3

ROSSE, Alexander: imprisoned for forgery, 2/73 & n. 3

ROTA CLUB, the: P's entry fee, 1/13 & n. 3; attends meetings, 1/14, 24, 61; debates on government, 1/17, 20–1

ROTHE (Roder), John/Johannes; kted Aug. 1660: marriage, 1/190 & n. 2, 196, 215; 7/203; sails to Holland, 1/216, 219

ROTHERHITHE [see also Taverns etc.: Half-way House]: P visits/passes through, 1/262; 2/12, 45, 112; 3/124, 128, 149, 160, 185, 188, 192, 214; 4/79, 151, 175, 233, 234, 296, 386; 5/47, 95; 6/40, 95, 158, 206; 7/69, 112, 114, 134, 176, 249; 8/39, 165, 325, 351; 9/25, 29, 468, 469; ship at, 4/23; launch, 5/353 & n. 3; plague, 6/163, 201; church (St Mary's) flooded, 7/4 & n. 6; burial, 9/200; Cherry Garden, 5/178, 180; Half-way tree, 3/95

ROTHERHITHE STAIRS: 5/29

ROTYR: see Roettier(s)

ROUEN (Roane): Charles II at, 1/156

ROULLES (Reulé), [Pierre], curé of St Barthélemy, Paris (d. 1666): sermon, 5/103 & n. 4

ROUNDTREE, [Ralph]: 2/118 & n. 1

ROUSE, Mr ——, ?tailor to the Queen: 4/245–6

ROWE, John, Independent divine (d. 1677): farewell sermon, 1/251–2 & n.

[ROWLEY, John], Vicar of Brampton, Hunts. (d. 1688): 8/471 & n. 5; ~ his wife, ib.

'ROXALANA': see Davenport

ROYAL AFRICA (Guinea) COMPANY, the [see also African House]: projected, 1/258 & n. 2; arms and motto, 4/152–3; election of assistants, 5/11; Duke of York criticises members, 5/300 & n. 4; forts overrun, 5/352–3 & n.; government negotiates with Dutch on its behalf, 8/426–7 & n.; petition in parliament against, 8/551 & n. 5; its five-guinea pieces, 9/313 & n. 4; Duke of York's business with, 9/350; meetings, 4/335; 5/48, 199–200; 8/181; P studies contract books, 5/14; dines with members, 5/52, 66, 124; also, 4/432 & n. 2

ROYAL EXCHANGE, the (the Exchange, the Old Exchange):

CHRON. SERIES: cartoon hung, 1/45; statue of Charles I, 1/89 & n. 3, 99, 113; Commonwealth legislation burnt, 2/108; plays advertised, 3/298; Dutchman whipped, 6/43 & n. 3; war proclaimed, 6/50 & n. 2; attendance reduced by Plague, 6/161, 168, 192, 205, 224, 268; increases, 6/278, 307; buildings destroyed in Fire, 7/276 & n.3; moves to Gresham College, 7/280; shops re-open, 7/404, 420; Upper Change rebuilt, 7/420; remainder rebuilt, 8/441, 497 & n. 1; 9/306 & n. 3; Clarendon's petition burnt, 8/577 & n. 5; Carr in pillory, 8/587

P'S BUSINESS AT [omitting the numerous occasions on which the business is unspecified]:

OFFICIAL: hires ships, 3/47; 5/250, 252, 255; begins to be known, 3/120; enquires about masts, 3/192; naval provisions, 4/293; ship insurance, 4/398; 5/126; foreign currency, 5/17, 259; lotteries, 5/270; deal contract, 5/277; freightage, 6/27; lighters, 6/74, 75; loan for Sandwich, 8/516; Brooke House Committee, 9/68; also, 5/229–30; 7/132, 405

PRIVATE: about Robert P's estate, 2/164; 3/118; meets Uncle Wight, 3/64, 78; 4/86; 9/430; and Mrs Bagwell, 5/350

P/EP SHOP(S) AT: for whisk, 1/299; gloves, 1/299; 2/80; 8/136; 9/265; linen, 4/12; stockings, 4/290; 6/73; pendants, 5/196; watch, 6/101; bands, 6/128; muff, 7/39; christening-bowl, 8/548; at sempstress's, 6/73, 124, 157, 334; for unspecified goods, 3/61, 239; 4/181, 332, 343; 6/76, 170, 174; 7/249, 292; 8/437; 9/403, 404

NEWS AND OPINION AT: L'Estrange gathers news, 5/348 & n. 1; shortage of, 7/242; maritime rights, 2/236; Franco-Dutch alliance, 3/7; Lawson's action at Algiers, 3/79; break with Spain, 3/115; news from Ireland, 4/100; from France, 4/162; Col. Turner's trial, 5/8–9, 23; Dutch in India, 5/41–2; shipping, 5/41–2, 49; 7/404, 408; 8/162, 374; mast storage abroad, 5/55; parliamentary news, 5/107, 131; 9/31–2, 399; Dutch in Guinea, 5/115, 127, 352; prospect of war, 5/134, 142; plague in Amster-

dam, 5/142; Batten's corruption, 5/140–1; expedition against Algiers, 5/141; negotiations with Dutch, 5/175; death of de Ruyter (rumour), 5/181; Dutch fleet movements, 5/186, 265, 333, 338; dismissals at dockyards, 5/194; gift to King from oriental potentate, 5/226; capture of Dutch Bordeaux fleet, 5/326, 341; Dutch off Margate, 6/8; loss of ships in Mediterranean, 6/10; and of Hamburg ships, 6/112; pursuit of Dutch after Battle of Lowestoft, 6/117; rumour of naval engagement, 6/157; French attack on merchantmen, 6/278; court news, 6/318; news of Plague, 6/328; 7/9; Four Days Fight, 7/142(2), 147, 153; Holmes's Bonfire, 7/248; pessimism about war, 7/361, 362; peace negotiations, 8/113, 124, 151, 157, 162–3, 231, 317, 355; views on peace terms, 8/162, 354, 362; Spanish-Portuguese peace, 8/191; relations between Dutch and Swedes, 8/231; Privy Council, 8/233–4, 518, 597; privateers from Ostend, 8/594–5; danger of war with France, 9/18

ROYAL FISHERY: see Fishery

ROYAL MEWS, the: P visits, 5/70 & n. 5; Spanish coach, 2/188

ROYAL MINT, the, Tower Hill: P visits, 4/143–6; 7/83; method of assay, 4/143 & nn.; frauds, 4/143–4 & n.; method of making coins, 4/144–5 & nn., 147

ROYAL SOCIETY, the ['Gresham College'; 'the Virtuosi'; the 'College of Virtuosoes'. For its premises, see Arundel House; Gresham College.]:

CHRON. SERIES: foundation, 2/22, n. 1; charter book, 6/6 & n. 1; meetings cancelled in Plague, 7/12; resumed, 7/21 & n. 1, 43, 51, 370, 389; moves to Arundel House, 8/7 & n. 2; gift of Arundel Library, 8/6–7 & n., 11; applies for grant of Chelsea College, 8/537 & n. 3; given site, 9/28 & n. 1; plans to build, 9/146 & n. 2, 248; deputation visits French ambassador, 9/333 & n. 3

P AS FELLOW: attends for first time, 2/21–2; promised introduction to, 3/72 & n. 3; admitted, 6/36, 48; stands

SABBATH OBSERVANCE:

translation of Corneille's *Pompée*, 7/176 & n. 2; Nell Gwyn his mistress, 8/334 & n. 2, 337, 371, 402, 503; King's indulgence towards, 9/336; at theatre, 9/54

SACKVILLE, [Frances], widow of Richard Sackville, 8th Earl of Dorset: 8/521

SACKVILLE, [Richard], 5th Earl of Dorset: case in Chancery, 1/48 & n. 1; at Rota Club, 1/61; alluded to: 3/34 & n. 2; ~ his wife [Frances], 1/48

SAFFRON WALDEN, Essex: P visits, 1/69–70; White Hart, 1/69 & n. 2; almshouses, 1/70 & n. 3

ST ALBANS, Earl of: *see* Jermyn

ST ANDREW, Holborn, church of: Stillingfleet preaches, 6/87 & nn.; alluded to, 9/548; parish: funeral at Quest House, 9/36

ST ANDREW'S DAY: observed at court, 4/401; 7/391; election day at Royal Society, 8/553; 9/379

[ST ANNE], church of, Blackfriars: Baxter preaches, 3/92 & n. 1

[ST. AUBIN'S], Jersey: pier, 4/195

ST BARTHOLOMEW [the Great, Smithfield], church of: sermon, 1/60

ST BARTHOLOMEW [?the Great, Smithfield], parish of: 1/269

ST BARTHOLOMEW'S DAY, 1662: test day for conformity, 3/166 & n. 1

[ST BOTOLPH], Bishopsgate, church of: portrait of Charles I, 5/285 & n. 1

ST BOTOLPH'S WHARF: in Fire, 7/271

ST BRIDE, Fleet St, church of: P attends service, 1/42; 2/89; 3/30, 77, 162; Herring expelled from living, 3/162; Tom P buried, 5/90; also, 8/6; parish: parish child, 4/282, 283; beadle, 4/283; charity, 4/410 & n. 2; indictment concerning Tom P's bastard, 5/114

ST CATHERINE CREE, church of: city corporation holds services, 8/389

ST CATHERINE'S DAY: 7/384

ST CATHERINE'S HILL, nr Guildford, Surrey: 2/211; 9/275

ST CHRISTOPHER'S: *see* St Kitt's

ST CLEMENT, Eastcheap, church of: P attends, 2/219

ST CLEMENT DANES church,

Strand: plague near, 6/140; tavern in churchyard, 8/541; alluded to: 1/32; 8/492

ST CLEMENT'S LANE: 2/219

ST DAVID'S DAY: Welshman hanged in effigy on, 8/89 & n. 1

[ST DIONIS BACKCHURCH]: sermons, 1/245 & n. 3; 5/356 & n. 2

ST DOMINGO: *see* San Domingo

ST DUNSTAN-IN-THE-EAST, nr Tower St, church of: P attends services, 4/268, 401; and funeral, 4/21; Sir J. Lawson buried, 6/145; ruins of after Fire, 9/172; alluded to: ?1/209; ?8/189

ST DUNSTAN - IN - THE - WEST, Fleet St, church of: repairs finished, 3/161 & n. 1; sermons, 3/161, 167; 8/389; service at 6 a.m., 5/203; P admires lady, 3/167; makes advances to girls, 8/389–90; alluded to: ?8/189

ST FAITH (St Faith's-under-St-Paul's), church of: destroyed in Fire, 7/279 & n. 1, 297, 309; 9/22–3, 305, 307

[ST GABRIEL], Fenchurch St, church of: 6/76 & n. 2

ST GEORGE'S DAY [*see also* Garter, Order of]: bonfires, 7/109; feast at Whitehall, 8/177

ST GILES-IN-THE-FIELDS, church of: P visits, 5/200; parish: under-clerk, 7/211 & n. 3; also, 8/460

ST GREGORY BY PAUL'S, church of: P attends service, 2/192, 211; 3/252

ST HELEN, Bishopsgate, church of: 7/329 & n. 1; parish: 7/329 & n. 1

ST HELEN'S POINT, Isle of Wight: 7/141

ST HELEN'S (Ellens) ROAD, off Isle of Wight: 7/279

ST IVES, Hunts.: 4/312; market, 3/220

ST JAGO: *see* Santiago

ST JAMES, Clerkenwell, church of: 5/100

ST JAMES'S DAY: holiday, 5/221; battle, 7/221 & n. 3; Parliament assembles, 8/293 & n. 3

ST JAMES'S FAIR/MARKET: *see* Fairs and Markets

[ST JAMES'S FIELDS]: building development, 4/295–6 & n.

ST JAMES'S GATE: 9/541

ST JAMES'S PALACE [Apartments occupied by individuals are indexed elsewhere under their names. P's visits on business are omitted.]: friary, 8/26–7 & nn.; gallery, 8/459; matted gallery, 8/181; guard, 1/38; Queen's chapel, services [see also Music: church; Sermons]: 3/202 & n. 1; 4/130; 5/63, 188; 7/87, 97, 99, 384; 8/116, 154, 427, 588–9; 9/126, 319, 515; also, 7/94

ST JAMES'S PARK [see also Gardens: Physic; Pall Mall]:

GENERAL: Echo, 1/38, 58; keeper 1/206; lake and canal, 1/246 & n. 2, 263–4; 2/51, 156, 171; 3/147; 7/207; gondolas, 2/177 & n. 5; inward park, 1/206; aviary, 2/157; skating, 3/272, 277, 282; riding, 3/288; sliding on lake, 4/37; hunting, 5/239; gates locked, 5/254; 6/147; Gravel Pits, 7/145; naval guns allegedly heard, 7/145, 150

PALL MALL (Pell Mell; the alley for the game): 1/246 & n. 2; keeper, 4/135; Duke of York plays, 2/64; 9/542; others play, 5/4; P/members of court stroll in, 4/229, 251–2; 5/55; 7/39, 61; 8/32–3, 92, 431; 9/319, 465; duel in, 3/171

P WALKS/MEETS FRIENDS IN [omitting occasions on which he merely passes through]: 1/53, 58, 80; 2/51, 62; 3/81, 147, 202, 208; 4/24, 70, 73, 100, 131, 135, 142, 158, 189, 192, 197, 203, 204, 229, 274, 288; 5/50, 55, 63, 102, 104, 133, 163, 174, 181, 186, 188, 198, 212, 215; 6/3, 34, 46, 60, 83, 199, 293; 7/5, 39, 46, 61, 84, 87, 97, 100, 107, 116, 148, 215, 216, 221, 223, 231, 240, 248, 265, 271, 375, 411; 8/21, 26, 32, 41, 43, 117–18, 128, 148, 210, 239, 374, 378, 427, 431, 464, 507; 9/105, 118, 151, 223, 256, 294, 295, 309, 319, 320, 401, 414, 415, 465, 483, 504, 515, 518(2), 560, 562; sleeps on grass, 7/207

KING/DUKE OF YORK AND OTHERS IN: watch waterfowl, 3/47; 8/68; Duke speaks to P, 3/47; 9/415; skates, 3/282; borrows P's cloak, 9/155; King speaks to P, 7/146; 9/105, 415; rides with Knights of the Garter, 8/184–5; Queen Mother in, 4/229; Queen in,

5/188; also, 1/173; 3/60; 4/251–2; 7/217; 8/507; 9/415

ST JOHN, Oliver (Lord St John), lawyer and politician (d. 1673): for free parliament, 1/44–5 & n.; defends Richard Cromwell, 1/74 & n. 6; emissary to King, 1/131, 132; at church, 3/220 & n. 1

[ST JOHN] RIVER, Nova Scotia: mining near, 8/426 & n. 1

ST JOHN (Jones), Clerkenwell, church of: 7/75

[ST JOHN THE BAPTIST'S DAY]: 9/249 & n. 3

ST JOHN'S ISLE [?Patmos]: P dreams about, 4/43

ST JOHN ST, Clerkenwell [see also Taverns etc.: Bottle of Hay; Theatre: Red Bull]: Newcastle's house, 8/197

ST KATHARINE, precinct of: 3/111; 4/350; 5/158 & n. 4; 6/278; 9/488

ST KATHARINE'S [STAIRS]: 6/278

ST KITT'S, Leeward Is.: French capture, 7/171 & n. 3; expedition to, 7/390 & n. 3

ST LAWRENCE JEWRY, church of: P admires, 6/34

ST LAWRENCE POULTNEY, church of: destroyed in Fire, 7/269; also, 7/235

ST MAGNUS, church of: destroyed in Fire, 7/268

ST MALO (Mellos), France: guard dogs, 7/133 & n. 1

ST MARGARET (Margetts), Westminster, church of: common prayer at, 1/215; House of Commons receives communion, 2/107; gallery, 8/236; sermons, 1/237; 7/123, 316; also, 7/142, 231; 8/167, 255, 400; 9/98–9, 168, 548; parish bellman, 1/19

ST MARGARET'S (Margetts), nr Chatham, Kent: P visits, 9/495

ST MARGARET'S HILL, Southwark: 4/76

ST MARTIN-IN-THE-FIELDS, parish of: plague in, 6/289, 304

ST MARTIN-INFRA-LUDGATE: 2/74

ST MARTIN-LE-GRAND [usually St Martin's]: 2/132; 6/332

[ST MARTIN OUTWICH] church of: P attends service, 7/235

ST MARTIN'S LANE, Westminster: 1/169; 2/101; 5/141
ST MARY AXE, parish of: 5/23
ST MARY-LE-BOW, church of: bells rung for Monck, 1/52; Court of Arches in, 4/33
ST MARY CREEK, nr Chatham: wet dock proposed, 4/225–6 & n., 259
ST MARY OVERIE, Southwark, church of: P admires monuments, 4/214 & n. 2
ST MARY, Whitechapel, church of: funeral at, 7/165 & n. 1
ST MATTHEW, Friday St, church of: disturbance in, 3/178 & n. 2
ST MELLOS: *see* St Malo
ST MICHAEL, Cornhill, parish of: burials, 6/152 & n. 3
ST MICHEL, [Alexandre], father of EP: good natured, 5/37; lodgings in ?Hind Court, 1/199 & n. 2; near Covent Garden, 3/232 & n. 2; 4/174, 390; in Long Acre, 5/50; occupation unknown to P, 3/86–7 & n.; P unwilling to meet, 4/173; EP ashamed of, 4/174; patent for smoky chimneys, 4/315 & n. 1; to serve against Turks, 5/4 & n. 4; ill, 6/219, 221; P sends money to, 6/221, 223; 8/281; rules paper for P, 7/111; pension from French church, 8/137 & n. 3; goes to France, 8/281 & n. 3; 9/40; grateful for P's charity, 9/40; EP visits, 1/5, 33; 2/218; 3/3, 86, 133, 143, 147, 232; 4/173, 315, 354, 390; 5/50, 183, 249, 250, 257, 333; 6/58; 7/34, 80; 8/163; also, 3/29; alluded to: 1/300; 3/215
ST MICHEL, Balthasar (Balty), brother of EP:
CHARACTER: P's opinion: unfavourable: 5/4, 37; 8/75, 83, 136; more favourable: 7/129, 154, 155, 326; 8/135, 165
CAREER: asks for employment, 1/104, 177; 2/164 & n. 4; 3/261–2; 4/390–1; 5/29; 6/140, 169; serves in Dutch army, 5/37, 44; 6/140; in Guards, 6/271, 318; 7/378; Muster-Master to fleet (1666), 7/82, 87, 90, 97, 101; income, 7/111; service in campaign, 7/110–11, 129, 130, 143, 154, 155, 208, 210, 232, 233, 242, 284, 326, 398; his success, 8/15, 19, 83; Muster-Master (1667), 8/128, 130, 131(2), 132, 141,

142, 148; profits, 8/148; service, 8/147, 148, 153, 154, 155(2), 162, 163, 165; 9/158; success, 9/158, 165, 185; Muster-Master (1668), 9/247–8; allowed deputy, 9/443; to help P with storekeeper's accounts, ib.; also, 1/105; 7/109, 110; 8/31
PRIVATE AFFAIRS: marries, 2/177; 3/110–11 & n.; unhappy, 4/439; fears wife unfaithful, 8/132–3, 134–5; his French servant, 2/177; gifts to EP, 1/46, 54; 5/45; recommends maids to, 3/257–8, 269, 270, 277; 279; 4/14, 16, 21, 40; sponges on, 3/285; 4/9; neglects parents, 7/291; to give allowance to, 8/148; at P's house in Fire, 7/284–9 passim; and in P's absence, 9/213; borrows money, 9/168; reads to P, 9/183, 206; ill, 7/339, 351, 352, 353, 359, 369, 370, 375, 389, 400, 417, 424; also, 1/286; 6/332; 8/136, 137; 9/175
LODGINGS/HOUSE: lodgings, 4/429; in plague-stricken district, 6/169; at Deptford, 9/195, 261, 349
SOCIAL: on *Naseby*, 1/105–6; at P's house, 3/8, 81, 260; 4/182; 7/302; 8/16, 138; 9/172, 194, 195, 402, 411, 431; at painters' studios, 7/108; 9/514–15; EP visits, 7/294; 8/74; also, 3/148, 232; 4/45
ST MICHEL, [Dorothea], (b. Kingsmill), wife of Alexandre; mother of EP: rejoins husband, 4/429; begs old clothes of EP, 5/103; EP sends her food, 6/7; suspects son's wife of infidelity, 7/291; pawns husband's possessions, 8/137; goes to France, 8/281 & n. 3; 9/40; living in Deptford, 9/403 & n. 1; prays for P, ib.; EP visits, 1/199&n. 2, 217; 2/31, 64; 3/133; 4/74, 83, 315, 354, 390, 427; 5/250, 257, 333; 6/131; 7/34, 39, 117; 8/177, 191, 260; 9/335, 403, 507, 517, 519, 543; alluded to: 1/300; 2/194; 3/87, 215; 7/389
ST MICHEL, [Esther] (b. Watts), wife of Balthasar:
P'S OPINION: 3/286; 4/48, 439; 6/140; 7/118
CHRON. SERIES: marries, 3/110&n. 4, 277 & n. 3; small stature, 3/286, 297; goes to Holland with husband, 5/37, 44; 6/140; still-born child, 7/138;

SAVILE, Henry, Groom of the Bed-chamber to the Duke of York: alleged affair with Duchess of York, 6/302 & n. 1; his part in Coventry's attempted duel with Buckingham, 9/462, 467; imprisoned, 9/466, 469; forbidden to attend Duke of York, 9/493; also, 9/491

SAVILL, ——, painter: P commissions portraits, 2/218 & n. 4; P/EP sit for, 2/221, 226, 227, 233, 235; 3/4; her dog added, 2/241; her portrait amended, 3/19; pictures paid for, 3/10; hung, 3/34; varnished, 3/106; miniature of P, 3/33, 35, 37, 39, 41, 49–50, 65, 76, 106; also, 2/234

SAVOY, Dowager-Duchess of: see Christina

SAVOY, Duchy of, envoy from: see [Piossasco]

SAVOY, the, Strand [see also French Church]: House of Lords Committee at hospital, 2/100 & n. 2; sermon at chapel, 2/29, 98; also, 1/214, 227; 3/160

[SAWYER, John], landlord of the Pope's Head tavern, Lombard St: 7/329 & n. 1

SAWYER, [Robert], lawyer, kted 1677; P's contemporary at Magdalene: as counsel, 7/386 & n. 3; 9/214; prospers, 8/567 & n. 4; ~ his wife [Mary] and child [Margaret], 8/567

SAXONY, Elector of: see John George II

SAYER(S), [John], Master-Cook, King's privy kitchen: 2/175

SCARBURGH, [Charles], physician; kted 1669 (d. 1694): on children's eyesight, 1/157; on stone, 4/59–60

SCAWEN (Scowen), [Robert], M.P. Cockermouth, Cumb. 1662–d. 70: P asks favour of, 1/257 & n. 2; also, 4/18; 8/248, 294, 480

SCHELLING: see Terschelling

SCHEVENINGEN (Scheveling), Holland: P at, 1/140, 143, 145, 148, 150; King's embarkation, 1/127, 135; house of entertainment, 1/140; church, 1/150 & n. 2

SCHOOLS [see also Eton College; Huntingdon; St Paul's School]: for boys: Twickenham, Mdx, 1/18, 20, 276; 7/209; Bromley, Kent, 6/223; Royal Latin school, Buckingham, 9/225 & n. 1; for girls: Bow, 8/448, 451; Chelsea, 4/45, 59, 82; Clerkenwell, 2/232; 4/132; Hackney, 8/174 & n. 4; 9/512; Putney, 8/188, 210; 9/526

SCHRAM, [Volkert], naval commander: commands squadron, 6/108 & n. 3

SCIENCE AND MATHEMATICS, P's interest in [For P as Fellow of the Royal Society, see Royal Society. See also Books; Clerk of the Acts: learns his trade; Scientific and Mathematical Instruments.]:

GENERAL: limited understanding, 3/131 & n.; 6/48; 8/247; 9/416

ARITHMETIC: learns multiplication table, 3/131 & n. 1, 134, 135; his arithmetic books, 4/406; discusses duodecimal system, 4/178 & n. 2; P teaches EP, 4/343, 344, 357, 360, 363, 364, 378, 402, 403, 404, 406

ASTRONOMY: instructs EP, 4/43; studies skies, 7/238–41 passim; discusses, 7/254? comet/meteor observed at Amsterdam, 5/134 & n. 1; comet of Nov. 1664–March 1665, 5/346 & n. 3, 348, 354–5, 355–6, 357; Hooke's lecture on, 6/48 & n. 1; that of April 1665, 6/75 & n. 1; of Aug. 1665, ?6/194 & n. 1; and of May 1668, 9/207–8 & n.

HIS OBSERVATIONS ETC. (MISC.): believes 'baboon' product of miscegenation, 2/160; watches demonstrations of Prince Rupert's drops, 3/9 & n. 3; of anatomy, 4/59–60 & nn.; injection of dog with opium, 5/151 & n. 1; dissection of eyes, 9/254–5; processes used at Royal Mint, 4/143–8 passim & nn.; shown hortus hyemalis, 6/289 & n. 6; and mechanism of watch, 6/337; observes phosphorescence in river, 6/241 & n. 3; wonders why guns heard in London not Dover, 7/145 & n. 4; comments on infant's manner of feeding at breast, 8/200

HIS CONVERSATIONS (MISC.): on inability of infants to focus eyes, 1/157; spontaneous generation, 2/105 & n. 4; authority of Scripture, ib.; levers, 2/112; snakes catching birds, 3/22 &

cook, 4/86, 90, 95; stays up all night cleaning kitchen, 4/253; scolded for leaving house dirty, 4/264; dismissed for stealing, 4/279; also, 4/100, 205, 236

JACK, FOOTBOY: arrives from Impington, 9/348; livery described, 9/372; reads to P, 9/372, 373; accompanies in London, 9/453, 530, 550, 557; also, 9/424, 439–40, 464, 469, 527, 530, 552

JANE, COOKMAID: enters service, 5/158–9 & n. 1, 191, 201; P pleased with, 5/225; dismissed by EP, 6/4(2), 26, 28; EP neglects to pay wages, 6/29, 30, 31

JANE (BIRCH). *see* Edwards

JANE (GENTLEMAN): *see* Gentleman

JINNY: parish child, engaged by EP, 4/282; runs away, ib.; dismissed, 4/283–4 & n.

LUCE, COOKMAID: arrives, 7/183; 'ugly and plain', ib.; falls downstairs, 7/188; drinks, 8/126; P kicks for carelessness, 8/164; found drunk and departs, 8/221–2

MARY, COOKMAID: arrives, 2/176; and leaves, 2/196

MARY, CHAMBERMAID: to replace Jane Birch, 4/34; works well, 4/40, 41; tries to corrupt cookmaid, 4/100; dismissed, 4/113

MARY, CHAMBERMAID: engaged by EP, 6/40, 51; at Woolwich during Plague, 6/149; EP quarrels with, 6/214, 246, 250, dismissed, 6/295, 296; engaged by E. Pearse, 6/317; 7/93, 103; also, 6/119, 143

MARY, COOKMAID: arrives, 7/121; and leaves, 7/183

MARY, UNDER-COOKMAID: arrives, 8/225; and leaves, 8/328; her love of gaming, ib.

MATT, CHAMBERMAID: EP tells of her good looks, 9/479, 481, 487; arrives, 9/502, 504; dismissed, 9/559

MERCER, MARY: *see* Mercer

NELL: arrives, 2/196; unwilling to sleep in room with P and EP, 2/213; 'a simple slut', 2/233; lazy, 3/8; dismissed, 3/57; alluded to: 2/241; ~ her mother, 2/196

NELL, COOKMAID: arrives, 8/419;

cooks well, 9/184; cuts P's hair, 9/201; dismissed, 9/332

NELL (PAYNE): *see* Payne

SARAH: enters service, 2/218 & n. 3, 222; ague, 3/46, 47, 51, 53, 65; combs P's hair, 3/96; washes his feet, 3/97; P pleased with, 3/113, 135; accompanies EP to Brampton, 3/65, 141, 151, 206; EP quarrels with, 3/135, 184; her proposed dismissal, 3/213, 258, 263, 273; departure, 3/274, 278; warns P against B. St Michel, 3/285; joins Penn's household, 3/295, 302; her gossiping, 4/7; dismissed, 4/92; also, 2/241; 3/95, 108, 110, 116, 208; 4/276; 6/141; ?7/268

SUSAN, COOKMAID: recommended by B. St Michel, 3/279; her cooking, 3/301; 4/34; ill, 4/41, 85, 86; replaced by Hannah, 4/86; twice returns temporarily, 4/150, 279; dismissed for drinking, 4/154, 280, 281

SUSAN, ?COOKMAID: 'an admirable slut', 5/55; the 'little girl', 4/438; 5/307, 318, 320; arrives, 4/284; EP angry with, 4/363; beaten for negligence, 5/13; 6/39; combs P's hair, 6/185; 7/95; at Woolwich with EP during Plague, 6/209, 282, 313; sent away with suspected plague, 7/115(3), 116(2); returns, 7/122; also, 5/165, 225, 257, 323, 360; 6/49, 143; 7/100, 108; ~ her father a sexton, 7/116; her mother, 7/116

WAYNEMAN: *see* Birch

WILL, FOOTBOY: enters service, 1/189, 193; combs P's hair, 1/222; dismissed for stealing, 1/233, 234, 237, 240; also, 1/203, 206; ~ his father, 1/233, 240

WILLET, DEB: *see* Willet

ANONYMOUS SERVANTS: coachman, 9/393, 464, 527; maids, 4/297, 304; 7/109, 111; 9/332, 510

SERVINGTON: *see* Cervington

SESSIONS HOUSE, Old Bailey: trials, 1/263, 266; 3/303; 4/294; funeral, 2/159 & n. 3; also, 8/316, 319

SEVERUS, Emperor A.D. 193–211: severity cited in sermon, 5/96 & n. 4

SEVILLE: high standard of coins minted at, 4/146

SEWERS, Commissioners of: 4/45–6 & n.; 5/353

SEX LIFE, P's [*See also* Pepys, Elizabeth: relations with P; Prostitutes; and (principally) Bagwell, Mrs ——; Burrows [Elizabeth]; Crisp, Diana; Daniel, Mrs ——; Knepp [Elizabeth]; Martin, Betty; Mitchell, Betty; Powell, Doll; Udall, Frances; Udall, Sarah; Welsh, Jane; Willet, Deb]: 1/222; 2/44; 4/204, 210, 230, 232; 6/191, 331; 7/365, 419; 8/588; 9/21-2, 57-8, 59, 184

SEYMOUR (Seamour), [Edward], M.P. Hindon, Wilts.; Commissioner for Prizes: conceited, 6/288; seizes prize-goods, 6/261 & n. 4, 262, 263-4; dines with W. Coventry, 5/11 & n. 2

SEYMOUR (Seamour), Capt. [Hugh], naval officer: wears hat in presence of Navy Board, 6/339; challenges Peter Pett to duel, 7/212 & n. 1; killed in action, 7/226 & n. 2, 231

SEYMOUR, Jane: *see* Jane (Seymour)

SEYMOUR, [John], Comptroller of Customs, London: 9/514 & n. 1

SEYMOUR, [John], servant to Sandwich: 9/331 & n. 1

SEYMOUR, William, 3rd/7th Duke of Somerset (1652–71): attends meeting of Royal Society, 8/243

SHA 'BĀN (Shavan Aga), Pasha of Algiers: 4/370 & nn., 386

SHADWELL, [Thomas], clerk in the Exchequer: 2/241

SHADWELL, [Thomas], dramatist and poet (d. 1692) [*see also* Plays]: at theatre, 9/310 & n. 3; theatre news from, 9/522

SHADWELL, Mdx: 7/284, 338

SHAFTESBURY, 1st Earl of: *see* Cooper

SHAFTO, [Robert], Recorder of Newcastle-upon-Tyne: 9/359

SHAKESPEARE [*see also* Plays]: cited by P, 6/191 & n. 3; quoted by Coventry, 7/265 & n. 1

SHALCROSS (Shelcrosse), [Thomas, draper]: 6/165-6

SHALES, Capt. [John], victualling agent, Portsmouth: business, 4/364, 371; gifts to P, 5/72, 152; recommended by P to Brouncker, 9/331 & n. 2

SHAR, Monsieur ——: *see* Esquier, d'

SHARP(E), [James], Archbishop of St Andrew's 1661–d.79: on *Naseby*, 1/128 & n. 2

SHATTERELL, [Robert], actor: 7/77

SHAVAN AGA: *see* Sha 'bān

SHAVING: *see* Dress and Personal Appearance

SHAW, Sir John, merchant and customs farmer: Clarendon's confidant, 5/219; pluralist, 8/398 & n. 3; complains about hemp, 9/214 & n. 1; also, 3/188; 6/126, 258

SHAW, Robin, clerk in the Exchequer 1660; later clerk to Ald. Backwell: political news from, 1/21; ill, 1/215, 257; death of first wife, 1/215 & n. 1; marries rich widow, 3/255-6 & n.; at Backwell's, 2/120; illness and death, 6/165, 169, 171; 7/215; social: 1/7, 8, 57, 259; 2/31

SHEERES, [Henry], military engineer, kted 1685: returns from Spain, 8/429, 443; stories of travels, 8/444, 451-2; 9/404, 509; engraving of Tangier, 9/419 & n. 2; paid for work at Tangier, 9/419, 429-30; gifts to P, 9/429-30, 536-7; teaches EP perspective, 9/534; EP fond of, 9/541; P jealous, 9/504, 522, 532, 533; his poetry, 9/504 & n. 1; leaves for Tangier, 9/541; also, 9/545 & n. 1; social: at theatre, 9/419, 435, 522; in May Day parade, 9/540; also, 9/420, 436, 437, 488, 509-10, 516-17, 539, 544

SHEERNESS, Kent: project for new yard, 6/194 & n. 2, 194-5; ships sail from, 7/189, 211, 212, 231; ship capsizes, 7/345; fortifications planned, 8/84, 98 & n. 2; King and Duke of York visit, 8/125, 126-7 & n.; capture by Dutch, 8/258, 259, 260; Dutch fleet off, 8/365; investigation into failure of defences, 8/496; 9/75

SHEFFIELD, John, 3rd Earl of Mulgrave, cr. Marquess of Normanby 1694, Duke of Normanby and Buckinghamshire 1703 (d. 1721): house, 9/317

SHELCROSSE: *see* Shalcross

SHELDON, Barbara: see Wood
SHELDON, Gilbert, Bishop of London 1660–3; Archbishop of Canterbury 1663–d.77:
CHARACTER: courage, 8/593 & n. 4
CHRON. SERIES: consecrated, 1/276 & n. 2; to be archbishop, 4/173 & n. 2; opposes indulgence to Presbyterians, 3/186 & n. 2; his nominations to benefices, 3/186 & n. 4, 190; injunction on sabbath observance, 3/196 & n. 3; his part in imprisonment of Calamy, 4/6 & n. 1; and in arrest of Catholic priest, 4/44; revokes licence for book on Catholicism, 4/111 & nn.; admires Stillingfleet's preaching, 6/87; appoints L. Jenkins judge, 8/133 & n. 2; slander against, 8/364 & n. 1; listens to mock sermon, 9/554; also, 8/151
POLITICAL: high standing with King, 4/137 & n. 2; inactive in Council, 5/73; attends cabinet, 5/317; good relations with Sandwich, 7/54, 56; dislike of Albemarle, 7/56; dismissed from Council, 8/585, 587, 593 & n. 4, 596, 600; 9/1–2
SOCIAL: at Lord Mayor's banquet, 4/355; his public dinners, 9/550 & n. 2, 554; also, 6/164, 188, 239
MISC.: presents naval papers to Coventry, 5/177 & n. 2
SHELDON, Ald. Sir Joseph, Sheriff 1666–7: fire at house, 8/320 & n. 1
SHELDON, William, Clerk of the Cheque, Woolwich:
CHRON. SERIES: poor bookkeeping, 3/136; instructed by P on call books, 4/80; houses EP in Plague, 6/128 & n. 2, 140, 143, 315; 7/3; P visits her, 6/153, 157, 162, 170, 174, 183, 185, 190, 200, 205, 206–9 passim, 212, 213, 214, 216, 219, 221, 222, 224, 226, 228, 242, 244, 246, 249–50, 262–3, 282, 303, 309, 341; EP stays with in Fire, 7/275, 280; also, 6/225
HIS HOUSE: P admires, 6/143; garden, 5/213
SOCIAL: 3/142; 4/79, 267, 284; 5/213, 307; 7/210
ALLUDED TO: 6/128, 140, 143, 253, 280; 7/5
SHELL HAVEN (Shield haven), Essex:

Dutch fleet in, 8/258, 351
SHELLS, shell-work: see Crafts
SHELSTON, [?Robert], grocer, [?of Leadenhall St]: gift to P, 1/95; asks for employment, 1/242; 2/32; social: 1/94; ~ his pretty wife [?Judith], 1/95
SHEPHEARD, ——, of Brampton, Hunts.: 3/223
SHEPPARD (Shepheard), [Robert], naval officer: 7/216
SHEPPEY, Isle of, Kent: 1/104
SHERES: see Sheeres
SHERGOLL, [Henry], doorkeeper to the Navy Office: 5/344
SHERWOOD FOREST, Notts.: report on, 4/158
SHERWYN, [Richard], Exchequer official: works on Tangier accounts, 6/14, 15, 17; 9/202; also, 1/31; 6/91–2
SHIPLEY (Shepley), [Edward], Sandwich's steward:
CHARACTER: P's regard, 6/32
AS STEWARD: on Dutch voyage with Sandwich, 1/95, 96, 104, 106, 136, 157, 163, 164, 166, 200, 258; financial business and accounts with P/Sandwich, 1/84, 209, 237, 297, 305; 2/3, 34, 56, 61, 67, 98, 105; 3/100, 116, 117, 121, 124, 126; 7/195, 199; 8/188; 9/211; accounts obscure, 3/131; to be transferred to Hinchingbrooke, 3/101 & n. 2; helps in parliamentary elections, 1/110–11, 112; shows P alterations at Hinchingbrooke, 3/220; unspecified business, 2/62, 108; 5/325; gifts to P/EP, 1/41; 4/22; 5/354; 7/15; P's gifts to, 1/166; 9/411; movements to and from Hinchingbrooke, 1/7, 23; 3/101, 131; 5/171, 191–2, 193, 325, 327; 6/32; 7/132, 193, 195, 371, 376; 8/220, 538, 539, 545; 9/455; dismissed, 9/475; also, 1/4, 21, 71, 73, 77, 78, 87, 93, 222, 266, 323, 324; 2/57, 83, 87; 7/371; 9/193
SOCIAL: at P's house, 1/6, 81, 203; 2/47; 3/99, 128; 6/62; 7/134; 8/223; 9/363; at Sandwich's London lodgings, 1/8, 9, 74, 76, 91, 206, 210, 216, 219, 220, 271; 2/37, 41, 48, 57, 66, 83, 87; 3/96, 120; at taverns, 1/15, 19, 85, 88, 201, 217, 234, 259, 265, 287, 295, 296, 301, 304, 307, 325; 2/33, 79, 89, 99, 109, 116, 119; 4/309, 312; 9/224; on

Swiftsure, 1/98, 100, 101; on *Naseby,*
1/103, 108, 114, 115, 116, 119, 120,
131, 162; at theatre, 1/297; 2/62;
Hinchingbrooke, 4/313; 8/472, 475;
Brampton, 8/470; 9/212; also, 1/11,
208, 215
MISC.: his clothes, 1/92, 324; breaks his
arm, 8/220
ALLUDED TO: 1/261, 270, 283; 2/228
SHIPMAN, Sir Abraham, Governor
of Bombay 1662–d. 64: 4/139
SHIPMAN, Mrs [?Dorothy], of Walthamstow: her dairy, 2/110; 8/226,
435; social: godmother, 2/109; at
Batten's wedding anniversary, 3/22;
also, 8/423
SHIPS:
DESIGN [*see also* Heemskerck, L. van;
Petty, Sir W.]: P studies Tudor
designs, 3/292; 8/84; Penn's views on
fo'cs'les, 7/195 & n. 1; Navy Board
discusses lowering of masts, 9/5 & n. 1
RATES: 3/128, n. 1; methods of calculating tonnage, 5/357–8 & n.; MS.
book of, 6/217
BUILDING AND REPAIR: sheathing, 4/232
& n. 3; project to build ten, 7/193 &
n. 5, 201
GUNS ETC. [*see also* Ordnance, Board
of]: trials, 7/183 & n. 1; 9/528 & n. 1;
brass, 6/52, 53; 7/227 & n. 2, 352 & n.
1; Elizabethan shot, 8/188; salutes,
1/95, 98, 105, 124, 131, 152, 153, 154,
163; 2/16, 121; 3/50, 175
TYPES [unusual types only are indexed,
together with entries which give
information about types]: billanders:
8/349; brigantines: 1/158; fireships:
preparation of, 8/358 & n. 1; frigates:
English compared with Dutch, 8/358;
galliots: 7/202, 205; gondolas: King's,
2/177 & n. 5; 8/56; herring busses:
2/198; 3/268–9, 274; ships' boats:
with eight oars, 3/150 & n. 1; sloops:
Dutch design, 8/358; yachts, royal
[*see also* below: *Anne; Bezan;
Catherine; Charles; Charlotte; Mary;
Merlin; Monmouth*]: 2/179 & n. 1;
bring over Queen-Mother from
France, 3/140; weather storm, 3/143–
4, 149 & n. 6; bring over Dunkirk
money, 3/164, 173, 262; also, 3/173,
7/417 [*see also Richmond*]

SHIP-MODELS: used for instruction,
3/149, 152, 158; P's collection, 3/163
& n. 1, 208; Navy Office collection,
3/103 & n. 1; others, 2/121, 192;
3/154; 4/256, 437; 8/279
SHIPS MENTIONED BY NAME IN TEXT OR
FOOTNOTES [Details are added where
possible from P's 'Register of Ships'
in *Cat.,* i. 266+, and *Lists of Men-of-
War 1650–1700,* pt i (1935) by R. C.
Anderson.]
Adventure (4th-rate; 32–44 guns;
built Woolwich 1646; sold 1688):
alluded to, 2/108; *Advice* (4th-rate;
40–50 guns; built Woodbridge 1650):
disabled, 6/19; [*Alexander* of Bristol]
(merchantman): captured, 8/16 & n.
4; *Amity* (30–8 guns; bought 1650;
sold 1667): paid off, 2/238–9 & n.;
Anne (Duke of York's yacht; 8–10
guns; sold 1686): building, 2/14 & n.
4; repaired, 5/146 & n. 1; seaworthi-
ness in storm, 3/143, 149; in action,
7/216; also, 2/104, 179; 3/63; *Antelope*
(4th-rate; 42–8 guns; built Woodbridge 1653): disabled, 6/19; *Assistance*
(4th-rate; 40–50 guns; built Deptford
1650; rebuilt 1699): P on board,
1/119, 124, 129; alluded to, 1/164, 168;
Assurance (4th-rate; 32–42 guns; built
Deptford 1646; sold 1698): sunk off
Woolwich, 1/313 & n. 2, 315;
weighed, 1/316, 319 & n. 4; P twice
merry in her, 1/316 & n. 2
Bear (36–44 guns; prize 1652; given
to Ordnance Office 1665): alluded to,
1/101; *Bear: see White Bear; Bezan*
(King's yacht; 4–6 guns; broken up
1687): built, 2/177, n. 4; beats
Jemmy in race, 3/188 & n. 1; also,
2/179; 6/188, 193, 228, 231, 241, 246,
247, 248, 273, 278, 287, 302, 333;
alluded to, 7/285; *Blackmoor* (pink;
12–14 guns; built Chatham 1656; sold
1667): brings prisoners from Holland,
3/45, 47; *Bradford: see Success; Breda*
(4th-rate; 40–8 guns; built Bristol
1654 as *Nantwich*): paid off, 3/185 &
n. 1; wrecked, 8/28 & n. 2; also,
7/224; *Bristol* (4th-rate; 44–50 guns;
built Portsmouth 1653; rebuilt 1693):
alluded to, 7/148
Cambridge (3rd-rate; 70 guns; built

Deptford 1666; wrecked 1694): her men come up from Portsmouth, 8/272 & n. 1, 275; *Catherine* (King's yacht; 8–10 guns; captured by Dutch 1673): built, 2/12 & n. 2, 14, 36, 76; beats *Mary* in race, 2/104; and *Bezan*, 6/194; victualled, 2/122; weathers storm in Channel, 3/140, 143, 146; drawing of, 4/301; returns from Flanders, 7/141–2, 145; also, 2/121, 179; 3/111 & n. 3, 126, 164; 4/99; 5/197; *Charity* (36–46 guns; prize 1653; captured by Dutch 1665): P on board, 2/121; *Charles* (yacht; 6 guns; built Woolwich 1662; given to Ordnance Office 1668): runs aground, 4/50; court-martial aboard, 9/497–8; *Charles: see Royal Charles; Charlotte* (yacht): P on board, 4/296; *Cheriton: see Speedwell; Chestnut* (8–10 guns; built Portsmouth 1656; wrecked 1665) paid off, 1/310; *Church* (20–6 guns; prize 1653; hulk at Harwich 1659): sold, 1/305 & n. 1; *Concord* (merchant-man; 28 guns): arrives from Mediterranean, 5/41–2 & n., 49; *Convertine* (4th-rate; 40–50 guns; Portuguese prize 1650; captured by Dutch 1666): alluded to, 3/31; *Coventry* (5th-rate; 20–6 guns; Spanish ship taken from royalists 1658): captured, 7/390 & n. 3; 8/511; *Crown* (merchantman): P on board, 5/30

Dartmouth (5th-rate; 22–32 guns; built Portsmouth 1655; wrecked 1690): paid off, 3/193 & n. 2; court martial concerning, 9/505; [*Defiance*] (3rd-rate; 66 guns): built, 6/7 & n. 2, 169; measured, 7/69 & n. 1; enquiry into her loss by fire, 9/481 & n. 1, 488, 494, 497–8 & nn.; also, 7/119; *Diamond* (40–50 guns; built Deptford 1651; captured by French 1693): in action, 6/82; overturns during careening, 7/345 & n. 2; *Dover* (40–50 guns; built Shoreham 1654; rebuilt 1695): to sail to Constantinople, 1/224; *Drake* (6th-rate; 12–16 guns; built Deptford 1652; condemned 1690): paid off, 3/58; *Dunbar: see Henry;* [*Dunkirk*] (E. Indiaman): mustered, 4/241 & n. 1; alluded to, 7/150 *Eagle* (merchantman; 44–56 guns):

hired to carry victuals to Tangier, 5/167 & n. 3, 276, 292; *Eagle* (hulk bought 1592; sold 1683): her boat, 3/150; *Edgar* (3rd-rate; rebuilt 1700): built at Bristol, 8/270 & n. 4; 9/231, 235 & n. 1; *Elias* (frigate; 5th-rate; 26–32 guns; Dutch prize c. 1646): brings timber from Forest of Dean, 4/20; and masts from N. America, 5/127 & n. 3; founders, 5/321 & n. 3; *Elizabeth* (ketch): 9/160; *Essex* (48–60 guns; built Deptford 1653): captured by Dutch, 7/154, 157

Fanfan (privateer; 6th-rate; 4 guns; built Harwich 1665 or 1666): made a pitch boat 1693): 8/341; *Fellowship* (hulk; 28 guns; taken from royalists 1643): sold, 3/185 & n. 2; *Flying Grey-hound* (privateer; 6th-rate; 24 guns; Dutch prize 1665; rebought by Navy Board 1668; sunk for foundation Sheerness 1673): *see* Prizes and Privateers (P); *Foresight* (4th-rate; 34–48 guns; built Deptford 1650; wrecked 1698): overturns during careening, 7/345 & n. 2; also, 3/153; *Fox* (14 guns; prize 1658; fireship and expended 1666): paid off, 2/93 & n. 3; *Franklin* (fly-boat; given away 1669): sunk as part of river defences, 8/270 & n. 4; *French Ruby* (3rd-rate; 66–75 guns; prize (*Rubis*) 1666; made 2nd-rate 1672; wrecked 1682): captured, 7/350 & n. 1; her guns, 7/352; to be altered, 7/352; 8/121

[*George*]: *see St George; Gift: see Great Gift; Gloucester* (3rd-rate; 50–62 guns; built Blackwall 1654; wrecked 1682): in action, 7/148; *Golden Hand* (fireship; 6 guns; Dutch prize 1665; founders 1673): to sail to Holland, 8/257 & n. 3; *Golden Phoenix* (Dutch E. Indiaman; 3rd-rate; 70 guns; sunk to block Thames 1667): captured by Sandwich, 6/219 & n. 1, 230–1 & n., 234; to be unloaded, 6/236; in river off Erith, 6/242, 249, 273; P on board, 6/300; *Grantham* (22–30 guns; built Southampton 1654; renamed *Guardland* 1660; fireship 1688; reconverted 1689; sold 1698): carries royalists to Flushing, 1/117; *Great Charity* (merchantman): captured by Dutch, 6/118

1/180; *Maria Sancta: see Sancta Maria;*
[*Martha and Mary*] (Margate hoy):
hired, 2/123 & n. 2; *Martin* (6th-rate;
12 guns; built Portsmouth 1652; sold
1667): paid off, 3/180 & n. 1; *Mary*
(*see also Speaker*): renamed, 1/154;
returns from Lisbon, 3/249; in action,
6/122, 129, 135; *Mary* (yacht; 8 guns;
wrecked 1675): presented to King by
Amsterdam, 1/222 & n. 1; admired by
P, 1/286-7 & n.; P on board, 4/272-3;
alluded to, 2/104, 179; 4/76, 157;
[*Mary Rose*] (E. Indiaman): built for
voyage to Bombay, 4/241 & n. 1;
Mathias (4th-rate; 38-52 guns; Dutch
prize 1653; burnt 1692): P hears
sermon on, 4/258; *Maybolt* (hoy;
prize 1666): granted to P, 8/464-5 &
n.; sold, 9/29; [*Merlin*] (yacht; 6-8
guns; built Rotherhithe 1666; sold
1698): court-martial held aboard,
9/505 & n. 1; ?also, 7/417; *Milford*
(5th-rate; 24-8 guns; built Wivenhoe
1654; accidentally burnt 1673): paid
off, 4/386 & n. 1; French demand
salute from in Mediterranean, 9/560
& n. 2; alluded to, 6/20; *Monmouth*
(yacht; 8 guns; sold 1895): built 7/38
& n. 3; guards chain across Medway,
8/310; sunk by order, 8/327-8; ?also,
7/417; [*Morning Star*] (E. Indiaman):
taken by Algerines, 9/492 & n. 5;
Mountagu (52-62 guns; built Portsmouth 1654 as *Lyme*; widened 1675;
rebuilt 1698): P admires, 2/93
Naseby (80-6 guns; built Woolwich
1655; renamed *Royal Charles* 1660;
captured 1667); Sandwich's affection
for, 1/100 & n. 2; P on board, 1/101-
54 passim; P's cabin, 1/101; his
window altered, 1/112; Sandwich's
bedchamber, 1/100; state-room,
1/114; and wine store, 1/116; her
roundhouse, 1/106; great cabin, 1/108
(2), 109, 111, 114, 118, 130, 133, 142,
153, 164; coach, 1/123, 128, 159,
160(2), 164; cook-room, 1/136;
cuddy, 1/137; scuttle, ib.; new flags
etc., 1/136, 142; renamed *Royal
Charles*, 1/154; story of fire when
King aboard, 1/176; alluded to, 1/78,
85; *Newbury* (52-62 guns; built Limehouse 1654; renamed *Revenge* 1660;

condemned 1678): alluded to, 1/109;
Newcastle (40-56 guns; built Ratcliffe
1653; wrecked 1703): P on board,
2/16; *Nonsuch* (frigate; 5th-rate; 36
guns; made 4th-rate 1669; 5th-rate
1691; captured 1695): built to Heemskerck's design, 9/171 & n. 2, 488 & n. 2;
Nonsuch (ketch; 8 guns; bought 1654;
sold 1667): to be fitted for voyage to
India, 2/62; runs aground, 6/8 & n. 3,
10 & n. 1, 19; alluded to, 1/121, 136;
Northwich [?error for *Norwich*]: allu-
ded to, 1/135; *Norwich* (24-30 guns;
built Chatham 1655; wrecked 1682):
P is shown over, 2/204; returns from
Tangier, 4/101; alluded to, 2/115
Old Success ('*Success*'; 34-8 guns;
French prize *Jules* 1650): formerly
Bradford, 1/154; paid off, 1/253-4 &
n.; 3/73; sold, 3/185 & n. 2; *Orange*
('*Urania*', Dutch prize *Oranje*; 5th-
rate; lost at sea, 1671): 6/122 & n. 5;
Oxford (5th-rate; 22-6 guns; built
Deptford 1656; blown up 1669): in
action, 6/20
Panther (privateer): 8/341; *Paradox*
(12-14 guns; taken from royalists
1649; sold 1667): paid off, 3/59;
alluded to, 1/114; *Phoenix* (32-40
guns; built Woolwich 1647): runs
aground, 6/8 & n. 3, 10 & n. 1, 19;
Phoenix of Riga (prize): 8/23-4, 123
& n. 1; *Phoenix* (Dutch E. Indiaman):
see *Golden Phoenix*; *Plymouth* (54-60
guns; built Wapping 1653; rebuilt
1705): to take ambassador to Constantinople, 1/217 & n. 3; also, 1/124,
134, 224; 6/141; *Portland* (4th-rate;
40-50 guns; built Wapping 1653;
burnt to avoid capture, 1692): disabled in action, 7/142; *Prince, Prince
Royal: see Royal Prince; Princess* (4th-
rate; 52-4 guns; built Lydney 1660;
broken up 1680): in Medway raid,
8/271-2; *Prosperous* (?horseboat; built
Chatham 1665; burnt by Dutch
1667): given to King by Penn, 8/441
& n. 3; *Providence* (fireship): plague
aboard, 6/189 & n. 2; lost at Tangier,
9/488-9 & n.; alluded to, 7/176
Rainbow (40-60 guns; built Deptford
1617; sunk at Sheerness 1680):
damaged in action, 7/149; alluded to,

4/110; *Reserve* (4th-rate; 34–48 guns; built Woodbridge 1650; rebuilt 1701): alluded to, 3/159, 163; *Resolution* (originally *Tredagh* q.v.): burnt in action, 7/221, 222, 226; her guns, 7/227; alluded to, 4/101; *Resolution* (3rd-rate; 70 guns; rebuilt 1698): to be built by Deane, 8/489 & n. 3; 'the best ship ... in the world', 9/262; Deane's drawing of, 9/262 & n. 4, 313, 330 & n. 3; alluded to, 9/178; *Revenge* (3rd-rate; 52–62 guns; built Limehouse 1654 as *Newbury*; condemned 1678): explosion on board, 7/345; *Richard:* renamed *Royal James*, 1/154; *Richmond: see Wakefield; Richmond* (yacht): to be taken into King's service, 9/301–2 & n.; *Rosebush* (24–34 guns; prize 1653; hulk at Harwich 1664; sold 1668): P dines on board, 2/36; to sail to Jamaica, 3/150 & n. 3; *Royal Catherine* (2nd-rate; 70–82 guns; rebuilt 1702): building, 4/91 & n. 1; 5/75, 110, 136, 232, 253; launched, 6/305, 306 & n. 3; admired by King, 6/306; with fleet, 6/80(2), 306; runs aground in Four Days Fight, 7/153–4; *Royal Catherine* (merchantman): 3/156; *Royal Charles* ('*Charles*'; *see Naseby*): formerly *Naseby*, 1/154; P on board, 1/154–72 passim; paid off, 1/167; Sandwich sails in from Portugal, 3/128; Cromwellian figurehead replaced, 4/418 & n. 2, 420; Duke of York's flagship in Battle of Lowestoft, 6/122; runs aground in Four Days Fight, 7/153–4; 8/359; captured and towed away by Dutch in Medway raid, 8/262–3 & nn., 266, 267, 283 & n. 1, 310 & n. 4, 343, 495, 501, 502; alluded to, 1/256; 3/128, 131; 7/141, 146; [*Royal Charles II*] (1st-rate; 96 guns; renamed *St George* 1687; 2nd-rate 1691; rebuilt 1701): launched, 9/101 & n. 2; *Royal James* ('*James*'; 70–82 guns; built Woolwich 1658 as *Richard*): renamed, 1/154; Sandwich's model of, 2/121 & n. 5, 192; Sandwich sails to Mediterranean in, 3/128; dispute over rating of, 3/128 & n. 1; in dock at Woolwich, 3/142–3; 4/64; launched after repairs, 4/103; P inspects, 4/131; Sandwich on board,

6/287, 301; dispute about pay, 7/93–4 & n., 97 & n. 1; burnt in Medway by Dutch, 8/266, 308; alluded to, 3/95; *Royal Oak* (2nd-rate; 76 guns; built Portsmouth 1664): in action, 6/122; burnt by Dutch in Medway, 8/266, 308; *Royal Oak* (E. Indiaman): to be launched, 2/14 & n. 3; wrecked in storm, 6/36 & n. 1; *Royal Prince* (1st-rate; 64–85 guns; built Woolwich 1641): P visits in dock, 2/69; launched after repair, 4/225 & n. 4; EP visits, 6/56; her reputation for powerfulness, 6/129 & n. 4; Sandwich's flagship, 6/129, 151, 228; damaged in Battle of Lowestoft, 6/135; runs aground in Four Days Fight, 7/153 & n. 1, 158, 352; 8/12 & n. 1, 359; alluded to, 6/65, 241, 287; 8/109; *Royal Sovereign* (1st-rate; 90–100 guns; built Woolwich 1637; cut down 1660 and 1685; burnt by accident 1696): P visits, 2/15–16 & n., 69; and admires, 2/16; 3/155; 6/194; inspected by P, 3/155; 4/228; and by Navy Board, 6/194; print of, 4/29 & n. 4; with fleet, 6/196, 208, 228; alluded to, 6/188, 189; *Rubis: see French Ruby; Ruby* (4th-rate; 40–8 guns; built Deptford 1651; captured by French 1707): in action, 7/148; *Rupert* (3rd-rate; rebuilt 1703): her repute, 7/119, 127; 8/142; in action, 7/142, 155; drawing of, 8/142 & n. 2; to go to sea, 8/485; alluded to, 7/143; 8/39, 95

St George ('*George*'; 2nd-rate; 62–70 guns; built Deptford 1622; made a hulk 1687): paid off, 2/227 & n. 5, ?239 & n. 1; in action, 6/122; *St John Baptist* (prize): captured, 9/147 & n. 3; *St Patrick* (4th-rate; 48 guns; built Bristol 1666): captured by Dutch, 8/47, 67; *Sancta Maria* (4th-rate; 50 guns, Dutch prize 1665; burnt by Dutch 1667): runs aground 8/310 & n. 1; *Satisfaction* (26–32 guns; prize 1646): wreck of, 3/213 & n. 1; 6/19; paid off, 3/225–6 & n.; [*Seaflow*] (merchantman): hired, 1/267 & n. 4; *Seven Oaks* (4th-rate; Dutch prize (*Zevenwolden*) 1665; recaptured 1666): in action, 7/154; *Slothany* (*Slot van Honingen*, Dutch E. Indiaman;

3rd-rate; 60 guns; hulk 1667; sold
1686): captured by Sandwich, 6/219
& n. 1, 230-1 & n., 234; to be
unloaded, 6/236; in river off Erith,
6/242, 249, 273; P on board, 6/300;
Sophia (26-34 guns; prize 1652;
sold 1667): paid off, 2/237; *Speaker*
(50-62 guns; built Woolwich 1650;
wrecked 1703): P admires, 1/115; renamed *Mary*, 1/154; alluded to, 1/86;
Speedwell (20-8 guns; built Deptford
1656; wrecked 1678): formerly *Cheriton*, 1/154; alluded to, 1/221; *Success:
see Old Success; [Surprise]* (merchantman): carries King to France (1651),
1/156 & n. 2; *Swallow* (ketch; 6 guns;
bought 1661; sold 1667): sermon on,
3/72; *Sweepstakes* (5th-rate; 36 guns;
built Yarmouth 1666; sold 1698):
in action, 7/148, 215 & n. 3; *Swiftsure*
(44-6 guns; built Deptford 1621;
rebuilt 1653): P and Sandwich on
board, 1/95-102 passim; reported
missing in action, 7/154-7 passim
   Tangier-Merchant (merchantman):
hired for Tangier, 4/20 & n. 2; 5/139;
Tholen (Dutch): burnt in action,
7/229 & n. 5; *Tredagh* (50-66 guns;
built Ratcliffe 1654; renamed *Resolution* 1660): carries Dowager Princess
Mary and Sandwich from Holland,
1/254
   Union (merchantman): hired for
Tangier, 5/340; *Unity* (4th-rate; 42
guns; Dutch prize 1665): in Medway
raid, 8/501; *Urania: see Orange
Vanguard* (40-60 guns; built Woolwich 1631; sold 1667): in action,
6/129; sunk in Medway raid, 8/310
Wakefield (22-6 guns; built Portsmouth 1656; fireship 1688; reconverted 1689; sold 1698): renamed
Richmond, 1/154; *Wexford:* alluded to,
8/81, 100; *Weymouth* (12-16 guns;
taken from royalists 1646): sold,
3/185 & n. 2; *White Bear* (1st-rate;
built 1563; rebuilt 1600): engraving
of, 8/84 & n. 3; *Wild Boar* (flyboat;
6th-rate; prize 1665): sold, 8/484 &
n. 1; *William* (merchantman): on
convoy duty, 5/340 & n. 2; *William
and Mary* (merchantman): hired for
Tangier, 4/368 & n. 4; *Winceby: see*

Happy Return; *Wolf* (6-16 guns;
Spanish prize 1656; sold 1663): paid
off, 1/290; *Worcester* (48-60 guns;
built Woolwich 1651; renamed *Dunkirk* 1660; rebuilt 1704): alluded to,
1/109
   Yarmouth (44-54 guns; built Yarmouth 1653; broken up 1680): in
action, 6/82 & n. 1; also, 1/137; *York*
(3rd-rate; 52-60 guns; built Blackwall 1654 as *Marston Moor*; wrecked
1703): in action, 7/176 & n. 3; *Young
Lion* (6th-rate; 10 guns; prize 1665;
sunk for foundation Sheerness 1673):
sold and bought back, 9/160 & n. 2

SHIPTON, MOTHER: prophecy of
Great Fire, 7/333 & n. 2

SHISH, Jonas, Assistant-Shipwright,
Deptford: his yard, 4/104; ketches,
ib.; builds *Charles*, 9/101 & n. 2;
business, 5/75, 217; 8/188; 9/29;
appointed Master-Shipwright, 9/128
& n. 1

SHOE LANE [*see also* Taverns etc.:
Gridiron]: cockpit, 4/427; also, 2/156;
9/297

SHOOTER'S HILL, Kent: gibbet,
2/72-3 & n.

SHORE, Jane, mistress of Edward IV:
Lady Castlemaine compared to, 3/68
& n. 4; alluded to in sermon, 5/97

SHOREDITCH: 4/432; 7/121; 8/212

SHORTGRAVE (Shotgrave), [Rich-
ard], operator to the Royal Society:
9/337

SHORTHAND: P learns Shelton's
system, vol. i, p. xxi; the system, vol.
i, pp. xlviii-lix & nn., lxxii, lxxvii,
lxxxvii & n. 91, xc; problems of
transcribing, vol. i, pp. lvii-lxvii &
nn.; P records use of, 5/174; 7/374;
8/448, 553; demonstrates it, 9/269;
Coventry reads psalms in, 2/76 & n.
3; prefers clerk with knowledge of,
8/207; used by Hewer, 7/374 & n. 1;
9/483

SHORT'S: *see* Taverns etc

SHOTERELL; *see* Shatterell

SHOTT, ——, woodmonger: P orders
firing from, 1/81; also, 1/33

SHREWSBURY, Earl and Countess
of: *see* Talbot

SHREWSBURY, [William], bookseller, Duck Lane: P visits/buys from, 9/161 & n. 1, 173, 260–1, 265, 268, 276, 284(2), 297, 327 & n. 2, 335, 345

SHREWSBURY, ——, wife of William: P kisses, 9/161; admires, 9/170, 173, 260, 265, 276; calls to see, 9/268, 284(2); tries to begin acquaintance with, 9/285; finds weeping, 9/297; pregnant, 9/335

SHROVE TUESDAY: club meets on, 1/78; cockshy, 2/44 & n. 1; fritters, 2/43–4; 6/32; Shrovetide verses by Eton boys, 7/59 & n. 6; also, 4/65; 5/62; 8/72; 9/457

SIAM: anecdotes of, 7/250–1 & n.

SICK AND WOUNDED, COMMISSION FOR THE: 8/407–8 & nn.

SIDLEY: see Sedley

SIDNEY, Algernon, republican (d. 1683): parliamentary commissioner in Baltic war (1659), 4/69 & n. 2; enmity to Sandwich, ib.

SIDNEY, Henry, Groom of the Bedchamber to the Duke of York and Master of the Horse to the Duchess, cr. Viscount 1689, Earl of Romney 1694 (d. 1704): alleged affair with Duchess of York, 6/302 & n. 1; 7/8 & n. 1, 323

SIDNEY, Col. [Robert]: 7/73

SIGNET OFFICE, Whitehall: 1/197

SILBURY HILL, Wilts.: P visits, 9/240 & n. 2

SIMCOTES (Symcottes), [John], physician, Huntingdon: 2/137 & n. 6

SIMON (Symons), [Thomas], engraver to the Mint: his engraving of Cromwell's head, 4/70 & nn.

SIMONS, Mr ——, servant to Lord Hatton: 2/221, 222

SIMPSON (Symson) [John], lawyer, kted 1678: 9/420

SIMPSON, John, minister of All Hallows, Thames St: King's arms set up in his church, 1/113 & n. 4

SIMPSON (Sympson), [Thomas], Master-Joiner of Deptford and Woolwich yards: work at P's house, Seething Lane: on dining room, 3/235 & n. 3; chimney pieces, 4/320; 9/266, 267, 279–80; cupboard, 4/353; bookcases, 7/214 & n. 4, 242, 252; helps arrange books etc., 7/258, 290; work

at Navy Office: alters P's closet, 5/143 & n. 1, 144, 145; other alterations, 8/523, 524; social: dines with P, 3/235; 7/258; 8/525

SINGLETON, John, court musician: King's affront, 1/297–8 & n.

SITTINGBOURNE, Kent: 1/172; 6/65

SIVILL: see Seville

SJAELLAND (Is.), Denmark: turkey from, 1/41 & n. 4

SKEFFINGTON, Sir John, P's contemporary at Magdalene; succ. as 2nd Viscount Massereene 1665 (d. 1695): 5/276–7 & n.

SKELTON, Bernard, P's schoolfellow; Fellow of Peterhouse, Cambridge 1659–64 (d. ?1690): university taxor, 3/218 & n. 2

SKINNER, [Thomas], merchant: dispute with E. India Company, 9/85 & n. 2, 182–4 passim & n., 196 & n. 1

SKINNERS' COMPANY: see London: livery companies

SKINNERS' HALL, Dowgate Hill: King's arms in, 1/106

SLANING (Slany), Anne, Lady Slaning (b. Carteret), wife of Sir Nicholas (d. 1691): marriage, 4/254 & n. 3; shares P's taste for cream and brown bread, 6/157; piety, 6/182; at Cranbourne, 7/54, 57

SLANING (Slany), Sir Nicholas, cr. bt 1663 (d. 1668): marriage, 4/254 & n. 3; admitted to Royal Society, 6/48

SLATER, [John], Navy Office messenger: employed as cook, 2/22; alluded to: 2/24, 28, 227

SLINGSBY, Sir Arthur, of Patrixbourne, nr Canterbury, Kent: pension, 4/274–5; partners King at tennis, 4/435; lottery, 5/214 & n. 2; social: 9/276

SLINGSBY, Henry, Deputy-Master of the Mint 1660, Master 1662: 'very ingenious', 6/22; shows P new coins, 2/38–9; 3/265; 4/70; conducts P and Mennes round Mint, 4/143–8; lease of houses etc. from King, 2/104 & n. 2; on amount of money current, 6/22–3; export of bullion, ib.; and revaluation, 7/304; social: 2/120

SLINGSBY, [Margaret], Lady Slingsby, widow of Sir Guildford Slingsby: 2/26

SLINGSBY, Col. Robert, ('the Comptroller'), cr. bt 1661, Comptroller of the Navy 1660–1:

CHARACTER: P's regard, 2/108, 120, 202

AS COMPTROLLER: appointed, 1/240 & n. 1; visits Deptford, 2/11, 12, 76; Woolwich, 2/11; and Portsmouth, 2/89; memorandum on state of navy, 2/20 & n. 3; disbanding business, 2/39; victualling business, 2/62, 104; acquires official logdings, 2/108, 110–11, 114, 119; plans to expand Navy Office, 2/143 & n. 4, 160–1; unspecified business, 1/290; 2/38, 184–5; also, 1/242, 254

SOCIAL: 1/253, 292; 2/24, 25–6, 30, 51, 76, 111, 131, 175, 179

MISC.: news from, 1/315, 318 & n. 2; 2/39; advises P to enter parliament, 2/42; King's debt to, 1/288 & n. 2; house and bowling-alley, 1/290; 2/15, 115; recites his verses, 1/302; projected order of Knights of the Sea, 1/314 & n. 2; created baronet, 2/61; unsuccessful parliamentary candidate, 2/76 & n. 1; illness and death, 2/200, 201, 202, 204

ALLUDED TO: 2/13, 25

~ his wife [Elizabeth], 2/24, 26, 76, 179; his daughter, 2/24; his sister, 1/290

SMALLWOOD, [Matthew], Canon of St Paul's 1660–71, Dean of Lichfield 1671–d.83: examiner at Apposition Day, St Paul's School, 5/38 & n. 3

SMALLWOOD, [William], barrister, Middle Temple: advises P in dispute with Trice, 2/217 & n. 3, 230; 4/352

[SMEGERGILL, alias Caesar, William], musician: plays lute, 5/344; 7/182; 8/118, 325, 333, 529, 530, 558; treble viol, 7/338; teaches lute/theorbo to Tom Edwards, 5/344; 6/86; 7/182, 226–7, 338, 375; to Lady Crew's page, 8/333; recommends gut string as fishing line, 8/119; stays in Westminster in Plague, 7/40–1

[SMETHWICK] (Smithys), [Francis]:

burning-glass, 9/113 & n. 5

SMITH, Sir George, merchant: to leave London during Plague, 6/205; city news from, 6/251–2; 7/174; social: Lady Robinson's crony, 6/290; entertains P and others, 6/187, 192 & n. 1, 307, 311–12; 7/4; also, 6/186, 257, 299; alluded to: 6/234; ~ his wife [Martha], 6/312

SMITH, Capt. Jeremy, naval commander, kted 1665; Navy Commissioner 1669–75: reputation, 4/196; 6/129; 7/158, 333, 344; 9/123, 137; P's opinion, 6/264; 9/382; leader of Albemarle's faction, 7/158, 333; pay, 4/325; conduct at Battle of Lowestoft, 6/122, 135; with fleet, 6/278; sails for Mediterranean, 7/9 & n. 5, 39–40, 45; at Cadiz, 7/46, 71; portrait by Lely, 7/102 & n. 3; commands *Loyal London*, 7/181, 215; accused by Holmes of failure to pursue enemy, 7/339–40 & n.; their duel, 7/348; charges against, 9/107, 118; to be land admiral at Portsmouth, 9/149; to command fleet, 9/123; appointed Navy Commissioner, 9/350, 551 & n. 2; also, 8/263–4; 9/383, 466; social: 8/479; 9/468, 469

SMITH, [John], herald painter: makes hatchment, 4/424–5 & n.

SMITH, John, first transcriber of the diary: vol. i, pp. lxxvi–lxxix, lxxxiii, lxxxviii, xc, xcii; edition of P's Tangier Journal, vol. i, p. lxxxv

SMITH, [Richard], boatswain, Woolwich yard: tells P of malpractices, 5/117

SMITH, [Robert], Navy Office messenger: to prosecute forger of pay tickets, 2/73 & n. 3; his part in Field case, 3/231 & n. 3, 262, 280; 4/16; helps to prepare King's yacht, 3/140; dines with Navy Board, 3/14; also, 1/253; 3/19; 7/250

SMITH, Sydney, author (d. 1845): opinion of diary, vol. i, p. lxxxiii

SMITH, [?Theophilus], mercer: 7/80 & n. 3

SMITH, [Thomas], formerly secretary to the Lord High Admiral and Navy Commissioner: chamber in Navy

and Frenchmen, 1/10; English natural affection for, 2/188 & n. 4; bullfights, 3/90; revenues 5/68; shortage of bullion, 6/23; stamp tax, 7/332 & n. 2; court, 7/201; 8/452; army, 7/201; 9/6 & n. 2, 396-7 & nn.; anecdote of friar, 8/67; dress at court, 8/79; effects of Inquisition on cloth industry, 8/79-80 & n.; beards, 8/453; customs, 8/111 & n. 3, 451-2 & nn.; the Pantéon at Escorial, 9/118 & n. 5; food: *oleo*, 9/509-10, 544; sauce, 9/443; also, 3/251

CHRON. SERIES: resents loss of Tangier, 3/33; English merchants fear break with, 3/115; Spanish reaction to raid on Santiago, 4/94 & n. 3; trade treaty with England (May 1668), 8/30, 45, 69 & n. 2, 74 & n. 2, 75, 107 & n. 2, 190 & n. 1, 246, 453 & n. 2

SPANISH NETHERLANDS: French threat to Flanders, 8/74, 75, 92 & n. 3, 107-8, 175; Louis XIV's claim, 8/186 & n. 2, 254 & n. 1; French invasion, 8/186, 432; 9/38 & n. 1; English troops for, 8/246 & n. 3; Flemish ships in Thames, 8/266; wars in (1650s), 9/396 & nn.; also, 3/246; 7/229

SPARGUS (asparagus) Garden, ?Whitehall: 9/172

SPARKE(S), [Edward], clergyman: 1/60

SPARLING, Capt. [Thomas], naval officer: on voyage to Holland, 1/102, 119, 168; gift to P, 1/164; changes Dutch money for, 1/168, 178-9; social: 1/167; ~ his harper, 1/119, 124, 153

SPAS: see Banbury; Barnet; Bath; Bourbon l'Archambault; Epsom; Tunbridge Wells

SPELMAN, [Clement], Cursitor Baron of the Exchequer 1663-79 (d. 1680): 6/65 & n. 3

SPELMAN (Spillman), Lady: 5/130

SPENCER, Dr [John], Fellow of Corpus Christi College, Cambridge 1655-67; Master 1667-93; Dean of Ely 1677-d.93 [see also Books]: his learning, 7/133 & n. 3

SPENCER, Robert, 2nd Earl of Sunderland, Secretary of State 1679-81, 1683-8 (d. 1702): breaks off

engagement with Lady Anne Digby, 4/208-9 & n.

SPICER, Jack, clerk in the Exchequer: Sandwich's money deposited with, 1/290, 291, 292, 294, 312; at Nonsuch in Plague, 6/235-6; deals with P's Tangier tallies, 7/32-3; counts money for P, 7/251; also, 1/43, 44, 317; 3/296-7; 9/78; social: at P's dinner for old Exchequer colleagues, 2/241; at taverns, 1/7, 8, 33, 57, 201, 229, 270; 2/4, 6, 50, 227; 6/162; 7/398; 8/590; also, 1/41, 257, 259

SPITAL (Spittle), [Square], Spital-fields: Spital sermons at, 3/57-8 & n.; 9/517

SPITALFIELDS: 9/528

SPITTS, the (roadstead off Sheppey): 1/104

SPONG, [John], Chancery clerk and optical-instrument maker: CHARACTER: P admires, 6/92-3; his 'plainness and ingenuity', 9/417; also, 3/120; 5/235

CHRON. SERIES: engrosses P's Chancery bill, 1/197-8, 198, 204; and his agreement with Barlow, 1/205; arrested as suspected plotter, 3/237-8 & n.; experiments with microscope, 5/235; 7/226; visits glass maker, 7/218-19; demonstrates magic lantern, 7/254 & n. 3; and pantograph, 9/340 & n. 1, 389-90 & nn., 417; supplies P with pantograph, 9/437, 443-4; also, 1/273 MUSICAL/SOCIAL: sings with P, 1/63, 205, 268, 272, 274; 3/99, 120; plays flageolet, 1/71; at music meeting, 5/290; dines with P, 8/105-6; 9/406, 524-5; also, 2/161

~ his mother, 1/272

SPORTS: see Games etc.

SPRAGGE, Capt. Edward, kted 1665; naval commander: at council of war, 6/230; influence in fleet, 7/158, 178, 179; protégé of Rupert, 7/178-9; responsibility for division of fleet, ib.; 8/148; enquiry into, 8/515; challenges Commissioner Pett to duel, 7/212; appointed to command in river, 8/149; squadron in action, 8/354, 359; conduct in Medway raid, 8/308, 351, 379, 501; 9/11; criticises officers of Ordnance, 8/496; enemy of

Sandwich, 8/549; influence with Buckingham, 9/382; jilted by Mrs Hollworthy, 8/141; also, 4/53; 8/485-6; 9/348; social: 7/12, 44; 9/560

SPRY, [Arthur], (d.1685) M.P. St Mawes, Cornwall 1660, 1661-79: 1/288 & n. 1

SPURRIER, Mr ——: 1/32

SPURSTOWE, [William], Presbyterian divine, Master of St Catharine Hall, Cambridge 1645-60 (d. 1666), preaches before King, 1/260 & n. 4

SQUIBB, [Arthur, jun.]: claims tellership in Exchequer, 1/31 & n. 1, 34 & n. 1, 36, 40, 43-5 passim, 49 & n. 1

STACEY, Doll, milliner at the New Exchange: P admires, 5/9, 51; marriage, 9/438; also, 5/55

STACEY, [John], tar merchant: cancels agreement, 4/187; informs P about tar, 5/80; stories of Lady Batten, 4/232; ~ his servant, 4/187

STA(I)NES, [Thomas], glazier: contracts, 5/44 & n. 4, 117 & n. 1, 118; house destroyed in Fire, 7/270

STAINES, Mdx: P at, 6/197, 198

STAMFORD, Lincs.: 5/233; 8/93

STANDING'S: see Taverns etc.

STANESBY (Stainsby), Capt. [John], naval officer: to be tried for cowardice, 6/104 & n. 4

STANGATE, Lambeth: 4/263; 7/104; 9/491

STANHOPE, Elizabeth, Countess of Chesterfield (b. Butler), wife of the 2nd Earl (d. 1665): affair with Duke of York, 3/248 & n. 2; 4/1, 19; leaves court, 4/1

STANHOPE, Philip, 2nd Earl of Chesterfield, Lord Chamberlain to the Queen 1662-5 (d.1713): fights duel, 1/20 & n. 1; quarrels with Ned Mountagu, 3/290; 4/25; leaves court, 4/1; plays tennis, 4/435; at Harwich, 8/255; ~ his coachman killed, 1/303

STANKES, Goody, [Joan], wife of Will: death, 9/309 & n. 2; social: 2/138; 3/220

STANKES, Will, of Brampton: P's bailiff, 2/136; 5/325; accompanies to Brampton court, 2/181; 3/222; reports to P, 4/108, 118, 119; dislikes London, 4/118; social: 2/138, 182; 4/308

STANLEY, Ben, P's old playfellow: landlord of New Exchange tavern, 4/384

STANLEY, [Edward], son of the 7th Earl of Derby; M.P. Lancashire 1661-4: death, 5/310-11 & n.

STANLEY, [William], Vicar of Walmer, Kent, 1648-d.80: prays for King, 1/129 & n. 1

[STANLEY, William], Mayor of Southampton: 3/71 & n. 2

STANTON: see Fenstanton

STAPELY, [Joseph], ropemaker, Wapping: 6/34 & n. 3; 9/518

STARKEY, [John], bookseller, Fleet St: P visits/buys books from, 8/156 & n. 1, 168, 341, 377, ?511, ?525, ?547, 597-8, ?599; 9/291

STARKEY'S [Philip], cookshop, Austin Friars: P entertained to dinner at, 7/44

STARKEY, [?Samuel, of Gray's Inn]: 9/464

STARLING, Ald. [Samuel]: 7/282 & n. 1

STATIONERS' HALL, Ludgate Hill: destroyed in Fire, 7/297, 309

STAYNER, Sir Richard, naval commander (often 'the Rear Admiral'): on Dutch voyage, 1/101, 104, 106, 110 & n. 1, 115, 124, 134, 135, 153, 154, 159, 164, 167; Sandwich's confidant, 1/110; 2/33; at Dover to help in parliamentary election, 1/110-11; knighted, 1/254; death and funeral, 3/249 & n. 1, 268 & n. 2

STEADMAN [Hugh]: see Taverns etc.: Mitre, Fleet St

STEELYARD, the, Thames St [see also Taverns etc.: Rhenish winehouse (Prior's)]: closed in Plague, 6/270; Fire in, 7/268, 269; also, 3/174; 4/25

STEFKINS, [Theodore], musician: 4/233 & n. 2

STELLINGWERF, [Augustus], naval commander: 6/108 & n. 3

STEPHENS (Stevens), [Roger], silversmith, Foster Lane: sells shears, 1/15; to clean plate, 2/22; changes silver lace, 5/239; values flagons, 5/301; also, 1/24, ?26, 281

STEPHENS, Mrs ——, of Portsmouth: 3/70, 73

STEPHENS, ——, lawyer, of the Temple: consulted about Downing's dispute with Squibb, 1/40, 48, 49
STEPNEY: Trinity House, 1/177; 7/381; 9/202; churchyard, 8/248; also, 3/5; 8/437
STERNE, Richard, Archbishop of York 1664–d. 83: preaches at Whitehall, 7/94 & n. 4
STERPIN, Kate: see Petit
STERRY, [Nathaniel], secretary to the plenipotentiaries in Denmark 1659: Swedish news from, 1/83
STEVENAGE, Herts.: P at, 2/183; 5/233, 298; 9/224; [Swan Inn], 8/475 & n. 1
STEVENS (Stephens), [Anthony], cashier to the Navy Treasurer: at pays, 2/93; 6/319; to go to Southampton, 3/70; business with, 6/332; 8/103; on theology, 2/94; also, 1/84, 191
STEVENTON, [?John], purser: abused by Mennes, 4/151; to surrender place, 9/381, 382 & n. 4; also, 8/381; 9/188
STEVENTON (Stephenton), St John, Clerk of the Cheque, Portsmouth dockyard: 3/74 & n. 2, 174
STEWARD, Capt. [Francis], naval officer: criticised, 7/174 & n. 2
STEWARD, Mrs ——: 5/126
STEWARD, STEWART: see Stuart
STILLINGFLEET, Edward, chaplain to the King, Rector of St Andrew, Holborn; Bishop of Worcester 1689–d. 99 [see also Books]: his preaching, 6/87 & nn.; preaches at funeral, 9/40, 49; his school, 8/17 & n. 6; also, 6/80; 9/548
STILLINGWORTH: see Stellingwerf
STILLYARD: see Steelyard
STINT, ——, solicitor: 3/280; 4/333
STIRTLOE (Sturtlow), Hunts.: P inherits land, 2/136, 193, 227; sells, 2/138; 3/27, 103, 226, 228; 4/119; also, 5/44, 91
STOAKES (Stokes), Capt. [John], naval officer: to employ B. St Michel, 1/104; Sandwich dislikes, 1/107; dispute with Winter, 1/175 & n. 1; to buy paper in France for Navy Board, 1/201; ship *Assurance* wrecked, 1/313

& n. 2, 316; and paid off, 2/238; stories of Gambia, 3/10–11 & n.; death, 6/35; social: 1/92, 159, 178; 2/210
STOCKDALE, [Robert]: 6/163, 185
STOCKS MARKET (the Stocks), Cornhill [see also Taverns etc.: Three Cranes]: destroyed in Fire, 9/307 & n. 3; also, 7/14 & n. 1, 164
[STOKE] NEWINGTON, Mdx: affray, 3/34; P's parents married [error], 5/360 & n. 2
STOKES [Capt.]: see Stoakes
STOKES, [Humphrey], goldsmith, Lombard St: business, 7/9–10, 244, 367; 8/582; house destroyed in Fire, 7/270; also, 7/361; ~ his pretty wife, 7/9–10, 362
STONE, Capt. [John], Commonwealth Exchequer official: advises in dispute concerning Downing, 1/40, 44, 45
STONE, [Symon], painter: his copy of ?Johnson's portrait of Lord Coventry, 7/183 & n. 3
STONE, Mrs [?Thomas]: 9/116 & n. 1
STONEHENGE, Wilts.: book on, 9/226 & n. 1; P visits, 9/229; also, 9/240
STORY, Capt. [Thomas], receiver of assessments and farmer of excise, Cambridgeshire: business with, 8/85 & n. 2; news from, 8/85–6 & n.
STOWELL, [?Robert]: 1/239
STRACHAN (Straughan), Capt. [John] navy agent, Leith: gift from King, 1/300–1 & n.; advice about ballast, 1/301; P's opinion, ib.
STRADLING, [George], chaplain to the Bishop of London, Dean of Chichester 1672–d.88: a slicenser of books, 4/111 & n. 2
STRADWICK: see Strudwick
STRAITS, the: see Mediterranean
STRAND, the [see also Taverns etc.: Bell; Bull; Castle; Cock; Fountain; Golden Lion; Half Moon]: mutiny, 1/38, 59; affray, 8/206; Maypole, 1/52, 300; 2/127; 4/167; 7/417; 8/206; conduit, 5/91; turnstiles, 9/366
STRAND BRIDGE: 1/52; 8/138; 9/199
STRAND STAIRS: 9/368

STUCKEY, [Valentine], of the Ward-
robe: 3/199
STUKELEY, Hunts.: manor, 3/176 &
n. 2
STURBRIDGE, Cambs.: P and EP at
fair, 2/181 & n. 3; alluded to: 5/250
SUFFOLK, Earl of: *see* Howard,
James
SUFFOLK ST: 9/450, 473, 474
SUNDERLAND, Earl of: *see* Spencer,
Robert
SURAT, India: Dutch capture English
factory, 5/49
SURINAM, Dutch Guiana: ceded to
France, 8/426
SURVEYOR-GENERAL OF THE
VICTUALLING, P as: *see* Clerk of
the Acts
SUTTON, [Abraham], Flanders mer-
chant: 3/178; 5/119
SVINESUND (Swinsound), Norway:
deals from, 3/118 & n. 3; 4/232
SWADDELL (Swaddle), [John], clerk
to Arlington: 9/172
SWAKELEYS, Ickenham, Mdx: house
described, 6/214–15; also, 6/266
SWAN, [Humphrey], broom and
reed merchant: 7/331 & n. 2
SWAN, Will, servant to Lord Widd-
rington: a hypocrite/fanatic, 1/179;
2/235; 3/117, 123, 250, 275; 9/264;
said to be writing book, 2/235 & n. 2;
legal business, 1/36, 40, 47, 48, 49; his
house, 1/40; also: 1/41; social: 1/43,
95; 9/269; ~ his wife, 1/40
SWANLEY, Capt. [John], naval officer: conduct in action criticised,
7/176 & n. 3
SWAYNE, [William], eating house
keeper, Westminster [*see also* Taverns
etc.]: 5/112; 7/49; ~ his wife, 5/112
SWEDEN [*see also* Brahe, N. N.;
Charles X; Barckmann, Sir J.;
Thynne, [T.]]: import of iron from,
4/412 & n. 2; copper mines alluded
to, 8/426; friendship to England
doubted, 5/354; 7/107 & n. 1;
rumoured declaration of war against
Dutch, 7/92; said to be friendly to
England, 7/221; rumoured seizure of
English mast-ships, 7/390 & n. 5;
rumoured quarrel with Dutch, 8/231
& n. 3; mediates in peace negotiations

between English and Dutch, 8/80 &
n. 4, 92, 155, 156, 177, 317, 349, 528
SWYNFEN, [John], M.P. Tamworth,
Staffs.: story of Bishop Bridgeman,
3/254 & nn.; eloquence, 8/2
SWYNFEN, [Richard], secretary to
the 2nd Earl of Manchester: 9/139–40
SYDENHAM, [Col. William]: expelled from parliament, 1/21 & n. 2
[SYDSERFF, Thomas], Bishop of
Galloway 1635, of Orkney 1661–
d.63: indiscriminate ordinations,
2/117–18 & n.
SYMCOTTES: *see* SIMCOTES
[SYMONDS, Thomas, of Hambledon,
Hants.]: 1/155 & n. 4
SYMONS, [Margaret] (b. Shering),
wife of Will: P admires, 1/175; 2/43;
beneficiary under Chetwynd's will,
3/275 & n. 2; death, 4/415; 5/7; foretells date of, 5/8; also, 2/171
SYMONS, [Thomas], army surgeon:
land purchase, 1/185 & n. 3
SYMONS, Will, Council under-clerk
1660: dismissed, 1/23; advises P on
Exchequer place, 1/80; recalls serving
eight governments in one year, 5/8 &
n. 2; political news from, 1/12, 64–5;
inherits estate, 1/230 & n. 1; pew in
Westminster Abbey, 1/252; asks for
loan, 1/311; executor of Chetwynd's
will, 3/275 & n. 2; social: at Rota
Club, 1/61; P's farewell party before
Dutch voyage, 1/92; clerks' club,
1/208; bawdy talk, 5/7; at his house,
1/175; at P's, 5/7–8; 7/123; at taverns,
1/38, 86, 174–5, 230, 244, 248; 2/28;
also, 1/26, 116; 3/3
SYMONS, Mr ——, dancing master:
to go to sea with Sandwich, 2/117
SYMONS, ——, murderer: 9/412
SYMSON: *see* Simpson
SYON HOUSE, Isleworth, Mdx:
6/267

TAAFFE, Theobald, 1st Earl of
Carlingford (d. 1677): court news
from, 3/75; also, 9/544
TAFFILETTA [Tāfīlalt]: *see* al-Rashīd
TAGUS, the: Sandwich's drawing,
4/286 & n. 1
TALBOT, [Anna Maria], Countess of
Shrewsbury, (b. Brudenell), wife of

Povey, 7/51, 71, 335(2); Belasyse, 7/190, 191, 330, 338, 423; 8/22–3; 9/202; Vernatti, 7/265, 338; Middleton, 9/325, 328

OTHER FINANCIAL BUSINESS: negotiations with bankers, 6/108, 115, 193, 266, 267, 268; 7/170, 174, 242; 9/78 & n. 1, 315 & n. 1, 325, 328; his accounts with, 6/204–5, 207; enquiries into expenditure by Brooke House Committee, 9/562; also, 6/144, 146; 7/66; 8/100, 103, 123, 203, 244, 329, 341, 348, 372, 383, 390, 407, 518, 520(2); 9/152, 214, 249

SHIPPING BUSINESS: freightage, 4/52 & n. 1, 85; 5/167(2) & n. 3, 175, 186, 199, 201, 255, 276, 292, 332–3, 335, 337 & n. 1, 338, 340 & n. 2, 341; hire, 5/252; 6/27, 28, 32, 70; ships' passes, 7/20 & n. 3, 36, 38, 64, 98, 167

VICTUALLING BUSINESS: Yeabsley's accounts, 7/110, 121; 8/515; payments to Gauden, 6/322, 325; 7/402; Andrews, 6/227, 337; and Lanyon, 8/102, 146, 252; empowered to order bread, 4/21; discusses victualling with Sandwich, 4/30; inspects oats, 5/179, 187; his expenses allowed, 5/200; drafts contract with Alsop and Lanyon, 5/195, 196, 202, 204, 213, 223, 226, 229, 236; with Andrews, 6/37, 98; discusses contract with Gauden, 6/171–2, 253–4; with Andrews, 6/185, 201, 226–7; with Yeabsley, 8/438, 483, 515; also, 7/9

MISC. BUSINESS: appointment of river agent, 4/93; supply of deals, 5/277(2), 279; advised not to press enquiries into mole, 5/343; canvas, 6/65–6 & n.; lighters, 6/146 & n. 2, 172; 7/227

PERQUISITES, PROFITS AND BRIBES: general: hopes for, 4/85; 5/167, 249, 252, 258, 267, 277(2) 332–3, 337, 338, 340; 6/7, 27, 28, 32, 37, 70, 109, 146, 157, 172, 204, 208, 251, 252–3; 8/513; receives c. £250 in one month, 5/276; Tangier 'one of the best flowers in my garden', 5/280; fears discovery, 5/340 & n. 2, 348; willing to admit to, 9/99; justifies gains, 5/195, 214, 279; and retainer, 8/593; insists on paying for candlestick, 9/429–30; money: from

Lanyon and partners (victuallers), £300 p.a., 5/210, 223, 224, 226, 227, 263, 267; £36, 6/57; £222, 6/202; £64, 6/227; £210, 6/337, 340; £200, 7/162, 168; from Gauden (victualler), £500, 6/322, 325; £500, 8/35, 37, 44; from Cholmley (contractor for mole), £200 p.a., 6/306; 8/592, 593; £100, 7/19; from Houblons (ship's pass), £200, 7/64, 66, 98, 167; from other merchants (hire and freightage), £26, 5/175; £50, 5/186, 199, 201–2; £30, 5/255, 276; £117, 5/340, 341; £200, 6/286; 7/24; £100, 7/227; from Fitzgerald, £20, 7/173; also, 4/93; 6/26, 37, 242(2); 7/402; 8/372; other gifts, 7/167

TANNER, Mr ——: plays violin with P, 1/78

TAPESTRY: see Textiles etc.

TASBOROUGH, [John], clerk to Povey: 6/73, 153

TATNELL, Capt. [Valentine], naval officer: enmity to Coventry, 9/108 & n. 2, 129; also, 9/147

TAUNTON, Som.: Blake's defence (1644–5), 5/169 & n. 3

TAVERNS, inns, alehouses and eating-houses [mentioned by name and in London, Westminster and immediate environs, i.e. Bow, Chelsea, Clerkenwell, Holloway, Islington, Knightsbridge, Lambeth, Mile End, Rotherhithe and Stroud Green. Those not in this area are indexed under place-names. Those not named are indexed under streets etc. In this list where P gives sufficient information the street location is added. Asterisks denote the occasions on which he had a meal elsewhere than in an eating-house. For other houses of refreshment, see Cakehouses; Cookshops; Coffee-houses; Gardens: pleasure-gardens; Milk-house; Whey-house. See also Entertainments.]

GENERAL: closed during church services, 1/54 & n. 1, 270; 6/5; brewhouse, 1/119; dining clubs, 1/208; 7/375; bar, 1/301; 8/345; convenience of ordinaries, 4/131; French taverns compared with English, ib.; P rarely visits in mornings, 9/220

Covent Garden: murder at, 1/307 &
n. 2; P visits, 2/193, 220; 7/425;
Fleece tavern, by Guildhall: trick
played on landlady, 2/43; P visits,
2/50; Fleece mum-house, Leadenhall
St: P visits, 3/94; 5/142, 191; Folly,
floating house of entertainment on
Thames: P visits, 9/161 & n. 7;
Fountain tavern, Old Bailey: alluded
to, 5/168; Fountain tavern, Strand: P
visits, 2/195, 221; Fox tavern, King
St, Westminster: P visits, 1/88*;
French ordinary, Westminster: 1/23
Game's: see Coach and Horses,
Aldgate; George inn, Holborn: EP
takes coach, 3/148; 'George's, old',
Lambeth (unident.): P and EP dine at,
2/178; alluded to, 4/217; Glasshouse
inn, Broad St: Monck at, 1/53, n. 5;
P visits, 4/88; 5/64*; Globe tavern,
Eastcheap: P visits, 4/20; Globe
tavern, Fleet St: business meetings,
4/350; 6/65; Goat tavern, Charing
Cross: P visits, 2/64, 75; Mountagu
children stay at, 2/75; (Golden)
Fleece: see Fleece; (Golden) Hoop:
see Hoop; Golden Lion tavern,
Charing Cross: P visits, 1/19; Golden
Lion tavern, Strand: P visits, 7/424;
Grange inn, Portugal Row: P visits,
3/57 & n. 5; Great/Old James: see
Old/Great James; Green Dragon,
Lambeth Hill: P visits, 1/19; Green
Man tavern, Stroud Green: alluded to,
8/465; 9/545; Greyhound tavern,.
Fleet St: P visits, 1/71; 2/17, 212;
Gridiron, alehouse, Shoe Lane:
?2/156; 2/178; Gun, Mile End: P
visits, 9/221

Half Moon tavern, Strand: P visits,
1/15, 59, 181, 194, 223; 4/179;
5/205(2); 7/425; alluded to, 4/429;
5/55; 6/121; Halfway House, nr
Rotherhithe: P visits, 2/45, 112; 3/86,
91, 115; 4/99, 112, 144, 151, 162;
5/80, 95, 111, 124, 138, 156, 176;
6/184, 310, 332; 7/115; 8/325; alluded
to, 4/79, 110; 5/155, 347; Hare's, Mrs:
see Trumpet; Harp and Ball tavern,
nr Charing Cross (Roberts's): P
visits, 1/23, 33, 86; 3/298; 6/87, 103,
115, 142, 144, 145, 155; 7/418; 9/163,
248, 474, 542; ~ Mary at, from

Wales, 6/144; P admires, 6/87, 103;
talks with, 6/142, 145(2) takes on
jaunt, 6/155; also, 6/115, 142, 145(2);
Harper's, King St, Westminster [see
also Harper, James; Harper, Mary;
Harper, Tom]: P buys gloves, 1/183;
other visits, 1/9*, 12, 14, 15, 21, 33, 34,
37, 38, 48, 56, 58, 59, 82, 83, 87, 88,
200, 201, 225–6, 251, 286, 325;
2/80–1, 87; Harv(e)y's, Salisbury
Court: P visits, 1/175; Heaven, eating
house, Old Palace Yard: P dines,
1/31, 234, 290; Hell, eating house,
New Palace Yard: P dines, 1/303;
Herbert's: see Swan, New Palace
Yard; Hercules Pillars ordinary, off
Fleet St: 1/264, 278; 2/6, 145; 4/87*,
356; 8/281; 9/54*, 169*, 171*, 177*,
182*, 183*, 197–8*, 249*, 295*,
299*, 356*, 366*, 373*, 390*, 421*,
442–3*, 445*, 456*, 531, 538*;
Hilton's, Axe Yard: soldiers quartered,
1/46; Hoop (Golden Hoop) tavern,
Thames St/Fish St Hill: P visits,
1/249–50, 287*; 2/9; Horn tavern,
Fleet St: P visits, 4/102; ?5/246 & n. 2;
Horseshoe tavern, nr Navy Office:
Betty Lane's foolish visit, 5/285
Jacob's (?Salutation, Charing
Cross): P visits, 1/58; Jamaica House,
Bermondsey: P visits, 8/167

Keeper's lodge ('the Lodge'), Hyde
Park, milk house: P visits, 9/142 &
n. 1, ?154, 156, 175, 184, 222, 260,
533–4, 541; King's Head, Bow: P
visits, 3/169*; King's Head tavern,
Chancery Lane: P visits, 6/139*; with
fellows of Royal Society, 9/146–7;
King's Head inn, Charing Cross:
renamed, 1/179; P visits, 1/179, 206;
3/238*; 4/23*, 37*, 58*, 130*, 216*,
345*, 349*, 371*, 394*, 408*, 419*,
435*; alluded to, 4/12, 196; King's
Head tavern, Fish St Hill: P visits,
5/309; King's Head, Islington ('the old
House'; Pitt's): P visits, 2/98, 125;
5/133; known to P in youth, 5/101;
King's Head, Lambeth Marsh: P
visits, 4/263; King's Head, nr Royal
Exchange: P visits, 4/384 & n. 3;
King's Head, nr Royal Exchange: P
visits, 4/384 & n. 3; King's Head,
Tower St: P's dirty dinner, 2/89*

Paul's Churchyard: P visits, 2/124*, 161; Saracen's Head, nr Wardrobe: P visits, 2/211; Ship tavern, Billiter Lane, Fenchurch St [see also [Brome], ——; Morris, [John]]: P visits to admire landlord's daughter, 8/156, 345, 443; 9/51, 284, 485–6; pays his debts, 8/443; also, 4/404; Ship tavern, [?King St], Westminster: alluded to, 1/95; Ship tavern, ?Temple Bar: P visits, 2/173; Ship tavern, Threadneedle St: P dines, 3/150; Short's alehouse, Old Bailey: P visits, 3/100; Spring Garden, Vauxhall, house at: P visits, 6/164; Standing's, Fleet St: P visits, 1/250, 290, 303; 2/17, 25, 180; Star tavern, Cheapside (Ringstead's): P visits, 1/14, 52, 307; 2/109, 238; 3/91; 4/424; Star Tavern, ?Tower St: P visits, 4/424; Steadman's: see Mitre tavern, Fleet St; Sugar Loaf, Temple Bar: P visits, 1/48, 49; 9/477*; Sun tavern, Chancery Lane: P visits, 1/24; Sun tavern, Fish St Hill: P visits, 1/84*, 88*, 212*, 321*; 2/208, 210*, 213–14*; 7/91*; Sun tavern, King St, Westminster: P visits, 1/57*, 73, 75, 181*, 192, 194, 207, 209, 211, 217, 229, 231, 235, 265, 292, 296, 304; 3/192; 9/271; P's old drawer George alluded to, 1/229; Sun tavern, Threadneedle St ('behind the Exchange'): aviary, 4/85; Buckingham at, 8/299; P visits, 1/80; 2/196, 219; 4/85*, 172; 5/35, 271; 6/27*, 30*, 39*, 44*, 77*, 86*; 7/36, 38*, 299; 8/49*, 108*, 135, 516*; alluded to, 8/302; Swan tavern, Chelsea: 7/94; Swan tavern, Dowgate: 'a poor house', 1/185; Swan tavern, King St, Westminster: P visits, 2/97; 7/305; Swan tavern (Herbert's), New Palace Yard [see also Udall, Frances; Udall, Sarah]: 'my old house', 6/253; P visits, 1/7, 16, 45, 244, 294, 320; 2/219*, 3/296; 5/128; 6/1, 6, 17*, 65, 75*, 103, 111, 132, 141, 145, 253, 310; 7/32, 62, 81*, 99, 103*, 117, 201, 317, 319*, 355, 392, 396, 413; 8/34, 35*, 68, 120, 124, 133, 158–9, 224, 400, 456, 588; 9/75, 136, 161; new maid, 9/551; alluded to, 9/86; Swan tavern, Old Fish St: P dines, 3/165; juggler,

ib.; Swan tavern, Westminster [probably the Swan in New Palace Yard, in some cases possibly that in King St]: P visits, 1/43, 49, 55, 74, 91, 196; 2/49, 117; 3/43, 299; 7/39; 108, 134, 173*, 231–2*, 278, 279, 398; 8/102, 295, 323, 367, 590; 9/36, 56*, 295, 560*; his assignations with Doll Lane, 7/385–6; 8/193, 422; 9/317(2); Swan-with-two-Necks, Tothill St: W. Joyce in custody of Black Rod, 5/111; Swayne's, eating-house, New Palace Yard: P meets Doll Lane, 7/49–50

Three Cranes tavern, Old Bailey: wedding party, 3/16; Three Cranes tavern, Poultry ('at the Stocks'): farewell party, 2/163; Three Mariners, Lambeth: P visits, 2/120; noted for ale, ib.; Three Tuns tavern, Charing Cross: the old Three Tuns, 1/185; P visits, 1/185, 253; 2/206, 227; 9/359–60*; landlord [—— Darling], 2/206; his sister, ib; daughter, 2/228; Three Tuns tavern, Crutched Friars: newly established, 7/373; affray, 8/208; parish dinners, 8/218; 9/559; P visits, 7/373; 8/218*, 220*; 9/222*, 559*; landlord [John Kent], 8/208; Three Tuns tavern, Guildhall yard: P visits, 1/50; Triumph tavern, Charing Cross: Portuguese ladies at, 3/92; Trumpet, King St, Westminster (Mrs Hare's): P visits, 1/214; 5/9, 242, 340; 6/18 [White Hart], post-house, Charing Cross: 6/197 & n. 2; [?White Hind] inn, Cripplegate: coaches at, 6/95 & n. 4; White Horse, King St, Westminster: horse stabled, 1/85; White Horse tavern, Lombard St [see also Browne, Frances]: P visits, 5/330*, 338*; 7/63*, 68*; alluded to, 8/82 & n. 1; White Lion, Islington: alluded to, 9/32; Will's alehouse, Old Palace Yard [see also Griffin, W.]: P visits, 1/5, 6, 7, 14, 15, 16, 20, 21, 26, 32, 33, 34, 37, 40, 43, 45, 56(2), 57, 61, 64, 71, 78, 87, 173, 174, 257, 290, 294; 2/4(2)*, 6, 31, 40; Wood's, Pall Mall: 'our old house for clubbing', 1/208; P visits, ib.; shut in Plague, 6/147–8; World's End, Knightsbridge: P visits, 9/549, 564

TAXATION [for P's taxes, see Finances (P)]:

music, 5/174–5 & n.; 6/88; composes songs, 6/80–1 & n.; to show P King Edgar's charter, 6/81 & n. 1; appointed Storekeeper, Harwich, 6/318 & n. 1; 9/151–2; anthem criticised by Duke of York, 9/251 & n. 3; MS. of play, 9/546–7 & n.; also, 5/238; 9/271
TAYLOR, [Thomas], master of Huntingdon grammar school: conducts Robert P's funeral service, 2/133 & n. 3; Sandwich's sons taught by, 8/472 & n. 1
TAYLOR, ——, of Brampton: 3/222
TAYLOUR, [John], clerk in the Exchequer: 2/241
TEDDEMAN, [Henry], 'old Teddiman', brother of Sir Thomas; naval officer: deprived of commission, 7/163 & n. 3, 222–3
TEDDEMAN (Tiddiman), Capt. Thomas, kted 1665, naval commander:
P'S HIGH OPINION, 9/184, 198
CHRON. SERIES: in Mediterranean, 1/119; 3/89(2); captures Dutch ships, 5/326 & n. 2; serves under Sandwich (1665), 6/147; action at Bergen, 6/195–6 & nn., 213, 229; conduct in Four Days Fight criticised, 7/148 & n. 5, 158; defended, 7/154 & n. 3; discusses fleet's lack of discipline, 7/345; to command Dover squadron, 8/149; illness and death, 9/184, 198; last words and funeral, 9/200 & n. 4; portrait, 7/102 & n. 3; house, 9/184; also, 1/108 & n. 2; 6/80, 230, 329
SOCIAL: 1/321; 2/45
TEDDINGTON, Mdx: 3/81
TEIL, Capt. [Jean-Baptiste] du, naval officer: deprived of commisison, 7/163 & n. 1, 222; 8/147
TEMPEST, [?Rowland]: sings with P, 9/58–9, 219, 261
TEMPLE, [Anne], Maid of Honour to the Duchess of York: at court ball, 7/372
TEMPLE, Col. [Edmund]: killed in duel, 9/111 & n. 1
TEMPLE, [James], goldsmith, Vyner's chief assistant: 'the fat blade', 6/246; information about currency etc., 6/325, 326; Cocke's imprest assigned on, 6/329; ill, 8/37; Royal African Co.

business, 9/350; funeral, 9/501, 502; social: 6/248, 311; 7/404; 9/15; ~ his son, 8/598; his wife, 8/284
TEMPLE, Sir Richard, M.P. Buckingham, Bucks.: undertaking to manage Commons, 4/191–2 & n., 200, 207–8, 208, 211; opposes triennial bill, 5/99 & n. 3; introduces new one, 9/77 & n. 2; attacks Coventry over sale of offices, 9/129, 173
[TEMPLE, Sandys], naval officer: captured by Dutch, 6/117–18 & n.
TEMPLE, the [see also Inner Temple; Middle Temple]: general: damaged in Fire, 7/279; dispute over immunity from city's jurisdiction, 9/465–6 & n., 511–12; church: P attends service, 1/302; 2/75; 3/64, 252; monuments, 7/338; Selden's tomb, 8/545 & n. 2; P walks in, 3/275; 4/176; in King's Bench court, 4/200; garden: 1/44; 3/167; 8/367; gate: 9/534; garden walks: 4/162; 8/61, 64
TEMPLE BAR: middle door in, 6/114 & n. 3
TEMPLE STAIRS: 8/232
TEMPLER, [Benjamin], Rector of Ashley, Northants., 1657–61, 1661–d. 87: on snakes, 3/22 & n. 2
TENERIFE, Canary Is.: 2/21 & n. 4
TERNE, [Christopher], physician and Fellow of the Royal Society (d. 1673): anatomy lecture, 4/59
TERNE, Capt. [Henry], naval officer: at Blake's funeral, 2/74; killed in action, 7/154; social: 4/386
TERRY, Mrs ——: 2/158
TERSCHELLING (the Schelling, Scelling): English raid, 7/247 & n. 1; 8/309
[TETTERSELL, Nicholas]: his part in Charles II's escape to France (1651), 1/156 & n. 2
TEVIOT (Tiviott), Lord: see Rutherford
TEXEL, (island and channel): naval engagement off (May 1665), 6/99; Dutch take refuge in, 6/123; Sandwich's fleet near, 6/165; Dutch fleet in, 6/248
TEXTILES and fabrics (see also Dress):
BAIZE (BAYS): 1/268; 4/360; 8/79
BIRD'S EYE : hood, 6/102 & n. 2

Queen at, 4/251, 272; 7/214 & n. 3;
King at, 7/228; Lady Sandwich made
ill by waters, 6/152; alluded to:
7/260
TUNIS: peace with, 3/263 & n. 4, 271
TURBERVILLE, [Daubigny], eye
specialist: P consults, 9/248 & n. 6;
249, 251, 255; sees eyes dissected,
9/254–5
TURENNE (Turin, Turein), Henri de
la Tour d'Auvergne, Vicomte, Marshal of France (d. 1675): anecdote of,
8/127 & n. 2; to command in Flanders
campaign, 8/186; Colbert his rival,
9/397 & n. 2
TURKEY/Turks: see Algiers; Ottoman Empire, the; Tangier; Tunis
TURKEY COMPANY: see Levant
Company
TURLINGTON, [John], spectacle
maker, Cornhill: P buys spectacles
from, 8/486 & n. 2; advice to P,
8/519; ~ daughter's advice to,
8/486
TURNER, Betty, daughter of John:
her good looks, 5/337–8; 9/409, 464,
481, 512; P glad to have goodlooking
kinswoman, 9/407; to go to school,
9/512, 526; social: at P's Twelfth
Night party, 9/409; dances a jig,
9/464; at Mulberry Garden, 9/509–10;
at her mother's house, 9/446, 482, 506;
at P's house, 9/463, 478, 519; at
theatre, 9/476; also, 9/510, 511, 521;
alluded to: 9/540
TURNER, Betty, daughter of Thomas
of the Navy Office:
CHRON. SERIES: plays badly on harpsichord, 4/120; sings worse than EP,
9/35; grown a fine lady, 8/389; in
dancing display, 8/392, 396; helps P
title books, 9/49; accompanies EP to
Brampton, 9/144, 145, 210; and to
West Country, 9/229, 231, 233, 234,
238; also, 9/123; ~ her sparrow, 9/225
SOCIAL: dances at P's house, 8/511;
9/42; and at Twelfth Night party,
9/12; at theatre, 9/133; at P's house,
8/557; 9/28, 29, 38, 126, 244, 250,
265, 301, 325, 380; also, 2/175; 9/54–5,
245, 259, 261
'TURNER, Betty' (error): see Mordaunt, [Elizabeth], Lady Mordaunt

TURNER, Charles, son of Jane: 3/88;
9/446
TURNER, [Elizabeth], wife of Thomas of the Navy Office:
P'S OPINION: shares Batten's dislike,
5/293; a gossip, 7/105, 121 &
n. 1
CHRON. SERIES: supports P in Field case,
4/53; loses lodgings, 7/105, 296 & n. 2,
359; which Brouncker claims, 8/24,
29, 31 & n. 4; his unkindness, 8/36,
40, 51; new lodgings, 8/51, 63, 398;
9/36, 200 & n. 8; her balsam, 7/37, 40;
her strong waters, 4/221; 9/145; tends
P's sprained ankle, 8/340; gives EP
shells, 7/105; joins her in collecting
May-dew, 8/240; and at bleacher's,
8/401; seeks employment for son
(Frank), 8/155, 172, 457; 9/38–9; consults P about son (Thomas), 9/279;
P's help in promoting husband,
9/334–5; P gives her gloves, 9/120;
caresses, 9/312, 314; also, 6/23; 7/274;
8/490, 580; 9/115–16
GOSSIP FROM: about court, 4/177;
Brouncker's ménage, 8/51, 75, 225–6;
Penn's, 8/63, 141–2, 155, 226–9, 423,
595; Batten's, 8/159; also, 8/315;
9/157
SOCIAL: visits Cambridge, 2/136; Deptford, 3/198; 8/435; Epsom, 8/335–40;
Barnet and Hatfield, 8/380–2; Mile
End, 9/180, 208; at Greenwich, 6/212,
299; 7/1; at dances in Navy Office,
8/29; 9/13; Battens', 2/24; 4/218, 221,
230; Penns', 8/3, 371; in garden at
Seething Lane, 8/391; 9/252, 261; at
theatre, 8/433; 9/170, 189; P/EP
visit(s)/dine(s) with, 4/278; 7/120;
8/395–6; 9/46, 222–3, 276; at P's
house, 7/67; 8/4, 282, 433, 437, 441,
447; 9/28, 123–4, 138, 144, 184, 198,
213, 244, 258, 265, 278, 306, 325,
380; also, 2/38, 175; 5/303; 7/53;
8/378, 389, 581; 9/245
TURNER, Frank, naval officer, son of
Thomas of the Navy Office: commission expires, 8/150, 155, 172, 228;
joins E. India Company, 8/457;
9/38–9; social: 8/437, 580
TURNER, 'Col'. [James], criminal:
arrested with wife for robbery, 5/10–
11 & n.; trial and conviction, 5/13, 17,

18–19; confesses, 5/20; execution described, 5/23 & nn.; also, 5/24
[TURNER, Sir James], Governor of Dumfries: imprisoned by rebels, 7/377 & n. 4
TURNER, Jane (Madam Turner; b. Pepys), wife of John, lawyer, and P's cousin:
P'S OPINION: 'a good woman', 2/40; values her friendship, 4/273; shapely legs, 6/28
CHRON. SERIES: P's operation at her house, 1/97 & n. 3; ill, 2/214 & n. 1, 219, 227, 235, 237; 3/8, 13, 30, 44, 62; visited by sons, 3/88; brother's death at her house, 4/424, 425, 426, 432; 5/10; warns P of Tom P's illness, 5/29; attends his death and funeral, 5/81, 84–7 passim, 89, 90, 91; in Yorkshire, 7/391–2, 403 & n. 2; London house destroyed in Fire, 7/386, 391; returns to London, 9/353; borrows P's coach horses, 9/529; to leave town, 9/530; P gives her wine, 4/187; oysters, 5/88; and eagle, 5/352; also, 1/225; 6/28 & n. 2, 49
SOCIAL: with P visits Parliament chamber, 1/39; at Roger P's wedding, 1/39–40; gives Shrove Tuesday dinner, 2/43–4; at P's stone feast, 2/60 & n. 1; 3/53; 4/94–5; 5/98; 6/67, 124; 9/484; visits Chatham and Rochester, 2/67–73; Greenwich, 4/272–3; attends funeral, 5/347; Roger P and family on visit to, 9/407, 446, 475, 477; at P's Twelfth Night party, 9/409; P's valentine, 9/449; P/EP visit/dine with, 1/11, 26, 54, 60, 173, 181–2, 196; 2/52, 59, 63, 90; 3/167, 208, 269; 4/124, 175, 276; 5/71, 124, 130; 9/380, 407, 416, 425, 426, 447, 450, 461, 465, 473, 482, 505, 526; at P's house, 1/10; 2/53; 4/5, 65; 5/19, 337; 7/389; 9/463–4, 481, 519; at theatre, 3/78; 4/32; 9/420, 422, 429, 435, 453, 475, 478, 486; also, 1/42, 72; 4/95; 9/510, 511, 512, 521, 530–1
MISC.: pew at St Bride's, 1/42; 2/89; 3/30, 77, 162; coach, 4/95; 5/87, 130
~ her sister Turner, 9/512; her servant John, 4/68
TURNER, John, chaplain to Sandwich and Rector of Eynesbury, Hunts.:

appointed chaplain, 1/295; sermon, 2/133; learning, 8/517; also, 2/74; ?5/64, 80; social: 8/511, 516
TURNER, John, lawyer, of the Middle Temple, Recorder of York 1662–85: P's admiration, 9/429; consulted on dispute with Trices, 2/210, 214, 226, 230; 3/83; 4/346–7; nominated as arbiter, 3/270, 274, 276; insists on living in Yorkshire, 7/391–2, 403; his Reader's Feast, 6/28, 49; social: 2/24, 25, 211; 9/380, 450; alluded to: 3/88; 9/461, 530; ~ his man Roger, 2/218
TURNER, Moses, son of Thomas: 9/39
TURNER, Theophila ('The'), daughter of John, lawyer:
CHRON. SERIES: ill-mannered, 1/268; new harpsichord, 2/40, 44, 63; disappointed of place at coronation, 2/59; ill, 3/8; in country, 4/272; grown fat, 5/337; in London to put brothers and sisters to school, 8/210 & n. 1; returns to Yorkshire, 8/259, 262; in London, 9/353; to buy coach, ib.; is bled, 9/476; bridesmaid to Jane Birch, 9/500; also, 1/251
SOCIAL: at P's father's, 1/3 & n. 3, 65; runs races, 1/40; at P's stone feast, 2/60; 3/53; 4/94–5; 5/98; 6/124; P's valentine, 4/65, 68; plays harpsichord, 5/88; in Hyde Park, 5/130; 9/530–1; at P's Twelfth Night party, 9/409; composes mock letter with P, 9/463–4; at Mulberry Garden, 9/510; at her mother's, 9/407, 437, 482, 506; at theatre, 3/78; 4/32; 9/416, 420, 422, 429, 435, 453, 486; at P's house, 1/10, 225; 2/53; 3/44; 5/85; 6/98; 9/478, 481; also, 5/347; 8/221; 9/425, 512, 521
ALLUDED TO: 6/312; 8/260, 261
TURNER, Thomas, of Navy Office; after 1668 Storekeeper at Deptford:
CHARACTER: P's low opinion, 3/137; 6/37; 7/31; 8/38
CHRON. SERIES: hopes for Clerkship of Acts, 1/183–4, 189; salary and allowance, 1/191, 228; 5/228; appointed Purveyor of Petty Provisions, 2/54 & n. 1; 5/320; alleged payment for, 8/228 & n. 2; visits Cambridge, 2/136;

GENERAL: P admires, 1/249; condition of roads, 3/246; efficiency of excise, 5/68-9 & n.

CHRON. SERIES: rumoured expedition to E. Indies, 2/46; opposes Charles II's marriage, 2/65 & n. 3; makes treaty with French (Apr. 1662), 3/7 & n. 5; commercial treaty with England (Sept. 1662), 4/223 & n. 2; fleet said to threaten Portugal, 3/61 & n. 2, 110 & n. 2; plague, 4/340 & n. 2; 5/186, 220 & n. 2; investors to lend to English government, 8/400 & nn.; naval preparations, 8/568; 9/26, 123; attempts to persuade French to break peace with England, 8/568; concludes Triple Alliance, 9/30 & n. 4, 35, 60, 61, 70; mediates with England in Franco-Spanish peace negotiations, 9/176

NAVAL ADMINISTRATION: Warren's account of, 4/398; P admires efficiency, 4/176; 5/354; yarn and cable making, 3/101; 6/35; seamen's wages, 6/45 & n. 1

PROVINCES: Holland: gift to Duke of York from E. India Company, 2/79; gift to Queen Catherine, 3/82; alms-boxes in taverns, 1/146 & n. 3; 3/204; Holland and Zeeland for war against England, 5/121; English prisoners of war in Zeeland, 8/407-8, 426

P'S VISIT TO (1660): preparations, 1/87-96; voyage, 1/96-137 & nn.; stay in Holland, 1/137-52 & nn.; plans to revisit (1668), 9/462, n. 3, 558

UNTHANK, [John], EP's tailor:

CHRON. SERIES: mourning, 1/248; petti-coats, 4/199; 5/114, 118; flowered tabby gown, 7/298, 302; Barker interviewed at, 7/314; EP godmother to child, 8/164, 180; dines with P, 1/223; also, 4/155; 5/221; ~ his wife, 8/164

EP VISITS [often using shop as rendez-vous with P]: 4/28, 373; 5/118, 128, 262, 331, 332; 6/7, 79-80; 7/252, 310, 305, 310, 326, 327, 371, 373; 8/113, 121, 146, 192, 208, 213, 218, 326, 341, 348, 354, 377, 397, 411, 447, 519, 520, 528, 537, 558, 563, 567, 574, 601; 9/9, 22, 64, 80, 113, 136, 142, 247, 248, 249, 250, 255, 258, 259, 262, 264,

271, 301, 304, 334, 373, 393, 400, 408, 421, 427, 440, 445, 455, 465, 470, 475, 494, 509, 516, 523, 532, 551, 555, 560, 561

ALLUDED TO: 4/371; 7/53; 8/124

UPNOR CASTLE, nr Chatham, Kent: inspected, 3/155 & n. 1; pay, 7/253; ineffective in Medway raid, 8/265 & n. 1, 266, 276, 308; new batteries, 8/308; alluded to: 8/267, 309; 9/498

URSLER, Barbara, bearded lady: 9/398 & n. 2

UTBER, [Riches], Capt., naval officer: Coventry's high opinion, 4/196; wounded in action, 7/155; critical of Sandwich, 8/549

UTBER(T), ——: 2/173

UTHWAYT, [John], Clerk of the Survey, Deptford: lazy bookkeeper, 3/129; to equip *Maybolt*, 8/503-4; also, 2/45; 3/198; 6/180; 7/162

UXBRIDGE, Mdx: 6/110; fields, 7/204

UXBRIDGE, TREATY OF (1645): 4/212 & n. 1

VALLIÈRE, DE LA, Françoise Louise, cr. Duchesse 1667 (d. 1710): Louis XIV's visits to, 4/26, 189; gifts to, 8/183 & n. 2; her child by, 4/189

VANDENA [?Vandenancker], Capt. ——, of the Rhenish winehouse, Westminster: 8/323

VANDEPUT, [Peter], merchant, kted 1684: at parish dinner, 9/179

VAN DYCK, Sir Anthony, painter (d. 1641): copy of self-portrait, 4/139 & n. 3; portrait of Queen-Mother, 6/222 & n. 2; of Charles I and family, 8/181 & n. 3

VANE, Sir Henry, jun., republican: suspended from parliament, 1/13 & n. 5, 51 & n. 2, 56; imprisoned in Scilly Is., 2/204 & n. 1; tried and executed, 3/88 & n. 3, 103-4 & n., 108-9 & n.; speech on scaffold, 3/108-9; his courage, 3/112, 116, 117, 127; book on trial, 4/40 & n. 2; P's opinion of him, ib.; association with Penn, 4/375-6 & n.; 6/66; 8/227 & nn.; ~ his wife [Frances, b. Wray, d. 1679], 8/227

VIVIAN, Mr ——, of Westminster: 1/248

VLIE ('Fly'), the, Zeeland: Dutch ships burnt in, 7/247 & n. 1

VOWS (P):
GENERAL: makes/renews/reads over/ writes out vows, 3/209, 245, 296, 301; 4/6, 16–17, 306, 338, 348, 360, 417, 438; 5/4–5, 249; 6/10, 13, 72–3, 103, 253; 7/65, 117, 118, 164; 8/3, 6, 527; reads over on Sundays, 3/141, 162, 167, 182, 296; 4/43, 74, 96, 112, 191, 202, 218, 247, 259, 268; 5/31, 54; 8/43, 70; his benefit from, 3/167, 245; 4/438; 5/74

PARTICULAR:
    AGAINST DRINK: 1/84; 2/142, 242 & n. 1; 3/98, 125, 207; 4/235; 6/336; 1; 3/98, 125, 132, 207; 4/235; 6/336; 7/15; observed, 4/341–2; excuses breaches, 3/298; 4/4, 280, 284, 354; 6/226; 8/130

    AGAINST THEATRE-GOING: 2/200, 242 & n. 1; 3/89, 93, 98, 125, 132, 207, 294; 4/8, 182; 5/3, 33; 8/399, 527; observed, 4/431, 433, 434; 5/2–3; 8/7, 225; 9/47; breaks and pays forfeit, 2/200; 3/230, 294; 4/56–7, 164; 7/401; 8/45; excuses breaches, 4/128–9; 5/78, 224 & n. 1, 232, 236, 240, 282; 8/122–3, 429

    AGAINST IDLENESS: 4/123; 5/25, 31, 195, 250; 7/15, 25, 63, 86; 8/171–2, 175; breaks, 5/284; 7/23; excuses breaches, 5/192, 193; 8/224

    AGAINST EXTRAVAGANCE: 3/40, 80, 302; observed, 5/14; breaks, 5/55; excuses breaches, 4/395; 5/128

    MISC.: to rise early, 1/308; 6/55; to allow EP dancing lessons, 4/149–50; to say family prayers twice weekly, 5/14; not to be alone with Betty Lane for more than quarter of an hour, 5/113; *laisser aller les femmes* for one month, 6/20, 29; observed, 6/35, 53; breaks, 7/205; excuses breaches, 7/303, 396; to draw up will, 6/187; to refrain from visiting Deb Willet, 9/545; sums paid in forfeits: 3/230; 4/123, 149–50, 431; 5/55, 193, 284; 6/29; 7/205, 401

VRIES, Tjerk Hiddes de; naval commander: killed in action, 7/229 & n. 3, 231

VYNER, [Abigail], Lady Vyner, wife of Sir George: her beauty, 8/174, 408

VYNER (Viner), Sir George, gold-smith-banker: 8/174

VYNER (Viner), [Mary], Lady Vyner, wife of Sir Robert: wealth and good looks, 6/215 & n. 2

VYNER (Viner), Ald. Robert, gold-smith-banker, Lombard St, kted 1665 cr. bt 1666
GENERAL: character, 6/108; wealth, 6/215; profit from recoinage, 6/326; credit after Fire, 7/323; cash reserves, 8/275–6 & n.

BUSINESS WITH P:
    OFFICIAL: consulted about canvas, 6/65; cashes/gives credit on tallies for navy/Tangier, 6/115, 121, 164(2), 224; 7/12, 174, 201, 205, 339; unwilling to lend to government, 6/266; 7/330–1; 8/276, n. 1; also, 6/108; 8/221

    PRIVATE: supplies plate, 7/37, 405, 409, 413, 415, 420; and christening-bowl, 8/548; P deposits money with, 7/34; withdraws, 7/66, 84, 85; buys guineas from, 7/346, 348

    UNSPECIFIED: 6/297, 311, 340; 7/323, 328, 366; 8/37, 38, 74, 83, 170

    P'S ACCOUNTS WITH: 8/87, 124, 151, 180, 203, 209, 233

OTHER BUSINESS: with Cocke, 6/334; Sandwich, 7/32; 8/581–2 & n.; J. Pearse, 8/270; Carteret, 8/598; also, 7/38; 8/196

MISC.: leaves London in Plague, 6/205; house at Ickenham, 6/214–15, 266; lodgings at African House, 7/323; concerned in rebuilding after Fire, 8/81; account of origin of Fire, 8/82; also, 6/163; ~ kinsman buried, 8/101

VYNER (Viner), Sir Thomas, gold-smith-banker, Lombard St: provides cash for fleet, 5/15; pays P freightage, 5/340; funeral, 6/114 & n. 1

WADE, [Thomas], of Axe Yard, victualling official: profits on Baltic voyage (1659), 1/83 & n. 1; attempts to discover treasure in Tower, 3/240–2, 244, 246, 248, 256, 285, 286; social: 1/16, 57

WADLOW, Capt. [John], landlord of the Devil tavern, Fleet St: in

Dutch off Harwich, 8/281 & n. 4; threaten colliers, 8/285 & n. 5; in Thames, 8/296, 298, 303; land near Harwich, 8/317 & nn., 322 & n. 2; off s. and e. coasts, 8/327 & n. 1, 345 & n. 1; invade Thames again, 8/349 & n. 1; beaten off, 8/350, 351; defeated in Second Battle of N. Foreland, 8/354 & n. 3, 357–60 & nn.; gunfire heard at Whitehall, 8/367; Dutch plans for next year, 8/568; also, 8/163, 170; other engagements: French expedition to W. Indies, 8/2 & n. 1; take Antigua, 8/38 & n. 1; defeated off Martinique, 8/430 & n. 1; English privateers in Caribbean, 8/75 & n. 1; Harman in W. Indies, 8/132 & n. 3, 147, 153, 156; English squadron in Mediterranean, 8/43; also, 8/47, 162

PUBLIC PESSIMISM: 7/395; 8/306; merchants', 7/371; P's, 6/6, 218; 7/371, 374, 376, 378, 395, 426; 8/68, 88, 113, 146, 249, 274, 289, 305, 306, 363, 366, 377, 532, 602; Lord Crew's, 6/6; 7/387; Coventry's, 6/291–2; Cocke's, 6/218; Houblon's, 7/371; Carteret's, 7/383; Evelyn's, 7/406; 8/248–9, 278, 377; 9/484; Batten's, 7/416; Ford's, ib.; Reymes's, 8/68; and Povey's, 8/289

PEACE NEGOTIATIONS: overtures to Dutch and French, 7/411; Dutch demands, 7/369–70 & n.; venue, 8/17 & n. 3, 61–2 & n., 69, 72–3, 74, 80 & n. 4, 92 & n. 2, 106 & n. 2; Breda agreed on, 8/124, 125–6; King's speech to Parliament, 8/52; appoints plenipotentiaries, 8/61 & n. 3; Arlington's part in, 8/68–9 & n.; French part in, 8/69 & n. 2, 106–7 & n., 113, 170 & n. 5, 297; negotiations with Spain, 8/74 & n. 2; Dutch terms, 8/88, 95–6 & n., 100, 113; Dutch fear French making separate treaty, 8/153; plenipotentiaries assemble, 8/138 & n. 4, 145 & n. 3, 155, 161, 189, 216, 218; rumoured terms, 8/176 & n. 1; Dutch demands high, 8/244, 249; draft treaty, 8/322, 323, 326 & n. 3, 327, 329–30; its severity, 8/335; treaty sealed, 8/352; announced to Parliament, 8/361; further Dutch demands, 8/375; peace ratified, 8/378, 396 & n.

1, 397 & n. 1; proclaimed in London, 8/399; terms concerning prisoners, 8/407–8 & nn., 425–6; and territorial disputes, 8/426; printed copies, 8/453 & n. 3

PUBLIC REACTION TO PEACE: need for recognised by court, 8/62; by P, 8/176, 323, 324, 328–9, 329; by bankers, 8/285; and by Albemarle and Council, 8/347; terms feared/disliked by merchants, 8/157–8, 354–5, 362, 398–9; by court and nation, 8/361–2, 398–9; by P, 8/396; by Downing, 8/425–6; opinion in United Provinces, 8/225, 345

PEACE ALLUDED TO: 8/63, 93, 120, 128, 139, 285, 289, 317, 326, 354, 384, 386, 388, 391

WARCUP, Edmund, magistrate, bailiff of Southwark: in prize-goods affair, 6/269 & n. 3; 7/203–4, 219; disgraced, 7/219 & n. 4; allergy to roses, 7/204; social: 7/23

WARD, [Lieut. James], naval officer: questioned by Brooke House Committee, 9/204 & n. 1

WARD, [Richard], Muster-Master: 8/15 & n. 3, 19

WARD, [Seth], Bishop of Salisbury 1667–d. 89, Fellow of the Royal Society: preaching admired by King, 8/116 & n. 5; praises Abraham Cowley, 8/383 & n. 3; P visits, 9/229 & n. 4

WARD, Mr ——, [?of the Exchequer]: 6/235

WARD, Mr ——: 2/7; ~ his wife, ib.

WARDOUR, [William], Clerk of the Pells in the Exchequer: 6/244

WARDROBE, the KING'S GREAT, Puddle Dock [see also Mountagu, E., 1st Earl of Sandwich; Newport, A.; Reymes, Col. B; Townshend, T.]: officers dine together, 3/172; give Christmas dinner for tradesmen, 3/294; houses belonging to, 4/422; debts and shortages, 8/417–18 & nn.; economies proposed, 9/7; reorganisation, 9/41 & nn.; moves to Hatton Garden after Fire, 8/597 & n. 1; the building: an orphanage during Interregnum, 1/180 & n. 1; Jane Shore's Tower, 2/118 & n. 2; Master's

Lodgings, 1/291; 2/95, 97; kitchen, 2/106; great chamber, 3/134; garden, 3/228; withdrawing room, 4/428
WARE, [?Thomas], of Westminster: 2/81
WARE, Herts.: P travels through, 1/66; 3/217, 225; 4/307; overnight at, 2/146, 180; alluded to: 7/137
[WARNER, John], Bishop of Rochesester 1637–d. 66: 1/259 & n. 3
WARRELL, ——: wins prize-fight, 9/516–17
WARREN, [Thomas], merchant: pays P for warrant exempting seamen from press, 6/77 & n. 2, 85, 100; and for pass for ship, 8/548–9
WARREN, William, kted 1661, timber merchant:
NAVY BOARD BUSINESS: contracts: 40,000 Norwegian deals, 4/232 & n. 4, 233, 264; £3000-worth of masts, 4/302, 303–4 & n., 341, 436; defended by P, 4/326; for 1000 Göteborg masts, 5/73, 195 & n. 2, 213–14, 215–16 & n.; 7/2–3 & n.; defended by P, 9/254, 255; New England masts, 5/239 & n. 1; 3000 loads of timber, 5/299 & n. 3, 300–1, 303 & n. 4, 304; Norway goods, 5/333 & n. 1; 6/330 & n. 2; provides lighters, 6/74; 7/155, 157, 161, 227; tenders for plank, 6/99; ships insured by Board, 6/328, 329, 331; buys prize ships, 7/79–80, 85, 87, 88, 89–90 & n.; criticises Batten and others, 4/201, 422–3; 5/130–1, 143, 229; criticised by Batten and others, 2/78; 4/314, 326, 421 & n. 3, 423–4, 437; 6/38; proposed alliance with Castle, 5/337 & n. 2; accounts discussed, 8/192, 200, 216, 234, 550; 9/384, 394; and scrutinised by Brooke House Committee, 9/73 & n. 2, 220, 254(2) & n. 1, 277, 378 & n. 2; also, 3/64; 7/354; 9/16, 390; unspecified business, 4/253, 287; 5/105, 293; 6/309, 332; 7/10, 45, 95, 376; 8/575; 9/106, 332, 345
TANGIER BUSINESS: supplies deals, 5/277; and lighters, 6/146 & n. 2, 286, 340; 7/24; unspecified, 6/264
BUSINESS ALLIANCE WITH P: P's regard, 4/422–3; 7/24, 307, 402; 8/12; their friendship, 5/337; 6/226; and 'firm

league', 6/32; advises P about deals, 3/118, 131; 4/201; mast prices, 3/192; timber measurement, 4/233; storage of masts, 4/420; 5/78; Field case, 4/364; Wood's masts, 5/71; private trading, 5/277; mast-dock, 6/162, 184; and prizes etc., 8/516, 575–6, 579; instructs P about Dutch admiralty, 4/398; shipbuilding, 5/109; trade and investments, 4/124–5, 398, 408; advises on gaining wealth and reputation, 4/423; 5/293; 6/7, 200, 328, 329, 331, 338; 7/24, 77; recommends Walsingham's *Manual,* 5/10 & n. 2; advises him about Tangier treasurership, 6/106; and against marrying Paulina to Gauden's son, 7/89; reluctant to join in Scottish timber scheme, 7/300, 301
GIFTS TO P: payments [for amounts, *see* Clerk of the Acts; Tangier]: for mast contract, 5/229–30, 270, 271; freightage bargain, 6/55, 70; deal with lighters, 6/286; arranging insurance, 7/25; help with purchase of ships, 7/89; undisclosed services, 6/328; 7/25, 85, 89–90, 243, 244; shares profits with/arranges loan for P, 7/89–90 & n., 243, 244; gloves etc., 4/39; 5/35; gifts alluded to: 6/208, 264; 7/177, 376; denies their existence to Brooke House Committee, 9/92; P willing for gifts concerning Tangier to be admitted, 9/99
SOCIAL: his conversation, 5/76, 130; 6/98, 151; 7/1; entertains P and others to dinner, 2/235; 6/273, 332; 7/41, 104, 223, 329; also, 2/192; 5/116, 130–1, 143; 6/44, 69, 273; 7/406
MISC.: supplies deals for Hinchingbrooke, 1/324; 2/8, 35, 79; rumoured knighthood, 2/78 & n. 2; elected alderman, 3/100–1 & n.; claims knowledge of secret moves towards Restoration, 4/398; illnesses, 5/130; 6/226; house (at Wapping), 3/119; 4/201; (at Rotherhithe), 6/340; 7/161 & n. 1; yard, 4/103, 201; masts captured by Dutch, 5/321 & n. 2; also, 5/233, 296
ALLUDED TO: 3/150
~ his man, 5/109
WARWICK, Earl of: *see* Rich

WARWICK, Sir Philip, secretary to Southampton, Lord Treasurer:
CHARACTER: P's regard, 5/70; 6/110; 7/382; 8/213
BUSINESS: advises P on marine insurance, 4/395; on presenting estimates, 5/327, 329, 330; views on revenue and trade, 5/68–70 & nn.; taxation, 5/327–8 & nn.; Additional Aid, 7/61, 130–1 & n.; state of nation, 7/61; exchanges confidences about national and naval finances, 6/46, 75; P discusses navy finances with, 4/81, 305, 317; 6/48, 83, 95, 257; 7/64, 125, 233, 313; applies to for money for Tangier, 6/91, 92, 119, 121, 123, 127; 7/116–17, 137, 233; 8/32, 46, 52, 100, 123, 203, 205; other Tangier business, 5/229; his emoluments, 5/69; unspecified business, 5/321; 6/9, 16, 70, 71; 7/38, 39; also, 6/3; 7/295; 8/198, 219
MISC.: his new house, 6/3; 7/64 & n. 1; his drawleaf table, 6/109; recalls Southampton's last words, 8/213; ~ his wife [Joan], 2/29; his clerk, 6/154
WARWICK HOUSE, Holborn: 1/75 & n. 4, 272
WARWICK LANE: 5/20
WASHING, SHAVING etc.: see Dress and Personal Appearance
WASHINGTON, Col. [Henry]: 1/264
WASHINGTON, Mrs [Henry], shopkeeper, Westminster Hall: 9/187; ~ her husband, ib.
WASHINGTON, [Richard], purser: 1/174, 190
WASHINGTON, ——, of the Exchequer: social: 1/21, 41, 79; 2/227
WATCHES and clocks:
WATCHES: P's silver, 6/83 & n. 2, 100, 101; alarm, 6/158 & n. 3; minute, 6/221 & n. 3; plain, 7/293; 'of many motions', 7/293 & n. 1; 9/4; EP's, 8/51, 146; Lady Penn's gold, 8/228; Brouncker dismantles and reassembles, 6/337; P. Carteret makes, 9/109; also, 5/272; 9/489
CLOCKS: King's bullet, 1/209 & n. 2; Queen's night, 5/188 & n. 4
WATERHOUSE, [Edward], physician: ordained, 9/215 & n. 1; his

preaching, 9/432–3 & n.
WATERHOUSE, [Nathaniel], Master of the Green Cloth 1654–9: 1/34 & n. 4
WATERMAN, [George], Sheriff 1664–5, kted June 1665, Lord Mayor 1671–2: entertains Navy Board, 6/78–9
WATERMEN: see London: livery companies; Travel (river)
WATERS, [Edmund]: see Taverns etc.: Sun, King St
WATKINS, [William], clerk in Privy Seal Office: troubled at P's appointment in Privy Seal, 1/207; dies, 3/76, 80; also, 1/173, 197
WATLING ST: Fire, 7/269
WATSON, [Francis]: patent for lacquer, 9/531–2 & n.
[WATTS, ——], father of Esther St Michel: unwilling to give jointure, 3/286
WATTS, ——, merchant: offers P £500 for Clerkship of Acts, 1/185
[WAYMOUTH, Robert], mastergunner: in court-martial, 9/498 & n. 2
WAYNEMAN: see Birch, W.
WAYTE, Wayth: see Waith
WEATHER [No attempt is made to index passing references to the daily weather or to short-term changes. This section is designed to list long-term spells, storms and P's comments.]:
GENERAL: effects of hot weather on plague, 3/10, 18 & n. 3; 6/305, 306; and theatre attendance, 8/171; damage to ships by lightning, 4/200–1; effects of thunder on beer, 4/365 & n. 2; on wine, 7/256; Fire preceded by drought, 7/269; Duke of York's method of forecasting, 9/150
CHRON. SERIES:
 1660: unusually bad spell (20 May; in Holland), 1/150–1; first rain after dry spell (16 June), 1/176
 1661: mild winter, 2/19–20 & n., 25, 39; thunderstorm (23 Apr.), 2/86; wet summer, with fear of famine, 2/112–13 & n.
 1662: unseasonably warm spell (Jan.), 3/10 & n. 3; storm (18 Feb.), 3/31–2 &

n., 35, 42; first snow and frost for three years (Nov.–Dec.), 3/267, 268, 270, 271, 274, 276, 279, 280

1663: first rain after drought (17 Feb.), 4/45; storm at Northampton (6 May), 4/139 & n. 1; wet spell of three months (Apr.–June), 4/200 & n. 1, 204, 205, 206, 220; storm at Deptford (25 Sept.), 4/317–18

1664: unusually thundery weather in England and France, 5/195–6; thunderstorm (16 Aug.), 5/243 & n. 3

1665: 'one of the coldest days . . . ever felt in England' (6 Feb.), 6/32; 'as hard a winter as any hath been these many years', 6/66–7 & n.; 'the hottest day that ever I felt in my life' (7 June), 6/120; 'very hot beyond bearing' (11 July), 6/155; 'as great a Storme as was almost ever remembered' (14 Nov.), 6/298 & n. 2

1666: the 'Great Storme' (23–4 Jan.), 7/21–2 & n.; 'all cry out for lack of rain' (18 March), 7/75 & n. 4; 'mighty hot' (29 Apr.), 7/112; 'wonderous hot' with sheet lightning (10 May), 7/121; thunderstorm (31 May), 7/138; showers after dry spell (26–7 June), 7/183, 184; 'the hottest night that ever I was in in my life' (7–8 July), 7/197; thunderstorm, ib.; drought continues (2 Sept.), 7/269; ends (9 Sept.), 7/283 & n. 2; hailstorm at Harwich (16 July), 7/207–8; storm (17–18 Sept.), 7/289 & n. 1

1667: the coldest day ever remembered (6, 7 March), 8/98 & n. 6, 102; dry spell ends (21 Apr.), 8/175 & n. 2; hot spell (May), 8/245; 'mighty hot' spell (July), 8/333; month's drought ends (27 July), 8/356

1668: heatwave (July), 9/262, 263, 264; 'summer weather' (27 Sept.– 1 Oct.), 9/319, 322, 325; the first frost (7 Dec.), 9/386

1669: 'mighty temperate' (14 March), 9/482; dry spell ends (18 Apr.), 9/526

WEAVER, [Elizabeth] (b. Farley), actress: mistress of Charles II, 9/19 & n. 4

WEAVER, [Richard], of Huntingdon: discusses Brampton business, 8/71;

death, 8/162 & n. 3; social: 2/213; ~ his wife, 9/451

WEDDINGS and MOCK-WEDDINGS: see Marriage

[WEEDON, Richard]: see Taverns etc: Dolphin, Tower St

WELD (Wilde), Dorothy: see Pickering

WELD (Wiles, Wild), [George], M.P. Much Wenlock, Salop (d. 1701): coxcomb, 3/242; 9/103; as Deputy-Governor of Tower, 3/242; at cock-fight, 4/428; enemy of Navy Board, 9/103–4; also, 8/307

WELL BANK, the, North Sea: Dutch fleet near, 6/219 & n. 2

WELLING: see Welwyn

WELLS, [John]; Storekeeper to the Navy: his MS. on ship-building, 5/108 & n. 2

WELLS, [William], Vicar of Brampton, Hunts: 3/220 & n. 2

WELLS, [Winifred], Maid of Honour to the Queen: story of alleged miscarriage, 4/37 & n. 4, 56; in riding-dress, 7/162; her beauty, 9/563

WELLS, Som.: Cathedral carvings, 9/239 & n. 2

WELSH, Jane, maidservant to Jervas, the Westminster barber: P attracted by, 5/212, 224, 246; 6/20; she breaks assignations, 5/260, 267–8, 273; 6/1, 5, 18–19; cold to P, 5/275, 340; he meets briefly, 5/287, 316, 332; 6/6, 9; Jervases try to marry off, 5/260; 6/16; deceived by bigamous fiddler, 6/9, 16–17, 22, 74–5; 7/103; to go to Ireland, 6/75

WELWYN (Welling), Herts.: P at, 2/183; 5/233–4, 296; Swan Inn, 5/296

WENDY (Wendby), [Thomas]: elected M.P. Cambridgeshire, 1/112 & n. 2

WENTWORTH, Thomas, 1st Earl of Strafford (d. 1641): attainder (1641), 8/518–19 & n.

WENTWORTH, Thomas, 1st Earl of Cleveland, Captain of Gentlemen Pensioners: death, 8/154 & n. 2

WENTWORTH, 'Squire', [Thomas]: to be tried for manslaughter, 3/34 & n. 2; defence, 3/36

WERDEN, Col. Robert, Groom of the Bedchamber to the Duke of York: 8/406

WEST INDIES: Myngs's fame in, 7/166; French expedition, 8/2 & n. 1; Spaniards suffer from English privateers, 8/75 & n. 1; Harman's expedition, 8/132 & n. 3, 147, 153, 156

WESTMINSTER: P hopes for clerkship of city, 1/79–80 & n.; flood, 1/93 & n. 1; horseferry, 3/289; Plague in: 6/132, 141, 144, 147–8, 154, 163, 210, 268 & n. 4, 289; no doctors left and only one apothecary, 6/268; streets empty, 7/3; crowds in street demand recall of parliament, 8/268

WESTMINSTER ABBEY:
GENERAL: bishops at, 1/259; regicides' bodies exhumed, 1/309 & n. 4; coronation service, 2/83–4; funerals, 1/249 & n. 2; 6/127 & n. 3; 9/158 & n. 2; Dean and Chapter allegedly harsh landlords, 8/198–9 & n.

P ATTENDS SERVICES: comments on restored prayer-book service, 1/190, 261; thin congregation, 1/257; and music, 1/283 & n. 1, 324; 6/18; sings in choir, 2/240; also, 1/201 & n. 1, 201–2, 251–2, 259, 276; 2/48, 83–4

HENRY VII'S CHAPEL: 1/201, 259; 7/160; 9/457

OTHER PLACES ETC. IN: cloisters: P makes assignations in, 5/260, 267–8, 273; also, 9/168; tombs, 5/268; 9/456–7 & n.; churchyard, 7/160; west door: P makes assignation at, 7/240; Deanery, 9/89

ALLUDED TO: 6/5; 7/345

WESTMINSTER BRIDGE: see Westminster Stairs

WESTMINSTER HALL:
GENERAL: 1/140; regicides' heads displayed, 2/31 & n. 4; coronation banquet, 2/84–5; to be repaired, 4/232; full again after Plague, 7/38; fire near, 7/263; as storehouse in Fire, 7/278

LAW COURTS: judges' procession, 1/272 & n. 3; new location, 2/101 & n. 3; Chancery Row, 1/61; [Common Pleas], 7/391 & n. 1

SHOPS: closed on fast day, 7/359; in early evening, 8/353; P/EP at: for pictures, 1/19; books/newsbooks/pamphlets, 1/275, 301; 2/4; 3/52, 296; 4/111; 6/162; 8/40, 86, 98, 422; caps, 2/39; 7/346; gloves, 7/156; 8/121; ribbon, 9/165; also, 3/5; 4/368; 7/129, 186, 295, 368–9, 393; 8/151

P VISITS [omitting passing visits – e.g. on his way to parliament – and casual visits to meet friends or shopgirls]: in term-time, 2/31, 124; 3/22, 253; 4/25; 5/40, 184; 8/177, 193, 291, 360; 9/552; absent from, 5/331; takes EP to see and be seen, 7/89; full when parliament in session, 8/360; empty at night, 8/583; 'walks'/'talks' in, 1/4–5, 7–8, 13, 17, 46–7, 50, 56, 58, 65, 74, 75; 2/130, 139, 170, 210, 227; 3/3, 11, 43, 49, 83, 173–4, 238; 4/44, 58, 62, 66, 68, 91, 113, 126, 135, 159, 170, 173, 191, 213, 222, 232, 242, 303, 348, 370, 431; 5/33, 34, 71, 111, 128, 138, 215, 246, 249, 338; 6/13, 17, 75, 115, 141, 186; 7/61, 81, 88, 98, 108, 116, 201, 229, 256, 291, 295, 296, 308, 313, 314, 319, 323, 337, 339, 342, 360, 378, 380, 381, 392, 396, 406, 413, 415; 8/1–2, 35, 46–7, 52(2), 102, 110, 111, 113, 120, 158, 181, 199, 203, 205, 223, 224, 248, 294, 299, 317, 323, 329, 341, 348, 462, 377, 393, 440, 479, 480, 491, 493, 497–8, 510, 529, 532, 544, 555, 557, 558, 564, 574, 575, 579, 588; 9/6, 55, 56, 60, 73–4, 76–7, 83, 85, 92–3, 105–6, 112, 112–13, 113, 114, 115, 116, 119, 121, 135–6, 136, 153, 163, 165, 174, 176, 177, 178, 182, 185, 186–7, 187, 190, 193, 197, 208, 220, 277, 317, 322, 348, 369, 462(2), 486, 513, 526, 527

WESTMINSTER PALACE [see also Exchequer; Old Palace Yard; New Palace Yard; Parliament; Westminster Hall]: Court of Exchequer Chamber, 8/181, 231; Court of Wards, 1/48; 7/324; 9/107; Inner Court, 7/304, 305; gate/gatehouse, 1/208; 4/114; 6/132; Star Chamber, 1/34

WESTMINSTER STAIRS: drowned man on, 2/227; also, 2/30; 3/196; ?7/103; ?8/180

WESTON, Charles, 3rd Earl of

over customs dues, 5/38, 50, 54, 72, 75, 76, 145; ill, 8/231–2; estrangement from P and EP, 8/232; 9/275, 330 & n. 2; portrait, 2/202; house: in London, 2/202; at St Catherine's Hill, nr Guildford, 2/211; 9/275; also, 2/117, 132; 3/64; 6/83; 7/366
MARRIAGE: ruled by wife, 3/276; complains of her relations, 3/295; and cooking, 5/49; unhappiness/quarrels with, 5/100, 191, 292
SOCIAL: gives fish dinner, 1/28 & n. 3; drunk, 1/220; at funeral, 2/159; P gives chine of beef to, 2/219; shares oysters with, 5/269, 274; at P's stone feast, 4/95; 5/98; at fish dinner, 5/53; views Clarendon House, 7/87; P critical of his entertainment, 7/366; P/EP visit(s)/dine(s) with etc., 1/194; 2/9, 19, 37, 162, 202, 208; 3/30, 178, 202, 228, 236; 4/106, 107–8, 269, 306; 5/1–2, 10, 19, 30, 94, 119, 125, 129, 188, 268, 315; 6/29; 7/345; 9/405, 449; at P's house, 2/28, 52, 215; 3/9, 14, 94; 4/427; 5/27, 77, 128, 162, 211, 256, 340; 6/133; 7/46, 71, 112, 134, 385; 9/334, 383, 403, 430; at the Mitre, Fenchurch St, 1/174, 195, 256; 2/36, 45, 58, 99, 107, 170; 3/61, 124, 166, 173, 183; 5/47, 235; also, 1/80, 194; 2/207; 4/291
ALLUDED TO: 9/375
~ his cousins, 9/406
WIGHT, [William], son of the foregoing: legacy from Robert P, 4/86
WIGS: see Dress (Men, etc.): hairdressing
WILDAY, ——, [?of Worcester]: 1/92
WILDE, Dorothy: see Pickering
WILDE (Wiles), Elizabeth: see Wyld
WILDE, Sir William, Recorder of London 1659–68 (d. 1679): 1/252
WILDMAN, Maj. [John], republican: association with Buckingham, 8/569–70 & n.; 9/347–8 & n.; nominated to Brooke House Committee, 8/569–70 & n., 571, 577 & n. 1
[WILFORD, Francis], Dean of Ely 1662–d. 67: sermon, 3/190 & n. 2
WILGRESS, Capt. [John], naval officer: commissioned, 1/101
WILKES, [Luke], Yeoman of the King's Wardrobe: 4/26

WILKES, [Luke] [?identical with the foregoing]; servant to Secretary Williamson: 7/289–90
WILKINS, John, Bishop of Chester 1668–d.72; Fellow of the Royal Society [see also Books]: P's regard, 6/95; sermons, 1/302; 6/34; examiner at St Paul's School, 4/33; 5/38; experiments on coaches, 6/94; 7/12, 20 & n. 2; asks P for information on naval terms, 7/148; congratulates P on parliamentary speech, 9/113; appointed bishop, 9/331 & n. 3; lodgings at Lincoln's Inn, ib.; rumoured appointment as Bishop of Winchester and Lord Treasurer, 9/485; Buckingham his patron, ib.; also, 8/541, 543, 555; alluded to: 7/72
WILKINSON, Capt. [Robert], naval officer: surrenders to Dutch, 6/117–18 & n.
WILKINSON, of the Six Clerks' Office in Chancery: 4/242, 345, 346, 351, 352
WILKINSON'S (the Crown), cookshop, King St, Westminster: P dines at 1/21, 91, 284; 2/102, 171, 229; 3/3, 87, 269, 382; 4/189; 9/81; buys/orders food from, 1/26, 39; 8/559; drinks at, 1/201; 6/109, also, 1/85,?190; 9/86; death of the landlord, 9/81
WILL, P's boy: see Servants
WILL'S: see Taverns etc.
WILLET, Deb, companion to EP:
APPEARANCE: good looks, 8/448, 451, 456, 465, 468; grave and genteel, 8/456–7
AS EP'S COMPANION: engaged, 8/448, 451, 456; at Cambridge and Brampton, 8/465–75 passim; combs P's hair, 8/531; 9/20, 37; helps to title books, 9/49, 72; EP angry with, 9/61, 119, 143; visits Brampton, 9/98, 125, 143, 145, 210; on West Country tour, 9/229, 231–6 passim, 238, 266, 273–4; visits Impington, 9/306
P'S AFFAIR WITH: P pleased with, 8/451, 453–4, 458(2), 468; EP jealous, 8/477, 481; P kisses, 8/585; 9/145; caresses, 9/143, 144, 274, 277, 282, 328; discovered by EP, 9/337–8; her rage and P's guilt, 9/338–46 passim; P fears she must leave, 9/346, 348–9; is prevented

from seeing, 9/353, 354, 356; her confession, 9/356; and dismissal, 9/357, 358, 361–3; P searches for, 9/364–7 passim; EP threatens to slit her nose, 9/367, 369; P never to see again, 9/368, 370, 371, 378; forced to accept Hewer as escort, 9/368, 373; sees in street, 9/387; EP makes jealous scenes, 9/384, 395, 422, 433, 480–1, 546; threatens him with hot tongs, 9/413–14; he meets by chance, 9/518–21 passim; she breaks assignation, 9/526; winks at P in street, 9/534; moves to Greenwich, 9/543; affair alluded to, 9/502, 564

SOCIAL: accompanies EP to theatre, 8/459, 463, 481(2), 486, 508, 516, 521(2), 525, 527, 594; 9/12, 14, 18, 19, 37, 54, 62, 81, 85, 89, 91, 93, 100, 107, 133(2), 137, 246, 249, 250, 263, 268–71 passim, 278, 280–1, 296, 304, 326; to tailor/shops etc., 8/460, 519, 520, 528, 558, 563–4, 567, 574, 601; 9/16, 22, 28, 29, 39, 46, 64, 66, 79, 100, 113, 124, 256, 258, 259, 301, 329, 330, 332(2), 334; to Islington, Mile End etc., 9/133, 254, 255, 271–2, 276; to S. Cooper's studio, 9/256, 258, 259, 260, 276; Vauxhall, 9/257, 268; Bartholomew Fair, 9/290, 293, 296, 299; dances, 8/493; 9/128, 289; plays cards, 8/594, 599; 9/17, 35, 107; fortune told, 9/278; also, 9/1, 23, 36, 139, 143, 262
~ her mother, 9/235

WILLIAM I, Prince of Orange (the Silent; d. 1584): tomb at Delft, 1/146 & n. 2

WILLIAM II, Prince of Orange (d. 1650): struggle against republicans, 6/146–7 & nn.

WILLIAM III, Prince of Orange (King of England 1689–1702): 'a pretty boy', 1/139; gives audience, 1/138, 139; on Naseby, 1/154; at aunt's wedding, 7/250 & n. 1; opposed by republicans, 6/147; his faction and the peace negotiations, 8/69 & n. 1, 92, n. 2, 106 & n. 1

WILLIAMS, [Abigail], 'Madam Williams', Lord Brouncker's mistress:
P's DISLIKE: Brouncker's doxy, 6/213; 8/5; whore, 6/234; 7/237; spiteful, 6/217; ugly, 6/251; impudent, 6/273,

303; 'a prating, vain, idle woman', 9/200; also, 7/76, 91, 221

CHRON. SERIES: P meets, 6/204 & n. 1; Brouncker's attachment, 6/212, 285; 7/68, 74; 8/314; swoons on hearing of rival, 7/237–8; at Erith, 6/244, 249; information on prize-goods affair, 6/299–300, 302, 303, 309; rebukes P for over-familiarity, 6/337; stories of her accepting bribes, 8/51–2, 75, 226; and of her poverty, 8/226, 302; angry with P over Carkesse affair, 8/203, 260; at St Olave's, 9/452; her closet, 7/76; 8/395; 9/199–200; also, 6/217; 8/97

SOCIAL: visits EP at Woolwich, 6/206; dines on East Indiaman, 6/273; birthday party for Brouncker, 6/285; visits P's house, 7/66–7; godmother to Knepp's son, 7/196; at Brouncker's house/lodgings, 6/236; 7/3; 8/431; 9/546; at hers, 7/14; 8/509; 9/106, 133, 331; at other houses/lodgings, 6/220, 228, 233; 7/18, 34, 38, 69, 364, 408; 8/394; 9/15, 505; at theatre, 8/395; 9/310, 381; also, 6/334; 7/3–4, 173; 9/109
~ her woman, 6/204

WILLIAMS, Col. [Henry], of Ramsey, Hunts.: changes name from Cromwell, 4/82–3 & n.; at Hinchingbrooke, 4/313

WILLIAMS, Dr John, physician: treats EP, 1/215, 276; 2/98, 125; 4/162(2), 350: consulted in dispute over Robert P's estate, 2/156, 160, 164, 176–80 passim, 210, 223; 3/12, 16, 100, 215; 4/126, 132, 350, 351, 364; illness, 2/193, 209; love affair, 6/144; garden and dog, 2/176; out of town, 3/118, 294; alluded to: 2/158; ~ his sister, 2/180; Jane, his maid at Cambridge, 1/216

WILLIAMS, [Vincent], Groom of the Chamber to the King: 7/218

WILLIAMSON, Joseph, Under-Secretary to Arlington and Keeper of State Papers, 1660–74; kted 1672; Secretary of State 1674–8:
CHARACTER: 4/35, 270; 5/323; 7/63, 169; 8/318, 556

CHRON. SERIES: manager of Fishery Corporation's lotteries, 5/323 & n. 2;

news from, 6/156; 7/229; 8/323; edits *Oxford Gazette*, 6/305 & n. 3; 7/116; at launch, 7/169; defeated in bye-election, 7/337 & n. 2; influence, 8/318; praises P's parliamentary speech, 9/105; consulted by P on defence of Navy Board, 9/483; reads P's memorandum to cabinet, 9/525; also, 7/205; 9/61, 486

SOCIAL: 6/68; 7/38; 9/352, 410–11, 543

WILLIAMSON, Capt. [Robert], naval officer: commissioned, 1/90

WILLOUGHBY, Francis, 5th Baron Willoughby of Parham, Governor of Barbados etc. 1663–6: drowned, 7/390 & n. 3

WILLOUGHBY, Maj. [Francis], Navy Commissioner, 1653–1660: on *Naseby*, 1/105; lodgings, 1/197

WILLS (P): his first (March 1660), 1/90 & n. 1; tears up EP's copy, 4/9; to make a second, 4/433; 5/20, 25, 26, 29; concludes and attaches memorandum (Jan. 1664), 5/31; alters on Tom's death, 5/192; draws up a third (Aug. 1665), 6/187, 189, 192; copies, 7/134; his fourth (June 1667), 8/266

WILLYS, Sir Richard, royalist: dismissed from governorship of Newark (1645), 6/30–1 & n.; plot betrayed (1659), 1/141 & n. 1, 221; marriage, 1/141

WILLYS, Sir Thomas, M.P. Cambridge borough 1660: defeated in county election (1660), 1/112 & n. 2; on corruption of navy, 4/37

WILMOT, John, 2nd Earl of Rochester: attempts to abduct Elizabeth Malet, 6/110 & n. 2, 119; 7/385; marries her, 8/44 & n. 4; his poverty, ib.; at court ball, 7/372; at theatre, 8/44; assaults T. Killigrew in King's presence, 9/451–2 & n.; also, 9/382

WILSON, Tom, Navy Office clerk; Surveyor of Victualling, London, 1665–7; Storekeeper, Chatham 1667–?76: practical joke, 4/226–7, 230; appointed Surveyor of Victualling, 6/272, 280 & n. 3; victualling business, 6/294, 305–6, 325; 7/135, 262, 265; 8/587; 9/8(2); Tangier accounts, 7/255; stories of Tom Fuller, 8/337; as Storekeeper, 8/447; ill, 9/300; P

visits at Chatham, 9/499; also, 8/229, 267; ∼ his wife [Jane], 9/499

WILSON, Mrs ——, Lady Castlemaine's lady-in-waiting: her beauty, 8/324–5; said to be pregnant by King, 9/186

WILTON HOUSE, Wilts.: P's comments on, 9/230; court to visit in Plague, 6/189 & n. 3

WILTSHIRE, excise farmers of: 9/529 & n. 2

WIMBLEDON, Surrey: Bristol's house at, 5/89

WIN: *see* Wynn

WINCHCOMBE, Glos.: tobacco cultivation, 8/442; also, 2/225

WINCHELSEA, Sussex: bye-election, 7/337 & n. 2

WINCHILSEA, Lord: *see* Finch, H.

WINDHAM: *see* Wyndham

WINDSOR, Thomas, 7th Baron Windsor, cr. Earl of Plymouth 1682; Governor of Jamaica 1661–4 (d. 1687): consults Navy Board, 3/62–3; attack on Santiago, Cuba, 4/41 & n. 5, 94 & n. 3; returns, 4/41 & n. 4, 54

WINDSOR, Berks.: painting by Danckerts, 9/423 & n. 1, 539; Poor Knights of, 1/78 & n. 1, 7/58 & n. 4; installation of Knights of Garter, 2/75 & n. 7; 4/108; St George's Chapel, 7/57–8 & nn.; royal tombs in, 7/58 & n. 6; castle, 7/58–9 & nn.; Garter Inn, 7/57 & n. 1, 59; also, 6/195, 198; 7/54

WINDSOR FOREST: P lost in, 6/197

WINE, (Wyne), [Arthur], purveyor of fish to the King's household: 1/287; 4/101

WINGATE, [Edward]. M.P. St Albans Herts. 1640–8: 9/518 & n. 2

WINTER, Sir John, secretary to the Queen Mother: P's regard, 3/165; 6/62; 8/114; lease of timber and iron in Forest of Dean, 3/112 & n. 2, 114; 4/193 & n. 3; stories of Forest, 3/165; business, 6/62 & n. 2; 8/114, 191 & n. 4

WINTER, [Thomas], timber merchant: 4/326 & n. 2, 381

WINTER, [William], merchant: dispute with Capt. Stoakes, 1/175 & n. 1; dines with P, 1/212

WINTER, —— (old Winter), the Algiers pirate: 3/124 & n. 1

WINTERSELL, [William], actor: P admires in Shirley's *Love in a maze*, 9/178 & n. 1

WISBECH, Cambs.: J. Day's estate, 4/231; description of town, church, library and Thurloe's house, 4/310–11 & nn.

[WISE, Henry], gardener: redesigns Navy Office garden, 3/17 & n. 3

[WISE, Lucy], 'Mother' of the Maids of Honour to the Duchess of York: 9/468

WISE, ——, viol maker, Bishopsgate St: P visits, 4/232, 233, ?242, 252, 255, ?261

WISEMAN, Sir Robert, Admiralty lawyer: on civil government of Tangier, 4/102 & n. 1; prize case, 8/131, 133

WITCHES and witchcraft: *see* Popular beliefs etc.

WITHAM, Capt. [Edward], army officer, Tangier: story of Teviot's death, 5/179–80; inspects oats, 5/179, 187; quarrel with Fitzgerald, 9/273 & n. 2

WITHERLEY (Wiverly), [Thomas], physician: Jane Turner's doctor, 5/85; diagnosis of Tom P, 5/85, 86, 87

WITHERS, [?Robert]: 7/278 & n. 3

WITT, Jan de, Grand Pensionary of Holland 1653–d.72: quarrel with Orangists, 6/146–7 & nn.; accompanies fleet, 6/198 & n. 2; power insecure, 7/216; (untrue) rumour of flight, 7/250 & n. 1, 255; peace negotiations, 8/69, 92 & n. 2; deceived by Downing's spies, 9/402; also, 8/347

WIVELL, [Edward], victualling agent, Dover: 1/174, 287

WIVERLY: *see* Witherley

WOLFE, [William], fishmonger, Fish St Hill: Fishery business, 5/309 & n. 2; house burnt in Fire, 7/270

[WOLLEY, Francis]: killed in duel, 1/20 & n. 1

WOLSTENHOLME (Wostenham), Sir John, Commissioner of the Customs (d.c.1670): 3/188

WOOD, Barbara, (b. Sheldon), niece of William Sheldon of Woolwich: 'odd looked', 7/250; marriage, 7/242, 250, 258–9, 398–9; with P at Fire,

7/270, 271; social: visits EP, 7/73 & n. 1, 75, 78, 89; also, 6/223, 279, 282, 314, 338; 7/126, 210; 8/375; alluded to: 6/315; 7/3

WOOD, Sir Henry, Clerk of the Board of the Green Cloth: stories of, 7/290 & n. 1; also, 4/348–9 & n.

WOOD(S), [John], Auditor of the Imprests in the Exchequer: allows salaries of Principal Officers of Navy, 3/279 & n. 2; examines accounts, 8/344; 9/22, 42(2), 58, 462, 529; ~ his clerk, Smith, 9/389, 393, 429

WOOD, [Mary], Lady Wood, wife of Sir Henry: pregnant, 4/348–9 & n.; dies of smallpox, 6/57–8 & n.

WOOD, [Thomas], Dean of Lichfield 1664–71, Bishop 1671–85: quarrel with Bishop, 9/45 & n. 2

WOOD, Capt. [Walter], naval officer: killed in action, 7/154

WOOD(S), William, timber merchant: ? his royalism, 1/102; a knave, 3/26; masts unsatisfactory, 3/227 & n. 5; 5/6 & n. 4, 50, 51, 52, 108, 123, 124, 135; contract for New England masts, 3/256, 268, 274; criticised by Warren and Deane, 4/287, 436; 5/29–30, 71; trickery, 5/117; corrupt understanding with Batten, 4/201; 5/108; Batten's executor, 8/569 & n. 4, 582, 584; also, 4/423–4; 5/79

WOOD, [William], son of the foregoing and husband of Barbara: marriage, 7/242, 250; rich, 7/250; a blockhead, 7/399; with P at Fire, 7/270, 271

WOOD, poor Mr ——: 2/36

WOOD'S: *see* Taverns etc.

WOODALL, Thomas, Surgeon in Ordinary to the King; killed in drunken quarrel, 8/90 & n. 3, 92

WOODCOCK, [Thomas], Fellow of Jesus College, Cambridge 1645–62; Rector of St Andrew Undershaft 1660–2: at The Hague, 1/144; preaches at St Olave's, 2/48; 3/91

WOOD(E)SON, [?George], of the Signet Office: 1/212, 217

WOODFINE, [?Thomas]: social: 1/19–20, 24, 91

WOODING, Ned: 2/72

WOODMONGERS' COMPANY:
see London: livery companies
WOODROFFE, [Edmund], clerk in
the Exchequer: 2/241; 6/235-6
[WOODSTOCK, ——], former hus-
band of Lady Batten: 4/233 & n. 1
WOOD ST [see also Taverns etc.:
Mitre]: furniture bought, 2/176; 4/6;
joiners, 5/251
WOOLLEY, [John], underkeeper of
Privy Council records: stationery
expenses, 8/176 & n. 2, 182-3
WOOLLEY, [Robert], broker: advises
P on Dutch prize-goods, 6/250, 254;
7/140; social: 5/94; 7/366, 385; 9/334;
~ his pretty wife, 7/345, 366; 9/334
WOOLWICH (Woolwige), Kent [see
also Acworth, W.; Bodham, W.;
Deane, A.; Falconer, J.; Pett, Christopher; Sheldon, W.; Ships: Royal
Catherine; Royal James]:
TOWN [for P/EP's stay in Plague, see
Sheldon, W.]: P/EP visit(s), 2/121;
4/149, 219; 5/45; Plague, 6/189, 282,
309-10; EP gathers May-dew, 8/240-
2 passim; White Hart, 3/150, 214;
4/64, 8/95; story of old woman,
9/221; also, 9/555
DOCKYARD: general: guard, 2/11, 13-
14; 7/275; thefts, 3/137 & n. 2; 4/236;
6/183-4; King visits, 3/265; corruption etc., 4/19, 79; quarrels between
Deane and Christopher Pett, 4/384,
?396; float, 5/130 & n.; purchase of
ground, 5/190-1 & n.; men laid off,
5/194 & n. 1; rope-stores, 5/325; projected mast-dock, 6/162 & n. 1, 184;
workmen sent to Fire, 7/274, 276;
fortifications, 8/266, 270, 284-5, 313
& n. 1, 350 & n. 1; war wounded
quartered at, 8/403; also, 3/170;
visits by P (sometimes with colleagues) on official business: inspects
wreck, 1/315, 316; studies or inspects
cordage/visits ropeyard, 2/14; 3/101,
136, 142, 145, 150, 156, 159, 179, 214;
4/64, 65, 79; 5/24, 130, 182 & n. 2,
190-1, 231, 253; 7/250; inspects
frames for Navy Office houses, 3/102
& n. 1; storehouses, 3/136 & n. 1, 188;
masts, 4/50; flags, 4/151; ironwork,
4/64; 5/75; new building, 4/284 & n.
2; hemp ship, 4/405; prize ship,

7/352 & n. 1; ballast wharf, 8/95; and
fortifications, 8/284-5; shipping business: 2/104, 112; 3/63, 150; 4/20,
102-3, 131; 5/136-7, 146-7, 155, 156,
165, 265, 305, 306; 7/153; 8/124, 257;
criticises survey, 3/150-1; musters
yard, 3/179 & n. 2, 214; 4/241 & n. 1;
reduces pay, 3/201; introduces new
call books, 3/289; also, 2/36; 3/19, 31;
4/67, 235, 254, 302, 425; 5/24, 39, 54,
95, 109, 192-3, 213, 262, 325, 357;
6/74, 93, 96, 111, 128; 7/149, 168;
8/84, 176; visits by P's colleagues on
official business: sale, 2/50 & n. 2;
musters, 3/188; pay, 3/201 & n. 1;
also, 1/313, 319; 2/36; 4/204
WOOTON: see Wotton, [William]
WORCESTER, Marquess of: see
Somerset
WORCESTER: Charles II's escape
after battle, 1/155-6 & n.; 8/526; King
Edgar's charter, 6/81 & n. 1
WORCESTER HOUSE, Strand,
Clarendon's residence 1660-6: P
visits, 1/198, 199, 225, 226; 2/157;
5/204-5; 7/107; Chancery cases at,
5/203-4, 205; Privy Council at, 5/114;
7/107; Great Hall, 1/226; 5/204;
garden, 5/205
[WORCESTER HOUSE], near Ewell,
Surrey: P visits, 6/312 & n. 2
WORSHIP, Mrs ——: at musical
evenings, 6/320-1, 323; 7/73; widowed, 8/58; dines with P, 8/157;
alluded to: 6/215
WORSHIP, Mrs ——, daughter of the
foregoing: sings well, 6/137, 215;
companion to Lady Vyner, 6/215; at
musical evenings, 6/320, 323; 7/73;
dines with P, 8/157
WOSTENHAM: see Wolstenholme
WOTTON, Charles Henry Kirk-
hoven, 3rd Baron Wotton, cr. Earl of
Bellomont (Ireland) 1680 (d. 1683):
house and garden, 9/281 & n. 4
WOTTON, Sir Henry, diplomatist
and poet, ambassador to Venice 1604-
12, 1616-19, 1621-4 (d. 1639): gives
picture of Venice to Eton, 7/60 & n. 2;
tomb and inscription, ib. & n. 5
WOTTON, [William], shoemaker,
Fleet St: work for P, 1/26, 81, 94;
3/204, 217; 4/28; 7/12; 9/295;

theatrical news from, 1/59; 3/204; 4/239, 347, 411; also, 1/24, 86; 3/94, 290; 4/426; 5/90; 8/136, 599; 9/452
WREN, Christopher, kted 1673: perspective machine, 7/51 & n. 4; 9/537-8 & n., 548; views Streeter's paintings, 9/434; appointed Surveyor of King's Works, 9/491 & n. 3; social: 8/64
WREN, Matthew, Bishop of Ely 1638–d.67: at Whitehall chapel, 1/186 & n. 5; also, 2/74
WREN, Matthew, secretary to Clarendon 1660–7; to the Duke of York 1667–72 [*see also* Books]:
EARLY CAREER: approves of P's memorandum on Fishery, 5/315; accused of corruption as Clarendon's secretary, 7/342 & n. 1; also, 6/79
SECRETARY TO THE DUKE OF YORK AS LORD HIGH ADMIRAL: appointment: 8/414, 419, 424; begins duties, 8/420, 431; resolved to attend Board regularly, 8/440; and not to sell offices, 8/447; business: warrant for *Maybolt*, 8/441, 479; shortage of money, 8/454; lists for parliament, 8/493; Albemarle's narrative, 9/5; bungles navy estimates in Commons, 9/93; appointment of B. St Michel as Muster-Master, 9/247; and of Navy Commissioners, 9/441; investigation of alleged embezzlement, 9/281 & n. 3, 291; P's report on faults of office, 9/287, 289–92 passim, 301, 305, 306, 308, 338, 344, 349, 360, 370, 374; appointment of storekeeper, 9/327; suspension of Anglesey, 9/340-1, 345; storekeeper's accounts, 9/474; also, 8/298; 9/382, 481; unspecified, 9/190, 406, 473, 486, 494; ~ lodgings at St James's, 9/330, 332
POLITICAL: critical of court party in Commons, 7/408; and of court, 9/319; news of Clarendon's fall, 8/24, 527, 563; attends conference on Clarendon's impeachment, 8/551; attempts to mediate between Clarendon and Buckingham, 9/361; account of Buckingham faction, 9/375, 447-8 & nn.; other news from parliament, 9/95, 416, 426; and from court, 9/140, 489, 491
SOCIAL: 7/38, 68, 404; 8/284-5, 394,

431; 9/280, 410–11, 550, 554
ALLUDED TO: 9/173, 273, 350, 518
WREN, ——, naval officer: 9/160
[WRICKLEMARSH, Kent]: T. Blount's house and vineyard, 6/94 & n. 3; alluded to: 6/213
WRIGHT, [Anne], Lady Wright, wife of Sir Henry: witty but conceited, 2/217 & n. 1; entrusted with Sandwich's letters, 1/32, 57; at investiture of peers, 2/79–80; views on fashion, 2/226, 230; social: sings to harpsichord, 2/104; plays billiards, 6/160; also, 1/26; 3/76; 4/25, 46, 47; 6/159; 7/17; 8/99; alluded to: 1/47, 176; ~ her little daughter, 6/160; her chaplain, 6/160; his death from plague, 6/174
WRIGHT, [?Anne], cousin of Sir Henry: at christening, 4/83; suggested as bride for J. Creed, 5/286
WRIGHT, Sir Henry, of Dagnams, Essex, Sandwich's brother-in-law: elected M.P. for Harwich, 1/98 & n. 3; goes to Holland, 1/135; at his London house, 1/41, 71, 84, 87, 93, 182, 288, 323; coach, 1/95; death, 4/411 & n. 3; also, 1/36; 2/153; social: 1/177; 3/12
WRIGHT, John, of Brentwood, Essex: recommends preacher, 1/86; on board *Royal Charles*, 1/171; maid ill of suspected plague, 6/181; ~ his pretty wife, 1/71; 6/181
WRIGHT, John Michael, painter (d. ?1700): P's opinion of his work, 3/113 & n. 4
WRIGHT, [?Laurence], physician: at The Hague, 1/149
WRIGHT, Nan: *see* Markham
WRIOTHESLEY, Thomas, 4th Earl of Southampton, Lord Treasurer 1660–d. 67:
CHARACTER AND REPUTATION: goodness and piety, 4/138; 8/213, 219, 222; honesty and loyalty, 4/389; 8/222; inefficiency, 6/218; 7/313; 8/179, 219, 230, 537; 9/40; Coventry's high opinion, 9/448, 489–90
AT THE TREASURY: appointed Commissioner, 1/170 & n. 3; takes office as Treasurer, 2/31 & n. 3; resignation/replacement rumoured, 4/137-8 & n.;

8/96 & n. 2; 9/476; *business: general*:
fixes revenue assignments, 3/297 & n.
1; warns King of bankruptcy, 5/69;
advice about customs administration,
5/70 & n. 2; wants Customs House
moved to Westminster, 7/280; faulty
drafting of poll bill, 8/66–7 & n.;
navy: correspondence with Navy
Board, 3/6 & n. 2, 179 & n. 4, 250,
258, 261, 277–81 passim & nn.;
allocates annual grant, 3/297; dis-
cusses/examines accounts, 4/121 & n.
2, 306; 6/72 & n. 1; 7/294 & n. 1, 295,
313, 356; expenses/debts, 5/325, 326;
7/48; parliamentary estimates, 5/327;
money for, 6/72, 78; 7/125, 383–4;
also, 2/221; 4/395; 8/140; *Tangier*:
signs P's commission as treasurer,
6/83–4 & n.; enquires into Peterborough's accounts, 6/90, 92; issues
tallies, 6/92, 95, 137, 139: 7/117, 118,
137; attends committee for first time,
6/139; attempts to borrow from
bankers, 6/119–20, 121; P applies to
for money, 6/154; 7/381–4 passim;
unspecified: 7/111, 120, 240
POLITICAL: advice to Clarendon, 4/367;
ally of Sandwich, 7/54; opposes
Dutch war, 9/489–90 & n.; advice to
King on indemnity bill (1660), 9/490
& n. 3; at Cabinet/Council, 5/317;
6/78, 104–5; 7/260, 312; Cabinet
meets at his house, 8/80, 117, 138, 149
HIS PROPERTY ETC.: house [in Blooms-
bury], 3/51; 5/83 & n. 1; 8/138;
garden, 7/191; estate at Titchfield,
Hants., 3/70; building scheme in
Bloomsbury, 5/286 & n. 2; presents
Stillingfleet to St Andrew's, Holborn,
6/87 & n. 1; long finger-nails, 4/389
ILLNESS AND DEATH: has gout, 4/389;
7/43; the stone, 8/189, 190, 191;
shown P's stone, 8/198; last illness,
8/180, 181, 193, 195, 197, 202–3, 205,
213, 216; death, 8/218; porter's grief,
ib.; last words, 8/222
SOCIAL: 4/106–7
WRITINGS (P) [i.e. personal memoranda, literary exercises etc.]: his
romance *Love a Cheate*, 5/31; 'boyish'
MSS, 5/360; monthly memorandums
of things to be done, 5/227 & n. 1,
284; MS. book of tales, 4/346, 406;

5/103; 8/95; projected lampoon on
Four Days Fight, 7/207 & n. 2; projected history of ?navy, ?war, 5/177–8
& n.; 9/26 & n. 1; *Memoires relating to
the state of the navy* (1690), vol. i, p.
xxxviii
WYARD (Wiard), ——, surgeon, of
Plymouth, Devon: 3/70; ~ his wife,
ib.
WYLD, Dorothy: *see* Pickering
WYLD (Wilde, Wiles), Elizabeth: at
P's stone-feast, 6/124; Roger P
thinks of marrying, 8/365 & n. 2
WYNDHAM, [Christabella], governess to future Charles II: influence,
6/316 & n. 3
WYNDHAM, Col. [Edmund], husband of Christabella: 6/300, 316
WYNDHAM, [John]: killed in action,
6/196
WYNN, [Rowland], E. India merchant: 9/193 & n. 1
WYNN (Win), [Thomas]: Chancery
case concerning, 5/140 & n. 1
[?WYNNE, Henry], mathematical-
instrument maker, Chancery Lane:
9/437 & n. 3

YARD, ——, merchant: 6/296
YARMOUTH, Great, Norf.: 6/315;
8/322 & n. 2
YATES, Mrs ——, of the Theatre
Royal: 8/430
YEABSLEY, [Thomas], victualler, of
Plymouth, Devon: Tangier victualling contract, 5/210 & n. 3, 214; 6/201;
7/156, 162, 163; 8/438, 513; his bill,
6/58; accounts, 6/203–4; 7/110, 115,
121, 167, 168; 8/461, 483, 491, 513,
515; alleged bribery of Lord Ashley,
7/128 & n. 3, 129, 137, 156; 8/445,
446; accused of cheating, 9/262, 297–
8; social: 8/511
YELLING, Hunts.: P at, 2/148
YELVERTON, Sir Henry, P's schoolfellow: presents address to Rump,
1/73 & n. 1; elected M.P. for Northamptonshire, 1/116; praises P's parliamentary speech, 9/122–3; 'a wise
man', 9/123; news from, ib.
YORK: 5/13, 233
YORK BUILDINGS, Westminster:
P's house, vol. i, p. xxxviii

LIST OF ILLUSTRATIONS IN VOLUMES I TO IX

BIBLIOGRAPHY

In the footnotes to the text of the diary, references to printed books are usually given in a deliberately brief form. Further details, where necessary, are therefore given here. Books listed under 'Editorial Abbreviations' in volumes i and x are not included. Titles are in some cases abbreviated. The place of publication is London unless otherwise stated.

Abbott, Wilbur C., *Conflicts with oblivion*, Cambridge, Mass. 1935

Adair, John E., *Roundhead General: Sir William Waller*, 1969

Adams, John Q., *Dramatic records of Sir Henry Herbert 1623–73*, New Haven, Conn. 1917

Addison, Sir William, *Audley End*, 1953
  English fairs and markets, 1953

Ailesbury, Earl of, *Memoirs* (ed. Buckley), 2 vols. Roxburghe Club 1890

Albion, Robert G., *Forest and sea power . . . 1652–1862*, Cambridge, Mass. 1926

Anderson, Matthew S., *Britain's discovery of Russia 1553–1815*, 1958

Anderson, Roger C., *Lists of men-of-war 1650–1700*, pt i, *English Ships 1649–1702* (Soc. Naut. Research), Cambridge 1939

Anderson, Roger C. and R., *Sailing Ships*, 1947

André, Louis, *Michel le Tellier et Louvois*, Paris 1943

Andrews, Charles M., *British committees of trade 1622–75*, Baltimore 1908

Andrews, William, *Bygone Punishments*, Hull 1890

Arber, Edward (ed.), *The Term Catalogues 1668–1709*, 3 vols., 1903–6

Arlington, Earl of, *Letters to Sir William Temple [1665–70]*, (ed. T. Bebington), 1701

Ashley, Maurice P., *Financial and commercial policy under the Protectorate*, Oxford 1934
  John Wildman, 1947

Ashton, John, *History of English lotteries*, 1893
  History of gambling in England, 1898
  Hyde Park, 1896

Atkinson, Thomas D. (intro. by J. W. Clark), *Cambridge described and illustrated*, 1897

Auerbach, Bertrand, *La France et le Saint-Empire Romain*, Paris 1912

Aylmer, Gerald E., *The King's servants: the civil service of Charles I*, 1961

Aylward, James de V., *The smallsword in England*, 1945

Bagwell, Richard, *Ireland under the Stuarts*, 3 vols, 1906–16

Baillie, Granville H., *Watches, their history, decoration and mechanism*, 1929

Bankoft, George, *The story of surgery*, 1947

Barber, Richard W., *Samuel Pepys Esquire*, 1970

Barbour, Violet, *Henry Bennet, Earl of Arlington*, Washington, D.C. 1914
    Capitalism in Amsterdam in the 17th century, Baltimore 1950

Barlow, Edward, *Journal* (ed. Lubbock), 2 vols, 1934

Barrett, Charles R. B., *The Trinity House of Deptford Strond*, 1893

Barrow, Albert S. ('Sabretache'), *Monarchy and the chase*, 1948

Barton, Margaret, *Tunbridge Wells*, 1937

Bastide, Charles, *The Anglo-French entente in the 17th century*, 1914

Baxter, Stephen B., *The development of the Treasury 1660–1702*, 1957

Beck, William and Ball, T. F., *London Friends' Meetings*, 1869

Beckett, Ronald B., *Lely*, 1951

Beloff, Max, *Public order and popular disturbances 1660–1714*, Oxford 1938

Bent, James T., *Genoa*, 1881

Bentley, Gerald E., *The Jacobean and Caroline stage*, 7 vols, Oxford 1941–68

Beresford, John J., *The Godfather of Downing St: Sir George Downing*, 1925

Beresford, William, *Lichfield*, 1883

Bernbaum, Ernest, *The Mary Carleton narratives 1663–73*, Cambridge, Mass, 1914

Bertin, Ernest, *Les mariages dans l'ancienne société française*, Paris 1879

Beveridge, Sir William (et al.), *Prices and wages in England*, vol. i, 1939

Bewes, Wyndham A., *Church Briefs*, 1896

Birch, Walter de G. (ed.), *Cartularium Saxonicum*, 3 vols, 1883–93
    (ed.), *Historical charters of London*, 1884

Black, William G., *Folk-Medicine*, 1883

Bloch, Marc, *Les rois thaumaturges*, Strasbourg 1924

Blundell, William, *Crosby Records: A Cavalier's notebook* (ed. Gibson), 1880

Boseley, Ira, *Ministers of the Abbey Independent Church 1650–60*, 1911

Bosher, Robert S., *The making of the Restoration settlement . . . 1649–62*, 1951

Boswell, Eleanore, *The Restoration court stage*, Cambridge, Mass. 1932

Bourel de la Roncière, Charles G., *Histoire de la marine française*, Paris 1899–

Brady, W. M., *The episcopal succession in England . . . 1400–1875*, 3 vols, Rome 1876–7

Braithwaite, William C., *The beginnings of Quakerism*, 1912
    The second period of Quakerism, 1919

Brand, John, *Popular Antiquities* (ed. Hazlitt), 2 vols, 1905

Brereton, Sir W., *Travels in England* etc. (ed. Hawkins), Chetham Soc., 1844

Brett-James, Norman G., *The growth of Stuart London*, 1935

Bridge, Sir Frederick, *Samuel Pepys, lover of musique*, 1903

Brittain, Frederick, *Latin in church: the history of its pronunciation*, Alcuin Club, 1955

Broodbank, Sir Joseph G., *History of the port of London*, 2 vols, 1921

Brooke, George C., *English coins from the 7th century to the present day*, 1950

Brown, Louise F., *Political activities of Baptists etc. during the Interregnum* Washington, D.C. 1912

The first Earl of Shaftesbury, N.Y. 1933

Brown, R. Allen: *see* Colvin

Browne, Sir Thomas, *Works* (ed. Keynes), 4 vols, 1964

Browning, Andrew, *Thomas Osborne, Earl of Danby 1632–1712*, 3 vols, Glasgow 1944–51

Bulstrode Papers [newsletters from the collection of Alfred Morrison], 1897

Bund, John W. Willis (ed.), *Diary of Henry Townshend*, 2 vols, Worc. Hist. Soc., 1920

Burton, Robert, *Anatomy of melancholy* (ed. Shilleto), 3 vols, 1893

Byrom, John, *Private Journal . . .* (ed. Parkinson), 4 vols, Chetham Soc., 1854–7

Callender, Sir Geoffrey, *Portrait of Peter Pett and the Sovereign of the Seas*, Newport (I. of W.) 1930

Carl, Philipp, *Repertorium der Cometen – Astronomie*, Munich 1864

Carlton, William J., *Shorthand Books* (*Descriptive catalogue of the library of S. Pepys*, pt iv), 1940

Carr, Cecil T. (ed.), *Select charters of trading companies 1500–1707*, Selden Soc., 1913

Carte, Thomas, *Ormond*, 3 vols, 1735–6

Cavendish, Margaret, *Life of the Duke of Newcastle* (ed. Firth), 1886

Chappell, William, *Popular music of olden time*, 2 vols, 1853–9

Chapuis, Alfred and Droz, E. (trans.), *Automata*, Neuchatel 1958

Charrington, John, *Catalogue of engraved portraits in the library of S. Pepys*, Cambridge 1936

Chatterton, E. Keble, *Ship-models*, 1923

Chavagnac, Gaspard de (i.e. G. Courtilz de Sandras), *Mémoires*, Paris 1900

Chester, Joseph L., *Marriage etc. registers of . . . the . . . abbey of St Peter, Westminster*, Harl. Soc., 1876

Chéruel, Adolphe, *Histoire de la France sous Mazarin*, 3 vols, Paris 1882

Chettle, George H., *The Queen's House, Greenwich*, 1937

Christie, William D., *Shaftesbury*, 2 vols, 1871

Clark, Alexander F. B., *Boileau and the French classical critics in England 1660–1830*, Paris 1925

Clark, Alice, *The working life of women in the 17th century*, 1919

Clark, Sir George N. (and A. M. Cooke), *History of the Royal College of Physicians*, 3 vols, Oxford 1964–72

War and society in the 17th century, Cambridge 1958

Clark, John W. and Gray, A., *Old plans . . . of Cambridge 1574–1798*, Cambridge 1921

Clarke, Martin L., *Classical education in Britain 1500–1900*, Cambridge 1959

Clarke Papers (ed. Firth), 4 vols, Camden Soc., 1891–1901

Clement, Pierre, *Lettres etc. de Colbert*, 8 vols, Paris 1861–82

Cleveland, John, *Poems* (ed. Morris and Withington), Oxford 1967

Cobbett, Richard S., *Memorials of Twickenham*, 1872

Cole, Charles W., *Colbert and a century of French mercantilism*, 2 vols, N.Y. 1939

Cole, Francis J., *Early theories of sexual generation*, Oxford 1930

Coleman, Donald C., *Sir John Banks*, Oxford 1963

Collinson, John, *History of Somerset*, 3 vols, Bath 1791

Colvin, Howard M., *Biographical dictionary of English architects 1660–1840*, 1954

(ed.), *The King's Works* (vol. ii, ed. R. Allen Brown et al.)

Cooper, Charles H., *Annals of Cambridge*, 5 vols, Cambridge 1842–53
Memorials of Cambridge, 3 vols, Cambridge 1860–6

Corbett, Sir Julian S., *Drake and the Tudor navy*, 2 vols, 1899
England in the Mediterranean 1603–1713, 2 vols, 1904
(ed.) *Fighting Instructions 1530–1816*, Navy Rec. Soc., 1905

Costello, William T., *The scholastic curriculum at early 17th-century Cambridge*, Cambridge, Mass. 1958

Cowper, Francis H., *A prospect of Gray's Inn*, 1951

Craig, Sir John, *The Mint*, Cambridge 1953

Crawfurd, Sir Raymond, *The King's Evil*, Oxford 1911

Creighton, Charles, *History of epidemics in Britain*, 2 vols, 1965

Croft-Murray, Edward F., *Decorative painting in England 1537–1837*, 2 vols, 1962–70

Cunnington, Cecil W. and P., *History of underclothes*, 1951

Curtis, Mark H., *Oxford and Cambridge in transition 1558–1642*, Oxford 1959

Cussans, John E., *History of Hertfordshire* 3 vols, 1870–81

Dale, Hylton B., *The fellowship of woodmongers*, [n.d.]

Danby, Henry C., *The draining of the fens*, Cambridge 1940

Davies, Godfrey, *The restoration of Charles II 1658–60*, San Marino, Calif. 1955

Davies, John S., *History of Southampton*, 1883

Davies, Kenneth G., *The Royal African Company*, 1957

Davies, Randall R. H., *Chelsea Old Church*, 1904

Dawson, Oliver S., *The story of Wanstead Park*, [n.d.]

Defoe, Daniel, *Tour* (ed. Cole), 2 vols, 1927

Desdevises du Dézert, Georges N., *L'Espagne de l'ancien régime*, 3 vols, Paris 1897–1904

Dews, Nathan, *History of Deptford*, 1884

Dietz, Frederick C., *English public finance 1558–1641*, 1932

Dingley, Thomas, *History from marble* (ed. Nichols), Camden Soc., 1867

Dutuit, Eugène, *Manuel de l'amateur d'estampes*, vols 1, 4, 6 only pub., Paris 1881–5

East, Robert, *Extracts from the records of Portsmouth*, Portsmouth 1891

Elder, John R., *Royal fishery companies of the 17th century*, Glasgow 1912

Esdaile, Arundell J. K., *List of English tales etc. published before 1740*, 1912

Esdaile, Katharine A., *English church monuments 1510–1840*, 1946
  English monumental sculpture since the Renaissance, 1927
  Temple Church monuments, 1933

Evans, Florence M. G., *The Principal Secretary of State 1558–1680*, Manchester
  1932

Evans, Willa McC., *Henry Lawes*, N.Y. 1941

Evelyn, *Diary and Correspondence* (ed. Wheatley), 4 vols, 1879
  Miscellaneous Writings (ed. Upcott), 1825

Fagan, Louis, *Descriptive catalogue of the engraved works of William Faithorne*,
  1888

Fanshawe, Herbert C., *History of the Fanshawe family*, Newcastle upon Tyne
  1927

Feavearyear, Sir Albert E., *The pound sterling*, Oxford 1931

Feiling, Sir Keith, *History of the Tory Party 1640–1714*, Oxford 1924

Fellowes, Edmund H., *Charles I, his death, his funeral, his relics*, Windsor 1950

Fiennes, Celia, *Journeys* (ed. C. Morris), 1947

Firth, Sir Charles H. and Lomas, S. C., *Notes on the diplomatic relations of
  England and France 1603–88*, Oxford 1906

Fisher, Frederick J. (ed.), *Essays in honour of R. H. Tawney*, Cambridge 1961

Fisher, Sir Godfrey, *Barbary Legend 1415–1830*, N.Y. 1957

Foord, Alfred S., *Springs, streams and spas of London*, 1910

Forbes-Leith, William, *The Scots men-at-arms in France*, 2 vols, Edinburgh 1882

Foss, Edward, *Judges of England* [1066–1864], 9 vols, 1848–64

Foster, Joseph, *Grantees of arms* (ed. Rylands), Harl. Soc. Pub. vol. 66, 1915

Foster, Sir Michael, *Lectures on the history of physiology*, Cambridge 1901

Foster, Sir William, *English factories in India* [1618–69], 13 vols, Oxford 1906–27
  John Company, 1926

Fox, George, *Journal* (ed. Penney, rev. Nickalls), Cambridge 1952
  Short Journal (ed. Penney), Cambridge 1925

Fox, Levi (ed.), *English historical scholarship in the 16th and 17th centuries*,
  Dugdale Soc., 1956

Foxcroft, Helen C., *Life and letters of the 1st Marquis of Halifax*, 2 vols, 1898

Foxon, David F., *Libertine literature in England 1660–1745*, 1964

Franklin, Kenneth J., *A short history of physiology*, 1933

Fraser, Peter, *The intelligence of Secretaries of State 1660–88*, Cambridge 1956

Fraser, Sir William, *Memorials of the Montgomeries*, Edinburgh 1859

Freeman, Andrew J., *Father Smith*, 1926

Frost, Maurice, *English and Scottish psalm and hymn tunes c. 1543–1677*, Oxford
  1953

Fulton, Thomas W., *The sovereignty of the sea*, 1911

Funke, Otto, *Zum Weltsprachenproblem in England im 17. Jahrhundert*, Heidelberg
  1929

Gardiner, Dorothy, *The story of Lambeth Palace*, 1930

Gardiner, Samuel R., *History of the Great Civil War 1642–9*, 4 vols, 1893

Gasztowtt, Anne-Marie, *Une mission diplomatique en Pologne 1665–8*, Paris 1916

Gatty, Charles T., *Mary Davies and the manor of Ebury*, 1921

Gelder, Hendrik E. van, *'s Gravenhage in zeven eeuwen*, Amsterdam 1937

George, John N., *English pistols and revolvers*, Onslow Co., N.C. 1938

George, Mary D., *English political caricatures to 1792*, Oxford 1959

Gérin, Charles, *Louis XIV et le Saint-Siège*, 2 vols, Paris 1894

Goddard, Edward H., *Wiltshire Bibliography*, [?Trowbridge] 1929

Gras, Norman S. B., *The evolution of the English corn market*, Cambridge, Mass. 1915

Gray's Inn: Pension Book 1569–1800 (ed. Fletcher), 2 vols, 1901–10

Green, Henry and Wigram, R., *Chronicles of Blackwall Yard*, 1881

Greville, Charles C. F., *Memoirs 1814–60* (ed. Strachey and Fulford), 8 vols, 1938

Gunning, Henry, *Reminiscences of Cambridge*, 2 vols, 1854

Gunther, Robert W. T., *Oxford Gardens*, Oxford 1912

Haley, Kenneth H. D., *The first Earl of Shaftesbury*, Oxford 1968

Hall, A. Rupert and Marie (eds), *Correspondence of Henry Oldenburg*, Madison 1965–

Handover, Phyllis M., *History of the London Gazette 1665–1965*, 1965

Hardacre, Paul H., *The Royalists during the Puritan Revolution*, The Hague 1956

Haring, Clarence H., *Buccaneers in the W. Indies in the 17th century*, 1910

Hart, Cyril E., *Commoners of the Dean Forest*, Gloucester 1951

   Free Miners of Dean, Gloucester 1953

Hartmann, Cyril H., *Clifford of the Cabal*, 1937

   The King my brother, 1954

   The King's friend, 1951

   La Belle Stuart, 1924

Hasted, Edward, *History and topographical survey of Kent*, pt i (ed. Drake), 1886

Hastings, James (ed.), *Encyclopaedia of religion and ethics*, Edinburgh 1908–26

Havran, Martin J., *Caroline Courtier: the life of Lord Cottington*, 1973

Hawkins, Edward et al., *Medallic illustrations of the history of Great Britain to the death of George II*, 2 vols, 1885

Hayes, Richard F., *Old Irish links with France*, Dublin 1940

Hazlitt, William C., *Old cookery books*, 1902

Herbert, Arthur S., *Historical catalogue of printed editions of the English Bible 1525–1961*, 1968

Hervey, George F. and Hems, J., *The Goldfish*, 1948

[Hill, Frank], *Sackville College*, East Grinstead 1913

Hill, George, *An historical account of the Macdonnells of Antrim*, Belfast 1873

Hind, Arthur M., *Wenceslaus Hollar and his view of London and Westminster*, 1922

Hinton, Raymond W. K., *Eastland trade and the commonweal in the 17th century*, Cambridge 1959

Hodges, Harold W. and Hughes, E. A. (eds), *Select naval documents*, Cambridge 1936

Holdsworth, Sir William, *History of English law*, 13 vols, 1922–52

Hole, Christina, *English home-life 1500–1800*, 1949

Holles, Gervase, *Memorials of the Holles family* (ed. Wood), Camden Soc., 1937

Hollond, John, *Two discourses of the Navy* (ed. Tanner), Navy Rec. Soc., 1896

Hooke, Robert, *Diary 1672–80* (ed. Robinson and Adams), 1935

Horden, John R. R., *Francis Quarles, a bibliography*, Oxford Bibliog. Soc., Oxford 1953

Hore, John P., *History of Newmarket and annals of the turf*, 3 vols, 1886

Horsefield, John K., *British monetary experiments 1650–1710*, 1960

Hoskins, Samuel E., *Charles II in the Channel Islands*, 2 vols, 1854

Houblon, Lady A. Archer, *The Houblon family*, 2 vols, 1907

Howell, James, *Epistolae Ho-Elianae or Familiar Letters* (ed. Jacobs), 2 vols, 1892

Howell, Roger, *Newcastle upon Tyne and the Puritan revolution*, Oxford 1967

Howell, Thomas B. and Howell, T. J. (eds), *A complete collection of state trials*, 34 vols, 1816–28

Hubaud, L-J., *Dissertation littéraire . . . sur deux petits poèmes*, Marseilles 1854

Hughes, George M., *History of Windsor Forest*, 1890

Hulton, Paul H. (ed.), *Drawings of England in the 17th century*, 2 vols, Walpole Soc., 1959

Humpherus, Henry, *History of the Watermen's Company*, 3 vols, [n.d.]

Hutchinson, J. R., *The press-gang afloat and ashore*, 1913

Huygens, Christiaan, *Oeuvres Complètes*, 22 vols, The Hague 1888–1950

Ingram, Bruce S. (ed.), *Three sea journals of Stuart times*, 1936

James, Percival R., *The baths of Bath in the 16th and 17th centuries*, Bristol 1938

Jewitt, Llewellyn, *Corporation plate and insignia of the cities and towns of England and Wales* (ed. Hope), 2 vols, 1895

Johnson, Basil H., *Berkeley Square to Bond Street*, 1952

Jones, E. Alfred, *Plate of St George's Chapel, Windsor Castle*, 1939

Jones, Philip E. (ed.), *The Fire Court*, 1966–

Jonge, Johan C. de, *Geschiedenis van het nederlandsche zeewesen*, 2 vols, Haarlem 1858–9

Josselin, Ralph, *Diary 1616–83* (ed. Hockliffe), Camden Soc., 1908

Josten, Conrad H. (ed.), *Elias Ashmole, his autobiographical notes etc.*, 5 vols, Oxford 1966

Judson, J. Richard, *Gerrit van Honthorst*, The Hague 1959

Jusserand, Jean A. J., *A French Ambassador*, 1892

Kaufman, Helen A., *Conscientious Cavalier: Bullen Reymes 1613–72*, 1962

Keevil, John J. et al., *Medicine and the navy, 1200–1900*, 4 vols, Edinburgh 1957–63

Kennedy, James, *The manor and parish of Hampstead*, 1906

Keynes, Sir Geoffrey (ed.), *Blood Transfusion*, Bristol 1949

Kingsford, Charles L., *The early history of Piccadilly*, Cambridge 1925

Kingston, Alfred, *East Anglia and the Great Civil War*, 1897

Kirby, Ethyn W., *William Prynne*, Cambridge, Mass. 1931

Kitchin, George, *Sir Roger L'Estrange*, 1913
Survey of burlesque and parody in English, Edinburgh 1931

Lafontaine, Henry C. de (ed.), *The King's Musick: records relating to music and musicians 1460–1700*, [1909]

Lambley, Kathleen, *The teaching of the French language in England in Tudor and Stuart times*, Manchester 1920

Lamont, William M., *Marginal Prynne, 1600–69*, 1963

Lane Poole, Rachel, *Catalogue of portraits in Oxford*, 3 vols, Oxford 1912–25

Lane Poole, Stanley, *The life of . . . Stratford Canning*, 2 vols, 1888

Lang, Jane, *The rebuilding of St Paul's after the Great Fire*, 1956

Latimer, John, *Annals of Bristol in the 17th century*, Bristol 1900

Laughton, Sir John K. (ed.), *State papers relating to the defeat of the Spanish Armada*, 2 vols, Navy Rec. Soc., 1894

Legrelle, Antoine, *La diplomatie française et la succession d'Espagne*, 4 vols, Paris 1888–92

Lemaire, Louis, *Le rachat de Dunkerque: documents inédits*, Dunkirk 1924

Lennard, Reginald V. (ed.), *Englishmen at rest and play 1558–1714*, Oxford 1931

Leuridant, Félicien, *Une ambassade du Prince de Ligne en Angleterre 1660*, Brussels 1923

Lewis, Michael A., *England's Sea-officers: the story of the naval profession*, 1939
The Spanish Armada, 1960

Lewis, Lady Theresa (ed.), *Lives of friends of Clarendon*, 3 vols, 1852

Liber Albus: the White Book of the City of London (ed. Henry T. Riley), 1861

Loisel, Gustave, *Histoire des ménageries*, Paris 1912

Lowe, Robert W., *Betterton*, 1891

Lower, Sir William, *A relation of the voyage etc. [of Charles II]*, The Hague 1660

Lubimenko, Inna, *Relations commerciales de l'Angleterre avec la Russie avant Pierre le Grand*, Paris 1934

Lufkin, Arthur W., *A history of dentistry*, 1948

Lyons, Sir Henry, *The Royal Society 1660–1940*, Cambridge 1944

McCloy, Shelby T., *French inventions of the 18th century*, Lexington, Ky 1952

McCulloch, John R. (ed.), *Select collection of early English tracts on commerce*, 1856

Macdonald, Hugh and Hargreaves, M., *Thomas Hobbes: a bibliography*, Bibliog. Soc., 1952

McDonnell, Sir Michael, *The registers of St Paul's School 1504–1748*, 1957
    The History of St Paul's School, 1909

McKisack, May, *The parliamentary representation of English boroughs during the Middle Ages*, 1932

McLachlan, Jean O., *Trade and peace with Old Spain 1667–1750*, Cambridge 1940

Maclure, Millar, *Paul's Cross sermons 1534–1642*, Toronto 1958

Madan, Francis F., *A new bibliography of the Eikon Basilike*, Oxford Bibliog. Soc., 1950

Madge, Sidney J. *The Domesday of Crown lands*, 1938

Magne, Emile, *Images de Paris sous Louis XIV*, Paris 1939

Marburg, Clara, *Mr Pepys and Mr Evelyn*, 1935

Markham, Christopher A. and Cox, J. C., *Records of Northampton*, 2 vols, 1898

Marples, Morris, *A history of football*, 1954

Martin, John B., *'The Grasshopper' in Lombard Street*, 1892

Matthews, Arnold G., *Calamy Revised*, Oxford 1934

Maxwell-Lyte, Sir Henry C., *Historical Notes on the Great Seal*, 1926

Mercier, Ernest, *Histoire de l'Afrique septentrionale*, 2 vols, Paris 1888

Millar, Sir Oliver, *Tudor, Stuart and early Georgian pictures in the collection of H.M. the Queen*, 1963

Mitchell, W. Fraser, *English pulpit oratory from Andrewes to Tillotson*, 1932

Monson, Sir William, *Naval Tracts* (ed. Oppenheim), Navy Rec. Soc., 5 vols, 1902–14

Mordaunt, John, Viscount Mordaunt, *Letter Book 1658–60* (ed. Coate), Camden Soc., 1945

Morison, Samuel E., *Harvard College in the 17th century*, 2 pts, Cambridge, Mass. 1936

Morley, Henry, *Memoirs of Bartholomew Fair*, 1859

Muddiman, Joseph G., *A history of English journalism [to 1666]*, 1908
    (ed.) *The trial of Charles I*, 1928

Mullinger, James B., *Cambridge characteristics in the 17th century*, Cambridge 1867

Neale, Sir John, *The Elizabethan House of Commons*, 1950

Needham, Raymond and Webster, A., *Somerset House*, 1905

Nef, John U., *The rise of the British coal industry 1550–1700*, 2 vols, 1932

Nethercot, Arthur H., *Abraham Cowley*, 1931

Nettel, Reginald, *Seven centuries of popular song*, 1956

Newton, Lady Evelyn C. Legh, *Lyme Letters 1660–1760*, 1925

Newton, Samuel, *Diary* (ed. Foster), Camb. Antiq. Soc., Cambridge 1890

Nicholls, Henry G., *The Forest of Dean*, 1858

Nicolson, Marjorie H. (ed.), *The Conway Letters 1642–84*, New Haven, Conn. 1930
    Pepys' diary and the new science, Charlottesville, Va. 1965

Notestein, Wallace (ed.), *The journal of Sir S. D'Ewes*, New Haven, Conn. 1923

Nuttall, Geoffrey F. and Chadwick, O., *From uniformity to unity 1662–1962*, 1962

O'Donoghue, Edward G., *Bridewell Hospital*, 1923

O'Donoghue, Freeman and Hake, H. M., *Catalogue of engraved portraits in the British Museum*, 6 vols, Oxford 1908–25

Ogg, David, *England in the reign of Charles II*, 2 vols, Oxford 1955

Oliver, Harold J., *Sir Robert Howard*, Durham, N.C. 1963

Ollard, Richard L., *The escape of Charles II after the battle of Worcester*, 1966
  Man of War: Sir Robert Holmes and the Restoration navy, 1969

Oman, Sir Charles, *The coinage of England*, 1931

Ornsby, George (ed.), *Correspondence of John Cosin*, 2 vols, Surtees Soc., Durham 1869–72

Osborne, Mary T., *Advice-to-a-painter poems 1633–1856*, Austin, Texas 1949

Overall, William H. and H. C. (eds), *Analytical index to the Remembrancia of the City of London 1579–1664*, 1878

Overton, John H., *Life in the English Church [1660–1714]*, 1885

Page, Frances M., *The estates of Crowland Abbey*, Cambridge 1934

Parkes, Joan, *Travel in England in the 17th century*, Oxford 1925

Parsons, Frederick G., *History of St Thomas's Hospital*, 3 vols, 1932–6

Pastor, Ludwig (trans.), *History of the Popes*, 1891–

Pearce, Ernest H., *Annals of Christ's Hospital*, 1901

Pearsall Smith, Logan, *The life of Sir Henry Wotton*, 2 vols, Oxford 1907

Pearson, Karl and Morant, G. M., *The portraiture of Oliver Cromwell*, 1935

Penn, William, jun., *My Irish journal 1669–70* (ed. Grubb), 1952

Penney, Norman (ed.), *Extracts from state papers relating to Friends 1654–72*, 1913

Percy, Thomas, *Reliques* (ed. Wheatley), 3 vols, 1876

Perrin, William G., *British Flags*, Cambridge 1922

Petitjean, Charles and Wickert, C., *Catalogue de l'œuvre gravé de R. Nanteuil*, Paris 1925

Petty, Sir William, *Economic Writings* (ed. Hull), 2 vols, Cambridge 1899

Petty-Southwell Correspondence 1676–87 (ed. Marquess of Lansdowne), 1928

Pevsner, Sir Nikolaus, *Buildings of England: Hertfordshire*, 1953
  (with Nairn, rev. Cherry), ib.: *Surrey*, 1971

Phillips, Frank T., *History of the Company of Cooks, London*, 1932

Picciotto, James, *Sketches of Anglo-Jewish history*, 1875

Pinks, William J., *The history of Clerkenwell*, 1881

Pinto, Vivian de Sola, *Sir Charles Sedley*, 1927

Playfair, Sir Robert, *The scourge of Christendom*, 1884

Plomer, Henry R. (with A. Esdaile), *Dictionary of printers and booksellers in England*, 2 vols, Bibliog. Soc., Oxford 1907–22

Plumb, J. H. (ed.), *Studies in social history: a tribute to G. M. Trevelyan*, 1955
Pontalis, Antonin L., *John de Witt* (trans.), 1885
Pool, Bernard, *Navy Board contracts 1660–1832*, 1966
Pooley, Charles, *Notes on the old crosses of Gloucestershire*, 1868
Porritt, Anne G. and E., *The unreformed House of Commons*, 2 vols, Cambridge 1903–9
Povah, Alfred, *Annals of St Olave, Hart St*, 1894
Powell, John R., *The navy in the English Civil War*, Hamden, Conn. 1962
Prestage, Edgar, *Diplomatic relations of Portugal 1640–68*, Watford 1925
Preston, Arthur E., *Christ's Hospital, Abingdon, almshouses, hall and portraits*, Oxford 1929
Purnell, Edward K., *Magdalene College*, Camb. Coll. Histories, 1904
Raven, Charles E., *English naturalists from Neckam to Ray*, Cambridge 1947
  John Ray, Cambridge 1942
Records of Lincoln's Inn: Black Books (ed. Baildon), 4 vols, 1897–1902
Reddaway, Thomas F., *The rebuilding of London after the Great Fire*, 1951
Redgrove, Herbert S. and I. M. L., *Joseph Glanvill and psychical research in the 17th century*, 1921
Reresby, Sir John, *Memoirs* (ed. Browning), Glasgow 1936
Rex, Mildred B., *University representation in England 1604–90*, 1954
Riemer, Jacob de, *Beschryving van 's Gravenhage*, 2 vols, Delft and The Hague 1730–9
Roberts, Clayton, *The growth of responsible government in Stuart England*, Cambridge 1966
Rogers, James E. T., *History of agriculture and prices in England 1259–1793*, 7 vols, Oxford 1866–1902
Rogers, Philip G., *The Dutch in the Medway*, 1970
Rohde, Eleanour S. (ed.), *The garden book of Sir T. Hanmer*, 1933
Rollins, Hyder E. (ed.), *A Pepysian garland*, Cambridge 1922
Roncière: *see* Bourel de la Roncière
Rose-Troup, Frances, *The Western rebellion of 1549*, 1913
Roseveare, Henry, *The Treasury*, 1969
Rouse Ball, Walter W., *Notes on the history of Trinity College, Cambridge*, 1899
Roxburghe Ballads (ed. William Chappell and J. W. Ebsworth), 9 vols, Hertford 1871–99
Russell, J. M., *History of Maidstone*, Maidstone 1881
Savile Correspondence (ed. William D. Cooper), Camden Soc., 1858
Sayle, Robert T. D., *The barges of the Merchant Taylors' Company*, 1933
  Lord Mayors' pageants of the Merchant Taylors' Company, Reading 1931
Scholes, Percy A., *The puritans and music in England and New England*, 1934
Scott, James R., *Memorials of the family of Scott of Scot's Hall*, 1876
Scott, Sir William R., *Joint-stock companies to 1720*, 3 vols, Cambridge 1910–12
Selden, John, *Table Talk* (ed. Pollock), 1927

Sergison Papers (ed. Merriman), Navy Rec. Soc., 1950

Shaw, William A., *The Knights of England*, 2 vols, 1906

Shrewsbury, John F. D., *The history of bubonic plague in the British Isles*, Cambridge 1970

Simon, André L., *Bottlescrew days: wine-drinking in England during the 18th century*, 1926
 History of the wine trade in England, 3 vols, 1907–9

Simpson, Claude M., *The British broadside ballad and its music*, New Brunswick, N.J. 1966

Singer, Charles J, et al. (eds), *History of Technology*, 5 vols, Oxford 1954–8

Slothouwer, D. F., *De paleizen van Frederik Hendrik*, Leiden [1946]

Smith, Adam, *The wealth of nations* (ed. Cannan), 2 vols, 1904

Smith, Frederick F., *History of Rochester*, Rochester 1928

Smith, H. Maynard (ed.), *The early life of John Evelyn*, Oxford 1920

Smyth, Charles H. E., *Church and parish: studies in the history of St Margaret's Westminster*, 1955

Smyth, John, *The Berkeley manuscripts: the lives of the Berkeleys* (ed. Maclean), 3 vols, Gloucester 1883–5

[*Somers Tracts*], ed. Walter Scott, 13 vols, 1809–15

Speaight, George G., *The history of the English puppet theatre*, 1955

Speed, John, *History of Southampton* (ed. Aubrey), Southampton Rec. Soc., 1909

Spencer, Hazelton, *Shakespeare Improved: the Restoration versions in quarto and on the stage*, Cambridge, Mass. 1927

Steinman, George S., *A memoir of Barbara, Duchess of Cleveland* (with Addenda), Oxford 1871–8

Stern, Walter M., *The porters of London*, 1960

Straker, Ernest, *Wealden Iron*, 1931

Straus, Ralph, *Carriages and coaches*, 1912

Strode, William, *Poetical Works* (ed. Dobell), 1907

Strong, Sir Roy, *Holbein and Henry VIII*, 1967

Stuart, Dorothy M., *The English Abigail*, 1946

Summers, Montague, *The Playhouse of Pepys*, 1935
 The Restoration Theatre, 1934

Summerson, Sir John, *Architecture in Britain 1530–1830*, 1953

Symonds, Richard, *Diary of the marches of the royal army* [1644–5] (ed. Long), Camden Soc., 1859

Swart, Koenraad W., *Sale of offices in the 17th century*, The Hague 1949

Sykes, Norman, *From Sheldon to Secker*, Cambridge 1969

Tanner, James R., *Samuel Pepys and the Royal Navy*, Cambridge 1920

Tate, William E., *The parish chest*, Cambridge 1951

Thompson, Edward M., *Correspondence of the family of Hatton 1601–1704*, 2 vols, Camden Soc., 1878

Thomson, Gladys S., *Life in a noble household 1641–1700*, 1937

Thomson, Mark A., *Constitutional history of England 1642–1801*, 1938

Thorn-Drury, George (ed.), *A little ark of 17th century verse*, 1921

Thorndike, Lynn, *History of magic*, 8 vols, London, 1923–58

Thornton, Archibald P., *West India policy under the Restoration*, Oxford 1956

Thurloe, John, *Collection of state papers* (ed. T. Birch), 7 vols, 1742

Tibbutt, Harry G., *Life and letters of Sir Lewis Dyve 1599–1669*, Beds. Hist. Soc., Streatley 1948

Tighe, Robert R. and Davis, J. E., *Annals of Windsor*, 1858

Townshend, Henry, *Diary* (ed. J. W. Willis Bund), Worc. Hist. Soc., 1920

Turnbull, George H., *Hartlib, Dury, and Comenius*, Liverpool 1947

Turner, Edward R., *The Privy Council 1603–1784*, 2 vols, Baltimore 1927–8

Turner, Francis C., *James II*, 1948

Turner, G. Lyon, *Original records of early nonconformity*, 3 vols, 1911–14

Uffenbach, Z. C. von, *London in 1710* (ed. Quarrell and Mare), 1934

Underwood, Edgar A. (ed.), *Science, medicine and history*, 2 vols, 1953

Varley, Frederick J., *Oliver Cromwell's latter end*, 1939

Vertue, George, *Notebooks*, 7 vols, Walpole Soc., Oxford 1930–55

Villari, Luigi, *The Republic of Ragusa*, 1904

Vincent, William A. L., *The state and school education, 1640–60, in England and Wales*, 1950

Wagner, Sir Anthony R., *Historical heraldry of Britain*, 1939
  Records and collections of the College of Arms, 1952

Walford, Edward, *Greater London, its history etc.* 2 vols, [n.d.]

Walpole, Horace, *Anecdotes of painting* (ed. Wornum), 3 vols, 1849
  Correspondence (ed. Lewis et al.), New Haven, Conn. 1937–

Wardale, John R. (ed.), *Clare College letters and documents*, Cambridge 1903

Warner, Sir George F. (ed.), *The Nicholas Papers*, 4 vols, Camden Soc., 1886–1920

Warnsinck, Johan C. M., *De retourvloot van Pieter de Bitter*, The Hague 1929

Watson, Foster, *English grammar schools to 1660*, Cambridge 1908

Weiss, D. G., *Samuel Pepys, curioso*

Westergaard, W. (ed.), *The First Triple Alliance 1668–72*, New Haven, Conn. 1947

Westrup, Sir Jack A., *Henry Purcell*, 1960

Wheatley, Henry B., *Samuel Pepys and the world he lived in*, 1880

Whitaker, Wilfred B., *Sunday in Tudor and Stuart times*, 1933

White, Eric W., *The rise of English opera*, 1951

Whitelocke, Bulstrode, *Memorials of the English affairs [1625–60]*, 4 vols, Oxford 1853

Whiting, Charles E., *Studies in English puritanism 1660–88*, 1931

Wickham Legg, John and Hope, W. H. St J. (eds), *Inventories of Christchurch Canterbury*, 1902

Wickham Legg, Leopold G., *English coronation records*, 1901

Wilks, George, *The Barons of the Cinque Ports*, Folkestone 1892

Willcox, William B., *Gloucestershire 1590–1640*, New Haven, Conn. 1940

Williams, J. B. (J. G. Muddiman), *History of English journalism to* [*1666*], 1908

Williams, Neville J., *Powder and paint*, 1957

Williamson, J. Bruce, *History of the Temple*, 1924

Willis, Robert and Clark, J. W., *Architectural history of Cambridge*, 4 vols, Cambridge 1886

Wilson, John H., *Nell Gwyn*, New York 1952
  A rake and his times: George Villiers, 2nd Duke of Buckingham, New York 1954

Winstanley, Denys A., *Unreformed Cambridge*, Cambridge 1935

Withington, Robert, *English Pageantry*, Cambridge, Mass. 1918

Wolf, Abraham, *History of science etc, in the 16th and 17th centuries*, 1950

Wood, Alfred C., *Nottinghamshire in the Civil War*, Oxford 1937

Woodfill, Walter L., *Musicians in English society from Elizabeth to Charles I*, Princeton, N.J. 1953

Woodruff, Charles E. and Danks, W., *Memorials of Canterbury*, 1912

Woodward, John, *Tudor and Stuart drawings*, 1951

Wright, Arthur R. (ed. Lones), *British calendar customs: England*, 3 vols, Folk Lore Soc., 1936–40

Wright, Lawrence, *Clean and decent*, 1962
  Warm and snug, 1960

Yonge, James, *Journal* (ed. Poynter), 1963

Young, Sidney, *Annals of the Barber-Surgeons of London*, 1890

Zook, George F., *The Company of the Royal Adventurers trading into Africa*, Lancaster, Pa. 1919

CORRECTIONS, VOLUMES I TO IX

[Some of these corrections have been made in the reprints issued since 1971. Oblique lines are used to separate the corrigenda from the corrections. A minus sign before a line number indicates its position above the bottom line.]

VOLUME I

Preface and Introduction
p. xiii, l. −7: X/XI
p. xxi, ll. 6–7: Boughton, North-amptonshire/Kimbolton, Huntingdonshire
p. xxxvi, l. 9: depts/debts
p. l, l. 13: September/October
p. lxii, l. 21: 16 March/8 March
p. lxix, l. −2 & n. 11, l. 4: January/December
p. lxxiv, l. −7: 'Cuppe'/'Cupp'
l. −6: 'tee'/'Tee'
p. lxxxix, l. 11: 15 May/18 May
p. xc, l. −6: than/that
p. cx, l. 16: Richard/William
p. cxliv, l. 15: *delete* 'about 3000'
l. −3: Fot/For

Text
p. 15, l. 4: *add* '[Crew]' *after* 'Walgrave'
p. 44, l. 6: *add* asterisk *after* 'Palace'
p. 56, l. −4: *add* '[Crew]' *after* 'Walgrave'
p. 85, 12 March, l. 1: rise/ris
p. 207, l. 12: *delete* asterisk

Select Glossary
BALLET: *delete* 'broadside' (recurrent)

CAUDLE: *add* 'made with wine' (recurrent)

Notes
p. 16, n. 1, l. 4: Henry/Herbert
p. 25, n. 4, l. 2: violonist/violinist
p. 49, n. 4, l. 1: *add* '[Girolamo Franzini],' *before 'Las'*
p. 54, n. 1, l. 5: Joseph/Joshua (recurrent)
p. 70, n. 4, l. 2: Much Munden/Great Munden
p. 80, n. 3, l. 1: n. 6/n. 5
p. 87, n. 1, l. 5: borough/county
p. 105, n. 3: *replace by* 'The 16th-century artillery forts of Walmer, Deal, and Sandown.'
p. 140, n. 4: *add* 'The *Novum Organum;'* *before* 'probably'
p. 183, n. 2, l. 4: 94/203
p. 197: *delete* note *a*
p. 267, n. 4, l. 4: it/she (recurrent)
p. 272, n. 3, l. 4: 1672/1673
p. 314, n. 2, l. 4: 14/114
p. 334, l. 6 (St Michel): Mary/Dorothea (recurrent)
l. 22 (Trice): half/step (recurrent)

VOLUME II

Text
p. 67, 7 April, l. −1: Battnes/Battens
p. 124, l. 3: her/him (MS. 'her')
p. 197, l. 14: *delete* semi-colon
p. 203, l. 2: Therobo/Theorbo
p. 240, 28 December, l. 3: *delete* 'too' (MS. 'into to')

Notes
p. 6, n. 3, l. 5: *delete* 'well'
p. 41, n. 2, l. −1: June/January
p. 43, n. 2: p. 62; 17 December 1665/pp. 62–3 & n.; vii. 32

p. 58, n. 5: James/Benjamin
p. 110, n. 2, l. 2: 4th/2nd
p. 132, n. 1, l. 3: 72/74
p. 137, n. 2, l. 1: Kt/cr. bt 1662
p. 146, n. 1: *delete* note
p. 160, n. 3, l. 1: sailed . . . 1662/in July returned from W. Africa
p. 165, n. 1, l. 3: Chapeton/Chapoton
p. 192, n. 5: Josias/James
p. 198, n. 3: George/?Richard
n. 4, last line: Committee/Corporation
p. 204, n. 1, l. 6: Yarrington/Yarranton

p. 217, n. 1, l. 3: Pepys/Sandwich
p. 239, n. 4: *replace by* 'This is said to be the first known instance of a record of a Marian apparition. The

saint was St Gregory Thaumaturgus (c. 213–c. 270): F. L. Cross, *Oxf. Dict. Christian Church* (Oxf. 1974), p. 601.'

VOLUME III

Text
p. 3, 5 January, l. 3: beef./beef,
p. 64, l. —9: Warren/Batten (MS. 'Warren')
p. 78, l. —5: Lue[ll]in/Luein
p. 83, last line: me,/met
p. 105, l. 2: form/from
p. 120, 25 June, l. 6: ships/shops
p. 158, l. 1: *add* superior 1 after 'perticularly'
p. 171, l. 17: Sandwiches/Sandwich (MS. 'Sandwiches')
p. 174, 23 August, l. 1: words/works
p. 194, l. 2: γχ/ούχ
p. 228, 19 October, l. 7: by/be
p. 237, l. 8: jealouses/jealousys
p. 243, l. 8: should not/should (MS. 'should not')
p. 285, l. 12: for/from (MS. 'for') 17 December, l. 4: if/it
p. 300,   l. 4: *delete* comma *after* 'Gauden'

Notes
p. 9, n. 3, l. 3: *delete* 'blown'
p. 14, n. 3, l. 6: five/c. fifty
p. 15, n. 2, l. 1: Huntingdon/Dover
p. 30, n. 3, last line: 216/214
p. 44, n. 2, l. 1: Olwin/Oliver
p. 52, n. 1, l. 5: 1686/1676
p. 85, n. 1, l. 2: 1682/1681
p. 113, n. 3, l. 8: 10 July 1664/vii. 359 & n. 3

p. 142, n. 3, l. 7: below,/above, l. 8: 13 February 1665 & n./p. 137 & n. 3
p. 159, n. 2: *replace by* 'Millicent, of Barham, Cambs., was said to be "the best extemporary fool" at James's court: A. Weldon, *Court . . . of James I* (1650), p. 92. James's monopolies had been notorious'.
p. 173, n. 1, ll, 1–2: i. 222 & n. 1/ii. 179 & n. 1
p. 194, n. 1, ll. 1–4: *Replace by* 'Dr R. Luckett writes: Pepys is loosely paraphrasing, or inaccurately recalling, Epictetus (*Encheiridion* I. i): τῶν ὄντων τὰ μέν ἐστιν ἐφ᾿ ἡμῖν, τὰ δὲ οὐκ ἐφ᾿ ἡμῖν ('Of things, some are in our power, others are not'). He accidentally writes οὐχ for οὐκ (he intended τὰ ἐφ᾿ ἡμῖν καὶ τὰ οὐκ ἐφ᾿ ἡμῖν); the slip is a natural one given the extensive use of ligatures in the seventeenth century. That it was a consequence of accident rather than ignorance is demonstrated by his correct rendering of οὐκ at iv. 16.'
p. 221, n. 1: 205/204 & n. 2
p. 232, n. 1, ll. 1–2: below, 15 October 1666 & n./above, ii. 195, n. 3
p. 235, n. 3, l. 3: some/two
p. 270, n. 4, l. 2: 1708/1713
p. 303, n. 2, l. 2: 221/222

VOLUME IV

Text
p. 16, l. 3: ἐφ ηνῖϋ/ἐφ᾿ ἡμιῦ
p. 61, 28 February, l. 4.: Batten/ Warren (MS. 'Batten')
p. 75, l. —4: *repunctuate* sees, and saith,
p. 98, l. 3: *add* '[?plain]' *after* 'most'
p. 118, l. —5: wood/woo'd
p. 133, l. 7: up,/up [to]
p. 144, l. —5: over/*over*
p. 145, l. 9: leade/gold (MS. 'leade')
p. 155, l. 3: fist/first

p. 298, 4 September, l. —5: place and/ placed at (MS. 'place and')
p. 366, l. 13: Lord it/Lord in
p. 367, l. —2: *add* '[him]' *after* 'have'
p. 369, l. 7: Hear/Here
p. 380, l. —2: rooms/room
p. 386, last line: *transpose* 'I pray' *to* beginning of l. 1 p.389
p. 405, 5 December, l. 3: *repunctuate* 'Allen home to dinner,'
p. 409, l. —1: *repunctuate* 'and I,'

p. 428, l. 3: this/these (MS. 'this')
p. 436, 29 December, l. 12: not/nor (MS. 'not')

Notes
p. 17, n. 1: *delete* note
p. 20, n. 2, l. 1: 7/6
p. 25, n. 1, ll. 3–4: Sir William Berkeley/Sir Charles Berkeley, jun.
p. 37, n. 3: *add* ',1660' *after* 'borough'
p. 41, n. 5, l. 4: St Jago/Santiago
p. 73, n. 1, l. 10: Solebay/Lowestoft
p. 75, n. 3, l. 6: 68/61
p. 91, n. 1: *replace first sentence by* 'The stempiece was the main vertical timber of the bow'.
p. 95, n. 3, l. −5: during the Interregnum/in the 1620s
p. 105, n. 2, l. −1: 1663/1652
p. 119, n. 2, l. 5: Sturtlow/Stirtloe
p. 126, n. 2, l. 12: not/nor
p. 159, n. 4: Should be n. 1, p. 160 and should read 'See below, p. 243 & n. 3'
p. 164, n. 2: milk/cold milk
p. 187, n. 3, l. 1: *add* 'eldest' *before* 'sons'
p. 210, n. 1: *add* '*Recte* manslaughter.' *before* 'See'
p. 235, n. 2: *replace* last sentence *by*

'PL 1075(11).'
p. 255, n. 1, last line: *Varii Sectiones*/ *Variæ Lectiones*
p. 304, n. 1, l. 8: 419/421
p. 308, n. 1: *replace* first sentence *by* 'Near Kettering, Northants.'
p. 312, n. 2: Huntingdon/Brampton
p. 319, n. 1: Hart St/Seething Lane
p. 320, n. 2: *delete* second sentence
p. 322, n. 1, ll. 10–11: *delete* 'and N. America'
p. 349, n. 1, ll. 5–6: *delete* 'appears . . . She'
p. 354, n. 1, l. 1: James/Benjamin
p. 363, n. 1, l. 2: 437/439
p. 372, n. 3, l. 2: excluded/extruded
p. 382, n. 3, l. 2: *replace* 'App. B, pp. 440–1' *by* 'pp. 387–8'
p. 423, n. 1: *replace by* 'Cf. B. J. Whiting, *Proverbs, sentences &c.* (Camb. Mass. 1968), item F635. The verse, in various forms, was in current use within living memory.'
p. 424, n. 2: 402/404; n. 3: 412/421
p. 435, n. 1: 393, n. 1/395, n. 2
p. 441, n. 2: *replace* 'Calabrian . . . Excelsior' *by* 'and *sal prunellæ*, with three ounces of Calabrian manna (dried sap of *Fraxinus ornus L.*)'

VOLUME V

Text
p. 7, last line: *add* '[her]' after 'commend'
p. 16, 15 January, para. 4, l. 1: with/that
p. 283, l. −6: *repunctuate* 'angry, . . . plain;'

Notes
p. 8, n. 2, ll. −3 & −2: The year date should be '1659/60'
p. 42, n. 2: *replace by* 'See above, iii. 17 & n. 1'
p. 53, n. 3, ll. 1–2: *replace by* 'At Tooting Bec (C. A. F. Meekings, ed., *Surrey Hearth Tax 1664*, 1942, p. 86).'
p. 56, n. 4: 405/407
p. 63, n. 1, l. 7: 1660/1661
p. 73, n. 5: *delete* 'trotting'
p. 116, n. 1, col. 1, l. −8: 24 May 1669/

December 1672
p. 117, n. 4, ll. 6–7: *delete* 'and . . . will'
p. 170, n. 3, l. 4: French/Spaniards
p. 184, n. 2, l. 2: *delete* 'groom-porter'
p. 189, n. 2: *replace by* 'Drawing the outline for the mould of a ship. Cf. PL2910.'
p. 190, n. 1, l. −1: hat/that
p. 237, n. 3, l. 2: *add* 'and arithmetic' *after* 'penmanship'
n. 4, l. 2: ll. 146–73/ll. 1461–3
p. 244, n. 2, l. −1: quarrel with his father/disgrace at court
p. 281, n. 1, l. 1: *delete* 'Sir'
p. 289, n. 2, ll. −5 to −2: *delete* 'Pepys . . . 162'
p. 316, n. 2: *replace by* 'Now the New Armouries'
p. 321, n. 3, l. 4: Holmes's/Nicholls's

p. 342, n. 1: Christopher Cisner/David Primerose
n. 2: *delete* queries
p. 346, n. 3, l. 11: November/

December
p. 353, n. 1, l. 4: Allin's/Holmes's
p. 361, n. 1, ll. 13–14: both ... 1680/ who died in 1680 and 1689

VOLUME VI

Text
p. 125, 12 June, l. 4: sleeve-bands/ sleeve-hands
p. 135, 23 June, l. —3: *add*, 'did give him' *after* 'Albimarle'; *delete* note *b*
p. 162, 19 July, l. 3: Falconer/Falconbridge

Notes
p. 24, n. 2, l. —1: *Office/Board*
p. 37, n. 2, l. 1: Harvey/Hervey (recurrent)
p. 41, n. 2: Charlotte/Lady Charlotte
p. 53, n. 5: v. 269 & n. 2/v. 323 & n. 2
p. 95, n. 2, l. 2: 32/34
n. 4: *delete* second sentence

p. 100, n. 5: iii. 17 & n. 2/iv. 379
n. 6: n. 1/n. 2
p. 101, n. 1, l. 5: son Samuel/cousin John
p. 102, n. 6: Wanstead/Walthamstow
p. 126, n. 1, l. 5: son/grandson
p. 149, n. 2: n. 1/n. 2
p. 152, n. 2, ll. 2–3: *delete* 'whom ... Cambridge'
p. 160, n. 1, ll. 4–5: probably ... Romford/St Peter's, South Weald
p. 163, n. 4: *alter to* 'were London merchants'
p. 166, n. 1: Greenwich tradesman/ Westminster draper
p. 279, n. 2, l. 3: *delete* 'iron'
p. 280, n. 1, l. 3: 255, n. 1/254, n. 2

VOLUME VII

Text
p. 44, l. 4: How/Hewer (MS. 'WH')
p. 107, l. —9: in/is (MS. 'in')
p. 150, l. —2: Ball/Bell (MS. 'Ball')
p. 183, l. 13: *repunctuate* 'work, so is'
p. 229, l. 11: him/it (MS. 'him')

Notes
p. 41, n. 2, l. 1: John/Edward, son of John
l. 2: *delete* 'son of'
l. 3: *delete* 'of the same name'
p. 54, n. 1, l. 3: lieutenants/rivals
p. 94, n. 6, l. 7: Herts./Hants.
p. 108, n. 4: p. 93, n. 1/p. 44, n. 2
p. 111, n. 2: iv./v.
p. 114, n. 3, l. 10: 1655/1665
p. 115, n. 2: n. 3/n. 4
p. 132, n. 3, l. —3: 220–1/385 & n. 2
p. 145, n. 7, l. 1: John/Samuel
p. 154, n. 3, l. 5: elder brother/cousin
p. 225, n. 2: Weilings/Wielings

p. 229, n. 3, l. 2: Koenders/Coenders
p. 243, n. 3, l. 3: possibly Edmond/ probably William
p. 245, n. 4, l. 4: 1662–6/1662–83
p. 271, n. 2: *alter to* 'Barbara Sheldon'
p. 290, n. 2, l. —1: 1641/?1652
p. 309, n. 1, last line: 4/3
p. 341, n. 2: *add* 'The Queen's birthday was in fact on 15 November: see below.'
p. 346, n. 1, l. 5: 1667/November 1666
p. 352, n. 5: *replace by* 'Clerk-Comptroller of the Green Cloth'
p. 375, n. 2, l. 6: Henry/William
p. 383, n. 3: *replace by* 'John Ashburnham, Groom of the Bedchamber'.
p. 385, n. 2, last line: 245 & n. 5/132 & n. 3
p. 386, n. 3, l. 5: 1654/1652
p. 391, n. 1, ll. 8–9: Henley, Som./ Bramshill, Hants.
p. 403, n. 3, l. —1: George/Charles

VOLUME VIII

Text

p. 27, l. −5: Ball/Hall (MS. 'Ball')
p. 29, l. −1: they ng/they not being
p. 73, 20 February, l. 14: *repunctuate* 'closet, all our business lack of money'
p. 111, l. −5: believe she/believes he
p. 215, 15 May, l. 13: Cholmely/ Chichely (MS. 'Ch.')
p. 239, l. 2: [?coach]/[water]
p. 270, l. 5: foretell/[did] foretell
p. 345, ll. 11 & 12: *add* comma *after* 'pretty'; *delete* comma *after* 'fast'
p. 495, l. 4: *add* comma *after* 'series'
p. 564, l. 12: Edwd/Richard (MS. 'Edwd')

Notes

p. 19, n. 2: Peter/John
p. 37, n. 2: John/James
p. 45, n. 1, l. 2: n. 3/n. 1
p. 56, n. 6: *replace by* 'Vicenzo Albrici'
p. 85, n. 3, l. −1: the borough/ Cambridge borough
p. 131, n. 1: *replace by* 'Sir William Turner.'
p. 144, n. 3, l. 3: n. 3/n. 4
p. 154, n. 2, l. 2: 1664/1665
p. 171, n. 5, l. 2: 15/13
p. 179, n. 2: *add* at beginning 'The New Armouries:'
p. 205, n. 2, l. 2: purchase/acquisition
p. 218, n. 3, l. 6: 1880/1884
p. 236, n. 2, l. −3: *Works/Writings*
p. 241, n. 1, ll. 1–3: had been a fellow ... Cambridge/had presumably been a private tutor to Brookes
p. 257, n. 5: *replace by* 'The defences of Gravesend.'
p. 265, n. 1, l. 8: *delete* 'the Presbyterian'
p. 267, n. 2: *replace by* 'Thomas Wilson, newly appointed storekeeper at Chatham.'
p. 269, n. 1: n. 2/n. 1
p. 275, n. 3: *replace by* 'Cf. below, ix. 500 & n. 1.'
n. 4, l. 2: n. 4/n. 5
p. 330, n. 5, l. 2: 3rd/1st
p. 347, n. 1: n. 5/n. 7
p. 367, n. 2: a lieutenant ... *Royal Charles*/captain of a frigate
p. 377, n. 2: [n.]4/n. 3
p. 381, n. 2: *replace by* 'In the High St.'
p. 384, n. 1, l. 2: Ferdinand III/ Leopold I
p. 418, n. 1: n. 4/n. 3
n. 3, l. −1: *delete* 'Sir'
p. 421, n. 3: *delete* note
p. 425, n. 3: who became messenger ... 1670/Groom of the Privy Chamber from 1660
p. 446, n. 6: *preface by* '?'
p. 464, n. 1, l. 5: n. 1/n. 2
p. 469, n. 1, l. 8: 1603/1626
p. 505, n. 2, l. 1: 1553/1552
p. 511, n. 3, l. −2: 1660/1666
p. 515, n. 4: 514 & n. 1/513 & n. 2
p. 526, n. 4, l. 3: Charles I/Charles II
p. 538, n. 3: Robert/John
p. 557, n. 2: n. 2/n. 4 *add* '(E)'
p. 582, n. 2, l. 2: *delete* '(Batten's son-in-law)'
p. 585, n. 6: *replace* second sentence *by* 'Ensum had died in 1666 ... Jackson'

VOLUME IX

Text

p. 12, l. −2: house/office (MS. 'house')
p. 78, l. −1: *add* comma *after* 'at it'
p. 148, last line: Aldersgate/Aldgate
p. 154, l. −9: House/[?Gate-]house
p. 158, l. 10: *delete* comma *after* 'coaches'
p. 180, l. −9: to anything/to [do] anything
p. 201, l. −2: bands/hands
p. 410, 8 January, ll. 13–14: no great/ great (MS. 'no great')
p. 411, 10 January, l. 1: *add* comma *after* 'Accidentally'

p. 429, 28 January, l. 1: afternoon/
morning (MS. 'afternoon')
p. 468, l. −1: Maids/Maid
p. 480, l. 15: Chancer/Chancery
p. 520, 15 April, l. 5: Aldersgate/
Aldgate
p. 531, 22 Apr. 1669, l. 6: given/give
p. 554, l. −9: the Bishop make himself/
the Bishop (MS. 'the Bishop make
himself')

Notes
p. 6, n. 1: discharged/dismissed
p. 83, n. 1, ll. 2, 4: 1666/1667
p. 108, n. 2, l. 4: n. 1/n. 2
p. 117, n. 3: Eliezer/Eliezer Jenkins
p. 147, n. 2: David/Daniel
p. 157, n. 2, ll. 5–6: Sir William . . .
Yorks./the late Ald. Robert Lowther
of London
p. 161, n. 2: *replace by* 'Mary Ham-
mon, Sir John Mennes's sister.'
p. 163, n. 5: *replace by* 'Of prize
goods.'
p. 184, n. 1: *delete* note

p. 207, n. 3: *delete* 'at Aubrey's
house'
p. 215, n. 3, ll. 1–3: *replace* first
sentence *by* 'Probably Viscountess
Lambart (d. 1649) an Irish acquain-
of Penn's. I owe this suggestion to
J. Ferris.'
p. 231, n. 2: n. 2/n. 1
p. 238, n. 4: 1620/1621
p. 241, n. 1: *replace by* 'All the Avebury
stones and most of those at Stonehenge were of local sarsen.'
p. 293, n. 1, l. 11: ib./id.
p. 341, n. 1, last line: 67, n. 3/64–5
p. 347, n. 1, l. 4: 1662/1661
p. 383, n. 3: 1659/?1652
p. 416, n. 1, ll. 4–5: first President/
first pre-Charter President
p. 430, n. 1, l. 1: Jennings/Jennens
n. 3, l. 2: Philip/Henry
p. 441, n. 4, l. 4: n. 4/n. 3
p. 460, n. 5, l. 5: *add* 'W. Chappell
and' *before* 'J. W. Ebsworth'
p. 506, n. 1, l. 11: 1633/1660
p. 507, n. 3: Charles . . . London/
Thomas Foulkes, Groom of the
Buckhounds

ACKNOWLEDGEMENTS, VOLUMES I TO IX

It is with deep regret that I have to record the death in 1975 of my co-editor, the late Professor William Matthews. It therefore falls to me at this point to acknowledge the debt to the large number of institutions and individuals who have assisted in the publication of the volumes of text since 1970, in addition to those whose names appear in the list of acknowledgements published in volume I:

To Magdalene College, the Trustees of the Leverhulme Foundation and the Goldsmiths' Company, for financial help without which it could not have been done.

To the late Prof. Edward Wilson of Cambridge for his translations of Pepys's Spanish; and to Esmond de Beer, Richard Ollard and MacDonald Emslie for help with the proofs.

To the archivists who have extended me every courtesy on my visits to their collections – at the Admiralty; the Berkshire County Record Office; the city of Bristol; Christ Church, Oxford; Eton College; the Goldsmiths' Company; Gray's Inn; Guildhall, London; the House of Lords; Huntingdon Borough and Huntingdonshire County Record Offices; the Mercers' Company; the Middle Temple; the National Maritime Museum; the North Yorkshire County Record Office; the University of Cambridge; the Dr Williams Library; Messrs Williams & Glyn; and the parish priests in charge of the parochial records at Brampton, Huntingdon, and St Olave's, Hart St.

To the officials I have consulted by letter – of the Victoria and Albert Museum; the Rijksmuseum, Amsterdam; the London Survey Committee of the Greater London Council; the Royal Geographical Society; the College of Heralds; the county record offices of Hertfordshire, Kent and Norfolk; the town libraries of Brentford and Chiswick, of Deal, Dover, Lambeth, Norwich, Portsmouth, Rochester, Shrewsbury, Walthamstow, Wandsworth and Woolwich; the county library of Wiltshire; the William Andrews Clark Library, Los Angeles; the Huntington Library, San Marino; St Paul's School; Westminster School and Canterbury Cathedral.

To the following for information on particular points – P. J. Adams, Dr S. O. Agrell, Lee Ash, Prof. V. Barbour, R. A. Barker, J. Berryman, M. F. Bond, Prof. W. H. Bond, Dr D. S. Brewer, Dr G. L. Broderick, Dr R. A. Brown, Prof. D. Chandaman, I. A. Crawford, Mrs P. E. Cunnington, J. Daniels, the late Prof. Alun Davies, G. Devey, Prof. G. Donaldson, Prof. K. Downes, Prof. J. D. Fage, C. Farthing, Dr P. J. Fitzpatrick, Dr D. Foxon, Miss D. Gifford, Mrs P. Glanville, the late

Prof. D. V. Glass, Dr J. Gmitro, G. H. Gollin, Sir J. Graham, Dr G. S. Graham-Smith, Rev. D. N. Griffiths, Dr R. Gwynn, Prof. J. R. Hale, Dr G. Hammersley, Miss F. Harman, C. E. Hart, Prof. R. Hatton, A. M. Hawker, Prof. H. T. Heath, R. L. Helps, P. Heselton, J. E. Hobbs, Miss C. Hole, Lord Hylton, Dr C. Imber, the late Sir G. Isham, Dr D. Johnson, Rev. M. O. W. Johnson, Dr C. H. Josten, Prof. H. A. Kaufman, Miss L. Kirk, Prof. E. H. Kossmann, Prof. W. A. Lamont, Dr P. Laslett, R. E. Latham, Prof. R. Leslie, B. Lillywhite, W. Lockwood, Sir R. Mackworth-Young, Dr G. C. R. Morris, the late Dr. A. N. L. Munby, Rev. Prof. G. F. Nuttall, J. C. T. Oates, Lt-Col. C. D. L. Pepys, R. L. Percival, J. Porteous, the late Maj.-Gen. M. W. Prynne, W. J. Rasbridge, M. Richardson-Bunbury, Dr P. Rickard, C. A. Rivington, Prof. C. Robbins, G. Roper, Dr V. A. Rowe, Dr I. Roy, the late J. Saltmarsh, Miss M. L. Savell, D. Scott, Dr A. Sharp, Maj.-Gen. H. B. Sitwell, R. S. Smailes, Prof. T. R. Smith, Sir R. Somerville, G. D. Squibb, P. Strong, Sir J. Summerson, Prof. G. H. Turnbull, Mrs S. Tyacke, Sir A. Wagner, Prof. R. R. Walcott, H. M. Walton, Rev. J. Watson, J. J. Wells, the late Prof. D. Whitelock, Dr T. D. Whittet, C. J. Whitwood, Col. F. B. Wiener, J. Wilson, Cmdr H. B. Wise, Prof. A. H. Woolrych, and Brig. P. Young.

And finally to the friends and correspondents who have commented on the volumes as they appeared and offered suggestions for their improvement – particularly John Ferris, J. J. van Herpen, Richard Luckett, Dr J. C. Mitchell, R. G. Pascoe, Dr T. D. Rogers and Capt. A. B. Sainsbury.

Robert Latham